*Computational
Economics
and Finance*

Hal R. Varian
Editor

Computational Economics and Finance

Modeling and Analysis with *Mathematica*®

Hal R. Varian
School of Information Management and Systems
University of California, Berkeley
Berkeley, CA 94720-4600
USA

Publisher: Allan M. Wylde
Publishing Associate: Keisha Sherbecoe
Product Manager: Walter Borden
Production Manager: Bill Imbornoni
Manufacturing Supervisor: Jacqui Ashri
Cover Designer: A Good Thing, Inc.

Library of Congress Cataloging-in-Publication Data
Varian, Hal R.
    Computational economics and finance : modeling and analysis
    with mathematica / Hal R. Varian
        p. cm.
    Includes bibliographical references.
    ISBN-13: 978-1-4612-7510-7   e-ISBN-13: 978-1-4612-2340-5
    DOI: 10.1007/978-1-4612-2340-5
    1. Econometric models–Computer progress.   2. Finance–Computer
programs.   3. Mathematica (Computer file).   I. Title
HB143.V37   1996   510'.285'536–dc20   92-37343

Printed on acid-free paper.

Softcover reprint of the hardcover 1st edition 1996
Published by TELOS®, The Electronic Library of Science, Santa Clara, California.
TELOS® is an imprint of Springer-Verlag New York, Inc.

Photocomposed pages prepared from the authors' *Mathematica* files.

9 8 7 6 5 4 3 2 1

THE ELECTRONIC LIBRARY OF SCIENCE

TELOS, The Electronic Library of Science, is an imprint of Springer-Verlag New York with publishing facilities in Santa Clara, California. Its publishing program encompasses the natural and physical sciences, computer science, mathematics, economics, and engineering. All TELOS publications have a computational orientation to them, as TELOS' primary publishing strategy is to wed the traditional print medium with the emerging new electronic media in order to provide the reader with a truly interactive multimedia information environment. To achieve this, every TELOS publication delivered on paper has an associated electronic component. This can take the form of book/diskette combinations, book/CD-ROM packages, books delivered via networks, electronic journals, newsletters, plus a multitude of other exciting possibilities. Since TELOS is not committed to any one technology, any delivery medium can be considered. We also do not foresee the imminent demise of the paper book, or journal, as we know them. Instead we believe paper and electronic media can coexist side-by-side, since both offer valuable means by which to convey information to consumers.

The range of TELOS publications extends from research level reference works to textbook materials for the higher education audience, practical handbooks for working professionals, and broadly accessible science, computer science, and high technology general interest publications. Many TELOS publications are interdisciplinary in nature, and most are targeted for the individual buyer, which dictates that TELOS publications be affordably priced.

Of the numerous definitions of the Greek word "telos," the one most representative of our publishing philosophy is "to turn," or "turning point." We perceive the establishment of the TELOS publishing program to be a significant step forward towards attaining a new plateau of high quality information packaging and dissemination in the interactive learning environment of the future. TELOS welcomes you to join us in the exploration and development of this exciting frontier as a reader and user, an author, editor, consultant, strategic partner, or in whatever other capacity one might imagine.

TELOS, The Electronic Library of Science
Springer-Verlag Publishers
3600 Pruneridge Avenue, Suite 200
Santa Clara, CA 95051

THE
ELECTRONIC
® LIBRARY
OF
SCIENCE

TELOS Diskettes

Unless otherwise designated, computer diskettes packaged with TELOS publications are 3.5″ high-density DOS-formatted diskettes. They may be read by any IBM-compatible computer running DOS or Windows. They may also be read by computers running NEXTSTEP, by most UNIX machines, and by Macintosh computers using a file exchange utility.

In those cases where the diskettes require the availability of specific software programs in order to run them, or to take full advantage of their capabilities, then the specific requirements regarding these software packages will be indicated.

TELOS CD-ROM Discs

For buyers of TELOS publications containing CD-ROM discs, or in those cases where the product is a stand-alone CD-ROM, it is always indicated on which specific platform, or platforms, the disc is designed to run. For example, Macintosh only; Windows only; cross-platform, and so forth.

TELOSpub.com (Online)

Interact with TELOS online via the Internet by setting your World-Wide-Web browser to the URL: *http://www.telospub.com*.

The TELOS Web site features new product information and updates, an online catalog and ordering, samples from our publications, information about TELOS, data-files related to and enhancements of our products, and a broad selection of other unique features. Presented in hypertext format with rich graphics, it's your best way to discover what's new at TELOS.

TELOS also maintains these additional Internet resources:

gopher://gopher.telospub.com
ftp://ftp.telospub.com

For up-to-date information regarding TELOS online services, send the one-line e-mail message:

send info to: info@TELOSpub.com.

Preface

In 1992 I edited *Economic and Financial Modeling with Mathematica*. In the Preface to that work I said "I have been pleased and impressed with the materials developed by the contributors to this book. But there is a lot more that can be done. If the demand for this book, and the supply of new applications are large enough we may well publish a second volume." As it turned out both conditions were satisfied: many readers bought the book and several authors came forth with new and exciting applications of *Mathematica*. The result is the book you hold in your hands.

Overview of the Book

As before, I have divided the book into three main sections: economics, finance, and statistics.

The first few chapters in economics have to do with various forms of optimization. Michael Carter leads off with a study of *Mathematica*'s capabilities for linear programming. He provides both a tutorial in using *Mathematica*'s built-in functions and goes on to describe extensions to these functions that make them much more useful for economic applications. Jean-Christophe Culioli follows with a very nice overview of nonlinear programming techniques that can be implemented in *Mathematica*. Whereas Culioli is primarily concerned with convex optimization problems, Paul Rubin shows how *Mathematica* can be used to get a complete solution to a certain class of non-convex problems.

Moving on to economic applications, Eduardo Ley examines "data envelopment analysis," which is a way to measure the efficiency of production units using linear programming techniques. I demonstrate another way of doing efficiency analysis that applies to both production and consumption decisions. William Sharkey shows how to use *Mathematica* to allocate fixed costs using some of the tools of cooperative game theory. Finally, Luke Froeb and Gregory Werden demonstrate the use of *Mathematica* for simulation of mergers in an oligopolistic industry.

Turning to financial applications, John Dickhaut, Steve Gjerstad, and Arijit Mukherji have written a nice set of tools for studying auctions, both theoretically and experimentally. Given the recent interest in auctions of the electromagnetic spectrum, I expect to see much further research in practical problems of auction design, and this chapter provides a very nice demonstration of how *Mathematica* can be used for this purpose.

Ward Hanson looks at yield management of perishable assets—how to price goods such as airline seats, hotel rooms, and other dated services. In addition to the mathematical analysis, this chapter also presents a neat example of how to integrate *Mathematica* with a spreadsheet using MathTalk.

Simon Benninga, Raz Steinmetz, and John Stroughair show how *Mathematica* can be used to compute option values in a variety of cases. Their treatment of binomial option pricing is especially interesting. Mark Fisher and David Zervos use *Mathematica* to fit yield curves, and Luke Froeb examines the use of *Mathematica* in spectral analysis of financial time series.

These two chapters provide a nice lead-in to the statistical applications that follow. Robert Stine shows how to use *Mathematica* to do "exploratory data analysis." This involves making use of both the computational and the graphical capabilities of the program. David Belsely provides a very nice illustration of the use of *Mathematica* for Monte Carlo problems. Although *Mathematica* is significantly slower than dedicated statistical packages, the ease and flexibility of its programming language more than makes up for this lack of speed. Finally, Colin Rose and Murray Smith provide a very useful set of tools for manipulating probability distributions.

Acknowledgments

The first volume of *Economic and Financial Modeling with Mathematica* owed its existence to Allan Wylde, Publisher of TELOS/Springer-Verlag, and the same is true of the second volume. His words of encouragement (and his persistence) were necessary ingredients to produce the final product.

I would also like to thank Leszek Sczaniecki at Wolfram Research who was kind enough to ask his staff to read preliminary versions of the chapters; they provided a number of useful comments and suggestions. Finally, Paul Wellin has done a wonderful job of converting the authors' highly eclectic manuscripts to a coherent set of chapters.

The most enjoyable part of the project has been working with the authors; their creativity and energy never ceases to amaze me. I hope that you, the reader, will be as pleased with the results as I am.

Hal R. Varian
Berkeley
May 1996

Contents

FINANCE

STATISTICS

Contributors

David A. Belsley {*belsley@bcvms.bc.edu*} received a B.A. from Haverford College and a Ph.D. in Economics from M.I.T. He taught at Dartmouth College prior to Boston College, where he is currently Professor of Economics. He is also Senior Research Associate at the Center for Computational Research in Economics and Management Science (CCREMS) at M.I.T. and is a consultant to both government and industry. His publications include numerous articles and monographs, including "Regression Diagnostics" and "Conditioning Diagnostics." His research encompasses regression diagnostics, estimation of simultaneous equations, Monte Carlo methods, computational economics, and applied econometric studies. He is the author of a number of *Mathematica* packages, including *Econometrics.m*. He is on the editorial boards of *Computational Economics*, *Computational Statistics and Data Analysis*, and the *International Journal of Forecasting*.

Simon Benninga {*mssimon@pluto.mscc.huji.ac.il*} has a B.A. (University of Michigan, 1969) and an M.Sc. (Hebrew University of Jerusalem, 1972) in mathematics. He received his Ph.D. in economics and finance at Tel-Aviv University in 1977. He is currently Professor of Finance at the School of Business of the Hebrew University. Benninga is the author of *Numerical Techniques in Finance* (MIT Press, 1989) and *Corporate Finance: A Valuation Approach* (with Oded Sarig, to be published by McGraw-Hill in 1996). The paper in this book was written while Benninga was a visiting Professor of Finance at the Wharton School.

Michael Carter {*m.carter@econ.caterbury.ac.nz*} studied at the University of Canterbury (M.Com., B.Sc.) and Stanford University (A.M., Ph.D. in economics). He spent five years in the Research School of Social Sciences at the Autralian National University before taking up his current position at the University of Canterbury in 1985. His publications cover many areas of economics, including industrial organization and game theory. He is currently writing a text on the foundations of mathematical economics.

J.-C. Culioli {*culioli@trovatore.ensmp.fr*} graduated from École Polytechnique, Palaiseau, France, in 1982. He received his Doctorat in automatic control and mathematics from École Nationale Supérieure des Mines de Paris in 1987. From 1982 to 1987 he was successively with Arthur Andersen (Paris La Defense), Électricité de France (Paris), and Schlumberger Montrouge Research. In 1988 and 1989, he was postdoctoral fellow with Oak Ridge National Laboratory Engineering Physics and Mathematics Division. Since 1990, he has been with the Centre Automatique et Systèmes, École des Mines de Paris, Fontainebleau. He teaches optimization at École Nationale Supérieure des Mines de Paris, automatic control at École Centrale Paris, and stochastic optimization University of Paris–Sorbonne. He wrote two introductory books on optimization and the *Mathematica* language, respectively. He is a member of SIAM and the French SMAI. His current research is in optimal control and optimization.

John Dickhaut {*jdickhaut@csom.umn.edu*} received his B.A. from Duke University and his Masters and Ph.D. (business) at The Ohio State University. He has taught at the University of Chicago, and the University of Minnesota where he is the Honeywell Professor of Accounting. He studies the performance of multiple-person models of behavior in the laboratory, especially those models with an economics foundation. He is currently a member of the editorial board of *The Journal of Accounting Research*, as well as a member of the Economic Science Association Advisory Board.

Mark Fisher {*mfisher@frb.gov*} received his B.A. in economics in 1975 from U.C. Santa Barbara, his M.B.A. in finance in 1979, and his Ph.D. in finance and economics in 1988 from the University of Chicago Graduate School of Business. He is currently an economist at the Federal Reserve Board in Washington in the Trading Risk Analysis section of the Division of Research and Statistics. His current research involves the term structure of interest rates and fixed-income derivatives.

Luke M. Froeb {*luke.froeb@macpost.vanderbilt.edu*} received his A.B. degree from Stanford in 1978, and a Ph.D. in economics from the University of Wisconsin in 1983. He worked at the Antitrust Division of the U.S. Department of Justice for six years where his dissatisfaction with traditional merger analysis led him to develop his merger simulation software. He is currently an Associate Professor at the Owen Graduate School of Management at Vanderbilt. His current research interests include antitrust and econometrics, and he is developing a *Mathematica* web server for use in his classes.

Steve Gjerstad {*gjerstad@u.arizona.edu*} received his B.Math. degree from the Institute of Technology at the University of Minnesota in 1986. He received his M.S. and Ph.D. in economics, also from the University of Minnesota, in 1992 and 1995. He is currently Visiting Associate Research Scientist in the Economic Science Laboratory at the University of Arizona. His research is in the area of individual choice models of games and auctions. His current research interests include experimental tests of competitive equilibrium in general equilibrium-type economies and the theory of multiple equilibria in exchange economies.

Ward Hanson {*hanson_ward@gsb.stanford.edu*} is on the faculty of the Graduate School of Business, Stanford University. He received his Ph.D. in economics from Stanford University, and has served on the faculty of the University of Chicago Graduate School of Business and the Krannert Graduate School of Business at Purdue. His current areas of interest are software economics, internet technology and its impacts on business, and sophisticated pricing strategies. He is especially interested in making *Mathematica*-based models accessible to a wide variety of users by combining packages with spreadsheet and Web-based front-ends.

Eduardo Ley {*edley@eco.uc3m.es*} received his *Licenciado* degree from the *Universidad Computense de Madrid*, and his M.A. in statistics and Ph.D. in economics from the University of Michigan in Ann Arbor. He has held visiting appointments at the Universidad Carlos III de Madrid and the University of Michigan. Presently he is a fellow at Resources for the Future in Washington, D.C. His research is directed primarily at public and environmental economics, and econometrics.

Arijit Mukherji {*arijit@atlas.socsci.umn.edu*} received his B. Com. degree from the University of Calcutta in 1983, qualified as a chartered accountant in India in 1984, and received his Ph.D. in business from the University of Pittsburgh in 1991. He is currently Assistant Professor of Accounting at the Carlson School of Management at the University of Minnesota. His publications are mainly in the area of the economics of information and incentives, and experiments on game theory. His current research interests include theories of learning in games, models of decentralization, and the theory of incomplete contracts.

Colin Rose {*colinr@extro.ucc.su.oz.au*} is director of the Theoretical Research Institute (Sydney). He received his B.Ec. (Hons.) and Ph.D. from Sydney University. He has published in the areas of international finance, economic theory, and mathematical statistics. He is currently working on irreversible investment models and collapsing exchange rate target zones, and is writing a book on the art of censoring and folding in economic analysis.

Paul A. Rubin {*rubin@msu.edu*} is Associate Professor of Management Science at the Eli Broad Graduate School of Management at Michigan State University. He received degrees in mathematics from Princeton University (A.B.) and Michigan State University (Ph.D.) before going where the bucks (allegedly) are. His primary research interest is in the application of mathematical programming techniques to problems in operations management.

William W. Sharkey {*wsharkey@fcc.gov*} received a B.S. degree in mathematics from the University of Michigan in 1969 and a Ph.D. in economics from the University of Chicago in 1973. He is currently Senior Economist with the Office of Plans and Policy at the Federal Communiations Commission in Washington, D.C. Previously he was a visiting professor at the École Polytechnique in Paris and the Institut d'Économie Industrielle in Toulouse, and was a member of the economics research group at Bellcore and at Bell Laboratories. His research interests include the economics of regulation, the economics of telecommunications, cooperative game theory, cost allocation, and the economics of networks. He is the author of *The Theory of Natural Monopoly*.

Murray D. Smith {*murrays@bullwinkle.econ.su.oz.au*} received his B.Ec. (Hons.) and Ph.D. degrees from Monash University. He has worked as a Lecturer in Econometrics at the University of New South Wales, and is currently a Senior

Lecturer in Econometrics at the University of Sydney. His research interests lie in the general area of econometric theory, with particular reference to exact finite sample distribution theory.

Raz Steinmetz has a B.Sc. in mathematics and computer science from Tel-Aviv University and an M.B.A. from the Wharton School, University of Pennsylvania (1993). He is a self-employed investment manager in New York City.

Robert A. Stine {*stine@stat.wharton.upenn.edu*} is Associate Professor of Statistics at the Wharton School of the University of Pennsylvania. He holds a B.S. in mathematics from the University of South Carolina and a Ph.D. in statistics from Princeton. His current research interests span topics in statistical computing, mixture models, and time series analysis.

John Stroughair {*clbilc@ark.ship.edu*} is a consultant with Oliver, Wyman & Co. He has a Ph.D. in physics from Case-Western Reserve University (1982) and an M.B.A. from the Wharton School, University of Pennsylvania (1993).

Hal R. Varian {*hal@sims.berkeley.edu*} received his S.B. degree from M.I.T. in 1969 and his M.A. in mathematics and Ph.D. in economics from U.C. Berkeley in 1973. He is currently the Dean of the School of Information Management and Systems at U.C. Berkeley. He is also a Professor in the Haas School of Business, a Professor in the Department of Economics at Berkeley, and holds the Class of 1944 Chair. His current research involves the economics of information technology.

Gregory J. Werden {*werdengj@aol.com*} received B.A. and M.A. degrees from the University of Cincinnati in 1973 and 1974, and M.A. and Ph.D. degrees from the University of Wisconsin in 1976 and 1977. He has since worked in the Antitrust Division of the U.S. Department of Justice. His current titles are Director of Research, Economic Analysis Group and Chief, Appellate Liaison Unit, Economic Litigation Section. In these positions he specializes in appellate antitrust litigation. He has been actively involved in research on antitrust issues, particularly market delineation and merger policy.

David Zervos {*david_zervos@il.us.swissbank.com*} received his B.S. in systems science and mathematics at Washington University (St. Louis) in 1987, his M.A. in economics from the University of Rochester in 1991, and his Ph.D. in economics from the University of Rochester in 1992. He is currently an Associate Director in the Quantitative Interest Rate Research Group at SBC Warburg in London. His current research involves term structure modeling, relative value trading, and fixed income derivative pricing.

Part I

Economics

Part 1

Economics

1 Linear Programming with *Mathematica*: The Simplex Algorithm

Michael Carter

Linear programming and the simplex algorithm are fundamental to the theory and practice of optimization. In this chapter, we exploit the symbolic manipulation capability of *Mathematica* to elucidate the simplex algorithm clearly and intuitively. This provides the foundation for the following chapter, in which we develop functions that enhance *Mathematica*'s in-built linear programming facility.

> *The subject of linear programming is surrounded by notational and terminological thickets. Both of these thorny defenses are lovingly cultivated by a coterie of stern acolytes who have devoted themselves to the field. Actually, the basic ideas of linear programming are quite simple.*
>
> Press, Teukolsky, Vetterling, and Flannery (1992, p. 431)

1.1 Introduction

In his book *Methods of Mathematical Economics*, Joel Franklin (1980) relates the story of a visit to the headquarters of the Mobil Oil Corporation in New York in 1958. The purpose of his visit was to study Mobil's use of computers. In those days, computers were rare and expensive and Mobil's installation had cost millions of dollars. Franklin recognized the person in charge; they had been post-doctoral fellows together. Franklin asked his former colleague how long he thought it would take to pay off this investment. "We paid it off in about two weeks," was the surprise response. Elaborating, he explained that Mobil was able to make massive cost savings by optimizing production decisions using linear programming, decisions that had previously been made heuristically.

It would be hard to exaggerate the importance of linear programming in practical optimization, in applications such as production scheduling, transportation and distribution, inventory control, job assignment, capital budgeting, and portfolio management. Franklin's anecdote highlights the enormous benefits that can accrue from optimizing recurrent decisions.

There are two main reasons for the practical success of linear programming. Many production processes and economic systems are linear or nearly so. Linear programming provides an appropriate mathematical model for such processes. Also, there exists a very efficient algorithm (the simplex algorithm) for solving most linear programming problems. The postwar conjunction of the availability of digital computers and the discovery of the simplex algorithm by George Dantzig paved the way for successful industrial application as exemplified by Mobil's experience.

Linear programming is also important to economists and game theorists. Although most economic models are nonlinear, linear models of exchange, production, and capital accumulation serve an important didactic role (Dorfman et al. 1958). Furthermore, an understanding of the simplex algorithm and the duality theorem enhances comprehension of nonlinear optimization, mastery of which is central to economic analysis. In game theory, the solution of zero-sum games is a linear programming problem and the minimax theorem is formally equivalent to the fundamental duality theorem of linear programming. The efficient solution of nonzero-sum games uses a modification of the simplex algorithm called the complementary pivot algorithm (Lemke and Howson 1964; Wilson 1992). Much of cooperative game theory reduces to the application of linear programming theory and techniques (Carter 1993).

Despite recent discoveries of alternative "interior point" algorithms, the simplex method and its variants remain by far the most common practical method for solving linear programming problems. The simplex algorithm is based upon a very simple intuitive idea of successive improvement. However, because most textbook treatments aim at describing a mathematical formulation suitable for implementation by conventional programming languages, their discussion tends to hide the intuitive simplicity of the algorithm. The symbolic manipulation capability of *Mathematica* enables the simplex algorithm to be elucidated more clearly and intuitively, and the significance of all the results understood.

Because our implementation of the simplex algorithm is designed for explanation rather than execution, our code emphasizes clarity rather than efficiency.

1.2   The Problem

To make the exposition easier to follow, we start with a simple specific example. A furniture maker can produce three products: bookcases, chairs, and desks. Each product requires machining, finishing, and some labor. The supply of these resources is limited. Unit profits and resource requirements are listed in the following table.

	Bookcases	Chairs	Desks	Capacity
Finishing	2	2	1	30
Labor	1	2	3	25
Machining	2	1	1	20
Net profit	3	1	3	

The problem of maximizing profit can be specified as the following linear program. Maximize

```
In[1]:=  profit = 3x[b] + x[c] + 3x[d];
```

subject to the

```
In[2]:=  constraints =
         { 2x[b] + 2x[c] +  x[d] <= 30,
            x[b] + 2x[c] + 3x[d] <= 25,
           2x[b] +  x[c] +  x[d] <= 20
         };
```

and $x_i \geq 0$.

For analysis, inequalities are more difficult to manipulate than equations. By introducing *slack variables*, we can transform the inequalities into a corresponding system of equations. This is called the *standard form*. The slack variables measure the unused capacity of a resource at any given production plan. For convenience, we label the spare capacities of finishing, labor, and machining s_f, s_l, and s_m, respectively.

```
In[3]:=  StandardLP[constraints_, labels_List] :=
            Transpose @
               {labels,constraints} /.
               {i_, lhs_ <= rhs_}:> s[i] == rhs - lhs
```

```
In[4]:=  StandardLP[constraints, {f,l,m}]
```

```
Out[4]=  {s[f] == 30 - 2 x[b] - 2 x[c] - x[d],
          s[l] == 25 - x[b] - 2 x[c] - 3 x[d],
          s[m] == 20 - 2 x[b] - x[c] - x[d]}
```

For example, if the furniture maker were to produce 1 bookcase, 2 chairs, and 3 desks, the unused capacities would be

```
In[5]:=  % /. {x[b] -> 1, x[c] ->2, x[d] -> 3}
```

```
Out[5]=  {s[f] == 21, s[l] == 11, s[m] == 13}
```

The linear programming problem can be succinctly summarized by prepending the objective function to the constraints. To ensure that the result is nicely formatted, we can set **$PrePrint** to apply **MatrixForm** automatically to any system of equations (*tableau*).

```
In[6]:=  TableauQ[_] := False
         TableauQ[{_Equal..}] := True
         $PrePrint = If[TableauQ[#], TableForm[#],#]&;
```

```
In[7]:=  problem=Prepend[StandardLP[constraints, {f,l,m}],
                z == profit]
```

```
Out[7]=  z == 3 x[b] + x[c] + 3 x[d]

         s[f] == 30 - 2 x[b] - 2 x[c] - x[d]

         s[l] == 25 - x[b] - 2 x[c] - 3 x[d]

         s[m] == 20 - 2 x[b] - x[c] - x[d]
```

We can also use **TableauQ** to preclude applying **StandardLP** to a system that is already in standard form.

```
In[8]:=  StandardLP[constraints_?TableauQ,labels_List] :=
             constraints
```

Programming Note: We use *Mathematica* functions, for example $x[b]$, $s[l]$, to represent variables rather than simple variable names such as $x1, x2$, or b, c, d. This facilitates manipulation in *Mathematica*, for example, in the use of pattern matching and automatic generation of variable names. It more closely resembles the subscript notation used in many presentations and would enable the use of more descriptive variable names such as $x[desks]$, if required. We adopt the convention of using $x[j]$ to denote decision variables and $s[i]$ to denote slack variables. We rely on this convention occasionally in the code.

We warn the reader that our use of global symbols such as $s[i]$ and z contravenes good programming practice. In production code, these would normally be hidden in a context so that they would not clash with user symbols. However, use of $s[i]$ to denote slack variables and z to denote the value of the objective function is conventional in the linear programming literature, and is appropriate given the pedagogical nature of this chapter.

1.3   Searching for a Solution

Are there any feasible solutions to the production problem? Yes, an obvious possibility is to produce nothing ($x_i = 0$), but it is not very profitable. Another feasible solution was cited in the previous section. The production plan

```
In[9]:=  productionPlan = {x[b] -> 1, x[c] -> 2, x[d] -> 3};
```

is feasible

In[10]:= **constraints /. productionPlan**

Out[10]= {True, True, True}

and produces a profit of

In[11]:= **profit /. productionPlan**

Out[11]= 14

A better plan is

In[12]:= **{profit, constraints} /.**
        (productionPlan = {x[b] -> 2, x[c] -> 4, x[d] -> 5})

Out[12]= {25, {True, True, True}}

Unfortunately, we cannot produce

In[13]:= **{profit, constraints} /.**
        (productionPlan = {x[b] -> 5, x[c] -> 4, x[d] -> 5})

Out[13]= {34, {True, False, True}}

because the requirements of 5 bookcases, 4 chairs, and 5 desks exceeds the available labor supply. If we eliminate the chairs, we can produce

In[14]:= **{profit, constraints} /.**
        (productionPlan = {x[b] -> 5, x[c] -> 0, x[d] -> 5})

Out[14]= {30, {True, True, True}}

This is the most profitable plan that we have considered so far, but is it the best? How can we tell? We could continue to explore various permutations, but it is not clear how we would know when we have reached the optimum plan or even that an optimum plan exists. Clearly, we need some systematic way in which to explore the various alternatives.

A sensible starting point would be to produce as much as possible of the most profitable item. Bookcases (x_b) and desks (x_d) are equally profitable. Arbitrarily, let us choose bookcases. What is the maximum number of bookcases x_b that can be produced with the available resouces? Inspection reveals that machining capacity is the limiting factor in the production of bookcases. Each bookcase requires 2 hours of machining. A total of 20 hours is available. Therefore we can produce a maximum of 10 bookcases.

Our first tentative production plan is

```
In[15]:= productionPlan = {x[b] -> 10, x[c] -> 0, x[d] -> 0};
```

This plan exhausts the machining capacity but leaves spare capacity in finishing and spare labor, resulting in a profit of $30.

```
In[16]:= problem /. productionPlan
```

```
Out[16]= z == 30

         s[f] == 10

         s[l] == 15

         s[m] == 0
```

Is this an optimal solution? It is not immediately obvious. Sure, we have spare resources. But we know that we cannot produce any more bookcases. Furthermore, because the machining constraint is binding, any output of the other goods can only be accomplished by contracting the production of bookcases. In other words, any production of chairs or desks involves a tradeoff against the production of bookcases. Is such a tradeoff profitable?

The tradeoff imposed by the limited supply of machining capacity is represented by the third constraint, which is called the *pivot row*.

```
In[17]:= pivotRow = First @ Cases[problem, s[m] == _]
```

```
Out[17]= s[m] == 20 - 2 x[b] - x[c] - x[d]
```

This equation imposes a constraint on the total production of bookcases that can be highlighted by solving this constraint for x_b.

```
In[18]:= RevisedPivotRow =
             Roots[pivotRow, x[b]] // ExpandAll
```

```
Out[18]=                  s[m]    x[c]    x[d]
              x[b] == 10 - ---- - ---- - ----
                            2       2      2
```

This equation expresses the machining constraint in terms of the production of bookcases. It reveals two important technological facts. The intercept is the number of bookcases that can be produced by devoting all of the machining resource to the production of bookcases. The coefficients on the other goods x_c and x_d indicate that, *while the machining constraint remains binding*, every chair and desk produced reduces the available output of bookcases by 1/2 unit. This is the technological tradeoff imposed by the machining constraint. The revised constraint reveals that (1) a maximum of 10 bookcases can be produced by concentrating on bookcases alone, and (2) every chair or desk produced would reduce the potential number of bookcases by 1/2. This is the fundamental technological tradeoff.

The *economics of this tradeoff* is revealed by substituting the technological tradeoff into the objective function. To do this, we first express the revised pivot row as a transformation rule

```
In[19]:= pivotRule = ToRules[RevisedPivotRow]
```

```
Out[19]=                  s[m]    x[c]    x[d]
           {x[b] -> 10 - ---- - ---- - ----}
                           2       2       2
```

and use this to transform the objective function

```
In[20]:= RevisedObjective = profit /. pivotRule //
                ExpandAll
```

```
Out[20]=        3 s[m]    x[c]    3 x[d]
           30 - ------ - ---- + ------
                   2       2       2
```

This revised objective function reflects the *economic position* at the tentative production plan ($x_b = 10, x_c = 0, x_d = 0$). The intercept 30 represents the net profit earned by this plan. The coefficients on x_c and x_d evaluate the marginal benefit of producing chairs or desks, while taking account of the need to reduce correspondingly the output of bookcases (the technological tradeoff). This reveals that the marginal benefit of substituting chairs for desks is negative, whereas the marginal benefit of producing a desk, *after accounting for the corresponding reduction in the output of bookcases*, is positive. Some substitution of desks for bookcases is desirable. Producing one less bookcase would enable the firm to produce 2 desks, increasing net profit by $3. At the margin, each desk is worth $3/2. Note that bookcases and desks have the same selling price, $3. The reason that it is more profitable to produce a combination of bookcases and desks (as opposed to bookcases alone) is that desks require less of the scarce machining capacity.

The coefficient of x_d, 3/2, measures the true opportunity cost of producing all 10 bookcases, which is the foregone opportunity to produce some desks. Similarly, the coefficient $-3/2$ on the slack variable s_m measures the opportunity cost of the machining constraint—the foregone potential output of bookcases and/or desks. Its inverse (negative) 3/2 is called the *shadow price* of machining capacity. It indicates that profit could be increased by 3/2 if this constraint were relaxed by one unit. Similarly, the coefficient 3/2 on the $x[d]$ can be interpreted as the *shadow price* of the nonnegativity constraint on this variable. Shadow prices play a central role in the solution of linear programming problems. As we demonstrate shortly, they guide the process of sequential improvement leading to the optimal solution. At the optimal solution, the shadow prices provide important information about the sensitivity of the solution to changes in the parameters of the problem.

The revised objective function reveals that our tentative plan $(10, 0, 0)$ is not optimal; some substitution of desks for bookcases is desirable. How many desks should we produce? Linearity implies that we should exploit any profitable substitution as far as resources allow. The impact on machining is implicitly taken account of by the pivot row. We should substitute desks for bookcases until we run out of some other resources. The impact of this substitution on resource requirements can be obtained by using the pivot rule to rewrite the other resource constraints.

```
In[21]:= RevisedConstraints = Rest[problem] /.
            {pivotRow :> RevisedPivotRow,
          otherRow_Equal :> (otherRow /. pivotRule)} //
                  ExpandAll
```

```
Out[21]= s[f] == 10 + s[m] - x[c]

                 s[m]   3 x[c]   5 x[d]
         s[l] == 15 + ---- - ------ - ------
                  2      2   .    2

                 s[m]   x[c]   x[d]
         x[b] == 10 - ---- - ---- - ----
                  2     2      2
```

The absence of x_d from the first equation indicates that substituting desks for bookcases will have no impact on the utilization of finishing capacity. (Although desks are less demanding of finishing than bookcases, the machining constraint allows us to substitute 2 desks for every bookcase.) The second equation reveals that substitution will utilize spare labor capacity because desks are considerably more labor intensive than bookcases. Each desk will utilize $5/2$ units of spare labor capacity. Available spare capacity is 15 units, allowing the substitution of 6 desks for 3 bookcases. Therefore our second tentative production plan is

```
In[22]:= productionPlan = {x[b] -> 7, x[c] -> 0, x[d] -> 6};
```

```
In[23]:= problem /. productionPlan
```

```
Out[23]= z == 39

         s[f] == 10

         s[l] == 0

         s[m] == 0
```

This plan exhausts both labor and machining capacity and produces a profit of \$39, compared to \$30 with the earlier plan. This certainly represents an improvement over our first production plan. Is this now an optimal solution? This is the same question we asked of the first production plan and we could repeat the same analysis from a new starting point. This is the pivotal step in linear programming. We now formalize this procedure.

1.4   Formalizing This Procedure–Pivoting

Let us review what we have just done. Faced with the linear programming problem

In[24]:= **problem**

Out[24]= z == 3 x[b] + x[c] + 3 x[d]

  s[f] == 30 - 2 x[b] - 2 x[c] - x[d]

  s[l] == 25 - x[b] - 2 x[c] - 3 x[d]

  s[m] == 20 - 2 x[b] - x[c] - x[d]

we proposed a tentative production plan that involved maximum production of the most profitable good, in this instance, bookcases. Examining the resource constraints, we deduced that machining capacity would most limit the production of bookcases. The insightful step was rewriting the specification of the problem to more clearly represent the technological and economic tradeoffs entailed by the maximum production of bookcases. This rewritten specification clearly indicated that the tentative production plan of 10 bookcases was not optimal, and also indicated the direction of improvement.

The tentative production plan $(10, 0, 0)$ producing as many desks as possible is a *basic feasible solution*. It is a basic solution in that no more than the minimal number of variables are nonzero. In this case, the basic variables are $x[b]$, $s[1]$, and $s[3]$. The process of moving from one basic feasible solution to another and rewriting the specification of the problem to fully reflect the technological and economic tradeoffs from the perspective of the new basic solution is called *pivoting*. This procedure was carried out in the preceding section and is summarized in the function **Pivot**.

```
In[25]:= Pivot[tableau_?TableauQ,x_[j_],s_[i_]] :=
            Module[{pivotRow},
            pivotRow = First @ Cases[tableau, s[i] == _];
            tableau /. {pivotRow :> Roots[pivotRow,x[j]],
              otherRow_Equal :> (otherRow /.
                Flatten @ Solve[pivotRow,x[j]])} //
                ExpandAll
         ]
```

The function **Pivot** returns the revised constraints together with the revised objective function. These summarize the optimization problem from the viewpoint of the tentative production plan (the basic feasible solution). The left-hand side of the revised constraints indicates the values of the positive decision variables and the positive slack variables, which measure spare resource capacity. The coefficient of the revised objective function measures the shadow prices of the fully used resources and the zero decision variables. In the linear programming literature, the revised objective function and constraints constitute what is called a *tableau*. The tableau is a very compact representation of the technological and economic tradeoffs that pertain at any tentative solution.[1]

In the production planning example, our first basic feasible solution was obtained by concentrating on the production of bookcases. The maximum number of bookcases was limited by the machining constraint. The revised specification at this basic solution is

```
In[26]:= tableau = Pivot[problem,x[b],s[m]]

Out[26]=              3 s[m]    x[c]    3 x[d]
            z == 30 - ------ - ---- + ------
                         2        2       2

            s[f] == 10 + s[m] - x[c]

                         s[m]   3 x[c]   5 x[d]
            s[l] == 15 + ---- - ------ - ------
                          2       2        2

                         s[m]   x[c]   x[d]
            x[b] == 10 - ---- - ---- - ----
                          2      2      2
```

Our next step was to substitute some desks for bookcases. The extent of the substitution was limited by the labor resource. Making this substitution leads to the revised tableau.

```
In[27]:= Pivot[tableau,x[d],s[l]] // TableForm

Out[27]=              3 s[l]   6 s[m]   7 x[c]
            z == 39 - ------ - ------ - ------
                         5        5        5

            s[f] == 10 + s[m] - x[c]
```

---

[1]In fact, the linear programming literature usually reserves the term "tableau" for the matrix of coefficients of the preceding equations. The full system of equations was called a *dictionary* by Strum (1972), whose approach was fully developed by Chvátal (1983).

$$x[d] \ == \ 6 \ - \ \frac{2\ s[l]}{5} \ + \ \frac{s[m]}{5} \ - \ \frac{3\ x[c]}{5}$$

$$x[b] \ == \ 7 \ + \ \frac{s[l]}{5} \ - \ \frac{3\ s[m]}{5} \ - \ \frac{x[c]}{5}$$

The revised objective function (top row) reveals that this is now an optimal production plan, because all the coefficients are negative. Any move that increases the currently zero variables (s_l, s_m, x_c) must reduce profit below \$39. There is no further profitable improvement. The optimal plan requires the production of 7 bookcases and 6 desks. It leaves spare finishing capacity of 10, which cannot be utilized profitably.

The procedure we have followed in seeking an optimal solution is one of sequential improvement. At each tentative production process, we looked for a profitable improvement. The potential for profitable improvement was summarized in the revised objective function. Having identified a potential improvement, we then made that improvement to the full extent possible (which is profitable because of linearity), while accounting for all the tradeoffs necessary to adhere to the binding constraints. Finally, we revised the formulation of the problem to account for any new tradeoffs inherent in the new tentative production plan. This stepwise improvement procedure is known as *pivoting*.

To automate the pivoting process, we need to identify the critical resource that limits the extent of any potential improvement, that is, the resource which most limits the extent to which the variable x_i can be increased. This is done by comparing the ratio of the available surplus (the constant term) of the resource to the unit requirements of the activity (the coefficient of x_i) and selecting the smallest. This is implemented in the function **LimitingResource**, which makes use of pattern matching to parse the components of each constraint. ExpansionRatios is a list comprising each resource (represented by the corresponding slack variable) and its expansion ratio. **MinPair** selects the mimimum element in this list.

```
In[28]:= MinPair[pairs_List] :=
            Fold[If[#1[[2]] <= #2[[2]],#1,#2]&,
            First[pairs],Rest[pairs]]
```

```
In[29]:= LimitingResource[tableau_,var_] :=
        Module[{ExpansionRatios},
        ExpansionRatios = (Rest[tableau] /.
        {resource_ == (b_ ? NumberQ) + a_. var + x_:>
                    {resource,b/Abs[a]}}/; a < 0,
          resource_ == a_. var + x_ :> {resource,0} /; a < 0,
          resource_ == x_   :> {resource,Infinity}});
        First @ MinPair[ExpansionRatios]
        ]
```

Programming Note: This calculation is applied only to the constraints
(Rest[tableau]). The usual convention in the linear programming literature is to put the objective function at the bottom of the tableau. We have
reversed this convention, putting the objective at the top, to facilitate separating
the objective function and the constraints when required.

For example, we previously found that the first resource (machining) was
the limiting factor in the production of bookcases, whereas labor is the critical
resource in making desks.

```
In[30]:= LimitingResource[problem,x[b]]
```

```
Out[30]= s[m]
```

```
In[31]:= LimitingResource[problem,x[d]]
```

```
Out[31]= s[1]
```

We use **LimitingResource** to augment the function **Pivot** to find the critical
resource limiting the extent of any potential improvement.

```
In[32]:= Pivot[tableau_?TableauQ,x_[j_]] :=
          Pivot[tableau,x[j],LimitingResource[tableau,x[j]]]
```

In the production planning example, bookcases and desks are equally profitable.
We arbitrarily chose to focus initially on bookcases. To illustrate the function
Pivot, let us investigate what would have happened if we had made the other
choice. Concentrating on the production of desks leads to

```
In[33]:= Pivot[problem, x[d]]
```

```
Out[33]= z == 25 - s[1] + 2 x[b] - x[c]


                65    s[1]   5 x[b]    4 x[c]
        s[f] == -- + ---- - ------ - ------
                3     3       3         3


                25    s[1]   x[b]    2 x[c]
        x[d] == -- - ---- - ---- - ------
                3     3       3        3


                35    s[1]   5 x[b]   x[c]
        s[m] == -- + ---- - ------ - ----
                3     3       3        3
```

The revised objective function indicates that this is not optimal, some substitution of bookcases for desks is indicated.

```
In[34]:= Pivot[%,x[b]]
```

```
Out[34]=              3 s[1]   6 s[m]   7 x[c]
             z == 39 - ------ - ------ - ------
                          5        5        5

             s[f] == 10 + s[m] - x[c]

                         2 s[1]    s[m]   3 x[c]
             x[d] == 6 - ------ + ---- - ------
                           5        5       5

                         s[1]   3 s[m]    x[c]
             x[b] == 7 + ---- - ------ - ----
                          5       5        5
```

The top row indicates that this is an optimal solution and indeed it is the same solution as that arrived at earlier.

Now consider the situation if we begin with the production of chairs. Concentrating on the production of chairs yields a profit of only $12.50.

```
In[35]:= Pivot[problem, x[c]]
```

```
Out[35]=      25   s[1]   5 x[b]   3 x[d]
         z == -- - ---- + ------ + ------
              2     2       2        2

         s[f] == 5 + s[1] - x[b] + 2 x[d]

                 25   s[1]   x[b]   3 x[d]
         x[c] == -- - ---- - ---- - ------
                 2     2      2       2

                 15   s[1]   3 x[b]   x[d]
         s[m] == -- + ---- - ------ + ----
                 2     2       2       2
```

This tableau indicates that producing chairs alone does not use the available resources very efficiently. Producing some bookcases or desks would be profitable. Substituting some desks for chairs yields

```
In[36]:= Pivot[%, x[d]]
```

```
Out[36]= z == 25 - s[1] + 2 x[b] - x[c]

                 65   s[1]   5 x[b]   4 x[c]
         s[f] == -- + ---- - ------ - ------
                 3     3       3        3
```

```
               25    s[1]     x[b]    2 x[c]
       x[d] == -- -  ---- -   ---- -  ------
                3     3        3        3

               35    s[1]    5 x[b]    x[c]
       s[m] == -- +  ---- -  ------ -  ----
                3     3        3        3
```

This looks better, but adding some bookcases would be even better. One more step gives the optimal solution.

In[37]:= **Pivot[%,x[b]]**

Out[37]=
```
                        3 s[1]    6 s[m]    7 x[c]
          z == 39 -     ------ -  ------ -  ------
                          5         5         5

          s[f] == 10 + s[m] - x[c]

                        2 s[1]    s[m]    3 x[c]
          x[d] == 6 -   ------ +  ---- -  ------
                          5        5        5

                        s[1]    3 s[m]    x[c]
          x[b] == 7 +   ---- -  ------ -  ----
                          5       5        5
```

From this experiment, it would seem that all paths of sequential improvement lead eventually to the optimal solution. Later, we consider whether this is always true. Our experiment also reveals that some paths are quicker than others. Starting with bookcases or desks, we require two steps to reach the optimal solution. Beginning with chairs required three steps. The remaining component of the simplex algorithm is a criterion for guiding the process of sequential improvement efficiently.

1.5   The Simplex Algorithm

As we have just seen, the process of sequential improvement leading to an optimal solution can follow different paths. The basic simplex algorithm uses the shadow prices at each stage to guide the process of sequential improvement. This has proved to be an extremely efficient procedure in practice.

The shadow prices are the negatives of the coefficients of the variables in the revised objective function. Consequently, any variable that has a negative shadow price has a positive coefficient in the revised objective function and offers potential for improvement. Arguably, the variable with the lowest (most negative) shadow price offers the greatest potential for improvement.

The function **ShadowPrice** determines the shadow price of any given variable. **ShadowPrices** extracts the shadow prices from the revised objective function, returning a list of variables and their shadow prices. (Because the names are so similar, we reassure *Mathematica* that we have not made a spelling mistake.)

```
In[38]:= Off[General::spell1];
         ShadowPrice[objective_,var_]:=
            -Coefficient[objective,var]
         ShadowPrices[objective_] :=
            {#, ShadowPrice[objective,#]}& /@
               Variables[objective]
         On[General::spell1];
```

```
In[39]:= ShadowPrices[First[Pivot[problem,x[b]]][[2]]]
```

$$
Out[39]= \left\{\left\{s[m],\ -\tfrac{3}{2}\right\},\ \left\{x[c],\ -\tfrac{1}{2}\right\},\ \left\{x[d],\ -(-\tfrac{3}{2})\right\}\right\}
$$

Candidates for pivoting are those variables that have negative shadow prices. **NextPivot** identifies the variable with the most negative shadow price, which becomes the pivot variable. It returns None if all shadow prices are positive. The function **Simplex** iterates the pivoting procedure until there is no further potential for improvement, stopping when there is no variable with a negative shadow price in the revised objective function. It returns the final tableau.

```
In[40]:= NextPivot[tableau_?TableauQ] := Module[
            {minshadow =
            MinPair[ShadowPrices[First[tableau][[2]]]]},
            If[minshadow[[2]] < 0,minshadow[[1]],None]
         ]
```

By augmenting the function pivot to select the next pivot when none is specified,

```
In[41]:= Pivot[tableau_?TableauQ] :=
            Pivot[tableau,NextPivot[tableau]]
```

the problem can be solved by repeated application of the function **Pivot**.

```
In[42]:= Pivot @ Pivot[problem]
```

$$
Out[42]= \quad z == 39 - \frac{3\ s[l]}{5} - \frac{6\ s[m]}{5} - \frac{7\ x[c]}{5}
$$

$$
s[f] == 10 + s[m] - x[c]
$$

```
                        2 s[l]    s[m]    3 x[c]
            x[d] == 6 - ------  + ----  - ------
                          5        5        5


                          s[l]    3 s[m]    x[c]
            x[b] == 7 + ----  - ------  - ----
                          5         5        5
```

If we provide an appropriate stopping rule, the simplex algorithm can be encoded surprisingly elegantly.

In[43]:= **Pivot[tableau_?TableauQ,None] := tableau**

In[44]:= **Simplex[tableau_?TableauQ] := FixedPoint[Pivot,tableau]**

In[45]:= **finalTableau = Simplex[problem]**

Out[45]=
```
                        3 s[l]    6 s[m]    7 x[c]
            z == 39 - ------  - ------  - ------
                          5         5         5


        s[f]  == 10 + s[m] - x[c]


                        2 s[l]    s[m]    3 x[c]
            x[d] == 6 - ------  + ----  - ------
                          5        5        5


                          s[l]    3 s[m]    x[c]
            x[b] == 7 + ----  - ------  - ----
                          5         5        5
```

We can easily equip **Simplex** to recognize alternative representations of the linear programming problem. For example, to match the calling sequence of **ConstrainedMax** we provide

In[46]:= **Simplex[objective_,constraints_] :=**
        Simplex[Prepend[StandardLP[constraints],
           z == objective]]

The output of the function **Simplex** is the *final tableau*, comprising the revised objective function and constraints at the optimal solution. The final tableau is a very compact summary of useful information regarding the optimal solution of a linear programming problem. It tells us the optimal values of the decision variables, the amounts of unused resources, and the optimal value of the objective function. It indicates whether the optimal solution is unique. It also includes the solution of a related linear program, the *dual*, and yields a wealth of information about the sensitivity of the optimal solution to changes in the specification of the problem. Mining this information is the subject of the companion piece on

Sensitivity Analysis (Chapter 2). To complete this chapter, we confront some potential problems with our implementation and extend the algorithm to deal with minimization and other problems.

1.6   Potential Problems

Our description of the simplex algorithm glossed over some potential problems that we now confront. Our algorithm began at a feasible solution, and then made a sequence of potential improvements until no further improvements could be made. Disregarding questions of efficiency, there are only two ways in which our procedure can fail to produce an optimal solution eventually: it will only fail if there is no optimal solution, or the algorithm gets stuck in an infinite loop and fails to terminate. There are two reasons why an optimal solution may not exist—either the feasible set is empty or the feasible set is unbounded. We consider each of these possibilities in turn.

Before proceeding, we need to augment the function **StandardLP** to provide default constraint labels when none are specified.

```
In[47]:= StandardLP[constraints_] :=
            StandardLP[constraints, Range[Length[constraints]]]
```

1.6.1   Unboundedness

At each pivoting step, we presumed that the amount of potential improvement would be limited by some resource. If this is not the case, we could repeat that improvement and obtain an infinite return. For example, consider the problem

$$\max x_1 + x_2$$

subject to

$$x[1] - x[2] \leq 0$$

Any nonnegative pair (x_1, x_2) is feasible provided $x_1 \leq x_2$. There is no limit to how big we can make the return. The feasible set is unbounded. Clearly there is no optimal solution.

To handle this possibility, we need to extend the function **Limiting-Resource** to recognize cases in which there is no critical resource and the feasible set is unbounded.

```
In[48]:= LimitingResource[tableau_,var_] :=
            Module[{ExpansionRatios},
            ExpansionRatios = (Rest[tableau] /.
            {resource_ == (b_ ? NumberQ) + a_. var + x_:>
                        {resource,b/Abs[a]}/; a < 0,
                resource_ == a_. var + x_ :> {resource,0} /; a < 0,
                resource_ == x_   :> {resource,Infinity}});
```

```
                      If[#[[2]] < Infinity,#[[1]],None] & @
                         MinPair[ExpansionRatios]
                    ]

In[49]:= problem = Prepend[StandardLP[{x[1] - x[2] <= 10}],
                    z == x[1] + x[2]]

Out[49]= z == x[1] + x[2]

         s[1] == 10 - x[1] + x[2]

In[50]:= LimitingResource[problem,x[2]]

Out[50]= None
```

We must also amend the function **Pivot** to recognize when the problem is unbounded.

```
In[51]:= Pivot[tableau_?TableauQ,x_[j_],None] := (
            Print["The problem is unbounded"];
            Return[tableau])

In[52]:= Simplex[problem]

         The problem is unbounded.

Out[52]= z == 10 - s[1] + 2 x[2]

         x[1] == 10 - s[1] + x[2]
```

1.6.2   Empty Feasible Set

The other reason why an optimal solution may fail to exist is that there may be no feasible solutions. In other words, the constraints are inconsistent. At first sight, this poses an insurmountable problem for applying the simplex algorithm, which requires an initial solution from which to make sequential improvements. In the preceding example, we used the trivial solution as a starting point. However, if the feasible set is empty, this is not feasible and hence not a valid starting point.

Fortunately, we can apply the simplex method to any problem to ascertain whether the feasible set is empty. Furthermore, this test also provides an initial feasible solution from which to initiate the search for an optimal solution.

Consider the following problem.

```
In[53]:= objective = x[1] - x[2] + x[3];
```

```
In[54]:= constraints =
          { 2x[1] -  x[2] + 2x[3] <=  4,
            2x[1] - 3x[2] +  x[3] <= -5,
           -x[1] +  x[2] - 2x[3] <= -1};
```

and $x_i >= 0$.

```
In[55]:= problem=Prepend[StandardLP[constraints],
                 z == objective]
```

```
Out[55]= z == x[1] - x[2] + x[3]

         s[1] == 4 - 2 x[1] + x[2] - 2 x[3]

         s[2] == -5 - 2 x[1] + 3 x[2] - x[3]

         s[3] == -1 + x[1] - x[2] + 2 x[3]
```

Note that the origin is not a feasible solution.

```
In[56]:= constraints /. {x[1] -> 0, x[2] -> 0, x[3] -> 0}
```

```
Out[56]= {True, False, False}
```

If there is no feasible solution, this is because the constraints are too restrictive. We investigate the consistency of the constraints by relaxing them until we find a feasible solution. We can ensure that the feasible set is nonempty by adding a sufficiently large positive quantity a_0 to the right-hand side of the constraints.

```
In[57]:= Relax[ineq_,epsilon_] := ineq /.
            {lhs_ <= rhs_ :> lhs<= rhs + epsilon,
             lhs_ == rhs_ :> lhs == rhs + epsilon}
```

```
In[58]:= Relax[constraints,a[0]]
```

```
Out[58]= {2 x[1] - x[2] + 2 x[3] <= 4 + a[0],
          2 x[1] - 3 x[2] + x[3] <= -5 + a[0],
          -x[1] + x[2] - 2 x[3] <= -1 + a[0]}
```

We can find the minimum value of a_0 which allows a feasible solution by solving the linear programming problem $\min_x a_0$ subject to the relaxed constraints. The original problem is feasible if and only if the minimum perturbation a_0 is zero. Moreover, the optimal solution to the relaxed problem is a feasible solution to the original problem, and provides a suitable starting point for the simplex algorithm.

The relaxed problem is

```
In[59]:= relaxed = Prepend[StandardLP[Relax[constraints,a[0]]],
                   z == -a[0]]
```

```
Out[59]= z == -a[0]

         s[1] == 4 + a[0] - 2 x[1] + x[2] - 2 x[3]

         s[2] == -5 + a[0] - 2 x[1] + 3 x[2] - x[3]

         s[3] == -1 + a[0] + x[1] - x[2] + 2 x[3]
```

We can readily obtain a feasible solution to this problem by pivoting on the perturbation a_0. The most stringent constraint is the one with the most negative intercept. The intercepts of the constraints are

```
In[60]:= Intercept[form_] := If[NumberQ[form],form,0]

In[61]:= Intercept[form_Plus] := Intercept[First @ form]

In[62]:= Rest[relaxed] /. lhs_ == rhs_ :> {lhs,Intercept[rhs]}

Out[62]= {{s[1], 4}, {s[2], -5}, {s[3], -1}}
```

The smallest (most negative) intercept is -5 associated with the second constraint.

```
In[63]:= MinPair[%]

Out[63]= {s[2], -5}
```

A feasible solution to the relaxed constraints can be generated by pivoting on a_0 using the second constraint.

```
In[64]:= Pivot[relaxed,a[0],s[2]]

Out[64]= z == -5 - s[2] - 2 x[1] + 3 x[2] - x[3]

         s[1] == 9 + s[2] - 2 x[2] - x[3]

         a[0] == 5 + s[2] + 2 x[1] - 3 x[2] + x[3]

         s[3] == 4 + s[2] + 3 x[1] - 4 x[2] + 3 x[3]
```

This indicates that the relaxed problem has a feasible solution with $a_0 = 5$ and $x_1 = x_2 = x_3 = 0$. Now we can apply the simplex algorithm to find the minimum feasible value of a_0.

```
In[65]:= phaseI = Simplex[%]

Out[65]= z == -a[0]

         s[1] == 3 + 2 a[0] - s[3] - x[1]
```

```
        8    4 a[0]    s[2]   3 s[3]    x[1]
x[3] == - - ------ + ---- + ------ - ----
        5     5        5       5        5
```

```
        11   3 a[0]   2 s[2]    s[3]   3 x[1]
x[2] == -- - ------ + ------ + ---- + ------
        5     5        5        5       5
```

The minimum value of a_0 is zero, and is achieved where $x_2 = 11/5$ and $x_3 = 8/5$. This is a feasible solution to the original problem, which indicates that the feasible set is not empty and which can serve as the starting point for applying the simplex algorithm to solve the original problem.

The revised constraints (in standard form) are obtained by setting $a_0 = 0$ in the phase I tableau.

In[66]:= **RevisedConstraints = Rest[phaseI] /. a[0]->0**

Out[66]= s[1] == 3 - s[3] - x[1]

```
        8    s[2]   3 s[3]    x[1]
x[3] == - + ---- + ------ - ----
        5    5       5        5
```

```
        11   2 s[2]    s[3]   3 x[1]
x[2] == -- + ------ + ---- + ------
        5    5         5       5
```

which indicates the initial feasible solution. The revised objective function, updated to recognize the tradeoffs at the initial feasible solution is

In[67]:= **RevisedObjective = objective /.**
             Flatten @ (ToRules /@ RevisedConstraints)

```
Out[67]=   3     s[2]   2 s[3]    x[1]
        -(-) - ---- + ------ + ----
         5     5       5        5
```

Together, these give the initial tableau for the original problem, to which the simplex algorithm can be applied. This is called phase II.

In[68]:= **InitialTableau = Prepend[RevisedConstraints,**
                 z == RevisedObjective]

```
Out[68]=        3     s[2]   2 s[3]    x[1]
        z == -(-) - ---- + ------ + ----
              5     5       5        5
```

```
        s[1] == 3 - s[3] - x[1]
```

$$x[3] == -\frac{8}{5} + \frac{s[2]}{5} + \frac{3\,s[3]}{5} - \frac{x[1]}{5}$$

$$x[2] == \frac{11}{5} + \frac{2\,s[2]}{5} + \frac{s[3]}{5} + \frac{3\,x[1]}{5}$$

```
In[69]:= Simplex[InitialTableau]
```

$$Out[69]= \quad z == \frac{3}{5} - \frac{2\,s[1]}{5} - \frac{s[2]}{5} - \frac{x[1]}{5}$$

$$s[3] == 3 - s[1] - x[1]$$

$$x[3] == \frac{17}{5} - \frac{3\,s[1]}{5} + \frac{s[2]}{5} - \frac{4\,x[1]}{5}$$

$$x[2] == \frac{14}{5} - \frac{s[1]}{5} + \frac{2\,s[2]}{5} + \frac{2\,x[1]}{5}$$

The optimal value of $3/5$ is obtained at $(0, 14/5, 17/5)$. We implement this two-stage procedure in the function **LP**.

```
In[70]:= LP[tableau_?TableauQ] := Module[{},
            smallest = MinPair[Rest[tableau] /.
            rhs_ == lhs_ :> {rhs,Intercept[lhs]}];
            If[smallest[[2]] >= 0,     (* origin feasible ? *)
            Simplex[tableau],    (* single phase *)

                        (* 2 phase required *)
            relaxed = Prepend[Relax[Rest[tableau],a[0]],
                    z == -a[0]];
            phaseI = Simplex @
                Pivot[relaxed,a[0],smallest[[1]]];
                If[Intercept[First[phaseI][[2]]]==0,
                        (* feasible? *)
                        (* phaseII *)
                RevisedConstraints = Rest[phaseI] /. a[0]->0;
                RevisedObjective = First[tableau][[2]] /.
                    Flatten @ (ToRules /@ RevisedConstraints) //
                        ExpandAll;
                Simplex @ Prepend[RevisedConstraints,
                    z == RevisedObjective],
                        (* infeasible *)
```

```
                      Print["The problem is infeasible"]
                      ]
                 ]
            ]
```

In[71]:= **LP[problem]**

```
Out[71]=        3   2 s[1]    s[2]    x[1]
           z == - - ------ - ---- - ----
                5     5        5       5


           s[3] == 3 - s[1] - x[1]


                  17   3 s[1]    s[2]   4 x[1]
           x[3] == -- - ------ + ---- - ------
                   5     5        5       5


                  14   s[1]    2 s[2]   2 x[1]
           x[2] == -- - ---- + ------ + ------
                   5     5       5        5
```

As with **Simplex**, we can easily provide an alternative invocation for **LP**.

In[72]:= **LP[objective_,constraints_] :=**
              LP[Prepend[StandardLP[constraints],
                    z == objective]]

In the following problem, the constraints are inconsistent and there is no feasible solution.

In[73]:= **constraints = {x[1] - x[2] <= -1,**
                 -x[1] - x[2] <= -33,
                 2x[1] + x[2] <= 2};
           objective = 3x[1] + x[2];

In[74]:= **LP[objective,constraints]**

```
           The problem is infeasible.
```

Actually, we have brushed over another potential problem. We have implicitly assumed that a_0 will be nonbasic at the solution of phase I. However, if phase I is degenerate, it is possible that a_0 remains basic with the value zero. This implies that, in the penultimate iteration, a_0 was equally as eligible as some other variable as the "critical resource." We need to ensure that a_0 is always driven out of the basis first. We can do this by amending the function **LimitingResource** to select a_0 whenever it is one of the critical resources. This can be achieved elegantly by sorting the expansion ratios prior to selecting the minimum. This will ensure that the artificial variable a_0 always comes before any slack s_i or decision x_j variable.

```
In[75]:= LimitingResource[tableau_?TableauQ,var_] :=
           Module[{ExpansionRatios},
           ExpansionRatios = (Rest[tableau] /.
           {resource_ == (b_ ? NumberQ) + a_. var + x_:>
                         {resource,b/Abs[a]}/; a < 0,
             resource_ == a_. var + x_ :> {resource,0} /; a < 0,
             resource_ == x_   :> {resource,Infinity}});
           If[#[[2]] < Infinity,#[[1]],None] & @
                MinPair[Sort @ ExpansionRatios]]
```

Programming Note: The user should be aware that the natural order of variable names is assumed at this point and avoid any variables that are alphabetically prior to a_0.

1.6.3 Degeneracy and Cycling

Provided an optimal solution exists, is our algorithm guaranteed to find it? Not necessarily. In rare examples, it is possible for the algorithm we have described to become stuck in an infinite loop. Cycling can be prevented by changing the way in which the pivoting variable is selected (amending the function **NextPivot**), at the cost of slower convergence in normal problems [see, for example, Chvátal (1983)]. Cycling is such a rare phenomenon that most computer implementations ignore the possibility.[2]

There we have it. Barring rare examples, the simplex algorithm as implemented here will either find the optimal solution of a maximization problem or demonstrate that no solution exists. Furthermore, the procedure can be extended easily to deal with minimization problems and equality constraints.

1.6.4 Minimization Problems

Because $\min_x f(x) = \max_x -f(x)$, any minimization can be converted into an equivalent maximization problem by reversing the sign of the objective function. Similarly, inequalities of the form $x \geq c$ can be converted into equivalent equations by subtracting a nonnegative surplus variable. For example, consider the problem of minimizing

```
In[76]:= objective =   30 x[1] + 25 x[2] + 20 x[3];
```

subject to

```
In[77]:= constraints = {2 x[1] +   x[2] + 2 x[3] >= 3,
                        2 x[1] + 2 x[2] +   x[3] >= 1,
                          x[1] + 3 x[2] +   x[3] >= 3};
```

---

[2]With rational data, *Mathematica* uses exact or infinite precision arithmetic. This *may* increase the incidence of cycling, because rounding error is thought to mitigate the incidence of cycling when using real arithmetic.

This problem is the *dual* of the production planning example. It is discussed further in the chapter on Sensitivity Analysis (Chapter 2).

We can easily extend the function **StandardLP** to transform $\geq$ inequalities

```
In[78]:= StandardLP[constraints_, labels_List] :=
            Transpose @
              {labels,constraints} /.
            {{i_, lhs_ <= rhs_}:> s[i] == rhs - lhs,
             {i_, lhs_ >= rhs_}:> s[i] == lhs - rhs}
```

```
In[79]:= StandardLP[constraints]
```

```
Out[79]= s[1] == -3 + 2 x[1] + x[2] + 2 x[3]

         s[2] == -1 + 2 x[1] + 2 x[2] + x[3]

         s[3] == -3 + x[1] + 3 x[2] + x[3]
```

Applying the two-phase procedure to the negative of the objective function, the solution of the dual problem is

```
In[80]:= LP[-objective,constraints]
```

```
Out[80]= z == -39 - 7 s[1] - 6 s[3] - 10 x[1]
```

$$x[2] == \frac{3}{5} - \frac{s[1]}{5} + \frac{2\,s[3]}{5}$$

$$s[2] == \frac{7}{5} + \frac{s[1]}{5} + \frac{3\,s[3]}{5} + x[1]$$

$$x[3] == \frac{6}{5} + \frac{3\,s[1]}{5} - \frac{s[3]}{5} - x[1]$$

Note that the optimal solution to the dual problem gives the final shadow prices of the production planning problem. The optimal value of the dual objective function, $39, is equal to the maximum profit of the production planning problem. This is an illustration of the duality theorem of linear programming.

1.6.5 Equalities and Artificial Variables

Often, linear programming problems involve equations as well as inequalities. For example, consider the problem of maximizing

```
In[81]:= objective = x[1] + 3 x[2];
```

subject to two inequalities and two equations.

```
In[82]:= constraints =
         { x[1] +  x[2] +  x[3] <= 10,
          2x[1] +  x[2] - 2x[3] >= 2,
           x[1] + 2x[2]         == 4,
           x[1]         - 2x[3] == -2};
```

One way to handle such problems is to replace every equation with a pair of inequalities as follows.

```
In[83]:= constraints /. lhs_ == rhs_ :> {lhs >= rhs,
                                         lhs <= rhs} //
             Flatten // TableForm
```

```
Out[83]= x[1] + x[2] + x[3] <= 10

         2 x[1] + x[2] - 2 x[3] >= 2

         x[1] + 2 x[2] >= 4

         x[1] + 2 x[2] <= 4

         x[1] - 2 x[3] >= -2

         x[1] - 2 x[3] <= -2
```

and solve as before

```
In[84]:= LP[objective,%]
```

```
Out[84]= z == 4 - s[2] - 2 s[4] - s[6]
```

$$s[1] == 3 - 2\ s[2] - \frac{s[4]}{2} - \frac{5\ s[6]}{2}$$

$$x[3] == 3 + s[2] + \frac{s[4]}{2} + \frac{3\ s[6]}{2}$$

$$x[1] == 4 + 2\ s[2] + s[4] + 2\ s[6]$$

$$s[3] == -s[4]$$

$$s[5] == -s[6]$$

$$x[2] == -s[2] - s[4] - s[6]$$

The optimal solution is $x_1 = 4$, $x_2 = 0$, $x_3 = 3$.

The drawback of this procedure is that it increases the dimensionality of the problem by introducing two slack variables for every equation. A more common approach to handling equations involves replacing these two slack variables with a single variable, called an *artificial variable*, which is allowed to adopt both positive and negative values. The artificial variable is driven to zero during the solution procedure. The variable a_0 introduced previously was an artificial variable. It would be relatively straightforward to amend **LP** to handle additional artificial variables. However, the effort is probably not warranted as in the next chapter we show how to take advantage of *Mathematica*'s inbuilt linear programming facility to obtain the final tableau of a linear programming problem.

Instead, we extend the function **StandardLP** to treat equations as above.

```
In[85]:= StandardLP[constraints_, labels_List] :=
            Transpose @ {labels,constraints} /.
            {{i_, lhs_ <= rhs_}:> s[i] == rhs - lhs,
             {i_, lhs_ >= rhs_}:> s[i] == lhs - rhs,
             {i_, lhs_ == rhs_}:> {sl[i] == rhs - lhs,
                     sg[i] == lhs - rhs}} // Flatten
```

```
In[86]:= StandardLP[constraints]
```

```
Out[86]= s[1] == 10 - x[1] - x[2] - x[3]

         s[2] == -2 + 2 x[1] + x[2] - 2 x[3]

         sl[3] == 4 - x[1] - 2 x[2]

         sg[3] == -4 + x[1] + 2 x[2]

         sl[4] == -2 - x[1] + 2 x[3]

         sg[4] == 2 + x[1] - 2 x[3]
```

```
In[87]:= LP[objective,constraints]
```

$$Out[87]= z == 4 - s[2] - 2\ sl[3] - sl[4]$$

$$s[1] == 3 - 2\ s[2] - \frac{sl[3]}{2} - \frac{5\ sl[4]}{2}$$

$$x[3] == 3 + s[2] + \frac{sl[3]}{2} + \frac{3\ sl[4]}{2}$$

$$sg[3] == -sl[3]$$

```
x[1] == 4 + 2 s[2] + sl[3] + 2 sl[4]

x[2] == -s[2] - sl[3] - sl[4]

sg[4] == -sl[4]
```

1.7 Acknowledgments

I gratefully acknowledge the assistance of John George, Department of Management, University of Canterbury in negotiating the thickets of linear programming. He is of course completely exonerated for any breach in my defenses. I also acknowledge my considerable debt to the book by Vašek Chvátal (1983), whose refreshing approach to linear programming illuminated my path, and to John Novak, Bill Sharkey, and Troels Petersen for improvements to the text and the code.

1.8 References

Carter, M. 1993. "Cooperative games." In *Economic and Financial Modeling with Mathematica*. H. Varian, Ed. New York, Springer-Verlag.

Chvátal, V. 1983. *Linear Programming*. San Francisco, Freeman.

Dorfman, R., P. A. Samuelson, and R. M. Solow. 1958. *Linear Programming and Economic Analysis*. New York, McGraw-Hill.

Franklin, J. 1980. *Undergraduate Texts in Mathematics: Methods of Mathematical Economics—Linear and Nonlinear Programming, Fixed Point Theorems*. New York, Springer-Verlag.

Lemke, C. E. and J. T. Howson. 1964. "Equilibrium points of bimatrix games." *SIAM Journal of Applied Mathematics*, **12**, 413–423.

Press, W. H., S. A. Teukolsky, W. T. Vetterling, et al. 1992. *Numerical Recipes in C: The Art of Scientific Computing*, 2nd ed. Cambridge, Cambridge University Press.

Strum, J. E. 1972. *Introduction to Linear Programming*. San Francisco, Holden-Day.

Wilson, R. 1992. "Computing simple stable equilibria." *Econometrica*, **60**, 1039–1070.

2 Linear Programming with *Mathematica:* Sensitivity Analysis

Michael Carter

2.1 Introduction

We describe a package designed to supplement *Mathematica*'s linear programming facility. Building on the foundation laid in the previous chapter, we first develop a set of tools for sensitivity analysis of the optimal solution. In order to utilize *Mathematica*'s efficient linear programming routine, we then develop a function that can deduce the final tableau from the output of `ConstrainedMax`.

With this function, the package can be applied to substantive problems, relying on *Mathematica*'s native code for intensive computation. To illustrate, we apply the package to analyze a classic problem of efficient nutrition.

The data in any real optimization problem are seldom known with absolute precision. Consequently, it is important to be able to estimate the sensitivity of the optimal solution to changes in the specification of the problem. Fortunately, it is possible to deduce a great deal about the sensitivity of the optimal solution to a linear programming problem from the final tableau. This is known as *sensitivity analysis*.

In the previous chapter we showed how linear programming problems can be solved using the simplex algorithm. The result is called the *final tableau*. In this chapter we build on this foundation, developing tools for sensitivity analysis. We first explore the anatomy of the final tableau, outlining the range of information which it embodies. We also show how this information is related to the solution of a related linear programming problem, called the *dual*. In following sections, we analyze more systematically the sensitivity of the optimal solution to changes in the parameters of the problem. First we elaborate the role of shadow prices in the analysis of changes in resource availability and derive bounds on their validity. Then we explore the sensitivity of the optimal solution to changes in the objective function.

Although the previous chapter outlined a complete implementation of the simplex algorithm, it was intended for pedagogical rather than computational purposes. *Mathematica*'s built-in linear programming facility is significantly more efficient at solving substantive problems, but its output is too concise to allow for sensitivity analysis. Therefore, in Section 2.5, we show how the final tableau can be reconstructed from the output of *Mathematica*'s built-in linear programming facility. The chapter concludes with a sensitivity analysis of a classic problem of nutrition, which was first posed by George Stigler before the simplex algorithm was available.

The functions developed in the preceding chapter are defined in the package **LinearProgramming**, which is included on the accompanying disk.

```
In[1]:=  <<c:/usr/lp/LinearProgramming.m
```

2.2   Interpreting the Final Tableau

The production planning problem introduced in the previous chapter required maximizing the function

```
In[2]:=  profit = 3x[b] + x[c] + 3x[d];
```

subject to the constraints

```
In[3]:=  constraints =
         { 2x[b] + 2x[c] +  x[d] <= 30,
            x[b] + 2x[c] + 3x[d] <= 25,
           2x[b] +  x[c] +  x[d] <= 20
           };
```

The optimal solution can be computed using the function **LP**, which yields the final tableau.

```
In[4]:=  finalTableau = LP[profit,
             StandardLP[constraints,{f,l,m}]]

Out[4]=              3 s[l]   6 s[m]   7 x[c]
            z == 39 - ------ - ------ - ------
                         5        5        5

            s[f] == 10 + s[m] - x[c]
```

```
                   2 s[l]    s[m]    3 x[c]
     x[d] == 6  -  ------  +  ----  -  ------
                     5         5        5


                   s[l]    3 s[m]    x[c]
     x[b] == 7  +  ----  -  ------  -  ----
                    5         5        5
```

The final tableau not only specifies the optimal solution to a particular problem, it also contains a wealth of information regarding the sensitivity of the optimal solution to changes in the parameters of the problem. It indicates whether the optimal solution is unique, and implicitly contains the solution of a host of related linear programming problems. In this section we explore the range of information contained in the final tableau.

Those variables that appear on the left hand of the final tableau are called *basic* variables. The right-hand side variables are the *nonbasic* variables.

```
In[5]:=  BasicVariables[tableau_?TableauQ] := First /@
            Rest[tableau]


In[6]:=  basic = BasicVariables[finalTableau]


Out[6]=  {s[f], x[d], x[b]}


In[7]:=  NonbasicVariables[tableau_] := Union @@
            (Variables[#[[2]]]& /@ tableau)


In[8]:=  nonbasic=NonbasicVariables[finalTableau]


Out[8]=  {s[l], s[m], x[c]}
```

The nonbasic variables are all zero at the optimal solution. Each belongs to a binding constraint—either a resource constraint ($s_i = 0$) or a nonnegativity constraint ($x_j = 0$). The basic variables are typically positive at the optimal solution. If not, that is, if one or more of the basic variables are zero, the solution is called *degenerate*. A degenerate solution indicates that one or more of the constraints are redundant in the sense that they could be relaxed without changing the solution. The values of the objective function and the basic variable can be highlighted by evaluating the final tableau with the nonbasic variables set to zero.

```
In[9]:=  SetAttributes[Zero,Listable];
         Zero[x_] := x -> 0


In[10]:= solution = finalTableau /. Zero[nonbasic]
```

```
Out[10]= z == 39

         s[f] == 10

         x[d] == 6

         x[b] == 7
```

The optimal plan produces 7 bookcases and 6 desks for a total profit of $39. The optimal values of the slack variables s_i measure the utilization of resources. In this case the optimal plan leaves spare finishing capacity of 10 units, but fully utilizes all the labor and machining capacity (because $s_l = s_m = 0$).

The first row of the final tableau is the revised objective function, which embodies the economic tradeoffs that pertain at the optimal solution. The coefficients of the nonbasic variables indicate the shadow prices of the binding constraints.

```
In[11]:= RevisedObjective = First[finalTableau]
```

$$Out[11]= \quad z == 39 - \frac{3 \, s[l]}{5} - \frac{6 \, s[m]}{5} - \frac{7 \, x[c]}{5}$$

We augment the definition of **ShadowPrices** to extract the shadow prices of the nonbasic variables from the final tableau.

```
In[12]:= ShadowPrices[tableau_?TableauQ] :=
            ShadowPrices[First[tableau][[2]]]
```

```
In[13]:= ShadowPrices[finalTableau]
```

$$Out[13]= \quad \left\{ \left\{ s[l], \ \frac{3}{5} \right\}, \ \left\{ s[m], \ \frac{6}{5} \right\}, \ \left\{ x[c], \ \frac{7}{5} \right\} \right\}$$

Shadow prices measure the economic consequences of marginal changes in resources.[1] The shadow prices of basic variables are always zero.

```
In[14]:= ShadowPrice[tableau_?TableauQ,var_] :=
            ShadowPrice[First[tableau][[2]],var]
```

```
In[15]:= ShadowPrice[finalTableau,s[f]]
```

```
Out[15]= 0
```

---

[1]Shadow prices may not be uniquely defined at degenerate solutions, taking different values depending upon whether the constraint is tightened or relaxed.

To determine the shadow prices of a set of variables, we define

```
In[16]:= ShadowPrices[tableau_?TableauQ,vars_List] :=
            {#,ShadowPrice[First[tableau][[2]],#]}& /@ vars
```

For example, the shadow prices of the resource constraints are

```
In[17]:= ShadowPrices[finalTableau,{s[f],s[l],s[m]}]
```

$$Out[17]= \{\{s[f], 0\}, \{s[l], \tfrac{3}{5}\}, \{s[m], \tfrac{6}{5}\}\}$$

The significance of the shadow prices is that they enable us to evaluate the impact of hypothetical changes in the parameters of the problem without solving the problem afresh. The reason was elucidated when discussing the simplex algorithm in the previous chapter. The revised objective function fully embodies the economic ramifications of all the technological constraints viewed from the perspective of the optimal solution. In this sense, the final tableau summarizes the solution of a whole family of related optimization problems. We elaborate this point in the following sections.

The changes in resource constraints may not be hypothetical. The marginal value of an additional hour of labor supply is $3/5. Consequently, if more labor can be obtained for less than an additional $3/5 per hour, it would be profitable to purchase extra labor. Similarly, if machining capacity can be let for more than $6/5, the furniture maker would increase total profit by reducing her own production and leasing some capacity. Shadow prices are the imputed values of the resources in terms of the objective function, and can be directly compared with market prices. The producer should buy those resources whose shadow price (value to her) is greater than the market price and sell those resources that the market values more highly than her own production opportunities.

The shadow prices can also be used to evaluate the profitability of new activities. Suppose that the furniture maker is contemplating adding a new product, an executive desk, to her range. Each executive desk would require 2 hours each of machining and finishing and 3 hours of labor. The economic cost of producing an executive desk (with fixed resources) is the value of the displaced production of bookcases and ordinary desks, which can be measured by the shadow prices of these resources. This cost is

$$\text{Cost of executive desk} = 2 \times 0 + 3\left(\frac{3}{5}\right) + 2\left(\frac{6}{5}\right) = \frac{21}{5}.$$

The executive desk will only be worthwhile provided it can be sold for a profit of at least $21/5 = \$4.20$.

The shadow prices attached to the resource constraints are in fact the solutions of a related linear programming problem called the *dual*. The dual of the production planning example poses the problem of finding the minimum price at which the furniture manufacturer would be willing to sell her resources (finishing, machining, and labor) given that the opportunity cost is determined by their alternative use in the production of bookcases, chairs, and desks for sale.

Formally specified, the dual of the production planning example is

$$\min 30x_1 + 25x_2 + 20x_3$$

$$\text{subject to } 2x_1 + x_2 + 2x_3 \geq 3$$

$$2x_1 + 2x_2 + x_3 \geq 1$$

$$x_1 + 3x_2 + x_3 \geq 3.$$

The solution represents the imputed or shadow prices of the resource. We solved this problem using LP in the section on minimization problems in the previous chapter, obtaining the solution $x_1 = 0, x_2 = 3/5, x_3 = 6/5$. The shadow prices of finishing, machining, and labor are $0, 3/5$, and $6/5$, respectively, which exactly correspond to the shadow prices derived from the original production planning example (the *primal*). Furthermore, we note that the minimal value obtained for the dual problem was \$39, which is exactly equal to the maximal profit obtained for the primal problem.

These observations illustrate the fundamental *duality theorem* of linear programming. If the primal linear programming problem has an optimal solution, then so does its dual and the optimal value of the objective function is the same for both problems. Furthermore, the optimal values of the decision variables in the dual problem are equal to the shadow prices of the resource constraints at the optimal solution of the primal problem. Therefore the final tableau for the primal problem includes the optimal solution of the related dual problem.

For a standard maximization problem, shadow prices are always nonnegative at the optimal solution. (Recall that the simplex algorithm terminates when the shadow prices are nonnegative. A negative shadow price indicates the possibility of a profitable substitution, by tightening a binding constraint.) The shadow prices of basic variables are always zero. However, it is not necessary that the shadow prices of nonbasic variables are strictly positive. A zero shadow price on a nonbasic variable indicates that the optimal solution is not unique, because that variable can be "pivoted" into the solution without changing the value of the objective function.

To illustrate, suppose the price of chairs is increased to $2(2/5)$. The original production plan of 7 bookcases and 6 desks remains optimal.

```
In[18]:= Simplex[3 x[b] + (12/5) x[c] + 3 x[d],
             StandardLP[constraints,{f,l,m}]]
```

```
Out[18]=              3 s[l]    6 s[m]
           z == 39 - ------ - ------
                        5         5

           s[f] == 10 + s[m] - x[c]
```

$$x[d] == 6 - \frac{2\,s[l]}{5} + \frac{s[m]}{5} - \frac{3\,x[c]}{5}$$

$$x[b] == 7 + \frac{s[l]}{5} - \frac{3\,s[m]}{5} - \frac{x[c]}{5}$$

However, the absence of the x_c from the revised objective function indicates that there are multiple optimal solutions. At this price, desks and chairs are equally profitable. Substituting chairs for desks reveals another optimal solution, producing 5 bookcases and 10 chairs. This substitution can be made by pivoting.

$In[19]:=$ **Pivot[%,x[c]]**

$Out[19]=$

$$z == 39 - \frac{3\,s[l]}{5} - \frac{6\,s[m]}{5}$$

$$x[c] == 10 - s[f] + s[m]$$

$$x[d] == \frac{3\,s[f]}{5} - \frac{2\,s[l]}{5} - \frac{2\,s[m]}{5}$$

$$x[b] == 5 + \frac{s[f]}{5} + \frac{s[l]}{5} - \frac{4\,s[m]}{5}$$

This is another example of degenerate optimal solution, in which the basic variable x_d is zero. Any convex combination of this and the previous solution will also be optimal.

$In[20]:=$ **% /. Zero[NonbasicVariables[%]]**

$Out[20]=$ z == 39

     x[c] == 10

     x[d] == 0

     x[b] == 5

In summary, the intercepts of the equations in the final tableau indicate the optimal value of the objective function and the values of the basic variables at which the optimum is obtained. The coefficients of the nonbasic variables in the first equation (the revised objective function) are the shadow prices, which indicate the economic consequences of marginal changes in the quantity of resources. Nonbasic variables with zero shadow prices indicate multiple optimal solutions. As we show in the following, the coefficients of the nonbasic variables in the remaining equations (the revised constraints) indicate how these consequences are obtained.

The final tableau is a very compact representation of the optimal solution to a linear programming problem. It embodies all the economic and technological tradeoffs that are pertinent at the optimal solution. It lists the maximal value of the objective function, and the values of the decision variables necessary to achieve this maximum. It also reveals the degree of utilization of resources, highlighting any unused capacity. It indicates whether the optimal solution is unique. The shadow prices appraise the imputed values of limited resources, assessing the profitability of any sale or purchase of additional resources. The tableau also indicates the optimal response to any change in resources. In this sense, it summarizes the solution to a whole family of related optimization problems. It is truly pregnant with information.

For future use, it is convenient to represent the final tableau as a set of transformation rules.

```
In[21]:= rules = ToRules /@ Rest[finalTableau] // Flatten


Out[21]= {s[f] -> 10 + s[m] - x[c],

                       2 s[l]    s[m]    3 x[c]
          x[d] -> 6 - ------ + ---- - ------,
                         5        5       5

                     s[l]    3 s[m]    x[c]
          x[b] -> 7 + ---- - ------ - ----}
                       5        5       5
```

2.3 Sensitivity with Respect to Resources

In this section, we examine more closely the sensitivity of the optimal solution to changes in the resource constraints. The shadow prices measure the impact on profit of changes in resource availability. For example, the shadow price of 3/5 on the labor constraint means that an additional hour of labor would increase profit by $3/5. To verify this, let us re-solve the production planning problem with an additional 5 hours of labor.

```
In[22]:= Simplex[profit,StandardLP[
             { 2x[b] + 2x[c] +  x[d] <= 30,
                x[b] + 2x[c] + 3x[d] <= 30,
               2x[b] +  x[c] +  x[d] <= 20
             },{f,1,m}]] /. Zero[nonbasic]
```

```
Out[22]= z  ==  42

         s[f]  ==  10

         x[d]  ==  8

         x[b]  ==  6
```

An additional 5 hours of labor would allow the furniture maker to produce 6 bookcases and 8 desks for a total profit of $42. Compared to the previous plan of 7 bookcases and 6 desks, this involves substituting 2 desks for 1 bookcase, increasing total profit by $3. Each additional hour of labor is worth $3/5 profit.

Similarly, an additional 5 units of machining time would allow the furniture maker to substitute 3 bookcases for a desk, increasing total profit by $6. Additional units of machining are worth $6/5 each. Again, this can be confirmed by re-solving the problem.

```
In[23]:= Simplex[profit,StandardLP[
              { 2x[b] + 2x[c] +  x[d] <= 30,
                 x[b] + 2x[c] + 3x[d] <= 25,
                2x[b] +  x[c] +  x[d] <= 25
                },{f,l,m}]] /. Zero[nonbasic]


Out[23]= z  ==  45

         s[f]  ==  5

         x[d]  ==  5

         x[b]  ==  10
```

The significance of the shadow price is that it indicates the impact on profit of a change in resources without re-solving the problem. We can also deduce how this is achieved, by evaluating the final tableau while allowing the appropriate slack variable to deviate from zero.

For example, increasing the labor resource is equivalent to allowing the slack variable s_l to assume negative values. Letting $\Delta_l = -s_l$ denote the increase in labor resources, we find that

```
In[24]:= finalTableau /. s[l] -> -Delta[l] /. Zero[nonbasic]


Out[24]=                3 Delta[l]
            z  ==  39 + ----------
                            5

         s[f]  ==  10
```

$$x[d] == 6 + \frac{2\ Delta[1]}{5}$$

$$x[b] == 7 - \frac{Delta[1]}{5}$$

Each additional unit of labor will increase profit by \$3/5, increase the number of desks by 2/5, and decrease the number of bookcases by 1/5. Consequently, an additional 5 hours of labor would allow

```
In[25]:= % /. Delta[1] -> 5
```

```
Out[25]= z == 42
```

$$s[f] == 10$$

$$x[d] == 8$$

$$x[b] == 6$$

which is consistent with the preceding result obtained by re-solving the production planning problem with a labor supply of 30 hours. In this way, we can estimate the impact of hypothetical changes in resources without re-solving the problem. For large problems, this can represent a considerable saving in computation.

More importantly, the shadow prices indicate which resource constraints are most critical. It is worthwhile devoting the greatest effort towards relaxing those constraints which carry the highest shadow price. Similarly, the decision maker should attempt to guard against disruption in the supply of the critical resources, and possibly look for alternative products or processes that reduce reliance on critical resources.

Typically, shadow prices have a limited range of validity, which can also be deduced from the final tableau. Just previously, we assessed the impact on the basic variables of small changes in labor supply, namely,

```
In[26]:= Rest[finalTableau] /. s[1] -> -Delta[1] /.
            Zero[nonbasic]
```

```
Out[26]= s[f] == 10
```

$$x[d] == 6 + \frac{2\ Delta[1]}{5}$$

$$x[b] == 7 - \frac{Delta[1]}{5}$$

An *optimal* response to an increase in labor supply $\Delta_l > 0$ has no effect on the utilization of finishing capacity, and requires the substitution of desks for bookcases. We observe that this substitution can profitably continue until the quantity of bookcases is reduced to zero, that is, while $\Delta_l \leq 35$. Similarly, an optimal response to a decrease in labor supply ($\Delta_l < 0$) requires substituting bookcases for desks, which substitution can profitably continue until it reduces the production of desks to zero, that is, while $\Delta_l \geq -15$. Therefore the range over which the shadow price of labor supply is valid is $-15 \leq \Delta_l \leq 35$, where Δ_l is the change in the supply of labor.

Consider a similar calculation for the machining constraint. The optimal response for small changes is

```
In[27]:= Rest[finalTableau] /. s[m] -> -Delta[m] /.
             Zero[nonbasic]
```

```
Out[27]= s[f] == 10 - Delta[m]

                    Delta[m]
         x[d]  == 6 - --------
                       5

                    3 Delta[m]
         x[b]  == 7 + ----------
                        5
```

This response will remain optimal provided it does not violate any of the other (resource and nonnegativity) constraints, that is, provided the basic variables remain nonnegative.

```
In[28]:= bounds=Cases[%,
            _ == b_  + a_. Delta[m]  :>
                 Sign[a] Delta[m] >= -b/Abs[a] ]
```

```
Out[28]=                                              35
         {-Delta[m] >= -10, -Delta[m] >= -30, Delta[m] >= -(--)}
                                                             3
```

Using the following function to simplify the inequalities

```
In[29]:= SimplifyInequalities[ineq_List,var_] :=
            Max @ Join[Cases[ineq, var >= a_ -> a],
                   Cases[ineq, -var <= a_ -> -a]] <=
            var <=
            Min @ Join[Cases[ineq, var <= a_ -> a],
                   Cases[ineq, -var >= a_ -> -a]]
```

the valid range is

```
In[30]:= SimplifyInequalities[bounds,Delta[m]]
```

```
Out[30]=     35
         -(--) <= Delta[m] <= 10
          3
```

We summarize this facility in the function **ShadowPriceRange**.

```
In[31]:= ShadowPriceRange[tableau_?TableauQ,s_[i_]] :=
            SimplifyInequalities[
                Select[Rest[tableau] /. s[i] -> -Delta[i] /.
                    Zero[NonbasicVariables[tableau]],
                !FreeQ[#,Delta[i]]&] /.
                _ == b_  + a_. Delta[i]   :>
                        Sign[a] Delta[i] >= -b/Abs[a],
            Delta[i]]
```

```
In[32]:= ShadowPriceRange[finalTableau,s[1]]
```

```
Out[32]= -15 <= Delta[1] <= 35
```

```
In[33]:= ShadowPriceRange[finalTableau,s[m]]
```

```
Out[33]=    35
         -(--) <= Delta[m] <= 10
           3
```

The preceding applies to the shadow prices of binding constraints. For nonbinding constraints (basic variables), the determination of the range of validity of the shadow prices is more straightforward. A surplus resource has a shadow price of zero, which is the imputed value of additional resources. The shadow price will remain zero as long as the constraint remains nonbinding, that is, provided the slack capacity is not reduced to zero.

In the production planning example, there is surplus finishing capacity of 10 units.

```
In[34]:= Cases[Rest[finalTableau] /. s[f] -> -Delta[f] /.
                    Zero[nonbasic],
                -Delta[f] == rhs_ :>  Delta[f] >= -rhs]
```

```
Out[34]= {Delta[f] >= -10}
```

```
In[35]:= SimplifyInequalities[%,Delta[f]]
```

```
Out[35]= -10 <= Delta[f] <= Infinity
```

Consequently, the shadow price of finishing capacity will remain zero for all increases in finishing capacity and any decreases in capacity of less than 10 units. That is, the range of validity of the shadow price of finishing capacity is $-10 \le \Delta_f \le \infty$. We extend the function **ShadowPriceRange** to deal with basic variables.

```
In[36]:= ShadowPriceRange[tableau_?TableauQ,s_[i_]] :=
            SimplifyInequalities[
                Select[Rest[tableau] /. s[i] -> -Delta[i] /.
                    Zero[NonbasicVariables[tableau]],
                !FreeQ[#,Delta[i]]&] /.
                {-Delta[i] == b_ :> Delta[i] >= -b,    (* basic *)
                     _ == b_ + a_. Delta[i] :> (* nonbasic *)
                        Sign[a] Delta[i] >= -b/Abs[a]},
            Delta[i]]
```

```
In[37]:= ShadowPriceRange[finalTableau,s[f]]
```

```
Out[37]= -10 <= Delta[f] <= Infinity
```

The function **SensitivityAnalysis** computes the shadow price and range of a given variable.

```
In[38]:= SensitivityAnalysis[tableau_?TableauQ,s_[i_]] :=
            {s[i],ShadowPrice[tableau,s[i]],
                ShadowPriceRange[tableau,s[i]]}
```

```
In[39]:= SensitivityAnalysis[finalTableau,s[f]]
```

```
Out[39]= {s[f], 0, -10 <= Delta[f] <= Infinity}
```

Provided we adhere to the convention of using $s[i]$ to denote slack variables, we can extend the domain of **SensitivityAnalysis** to compute the shadow prices and ranges of all slack variables.

```
In[40]:= SensitivityAnalysis[tableau_?TableauQ] :=
            SensitivityAnalysis[tableau,#]& /@
            Cases[Join[BasicVariables[tableau],
                NonbasicVariables[tableau]],s[i_]]
```

```
In[41]:= SensitivityAnalysis[finalTableau] // TableForm
```

```
Out[41]= s[f]   0    -10 <= Delta[f] <= Infinity

                3
                -
         s[1]   5    -15 <= Delta[1] <= 35

                6      35
                -    -(--) <= Delta[m] <= 10
         s[m]   5       3
```

It is important to note that these ranges are only valid for changes in one constraint at a time. Although the shadow prices are valid for marginal changes in more than one constraint, computation of the range of validity for simultaneous changes requires further calculation.

2.4   Sensitivity with Respect to Prices

In the production planning example, no chairs are produced because they are not sufficiently profitable. How much would the profitability of chairs have to rise to make their production worthwhile? We can address this question by varying the profit margin of chairs. For example, if the net profit of chairs becomes $1 + \Delta_c$, the profit function is

```
In[42]:= Deltaprofit = 3 x[b] + (1 + Delta[c]) x[c] + 3 x[d]

Out[42]= 3 x[b] + (1 + Delta[c]) x[c] + 3 x[d]
```

At the current optimal production plan, the revised objective function is

```
In[43]:= RevisedObjective = Collect[Deltaprofit /.
            rules,nonbasic]

Out[43]=        3 s[l]   6 s[m]         7
          39 - ------ - ------ + (-(-) + Delta[c]) x[c]
                  5        5           5
```

This reveals that production of chairs will not be profitable provided the coefficient of x_c is negative. Alternatively, production of chairs is not profitable provided the shadow price of chairs is positive, that is, $\Delta_c \leq 7/5$.

```
In[44]:= ShadowPrice[RevisedObjective,x[c]]

Out[44]= 7
         - - Delta[c]
         5
```

The net profit of chairs would have to rise to $1 + (7/5) = 2(2/5)$ for their production to be profitable. This could be brought about either with an increase in their selling price or a decrease in their cost.

We can verify this conclusion by solving the production planning problem with different profit margins for chairs. For example, doubling the net profit of chairs does not change the optimal solution.

```
In[45]:= Simplex[3 x[b] + 2 x[c] + 3 x[d],
            StandardLP[constraints,{f,l,m}]]
```

$Out[45]=$
$$z == 39 - \frac{3\ s[l]}{5} - \frac{6\ s[m]}{5} - \frac{2\ x[c]}{5}$$

$$s[f] == 10 + s[m] - x[c]$$

$$x[d] == 6 - \frac{2\ s[l]}{5} + \frac{s[m]}{5} - \frac{3\ x[c]}{5}$$

$$x[b] == 7 + \frac{s[l]}{5} - \frac{3\ s[m]}{5} - \frac{x[c]}{5}$$

However, at a net profit of $3, chairs become more profitable than desks. Again, the solution is degenerate.

$In[46]:=$ **Simplex[3 x[b] + 3 x[c] + 3 x[d],**
              StandardLP[constraints,{f,l,m}]]

$Out[46]=$
$$z == 45 - \frac{3\ s[f]}{5} - \frac{3\ s[l]}{5} - \frac{3\ s[m]}{5}$$

$$x[c] == 10 - s[f] + s[m]$$

$$x[d] == \frac{3\ s[f]}{5} - \frac{2\ s[l]}{5} - \frac{2\ s[m]}{5}$$

$$x[b] == 5 + \frac{s[f]}{5} + \frac{s[l]}{5} - \frac{4\ s[m]}{5}$$

Similarly, we might ask how much the price of desks would have to fall (or marginal costs rise) to render their production unprofitable. Letting Δ_d denote the change in the net profit of desks, the profit function is

$In[47]:=$ **Deltaprofit = 3 x[b] + x[c] + (3 + Delta[d]) x[d]**

$Out[47]=$ 3 x[b] + x[c] + (3 + Delta[d]) x[d]

and the revised objective function is

$In[48]:=$ **RevisedObjective = Collect[Deltaprofit /.**
              rules,nonbasic]

```
Out[48]=                                  3     2 Delta[d]
           39 + 6 Delta[d] + (-(-) - ----------) s[l] +
                                  5          5

                  6     Delta[d]              7     3 Delta[d]
           (-(-) + --------) s[m] + (-(-) - ----------) x[c]
             5        5                 5          5
```

```
In[49]:= ShadowPrices[RevisedObjective]
```

```
Out[49]=                                  3     2 Delta[d]
           {{Delta[d], -6}, {s[l], - + ----------},
                                   5        5

                  6     Delta[d]              7     3 Delta[d]
           {s[m], - - --------}, {x[c], - + ----------}}
                  5       5                  5        5
```

The first component (Δ_d, -6) indicates the direct effect on profit of a change in the price of desks. At the optimal production of 6 desks, every \$1 increase in the price of desks increases profit by \$6. The remaining terms can be interpreted as follows. Whatever the change Δ_d in the net profit of desks, the production plan $(7, 0, 6)$ remains optimal provided all these shadow prices are positive. Inspection reveals this will be true provided $-3/2 \leq \Delta_d \leq 6$. Let us program that evaluation.

First we select those shadow prices that depend upon Δ_d and convert them into inequalities, which can be simplified by the function SimplifyInequalities.

```
In[50]:= Cases[ShadowPrices[RevisedObjective],
              {_,b_ + a_. Delta[d]}  :> Sign[a] Delta[d] >=
              -b/Abs[a] ]
```

```
Out[50]=                 3                                            7
           {Delta[d] >= -(-), -Delta[d] >= -6, Delta[d] >= -(-)}
                         2                                      3
```

```
In[51]:= SimplifyInequalities[%,Delta[d]]
```

```
Out[51]=   3
           -(-) <= Delta[d] <= 6
            2
```

We summarize this facility in the function PriceRange.

```
In[52]:= PriceRange[tableau_?TableauQ,objective_,x_[i_]] :=
         Module[{RevisedObjective},
         RevisedObjective =
           Collect[objective /.
           a_. x[i] -> (a + Delta[i]) x[i] /.
```

```
                     (ToRules /@ Rest[tableau] // Flatten),
                     NonbasicVariables[tableau]];
             SimplifyInequalities[Cases[ShadowPrices[
                 RevisedObjective], {_,b_ + a_. Delta[i]}  :>
                 Sign[a] Delta[i] >= -b/Abs[a] ],
                 Delta[i]]
             ]
```

To determine the sensitivity to price changes, we have to know the original objective function, which was

```
In[53]:= objective = 3 x[b] + x[c] + 3 x[d]

Out[53]= 3 x[b] + x[c] + 3 x[d]

In[54]:= PriceRange[finalTableau,objective,x[d]]

Out[54]=    3
         -(-) <= Delta[d] <= 6
            2
```

To verify this conclusion, observe that increasing the profit margin of desks by $5 to $8 does not change the optimal production plan.

```
In[55]:= Simplex[3 x[b] +  x[c] + 8 x[d],
             StandardLP[constraints,{f,1,m}]]

Out[55]=              13 s[l]   s[m]    22 x[c]
          z == 69 - ------- - ---- - -------
                        5        5        5

          s[f] == 10 + s[m] - x[c]

                     2 s[l]   s[m]    3 x[c]
          x[d] == 6 - ------ + ---- - ------
                        5        5        5

                     s[l]   3 s[m]   x[c]
          x[b] == 7 + ---- - ------ - ----
                        5        5       5
```

However, if the net profit of desks falls by 50%, it is just as profitable to concentrate on bookcases alone.

```
In[56]:= Simplex[3 x[b] +  x[c] +  (3/2) x[d],
             StandardLP[constraints,{f,1,m}]]
```

```
Out[56]=                3 s[m]    x[c]
              z == 30 - ------ - ----
                          2        2

              s[f] == 10 + s[m] - x[c]

                           s[m]    3 x[c]    5 x[d]
              s[l] == 15 + ---- - ------ - ------
                            2        2         2

                           s[m]    x[c]    x[d]
              x[b] == 10 - ---- - ---- - ----
                            2       2       2
```

although the previous plan is equally profitable.

In[57]:= **Pivot[%,x[d]]**

```
Out[57]=                3 s[m]    x[c]
              z == 30 - ------ - ----
                          2        2

              s[f] == 10 + s[m] - x[c]

                          2 s[l]    s[m]    3 x[c]
              x[d] == 6 - ------ + ---- - ------
                            5        5        5

                          s[l]    3 s[m]    x[c]
              x[b] == 7 + ---- - ------ - ----
                           5        5        5
```

With a lower profit margin, desks are not profitable.

In line with the facilities developed in the previous section, we extend the function **SensitivityAnalysis** to tabulate the net profit and applicable range of any decision variable x_i.

In[58]:= **SensitivityAnalysis[tableau_?TableauQ,objective_Plus,**
         x_[i_]] := {x[i], Coefficient[objective,x[i]],
              PriceRange[tableau,objective,x[i]]}

In[59]:= **SensitivityAnalysis[finalTableau,objective,x[d]]**

```
Out[59]=                  3
              {x[d], 3, -(-) <= Delta[d] <= 6}
                        2
```

Its domain can then be extended to cover all the variables in the problem.

```
In[60]:= SensitivityAnalysis[tableau_?TableauQ,objective_Plus] :=
         Join[SensitivityAnalysis[tableau,objective,#]& /@
         Variables[objective],
           SensitivityAnalysis[tableau,#]& /@
         Cases[Join[BasicVariables[tableau],
           NonbasicVariables[tableau]],s[i_]]]
```

The function **SensitivityAnalysis** extracts from the final tableau the net profits associated with each decision variable, the shadow price of each resource constraint, and their respective ranges of validity.

```
In[61]:= SensitivityAnalysis[finalTableau,objective] //
         TableForm
```

$$Out[61]= \quad x[b] \quad 3 \quad -2 <= Delta[b] <= 3$$

$$x[c] \quad 1 \quad -Infinity <= Delta[c] <= -\frac{7}{5}$$

$$x[d] \quad 3 \quad -(\frac{3}{2}) <= Delta[d] <= 6$$

$$s[f] \quad 0 \quad -10 <= Delta[f] <= Infinity$$

$$s[l] \quad \frac{3}{5} \quad -15 <= Delta[l] <= 35$$

$$s[m] \quad \frac{6}{5} \quad -(\frac{35}{3}) <= Delta[m] <= 10$$

This does not exhaust the information that can potentially be extracted from the final tableau. Before leaving this topic, we briefly outline some of the ways in which sensitivity analysis could be extended. We could compute the impact of changes in the technology, that is, in the resource coefficients of the various activities. For example, what would be the effect on the optimal solution if the labor required for producing a desk was reduced from 3 to 2 hours? We could also consider the impact of multiple changes. What would be the impact of a simultaneous rise in the price of desks and chairs? What would be the effect of adding an additional shift, increasing finishing, machining, and labor capacity simultaneously? All these questions could be addressed utilizing information in the final tableau.

2.5   Computing the Final Tableau

Although the preceding discussion presents a complete implementation of the simplex algorithm for solving linear programming problems, it is not the most efficient way of doing so. Fortunately, *Mathematica* contains built-in functions for linear programming—**ConstrainedMax**, **ConstrainedMin**, and **LinearProgramming**. However, the output from these built-in functions is brief and concise. In this section, we show how the output of the built-in functions can be mined to yield the final tableau and hence all the sensitivity information that can be deduced from this tableau.

The usage message for **ConstrainedMax** reads

```
In[62]:= ?ConstrainedMax
```

ConstrainedMax[f, {inequalities}, {x, y, ...}] finds the global
    maximum of f in the domain specified by the inequalities. The
    variables x, y, ... are all assumed to be non-negative.

Let us apply this function to the production planning example which involved maximizing

```
In[63]:= profit = 3x[b] + x[c] + 3x[d];
```

subject to the

```
In[64]:= constraints =
        { 2x[b] + 2x[c] +  x[d] <= 30,
           x[b] + 2x[c] + 3x[d] <= 25,
          2x[b] +  x[c] +  x[d] <= 20
          };
```

and $x_i \geq 0$.

In reconstructing the final tableau, it is more convenient to apply **ConstrainedMax** to the standard form.

```
In[65]:= SFconstraints = StandardLP[constraints,{f,l,m}]
```

```
Out[65]= s[f] == 30 - 2 x[b] - 2 x[c] - x[d]

         s[l] == 25 - x[b] - 2 x[c] - 3 x[d]

         s[m] == 20 - 2 x[b] - x[c] - x[d]
```

To find the variables, we extend the definition of the inbuilt function **Variables** to handle equations.

```
In[66]:= Unprotect[Variables];
         Variables[equation_Equal] := Variables[List @@ equation]
         Protect[Variables];
```

The variables are

```
In[67]:= vars = Union @@ Variables /@ SFconstraints
```

```
Out[67]= {s[f], s[l], s[m], x[b], x[c], x[d]}
```

ConstrainedMax yields

```
In[68]:= solution=ConstrainedMax[profit, SFconstraints,vars]
```

```
Out[68]= {39, {s[f] -> 10, s[l] -> 0, s[m] -> 0, x[b] -> 7,
          x[c] -> 0, x[d] -> 6}}
```

The output of **ConstrainedMax** is the optimal value of the objective function and the values of all the variables.

The first step is to separate the basic and nonbasic variables. Provided the optimal solution is not degenerate,[2] this is straightforward. The basic variables are nonzero, whereas all the zero variables are nonbasic. Because this example is not degenerate, the nonbasic variables are

```
In[69]:= zerovars = Cases[solution[[2]], Rule[x_,0] -> x]
```

```
Out[69]= {s[l], s[m], x[c]}
```

and the rest are basic variables.

```
In[70]:= basic = Complement[vars,zerovars]
```

```
Out[70]= {s[f], x[b], x[d]}
```

The constraints of the final tableau are obtained by solving the original constraints for the basic variables.

```
In[71]:= FromRules[rules_List] := Apply[Equal,rules,1]
```

```
In[72]:= rules = Flatten @ Solve[SFconstraints,basic];
          FromRules[rules] // ExpandAll
```

$$Out[72]= s[f] == 10 + s[m] - x[c]$$

$$x[b] == 7 + \frac{s[l]}{5} - \frac{3\,s[m]}{5} - \frac{x[c]}{5}$$

---

[2]We treat degeneracy in the following.

```
                    2 s[l]     s[m]    3 x[c]
      x[d] == 6 -  ------  +  ----  -  ------
                      5         5        5
```

where **FromRules** converts a list of transformation rules back into equations.

Programming Note: It is necessary to use **Solve** rather than **Roots** to solve the constraints for the basic variables, because **Roots** only applies to a single equation. This provides a list of transformation rules, to which we must apply **FromRules**, which is the inverse of the built-in function **ToRules**.

The revised objective function is

```
In[73]:= profit /. rules // ExpandAll
```

```
Out[73]=        3 s[l]    6 s[m]    7 x[c]
           39 - ------ - ------ - ------
                  5         5         5
```

Thus the final tableau can be reconstructed.

```
In[74]:= finalTableau =
            Prepend[FromRules[rules],
               z == profit /. rules] // ExpandAll
```

```
Out[74]=            3 s[l]    6 s[m]    7 x[c]
           z == 39 - ------ - ------ - ------
                       5         5         5

           s[f] == 10 + s[m] - x[c]

                        s[l]    3 s[m]    x[c]
           x[b] == 7 + ----  - ------  - ----
                         5        5        5

                        2 s[l]    s[m]    3 x[c]
           x[d] == 6 - ------  + ----  - ------
                          5        5        5
```

We collect this procedure in the function **FinalTableau**.

```
In[75]:= FinalTableau[objective_,constraints_] :=
            Module[{SFconstraints,vars,solution,zerovars,
                basic,rules},
            SFconstraints = StandardLP[constraints];
            vars = Union @@ Variables /@ SFconstraints;
            solution = ConstrainedMax[objective,SFconstraints,
                vars];
            zerovars = Cases[solution[[2]], Rule[x_,0] -> x];
            basic = Complement[vars,zerovars];
            rules = Flatten @
                Solve[SFconstraints,basic];
```

```
                  Prepend[FromRules[rules],
                  z == objective /. rules] // ExpandAll
              ]
```

```
In[76]:= FinalTableau[profit,SFconstraints]
```

```
Out[76]=            3 s[l]   6 s[m]   7 x[c]
            z == 39 - ------ - ------ - ------
                        5        5        5


            s[f] == 10 + s[m] - x[c]


                      s[l]   3 s[m]   x[c]
            x[b] == 7 + ---- - ------ - ----
                        5        5      5


                      2 s[l]   s[m]   3 x[c]
            x[d] == 6 - ------ + ---- - ------
                        5         5      5
```

2.5.1 Degeneracy

Linear programming problems are degenerate when some of the basic variables are zero at the optimal solution. To handle degeneracy, we have to modify **FinalTableau** to select a suitable basis for inverting the initial tableau.[3] All nonzero variables are basic. To these we add a sufficient number of zero variables to complete the basis. However, not all the nonzero variables can be basic, and some trial and error is required.

To illustrate degeneracy, consider the following example.

```
In[77]:= objective = x[1];
```

```
In[78]:= constraints = { x[1]   <= 1,
              x[1] + x[2]         <= 1,
              x[1] + x[2] + x[3] <= 1};
```

```
In[79]:= SFconstraints = StandardLP[constraints]
```

```
Out[79]= s[1] == 1 - x[1]

         s[2] == 1 - x[1] - x[2]

         s[3] == 1 - x[1] - x[2] - x[3]
```

---

[3]A basis comprises m distinct variables, the coefficients of which are linearly independent (where m is the number of rows in the standard form).

```
In[80]:= vars = Union @@ Variables /@ SFconstraints
```

```
Out[80]= {s[1], s[2], s[3], x[1], x[2], x[3]}
```

The optimal solution is

```
In[81]:= solution=ConstrainedMax[objective, SFconstraints, vars]
```

```
Out[81]= {1, {s[1] -> 0, s[2] -> 0, s[3] -> 0, x[1] -> 1,
             x[2] -> 0, x[3] -> 0}}
```

The only nonzero variable is $x_1 = 1$. The remaining five variables are all zero.

```
In[82]:= zerovars = Cases[solution[[2]], Rule[x_,0] -> x]
```

```
Out[82]= {s[1], s[2], s[3], x[2], x[3]}
```

```
In[83]:= nonzerovars = Complement[vars,zerovars]
```

```
Out[83]= {x[1]}
```

Any basis must include x_1 and two of the five zero variables. However, not all selections of zero variables form a basis. For example, the set $\{x_1, s_1, s_2\}$ forms a basis because the constraints are solvable for these basis variables:

```
In[84]:= Solve[SFconstraints, {x[1], s[1], s[2]}]
```

```
Out[84]= {{s[1] -> s[3] + x[2] + x[3], s[2] -> s[3] + x[3],
             x[1] -> 1 - s[3] - x[2] - x[3]}}
```

However, the sets $\{x_1, x_2, s_1\}$ and $\{x_1, x_3, s_3\}$ do not form a basis, and cannot be used to solve for the final tableau. For example,

```
In[85]:= Solve[SFconstraints, {x[1], x[2], s[1]}]
```

```
Out[85]= {}
```

The empty set { } indicates no solution. To find a basis, we simply iterate through subsets of zero variables until we find a set that, together with the nonzero variables, forms a basis. To extract subsets of the appropriate size, we adopt the function **KSubsets** from the standard package DiscreteMath`Combinatorica`, which we repeat here for convenience.

```
In[86]:= KSubsets[l_List,0]  := { {} }
         KSubsets[l_List,1]  := Partition[l,1]
         KSubsets[l_List,k_Integer?Positive] := {l} /;
             (k == Length[l])
```

```
KSubsets[l_List,k_Integer?Positive] := {}  /;
    (k > Length[l])

KSubsets[l_List,k_Integer?Positive] :=
        Join[
                Map[(Prepend[#,First[l]])&,
                KSubsets[Rest[l],k-1]],
                KSubsets[Rest[l],k]
            ]
```

In the example, the subsets of size 2 of zero variables are

```
In[87]:= KSzerovars = KSubsets[zerovars,2]

Out[87]= {{s[1], s[2]}, {s[1], s[3]}, {s[1], x[2]}, {s[1], x[3]},
          {s[2], s[3]}, {s[2], x[2]}, {s[2], x[3]},
          {s[3], x[2]}, {s[3], x[3]}, {x[2], x[3]}}
```

FindBasic successively tries the elements of this set until it constructs a suitable basis.

```
In[88]:= FindBasic[SFconstraints_,nonzerovars_,KSzerovars_]:=
            Module[{rules},
              rules = Solve[SFconstraints,
                  Join[nonzerovars,First[KSzerovars]]];
              If[rules != {},rules,
              FindBasic[SFconstraints,nonzerovars,
                  Rest[KSzerovars]]]
            ]

In[89]:= FindBasic[SFconstraints,nonzerovars,KSzerovars]

Out[89]= {{s[1] -> s[3] + x[2] + x[3], s[2] -> s[3] + x[3],
          x[1] -> 1 - s[3] - x[2] - x[3]}}
```

In this case, the first selection $\{s_1, s_2\}$ is independent and sufficient to complete the basis. However, if we reorder the subsets

```
In[90]:= RotateLeft[KSzerovars,2] // Short

Out[90]= {{s[1], x[2]}, {s[1], x[3]}, {<<2>>}, <<6>>,
          {s[1], s[3]}}

In[91]:= FindBasic[SFconstraints,nonzerovars,%]

Out[91]= {{s[1] -> s[2] + x[2], x[3] -> s[2] - s[3],
          x[1] -> 1 - s[2] - x[2]}}
```

FindBasic deduces that the first pair $\{s_1, x_2\}$ is not basic, and chooses the second pair $\{s_1, x_3\}$. Because the function **KSubsets** orders the subsets lexicographically,

FindBasic will select slack variables s_j before decision variables x_j. The former are more likely to be basic, and **FindBasic** is likely to find a basis quickly.

A minor modification equips **FinalTableau** to handle degeneracy.

```
In[92]:= FinalTableau[objective_,constraints_] :=
            Module[{SFconstraints,vars,solution,zerovars,
               nonzerovars,rules},
            SFconstraints = StandardLP[constraints];
            vars = Union @@ Variables /@ SFconstraints;
            solution = ConstrainedMax[objective,SFconstraints,
               vars];
            zerovars = Cases[solution[[2]], Rule[x_,0] -> x];
            nonzerovars = Complement[vars,zerovars];
            rules = Flatten @ FindBasic[SFconstraints,
            nonzerovars,KSubsets[zerovars,Length[SFconstraints]-
            Length[nonzerovars]]];
            Prepend[FromRules[rules],
            z == objective /. rules] // ExpandAll
         ]
```

```
In[93]:= FinalTableau[objective,constraints]
```

```
Out[93]= z == 1 - s[3] - x[2] - x[3]

         s[1] == s[3] + x[2] + x[3]

         s[2] == s[3] + x[3]

         x[1] == 1 - s[3] - x[2] - x[3]
```

2.5.2 Nonexistence

To make **FinalTableau** robust, we need to equip it for the possibility that no solution exists, either because the feasible set is empty or unbounded. This will become evident when **ConstrainedMax** attempts to solve the problem and *Mathematica* generates an error message. The easy way to provide for this possibility uses the built-in function **Check** to monitor **ConstrainedMax**, and to abort if an error message is detected.

```
In[94]:= FinalTableau[objective_,constraints_] :=
            Module[{SFconstraints,vars,solution,zerovars,
               nonzerovars,rules},
            SFconstraints = StandardLP[constraints];
            vars = Union @@ Variables /@ SFconstraints;
            solution =
            Check[ConstrainedMax[objective,SFconstraints,vars],
               nonexistent];
```

```
                              (* stop if no solution exists *)
                  If[solution == nonexistent, Return[]];
                        (* else *)
                  zerovars = Cases[solution[[2]], Rule[x_,0] -> x];
                  nonzerovars = Complement[vars, zerovars];
                  rules = Flatten @ FindBasic[SFconstraints,
                  nonzerovars,
              KSubsets[zerovars, Length[SFconstraints]-
                  Length[nonzerovars]]];
                  Prepend[FromRules[rules],
              z == objective /. rules] // ExpandAll
          ]
```

To illustrate, we saw in the previous chapter that the following problem is unbounded

In[95]:= **FinalTableau[x[1] + x[2],{x[1] - x[2] <= 10}]**

ConstrainedMax::nbdd: Specified domain appears unbounded.

whereas the next problem is infeasible.

In[96]:= **FinalTableau[3x[1] + x[2],**
                { x[1] - x[2] <= 1,
                 -x[1] - x[2] <= -33,
                  2x[1] + x[2] <= 2}]

ConstrainedMax::nsat: The specified constraints cannot be satisfied.

For simplicity, we rely on the native *Mathematica* error messages. They could easily be converted to something more informative if required.

2.6   A Classic Example

One of the first applications of the simplex algorithm was to the determination of an adequate diet of minimum cost. The nutrition problem had been posed by George Stigler (1945), who gave a heuristic analysis. As a first step in his analysis of the problem, Stigler eliminated all foods whose nutritional contribution was dominated by other commodities. This reduced the list of eligible foods from 77 to 15. A further 6 foods were eliminated because they were dominated by a linear combination of the remaining foods. He then derived an approximate solution by inspection.[4] In 1947, J. Laderman of the National Bureau of

---

[4]Stigler did not anticipate the development of the simplex algorithm two years later, stating "... there does not appear to be any direct method of finding the minimum of linear function subject to linear conditions" (p. 310). However, his approximate solution turned out to be only 27 cents per year more costly than the optimum!

Standards utilized the problem to test the newly developed simplex algorithm. Using desk calculators, the solution of the system involving 9 equations and 77 unknowns required 120 person-days to calculate (Dantzig, 1963, p. 551). In 1953, the problem was solved by Dantzig on an IBM 701 computer in about 4 minutes.

The reduced problem, comprising 9 foods and 9 constraints, poses a worthwhile test for our linear programming functions. The data for the problem, the nutritive value per dollar of expenditure of the 9 foods, and the minimum daily allowance of nutrients, are listed in the following table.

	Calories (1000)	Protein (grams)	Calcium (grams)	Iron (mg)
Daily Allowance	3	70	0.8	12
Wheat Flour	44.7	1411	2.0	365
Evaporated Milk	8.4	422	15.1	9
Cheese (Cheddar)	7.4	448	16.4	19
Liver (Beef)	2.2	333	0.2	139
Cabbage	2.6	125	4.0	36
Spinach	1.1	106		138
Sweet Potatoes	9.6	138	2.7	54
Lima Beans (Dried)	17.4	1055	3.7	459
Navy Beans (Dried)	26.9	1691	11.4	792

	Vitamin A (1000 IU)	Thiamine (B_1) (mg)	Riboflavin (mg)	Niacin (mg)	Ascorbic Acid (mg)
Daily Allowance	5	1.8	2.7	18	75
Wheat Flour		55.4	33.3	441	
Evaporated Milk	26	3.0	23.5	11	60
Cheese (Cheddar)	28.1	0.8	10.3	4	
Liver (Beef)	169.2	6.4	50.8	316	525
Cabbage	7.2	9.0	4.5	26	5369
Spinach	918.4	5.7	13.8	33	2755
Sweet Potatoes	290.7	8.4	5.4	83	1912
Lima Beans (Dried)	5.1	26.9	38.2	93	
Navy Beans (Dried)		38.4	24.6	217	

We encode these data as follows. (We turn off spellchecking to avoid *Mathematica* warning us that Flour is very similar to Floor).

```
In[97]:= Off[General::spell1];
         foods = {Flour,Milk,Cheese,Liver,Cabbage,Spinach,
                    Potatoes,Lima, Navy};
         On[General::spell1];
```

```
In[98]:= nutritiveValues =
        {{44.7,8.4,7.4,2.2,2.6,1.1,9.6,17.4,26.9},
         {1411,422,448,333,125,106,138,1055,1691},
         {2,15.1,16.4,0.2,4,0,2.7,3.7,11.4},
         {365,9,19,139,36,138,54,459,792},
         {0,26,28.1,169.2,7.2,918.4,290.7,5.1,0},
         {55.4,3,0.9,6.4,9,5.7,8.4,26.9,38.4},
         {33.3,23.5,10.3,50.8,4.5,13.8,5.4,38.2,24.6},
         {441,11,4,316,26,33,83,93,217},
         {0,60,0,525,5369,2755,1912,0,0}};

In[99]:= allowances = {3,70,0.8,12,5,1.8,2.7,18,75};
```

Because the nutritive values of the various foods are given per dollar of expenditure, the cost function is total expenditure.

```
In[100]:=cost = Plus @@ x /@ foods

Out[100]=x[Cabbage] + x[Cheese] + x[Flour] + x[Lima] +
           x[Liver] + x[Milk] + x[Navy] + x[Potatoes] +
           x[Spinach]
```

where x_{Flour} is the expenditure on Flour, and so on. The nutritional constraints are

```
In[101]:=constraints = nutritiveValues.(x /@ foods) >=
            allowances // Thread;
```

Computing the final tableau as before we get

```
In[102]:=finalTableau=FinalTableau[-cost,StandardLP[constraints,
            {Cals,Prot,Ca,Fe,A,B1,B2,Nia,C}]]

General::spell1:
   Possible spelling error: new symbol name "Prot"
     is similar to existing symbol "Plot".

Out[102]=z == -0.108662 - 0.000400233 s[A] - 0.016358 s[B2] -
           0.000144118 s[C] - 0.0317377 s[Ca] -
           0.00876515 s[Cals] - 0.234905 x[Cheese] -
           0.103139 x[Lima] - 0.0436664 x[Milk] -
           0.349929 x[Potatoes]

         s[B1] == 2.32044 + 0.00178173 s[A] + 0.0600855 s[B2] +
           0.00070545 s[C] + 0.469462 s[Ca] + 1.17361 s[Cals] -
           16.1528 x[Cheese] + 2.43788 x[Lima] -
           15.4478 x[Milk] - 6.3254 x[Potatoes]
```

```
s[Fe] == 48.4669 + 0.231077 s[A] + 1.96333 s[B2] -
    0.0384643 s[C] + 55.254 s[Ca] + 4.23072 s[Cals] -
    945.189 x[Cheese] + 104.768 x[Lima] -
    910.712 x[Milk] - 140.033 x[Potatoes]

s[Nia] == 9.31598 - 0.0721403 s[A] + 6.22203 s[B2] +
    0.00263721 s[C] - 7.52855 s[Ca] + 5.56742 s[Cals] +
    24.2095 x[Cheese] - 213.331 x[Lima] -
    66.5855 x[Milk] + 32.2098 x[Potatoes]

s[Prot] == 77.4135 + 0.166875 s[A] + 5.18424 s[B2] -
    0.0527498 s[C] + 80.247 s[Ca] + 24.1134 s[Cals] -
    1104.58 x[Cheese] + 139.623 x[Lima] -
    1115.29 x[Milk] - 285.804 x[Potatoes]

x[Flour] == 0.0295191 - 0.000114638 s[A] -
    0.000828639 s[B2] + 0.0000321396 s[C] -
    0.0586491 s[Ca] + 0.0256128 s[Cals] +
    0.784067 x[Cheese] - 0.196422 x[Lima] +
    0.690979 x[Milk] - 0.111181 x[Potatoes]

x[Navy] == 0.0610286 + 0.000221774 s[A] -
    0.000205663 s[B2] - 0.0000712074 s[C] +
    0.0981656 s[Ca] - 0.00423899 s[Cals] -
    1.58266 x[Cheese] - 0.282729 x[Lima] -
    1.44335 x[Milk] - 0.151564 x[Potatoes]

x[Spinach] == 0.00500766 + 0.00114747 s[A] -
                                           -7
    0.00394299 s[B2] -  9.3211 10    s[C] +
    0.00176352 s[Ca] + 0.00285849 s[Cals] -
    0.0417057 x[Cheese] + 0.0885074 x[Lima] +
    0.0122415 x[Milk] - 0.342698 x[Potatoes]

x[Cabbage] == 0.0112144 - 0.00056002 s[A] -
    0.000069798 s[B2] + 0.000187016 s[C] +
    0.0000312175 s[Ca] + 0.0000506004 s[Cals] +
    0.0155691 x[Cheese] + 0.00452643 x[Lima] +
    0.00408336 x[Milk] - 0.19497 x[Potatoes]

x[Liver] == 0.00189256 - 0.000294355 s[A] +
                                         -6
    0.0214051 s[B2] - 2.89874 10    s[C] -
    0.00957355 s[Ca] - 0.0155178 s[Cals] +
    0.0596362 x[Cheese] - 0.510744 x[Lima] -
    0.220284 x[Milk] + 0.150343 x[Potatoes]
```

This is too much information to be readily absorbed. We can focus attention on the optimal solution values by setting the nonbasic variables to zero.

```
In[103]:=finalTableau /. Zero[NonbasicVariables @ finalTableau]
```

```
Out[103]=z == -0.108662

        s[B1]  == 2.32044

        s[Fe]  == 48.4669

        s[Nia] == 9.31598

        s[Prot] == 77.4135

        x[Flour] == 0.0295191

        x[Navy] == 0.0610286

        x[Spinach] == 0.00500766

        x[Cabbage] == 0.0112144

        x[Liver] == 0.00189256
```

The minimum cost diet is not exciting fare, comprising just five foods: wheat flour, liver, cabbage, spinach, and navy beans. Nutritional requirements could be met at a cost (in 1939 prices) of 10.9 cents per day or $39.66 dollars per year. This is only 27 cents (per year) less than the diet computed heuristically by Stigler. Only five of the nine nutritional constraints are binding.

More useful information is provided by a sensitivity analysis.

```
In[104]:=SensitivityAnalysis[finalTableau,-cost]
```

```
Out[104]= {
  {x[Cabbage], -1, -0.714676 <= Delta[Cabbage] <= 0.770615},
  {x[Cheese], -1, -Infinity <= Delta[Cheese] <= 0.234905},
  {x[Flour], -1, -0.525087 <= Delta[Flour] <= 0.063195},
  {x[Lima], -1, -Infinity <= Delta[Lima] <= 0.103139},
  {x[Liver], -1, -0.198228 <= Delta[Liver] <= 0.764211},
  {x[Milk], -1, -Infinity <= Delta[Milk] <= 0.0436664},
  {x[Navy], -1, -0.0302534 <= Delta[Navy] <= 0.323308},
  {x[Potatoes], -1, -Infinity <= Delta[Potatoes] <= 0.349929},
  {x[Spinach], -1, -1.0211 <= Delta[Spinach] <= 0.348796},
  {s[B1], 0, -2.32044 <= Delta[B1] <= Infinity},
  {s[Fe], 0, -48.4669 <= Delta[Fe] <= Infinity},
  {s[Nia], 0, -9.31598 <= Delta[Nia] <= Infinity},
  {s[Prot], 0, -77.4135 <= Delta[Prot] <= Infinity},
  {s[A], 0.000400233, -6.42952 <= Delta[A] <= 4.36409},
```

```
{s[B2], 0.016358, -1.27002 <= Delta[B2] <= 0.0884161},
{s[C], 0.000144118, -652.89 <= Delta[C] <= 59.9651},
{s[Ca], 0.0317377, -0.197686 <= Delta[Ca] <= 0.62169},
{s[Cals], 0.00876515, -0.121961 <= Delta[Cals] <=
    1.15251}}
```

In interpreting these ranges, remember that the price of each food is -1, because the objective is to minimize cost. Therefore an algebraic increase corresponds to a fall in the real price. For example, the sensitivity analysis reveals that the valid price range of cheese is $-\infty \leq \Delta_{Cheese} \leq 0.234905$. This implies that the price of cheese would have to fall nearly 25% before it would enter the optimal diet. A 3% rise in the price of navy beans would eliminate them from the optimal diet, whereas spinach would be retained even if the price doubled.

Because the nutritional constraints are measured in different units, it is worthwhile converting the shadow prices of the nutritional constraints to elasticities. Economists use elasticities to relate the percentage change in one variable to the percentage change in another, giving a measure of responsiveness that is independent of the units of measurement.

The nutritional requirements are

```
In[105]:=requirements = StandardLP[constraints,
            {Cals,Prot,Ca,Fe,A,B1,B2,Nia,C}] /.
         lhs_ == rhs_ :> {lhs, Abs @ Intercept[rhs]}
```

```
Out[105]={{s[Cals], 3}, {s[Prot], 70}, {s[Ca], 0.8},
          {s[Fe], 12}, {s[A], 5}, {s[B1], 1.8}, {s[B2], 2.7},
          {s[Nia], 18}, {s[C], 75}}
```

and their shadow prices are

```
In[106]:=shadowP = ShadowPrices[finalTableau,#[[1]]]& /@
                   requirements]
```

```
Out[106]={{s[Cals], 0.00876515}, {s[Prot], 0},
          {s[Ca], 0.0317377}, {s[Fe], 0}, {s[A], 0.000400233},
          {s[B1], 0},    {s[B2], 0.016358}, {s[Nia], 0},
          {s[C], 0.000144118}}
```

The cost of the optimal diet is

```
In[107]:=minimumCost = Intercept[First[finalTableau][[2]]] //
             Abs
```

```
Out[107]=0.108662
```

The *elasticity* of the cost of the optimal diet with respect to changes in the *calorie* requirement is

$$\text{Elasticity} = 100 \frac{\text{Shadow price/Minimum cost}}{1/\text{Nutritional requirement}}$$

$$= 100 \frac{0.00876515/0.108662}{1/3}$$

$$= 24.1993\%.$$

This calculation is made by the function **Elasticity**.

```
In[108]:=Elasticity[{var_,requirement_},{var_,shadowPrice_}] :=
         {var,100(shadowPrice/minimumCost)requirement}
```

The elasticities of cost with respect to changes in the nutritional requirements can be computed by threading this function over the lists of requirements and shadow prices.

```
In[109]:=Thread[Elasticity[requirements,shadowP]] //
              TableForm
```

```
Out[109]=s[Cals]    24.1992

         s[Prot]    0

         s[Ca]      23.3661

         s[Fe]      0

         s[A]       1.84164

         s[B1]      0

         s[B2]      40.6458

         s[Nia]     0

         s[C]       9.94716
```

The elasticities are zero for the nonbinding constraints. The cost of the optimal diet is very sensitive to the vitamin B2 requirement. A 1% increase in this requirement would increase the cost of the minimum diet by 40%. At the other end of the scale, the cost of the optimal diet is relatively insensitive to the vitamin A requirement, and quite insensitive to the vitamin B1 requirement (which is not binding).

Finally, some interesting information was obtained by timing the computation of the final tableau. On my 50 MHz DX, calculating the final tableau took

51 seconds. Of this, only 0.4 seconds were required to solve the problem using **ConstrainedMax**. Solving the system in terms of the basic variables took considerably longer, 2.9 seconds. Most of the time (48 seconds) was required simply to transform the systems of equations in the final tableau using **ExpandAll**! Because **ExpandAll** is used repeatedly in **Simplex**, we would expect the algorithm implemented in the previous chapter (**LP**) to be very slow. I am not sure how slow, because the following calculation was aborted after 46 hours.

```
In[110]:=LP[Prepend[StandardLP[requirements,
            {Cals,Prot,Ca,Fe,A,B1,B2,Nia,C}],
          - cost]] // Timing
```

```
Out[110]=$Aborted
```

2.7 Conclusion

This chapter describes a package designed to supplement *Mathematica*'s inbuilt linear programming facilities. We presented a set of tools for sensitivity analysis of the optimal solution using the final tableau. We also developed a function that can be used to deduce the final tableau from the Spartan output of *Mathematica*'s built-in linear programming function **ConstrainedMax**, obtaining all the information usually provided by a good linear programming package. This enables the package to be applied to a substantive problem, relying on *Mathematica*'s native code for intensive computation. As an illustration, we undertook a sensitivity analysis of a classic example in the linear programming literature.

2.8 Acknowledgments

I gratefully acknowledge the assistance of John George, who pointed out some of the subtleties of linear programming, and John Novak, Troels Petersen, and Bill Sharkey, who made significant improvements to the text and code.

2.9 References

Dantzig G. 1963. *Linear Programming and Extensions*. Princeton, NJ, Princeton University Press.
Stigler G. 1945. "The Cost of Subsistence." *Journal of Farm Economics*, 303–314.

3 Optimization with *Mathematica*

J.-C. Culioli

3.1 Introduction

3.1.1 Preliminary Comments

In the following presentation we refer to finding *minima* or *maxima* of functions, possibly subject to linear and/or nonlinear equality and/or inequality constraints. When we refer to such minima/maxima, we evidently assume that they exist. Most of the time, we also speak of *the* (instead of *a*) minimum/maximum of a given function. The idea is that *we will be glad enough to find any local solution*. Numerical optimization programs are usually not designed to prove existence or uniqueness of such solutions. This difficult mathematical task, strongly related to the modeling effort, is left to the user.

In order to keep a systematic point of view, we mostly talk about finding minima.

Note: Recall that the problem: *Find Max* $g(x)$ is equivalent to the problem: *Find* $-Min(-g(x))$

From a mathematical point of view, this presentation is *very informal*. Although Optimization Theory and the methods for building efficient algorithms are based on very firm mathematical grounds, practical end-users can read this paper and use the following routines even if they have very limited calculus and linear algebra knowledge.

Some very good books [Bertsekas (1982), Fletcher (1980), and Luenberger (1984)] on optimization are listed at the end of this chapter. We have also listed two books where many test-problems have been collected. Most of the examples given in the sequel are in fact typical test-problems.

Note: this chapter describes some built-in and new functions using as an illustration the *Mathematica* 2.2 version on a PowerBook 170 Macintosh computer. Readers should be warned that some results or comments given in the following might be either soon obsolete (especially timing considerations) or slightly different (due to machine-dependent numerical precision).

3.1.2   How *Not to* Use *Mathematica* for Optimization

3.1.2.1   A Nonlinear Criterion Subject to Constraints

Suppose that we want to mimimize the following criterion

```
In[1]:=  criterion =  1/2 u0^2 + 1/6 (u1^2 + u2^2 + u3^2) ;
```

subject to inequality constraints:

$$u0 \geq 2, \ u0 + u1 \geq 5, \ u0 + u2 \geq 2, \ u0 + u3 \geq 1.$$

One method for solving such a problem could be to transform inequality constraints into equality constraints with the use of slack variables, and then to apply Lagrange's rule to the Lagrangian

```
In[2]:=  Lag = criterion  +           (* The Lagrangian  *)
              p(u0-v0^2 - 2) +          (* u0    >= 2  becomes
                                         u0 - v0^2 = 2 *)
              p1(u0 + u1 -v1^2 - 5) +   (* u0 + u1   >= 5   becomes
                                         u0 + u1 - v1^2 = 5*)
              p2(u0 + u2 -v2^2 - 2) +   (* u0 + u2   >= 2   becomes
                                         u0 + u2 - v2^2 = 2*)
              p3(u0 + u3 -v3^2 - 1);    (* u0 + u3   >= 1   becomes
                                         u0 + u3 - v3^2 = 1*)
```

which is a combination of the criterion and some linear penalties of the constraints. The $p, p1, p2, p3$ variables are the classical *Lagrange multipliers*.

For later use, we define a vector containing all the variables: $u0$ to $u3$ are called "primal variables," p to $p3$ are sometimes also called "dual variables," and $v0$ to $v3$ are the "slack variables" that enable us to transform inequalities into equalities.

```
In[3]:=  var = {u0,u1,u2,u3,p,p1,p2,p3,v0,v1,v2,v3};
```

3.1.2.2   Optimality Conditions

The optimality conditions simply state that the gradient of the Lagrangian should be zero at any stationary point (and the minimum subject to the constraints is one of them).

```
In[4]:=  system = Map[D[Lag,#]==0&,var]
            (* system of optimality conditions *)

Out[4]=
                        u1            u2            u3
       {p + p1 + p2 + p3 + u0 == 0, p1 + -- == 0, p2 + -- == 0,  p3 + -- == 0,
                        3             3             3
```

$$-2 + u0 - v0^2 == 0, \quad -5 + u0 + u1 - v1^2 == 0, \quad -2 + u0 + u2 - v2^2 == 0,$$

$$-1 + u0 + u3 - v3^2 == 0, \quad -2\ p\ v0 == 0, \quad -2\ p1\ v1 == 0, \quad -2\ p2\ v2 == 0,$$

$$-2\ p3\ v3 == 0\}$$

In[5]:=   **Length[%]**

Out[5]=   12

If we are cautious, we might think that such a nonlinear set of 12 equations in 12 unknowns is not going to give a unique solution, but probably quite a few. This is why Short[ ] might be useful (the reader is urged to try this without it).

In[6]:=   **Short[sol = Solve[system,var],5]**

Out[6]=

$$\{\{p \to -(\tfrac{7}{3}),\ u1 \to 0,\ u2 \to 0,\ u3 \to -1,\ p2 \to 0,\ p3 \to \tfrac{1}{3},\ p1 \to 0,$$

$$v1 \to -I\ \mathrm{Sqrt}[3],\ u0 \to 2,\ v0 \to 0,\ v2 \to 0,\ v3 \to 0\},\ <<79>>,$$

$$\{u1 \to \tfrac{19}{5},\ u2 \to 0,\ u3 \to -(\tfrac{1}{5}),\ p \to 0,\ p1 \to -(\tfrac{19}{15}),\ p3 \to \tfrac{1}{15},\ p2 \to 0,$$

$$v0 \to \frac{2\ I}{\mathrm{Sqrt}[5]},\ v2 \to \frac{2\ I}{\mathrm{Sqrt}[5]},\ u0 \to -\tfrac{6}{5},\ v1 \to 0,\ v3 \to 0\}\}$$

There are in fact 81 candidate solutions (a lot of them having imaginary parts!), and we "just" have to pick the good one among those that minimize the criterion, that is, 16 of them.

In[7]:=   **criterion /. sol**

Out[7]=

$$\{\tfrac{13}{6}, \tfrac{13}{6}, \tfrac{13}{6}, \tfrac{13}{6}, \tfrac{13}{6}, \tfrac{13}{6}, 2, 2, 2, 2, 2, 2, 2, 2, 2, 2, 2, 2, \tfrac{11}{3}, \tfrac{11}{3}, \tfrac{11}{3}, \tfrac{7}{2},$$

$$\tfrac{7}{2}, \tfrac{7}{2}, \tfrac{7}{2}, \tfrac{7}{2}, \tfrac{7}{2}, 0, 0, 0, 0, 0, 0, 0, 0, 0, 0, 0, 0, 0, 0, 0, 0, \tfrac{1}{8}, \tfrac{1}{8}, \tfrac{1}{8}, \tfrac{1}{8},$$

$$\frac{1}{8}, \frac{1}{8}, \frac{1}{8}, \frac{1}{8}, \frac{8}{15}, \frac{8}{15}, \frac{8}{15}, \frac{8}{15}, \frac{1}{2}, \frac{1}{2}, \frac{1}{2}, \frac{1}{2}, \frac{1}{2}, \frac{1}{2}, \frac{1}{2}, \frac{1}{2}, \frac{16}{5}, \frac{16}{5}, \frac{16}{5}, \frac{16}{5}, \frac{29}{9}, \frac{29}{9},$$

$$\frac{25}{8}, \frac{25}{8}, \frac{25}{8}, \frac{25}{8}, \frac{25}{8}, \frac{25}{8}, \frac{25}{8}, \frac{25}{8}, \frac{47}{15}, \frac{47}{15}, \frac{47}{15}, \frac{47}{15}\}$$

This proves that it is generally not a good idea to transform a quite innocuous minimization problem into a combinatorial problem. Of course, instead of using slack variables, one can use Karush, Kuhn, and Tucker conditions [See Luenberger (1984), for example], but these conditions also have a combinatorial nature and one has to use an "active constraints" algorithm that is a kind of "educated guess algorithm." Here we follow another track.

3.1.3   Outline of the Chapter

Four built-in functions are available for optimization in *Mathematica:*

- **FindMinimum**, which finds the unconstrained minimum of a nonlinear function of several variables;
- **ConstrainedMin** (resp., **Max**), which finds the minimum (resp., max) of a linear function with *linear (in)*equality constraints;
- **LinearProgramming**, which is the basic linear solver for min $c.x$ subject to $A.x \geq b$ and $x \geq 0$.

Obviously, routines for linear or nonlinear functionals subject to nonlinear (in)equalities are lacking. Several requests have been made on math.sci.symbolic and the MathGroup on this subject.

Here we show that these routines can be programmed very easily in *Mathematica.*

In the sequel, we

- show how to track solutions of difficult smooth unconstrained problems,
- show how to solve linear problems,
- show how to solve nonlinear problems only with **FindMinimum**,
- describe the package `MultiplierMethod.m` dedicated to nonlinear problems with general constraints, and
- test this package on classical test problems.

3.1.4   Optimality Conditions (and Their Use to Trap Candidates)

3.1.4.1   Unconstrained Optimization

In unconstrained optimization, there are some easy tests that enable checking if one has found a good candidate for a *local minimum.*

If the function is twice differentiable, *for a minimum*, its *gradient should vanish* at such candidate point and the second derivative should be nonnegative: the *Hessian matrix should be at least positive semidefinite* (that is, with nonnegative eigenvalues). For a maximum, the gradient should also vanish but the Hessian matrix should be negative semidefinite. These necessary conditions are called first-order and second-order conditions.

We thus need the two following functions that compute the gradient and the Hessian of a function.

```
In[8]:=  Grad[function_,var_List]:= D[function,#]& /@ var ;
         Hessian[function_,var_List]:= Grad[Grad[function,var],
            var]
```

For example, the quadratic convex function $(x, y) \to (x - a)^2 + (y - b)^2$ attains its minimum at $(x = a, y = b)$, and

```
In[9]:=  function =  (x-a)^2 + (y-b)^2;
         candidate = {x -> a, y -> b};
```

```
In[10]:= Grad[function,{x,y}] /. candidate
```

```
Out[10]= {0, 0}
```

```
In[11]:= Hessian[function,{x,y}] /. candidate
```

```
Out[11]= {{2, 0}, {0, 2}}
```

which is positive definite. These results do not depend on the values of a or b. On the other hand, the quadratic function $(x, y) \to (x - a)^2 - (y - b)^2$ is nonconvex and the candidate $(x = a, y = b)$ is a saddle-point:

```
In[12]:= function =  (x-a)^2 - (y-b)^2;
         Grad[function,{x,y}] /. candidate
```

```
Out[12]= {0, 0}
```

```
In[13]:= Hessian[function,{x,y}] /. candidate
```

```
Out[13]= {{2, 0}, {0, -2}}
```

If a minimization algorithm eventually finds a saddle-point, it should warn the user that it is not a minimum. For example, if one accidently starts with such a point, the program may very well not go any further.

```
In[14]:= a= 1; b = -1; FindMinimum[function,{x,1},{y,-1}]
```

```
FindMinimum::fmgz:
   Warning: FindMinimum encountered a vanishing gradient. The
      result returned may not be a minimum; it may be a maximum
      or a saddle point.
```

Out[14]= {0., {x -> 1., y -> -1.}}

Now, if such a starting point is perturbed, one will quickly know if the candidate was a good one.

```
In[15]:= a= 1; b = -1;
         FindMinimum[currentpoint = {x,y};
               function,{x,1.001},{y,-1.001}]
```

```
FindMinimum::fmlim: The minimum could not be bracketed in 30
   iterations.
```

Out[15]= FindMinimum[currentpoint = {x, y};
               function, {x, 1.001}, {y, -1.001}]

```
In[16]:= currentpoint
```

Out[16]=
$$\{-9.18505 \ 10^9 \ , \ -9.18505 \ 10^9 \}$$

Note: On another computer, it is possible, due to different machine precision, to obtain a slightly different output on the foregoing inputs.

Here **FindMinimum** is telling us that the sequence of points it is generating is not converging and it even does not return any candidate! This is why we used this great "currentpoint" trick that was taught to us by J. Keiper.

Note that this trick is very useful for looking at the evolution of the **FindMinimum** algorithm. Try, for example,

```
list={}; FindMinimum[list = {list,x}; (x-1)^4, {x,5}];
ListPlot[Flatten[list],PlotJoined->True]
```

If we think that the algorithm did not return a solution because there were not enough iterations, we can increase the number of iterations with the **MaxIterations** option, and get the following candidate.

```
In[17]:= {cost, candidate} =
         FindMinimum[function,{x,1.001},{y,-1.001},
         MaxIterations -> 50]
```

Out[17]=
$$\{-1.40737 \ 10^{15} \ , \ \{x \ -> \ -5.28302 \ 10^{16} \ , \ y \ -> \ -5.28302 \ 10^{16} \ \}\}$$

```
In[18]:= Grad[function,{x,y}] /. candidate
```

Out[18]=
$$\{-1.0566 \ 10^{17} \ , \ 1.0566 \ 10^{17} \ \}$$

But clearly this is not a minimum. As could be checked, this candidate is in fact a limit point of the algorithm and **FindMinimum** stops because the candidate has hit some built-in boundary, which is standard in nonconvex optimization.

3.1.4.2 Constrained Optimization

In constrained optimization, such as

$$\min f(x) \ \text{s.t.} \ g(x) = 0 \ \text{and} \ h(x) \le 0,$$

optimality conditions can be written with the use of auxiliary variables (p, q), often called:

- dual variables,
- (Karush) Kuhn Tucker parameters,
- Lagrange multipliers, and so on.

First-order conditions are, for example,

If x^* is a solution, then there exist p and $q \ge 0$,

such that

$$f'(x^*) + p.g'(x^*) + q.h'(x^*) = 0 \quad \text{(KKT conditions)},$$

and

$$g(x^*) = 0, \quad h(x^*) \le 0, \quad \text{(feasibility)},$$

and

$$q.h(x^*) = 0 \quad \text{(complementary slackness)}.$$

With the help of the Lagrangian function L defined by

$$L(x, p, q) = f(x) + p.g(x) + q.h(x),$$

these conditions can be written

$$L_x'(x, p, q) = 0, \ L_p'(x, p, q) = 0, \ L_q'(x, p, q) \le 0, \quad \text{and} \quad q.L_q'(x, p, q) = 0.$$

With a triple (x^*, p^*, q^*) that satisfies all these conditions, we know that we already have a good candidate. But exactly as in the unconstrained case, we need *curvature* information to be sure: if the Hessian of L (reduced to the constraints

$g(x) = 0$ and $h(x) \leq 0$ that are active—equalities—around x^*) is positive, then x^* is a local minimum. This condition is more involved to test, although it is an excellent programming exercise.

3.2 Linear Programming

For more on this particular subject, read in this book Chapter 1 by Michael Carter on "Linear Programming with Mathematica: the Simplex Algorithm."

3.2.1 ConstrainedMin(Max) and LinearProgramming

These commands help solve linear programs with linear (in)equality constraints such as, for example,

$$\min x1 + 2x2 - x3 + 3x4,$$

subject to $x1 - x2 \geq 2$, $x2 + x3 + x4 \geq 4$, and $xi \geq 0$, $(i = 1, \ldots, 4)$.

The last constraint is very important because it is a constraint *always* used in the function **LinearProgramming**. Historically, *all linear programming variables are usually assumed positive* and if some problem involves variables yi which are not sign-constrained, we replace them with the standard trick $yi = xi - zi$ where $xi \geq 0$ and $zi \geq 0$.

Note that this "sign limitation" is purely technical and due to the standard implementation of the simplex algorithm. Most commercial packages (including the most recent interior point methods) accept signed or unsigned variables.

The main difference among these linear programming built-in functions is the type of arguments they handle and the expression they return.

ConstrainedMax and **ConstrainedMin** take as first argument the linear cost to maximize or minimize. The second argument is a list of equalities and/or inequalities of *any* type (>= or <= or ==). The third argument is the list of variables. They return the optimal cost and a replacement rule, such as **FindMinimum**. For example,

```
In[19]:= vars = Table[x[i],{i,4}];      (* define the variables *)
         cost = x[1] + 2 x[2]- x[3]+ 3 x[4];
         constraints = {x[1] - x[2] >= 4,
                        x[2] + x[3] + x[4]   >= 4,
                        x[3] <= 3.1, x[1] - x[3] == 1};
         ConstrainedMin[cost, constraints, vars]

Out[19]= {3.6, {x[1] -> 4.1, x[2] -> 0.1, x[3] -> 3.1,
               x[4] -> 0.8}}
```

or equivalently,

```
In[20]:= ConstrainedMax[-cost, constraints, vars]
```

```
Out[20]= {-3.6, {x[1] -> 4.1, x[2] -> 0.1, x[3] -> 3.1,
          x[4] -> 0.8}}
```

One can also use equality constraints with **ConstrainedMin**.

```
In[21]:= A = {{1,2,-1,3},{1,0,2,1}}; b = {4,2};
         Thread[A.vars - b == 0]
```

```
Out[21]= {-4 + x[1] + 2 x[2] - x[3] + 3 x[4] == 0,
          -2 + x[1] + 2 x[3] + x[4] == 0}
```

```
In[22]:= ConstrainedMin[cost, Thread[ A.vars - b == 0], vars]
```

```
Out[22]= {4, {x[1] -> 2, x[2] -> 1, x[3] -> 0, x[4] -> 0}}
```

```
In[23]:= A.vars /. %[[2]]
```

```
Out[23]= {4, 2}
```

On the other hand, **LinearProgramming** solves

$$\min c.x \quad \text{subject to} \quad A.x \geq b, x \geq 0$$

and takes as arguments the *cost vector c*, the *constraint matrix A*, and the *r.h.s vector b*. One way to use it with equalities is to transform each equality $x + y = e$ into *two* inequalities $x + y \geq e$ and $-x - y \geq -e$.

3.2.2 Solving an Assignment Problem

3.2.2.1 The Problem

$$\min \sum_i \sum_j c(i, j) x(i, j)$$

with each $c(i, j)$ a given cost, subject to the constraints

$$\sum_i x(i, j) = \sum_j x(i, j) = 1, \quad x(i, j) \geq 0, \quad (i = 1, \ldots, n, \quad j = 1, \ldots, n).$$

In other words, one wants to assign n jobs to n machines in an efficient manner [$c(i, j)$ is, for example, the cost of processing job j by machine i], and only one job per machine can be assigned.

3.2.2.2 Solution by Linear Programming (Not the Most Efficient, but...)

In[24]:= **Clear[A,b]**

To rewrite the problem as a general linear program, we consider the variable matrix $x(i,j)$ as a column vector $\{x(1,1),\ldots,x(1,n),x(2,1),\ldots,x(2,n),\ldots,x(n,n)\}$. We then need to build the A matrix that corresponds to the $\sum_i x(i,j) = \sum_j x(i,j) = 1$ equalities. For this we use the following function that codes the fact that there is only one job assigned to each machine and only one machine for each job.

In[25]:= **cond[i_,j_,n_] := If[i> n, If[Mod[i,n]==Mod[j,n],1,0],**
                          If[(j<= n i) && (j > n (i-1)),1,0]];
          A[n_] := Drop[Table[cond[i,j,n], {i,2 n},{j,n^2}], 1];
          b[n_] := Drop[Table[1,{2 n}],1];

Note: The function **cond** could certainly be more aesthetically produced using some functions of the standard package LinearAlgebra`Matrix `Manipulation. This would be a nice exercise for an interested reader.

We also dropped the first row of the matrix A and of the vector b because it is clear that A is not of full rank.

In[26]:= **A[4] // MatrixForm**

Out[26]=

0	0	0	0	1	1	1	1	0	0	0	0	0	0	0	0
0	0	0	0	0	0	0	0	1	1	1	1	0	0	0	0
0	0	0	0	0	0	0	0	0	0	0	0	1	1	1	1
1	0	0	0	1	0	0	0	1	0	0	0	1	0	0	0
0	1	0	0	0	1	0	0	0	1	0	0	0	1	0	0
0	0	1	0	0	0	1	0	0	0	1	0	0	0	1	0
0	0	0	1	0	0	0	1	0	0	0	1	0	0	0	1

Let us now solve a small-size assignment problem (only 49 variables). Here is the cost matrix

In[27]:= **n = 7;**
          cost = Table[Random[Integer,{1,1000}]/100.,{i,n^2}];
          Partition[cost,n] // MatrixForm

Out[27]=

5.81	4.06	4.9	3.25	1.53	1.03	9.1
8.32	1.63	3.08	0.38	4.06	5.77	0.34
8.62	8.11	6.21	2.5	9.7	9.83	8.
2.57	9.9	8.09	5.87	4.72	6.13	5.95
4.41	8.58	6.58	0.49	9.92	7.57	2.89
6.61	8.98	6.68	9.71	1.23	4.09	5.95
5.18	4.87	8.82	0.82	7.55	0.61	9.27

We convert equalities into couples of inequalities,

In[28]:= **AA = Join[A[n],-A[n]]; bb = Join[b[n],-b[n]];**

and solve the assignment problem

```
In[29]:= Timing[ sol = LinearProgramming[cost, AA, bb]; ]

Out[29]= {45.4333 Second, Null}
```

A better way (mentioned to us by an expert anonymous reviewer) of converting all equalities into inequalities is to replace the $(-A[n], -b[n])$ by $(-Plus@@A[n], -Plus@@b[n])$, giving a completely equivalent mathematical problem: because we are adding n positive variables and assuming that their sum is negative, all these variables must be equal to zero!

```
In[30]:= AAnew = Append[A[n],- Plus @@ A[n]];
         bbnew = Append[b[n],- Plus @@ b[n]];
         Timing[ Short[ sol = LinearProgramming[cost, AAnew,
            bbnew],3 ] ]

Out[30]= {23.5167 Second, {0, 1, 0, 0, 0, 0, 0, 0, 0, 0, 0, 0,
            0, 1, 0, 0, 1, 0, 0, 0, 0, 1, 0, 0, 0, 0, 0, 0, 0,
            0, 0, 1, 0, 0, 0, 0, 0, 0, 0, 1, 0, 0, 0, 0, 0, 0,
            0, 1, 0}}
```

The information contained in such listings of figures is not very easy to grasp. On the contrary, because we know that solutions have the property of either being $x(i, j) = 0$ or $x(i, j) = 1$, it is much better to use **ListDensityPlot** that will enlighten the $x^*(i, j) = 1$ solutions and darken the others.

```
In[31]:= ShowMe[xlist_,n_]:= With[{y = Partition[xlist,n]},
         ListDensityPlot[y]];
         ShowMe[sol,n]
```

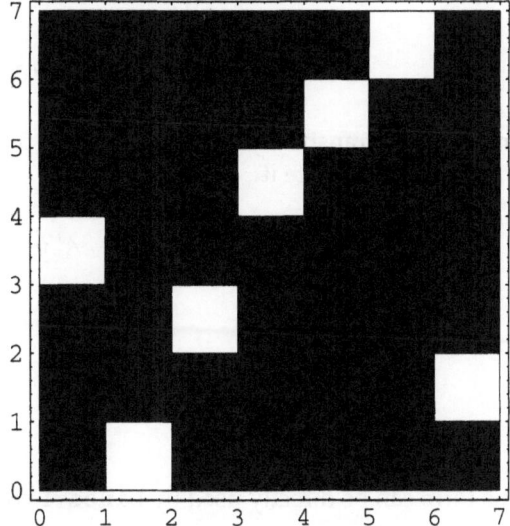

```
Out[31]= -DensityGraphics-
```

Clearly, there is only one 1 per row and per column, and the overall cost is simply

```
In[32]:= cost.sol
```

```
Out[32]= 15.51
```

It should be noted that the simplex algorithm (as programmed in **Linear-Programming**) is not the right type of algorithm for the assignment problem because it is very "degenerate," a defect that means that very few components of the solution are nonzero; here only n among the $x^*(i,j)$ are equal to 1 and $(n^2 - n)$ of them are zero. Large scale assignment problems are nowadays solved by graph algorithms (such as the Hungarian method).

3.2.3 Obtaining Dual Variables

LinearProgramming returns the *solution vector*. One has to build the minimum, possibly with replacement rules, and more subtly, the associated dual parameters that are well known to convey very useful sensitivity information (See Michael Carter's chapter on Sensitivity Analysis in this book).

One possibility of finding these dual parameters is, of course, to solve the associated "dual problem." For example, to

$$\min c.x \quad \text{s.t.} \quad Ax = b, x \geq 0$$

is associated the dual linear program

$$\max b.y \quad \text{s.t.} \quad A'.y \leq c,$$

where A' is the transpose of A. But this new problem is without the *positivity constraint*. So we rewrite it

$$\max b.(y - z) \quad \text{s.t.} \quad A'.y - A'.z \leq c$$

with $y \geq 0$ and $z \geq 0$, or

$$-\min b.(z - y) \quad \text{s.t.} \quad A'.z - A'.y \geq -c$$

with $y \geq 0$ and $z \geq 0$.

This form can be directly used by **LinearProgramming**.

```
In[33]:= Transpose[A[3]]   //MatrixForm
```

```
Out[33]= 0   0   1   0   0
         0   0   0   1   0
         0   0   0   0   1
         1   0   1   0   0
         1   0   0   1   0
         1   0   0   0   1
         0   1   1   0   0
         0   1   0   1   0
         0   1   0   0   1
```

```
In[34]:= Transpose[Join[A[3],-A[3]]] //MatrixForm
```

```
Out[34]= 0   0   1   0   0   0   0   -1   0   0
         0   0   0   1   0   0   0   0   -1   0
         0   0   0   0   1   0   0   0   0   -1
         1   0   1   0   0   -1  0   -1   0   0
         1   0   0   1   0   -1  0   0   -1   0
         1   0   0   0   1   -1  0   0   0   -1
         0   1   1   0   0   0   -1  -1   0   0
         0   1   0   1   0   0   -1  0   -1   0
         0   1   0   0   1   0   -1  0   0   -1
```

Recall that we had sol = LinearProgramming[cost, AA, bb]

```
In[35]:= Timing[ dual = LinearProgramming[bb,Transpose[AA],
            -cost]  ]
```

```
Out[35]= {37.9667 Second, {2.43, 0, 1.72, 0, 0, 0, 0, 0, 0, 0,
            1.09, 0, 0, 0, 1.85, 0, 0.12, 2.32, 0.45, 4.29,
            4.06, 4.36, 0.37, 0, 0.16, 2.77}}
```

Now we can compare "primal" and "dual" costs

```
In[36]:= {cost.sol, -bb.dual}
```

```
Out[36]= {15.51, 15.51}
```

Of course, it would be even nicer to obtain both solutions from only one run of **LinearProgramming**, and this will be provided in a future version of *Mathematica*.

Until then, it is always possible to recover the dual variables associated with the original problem.

```
In[37]:= dualvar = Drop[dual - RotateRight[dual,2 n-1],
            -(2 n - 1)]
```

```
Out[37]= {2.43, -1.85, 1.72, -0.12, -2.32, -0.45, -4.29, -4.06,
            -4.36, -0.37, 1.09, -0.16, -2.77}
```

Note that it is an interesting exercise to check exactly what this command does. Another exercise would be to use the smarter trick of transforming the $(-A, -b)$ constraint into a single constraint: show how to obtain the original dual variables from the solution of

```
dualnew = LinearProgramming[bbnew, Transpose[AAnew],
    -cost]
```

(Hint: try `Last[dualnew]-dualnew` and compare with `dualvar`)

3.3 Unconstrained Nonlinear Programming

3.3.1 FindMinimum

In order to test the **FindMinimum** function, let us see what the online documentation can teach us.

```
In[38]:= ?FindMinimum
```

```
FindMinimum[f, {x, x0}] searches for a local minimum in f,
    starting from the point x=x0.
```

In fact, **FindMinimum** can even search a minimum in a bounded region, and it will give a warning if the unbounded minimum is out of that region

```
In[39]:= FindMinimum[x1^2,{x1,1.5,1,3}]
```

```
FindMinimum::regex:
    Reached the point 0.5 {-1.} + {1.5} which is outside the
    region {{1., 3.}}.
```

```
Out[39]=                          2
            FindMinimum[x1 , {x1, 1.5, 1, 3}]
```

Indeed,

```
In[40]:= FindMinimum[x1^2,{x1,1.5}]
```

```
Out[40]= {0., {x1 -> 0.}}
```

FindMinimum can deal with functions of several variables. For example, the classical *Rosenbrock banana test-problem*, with unique solution {1, 1} and minimum value 0:

```
In[41]:= Rosenbrock[x1_,x2_] := 100(x2 - x1^2)^2 + (1-x1)^2;
         FindMinimum[Rosenbrock[x1,x2],{x1,-2},{x2,2}]
```

Out[41]=
$$\{1.50609 \ 10^{-13}, \ \{x1 \rightarrow 1., \ x2 \rightarrow 1.\}\}$$

As simple as it may seem, the Rosenbrock function is difficult to optimize in the sense that local information conveyed by the gradient—which is usually used for constructing a converging sequence to a possible solution—has only a very limited use (in other words, the local curvature changes rapidly).

Geographically speaking, the graph of the Rosenbrock function is similar to a very deep valley where water coming from steep slopes flows rapidly, while the river itself moves very slowly towards a lake.

In[42]:= **Plot3D[Rosenbrock[x1,x2],{x1,-.5,2}, {x2,-.5,1.5},**
      PlotRange -> {0,50}, PlotPoints -> 30, ClipFill->None]

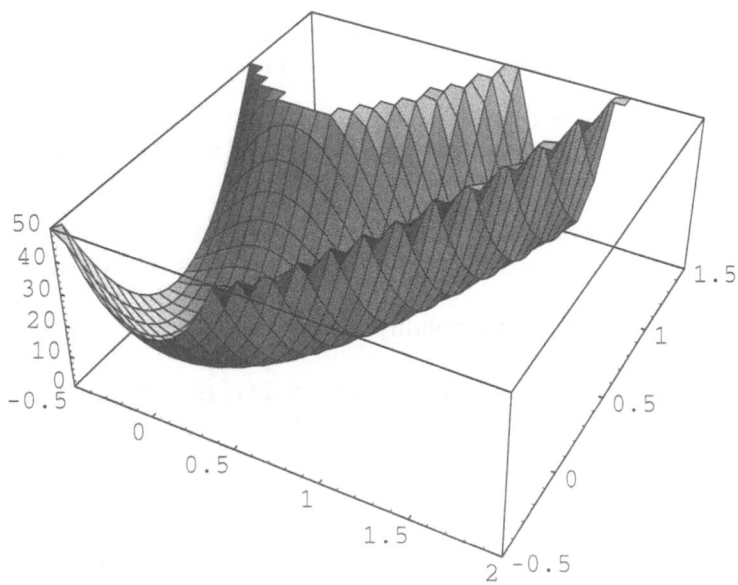

Out[42]= -SurfaceGraphics-

Note: the reader might be interested in trying **ContourPlot[Rosenbrock[x1,x2], x1,-.5,2, x2,-.5,1.5, Contours -> 30]** to help visualize the "valley."

Note that for very special points it is possible that **FindMinimum** will not give the solution with very good accuracy.

In[43]:= **FindMinimum[Rosenbrock[x1,x2],{x1,0.001},{x2,0.001}]**

Out[43]=   -10
                {8.29368 10   , {x1 -> 1.00003, x2 -> 1.00006}}

But this can be corrected either by changing the `AccuracyGoal` or by *avoiding any special pattern* such as $x1 = x2$ or any special value such as $x1$ or $x2 = 0$ in the initial points.

In[44]:= **FindMinimum[Rosenbrock[x1,x2],{x1,0.001},{x2,0.001},**
           AccuracyGoal-> 8]

Out[44]=   -15
                {4.35139 10   , {x1 -> 1., x2 -> 1.}}

Another typical example of a function that is not very easy to optimize is the Wood function that involves four variables.

In[45]:= **Wood[x1_,x2_,x3_,x4_] := 100(x2 - x1^2)^2 +**
           (1-x1)^2 + 90(x4 - x3^2)^2 + (1-x3)^2 +
           10.1 ((1-x2)^2 + (1-x4)^4) + 19.8 (1- x2)(1-x4)

In[46]:= **{cost, solution} =**
           FindMinimum[Wood[x1,x2,x3,x4], {x1,-3},{x2,-1},
           {x3,-3},{x4,-1}]

Out[46]= {-2.06026, {x1 -> 1.28153, x2 -> 1.64341,
              x3 -> 0.580138, x4 -> 0.332558}}

We can check the validity of the candidate

In[47]:= **Grad[Wood[x1,x2,x3,x4],{x1,x2,x3,x4}] /. solution**

Out[47]= {-0.00256793, 0.00229724, -0.00380926, 0.00697934}

In[48]:= **Hessian[Wood[x1,x2,x3,x4],{x1,x2,x3,x4}] /. solution**

Out[48]= {{1315.41, -512.611, 0, 0}, {-512.611, 220.2, 0, 19.8},
              {0, 0, 245.765, -208.85}, {0, 19.8, -208.85, 233.992}}

In[49]:= **Eigenvalues[%]**

Out[49]= {1517.94, 449.169, 38.9745, 9.28113}

So indeed we are close to a minimum because the gradient is almost zero and the second derivative matrix is positive definite (so the function is locally strongly convex) but we are not exactly at the minimum. To improve the solution, one way is to look for a zero of the gradient near the best obtained solution. To do this, we use the **FindRoot** function.

```
In[50]:= eqns = Grad[Wood[x1,x2,x3,x4],{x1,x2,x3,x4}]==0

Out[50]=                          2
          {-2 (1 - x1) - 400 x1 (-x1  + x2),


                                 2
            -20.2 (1 - x2) + 200 (-x1  + x2) - 19.8 (1 - x4),


                               2
            -2 (1 - x3) - 360 x3 (-x3  + x4),


                                       3           2
            -19.8 (1 - x2) - 40.4 (1 - x4)  + 180 (-x3  + x4)} == 0

In[51]:= newsolution = Apply[FindRoot[eqns,##]&,
             Apply[List,solution,1]]

Out[51]= {x1 -> 1.28153, x2 -> 1.64342, x3 -> 0.580097,
            x4 -> 0.332492}
```

Note that this evaluation was immediate! Only a few digits have changed in $x3$ and $x4$, but now,

```
In[52]:= Grad[Wood[x1,x2,x3,x4],{x1,x2,x3,x4}] /. newsolution

Out[52]=            -14               -15             -14
          {1.92381 10    , -7.50962 10    , 3.48457 10    ,


                        -14
            -5.34824 10    }

In[53]:= Hessian[Wood[x1,x2,x3,x4],{x1,x2,x3,x4}] /. newsolution

Out[53]= {{1315.41, -512.612, 0, 0}, {-512.612, 220.2, 0, 19.8},
            {0, 0, 245.737, -208.835},
            {0, 19.8, -208.835, 234.003}}

In[54]:= Eigenvalues[%]

Out[54]= {1517.95, 449.146, 38.9791, 9.28369}
```

we have a new solution which is much better inasmuch as the gradient of the Wood function is equal to 0 with a very good precision and the Hessian matrix is positive definite.

The reader will have noted the two interesting constructions **Apply[List [solution,1]]** and **Apply[FindRoot[eqns,##]&, {{x1,val1},...,**

{xn,valn}}] that enable to call and (call again) **FindRoot**, **FindMinimum**, and so on, easily with several variables.

As another use of this syntax, let us build an *n*-dimensional Rosenbrock Banana. The variables will be *xi*. We first need to produce these variables.

```
In[55]:= x[i_]:= ToExpression[ToString[x]<>ToString[i]]
```

```
In[56]:= nvars = 5; vars = Table[x[i],{i,nvars}]
```

```
Out[56]= {x1, x2, x3, x4, x5}
```

The test function is given by the general formula

```
In[57]:= testfunction= (1-x[1])^2 + 100 Sum[(x[i+1]-x[i]^2)^2,
            {i,1,nvars-1}]
```

$$Out[57] = (1 - x1)^2 + 100\ ((-x1^2 + x2)^2 + (-x2^2 + x3)^2 +$$
$$(-x3^2 + x4)^2 + (-x4^2 + x5)^2\ )$$

We know that the solution is *vars* = $\{1, 1, \ldots, 1\}$ and take typical alternating initial values

```
In[58]:= var0 = Table[2 (-1)^i,{i,nvars}]
```

```
Out[58]= {-2, 2, -2, 2, -2}
```

```
In[59]:= {cost,solution} = FindMinimum[testfunction,##]& @@
            Transpose[{vars,var0}]
```

```
FindMinimum::fmcv:
   FindMinimum failed to converge to the prescribed accuracy
      within 30 iterations.
```

```
Out[59]= {0.0144934, {x1 -> 0.88007, x2 -> 0.774691,
            x3 -> 0.600418, x4 -> 0.359653,
            x5 -> 0.128822}}
```

FindMinimum tells us that 30 iterations are not enough. In fact, we need more than 90 to get a correct evaluation of the optimal cost, and the improvement is approximately linear as a function of iteration number, especially for the farthest variables ($x[nvar]$, for example). ·

```
In[60]:= {cost, candidate} = FindMinimum[testfunction,
            ##,MaxIterations->60]&  @@ Apply[List,solution,1]

Out[60]= {0.00219232, {x1 -> 0.953224, x2 -> 0.908456,
            x3 -> 0.825211, x4 -> 0.680909, x5 -> 0.463638}}
```

Now let us try the candidate.

```
In[61]:= Grad[testfunction,vars] /. candidate

Out[61]= {-0.0250974, -0.00666709, 0.00518705, -0.012953,
            0.0000434104}
```

```
In[62]:= Hessian[testfunction,vars] /. candidate

Out[62]= {{728.98, -381.289, 0, 0, 0},
            {-381.289, 860.266, -363.382, 0, 0},
            {0, -363.382, 744.805, -330.085, 0},
            {0, 0, -330.085, 570.91, -272.364},
            {0, 0, 0, -272.364, 200}}
```

```
In[63]:= Eigenvalues[%]

Out[63]= {1367.01, 938.424, 548.588, 250.911, 0.0226243}
```

It is close to the solution but we need to improve it.

3.3.2 A Bunch of NewtonMin Functions

Let us build a **NewtonMinStep** function that will perform one Newton step
to minimize the quadratic approximation of testfunction in the vicinity of
our candidate solution. For this, we need a function that computes the *quadratic
approximation* of a function (the truncated order 2 Taylor series), as a function of
the following parameters.

  (i) the expression to approximate,
  (ii) the variables, and
  (iii) the point at which the approximation is done.

```
In[64]:= QuadApprox[f_,x_,x0_]:= Module[ {rep = Thread[x -> x0],
            gradf, hessf}, gradf = Grad[f,x] /. rep;
          hessf = Hessian[f,x] /. rep;
          (f /. rep ) + gradf.(x - x0) + 1/2 (x-x0).hessf.(x-x0) ]
```

For example, we have

```
In[65]:= quadfun = Expand[ QuadApprox[testfunction,vars,vars /.
            candidate] ]
```

```
Out[65]=                                    2
       219.596 - 348.522 x1 + 364.49 x1  - 118.199 x2 -


                                    2
       381.289 x1 x2 + 430.133 x2  - 59.7419 x3 -


                                    2
       363.382 x2 x3 + 372.402 x3  + 9.91676 x4 -


                                    2
       330.085 x3 x4 + 285.455 x4  + 92.7275 x5 -


                              2
       272.364 x4 x5 + 100 x5
```

The next step of the Newton algorithm is to find the minimum of this quadratic function, for example, with **FindMinimum**.
Note: Do you see how horrible this is ?

```
In[66]:= {cost, candidate}  =  FindMinimum[quadfun,##]& @@
             Transpose[{vars,var0}]


Out[66]= {0.000435919, {x1 -> 0.9907, x2 -> 0.98004,
             x3 -> 0.955337, x4 -> 0.895736, x5 -> 0.756192}}
```

There is clearly an improvement towards all 1s.
We can perform a few such steps in the following way.

```
In[67]:= Timing[ Table[ qf = QuadApprox[testfunction,vars,
         (vars /. candidate)];
         {cost, candidate} =
         FindMinimum[qf,##]& @@ Transpose[{vars,var0}],{6}] //
         TableForm  ]


Out[67]= {54.65 Second,                        x1 -> 0.986699}
                                               x2 -> 0.973486
                                               x3 -> 0.94756
                                               x4 -> 0.897635
                          0.000467902          x5 -> 0.805745


                                               x1 -> 0.993898
                                               x2 -> 0.987751
                                               x3 -> 0.975435
                                               x4 -> 0.950696
                          0.0000815997         x5 -> 0.901007
```

	x1 -> 0.993899
	x2 -> 0.987805
	x3 -> 0.975743
	x4 -> 0.952066
0.0000384169	x5 -> 0.906427

	x1 -> 0.999629
	x2 -> 0.999224
	x3 -> 0.998318
-6	x4 -> 0.996128
2.26856 10	x5 -> 0.99033

	x1 -> 0.999539
	x2 -> 0.999075
	x3 -> 0.99815
-7	x4 -> 0.996302
2.28902 10	x5 -> 0.992618

	x1 -> 0.999998
	x2 -> 0.999996
	x3 -> 0.999991
-10	x4 -> 0.999979
8.63328 10	x5 -> 0.999945

Of course, the Newton optimization algorithm can be programmed much more efficiently in the following way. Let

$$f(x^k) + g^k.(x - x^k) + \frac{1}{2}(x - x^k).h^k.(x - x^k)$$

be the (assumed positive) quadratic approximation of $f(x)$ around x^k. Then the minimum is attained at

$$x^{k+1} = x^k + \delta \qquad \text{such that } g^k + h^k.\delta = 0.$$

So we simply need to solve a *linear system* in δ.

```
In[68]:= Clear[NewtonMin]

In[69]:= NewtonMin[fn_,var_List,var0_List,itermax_Integer,
            coef_]:=
        Module[{dfn = Grad[fn,var], d2fn = Hessian[fn,var],
            vark = var0, deltak, pts},
        sk := Thread[var->vark];
        pts = Table[
        deltak = LinearSolve[d2fn /.sk,-(dfn /.sk)];
        vark = vark + coef deltak;   (* coef = damping <= 1 *)
        {fn /. sk, sk},    (* -> serves only display purposes *)
        {itermax}]]
```

Let us show the last 3 iterations of 30 Newton steps.

```
In[70]:= Timing[ Take[NewtonMin[testfunction,vars,var0,30,1.],
            -3]// TableForm ]
```

```
Out[70]= {17.8333 Second,                     x1 -> 0.999158}
                                              x2 -> 0.998246
                                              x3 -> 0.996231
                                              x4 -> 0.991463
                         0.00153185           x5 -> 0.979229

                                              x1 -> 0.998962
                                              x2 -> 0.997919
                                              x3 -> 0.99584
                                   -6         x4 -> 0.991695
                         1.08198 10           x5 -> 0.98346

                                              x1 -> 0.99999
                                              x2 -> 0.999978
                                              x3 -> 0.999952
                                   -7         x4 -> 0.999888
                         4.81048 10           x5 -> 0.999708
```

Certain remarks are in order:

(1) As previously implemented, NewtonMin is not a minimization routine!
    Indeed, it does not try to follow descent paths and could very well give
    the maximum of a concave function or a saddle-point.

```
In[71]:= Last[NewtonMin[x^2 - y^2,{x,y},{1,3},2,1]]
```

```
Out[71]= {0, {x -> 0, y -> 0}}
```

This is because it only tries to find a root to the system of equations
Grad[f,x] == 0, exactly as we did with the preceding FindRoot function.

(2) An apparently less efficient implementation (in the number of iterations,
    but much easier to program) of NewtonMin (or Max...) could thus be

```
In[72]:= FindRootNewtonMin[function_,vars_List,var0_List]:=
            With[{optim = Grad[function,vars]},
            FindRoot[optim,##]& @@ Transpose[{vars,var0}] ]
```

```
In[73]:= FindRootNewtonMin[testfunction,vars,var0] //Timing
```

```
FindRoot::cvnwt:
    Newton's method failed to converge to the prescribed
        accuracy after 15 iterations.
```

Out[73]= {2.76667 Second, {x1 -> -0.568664, x2 -> 0.323744,
            x3 -> 0.0955945, x4 -> 0.00119958,
            x5 -> -0.0034455}}

It takes roughly 250 iterations and a damping factor less than one to ensure convergence to the solution.

In[74]:= **Timing[FindRoot[Grad[testfunction,vars],##,**
            MaxIterations -> 250, DampingFactor-> .9]& @@
            Transpose[{vars,var0}]]

Out[74]= {10.9333 Second, {x1 -> 1., x2 -> 1., x3 -> 1.,
            x4 -> 1., x5 -> 1.}}

But it *is* fast!

3.4 General Nonlinear Programming

3.4.1 The General Nonlinear Problem

The general nonlinear programming problem is

$$\min f(x) \quad \text{s.t.} \quad g(x) = 0 \quad \text{and} \quad h(x) \le 0,$$

where f, g, and h are nonlinear (possibly vectorial) functions.

In[75]:= **Needs["Optimize'MMethod'"]**

Needs::nocont: Warning:Context Optimize'MMethod'
    was not created when Needs was evaluated.

Note: The former command assumes that one has installed the **Optimize 'MMethod.m** package in the Package Folder. This package is fully described and tested at the end of the chapter and is also available on MathSource under the current name **MultiplierMethod**.

3.4.2 The Penalization Attack

For example, let us consider:

$$\min y + x^2 \quad \text{s.t.} \quad x + y = 3.5, \quad -x + 2 \le 0, \quad -y + 1 \le 0$$

Any scalar *equality* constraint $g(x) = 0$ can be penalized by adding the term $kg(x)^2$ to the objective function $f(x)$. *Inequality* constraint $h(x) \le 0$ can be penalized by adding the term $k \max(0, h(x))^2$.

```
In[76]:= k0 = k1 = k2 = 1000;
         penal := y + x^2 + k0 (x + y - 3.5)^2 +
                  k1 Max[0,-x+2]^2 + k2 Max[0,-y+1]^2;
```

So let us just solve it.

```
In[77]:= FindMinimum[penal, {x,4.},{y,6.}]
```

```
FindMinimum::fmgs:
   Could not symbolically find the gradient of penal. Try giving
      two starting values for each variable.
```

```
Out[77]= FindMinimum[penal, {x, 4.}, {y, 6.}]
```

Oops!

```
In[78]:= D[Max[0,x]^2,x]
```

```
Out[78]=                               (0,1)
              2 Max[0, x] Max       [0, x]
```

The derivative of $\max(0, h(x))^2$ is not known in 0, so one possibility is to give two initial values for each variable, that is, to use the *secant-version* of **FindMinimum**, hoping that we will never go too close to 0.

```
In[79]:= FindMinimum[penal, {x,4.,5.},{y,6.,7.}]
```

```
Out[79]= {5.4975, {x -> 1.9985, y -> 1.501}}
```

Another possibility is to tell **FindMinimum** what the gradient should be.

```
In[80]:= Grad[penal,{x,y}]
```

```
Out[80]=                                                              (0,1)
           {2 x + 2000 (-3.5 + x + y) - 2000 Max[0, 2 - x] Max       [0, 2 - x],

                                                         (0,1)
            1 + 2000 (-3.5 + x + y) - 2000 Max[0, 1 - y] Max       [0, 1 - y]}
```

```
In[81]:= grad := Grad[penal,{x,y}] /.
             Derivative[0,1][Max][0,u_]:> 1
```

```
In[82]:= grad
```

```
Out[82]= {2 x + 2000 (-3.5 + x + y) - 2000 Max[0, 2 - x],
             1 + 2000 (-3.5 + x + y) - 2000 Max[0, 1 - y]}
```

With this explicit definition of the gradient, we get

```
In[83]:= FindMinimum[ penal, {x,4.},{y,6.},Gradient -> grad ]
```

```
Out[83]= {5.4975, {x -> 1.9985, y -> 1.501}}
```

Both methods take approximately the same time. Increasing the penalty helps get closer to the solution but only to a certain point, due to numerical difficulties and "nonexact penalization."

```
In[84]:= k0 = k1 = k2 = 100000;
         {cost,sol} = FindMinimum[ penal, {x,4.},{y,6.},
         Gradient -> grad ]
```

```
Out[84]= {5.49998, {x -> 1.99999, y -> 1.50001}}
```

Once we have good approximations of the solutions, it is also possible to find the dual parameters. Indeed $p = 2kg(x^*)$ and $q = 2k \max(0, h(x^*))$ are known to be good approximations of p^* and q^*.

```
In[85]:= p0 = 2 k0 (x+y-3.5)   /. sol
```

```
Out[85]= -1.00007
```

```
In[86]:= {q1,q2} = { Max[2 k1 (-x +2),0], Max[2 k2 (-y +1),0]} /.
         sol
```

```
Out[86]= {2.92777, 0}
```

Let us check this with the **MultiplierMethod** function (described in the next section):

```
In[87]:= SetOptions[MultiplierMethod,InnerIterations->5]
```

```
Out[87]= {Augmentation -> 10., CheckConvergence -> True,
          DualParameter -> False, InnerIterations -> 5,
          OuterIterations -> 30, ConvergenceGoal -> 6}
```

```
In[88]:= MultiplierMethod[ y + x^2, {x + y - 3.5},{-x+2,-y +1},
         {x,y},{4.,6.}, DualParameter -> True]
```

```
Out[88]=                                            -13
         {5.5, {x -> 2., y -> 1.5}, {-2.0646 10    },

                                         -8
          {MMethod'p1 -> -1.}, {2.48065 10  , -0.5},

          {MMethod'q1 -> 3., MMethod'q2 -> 0.}}
```

Note that we get as output:

- the optimal value 5.5,
- the primal solution x and y,
- the equality constraint satisfaction,
- the associated Lagrange multiplier $p1$,
- the inequality constraints satisfaction, and
- the dual Kuhn and Tucker parameters $q1$ and $q2$.

Let us now give the `MultiplierMethod.m` package.

3.4.3 Description of the MultiplierMethod.m Package

3.4.3.1 Principle

It is based on the Uzawa algorithm, which is a dual gradient ascent algorithm. Roughly speaking, it is based on the classical theory of economics.

Suppose you are the only producer of Martian Chocolate and that you can supply a quantity Q to the Market. Martian Chocolate is very expensive but also very sensitive to Earth's atmospheric conditions. Whatever you do not sell is lost (no stocks).

If the demand D is larger than Q, you will raise your price because some people (for whatever reasons) will probably accept paying a higher price. But if your price is too high, nobody will want such an expensive chocolate. There is thus an equilibrium price q that will "clear the market." This q is the price associated with the constraint $D = Q$.

The idea of the Uzawa algorithm is the following.

You pick a price, announce it, get orders that sum up to D, but you do not deliver, and:

- if $D > Q$, you pretend the shuttle from Mars is not back yet and there may be a shortage, and you have to increase the price;
- if $D < Q$, you explain you optimized the space journey and gained $x\%$ that you would like to take off the regular price.

And you go back to the Market until it is "potentially" cleared, that is, until you have found the right price p that sells all the chocolate. Then you sell all your chocolate.

`MultiplierMethod.m` is based on this principle:

- predict p^k and q^k prices associated with $g(x) = 0$ and $h(x) \leq 0$;
- minimize $f(x) + p^k.g(x) + q^k.h(x)$ (solve the customers' problems) which gives x^k;

- update

$$p^{k+1} = p^k + c_1 g(x^k) \quad \text{and} \quad q^{k+1} = q^k + c_2 \max(0, h(x^k))$$

(can you guess why there is a max?), where c_i are positive numbers, until convergence.

These steps can be shown to be equivalent to some gradient ascent step on the dual function

$$H(p, q) = \min_x \{ f(x) + p.g(x) + q.h(x) \}$$

The *augmented* Lagrangian *"plus"* is that we are better minimizing

$$f(x) + p^k g(x) + q^k h(x) + \frac{c_1}{2} g(x)^2 + \frac{c_2}{2} \max(0, h(x))^2,$$

instead of $f(x) + p^k.g(x) + q^k.h(x)$ at each iteration. This apparently small difference improves many aspects, including stability, precision, convergence, and so on [see the references and, in particular, Bertsekas (1982) and Luenberger (1984)].

3.4.3.2 Title, Author, Comments, References, Documentation

This part of the code does not call for any explanation.

```
In[89]:= (* :Title: MultiplierMethod *)

(* :Context: Optimize'MultiplierMethod' *)
(* :File:    Optimize'MMethod' *)

(* :Author: Jean-Christophe Culioli *)
(* :Email: culioli@cas.ensmp.fr      *)
(* :Affiliation:  Centre Automatique et Systemes,  *)
(*                Ecole des Mines de Paris, FRANCE *)

(* :Summary:
     This package provides the function MultiplierMethod
     for minimization of an objective function subject to
     equality and / or inequality constraints
*)

(* :Package Version: 1.1.1 *)

(* :Mathematica Version: 2.2 *)

(* :Copyright: Copyright 1994, J.-C Culioli,
          Ecole des Mines de Paris, France
```

This package may be copied in its entirety for nonprofit purposes
only. Sale, other than for the direct cost of the media, is
prohibited. This copyright notice must accompany all copies. *)

(* :History: V. 1.0, 10 September 94, by JCC *)
(* :History: V. 1.1, 17 September 94, by JCC : changed the use of
FindRoot for inner optimization to FindMinimum with specified
gradient, using the rule: Derivative[0, 1][Max][0., theta_]:> 1.
Suppressed any approximation to the Max[0,x] function. Slightly
slower on some problems but much more robust.*)
(* :History: V. 1.1.1, 2 October 95, by JCC : minor changes,
including the file name for DOS compatibility and the MMethod'
subcontext*)

(* :Keywords:
    optimization, objective function, minimize, constraints,
    linear and nonlinear constraints, equalities, inequalities,
    augmented Lagrangian, Uzawa algorithm, Primal-Dual method. *)

(* :Limitations: (Theoretical) The problem solved is Min f(x)
    subject to g(x) = 0, h(x) <= 0 where f and h are convex and
    g is affine -- no proof of convergence to a solution in most
    other cases *)

(* :Limitations: (Practical) This program does not check for
optimality of the returned "solution" which should thus be
considered as a simple "candidate". Some information about
possible infeasibility or KKT conditions not met are given. Note
that the CheckConvergence option only controls convergence,
neither optimality nor feasibility. *)

(* :Discussion: The method is a gradient ascent algorithm
(Uzawa algorithm) applied to the dual functional with Augmented
Lagrangian. It is often called the Multiplier Method and due to
Hestenes, Powell. See for example D. G. Luenberger, "Linear and
Nonlinear Programming", Addison-Wesley, second. ed., 1989. *)

(* :Implementation: The use of FindMinimum as an internal
algorithm lead us to cancel all messages and to imitate its usual
output even when internal convergence messages FindMinimum::fmlim
prevents the output. As a complement, one advantage of this is
that we can set the InnerIterations option to 1, thus mimicking
Arrow-Hurwicz algorithm !*)

3.4.3.3   Usages, Messages, Options

Here we mostly give information on the function and the options. We also
define the gradient for the Max[x, 0]^2 function, a function pos[ ] to project
a vector onto the positive orthant, and a function phi[ ] which computes the

augmented Lagrangian term. Then we create indexed dual variables within the "`MMethod'`" context.

```
In[90]:= BeginPackage["Optimize'MultiplierMethod'"]

ison = Off[FindMinimum::fmcv,FindMinimum::fmlim,
           General::spell,General::spell]


MultiplierMethod::usage = "MultiplierMethod[f,g,h,x,x0] finds
a local solution to a minimization algorithm where:
f is the criterion to be minimized, g is the list (possibly empty)
of equality constraints [with assumed zero right hand side],
h is the list (possibly empty) of inequality constraints
[with assumed zero right hand side in the <= direction],
x = {x1,x2,...} is a generic list of the variables, x0 is an
initial vector  for x. It returns a list {f*,{x1 -> x1*, etc}}
like FindMinimum. With the option DualParameter -> True it can
also provide information on  feasibility and Lagrange and/or
Karush Kuhn & Tucker multipliers.";

OuterIterations::usage = "OuterIterations is an option for
MultiplierMethod specifying  the maximum number of outer
iterations (gradient ascent for the dual parameters). The default
setting is OuterIterations -> 30.";

InnerIterations::usage = "InnerIterations is an option for
MultiplierMethod specifying  the maximum number of inner
iterations. The default setting is InnerIterations -> 10 .";

DualParameter::usage = "DualParameter is an option for
MultiplierMethod. With the default setting DualParameter -> False,
no information is provided on the dual parameters (Lagrange and/or
Karush, Kuhn & Tucker multipliers). With DualParameter -> True,
feasibility information and the dual parameter are appended to the
primal solution with the following format {f*,{x -> x*,...},g*,
{p -> p*,...},h*,{q -> q*,...}} where p's and q's are
automatically created variables.";

CheckConvergence::usage = "CheckConvergence is an option for
MultiplierMethod. With the setting CheckConvergence -> False,
convergence of the algorithm is not checked... and control is left
to the user with the OuterIterations option. With the default
CheckConvergence -> True, the stopping test is
Function[{u,v},Max[Abs[u-v]]< 10^-k  where k is the value of
the ConvergenceGoal option. The total number of iterations is
however limited to OuterIterations";

Augmentation::usage = "Augmentation is an option for
MultiplierMethod. It gives the value of the augmentation parameter
```

```
for the augmented Lagrangian. The default setting is
Augmentation -> 10. It should be decreased in case of initial
explosion and increased in case of slow convergence.";

ConvergenceGoal::usage = "ConvergenceGoal is an option for
MultiplierMethod. It gives the precision of the convergence test.
Its default setting is 6 which is very low but quick. It should be
increased to 10 or more for better precision.";

MultiplierMethod::parchange =
"Inappropriate parameter: '1' -> '2', changed to '3'.";

MultiplierMethod::nonKKT=
"Karush, Kuhn & Tucker conditions not satisfied better than '1'.";

MultiplierMethod::nonadmissible=
"current point '1' from admissible.";

MultiplierMethod::nonposq=
"non admissible Karush Kuhn & Tucker multipliers."

MultiplierMethod::nonslackness=
"complementary slackness not satisfied.";
```

`In[91]:=` `Begin["'private'"]`

```
Grad[function_,var_List]:= D[function,#]& /@ var ;
pos[x_List]:=Map[Max[0.,#]&,x];
phi[h_,q_,c_]:= Plus @@ ( 1/(2. c) (pos[q + c h]^2 - q^2) );
pvar[i_]:= ToExpression[ToString["MMethod'p"]<>ToString[i]];
qvar[i_]:= ToExpression[ToString["MMethod'q"]<>ToString[i]];

Options[MultiplierMethod] = {Augmentation -> 10.,
CheckConvergence -> True, DualParameter -> False,
InnerIterations -> 10, OuterIterations -> 30,
ConvergenceGoal -> 6};
```

3.4.3.4 The Program

The program is a succession of MultiplierMethodStep steps that are ascent steps on the dual functional or more simply successive updatings of the p and q price ("dual") vectors. The rest of the code is mostly declarations, test calls, and option switches.

`In[92]:=` `MultiplierMethod[f_,g_List,h_List,x_List,x0_List,opts___]:=`
```
Module[
{xk = x0,                        (*  primal variables *)
p, pk = Table[0.,{Length[g]}],   (* dual "<=" variables *)
q, qk = Table[0.,{Length[h]}],   (*   dual "=" variables *)
```

```
     AugmLag,                         (* augmented Lagrangian *)
     c, maxiter, mode, cvgoal,        (* options values *)
     repx, repp, repq},              (*   solutions  *)

     {c, maxiter, mode, cvgoal} = {Augmentation, OuterIterations,
     CheckConvergence, ConvergenceGoal}  /. {opts} /.
     Options[MultiplierMethod];

     p = Map[pvar,Range[Length[g]]];     (* building auxiliary *)
     q = Map[qvar,Range[Length[h]]];         (* variables *)

     AugmLag = f + p.g + c/2. g.g +  phi[h,q,c];

     If[ !NumberQ[cvgoal] || cvgoal < 0 || cvgoal > $MachinePrecision,
     Message[MultiplierMethod::parchange,ConvergenceGoal,cvgoal,
             cvgoal = ConvergenceGoal /. Options[MultiplierMethod]] ];

     Which[
         mode === False,  {xk, pk, qk} =
             Nest[MultiplierMethodStep[AugmLag,g,h,c,x,p,q,#]&,
                 {xk,pk,qk}, maxiter],
         mode === True,   {xk, pk, qk} =
             FixedPoint[MultiplierMethodStep[AugmLag,g,h,c,x,p,q,#]&,
                 {xk,pk,qk}, maxiter,
                 SameTest -> Function[{u,v},Max[Abs[u-v]]< 10^-cvgoal]
],
         True, Message[MultiplierMethod::opttf,CheckConvergence,mode]
         ];

     repx =Thread[x -> xk]; repp =Thread[p -> pk];
     repq =Thread[q -> qk];
     OptimalityConditions[f,g,h,x,p,q,repx,repp,repq];

     dualinfo = DualParameter /. {opts} /. Options[MultiplierMethod];
     Which[
         dualinfo === False,  {(f /. repx), repx},
         dualinfo === True, {(f /. repx), repx, (g /. repx), repp,
         (h /. repx), repq},
         True, Message[MultiplierMethod::opttf,DualParameter,dualinfo]
         ]

     ]
```

3.4.3.5   One Step of Dual Ascent

This is the heart of the program. We update prices. For this, we need to compute the "demands" (the satisfaction of the constraints). This demand is computed by solving an unconstrained minimization problem using **FindMinimum** (any other routine would do here).

```
In[93]:= MultiplierMethodStep[AugmLag_,g_,h_,c_,x_,p_,q_,{xk_,pk_,qk_}]:=
         Module[
         {iter = InnerIterations /. Options[MultiplierMethod],
         lastx, lagk, gradk, repk},
         lagk = (AugmLag /. Thread[p -> pk] ) /. Thread[q -> qk];
         gradk = Grad[lagk,x] //. Derivative[0, 1][Max][0., theta_]:> 1;
         FindMinimum[lastx = x; lagk, ##, MaxIterations -> iter,
         Gradient -> gradk ]& @@ Transpose[{x,xk}];
         repk = Thread[x -> lastx];    (* forcing output even if
                                         it is prevented by FindMinimum *)
         {x, pk + c g , pos[qk + c h]  } /. repk  ];
```

3.4.3.6 Optimality Conditions Checking

These are the optimality tests, as described at the beginning of this chapter.

```
In[94]:= OptimalityConditions[f_,g_,h_,x_,p_,q_,repx_,repp_,repq_]:=
         Module[ {toladm, tolKKT, tolslack, KKT,admissible,nadm,posq,
         slackness},

         toladm = tolslack = tolKKT = 10^-5;
         KKT = Grad[f,x] + Grad[g,x].p + Grad[h,x].q  /. repx /. repp /.
         repq;
         If[Max[Abs[KKT]] > tolKKT,
         Message[MultiplierMethod::nonKKT,Sqrt[KKT.KKT]]];

         admissible = {g , posit[h]} /. repx ;
         If[(nadm = Max[Abs[admissible]]) > toladm,
         Message[MultiplierMethod::nonadmissible,nadm]];

         posq = Apply[And,Positive[q]];
         If[!posq,Message[MultiplierMethod::nonposq]];
             (* should never happen *)

         slackness = q.h /. repq ;
         If[Max[Abs[slackness]] > tolslack,
         Message[MultiplierMethod::nonslackness]];
         ]

         End[]

         On[ison]

         EndPackage[]
```

3.4.4 Testing MultiplierMethod.m

We test here **MultiplierMethod** with several easy and hard test problems.
In order to reduce the computing time, we first reduce the number of "inner"

iterations to 5 instead of 10. This is the number of steps that **FindMinimum** performs to find a minimum of the "inner" unconstrained problem. It is usually a loss of time to compute this minimum too precisely because

- at the beginning of the algorithm it will be very far from the true solution; and
- at the end (close to convergence), very few steps will be needed to improve its precision. The default `InnerIterations ->10` is a reasonable value, especially if the number of variables is large.

Each test is performed on a Macintosh Powerbook 170, a quite slow machine. The reader will thus not be surprised to find a 10 to 20 factor improvement on the PowerMac, UNIX, or Pentium machine.

```
In[95]:= SetOptions[MultiplierMethod,InnerIterations ->5]
```

```
Out[95]= {Augmentation -> 10., CheckConvergence -> True,
          DualParameter -> False, InnerIterations -> 5,
          OuterIterations -> 30, ConvergenceGoal -> 6}
```

3.4.4.1 Trivial 1

```
In[96]:= f = x1^2    ; g ={} ; h = {-x1+1};
         MultiplierMethod[f,g,h,{x1},{5.}] // Timing
```

```
Out[96]= {7.96667 Second, {1., {x1 -> 1.}}}
```

3.4.4.2 Trivial 2

```
In[97]:= f = (x1-2)^2    ; g ={x1 -1} ; h = { };
         MultiplierMethod[f,g,h,{x1},{5.}] // Timing
```

```
Out[97]= {7.36667 Second, {1., {x1 -> 1.}}}
```

3.4.4.3 Trivial 3

```
In[98]:=  f = x1^2 + (x2-2)^2  ; g ={x1 + x2 -5/2} ;
          h = {-x1 + .25 , -x2 + 2};
          MultiplierMethod[f,g,h,{x1,x2},{5.,10.}] // Timing
```

```
Out[98]=  {36.6 Second, {0.125, {x1 -> 0.25, x2 -> 2.25}}}
```

3.4.4.4   Quadratic Programming

```
In[99]:=  f = x1^2 + (x2-4)^2 ; g ={x1-x2} ; h = {5 x2};
          MultiplierMethod[f,g,h,{x1,x2},{1.,2.}] // Timing
```

```
Out[99]=                                              -8
          {17.6833 Second, {16., {x1 -> 2.14616 10   ,

                         -10
            x2 -> 8.57096 10    }}}
```

```
In[100]:= MultiplierMethod[f,g,h,{x1,x2},{1.,2.},
            ConvergenceGoal -> True, DualParameter -> True] //
            Timing
```

```
MultiplierMethod::parchange:
   Inappropriate parameter: ConvergenceGoal -> True,
     changed to 6.
```

```
Out[100]=                                             -8
          {19.2333 Second, {16., {x1 -> 2.14616 10   ,

                         -10              -8
            x2 -> 8.57096 10    }, {2.06045 10   },

                                      -8               -9
            {MMethod'p1 -> -4.29233 10   }, {4.28548 10   },

            {MMethod'q1 -> 1.6}}}
```

3.4.4.5   Quadratic Programming: Equality Only

```
In[101]:= u = {u1,u2,u3};
          j = (u1-u2)^2 + u3;
          g = {{1, 1,1},{0,1,-2}}. u + {5,-1};  h = {};
          MultiplierMethod[j,g,h,u,{1.,2.,0.},
            DualParameter -> True] // Timing
```

```
Out[101]= {10.25 Second, {-1.41, {u1 -> -1.74, u2 -> -1.84,

                             -9               -10
            u3 -> -1.42}, {-1.30319 10   , -4.03212 10    },

            {MMethod'p1 -> -0.2, MMethod'p2 -> 0.4}, {}, {}}}
```

3.4.4.6   Quadratic Programming: Inequality Only

```
In[102]:= f = 2 x1^2 + x1 x2 + x2^2 - 12 x1 - 10 x2;
          g = {};   h = {x1 + x2 - 4, -x1, -x2};
          MultiplierMethod[f,g,h,{x1,x2},{0,0},
              DualParameter -> True]  // Timing
```

```
Out[102]= {25.3167 Second, {-28.5, {x1 -> 1.5, x2 -> 2.5}, {},

                              -8
                  {}, {7.21123 10  , -1.5, -2.5}, {MMethod`q1 -> 3.5,

                  MMethod`q2 -> 0., MMethod`q3 -> 0.}}}
```

3.4.4.7   Quadratic Programming with Two Equalities and One Inequality

```
In[103]:= u = {u1,u2,u3};
          j = (u1-u2)^2 + 5 u3;
          g = {{1, 1,1},{0,1,-3}}. u + {5,-1};   h = {-u1};
          MultiplierMethod[j,g,h,u,{1.,2.,0.},
              DualParameter -> True]  // Timing
```

```
Out[103]=                                                     -8
          {74.6333 Second, {4.75, {u1 -> -4.71815 10  , u2 -> -3.5,

                                   -8            -9
          u3 -> -1.5}, {1.33134 10  , 5.49807 10  },

          {MMethod`p1 -> 4., MMethod`p2 -> 3.},

                    -8
          {4.71815 10  }, {MMethod`q1 -> 11.}}}
```

3.4.4.8   A Few Tests From the Books by W. Hock and K. Schittkowski (1980) and K. Schittkowski (1987)

TP1 p. 24 (The Rosenbrock Problem)

```
In[104]:= f = 100 (x2 - x1^2)^2 + (1-x1)^2; g = {};
          h = {-x2 -1.5};
          MultiplierMethod[f,g,h,{x1,x2},{-2.,1.}] // Timing
```

```
Out[104]=                                -28
          {26.0667 Second, {6.08557 10  ,

              {x1 -> 1., x2 -> 1.}}}
```

TP2 p. 25

```
In[105]:= f = 100 (x2 - x1^2)^2 + (1-x1)^2; g = {};
          h = {-x2 +1.5};
          MultiplierMethod[f,g,h,{x1,x2},{-2.,1.}]   // Timing

Out[105]= {17.4833 Second, {4.94123,

             {x1 -> -1.22103, x2 -> 1.5}}}
```

TP216 p. 40

```
In[106]:= f = 100 (x1^2 - x2)^2 + (x1 - 1)^2;
          g = { x1 (x1-4) - 2 x2 + 12 }; h = {};
          MultiplierMethod[f,g,h,{x1,x2},{-1.2,1.},
             DualParameter -> True]  // Timing

Out[106]=
          {15.2 Second, {0.999375, {x1 -> 1.99938, x2 -> 4.},

                             -11
             {-2.92342 10    }, {MMethod'p1 -> 0.249883},

             {}, {}}}
```

TP217 p. 41

```
In[107]:= f = -x2; g =  { x1^2 + x2^2 - 1 };
          h = {-x1, -1 - x1 + 2 x2};
          MultiplierMethod[f,g,h,{x1,x2},{10.,10.}] // Timing

Out[107]= {24.8 Second, {-0.8, {x1 -> 0.6, x2 -> 0.8}}}

In[108]:= MultiplierMethod[f,g,h,{x1,x2},{10.,10.},
          ConvergenceGoal -> 3, Augmentation -> 1] // Timing

MultiplierMethod::nonadmissible: current point 0.0000659054
   from admissible.

Out[108]= {22.85 Second, {-0.799999, {x1 -> 0.599947,
             x2 -> 0.799999}}}
```

TP230 p. 54 Chamberlain Problem

```
In[109]:= f = x2;  g =  {};
          h = - {-2 x1^2 + x1^3 + x2 , -2(1-x1)^2 +
             (1-x1)^3 + x2};
          MultiplierMethod[f,g,h,{x1,x2},{0.,0.}]    // Timing
```

Out[109]= {13.4833 Second, {0.375, {x1 -> 0.5, x2 -> 0.375}}}

TP234 p. 58

```
In[110]:= f = (x2-x1)^4 -(1-x1); g = {};
          h = {x1 - 2, x2 - 2, -x1 + .2, -x2 + .2,
              x1^2 + x2^2 -1};
          MultiplierMethod[f,g,h,{x1,x2},{0.,0.}] // Timing
```

Out[110]= {19.5667 Second, {-0.8, {x1 -> 0.2, x2 -> 0.200324}}}

TP321 p. 142. . . difficult. . .

```
In[111]:= f = (x1-20)^2 + (x2 + 20)^2;
          g = {x1^2 /100. + x2^2 -1}; h = {};
          MultiplierMethod[f,g,h,{x1,x2},{0.,0.}] // Timing
```

MultiplierMethod::nonadmissible: current point 0.0418276 from
    admissible.

Out[111]= {71.8333 Second, {491.857, {x1 -> 10.0121,
              x2 -> -0.198496}}}

TP322 p. 143. . . difficult. . .

```
In[112]:= f = (x1-20)^2 + (x2 + 20)^2;
          g = {x1^2 /100. + 100. x2^2 -1}; h = {};
          MultiplierMethod[f,g,h,{x1,x2},{0.,0.}] // Timing
```

MultiplierMethod::nonKKT:
    Karush, Kuhn & Tucker conditions not satisfied better than
    0.00410777.

MultiplierMethod::nonadmissible: current point 0.0244129 from
    admissible.

Out[112]= {53.9167 Second, {497.547, {x1 -> 10.1193,
              x2 -> -0.00204762}}}

TP339 p. 160 Container Problem. . . difficult. . .
    The optimal solution is known to be **{3.36168, {x1 -> 2.380, x2 -
> 0.3162, x3 -> 1.943}}**

```
In[113]:= f = 1/(5. x1 x2 x3) + 4./x1 + 3./x3;
          h = {2. x1 x3 + x1 x2 -10., -x1,-x2,-x3,x1-5,
              x2-5,x3-5};
          g = {};
          MultiplierMethod[f,g,h,{x1,x2,x3},{1.,1.,1.}] //
          Timing
```

```
Out[113]= {55.85 Second, {3.36168, {x1 -> 2.37976,
               x2 -> 0.316228, x3 -> 1.94294}}}
```

TP340 p. 161 Pascal Problem

```
In[114]:= f = -x1 x2 x3;  h =  {-1.8 + x1 + 2 x2 + 2 x3, x1-1};
          g = {};
          MultiplierMethod[f,g,h,{x1,x2,x3},{1.,1.,1.},
             DualParameter -> True]
```

```
Out[114]=
          {-0.054, {x1 -> 0.6, x2 -> 0.3, x3 -> 0.3}, {}, {},

                     -9
          {-9.3924 10   , -0.4},

          {MMethod'q1 -> 0.09, MMethod'q2 -> 0.}}
```

3.4.5   Conclusion

Let us go back to the Rosenbrock Banana *unconstrained* problem. We can solve it with **MultiplierMethod**. We just need to define f and g as empty lists:

```
In[115]:= MultiplierMethod[100(x1^2-x2)^2 + (x1-1)^2,
          {},{},{x1,x2},{-2.,3.}] // Timing
```

```
Out[115]=                                   -28
          {28.1667 Second, {5.71722 10    ,

          {x1 -> 1., x2 -> 1.}}}
```

To compare, FindMinimum gives:

```
In[116]:= FindMinimum[100 (x1^2-x2)^2 + (x1-1)^2,{x1,-2},
             {x2,3}] // Timing
```

```
Out[116]=                                   -10
          {10.8667 Second, {8.26483 10    , {x1 -> 0.999989,
               x2 -> 0.999976}}}
```

We can also solve linear problems with **MultiplierMethod**. This experiment is left to the reader (try a small dimension assignment problem).

To finish, let us now solve the "difficult" problem of the Introduction.

```
In[117]:= f = 1/2 u0^2 + 1/6 (u1^2+u2^2+u3^2) ;
          u = {u0,u1,u2,u3};
          g = {};  (* no equality constraint *)
          h = {-u0 + 2, - u0 - u1 + 5, - u0 - u2 + 2 ,
               - u0 - u3 + 1};
          MultiplierMethod[f,g,h,u,Table[2,{4}]] // Timing
```

```
Out[117]= {52.3333 Second, {3.5, {u0 -> 2., u1 -> 3.,

                          -14                      -14
              u2 -> -1.63065 10    , u3 -> -1.52347 10   }}}
```

It does take some time, but there is no need to pick the solution from among a set of candidates.

3.5 Acknowledgments

I would like to thank the two reviewers who contributed to several improvements of this chapter.

3.6 References

D. P. Bertsekas. 1982. *Constrained Optimization and Lagrange Multipliers Method.* Boston, Academic Press.

R. Fletcher. 1980. *Practical Methods for Optimization.* New York, John Wiley & Sons.

W. Hock & K. Schittkowski. 1980. "Test Examples for Nonlinear Programming Codes." *Lecture Notes in Economics and Mathematical Systems,* **N 187**. New York, Springer-Verlag.

D. Luenberger. 1984. *Introduction to Linear and Nonlinear Programming.* Reading, MA, Addison-Wesley.

K. Schittkowski. 1987. "More Test Examples for Nonlinear Programming Codes." *Lecture Notes in Economic and Mathematical Systems,* **N 282**. New York, Springer-Verlag.

Part of the material presented here is also available in a French book, *Introduction l'Optimisation*, Ed. Ellipses, Paris, 1994, by J.-C. Culioli.

4 Optimizing with Piecewise Smooth Functions

Paul A. Rubin

4.1 Introduction

In this chapter, we introduce a *Mathematica* package designed to deal with piecewise smooth functions of a single variable, and illustrate its use on several lot-sizing problems arising in materials management. These problems exemplify the effect of economies or diseconomies of scale in managerial decision making. Incorporating scale effects in decision models often involves the use of functions that are piecewise smooth with a finite number of singularities, in the form of jump discontinuities in either the function or one of its derivatives. Introductory texts frequently suggest dealing with discontinuities by solving the problem over each domain interval separately and then comparing the solutions. As the number of subdomains to be considered grows, it becomes desirable to treat multiple domains automatically, rather than manually.

4.2 How Piecewise Smooth Functions Can Arise

Before delving into the use of *Mathematica* to solve problems involving piecewise smooth functions, we first show how they may occur in practice. The models discussed in the following arise in materials management, but similar situations are found in labor and capacity planning and a variety of other contexts.

4.2.1 Lot-Sizing

Lot-sizing problems involve the selection of a quantity of material to order, manufacture, or ship on a repetitive basis. Materials managers most often deal with integer quantities of material, but it is usually convenient (and adequately accurate) to treat material lot sizes as divisible, and then round results to an adjacent feasible (integer) amount. One example is the economic order quantity model for material purchases.

Assume that a firm consumes D units of a particular item annually, at a uniform rate, and that the item costs P dollars per unit to purchase. Assume further that there is a fixed charge of S dollars each time an order is placed, an inventory holding charge of hP dollars per unit per year, and a known lead time between placement and delivery of a replenishment order. Under these assumptions, it is convenient to order a fixed amount Q at regular intervals, timed so that the order is delivered just as the inventory level is dropping to zero. The total annual cost is then

$$TC(Q) = DS/Q + PD + hPQ/2,$$

where the terms on the right capture order placement, purchase, and inventory holding costs, respectively (average annual inventory is one-half the order size). TC is a convex function, minimized at

$$Q^* = \text{Sqrt}[2DS/(hP)],$$

which is known as the *economic order quantity* (EOQ). Because Q^* has no particular reason to be an integer, in practice we would normally take an adjacent integer quantity as our order size. Figures 1a and 1b show an example, drawn from Tables 9 and 10 of Rubin and Benton (1993), with the following parameters: $D = 12{,}500$, $P = \$35.50$, $S = \$125$, and $h = 0.36$. The EOQ is $Q^* = 494.49$; a purchase lot size of either 494 or 495 would be the practical choice.

4.2.1.1   Figure 1a, b

```
In[1]:= Clear[ demand, setup, holding, totalCost ];
        demand = 12500; setup = 125; holding = 0.36;
        totalCost[ quantity_, price_ ] :=
          demand setup/quantity + demand price +
          holding price quantity/2
        Plot[ totalCost[ q, 35.5 ], {q, 1, 1000},
            PlotRange -> {0, 10^6},
            AxesLabel -> {"Quantity", "Cost"} ];
        Plot[ totalCost[ q, 35.5 ], {q, 300, 700},
            PlotRange -> {450000, 450500},
            AxesLabel -> {"Quantity", "Cost"} ];
```

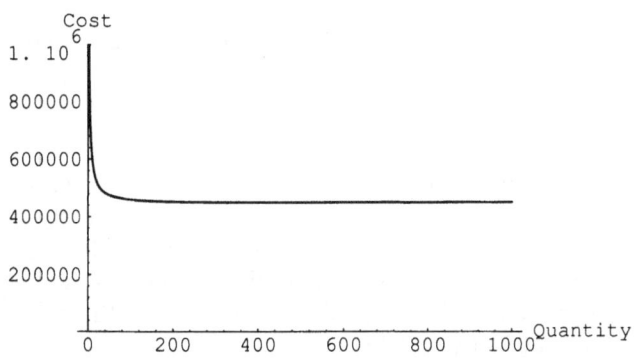

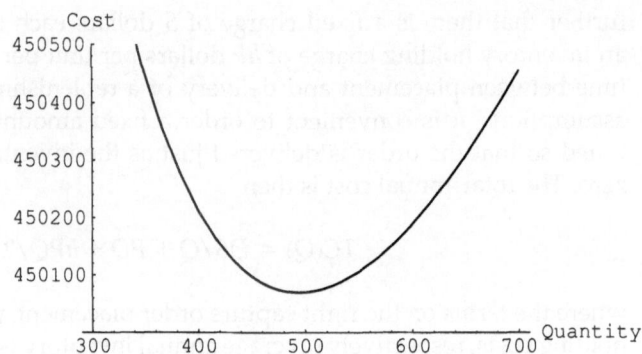

4.2.2   Economies and Diseconomies of Scale

The introduction of economies or diseconomies of scale tends to produce discontinuities in either the cost functions of a lot-sizing problem or their derivatives. For purchasing problems, the most common changes involve discounts offered by vendors for bulk purchases. In transportation problems, there may be similar discounts offered for larger shipments; in particular, carriers frequently offer more attractive tariffs (rates) for truckload shipments, volumes large enough to warrant devoting a truck exclusively to that shipment. The sizing of production lots is more likely to involve diseconomies of scale as, for instance, when the tradeoff between setup and holding costs in a make-to-stock environment leads to lot sizes exceeding the available primary storage capacity, requiring the use of costlier secondary storage sites.

Returning to the EOQ model, suppose that the vendor offers a decreasing sequence of unit prices $P_1 > P_2 > \cdots > P_M$ for orders meeting or exceeding an increasing sequence of qualifying amounts (*breakpoints*) $1 = Q_1 < Q_2 < \cdots < Q_M < Q_{M+1} = \infty$. We assume that each discounted price applies to the entirety of a qualifying order (an *all-units discount*). The total cost function must now be rewritten as

$$TC(Q) = DS/Q + P(Q)D + hP(Q)Q/2,$$

where $P(Q) = P_m$ if and only if $Q_m \leq Q < Q_{m+1}$. This function is discontinuous at the breakpoints Q_m. The conventional approach to calculating the EOQ involves minimizing the function separately over each subinterval of its domain [see, for instance, Love (1979), pp. 48–51]. Figure 2 shows the problem depicted in Figure 1, with the addition of the following discount schedule: $P_1 = \$35.50$, $P_2 = \$33.72$, $P_3 = \$31.45$, $P_4 = \$28.50$; $Q_1 = 1$, $Q_2 = 600$, $Q_3 = 1,000$, $Q_4 = 2,000$.

4.2.2.1 Figure 2

```
In[2]:= qtylist = {1, 600, 1000, 2000, 3000};
        qint = Partition[ qtylist, 2, 1 ];
        plist = {35.5, 33.72, 31.45, 28.5};
        Show[
          Table[
            Plot[ totalCost[ q, plist[[i]] ],
              Evaluate[ Prepend[ qint[[j]], q ] ],
              DisplayFunction -> Identity,
              PlotRange -> {300000, 600000},
              PlotStyle ->
                If[ i == j,
                Thickness[ 0.01 ],
                Dashing[ {0.01} ]
                ]
          ], {i, 4}, {j, 4}
          ],
          DisplayFunction -> $DisplayFunction,
          AxesLabel -> {"Quantity", "Cost"}
        ];
```

The alternative to an all-units discount is to apply each discounted price only to units in excess of the qualifying amount (an *incremental discount*). With incremental discounts, the function $TC(Q)$ remains continuous, albeit not convex, but becomes nondifferentiable at the breakpoints. Its formula remains the same, but $P(Q)$ is now the *average* price per unit when the order size is Q. Figures 3a and 3b illustrate this, applying the price schedule used in Figure 2 incrementally.

4.2.2.2 Figure 3a, b

```
In[3]:= (* define purchase cost of an order at various prices *)
        Clear[ purchase ];
        purchase[ 1 ][ q_ ] = plist[[1]] q;
```

```
Do[
  purchase[ i ][ q_ ] =
    purchase[ i-1 ][ qtylist[[i]] ] +
      plist[[i]](q - qtylist[[i]]),
  {i, 2, 4}
];
Show[
  Table[
    Plot[ purchase[ i ][ q ]/q,
      Evaluate[ Prepend[ qint[[j]], q ] ],
      DisplayFunction -> Identity,
      PlotRange -> {30, 36},
      PlotStyle ->
        If[ i == j,
        Thickness[ 0.01 ],
        Dashing[ {0.01} ]
        ]
    ], {i, 4}, {j, 4}
  ],
  DisplayFunction -> $DisplayFunction,
  AxesLabel -> {"Quantity", "Average Price"}
];
Show[
  Table[
    Plot[ totalCost[ q, purchase[ i ][ q ]/q ],
      Evaluate[ Prepend[ qint[[j]], q ] ],
      DisplayFunction -> Identity,
      PlotRange -> {300000, 600000},
      PlotStyle ->
        If[ i == j,
        Thickness[ 0.01 ],
        Dashing[ {0.01} ]
        ]
    ], {i, 4}, {j, 4}
  ],
  DisplayFunction -> $DisplayFunction,
  AxesLabel -> {"Quantity", "Cost"}
];
```

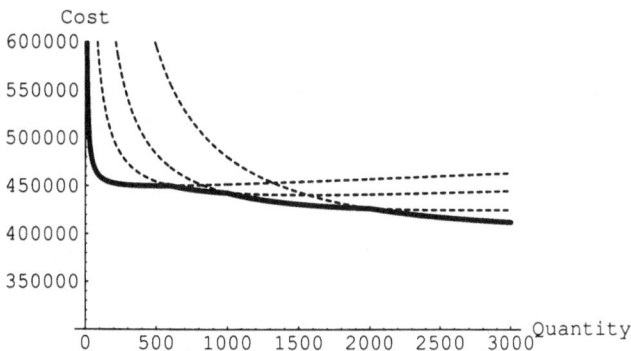

4.3   Dealing with Piecewise Smooth Functions in *Mathematica*

Mathematica's capacity for numerical optimization, together with its symbolic algebra capabilities, makes it a useful tool in solving standard lot-sizing problems. For instance, someone unfamiliar with the EOQ formula cited earlier could easily find the EOQ for the example given in Figure 1.

```
In[4]:=  FindMinimum[ totalCost[ q, 35.5 ], {q, 1} ]
```

```
Out[4]=  {450070., {q -> 494.487}}
```

Economies and diseconomies of scale present some difficulty, however, because *Mathematica* lacks intrinsic support for piecewise smooth functions. The standard package Calculus`DiracDelta` contains a function, **UnitStep**, which can be used to introduce discontinuous shifts in behavior in a function at a finite number of breakpoints. It is limited, however, in supporting only domain intervals closed on the left: **UnitStep[x-a]** takes value 1 for $x \geq a$ and 0 for $x < a$. Moreover, **FindMinimum** is not designed to work correctly with such discontinuous functions. The *Mathematica* kernel also contains a function **Interval** that can be used to declare intervals, but it is limited to supporting intervals closed at both ends.

Included on the diskette accompanying this book is a package PWS ` (file name PWS.M), which adds support for piecewise smooth functions to *Mathematica*. It uses a small utility package, Utilities`Message`, to manage some diagnostic messages *Mathematica* would otherwise be prone to print. This package is also included on the diskette (in file MESSAGE.M), and should be loaded to the same directory as the standard Utility`... packages which ship with *Mathematica*. Finally, a notebook (WALKTHRU.MA) contained on the diskette provides a tour of the capacities in the PWS ` package.

4.3.1   Describing Intervals

To support piecewise smooth functions, the first step was to provide a more general implementation of intervals. The standard interval notation in *Mathematica* is a set of endpoints, e.g., $\{a, b\}$. Inasmuch as we may encounter four different kinds of intervals (open or closed at either end), this provides insufficient flexibility. To distinguish types of intervals, we maintained the tacit *Mathematica* convention that $\{a, b\}$ represents the closed interval $[a, b]$, and added two new functions: **IA[x]**, representing a number "infinitesimally above" x, and **IB[x]**, representing a number "infinitesimally below" x. We refer to them collectively as "infinitesimals." The open interval (a, b) can now be represented as **{IA[a], IB[b]}**, whereas the semiopen intervals $[a, b)$ and $(a, b]$ would be represented respectively as **{a, IB[b]}** and **{IA[a], b}**.

Package PWS ` provides a fairly robust implementation of infinitesimals. For instance, arithmetic and comparison operators act correctly on them when the result is determinable. The notebook WALKTHRU.MA supplies details of the behavior of infinitesimals.

4.3.2   Piecewise Smooth Functions

Package PWS ` introduces two new heads, **PWS** and **PWSf**, to designate piecewise smooth functions. A standard piecewise smooth function expression consists of the head **PWS** and a list of pairs $\{subdomain, subfunction\}$, where the first element (*subdomain*) is an interval or singleton, using infinitesimals as needed, and the second element (*subfunction*) is the function to be evaluated when the argument falls in that interval. The subdomains must form a partition of the domain of the piecewise smooth function, and the subfunctions must each be smooth on their respective subdomains. It is not necessary to sort the ordered pairs. Package PWS ` includes a function, **PWSForm**, which prints **PWS** and **PWSf** functions in a tabular format for easier reading.

Subdomain specifications of a piecewise smooth function may contain symbols not yet assigned numeric values. The function will evaluate correctly only when its argument falls within a subdomain whose endpoints reduce to numbers. Operations, such as plotting, which potentially involve arguments in the ambiguously specified subdomains cannot be carried out. We call a piecewise smooth function *frozen* if its subdomains are fully determined. The head **PWSf** is used in place of **PWS** to distinguish frozen functions. The preferred way to create a frozen function is to create a standard piecewise smooth function using **PWS** and then apply the function **PWSFreeze** to convert it to a frozen function. Freezing is generally not necessary, as long as the PWS function's subdomains all evaluate to intervals with numeric (or infinitesimally adjusted) endpoints; the primary benefit of freezing is that **PWSFreeze** performs a consistency check to verify that the subdomains form a valid partition.

4.3.3   Using Piecewise Smooth Functions

PWS` extends several of *Mathematica*'s kernel commands and operators to function with piecewise smooth arguments. Arithmetic can be done between pairs of piecewise smooth functions, or between piecewise smooth functions and standard expressions, yielding piecewise smooth results. (PWS` makes no attempt to verify that a standard expression being combined with a **PWS** or **PWSf** function is itself smooth.) Most kernel functions that operate on scalar functions, including differentiation, integration, and optimization, can also be applied to piecewise smooth functions. Unary operators can be distributed across the subfunctions of a piecewise smooth function, and binary operators can be applied to pairs of piecewise smooth functions.

PWS` does not modify every kernel function, although most relevant extensions are included. Moreover, PWS` does not extend any functions defined in standard *Mathematica* packages. More thorough details on the use of the package can be found in the structured walk-through notebook.

4.3.4   Digression: Design Philosophy

One of *Mathematica*'s cardinal virtues is that it is extensible. The user is not limited to the capabilities of the kernel; new data types and new operators can be defined. There are effectively three approaches to extending *Mathematica*, each with its advantages and disadvantages.

4.3.4.1   Adding New Functions

The easiest (and arguably safest) approach is to define new functions, with entirely new names, preferably assembled in a package to isolate their internal workings from other contexts. By using new names (such as "**myPlot**" for an augmented plotting function), possible problems associated with altering the behavior of kernel functions (such as **Plot**) are avoided. There are possible drawbacks to this approach when the new functions are related in purpose to existing functions. First, it requires the user to remember new function names, and to recognize when the new function should be used in place of the kernel version. Should the user employ **Plot** or **myPlot** to plot a particular function? Second, if the user is writing code that will perform the operation on future arguments whose type is unknown at the time the code is written, it forces the user to provide for testing of the argument and selection of the correct function, and may cause problems with application of the function results (for instance, if the two versions do not return results in the same format).

4.3.4.2   Up-Values

The second approach is to use the name of an existing function, but associate the extended definition to arguments of a specific type (head) through up-values. This modifies the behavior of the kernel function, but only on arguments of the designated type (presumably a new type not found in the kernel). Moreover, the code for the modifications can easily be removed from memory without affecting normal operation of the kernel function. This approach, like the first, provides a high degree of safety. Unfortunately, *Mathematica*'s syntax places limitations on where in an argument an expression can appear if it is to be assigned an up-value.

4.3.4.3   Extending Kernel Functions

The third approach is to unprotect the kernel function and add directly to its definition. This provides the same ease of use associated with the second approach: the user employs a familiar function, and does not need to remember a new function name or select between the old and new functions. It also proves to be the most dangerous approach, primarily in that it may change the behavior of the kernel function in unanticipated ways.

In building PWS`, we used a mixture of these approaches. Entirely new functions, such as **IA** and **IB**, were coded with new names. Extensions of standard operations, such as addition (**Plus**), were done with up-values wherever permitted. A few functions, such as **Max** and **Min**, could not be extended with up-values for syntax reasons. Those cases were handled by unprotecting the kernel functions and adding to their definitions, taking care that the extensions applied only to expressions involving new heads (**IA**, **IB**, **PWS**, or **PWSf**).

4.4   Application of the Package

To illustrate the use of the package PWS`, let us revisit the earlier example of an EOQ problem with quantity discounts.

4.4.1   Single EOQ with All-Units Discounts

We start by entering the problem parameters.

```
In[5]:= << pws.m   (* load the package *)

In[6]:= Clear[ demand, setup, holding, price, totalCost ];
        demand = 12500; setup = 125; holding = 0.36;
```

Next we specify the price function as a piecewise-smooth function. Note that subdomain intervals are closed on the left: an order for exactly a breakpoint amount qualifies for the discount. The ampersands ("&") are necessary to distinguish constants (35.5) from constant-valued functions (35.5&).

```
In[7]:= price =
            PWSFreeze[
                PWS[ {{{1, IB[600]}}, 35.5&},   (* note use of '&' *)
                {{600, IB[1000]}}, 33.72&},
```

```
            {{1000, IB[2000]}, 31.45&},
            {{2000, Infinity}, 28.5&}}
         ]
      ];
```

Having defined price as a piecewise smooth function, we can reconstruct total cost as a piecewise smooth function. A bit of care must be taken in grouping the expressions in the formula, because *Mathematica* does not recognize that arithmetic expressions involving numbers and pure functions produce pure function results. To *Mathematica*, "**(holding #/2&)**" is a function but "**holding (#/2&)**" is not.

```
In[8]:=  totalCost =
            (demand setup/#)& + demand price +
            (holding #/2&) price ;
         totalCost // PWSForm
         Plot[ totalCost[ q ], {q, 1, 3000},
             PlotRange -> {350000, 550000},
             AxesLabel -> {"Quantity", "Cost"} ];
```

```
Frozen Piecewise Smooth Function:
   Domain                         Function
                                               1562500
                               443750. + ------- + 6.39 #1 &
   {1, IB[600]}        ==>                      #1


                                               1562500
                               421500. + ------- + 6.0696 #1 &
   {600, IB[1000]}     ==>                      #1


                                               1562500
                               393125. + ------- + 5.661 #1 &
   {1000, IB[2000]}    ==>                      #1


                                               1562500
                               356250. + ------- + 5.13 #1 &
   {2000, Infinity}    ==>                      #1
```

To calculate the EOQ with discount, we simply apply the **FindMinimum** kernel function, which has been extended to frozen piecewise smooth functions. The syntax for applying **FindMinimum** to a **PWSf** function deviates slightly from its normal syntax, in that an initial argument value is not employed. Also, the extended **FindMinimum** will not tolerate an unbounded subdomain, so we replace the upper domain limit Infinity with a large finite number.

```
In[9]:=  tC = totalCost /. Infinity -> 9999;
         FindMinimum[ tC[ q ], {q} ]

Out[9]=  {{367291., {q -> 2000}}}
```

This EOQ happens to be an endpoint of the final interval. We next examine a second item, with data drawn from the same source. Only the annual demand (5,640 units) and the price schedule ($41.20, $41.10, $41.07, $41.00) are different. For this item, the EOQ is an interior point of the first subdomain.

```
In[10]:= demand = 5640;
         price =
           PWSFreeze[
             PWS[ {{{1, IB[600]}, 41.20&},
               {{600, IB[1000]}, 41.10&},
               {{1000, IB[2000]}, 41.07&},
               {{2000, Infinity}, 41.00&}}
             ]
           ];
         totalCost =
           (demand setup/#)& + demand price +
           (holding #/2&) price;
         Plot[ totalCost[ q ], {q, 1, 3000},
               PlotRange -> {220000, 270000},
               AxesLabel -> {"Quantity", "Cost"},
               PlotStyle -> {{}, {Dashing[{0.01}]}}
         ];
         tC = totalCost /. Infinity -> 9999;
         FindMinimum[ tC[ q ], {q} ]
```

```
Out[10]= {{236941., {q -> 308.328}}}
```

4.4.2 Discounts on Purchase Price and Freight Costs

Hwang et al. (1990) constructed a model and solution algorithm for purchases of a single item when the vendor offers all-units discounts, the buyer pays shipping charges, and the carrier also offers all-units discounts. In their numerical example, annual demand was 3,000 units, order placement cost was $700, and annual inventory holding cost was 20% of purchase price. The vendor charged $20 per unit for orders of up to 1,500 units, $19 per unit for orders up to 4,000 units, and $18.50 per unit for larger orders. (Orders for exactly 1,500 or 4,000 units did not qualify for the lower price.) The carrier used transportation lots of 500 units each. For orders of 12,500 units (25 lots) or fewer, the carrier charged $400 per full or partial lot, discounting the entire charge 2% for each lot beyond the first. Thus a shipment of 25 lots would receive a 48% discount, reducing the average cost to $208 per lot. Beyond 25 lots, additional lots cost a flat $8 each.

To solve this problem in *Mathematica*, we can develop separate piecewise smooth functions for the purchase costs (including order setup and inventory holding) and the transportation costs, then combine them to form a piecewise smooth total cost function. Our solution, an order quantity of 1,600 units, matches that obtained by Hwang et al. using their algorithm.

```
In[11]:= demand = 3000; holding = 0.2; setup = 700;
         price =
           PWSFreeze[
             PWS[
               {{{1, 1500}, 20&}, {{IA[ 1500 ], 4000}, 19&},
                {{IA[ 4000 ], Infinity}, 18.5&}}
             ]
           ];
         purchase = demand setup/#& + demand price +
                 (holding #/2&) price;
         tariff1 =
           Table[ {{IA[ 400(j - 1) ], 400 j},
               Evaluate[ 400 j (1 - .02(j - 1)) ]&},
               {j, 25}
           ] /. IA[ 0 ] -> 1;
         tariff2 =
           Table[ {{IA[ 10000 + 400 (j - 1) ], 10000 + 400 j},
               Evaluate[ 5200 + 8 j ]&},
               {j, 10}
           ];
         tariff =
           PWSFreeze[ PWS[ Join[ tariff1, tariff2 ] ] ];
         totalCost = purchase + (demand/#&) tariff;
         Plot[ totalCost[ q ], {q, 1, 5600},
               AxesLabel -> {"Quantity", "Cost"},
               PlotStyle -> {{}, {Dashing[{0.01}]}},
               PlotRange -> {60000,74000}
         ];
```

```
Plot[ totalCost[ q ], {q, 200, 1800},
      AxesLabel -> {"Quantity", "Cost"},
      PlotStyle -> {{}, {Dashing[{0.01}]}},
      PlotRange -> {63000,70000}
];
FindMinimum[ totalCost[ q ], {q} ]
```

Out[11]= {{64172.5, {q -> 1600}}}

4.4.3   Discounts and Over-Declared Shipments

Russell and Krajewski (1991) also considered the case of a single item with known demand and all-units discounts on both purchase price and freight rate. Their model differed from that of Hwang et al. (1990) in recognizing the ability of the purchaser to exploit freight discounts by overstating the size of a shipment. If an order quantity is sufficiently close to the next higher breakpoint in the carrier's tariff schedule, the purchaser can reduce its shipping cost by inflating the declared weight. According to Russell and Krajewski, "[o]ver-declared shipments are universally accepted by carriers[.]" Russell and Krajewski incorporate this in an EOQ model, and supply an algorithm for finding the optimal order quantity.

We can solve their numerical example using the PWS` package. The purchasing portion of the example follows a familiar pattern, with prices ranging from

$6.21 to $5.76 per unit. They add one new datum, the weight of the product (3.8 pounds per unit).

```
In[12]:= Clear[ demand, setup, holding, price, totalCost ];
         demand = 7000; setup = 20; holding = 0.36; weight = 3.8;
         price =
           PWSFreeze[
             PWS[ {{{1, IB[750]}, 6.21&},
                  {{750, IB[1125]}, 5.94&},
                  {{1125, IB[2250]}, 5.88&},
                  {{2250, Infinity}, 5.76&}}
             ]
           ];
```

The nominal freight rates start with a flat charge of $65.60 for orders less than 216.5 pounds, and then range from $30.30 to $6.58 per hundredweight (CWT), with breaks at 5, 10, 20, 50, 100 and 200 CWT.

```
In[13]:= breakpoints =        (* convert from pounds to units *)
             {weight, 216.5, 500, 1000, 2000, 5000,
              10000, 20000, Infinity}/weight;
         (* start with rates in $/CWT *)
         rates = {30.30, 24.92, 18.87, 15.39, 10.67,
                  8.87, 6.58 };
         (* convert to $/unit and convert to functions *)
         rates = (rates weight/100) /. r_?NumberQ -> (r # &);
         (* add the initial flat charge *)
         rates = Prepend[ rates, 65.60 & ];
```

Before forming a piecewise smooth function for the freight tariffs, we must determine the order quantities at which over-declaring becomes desirable. We build the full tariff schedule starting from the highest quantity/lowest price range and working backward. Because the nominal cost of a shipment is monotonically increasing within each subdomain, we can skip over any breakpoints whose cost would exceed the cost of a shipment declared at the next higher breakpoint. Once we find an improved breakpoint, we can let *Mathematica* solve for the quantity at which to over-declare. The horizontal segments in the following plot represent over-declared shipments.

```
In[14]:= x = Transpose[ {Rest[ Reverse[ breakpoints ] ],
                 Reverse[ rates ]} ];
         tariff = {{Take[ breakpoints, -2 ], Last[ rates ]}};
         cost[ {qty_, rate_} ] := rate[ qty ];
           (* temporary function *)
         Clear[ q ];
```

```
While[
    z = cost[ x[[1]] ];   (* cost to beat *)
    q0 = IB[ x[[1, 1]] ];
    (* upper end of next interval *)
    (* weed out any meaningless breaks *)
    x = Select[ Rest[ x ], cost[ # ] < z& ];
    x != {},
        (* find where over-declaring becomes viable *)
        w = First[ q /. Solve[ x[[1, 2]][ q ] == z, q ] ];
        tariff = Join[ {{{x[[1, 1]], IB[ w ]}, x[[1, 2]]},
                  {{w, q0}, Evaluate[ z ]&}},
                tariff
            ]
];
If[ breakpoints[[1]] < q0,
    PrependTo[ tariff,
             {{breakpoints[[1]], q0}, Evaluate[ z ]&}
        ]
];  (* over-declare smallest shipments if needed *)
tariff = PWSFreeze[ PWS[ tariff ] ];
Plot[ tariff[ q ], {q, 1, 7000},
        AxesLabel -> {"Quantity", "Shipping Cost"} ];
```

Having constructed the modified tariff schedule and converted it to a piecewise smooth function, we proceed as with the Hwang et al. (1990) problem: write a piecewise smooth function for the purchase and holding costs; add the two functions to get a piecewise smooth total cost function (which we plot); and use **FindMinimum** to locate the EOQ. The optimal order quantity, approximately 2,475 units, is an interior minimum in one of the subdomains.

```
In[15]:= purchase = demand setup/#& + demand price +
            (holding #/2&) price;
        totalCost = purchase + (demand/#&) tariff;
        Plot[ totalCost[ q ], {q, 1, 6000},
            PlotRange -> {44000, 56000} ];
        tC = totalCost /. Infinity -> 99999;
        FindMinimum[ tC[ q ], {q} ]
```

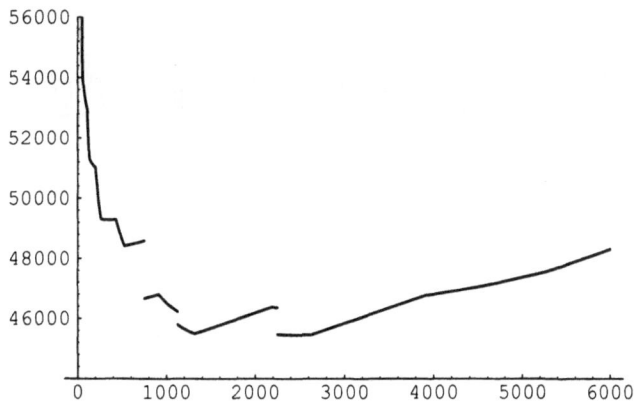

Out[15]= {{45451.3, {q -> 2474.6}}}

4.5 Conclusion

Piecewise smooth functions arise in many applications, not limited to materials management. *Mathematica*'s extensibility allows us to add support for piecewise smooth functions and thus to apply *Mathematica*'s sophisticated plotting and optimization capabilities to problems involving such functions. The package included with this chapter makes a start at building that support. Several further extensions suggest themselves. One such is a provision to find the pointwise minimum or maximum of two piecewise smooth functions, further subdividing domains as needed.

4.6 References

Hwang, H., D. H. Moon, and S. W. Shinn. 1990. "An EOQ Model with Quantity Discounts for Both Purchasing Price and Freight Cost." *Computers & Operations Research*, **17**, 73–78.

Love, S. 1979. *Inventory Control*. New York, McGraw-Hill.

Rubin, P. A. and W. C. Benton. 1993. "Jointly Constrained Order Quantities with All-Units Discounts." *Naval Research Logistics*, **40**, 255–278.

Russell, R. M. and L. J. Krajewski. 1991. "Optimal Purchase and Transportation Cost Lot Sizing for a Single Item." *Decision Sciences*, **22**, 940–952.

5 Data Screening and Data Envelopment Analysis

Eduardo Ley

5.1 Introduction

In this chapter we advocate the use of outlier detection techniques when performing Data Envelopment Analysis (DEA). We provide two separate packages: DEA.m implementing some basic DEA methods; and outlier.m implementing some outlier-detection methods (Hadi 1992, 1994). The two packages are completely independent.

5.2 Data Envelopment Analysis

Data envelopment analysis (DEA) uses a sequence of linear programs to construct a transformation frontier and to compute efficiency measures relative to this reference technology. This work is a generalization of the techniques developed in Farrell (1957); see Färe et al. (1985) for a detailed exposition of different generalizations and alternative measures of the Farrell input-based measure of technical efficiency. See Lovell (1994) for a modern introduction to this literature and the references cited therein for a historical perspective. See Charnes et al. (1991) for an also up-to-date but more technical exposition. Charnes et al. (1978) and Banker et al. (1984) are classic papers in the DEA literature.

Suppose that we have observations on n decision units each using m inputs to produce s outputs. We can construct a reference technology and then evaluate each unit's efficiency relative to this technology. Denote by x_{ij} the amount of input i used by unit j, and by y_{kj} the amount of output k produced by unit j. We shall arrange our observed data in the following way:

$$
P = \begin{pmatrix} y_{11} & y_{12} & \cdots & y_{1n} \\ y_{21} & y_{22} & \cdots & y_{2n} \\ \vdots & \vdots & \ddots & \vdots \\ y_{s1} & y_{s2} & \cdots & y_{sn} \\ x_{11} & x_{12} & \cdots & x_{1n} \\ x_{21} & x_{22} & \cdots & x_{2n} \\ \vdots & \vdots & \ddots & \vdots \\ x_{m1} & x_{m2} & \cdots & x_{mn} \end{pmatrix} = \begin{pmatrix} \mathbf{y}_1 & \mathbf{y}_2 & \cdots & \mathbf{y}_n \\ \mathbf{x}_1 & \mathbf{x}_2 & \cdots & \mathbf{x}_n \end{pmatrix} = \begin{pmatrix} Y \\ X \end{pmatrix}.
$$

P is then an $(s+m) \times n$ matrix; each of its columns p_j contains the data associated with unit j. Let $\lambda = (\lambda_1, \lambda_2, \ldots, \lambda_n)'$ be an *intensity* vector, and denote by 0_d a column vector of d zeroes.

5.2.1 Input-Oriented Efficiency Measure

The *input-oriented* efficiency measure θ_o associated with unit o can be obtained by solving the following linear program,

$$
\theta_o \equiv \min_{\theta, \lambda} \quad (1, 0_n') \begin{pmatrix} \theta \\ \lambda \end{pmatrix}
$$

$$
\text{subject to} \quad \begin{pmatrix} 0_s & Y \\ \mathbf{x}_o & -X \end{pmatrix} \begin{pmatrix} \theta \\ \lambda \end{pmatrix} \geq \begin{pmatrix} \mathbf{y}_o \\ 0_m \end{pmatrix} \tag{5.1}
$$

$$
\theta, \lambda \geq 0
$$

which assumes the existence of constant returns to scale. This assumption may be relaxed by adding any of the constraints

$$
\sum_{i=1}^n \lambda_i \begin{cases} = 1 & \Rightarrow \text{variable returns to scale;} \\ \leq 1 & \Rightarrow \text{nondecreasing returns to scale.} \end{cases}
$$

Thus for variable returns to scale we just need to replace the constraints in (5.1) by

$$
\begin{pmatrix} 0_s & Y \\ \mathbf{x}_o & -X \\ 0 & -1_n' \\ 0 & 1_n' \end{pmatrix} \begin{pmatrix} \theta \\ \lambda \end{pmatrix} \geq \begin{pmatrix} \mathbf{y}_o \\ 0_m \\ -1 \\ 1 \end{pmatrix},
$$

and by dropping the last row of the constraints we can handle the nondecreasing returns to scale case.

Assuming again constant returns to scale, the *dual program* is given by:

$$z_o \equiv \max_{u,v} \quad (\mathbf{y}'_o, 0'_m) \begin{pmatrix} u \\ v \end{pmatrix}$$

$$\text{subject to} \quad \begin{pmatrix} 0'_s & \mathbf{x}'_o \\ 0'_s & -\mathbf{x}'_o \\ -Y' & X' \end{pmatrix} \begin{pmatrix} u \\ v \end{pmatrix} \geq \begin{pmatrix} 1 \\ -1 \\ 0_n \end{pmatrix} \tag{5.2}$$

$$u \geq 0, \quad v \geq 0,$$

where $u = (u_1, \ldots, u_s)'$ and $v = (v_1, \ldots, v_m)'$ are known as *virtual multipliers* or *shadow prices*. See programs (3.5) and (3.6) in Lovell (1994) for a more detailed discussion. [Note that the primal program here corresponds to Lovell's dual and vice versa, i.e., program (5.1) in this chapter corresponds to Lovell's (3.6) and (5.2) to Lovell's (3.5).]

5.2.2   Output-Oriented Efficiency Measure

The *output-oriented* efficiency measure, η_o, associated with unit o can be obtained by solving

$$\eta_o \equiv \max_{\eta,\mu} \quad (1, 0'_n) \begin{pmatrix} \eta \\ \mu \end{pmatrix}$$

$$\text{subject to} \quad \begin{pmatrix} 0_m & -X \\ -\mathbf{y}_o & Y \end{pmatrix} \begin{pmatrix} \eta \\ \mu \end{pmatrix} \geq \begin{pmatrix} -\mathbf{x}_o \\ 0_s \end{pmatrix} \tag{5.3}$$

$$\eta, \mu \geq 0,$$

where μ is an intensity vector. This formulation again assumes constant returns to scale. As before, to allow for variable returns to scale one adds $\sum_i \mu_i = 1$, and $\sum_i \mu_i \leq 1$ will assume nondecreasing returns to scale. The dual program of (5.3) also has a pricing interpretation as in the input-oriented case. [See programs (3.2) and (3.3) in Lovell (1994) for a more detailed exposition.]

5.2.3   Interpretation

DEA first constructs a reference technology based on the observed input-output combinations of the different units and then it evaluates each unit with reference to this technology. The measures obtained by programs (5.2) and (5.3) give us the maximum radial[1] contraction of the input vector without reducing the output vector or the maximum radial expansion of the output vector without increasing the input vector, respectively.

If $\theta_o < 1$ in (5.1)—that is, unit o has an input-oriented efficiency measure that is less than one—then it would be possible to reduce *all* the inputs utilized by

---

[1] Alternative *nonradial* efficiency measures can be found in Färe et al. (1985).

unit o by $((1 - \theta) \times 100)\%$ without reducing any of its outputs. In addition, strictly positive slack variables indicate the possibility of increasing output— that is, any strictly positive element of $Y\lambda_o - \mathbf{y}_o$ is associated with an increase in the pertinent output.

When an output-based measure is used, if $\eta_o > 1$ in (3)—that is, unit o has an output-oriented efficiency measure that is greater than one— then it would be possible to augment *all* the outputs produced by unit o by $((\eta - 1) \times 100)\%$ without increasing the use of any of its inputs. Here also, the presence of strictly positive slack variables associated with the constraints $\mathbf{x}_o - X\mu_o \geq 0$ indicate the possibility of further savings by reducing the amount of the pertinent inputs.

5.3 The Dea.m Package

Let us illustrate the package with a small dataset from Dieck (1986). The data consist of 5 units each using 2 inputs to produce 1 output.

```
In[1]:= P = {{2,4,2,3,2}, {6,12,8,12,2}, {6,8,2,8,8}};
```

Once Dea.m has been loaded, we can obtain the values of θ and λ for all units by using **IEfficiencyCRS[m,s,P]** which returns an $n \times (n + 1)$ matrix with row i consisting of the optimal (θ_i, λ_i) for $i = 1,\ldots,n$ assuming constant returns to scale.

```
In[2]:= ie = IEfficiencyCRS[1,2,P]; MatrixForm[ie]
```

Out[2]=	0.833333	0	0.375	0	0	0.25
	1.	0	1.	0	0	0
	1.	0	0	1.	0	0
	0.75	0	0.75	0	0	0
	1.	0	0	0	0	1.

Each row of the preceding matrix corresponds to a production unit. The first element of row i, θ_i, is the input-efficiency measure of unit i; the rest of the row contains unit i's intensity vector λ_i. This vector tells us how to combine (weight) the input vectors of all units to achieve the level of output of unit i. Units 1 and 3 are inefficient because $\theta_1 = 0.83$ and $\theta_4 = 0.75$. We could reduce unit 1's inputs by 17% and still get the same output. We would achieve this by combining the activities of units 2 and 5 using their weights in λ_1—that is, 0.375 and 0.25.

If we were only interested in unit j's (θ_j, λ_j) then **IEfficiencyCRS[j,m,s,P]** can be invoked instead. (Of course, we could also just refer to row j of **ie**.) For unit 4,

```
In[3]:= ie4 = IEfficiencyCRS[4,1,2,P]
```

```
Out[3]= {0.75, 0, 0.75, 0, 0, 0}
```

which means that by using 75% of unit 4's inputs we could obtain the same output by using unit 2's input-output combination at a 75% intensity level.

An alternative form of this command is **IEfficiencyCRS**$[X, Y]$ when the input and output data are separated in matrices Y and X, or **IEfficiencyCRS**$[j, Y, X]$. Using **OEfficiency** instead of **IEfficiency** in all the preceding commands will compute the output-based efficiency measures (η_i, μ_i) for $i = 1, \ldots, n$. For instance,

```
In[4]:=  Y = TakeRows[P,1]; X = TakeRows[P,-2];
         MatrixForm[OEfficiencyCRS[X,Y]]
```

```
Out[4]=  1.2        0      0.45      0      0      0.3
         1.         0      1.        0      0      0
         1.         0      0         1.     0      0
         1.33333    0      1.        0      0      0
         1.         0      0         0      0      1.
```

Finally, because we have matrices with (θ_i, λ_i) (or (η_i, μ_i)) as rows, computing savings in inputs (outputs) and increases in outputs (inputs) is straightforward using *Mathematica*'s built-in functions for picking up parts of lists and for performing inner products. For example, for unit 4 the input savings are:

```
In[5]:=  (1-Part[ie4,1])*Part[Transpose[X],4]
```

```
Out[5]=  {3., 2.}
```

and the potential increase in output (for the input-based efficiency analysis) turns out to be zero.

```
In[6]:=  Y.Part[ie4, Range[2,6]] - Part[Transpose[Y],4]
```

```
Out[6]=  {0.}
```

Replacing 'CRS' by 'NDRS' or 'VRS' in all the preceding commands shown will change the assumption of constant returns of scale by nondecreasing returns or variable returns to scale, for example, **IEfficiencyVRS**$[X, Y]$ will compute the input-oriented efficiency measures under the assumption of variable returns to scale. [See Lovell (1994) or Färe et al. (1985) for the relationship between the resulting measures of inefficiency under the different assumptions.]

5.4   Identifying Multiple Outliers

DEA is often criticized on the basis of its sensitivity to extreme observations. In this section we introduce Hadi's (1992, 1994) method for identifying multiple outliers in multivariate data. Hadi's method is a general—that is, non-DEA specific—method that can be used to identify subset(s) of observations that are outlying in the k-dimensional scatter of points generated by the $n \times k$ data matrix

$Z \equiv (z_1, \ldots, z_n)'$; where $z_i = (z_{i1}, \ldots, z_{ik})$. (In the preceding DEA programs, we have $P' = Z$ and $k = s + m$.) Because only minimal assumptions are made (i.e., just that the data has been generated from an elliptical distribution), it is especially suitable for screening data that are going to be used in DEA. Wilson (1993, 1994) has developed methods for identifying influential observations in a DEA context. We relate Hadi's and Wilson's methods in the next section.

Assume that the two central moments of the distribution that generated Z are μ and Σ. Then we could measure the distance of observation i, z_i, from μ as

$$\delta_i(\mu, \Sigma) = (z_i - \mu)'\Sigma^{-1}(z_i - \mu). \tag{5.4}$$

This is known as the (sample squared) *Mahalanobis distance* (replacing the population moments by sample moments) which can be used to determine observation i's proximity to the center of the data. Of course, in most practical situations one does not know (μ, Σ). The problem with contaminated data is then to obtain robust estimators of μ and Σ while using an expression such as (5.4) to identify outliers [and therefore to determine which observations to leave out when estimating $(\mu, \Sigma)!$]. Hadi's method starts using the median as an estimator for μ. Observations are ranked according to their distances from the median (using their variance from the median as a measure of dispersion). Then (μ, Σ) are again estimated; this time the estimate of μ is computed as an arithmetic mean of the observations closest to the previous estimate of μ—this set of observations constitutes the *basic set*. The basic set is gradually expanded by embracing a larger number of the closer observations to the estimated center of the data and new estimates of (μ, Σ) are obtained. This process continues until the last cases added are "too far" from the estimated center of the data, or we run out of observations.

The algorithm [see Hadi (1992, 1994) for details of special cases] generally proceeds as follows.

[S_0] **Step 0:**

- Let $c = (1 + 2/(n - 1 - 3k) + (k + 1)/(n - k))^2$.
- Compute the median for each variable; $M = (M_1, \ldots, M_k)'$.
- Compute the variance from the median: $S = (n - 1)^{-1} \sum_{i=1}^n (z_i - M)(z_i - M)'$.
- Let h be the integer part of $(n + k + 1)/2$. Sort observations according to $d_i \leftarrow (z_i - M)'S^{-1}(z_i - M)$ in ascending order; take the first h observations.
- Compute the variance of these observations: $S_h \leftarrow (h-1)^{-1} \sum_{i=1}^h (z_{(i)} - \bar{z}_h)(z_{(i)} - \bar{z}_h)'$, where $\bar{z}_h \leftarrow h^{-1} \sum_{i=1}^h z_{(i)}$; and the subscript "$(j)$" denotes the jth ranked observation according to d_i.
- Compute $d_i \leftarrow (z_i - \bar{z}_h)'S_h^{-1}(z_i - \bar{z}_h)$ for all observations and sort the data in ascending order according to d_i.
- Let $b \leftarrow (k + 1)$.

- Divide the data into two subsets: *basic*, the first b observations and *nonbasic*, the rest.

[S_1] **Step 1:**

- Compute $\bar{z}_b$ and S_b of the observations in the basic subset.
- Compute $d_i \leftarrow (z_i - \bar{z}_b)'S_b^{-1}(z_i - \bar{z}_b)$ and sort the data in ascending order according to d_i.
- Let $b \leftarrow (b + 1)$.
- Divide the data into two subsets: *basic*, the first b observations and *nonbasic*, the rest.

[S_2] **Step 2:**

- Repeat S_1 until $b = h$, then proceed to S_3.

[S_3] **Step 3:**

- Compute $\bar{z}_b$ and S_b of the observations in the basic subset.
- Compute $d_i \leftarrow (z_i - \bar{z}_b)'S_b^{-1}(z_i - \bar{z}_b)$ and sort the data in ascending order according to d_i.
- If $d_{(r+1)} \geq c \cdot \chi_k^2(\alpha)$ then STOP and declare all observations with $d_i \geq c \cdot \chi_k^2(\alpha)$ as outliers at the $\alpha\%$ significance level. Otherwise, proceed. [Here again, the subscript "(i)" denotes the ith order statistic.]
- If $b = n$ then STOP and declare no outliers at the α significance level.
- Let $b \leftarrow (b + 1)$ and go to S_3.

5.4.1   The outliers.m Package

We implement Hadi's method in the `outliers.m` package. The function `IdentifyOutliers[`α`, Z]` returns a list with three elements: the mean of the final basic subset, its covariance matrix, and the threshold t-distance $\sqrt{c \cdot \chi_k^2(\alpha)}$, at the α significance level. We illustrate the use of the package using the body-brain weight data [see Jerison (1973)]. The data consist of 28 observations of pairs of body and brain weights for different species and they are also used in Hadi (1992).[2]

```
In[7]:=   Get[StringJoin[MyPath,"packages:outliers.m"]];
          braindata = ReadList[StringJoin[MyPath,"data:brain.dat"],
             {Number, Number}];
          {m,s,cv} = IdentifyOutliers[.05, braindata];
```

---

[2]Set `MyPath` to the appropriate directory path in the computer.

Out[7]=
```
    *** Number of Observations: 28. Number of Variables: 2
    *** Significance Level: 5.%
    Median is {1.73082, 2.13315}
    => Initial Iterations (Be patient!)
    => Size of Basic Set is 16 observations.
    => Observations outside Basic Set are:
    {26, 19, 7, 20, 27, 10, 24, 17, 14, 16, 6, 25}
    => Testing Forward
    ... Basic Set increased to 17 observations.  Last obs moved in is 26
    ... Basic Set increased to 18 observations.  Last obs moved in is 19
    ... Basic Set increased to 19 observations.  Last obs moved in is 20
    ... Basic Set increased to 20 observations.  Last obs moved in is 7
    ... Basic Set increased to 21 observations.  Last obs moved in is 27
    ... Basic Set increased to 22 observations.  Last obs moved in is 10
    ... Basic Set increased to 23 observations.  Last obs moved in is 24
    ... Basic Set increased to 24 observations.  Last obs moved in is 17
    ... Basic Set increased to 25 observations.  Last obs moved in is 14
    ... Basic Set increased to 26 observations.  Last obs moved in is 16
    => Testing Backward
    ... Basic Set decreased to 25 observations.  Obs 16 moved out.
    => Size of final basic set is... 25. (89.%)
    => OUTLIERS:
    ... Observation 16; distance is... 5.77598
    ... Observation 6; distance is... 6.3528
    ... Observation 25; distance is... 6.92187
        (Threshold distance is... 3.98089)
```

Note that, in general, it is possible that some observations leave the basic set at each step. Once a new observation is added, the new mean and covariance matrix determine the new distances. We only report the last observation added at each step because anything more sophisticated would require quite an additional programming effort.

Mathematica's graphing capabilities become very useful to gain further insights. (If the dataset contained more than two variables, we could choose two variables and fix the rest at either the median or the mean of the final basic set.) Here we show how to plot the observations along with constant-distance contours and the threshold contour.

```
In[8]:=  <<Graphics'ImplicitPlot';
         QuadraticForm[x1_,x2_,m_,s_] :=
             ({x1-m[[1]],x2-m[[2]]}).Inverse[s].({x1-m[[1]],
             x2-m[[2]]});
         plot1 = ContourPlot[QuadraticForm[x1,x2,m,s],
             {x1,m[[1]]-3Sqrt[s[[1]][[1]]],m[[1]]+
             3Sqrt[s[[1]][[1]]]},
             {x2,m[[2]]-3Sqrt[s[[2]][[2]]],m[[2]]+
             3Sqrt[s[[2]][[2]]]},
             DisplayFunction-> Identity, PlotPoints-> 100];
```

```
plot2 = ListPlot[braindata, Frame-> True, Axes-> False,
    DisplayFunction-> Identity,
    PlotStyle-> GrayLevel[1]];
plot3 = ImplicitPlot[QuadraticForm[x1,x2,m,s]==cv^2,
    {x1,m[[1]]-4Sqrt[s[[1]][[1]]],m[[1]]+
    4Sqrt[s[[1]][[1]]]},
    {x2,m[[2]]-4Sqrt[s[[2]][[2]]],m[[2]]+
    4Sqrt[s[[2]][[2]]]},
    PlotStyle -> GrayLevel[0.75],
    DisplayFunction-> Identity, PlotPoints-> 100];
Show[{plot1,plot2,plot3},
    DisplayFunction->$DisplayFunction]
```

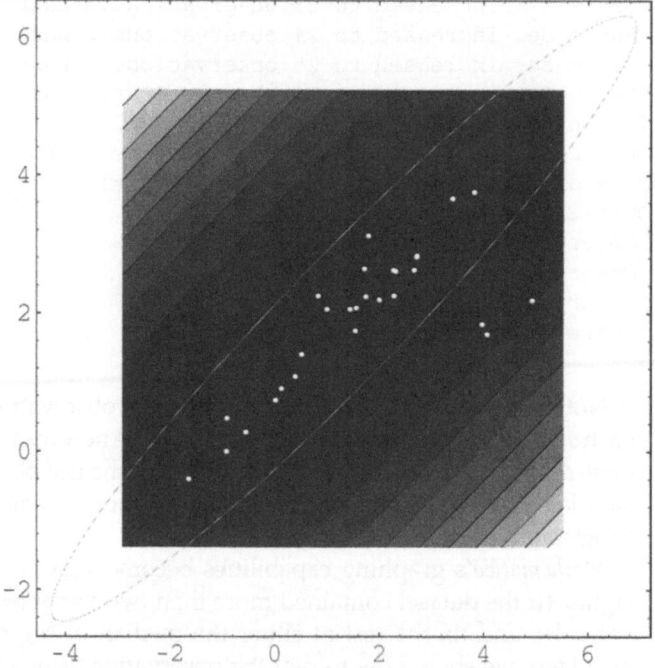

Out[8]=   -Graphics-

5.5   An Illustration Using Both Packages

Wilson (1993, 1994) presents methods for detecting outliers in DEA models. Wilson's methods are an extension to the multiple output case of the procedure developed in Andrews and Pregibon (1978). In Example 2, Wilson (1993) uses the data in Charnes et al. (1981) containing 70 observations (schools) on three outputs (reading scores, math scores, and Coppersmith scores) and five inputs (education level of mother, occupation index, parental visit index, counseling index, and number of teachers).[3]

Regarding this example, Wilson (1993) finds "that observations 44 and 59 are outliers." Also, "... Hence, observations 33, 35, 66, and 67 may also be outliers." And later, "... Thus a third group of outliers consisting of observations 1, 50, and 54 is suggested." Therefore using Wilson's methods, especially the visual inspection of his Figure 2, there are three groups of observations that could potentially be classified as outliers. These are:

$$G_1 = \{59, 44\}$$

$$G_2 = \{59, 44, 66, 67, 33, 35\}$$

$$G_3 = \{59, 44, 66, 67, 33, 35, 50, 54, 1\}$$

Using Hadi's method on the same dataset at the three most popular significance levels, $\alpha = 0.01, 0.05, 0.1$, we would declare as outliers the observations that are precisely in Wilson's G_1, G_2, and G_3, respectively.

5.6 Acknowledgments

I thank Arijit Mukherji, Colin Rose, and Murray Smith for useful comments, and Ali Hadi and Paul Wilson for sharing computer code and data with me.

5.7 References

Andrews, D. F. and D. Pregibon. 1978. "Finding the Outliers that Matter." *Journal of the Royal Statistical Society*, Series B, **40**, 85–93.

Banker, R. D., A. Charnes, and W. W. Cooper. 1984. "Some Models for Estimating Technical and Returns to Scale Inefficiencies in Data Envelopment Analysis." *Management Science*, **30**, 9, 1078–1092.

Charnes, A., W. W. Cooper, and E. Rhodes. 1978. "Measuring the Efficiency of Decision Making Units." *European Journal of Operations Research*, **2**, 6, 429–444.

Charnes, A., W. W. Cooper, and E. Rhodes. 1981. "Evaluating Program and Managerial Efficiency: An Application of Data Envelopment Analysis to Program Follow Through." *Management Science*, **27**, 6, 668–697.

Charnes, A., W. W. Cooper, and R. M. Thrall. 1991. "A Structure for Classifying and Characterizing Efficiency and Inefficiency in Data Envelopment Analysis;" *The Journal of Productivity Analysis*, **2**, 197–237.

Dieck, M. J. 1986. "Data Envelopment Analysis Software for Microcomputers: CCR1, Additive, MiniMax, Summary Window." Center for Cybernetic Studies Research Report #538, University of Texas at Austin.

Färe, R., S. Grosskopf, and C. A. K. Lovell. 1985. *The Measurement of Efficiency of Production*. Boston, Kluwer-Nijhoff Publishing.

---

[3]These data are provided in `ccr.dat`.

Farrell, M. J. 1957. "The Measurement of Productive Efficiency." *Journal of the Royal Statistical Society*, Series A, **120**, 3, 253–281.

Fried, H., C. A. K. Lovell, and S. Schmidt. 1993. *The Measurement of Productive Efficiency: Techniques and Applications*. Oxford, Oxford University Press.

Hadi, A. S. 1992. "Identifying Multiple Outliers in Multivariate Data." *Journal of the Royal Statistical Society*, Series B, **54**, 3, 761–771.

Hadi, A. S. 1994. "A Modification of a Method for the Detection of Outliers in Multivariate Samples." *Journal of the Royal Statistical Society*, Series B, **56**, 2, 393–396.

Jerison, H. J. 1973. *Evolution of the Brain and Intelligence*. New York, Academic Press.

Lovell, C. A. K. 1994. "Linear Programming Approaches to the Measurement and Analysis of Productive Efficiency." *TOP*, **2**, 2, 175–223.

Wilson, P. W. 1993. "Detecting Outliers in Deterministic Nonparametric Frontier Models with Multiple Outputs." *Journal of Business and Economic Statistics*, **11**, 3, 319–323.

Wilson, P. W. 1994. "Detecting Influential Observations in Data Envelopment Analysis." Mimeo, University of Texas at Austin.

6 Efficiency in Production and Consumption

Hal R. Varian

The standard economic models of firms and consumers emphasize optimizing behavior. Firms are assumed to minimize costs or maximize profits, whereas consumers are assumed to maximize utility. However, no one is perfect—even *homo economicus*. When analyzing real choice data it is necessary to allow for departures from this model of strict optimization.

In this chapter we consider some measures of choice efficiency. In general an efficiency measure should have the property that a value of 1 corresponds to 100 percent efficiency: full optimization. A value of 0 would correspond to behavior that is totally independent of efficient choice. Values between 0 and 1 should be interpretable as partial efficiency.

It turns out that there are relatively natural ways to construct such measures for economic choices and that *Mathematica* is a convenient computational engine for this task.

6.1 Cost Minimization

Consider a firm that chooses factor inputs to minimize costs. Let w be a vector of factor prices, x a vector of factor choices, $f(x)$ a production function, and y a target level of output. Then the hypothesized model is:

$$\min_x wx$$

such that $f(x) \geq y$.

Suppose that we have n observations of firm choices (w^t, x^t, y^t) for $t = 1, \ldots, n$. The following *Weak Axiom of Cost Minimization* (WACM) is necessary and sufficient for the data to be consistent with the cost minimization model:

WACM: $w^t x^t \leq w^t x^s$ for all s for which $y^s \geq y^t$

This condition is rather intuitive; it says that the observed choice must cost no more than any other choice that generates at least as much output. See Varian (1993) for further discussion.

If we have some data that violate WACM, we may want to see "how close" a specific observation t comes to satisfying WACM. A natural thing to do is to compute the following efficiency index:

$$e^t = \min_{y^s \geq y^t} \frac{w^t x^s}{w^t x^t}$$

If $e^t < 1$, then there is some observation that produces at least as much output as the tth observation and costs less than the tth observation. If $e^t = 1$, no such observation exists.

It is easy to compute this efficiency index using *Mathematica*. Suppose that we have n observations on k factors which we arrange in an array of dimension $n \times k$. The following function measures the efficiency of observation i relative to observation j.

```
In[1]:=  efficOf[i_,j_,w_,x_] :=
            (w[[j]].x[[i]])/(w[[j]].x[[j]])
```

This function returns the list of $n \times k$ efficiency measures.

```
In[2]:=  eff[w_,x_,y_] := Map[Union,
            Table[If[y[[i]] <= y[[j]],
            Min[efficOf[j,i,w,x],1],1],
            {i,1,Length[y]},{j,1,Length[y]}]]
```

Finally, the following function takes the minimum of the efficiency measures just computed to calculate the actual list of efficiencies.

```
In[3]:=  costEfficiency[w_,x_,y_] := Map[Min,eff[w,x,y]]
```

6.1.1   Example of Cost Efficiency Measurement

We illustrate the use of these tools with a dataset developed by Brooks (1993). These data describe the operation of a sample of Veteran's Administration pharmacies. There is a standard index of services for these pharmacies that serves as an output and several inputs. Inputs fall into two main categories: labor (pharmacist time, technician time) and capital (pill counting machines, office equipment, etc.).

First we set the directory and read in the data.

```
In[4]:=  SetDirectory["/Users/hal/Math/Efficiency"]
         <<cost.dat;

Out[4]=  /Users/hal/Math/Efficiency
```

Now we compute the efficiencies.

```
In[5]:=  effAll = costEfficiency[w,x,y]

Out[5]=  {0.84057, 0.525841, 0.907895, 0.682745, 1, 0.50789,
          0.595672, 0.654224, 0.590418, 0.746752, 0.595972,
          0.751879, 1, 1, 1, 0.870959, 0.990814, 0.77547,
          0.659193, 0.57482, 0.472514, 0.698577, 0.863941,
          0.768098, 0.693701, 0.754345, 1, 0.461564, 0.833214,
          0.841046, 0.718124, 1, 1, 0.790207, 1., 1, 0.638938,
          0.781148, 0.846167, 0.707507, 1, 1, 0.466252,
          0.66688, 0.583254, 0.617269, 0.641974, 0.83834,
          0.890836, 0.85853, 1, 0.780865, 0.631422, 0.658296,
          1, 0.846318, 0.707987, 0.648803, 0.571282, 0.653275,
          0.576511, 0.574738, 0.505807, 0.965922, 0.673734, 1,
          1, 0.999572, 0.581691, 0.603172, 0.6211, 0.806635, 1,
          0.676993, 0.484738, 1, 0.755765, 0.94052, 0.672726,
          0.727269, 0.812183, 1., 1, 0.679689, 0.770955}
```

Note that the only thing that is controlled for in these efficiency measures is the factor prices. Nothing is done about type of hospital, patient mix, and so on. Clearly some of the observed "inefficiency" is likely to be due to such factors.

We can use the same technique to measure efficiency with respect to a subset of the factor inputs. Here we extract just the labor inputs and measure the efficiencies with respect to those labor choices only.

```
In[6]:=  wlabor=Transpose[{Transpose[w][[1]],Transpose[w][[2]]}];
         xlabor=Transpose[{Transpose[x][[1]],Transpose[x][[2]]}];

In[7]:=  effLabor=costEfficiency[wlabor,xlabor,y]

Out[7]=  {0.81052, 0.521896, 0.87362, 0.672513, 1, 0.50412,
          0.596858, 0.652904, 0.587924, 0.741708, 0.588623,
          0.737364, 1, 1, 1, 0.855984, 0.95915, 0.772125,
          0.652891, 0.564115, 0.46887, 0.682503, 0.864779,
          0.757165, 0.694296, 0.727773, 1., 0.454564, 0.834703,
          0.810626, 0.718089, 1, 1, 0.802351, 1, 0.960112,
          0.663749, 0.788278, 0.84386, 0.702435, 1, 1.,
          0.469225, 0.653222, 0.574132, 0.639108, 0.636164,
          0.809674, 0.857015, 0.839908, 1, 0.765367, 0.623384,
          0.689988, 1, 0.833604, 0.683464, 0.616643, 0.566365,
          0.638567, 0.570566, 0.568162, 0.515951, 0.947074,
          0.665469, 1, 1, 0.999564, 0.576357, 0.592193, 0.60788,
          0.785772, 1, 0.668115, 0.474429, 1, 0.750681,
          0.900582, 0.669416, 0.717449, 0.819808, 1, 1,
          0.661303, 0.767011}
```

The two series look fairly similar. We do a scatterplot to compare the two lists of efficiency measures.

$In[8]:=$ **ListPlot[Transpose[{effAll,effLabor}]]**

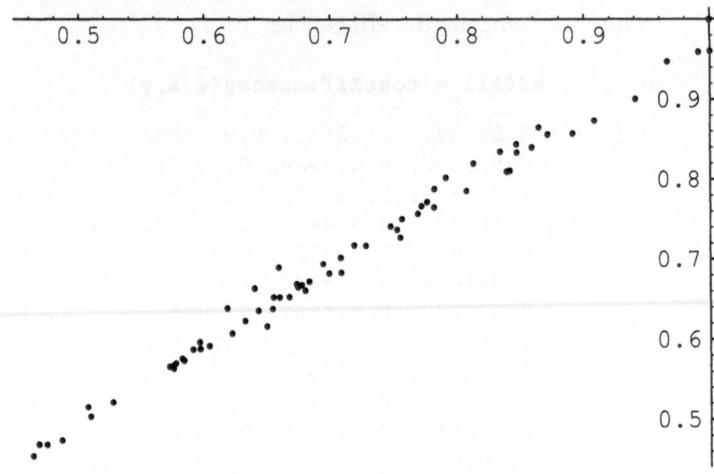

$Out[8]=$ -Graphics-

Note that the two series are very highly correlated; that is, firms that have low labor efficiency also appear to have low overall efficiency.

6.2   Utility Maximization

We now turn to consumer behavior. Consider a consumer who chooses a vector of consumption goods x, facing a price vector p, and having income m so as to maximize utility:

$$\max_x u(x)$$

such that $px \leq m$.

Define the direct revealed preference relation by $x^t R^D x^s$ if and only if $p^t x^t \geq p^t x^s$. The terminology is rather intuitive: x^t is directly revealed preferred to x^s if x^t is purchased when x^s was affordable. The revealed preference relation R is defined to be the transitive closure of the relation R^D. That is, $x^t R x$ if and only if there is some chain of observations $(x^s, x^r, \ldots, x^v)$ such that $x^t R^D x^s, x^s R^D x^r, \ldots, x^v R^D x$. Finally, some observed choices (p^t, x^t) are consistent with the utility maximization model if and only if they satisfy the *Generalized Axiom of Revealed Preference* (GARP):

GARP: If $x^t R x^s$, then it is not the case that $p^s x^s > p^s x^t$.

In words: if x^t was chosen when x^s was affordable, then x^s cannot be chosen when x^t is affordable.

6.2.1 Computing the Transitive Closure of a Preference Relation

As before we assume that the data come as two $n \times k$ matrices of prices and quantities.

The **rdMatrix** has a 1 in the (i, j) entry if observation i is directly revealed preferred to observation j.

```
In[9]:=  rdMatrix[p_,x_] := Module[{i,j,n},
                              n=Length[x];
                              Table[If[p[[i]].x[[i]] >=
                                p[[i]].x[[j]],1,0],
                                {i,1,n},{j,1,n}]]
```

We need to compute the transitive closure of this matrix. A possible way to do this is to raise the matrix to the nth power and then look at the sign of each entry. It is not hard to see that the (i, j) entry of the nth power matrix will be positive if and only if there is some chain of entries connecting i to j in the original matrix that are positive. This is very simple to implement in *Mathematica*.

```
In[10]:= tClosure[m_] := Sign[MatrixPower[m,Length[m]]]
```

See the appendix for another way to compute the transitive closure.

6.2.2 Example

Here is an example with three observations where the direct revealed preference relation involves no cycles, but the revealed preference relation does.

```
In[11]:= p={{1,2,8},{4,1,8},{3,1,2}};
         x={{2,1,3},{3,4,2},{2,6,2}};
```

```
In[12]:= m=rdMatrix[p,x]
```

```
Out[12]= {{1, 1, 0}, {0, 1, 1}, {1, 0, 1}}
```

```
In[13]:= tClosure[m]
```

```
Out[13]= {{1, 1, 1}, {1, 1, 1}, {1, 1, 1}}
```

6.2.3 Checking GARP

Once we compute the transitive closure, it is easy to check GARP. A convenient way to do this is to compute a "consumption efficiency index" analogous to the cost efficiency index we computed previously. Here is a function that returns the observations revealed preferred to observation i, given the revealed preference relation summarized by the matrix m.

```
In[14]:= ObsRP[i_,m_] := Complement[
                Table[If[m[[j,i]]>0,j,i],
                    {j,1,Length[m]}],{0}]
```

The function **consEfficiency** computes the minimum expenditure necessary to purchase an observed choice that is revealed preferred to a given observation.

```
In[15]:= consEfficiency[p_,x_] :=
            Module[{m,n},
                m=tClosure[rdMatrix[p,x]];
                n=Length[x];
                Table[Min[x[[ObsRP[i,m]]].p[[i]]/p[[i]].x[[i]]],
                    {i,1,n}]]
```

Here is an example of how this function is used.

```
In[16]:= p={{1.,2.},{2.,1.}};
         x={{1.,2.},{2.,1.}};
```

```
In[17]:= consEfficiency[p,x]
```

```
Out[17]= {0.8, 0.8}
```

This shows that each of the two choices is only 80% efficient.

6.3   The Token Economy

Battalio et al. (1973) collected a set of data on the consumption choices of 38 patients at Central Islip State Hospital. As part of their therapeutic treatment, the patients worked for tokens that could be retrieved for items such as cigarettes, candy, milk, locker rental, clothes, admission to a dance, and the like. During a seven-week period, the relative prices of various groups of these goods were doubled or halved. Because the prices of some of the goods were halved some weeks and doubled other weeks, prices varied by a factor of four. Data were collected on how the expenditures of each individual responded to the price changes. These data have been examined by Battalio et al. (1973) and Cox (1994) using revealed preference techniques.

Here are the prices and choices for subject number 8 in these experiments.

```
In[18]:= p={{1.,1.,1.},{0.5,2.,1.},{1.,1.,1.},{2.,0.5,1.},
            {2.,0.5,1.},{1.,1.,1.},{1.,1.,1.}};
         x={{30,9,9},{34,10,0},{10,4,0},{4,8,5},{2,15,0},
            {0,15,9},{4,7,12}};
```

Here is the consumption efficiency of this consumer's choices.

```
In[19]:= consEfficiency[p,x]
```

```
Out[19]= {1., 1., 1., 0.970588, 1., 0.708333, 0.73913}
```

Most of the consumers in the Battalio study were quite efficient. There were 256 choices made during the seven-week experiment. Of the inefficient choices, 8 were 97–99% efficient, 4 were 93–96% efficient, 1 was 91% efficient, and one was 81% efficient.

6.4 Afriat's Efficiency Index

The preceding efficiency index measures the consumption efficiency of each observation. Afriat's efficiency index, described in Afriat (1967), measures the overall efficiency of a set of consumption choices. Following Afriat, we say that an observation r is directly revealed preferred to an observation s at efficiency level e if $ep^r x^r \geq p^r x^s$. (Although Afriat does not require it, we adopt the convention that it is always the case that $x^r R^D x^r$; i.e., an observation is always directly revealed preferred to itself.) Obviously $e = 1$ is the standard revealed preference comparison and $e = 0$ is vacuous. For a given e we can construct the analogue of the direct revealed preference measure, compute its transitive closure R_e, and then check the analog of $GARP_e$: if $x^s R_e x^t$, then $ep^t x^t < p^t x^s$.

The following function computes the direct revealed preference relation associated with efficiency level e:

```
In[20]:= rdEMatrix[p_,x_,e_] := Module[{i,j,n},
            n=Length[p];
            Table[If[(e*p[[i]].x[[i]] >= p[[i]].x[[j]])
              || i==j,1,0],
            {i,1,n},{j,1,n}]]
```

We can use the **tClosure** function defined earlier to compute the transitive closure of this matrix. We then check to see if GARP is satisfied (at the given efficiency level) using the function **GARPOK**. This function returns a matrix with a False in the (i, j) entry if $x^i R x^j$ and $ep^j x^j > p^j x^i$; otherwise, it returns True. If **GARPOK** returns all True entries, the data are consistent with GARP at efficiency level e.

```
In[21]:= GARPOK[p_,x_,m_,e_] := Module[{i,j,n},
              n=Length[m];
              Table[
                If[m[[i,j]]==1 && (e*p[[j]].x[[j]]
                  > p[[j]].x[[i]]),False,True],
                {j,1,n},{i,1,n}]]
```

We use the **GARPOK** function to define a couple of other useful functions. This function returns the list of observations that violate GARP (at efficiency level e).

```
In[22]:= ViolationList[p_,x_,e_] :=
            Module[{m},
                m = tClosure[rdEMatrix[p,x,e]];
                Union[Flatten[Position[GARPOK[p,x,m,e],False]]]]
```

This function just counts the number of violations.

```
In[23]:= NumberViolations[p_,x_,e_] :=
            Length[ViolationList[p,x,e]]
```

We will try these functions on the example we used in the last section.

```
In[24]:= p={{1.,2.},{2.,1.}};
          x={{1.,2.},{2.,1.}};
```

```
In[25]:= MatrixForm[GARPOK[p,x,tClosure[rdEMatrix[p,x,.81]],.81]]
```

```
Out[25]= True    False
         False   True
```

```
In[26]:= MatrixForm[GARPOK[p,x,tClosure[rdEMatrix[p,x,.79]],.79]]
```

```
Out[26]= True    True
         True    True
```

This shows that the Afriat efficiency measure is between .79 and .81. We can automate the process of finding the maximal value of e such that the data satisfy GARP by using the following binary search.

```
In[27]:= AfriatEfficiency[p_,x_,maxSteps_] :=
            Module[{step,e},
            e=1/2;
              For[step=1,step<=maxSteps,step++,
                If[NumberViolations[p,x,e] > 0,
                    e=e-2^(-(step+1)),
                    e=e+2^(-(step+1))];
                Print[N[e]]]]
```

```
In[28]:= AfriatEfficiency[p,x,10]
```

```
0.75
0.875
0.8125
0.78125
0.796875
0.804687
0.800781
0.798828
0.799805
0.800293
```

As we saw before, these choices are about 80% efficient.
Here are the Battalio et al. data for subject 8 again:

```
In[29]:= p={{1.,1.,1.},{0.5,2.,1.},{1.,1.,1.},{2.,0.5,1.},
         {2.,0.5,1.},{1.,1.,1.},{1.,1.,1.}};
         x={{30,9,9},{34,10,0},{10,4,0},{4,8,5},{2,15,0},
         {0,15,9},{4,7,12}};

In[30]:= AfriatEfficiency[p,x,10]

0.75
0.875
0.9375
0.96875
0.984375
0.976562
0.972656
0.970703
0.969727
0.970215
```

It appears that subject 8 is about 97% efficient in her choices.

6.5 Drawing Budget Sets

Here are some functions to draw a set of budgets and illustrate the observations
that violate revealed preference.

```
In[31]:= DrawABudget[{p1_,p2_},{x1_,x2_}] := Module[
            {w,t},
            w=p1*x1 + p2*x2;
            Plot[w/p2 - p1*t/p2,{t,0,w/p1},
            AspectRatio->1,DisplayFunction->Identity]]
         DrawBudgets[p_,x_] := Table[{DrawABudget[p[[i]],x[[i]]],
                               Graphics[Point[x[[i]]]]},
                               {i,1,Length[p]}]

         PlotViolations[p_,x_] :=
             ListPlot[x[[ViolationList[p,x,1]]],
             AspectRatio->1, DisplayFunction->Identity,
             PlotStyle->{Hue[0],PointSize[.02]}]

         DrawViolations[p_,x_] := Show[DrawBudgets[p,x],
                               PlotViolations[p,x],
                               Prolog->PointSize[.02],
                               DisplayFunction->$DisplayFunction]
```

6.5.1 Example

To illustrate the use of **DrawViolations**, we examine some experimental data
generated by Andreoni and Miller (1994). They presented subjects with a choice
between taking some money for themselves or donating money to a group.

If the subjects chose to donate, the experimenters would match the donations at various rates, thereby changing the "price" of the donations. Andreoni and Miller were interested in whether the subjects' contributions varied with the price of contributions in the way predicted by the theory of economic choice.

Here is the choice behavior exhibited by one of their subjects:

```
In[32]:= p={{1.0,0.5},{0.5,1.0},{2.0,1.0},{1.0,2.0},{1.0,1.0},
         {1.0,0.5},{0.5,1.0},{2.0,1.0},{1.0,2.0}};
       x={{30.,16.},{76.,0.},{22.5,5.0},{30.0,10.0},
         {40.0,10.0},{40.0,20.0},{100.0,0.0},{35.5,5.1},
         {60.8,7.6}};
```

```
In[33]:= DrawViolations[p,x]
```

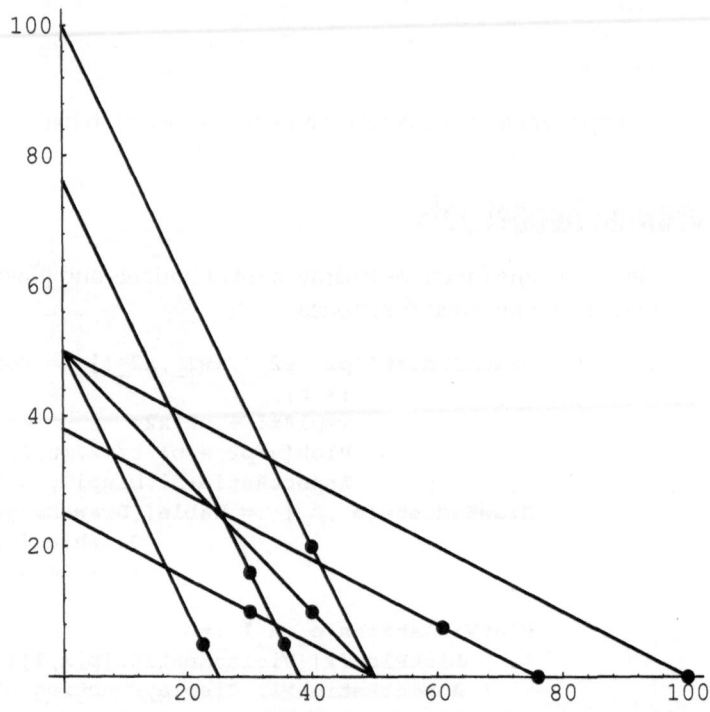

```
Out[33]= -Graphics-
```

(The violations are illustrated in red on the screen but they come through as grey on the monochrome printed page.)

6.6   Appendix

In the text we computed the transitive closure of the direct revealed preference relation by computing the matrix power of the direct revealed preference matrix. We did this using the internal *Mathematica* function **MatrixPower**. Raising an

$n \times n$ matrix to the power n would require n^4 operations if done in the most straightforward way. Another, seemingly more efficient, way to compute the transitive closure is given by Warshall's algorithm [See Warshall (1962).]

```
In[34]:= Warshall[mat_] := Module[{i,j,k,n,m},
            m=mat;
            n=Length[m];
            For[k=1,k<=n,k++,
                For[i=1,i<=n,i++,
                    For[j=1,j<=n,j++,If[m[[i,k]]==1 && m[[k,j]]==1,
                    m[[i,j]]=1]]]];m]
```

Note that Warshall's algorithm involves only n^3 operations. Despite this, Warshall's algorithm is much slower than using the internal **MatrixPower** function. For example, here is a random 10×10 matrix:

```
In[35]:= m = Table[Random[Integer,{0,1}],{i,1,10},{j,1,10}];
```

Here is how long Warshall's algorithm takes to compute the transitive closure.

```
In[36]:= Timing[Warshall[m]][[1]]
```

```
Out[36]= 1.31667 Second
```

Here is how long **MatrixPower** takes:

```
In[37]:= Timing[tClosure[m]][[1]]
```

```
Out[37]= 0.0166667 Second
```

The **MatrixPower** routine is about 100 times faster! This illustrates an important point about *Mathematica* programming: always use the built-in functions when possible.

6.7 Summary

Calculating choice efficiency for consumption and production data is very easy using *Mathematica*. In addition the data can be graphed, manipulated, and analyzed in a variety of other ways.

6.8 References

Afriat, S. 1967. "The Construction of a Utility Function From Expenditure Data." *International Economic Review*, 7, 67–77.

Andreoni, J. and J. H. Miller. 1994. "Giving According to GARP: An Experimental Study of Rationality and Altruism." CMU Working Paper.

Battalio, R. C. et al. 1973. "A Test of Consumer Demand Theory Using Observations of Individual Consumer Purchases." *Western Economic Journal*, **11**, 411–428.

Brooks, John. 1993. "Measuring Cost Efficiency in VA Hospital Pharmacies: An Applied Critique of the Methods." Ph.D. dissertation, University of Michigan.

Cox, J. C. 1994. "On Testing the Utility Hypothesis." Technical report, University of Arizona.

Houtman, M. and J. A. Maks. 1985. "Determining all Maximial Data Subsets Consistent With Revealed Preference." *Kwantitatieve Methoden*, **19**, 89–104.

Warshall, S. 1962. "A Theorem on Boolean Matrices," *Journal of the American Association of Computing Machinery*, **9**, 11–12.

Varian, H. 1993. *Microeconomic Analysis*, 3rd ed. New York, W. W. Norton & Co.

7 Cost Allocation

William W. Sharkey

7.1 Introduction

The need for cost allocation arises from the existence of costs that are shared among two or more outputs produced by a single firm. If there are n distinct outputs and $C(q_1, \ldots, q_n)$ represents the cost of producing any output bundle $q = \{q_1, \ldots, q_n\}$, there are shared costs whenever the marginal cost of some output i depends on another output j, that is,

$$\frac{\partial^2 C}{\partial q_i \partial q_j} \neq 0.$$

In the absence of shared costs it is possible to decompose the cost function into n component cost functions such that

$$C(q) = \sum_{i=1}^{n} C^i(q_i).$$

Clearly in this situation there is no need for cost allocation.

The concepts of incremental cost and stand-alone cost are of fundamental importance in the definition and analysis of cost allocation methodologies. Incremental costs are costs that can be directly attributed to an increase in the output of a good or service. In the case of a small increase in output, incremental cost corresponds to marginal cost. The stand-alone cost of a service, or set of services, is the total cost of providing those services on a stand-alone basis, that is, by a set of facilities specifically designed to produce only those services. Incremental costs and stand-alone costs are related in a simple algebraic manner. If $N = \{1, \ldots, n\}$ represents the set of outputs produced by a firm and S is any subset of these outputs, then $N \setminus S$ represents the complement of S in N—that is, the set of outputs contained in N and not in S. If the firm is producing an aggregate output bundle q, and we write q^S and $q^{N \setminus S}$ for the output bundles corresponding to the outputs in S and $N \setminus S$, respectively, the incremental cost of producing q^S is the total cost of producing q minus the stand-alone cost of producing $q^{N \setminus S}$—that is, $C(q^N) - C(q^{N \setminus S})$.

Traditionally, cost allocation has been interpreted as the application of a "fully distributed cost" methodology to the costs that remain after each output is assigned its incremental cost, that is, to

$$C(q) - \sum_{i=1}^{n} \left[C(q) - C(q^{N \setminus i}) \right].$$

These costs can be allocated in a variety of ways, but the most common methods of allocation rely on relative outputs, relative revenues, or relative incremental costs. That is, if x_i represents service i's measured level of the appropriate observable quantity (output, revenue, or incremental cost) then service i is allocated a fraction

$$\frac{x_i}{\sum_{j \in N} x_j}$$

of the nonattributable costs.

Fully distributed cost methods have been widely criticized by economists and accountants. They are based neither on optimization nor on a concept of fairness. Because there are many plausible methods, and the choice among methods can lead to significant differences in the final allocation, the fully distributed cost approach invites rent-seeking behavior by interest groups affected by the final pricing rule chosen. The remainder of this chapter describes methods of pricing and cost allocation that may be used in place of fully distributed cost methods, and the way in which *Mathematica* can be used to compute many specific pricing and cost allocation rules. Section 7.1 describes the basic game theoretic and optimization frameworks that are used throughout the chapter. Section 7.2 describes cost allocation methods in both discrete and continuous situations. Section 7.3 introduces the demand side, and describes methods for computing demand-compatible allocation rules, and optimal pricing rules. Section 7.4 continues the analysis of optimal pricing by considering nonlinear pricing methods.

7.1.1   Setup

This chapter is designed to be used in conjunction with the package Pricing which accompanies it (in the file Pricing.m). Before attempting to evaluate any of the following functions it is necessary to load and evaluate the package. This can be accomplished using the **Get [ ]** command, or equivalently

```
In[1]:=  <<Pricing.m
```

It is necessary to either specify a full path name for the package, or place the package in a location that will be automatically searched.

A listing of functions defined in the package `Pricing` can be obtained as follows:

```
In[2]:=  ?Pricing'*
```

AssignmentGame	NucleolusPrice
AumannShapleyPrice	PerCapitaNucleolus
BalancedCover	Profit
CESCostFunction	ProfitMaxNonlinear
CESDemandSystem	ProfitMaxPrice
CobbDouglasDemandSystem	ProfitMax2Part
Core	QuadraticCostFunction
CoreSelection	RamseyPrice
Cost	RealValuedGame
CostFunction	SCRB
CSValue	ShapleyValue
Demands	ShapleyValuePrice
DemandSystem	SpanningTreeGame
Dual	StableAssignments
Game	StandAloneGame
IndirectUtility	SubadditiveCover
IntegerGame	Subsets
KTMax	SubsidyFreePrices
LinearDemandSystem	SubsidyFreePriceSelection
MonotonicCover	SurplusMaxNonlinear
MultilinearExtension	SurplusMax2Part
NonlinearDemandSystem	Utility
Nucleolus	Values

Brief documentation about individual functions can also be obtained:

```
In[3]:=  ?CostFunction

CostFunction[x,F] defines a cost function where x is an
    arbitrary output vector and F[x] is the cost of producing x.
```

7.1.2 Game Theoretic Preliminaries

Discrete cost allocation problems are treated as cooperative games. Many of the game theoretic methods and tools used here were originally developed by Carter (1993). A cooperative game is defined by a set of players N and a coalitional worth function v. The objective of cooperative game theory is to define solutions that allocate the surplus $v(N)$ of the "grand coalition" among its members. This is the same as the objective of cost allocation theory, which is to allocate the cost of producing a collection of commodities when cost cannot be attributed to individual commodities in a nontrivial way. Formally, a (transferable utility) game is defined by a pair (N, v) where $v : 2^N \rightarrow \Re$ and $v(\emptyset) = 0$.

In order to define a game it is necessary to specify a set of players N and a coalitional worth function v which defines the worth of every subset of players in N. In *Mathematica* a game is an object of the form **Game[N_,v_]** where N is a list of players and v is a list of coalitional values. By convention, the list v defines the values of subsets of N arranged in a pre-sorted canonical order determined by the *Mathematica* function **Subsets[ ]** illustrated in the following example.

```
In[4]:=  Subsets[N_List] := Sort[Flatten /@ Distribute[{{},{#}} &
             /@ Sort[N], List]];
```

```
In[5]:=  T = {c,a,b};
         Subsets[T]
```

```
Out[5]=  {{}, {a}, {b}, {c}, {a, b}, {a, c}, {b, c}, {a, b, c}}
```

Some of the examples in this chapter make use of the function **IntegerGame[n_]** which defines an n-player game by assigning a pseudorandom integer as the worth of each nonempty coalition. Later in Section 7.2.4 we consider some more interesting classes of economic games.

```
In[6]:=  IntegerGame[n_] := Game[Range[n],
             Prepend[Table[Random[Integer,{1,10}],{2^n-1}],0]]
```

```
In[7]:=  game1 = IntegerGame[4]
```

```
Out[7]=  Game[{1, 2, 3, 4}, {0, 4, 1, 4, 3, 1, 1, 3, 3, 3, 10, 3,
             8, 10, 7, 8}]
```

Several utility functions are available for displaying and manipulating the contents of a game object. The function **Values[ ]** returns an ordered list of pairs of coalitions and their values.

```
In[8]:=  ThreeCityGame = Game[{Paris,Lyon,Toulouse},
             {0,0,1,0,2,1,3,3}]
```

```
Out[8]=  Game[{Paris, Lyon, Toulouse}, {0, 0, 1, 0, 2, 1, 3, 3}]
```

```
In[9]:=  Values[ThreeCityGame]
```

```
Out[9]=  {{{}, 0}, {{Lyon}, 0}, {{Paris}, 1}, {{Toulouse}, 0},
             {{Lyon, Paris}, 2}, {{Lyon, Toulouse}, 1},
             {{Paris, Toulouse}, 3}, {{Lyon, Paris, Toulouse}, 3}}
```

Many of the operations on games make use of the function **Dual[ ]**. The dual of a game (N, v) is the game $(N, v^\#)$ where $v^\#(S) = v(N) - v(N \setminus S)$. In a cost allocation framework, if the function v represents the "stand-alone cost" of a group of objects, then the function $v^\#$ represents the "incremental cost." Clearly **Dual[Dual[v]]** $= v$.

```
In[10]:= Dual[g_Game] := Game[First[g],
             (g[[2,-1]]-g[[2,Length[Last[g]]+1-#]]) & /@
             Range[Length[Last[g]]]]

In[11]:= Dual[game1]

Out[11]= Game[{1, 2, 3, 4}, {0, 1, -2, 0, 5, -2, 5, 5, 5, 7, 7,
             5, 4, 7, 4, 8}]

In[12]:= Dual[ThreeCityGame]

Out[12]= Game[{Paris, Lyon, Toulouse}, {0, 0, 2, 1, 3, 2, 3, 3}]
```

If g = **Game[N, v]**, the functions **MonotonicCover[g]** and **Subadditive-Cover[g]** return a game g' in which the worth function v' is respectively the smallest monotonic (subadditive) function such that $v' \geq v$ ($v' \leq v$).

```
In[13]:= MonotonicCover[g_Game] := Module[{w},
             w[S_] := Max[v[#,g] & /@ Subsets[S]];
             Game[First[g],w[#] &/@ Subsets[First[g]]]
             ];

In[14]:= SubadditiveCover[g_Game] := Module[{w},
             w[{}] = 0;
             w[S:{_}] := v[S,g];
             w[S:{_,__}] := Min[v[#,g]+v[Complement[S,#],g]&/@
                 Subsets[S]];
             Game[First[g],w[#] &/@ Subsets[First[g]]]
             ];

In[15]:= RealValuedGame[n_] := Game[Range[n],
             Prepend[Table[Random[],{2^n-1}],0]]

In[16]:= game2 = RealValuedGame[3]
         MonotonicCover[game2]
         SubadditiveCover[game2]

Out[16]= Game[{1, 2, 3}, {0, 0.646182, 0.262308, 0.00695034,
             0.288818, 0.594633, 0.841293, 0.618086}]

         Game[{1, 2, 3}, {0, 0.646182, 0.262308, 0.00695034,
             0.646182, 0.646182, 0.841293, 0.841293}]

         Game[{1, 2, 3}, {0, 0.646182, 0.262308, 0.00695034,
             0.288818, 0.594633, 0.269258, 0.295769}]
```

7.1.3   Optimization Preliminaries

The optimization framework of this chapter uses the function **KTMax[ ]**, due to Kaplan and Mukherji (1993). It has been slightly modified to allow for equality as well as inequality constraints in order to speed up the computation of large problems when it is known that certain constraints must hold as equalities. The constraints can be specified in the form "lhs $\geq$ rhs," "lhs $\leq$ rhs" or "lhs", where in the last case the right-hand side is assumed equal to zero and inequalities are assumed to be "$\geq$". For every subset of inequality constraints **KTMax[ ]** generates a Lagrangean for the system, sets its partial derivatives with respect to the variables equal to zero, and then solves the system. It stores this solution if it is feasible with respect to the remaining constraints, and then works through all possible sets of binding constraints to identify the feasible solution that maximizes the value of the objective function. Using problem specific information to represent as many constraints as possible as equalities—that is, binding at an optimum—will result in faster computations.

This function is demonstrated in the following simple example.

```
In[17]:= obj = z1 + z2;
         vars = {z1,z2};
         ineq = {};
         eq = {z1^2 + z2^2 == 2};
         KTMax[obj,vars,ineq,eq]

Out[17]= {2., {{z1 -> 1., z2 -> 1., lam[1] -> -0.5}}}
```

In some problems involving unbounded constraint sets with infinite valued solutions, **KTMax[ ]** will return a local solution to the first-order conditions that is not a global maximum, as in the following example.

```
In[18]:= obj = z1^2 + z2^2;
         vars = {z1,z2};
         ineq = {};
         eq = {z1 + z2 == 2};
         KTMax[obj,vars,ineq,eq]

Out[18]= {2., {{z1 -> 1., z2 -> 1., lam[1] -> -2.}}}
```

KTMax[ ] uses the *Mathematica* function **NSolve[ ]** to solve the first-order conditions of the Lagrangean corresponding to the specified objective and constraints. An alternative is to use the *Mathematica* function **FindRoot[ ]**, which uses Newton's method to find a local solution to a set of equations

$$f_1(x_1,\ldots,x_n) = 0,\ldots, f_n(x_1,\ldots,x_n) = 0,$$

starting at $x_1 = x_1^0,\ldots,x_n = x_n^0$. **FindRoot[ ]** will always find a local optimum (where the functions f_i represents the first-order conditions for a Lagrangean) assuming a local optimum exists. For nonlinear problems, there can be many local optima, so the outcome is likely to depend on the assigned starting values. Of course, second-order conditions need to be verified as well.

```
In[19]:= lagran = z1 + z2 + lam*(2 - z1^2 - z2^2);
         eqn = {D[lagran,z1]==0,D[lagran,z2]==0,
```

```
            D[lagran,lam]==0};
     FindRoot[eqn,{z1,2},{z2,0},{lam,1}]
```

Out[19]= {z1 -> 1., z2 -> 1., lam -> 0.5}

7.2 Cost Allocation Pricing

The objective of this section is to demonstrate how *Mathematica* can be used
to easily compute many of the methods commonly recommended by cost allocation theory. No attempt is made to present a comprehensive discussion of
cost allocation methods actually used, because the number of such methods
is very large. However, the main (game theoretic) methods are covered in this
chapter and the package Pricing. These include the Shapley value for discrete
games and the Aumann-Shapley pricing rule for continuous games, which are
described in Section 7.2.2, and the core and nucleolus which are described in
Section 7.2.3. Although basic definitions are provided, no attempt is made to
fully motivate the game theoretic aspects of these methods. The reader who
is unfamiliar with the underlying cooperative game theoretic framework may
wish to consult Young (1994) or Moulin (1988).

7.2.1 Continuous Cost Allocation Problems

Discrete cost allocation problems are just games. In a continuous cost allocation
problem, however, it is assumed that each output can be produced in an arbitrary
nonnegative quantity. Hence continuous cost allocation problems require the
definition of a cost function. Formally, a continuous cost allocation problem is
defined by a pair (F, α) where $\alpha \in \mathfrak{R}_{+}^{N}$, $F : X_{\alpha} \rightarrow \mathfrak{R}^{N}$ with $F(0) = 0$, where
$X_{\alpha} = \{x \in \mathfrak{R}_{+}^{N} \mid x \leq \alpha\}$.

In *Mathematica* a cost function is defined as an object of the form Cost-
Function[x_,F_] where x is an arbitrary output vector and $F(x)$ is the cost of
producing x. Cost[x_,c_] gives the cost of producing output vector x given
cost function c. A cost allocation problem is therefore a pair consisting of a
CostFunction and an output vector.

In[20]:= **costfunction1 = CostFunction[{x1,x2,x3},x1^2+(x2+x3)^3]**

Out[20]=   2   3
         CostFunction[{x1, x2, x3}, x1 + (x2 + x3)]

In[21]:= **Cost[{z1,z2,z3},costfunction1]**

Out[21]=   2   3
         z1 + (z2 + z3)

In[22]:= **Cost[{1,2,3},costfunction1]**

Out[22]= 126

Two examples of general classes of cost functions are the functions **CESCost-Function[ ]** and **QuadraticCostFunction[ ]** defined in the following. Cost functions in two or three variables can be displayed using the built-in *Mathematica* functions **Plot[ ]** and **Plot3D[ ]**, respectively.

```
In[23]:= CESCostFunction[a_?VectorQ,b_?VectorQ,c_?NumberQ] :=
            Module[{q,x},q = Array[x,Length[a]];
            CostFunction[q,(Plus @@ (a*q^b))^(1/c)]/.x->"x"
            ];

In[24]:= QuadraticCostFunction[f_?NumberQ,m_?VectorQ,
            M_?MatrixQ] := Module[{q,x},q = Array[x,Length[m]];
            CostFunction[q,f + m.q + q.M.q]/.x->"x"
            ];

In[25]:= costfunction2 = CESCostFunction[{10,10},{2,2},3]
         Plot3D[Cost[{x1,x2},costfunction2],{x1,0,1},{x2,0,1},
            BoxRatios->{1,1,1},ViewPoint->{1.3,-2.4,2}]
```

$$Out[25] = \text{CostFunction}[\{x[1], x[2]\}, (10\ x[1]^2 + 10\ x[2]^2)^{1/3}]$$

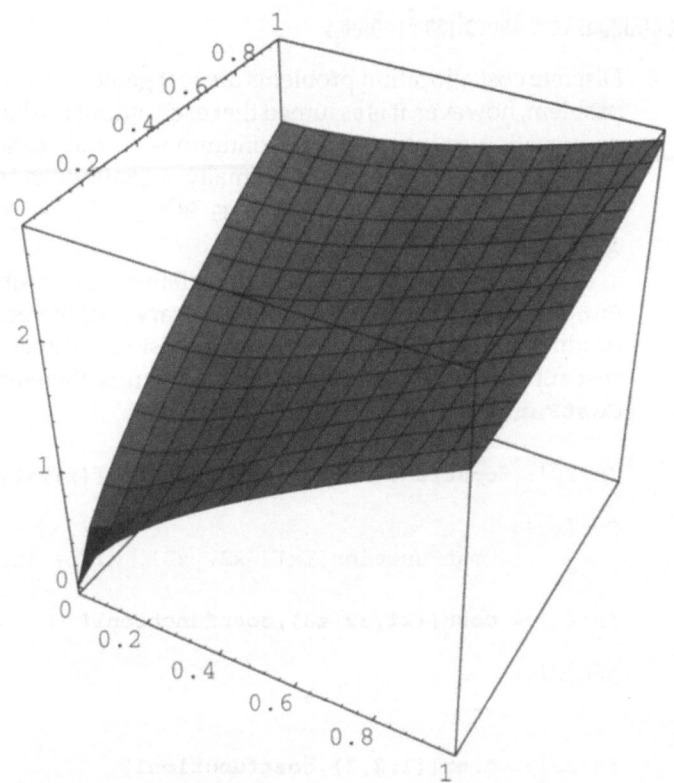

```
Out[25]= -SurfaceGraphics-
```

Associated with any continuous cost allocation problem there is a related discrete problem given by the function **StandAloneGame[ ]**. **StandAloneGame[alpha, CostFunction[x,F]]** generates the game, **Game[N,v]**, where $N = \{1, \ldots, |N|\}$, $v[S] = F[\alpha^S]$, and α^S is defined by

$$\alpha_i^S = \begin{cases} \alpha_i & \text{if } i \in S \\ 0 & \text{if } i \notin S \end{cases}.$$

In[26]:= **costfunction3 = CESCostFunction[{1,2,3},{.4,.5,.6},2]**

Out[26]= CostFunction[{x[1], x[2], x[3]},

$$\text{Sqrt}[x[1]^{0.4} + 2 \, x[2]^{0.5} + 3 \, x[3]^{0.6}]]$$

In[27]:= **game3 = StandAloneGame[{1,1,1},costfunction3]**

Out[27]= Game[{1, 2, 3}, {0, 1, Sqrt[2], Sqrt[3], Sqrt[3], 2, Sqrt[5], Sqrt[6]}]

Given a discrete cost allocation problem defined by **Game[N,v]** and a designated output vector α, one can define a continuous cost allocation problem by using the multilinear extension due to Owen (1972). The function **MultilinearExtension[alpha_,g_Game]** generates **CostFunction[x,F]**, where F is given by

$$F(x) = \sum_{S \subseteq T} \prod_{i \in S} \left(\frac{x_i}{\alpha_i}\right) \prod_{i \notin S} \left(1 - \frac{x_i}{\alpha_i}\right) v(S).$$

The multilinear extension represents only one of many ways to extend a discrete game to a continuous one. As the following example demonstrates, two different cost functions can give rise to identical stand-alone games.

In[28]:= **costfunction4 = MultilinearExtension[{1,1,1},game3]**

Out[28]= CostFunction[{q[1], q[2], q[3]},
        q[1] (1 - q[2]) (1 - q[3]) +
        Sqrt[2] (1 - q[1]) q[2] (1 - q[3]) +
        Sqrt[3] q[1] q[2] (1 - q[3]) +
        Sqrt[3] (1 - q[1]) (1 - q[2]) q[3] +
        2 q[1] (1 - q[2]) q[3] +
        Sqrt[5] (1 - q[1]) q[2] q[3] +
        Sqrt[6] q[1] q[2] q[3]]

In[29]:= **StandAloneGame[{1,1,1},costfunction4]**

Out[29]= Game[{1, 2, 3}, {0, 1, Sqrt[2], Sqrt[3], Sqrt[3], 2, Sqrt[5], Sqrt[6]}]

```
In[30]:= Cost[{.5,.5,.5},costfunction3]
         Cost[{.5,.5,.5},costfunction4] //N
```

Out[30]= 2.03748

Out[30]= 1.57048

7.2.2 Axiomatic Pricing

7.2.2.1 Discrete Problems

The Shapley value is the linear function φ defined by

$$\varphi_i(v) = \sum_{S \subseteq N \setminus i} \frac{1}{n} \frac{1}{\binom{n-1}{|S|}} [v(S \cup i) - v(S)]$$

for each $i \in N$. Shapley (1953) demonstrated that φ is the unique operator that satisfies a set of plausible axioms. [Loosely speaking, this axiomatization states that a function is efficient (cost sharing), symmetric, additive, and monotonic, if and only if it is the function φ previously defined.]

To define an alternative expression for the Shapley value, let Ω represent the set of all orderings of players $i \in N$. For any ordering $R = (j_1, \ldots, j_n)$ with $i = j_k$, let $X_i(R) = \{j_1, \ldots, j_{k-1}\}$ be the set of predecessors of i. Then $\Delta_i(R, v) = v(X_i(R) \cup i) - v(X_i(R))$ represents the marginal contribution of player i in the ordering R and

$$\varphi_i(v) = \sum_{R \in \Omega} \frac{1}{n!} \Delta_i(R, v)$$

for each $i \in N$.

In the first representation φ represents the expected marginal contribution of player i to $S \subset N \setminus i$, where S is chosen with probability

$$\frac{1}{n} \frac{1}{\binom{n-1}{|S|}},$$

that is, each size is equally likely and each coalition of a given size is equally likely. In the second representation φ represents player i's expected marginal contribution in a random order where each order is chosen with probability $1/n!$, that is, each ordering is equally likely. Thus in both interpretations the Shapley value has a natural interpretation as "average incremental cost."

A third representation of the Shapley value is given in terms of the potential function as defined in Hart and Mas-Colell (1989). The potential function Π^v is defined recursively by $\Pi^v(\emptyset) = 0$ and

$$\Pi^v(N) = \frac{1}{n}\left[v(N) + \sum_{i \in N}\Pi^v(N \setminus i)\right].$$

Hart and Mas-Colell proved that the Shapley value is the discrete derivative of the potential, that is,

$$\varphi_i(v) = \Pi^v(N) - \Pi^v(N \setminus i)$$

for each $i \in N$.

In some circumstances the symmetry property satisfied by the Shapley value may not be appropriate for a cost allocation rule. For example, in allocating the cost of a common input used by several departments in an organization, it might be appropriate to take account of the number of members in each department. The weighted Shapley value φ^w is the natural extension of the value to nonsymmetric situations, and it is defined by

$$\varphi_i^w(v) = \sum_{R \in \Omega} q^w(R)\,\Delta_i(R, v)$$

for each $i \in N$, where w is a vector of positive numbers and

$$q^w(R) = \left[\frac{w_{j_1}}{w_{j_1}}\right]\left[\frac{w_{j_2}}{w_{j_1} + w_{j_2}}\right]\cdots\left[\frac{w_{j_{n-1}}}{\sum_{i=1}^{n-1} w_{j_i}}\right]\left[\frac{w_{j_n}}{\sum_{i=1}^{n} w_{j_i}}\right].$$

Weighted Shapley values have been characterized axiomatically by Kalai and Samet (1985).

The function **ShapleyValue[g_]** computes the Shapley value of a discrete game g using the potential function. When this function is called with an argument consisting of a list of positive numbers of the appropriate length, the weighted Shapley value is returned. The recursive definition of the (weighted) potential function is efficiently handled by *Mathematica*.

```
In[31]:= game4 = MonotonicCover[game1]

Out[31]= Game[{1, 2, 3, 4}, {0, 4, 1, 4, 3, 4, 4, 4, 4, 3, 10, 4,
            8, 10, 10, 10}]

In[32]:= ShapleyValue[game4]

Out[32]=  7   7    41   17
         {-,  --,  --,  --}
          4   12   12   4
```

```
In[33]:= ShapleyValue[{1,2,3,4},game4]
```

```
Out[33]=  2371   184   1801   2803
         {----,  ---,  ----,  ----}
          840    315    840    630
```

An alternative value that is of interest in a cost allocation framework is the coalition structure value, due to Owen (1977) and Hart and Kurz (1983). This value is defined in terms of an exogenously given partition of the set of players. It can be interpreted as a "random order value" (the second representation of the Shapley value) in which players arrive randomly, but with the restriction that all members of a coalition specified by the partition arrive successively. This process is equivalent to first randomly ordering the coalitions of the partition, and then randomly ordering the members within each coalition. The function **CSValue[P_,g_]** computes the coalition structure value associated with partition *P* in game *g*.

```
In[34]:= CSValue[{{1,2},{3,4}},game4]
```

```
Out[34]=  7   1   13   19
         {-,  -,  --,  --}
          4   4    4    4
```

The separable cost-remaining benefit method of cost allocation (used by the Tennessee Valley Authority for the analysis of public water projects) is described by the function **SCRB[ ]**. Those who wish to study methods not included in this package should be able to write the appropriate code using a straightforward method such as the **SCRB[ ]** method as a guide.

```
In[35]:= SCRB[g_Game] := Module[{N,separablecost,
            nonseparablecost,alternativecost,remainingbenefit},
            N = Sort[First[g]];
            separablecost = (v[N,g] - v[Complement[N,{#}],g])
              &/@ N;
            nonseparablecost = v[N,g] - Plus @@ separablecost;
            alternativecost = v[{#},g] &/@ N;
            remainingbenefit = alternativecost - separablecost;
            separablecost + nonseparablecost*remainingbenefit/
              Plus @@ remainingbenefit
            ];
```

```
In[36]:= SCRB[game4]
```

```
Out[36]=     1      9
         {2,  -,  3,  -}
             2      2
```

7.2.2.2 Continuous Problems

Most real cost allocation problems, and all of the literature on efficient pricing described in Sections 7.3 and 7.4, are based on problems in which commodities are produced in arbitrary quantities by a (usually) continuous cost function. There are many plausible but ad hoc methods for setting prices in a continuous framework. Two examples are given by the functions **SymmetricPrice[ ]**, which assigns the price

$$p_i(q) = \frac{F(q)}{\sum q_i}$$

to each commodity, and **SymmetricSharePrice[ ]** which assigns

$$p_i(q) = \frac{F(q)}{nq_i}.$$

```
In[37]:= SymmetricPrice[output_,c_CostFunction] :=
            Table[Cost[output,c]/Plus@@output,{Length[output]}]

         SymmetricSharePrice[output_,c_CostFunction] :=
            (1/Length[Select[output,Positive]])*
               Table[Cost[output,c],{Length[output]}]/
               (output/.x_/;x==0->Infinity)

In[38]:= SymmetricPrice[{.1,.2,.3},costfunction1]
         SymmetricSharePrice[{.1,.2,.3},costfunction1]


Out[38]= {0.225, 0.225, 0.225}


Out[38]= {0.45, 0.225, 0.15}
```

The preceding pricing rules are arbitrary just as fully distributed cost rules are arbitrary. In the remainder of this section we illustrate pricing methods that can be justified in terms of axioms or properties that appear to be reasonable on the class of problems under consideration. For continuous problems the Aumann-Shapley mechanism is a well-known example. Given a cost function F and an output vector α, the Aumann-Shapley price mechanism is given by the function

$$P_i^{AS}(F, \alpha) = \int_0^1 \frac{\partial F}{\partial x_i}(\tau\alpha)d\tau$$

for each $i \in T$. Billera and Heath (1982) and Mirman and Tauman (1982) have characterized Aumann-Shapley pricing in terms of the following set of axioms: cost sharing, monotonicity, additivity, rescaling invariance, and symmetry.

Given a vector of positive weights w, the weighted Aumann-Shapley price mechanism is given by

$$P_i^{WAS}(F, \alpha) = \int_0^1 \frac{\partial F}{\partial x_i}(\tau^{w_1}\alpha_1, \ldots, \tau^{w_n}\alpha_n) w_i \tau^{w_i-1} d\tau$$

for each $i \in N$. Weighted Aumann-Shapley pricing is characterized axiomatically in McLean and Sharkey (1996), and McLean et al. (1995). These functions are implemented by the *Mathematica* function **AumannShapleyPrice[ ]** which is illustrated in the following.

```
In[39]:= AumannShapleyPrice[{1,1,1},costfunction1]
```

```
Out[39]= {1., 4., 4.}
```

```
In[40]:= AumannShapleyPrice[{2,1,3},{1,1,1},costfunction1]
```

```
Out[40]= {1., 2.62857, 5.37143}
```

Although the Aumann-Shapley axioms represent, in some sense, natural analogues of the Shapley value axioms in a continuous framework, it can be seen from its definition that Aumann-Shapley pricing is defined only on the class of continuously differentiable cost functions. In particular, the cost function must be continuous at the origin, so that there are no "fixed costs." The function **AumannShapleyPrice[ ]** should not be applied to discontinuous cost functions because the resulting price allocation will not in general satisfy the cost sharing axiom (i.e., revenue will not equal total cost). Samet et al. (1984) discuss the application of Aumann-Shapley pricing to piecewise continuously differentiable cost functions.

An alternative to the Aumann-Shapley pricing rule can be derived from the Shapley value of the stand-alone game associated with any continuous problem. This pricing rule is defined on the class of all cost functions including those with fixed costs. The weighted Shapley value price mechanism associated with a cost allocation problem (F, α) and weight vector w is defined by

$$P_i^{WSV}(F, \alpha) = \begin{cases} \dfrac{\phi_i^w(v_{(F,\alpha)})}{\alpha_i} & \text{if } \alpha_i > 0 \\ 0 & \text{if } \alpha_i = 0, \end{cases}$$

where $v_{(F,\alpha)}$ is the stand-alone game associated with (F, α). For a characterization of weighted Shapley value pricing and some related pricing methods see McLean and Sharkey (1995), and McLean et al. (1995).

The Shapley value price for any commodity produced in positive quantity is the Shapley value "revenue" from the stand-alone game divided by quantity. If $\alpha_i = 0$ in the problem (F, α), the corresponding Shapley value price is normalized to zero, because any price multiplied by a zero quantity would lead to the correct Shapley value revenue which is equal to zero in this case.

In[41]:= **ShapleyValuePrice[{2,1,3},{1,1,1},costfunction1]//N**

Out[41]= {1., 2.5, 5.5}

In general the Shapley value and Aumann-Shapley pricing mechanisms do not coincide. For the CES cost function defined in Section 7.2 we have:

In[42]:= **ShapleyValuePrice[{1,1,1},costfunction3] //N**
            AumannShapleyPrice[{1,1,1},costfunction3]

Out[42]= {0.502105, 0.827246, 1.12014}

Out[42]= {0.541293, 0.833333, 1.07486}

A class of functions where Shapley value pricing and Aumann-Shapley pricing do coincide is the class of "multilinear cost functions"—functions that can be expressed as the multilinear extension of some stand-alone game. This is illustrated in the following example, using the previously defined multilinear extension of the stand alone game corresponding to a CES cost function.

In[43]:= **ShapleyValuePrice[{1,1,1},costfunction4] //N**
            AumannShapleyPrice[{1,1,1},costfunction4]

Out[43]= {0.502105, 0.827246, 1.12014}

Out[43]= {0.502105, 0.827246, 1.12014}

7.2.3 Subsidy Free Pricing

Subsidy free prices are those such that no group of customers pays more than the stand-alone cost of serving it. In a discrete cost allocation problem, subsidy free prices are precisely the core of an appropriate game, except that in a cost allocation framework, the inequalities that define the core are the reverse of the usual case for a game. These inequalities are given by the following system:

$$\sum_{i \in N} x_i = v(N)$$
$$\sum_{i \in S} x_i \leq v(S) \quad \text{for all } S \subset N.$$

The (cost sharing) core of a game v is equal to the (surplus sharing with inequalities reversed) core of the dual game $v^{\#}$ associated with v.

The function **Core[ ]** computes the extreme points of the core using a simplex algorithm. The computational complexity of core computations is substantially greater than in the case of value computations.

The function `CoreSelection[w_,g_]` chooses a particular extreme point in the core by solving the linear program

$$\operatorname*{Max}_{x} w \cdot x$$

subject to the core constraints. By varying the weight vector w it is possible to select core allocations that favor individual players or groups of players.

```
In[44]:= game5 = Game[{1,2,3},{0,2,2,2,3,3,3,3}]
```

```
Out[44]= Game[{1, 2, 3}, {0, 2, 2, 2, 3, 3, 3, 3}]
```

```
In[45]:= Core[game5]
```

```
Out[45]= {{0, 1, 2}, {0, 2, 1}, {1, 0, 2}, {1, 2, 0}, {2, 0, 1},
          {2, 1, 0}}
```

```
In[46]:= CoreSelection[{1,2,3},game5]
```

```
Out[46]= {2, 1, 0}
```

In some cases the core is the empty set as in the following example:

```
In[47]:= Core[Game[{1, 2}, {0, 1, 1, 3}]
```

```
ConstrainedMax::nsat:
   The specified constraints cannot be satisfied.
```

```
Out[47]= {}
```

The nucleolus of a cost allocation game v is defined as the allocation that minimizes the maximum "unhappiness" lexicographically across coalitions, where unhappiness is given by $U(S,x) = x[S] - v[S]$. This is equivalent to minimizing the maximum "excess" in the dual game $v^{\#}$, where excess is given by $E[S,y] = v^{\#}[S] - x[S]$. The nucleolus treats every coalition, regardless of size, equally in its lexicographic minimization.

An alternative solution concept, the per capita nucleolus, weights coalitions according to their size by minimizing the maximum of

$$\frac{v^{\#}(S)}{|S|} - x(S).$$

That is, the per capita nucleolus favors small coalitions relative to the nucleolus.

```
In[48]:= game6 = Game[{1,2,3},{0,2,1,1,2,2,2,5/2}]
```

$$Out[48]= Game[\{1, 2, 3\}, \{0, 2, 1, 1, 2, 2, 2, \frac{5}{2}\}]$$

```
In[49]:= Nucleolus[game6]
         PerCapitaNucleolus[game6]
```

$$Out[49]= \{1, \frac{3}{4}, \frac{3}{4}\}$$

$$Out[49]= \{\frac{7}{6}, \frac{2}{3}, \frac{2}{3}\}$$

In a continuous problem, the functions **SubsidyFreePrices[ ]**, **SubsidyFreePriceSelection[ ]** and **NucleolusPrice[ ]** compute pricing rules for continuous cost allocation problems by applying the functions **Core[ ]**, **CoreSelection[ ]**, and **Nucleolus[ ]** to the appropriate standalone game. As in the case of the Shapley value, these functions compute a price by dividing "revenue" by "output," and so care must be taken to ensure that they are well defined at commodity vectors with zero components.

```
In[50]:= costfunction5 = MultilinearExtension[{1,1,1},game6]
```

$$Out[50]= CostFunction[\{q[1], q[2], q[3]\},$$

$$2\,q[1]\,(1 - q[2])\,(1 - q[3]) +$$

$$(1 - q[1])\,q[2]\,(1 - q[3]) +$$

$$2\,q[1]\,q[2]\,(1 - q[3]) +$$

$$(1 - q[1])\,(1 - q[2])\,q[3] +$$

$$2\,q[1]\,(1 - q[2])\,q[3] + 2\,(1 - q[1])\,q[2]\,q[3] +$$

$$\frac{5\,q[1]\,q[2]\,q[3]}{2}]$$

```
In[51]:= SubsidyFreePrices[{1,1,1},costfunction5]
```

$$Out[51]= \{\{\frac{1}{2}, 1, 1\}, \{1, \frac{1}{2}, 1\}, \{1, 1, \frac{1}{2}\}, \{\frac{3}{2}, \frac{1}{2}, \frac{1}{2}\}\}$$

```
In[52]:= SubsidyFreePriceSelection[{1,2,3},{1,1,1},costfunction5]

Out[52]=   3   1   1
         {-,  -,  -}
           2   2   2

In[53]:= NucleolusPrice[{1,1,1},costfunction5]

Out[53]=      3   3
          {1,  -,  -}
              4   4
```

7.2.4   Examples

One interesting class of discrete cost allocation problems is based on a minimum cost spanning tree game. In the minimum cost spanning tree problem, the players represent a set of "customer" nodes in a network (e.g., for delivery of cable television to homes) and there is a single supplier node. The cost associated with any coalition is given by the cost of the minimal cost network connecting every member of S to the supplier. A minimum cost spanning tree game is defined by a symmetric matrix M in which the elements m_{ij} represent the cost of connecting nodes i and j if $i \neq j$. The diagonal elements of M are assumed to be equal to zero, and are ignored in all computations involving M. By convention, the player set is given by $T = \{1, \ldots, m - 1\}$ where $\{m\}$ represents the supplier node. It is well known that minimum cost spanning tree games have nonempty cores. [See Sharkey (1995) for a survey of these results.] Given a cost matrix M, the function **MCST[ ]** computes the cost of the minimum cost spanning tree, and **SpanningTreeGame[ ]** uses this function to define a discrete cost allocation game.

```
In[54]:= c = Table[Random[Integer,{1,5}],{5},{5}];
         M = c + Transpose[c] - IdentityMatrix[5]*
             (c + Transpose[c])
         game7 = SpanningTreeGame[M]
         Core[game7]

Out[54]= {{0, 8, 3, 4, 5}, {8, 0, 3, 6, 5},
          {3, 3, 0, 4, 6}, {4, 6, 4, 0, 3}, {5, 5, 6, 3, 0}}

         Game[{1, 2, 3, 4}, {0, 5, 5, 6, 3, 10, 8, 7, 8, 8, 7,
            11, 12, 10, 10, 13}]

         {{3, 3, 4, 3}, {3, 3, 5, 2}, {3, 5, 2, 3},
          {3, 5, 3, 2}, {4, 3, 3, 3}, {4, 5, 1, 3},
          {5, 3, 3, 2}, {5, 5, 1, 2}}
```

A class of problems involving surplus sharing rather than cost sharing is the class of assignment problems. An assignment problem is defined by a (not necessarily square) matrix A in which the rows correspond to players of one type (e.g., men) and the columns correspond to players of another type (e.g., women).

Thus the players in the game are given by $N = \{M, F\}$ where $M = \{1, \ldots, m\}$ corresponds to the rows of A and $F = \{m + 1, \ldots, m + f\}$ corresponds to the columns. The value of a coalition consisting of man "i" and woman "j" is given by A_{ij}. The value of an arbitrary coalition is defined by the "optimal" assignment of men and women contained in the coalition. [See Shapley and Shubik (1972) for more details and results on assignment games.]

Assignment problems have a particular structure in which the stable core allocations can be determined directly as the "dual set," that is, the extreme points of the (linear programming) dual of the assignment problem for the entire set of players. Computation of this set, through the function **StableAssignments[ ]** is much faster than computation of the extreme points of the core. (It is not even necessary to explicitly compute the worth function v for coalitions other than the grand coalition in order to compute the stable assignments.)

```
In[55]:= A = Table[Random[Integer,{1,5}],{2},{2}]
         StableAssignments[A]

Out[55]= {{5, 2}, {3, 2}}

         {{0, 0, 5, 2}, {2, 0, 3, 2}, {2, 2, 3, 0},
          {4, 2, 1, 0}}

In[56]:= game8 = AssignmentGame[A]
         Core[Dual[game8]]

Out[56]= Game[{1, 2, 3, 4}, {0, 0, 0, 0, 0, 0, 5, 2, 3, 2, 0,
          5, 2, 5, 3, 7}]

         {{0, 0, 5, 2}, {2, 0, 3, 2}, {2, 2, 3, 0},
          {4, 2, 1, 0}}
```

7.3   Demand Compatible and Ramsey Pricing

7.3.1   Demand Compatible Pricing

This section illustrates a method by which cost allocation pricing can be shown to be compatible with consumer demand functions. Any number of commodities can be produced, but individual customer characteristics cannot be observed, so that demand is characterized as a single aggregate consumer. A demand system (for analysis of uniform pricing) is defined as an object of the form **Demand-System[p_,V_,Q_]** where p is a price vector, V[p] is an indirect utility function and Q[p] is a vector of demand functions. In the package Pricing there are three functions that may be used to generate demand systems for the analysis of uniform pricing. Each demand system assumes an indirect utility function of a specific form and solves for the demand equations by differentiating this function (using Roy's identity). The functions **CESDemandSystem[ ]** and **CobbDouglasDemandSystem[ ]** compute demand functions that are consistent with utility maximization given a CES utility function and Cobb-Douglas utility function, respectively. **LinearDemandSystem[ ]** generates a demand system that ignores income effects.

```
In[57]:= CESDemandSystem[a_?VectorQ,b_?VectorQ,c_?AtomQ,
            m_?AtomQ] := Module[{price,p,V,Q},
            price = Array[p,Length[b]];
            V[x_] := m*(a.(x^b))^(-1/c);
            Q[price] = Map[-D[V[price],#]&,price]/
              (V[price]/m);
            DemandSystem[price,V[price],Q[price]]/.p->"p"
            ];
```

```
In[58]:= demandsystem1 = CESDemandSystem[{1,1},{r,r},r,y]
```

```
Out[58]=                                              y
            DemandSystem[{p[1], p[2]}, -------------------,
                                          r       r 1/r
                                       (p[1]  + p[2] )


                 -1 + r            -1 + r
            y p[1]            y p[2]
          {-------------,  -------------}]
              r      r       r      r
           p[1]  + p[2]    p[1]  + p[2]
```

```
In[59]:= demandsystem2 = LinearDemandSystem[1000,{10,20,30,40},
            1.1*IdentityMatrix[4]-Table[.1,{4},{4}]]
```

```
Out[59]= DemandSystem[{p[1], p[2], p[3], p[4]},

           1000 - 10 p[1] - 20 p[2] - 30 p[3] +

           p[1] (1. p[1] - 0.1 p[2] - 0.1 p[3] - 0.1 p[4]) +

           p[2] (-0.1 p[1] + 1. p[2] - 0.1 p[3] - 0.1 p[4]) +

           p[3] (-0.1 p[1] - 0.1 p[2] + 1. p[3] - 0.1 p[4]) -

           40 p[4] +

           p[4] (-0.1 p[1] - 0.1 p[2] - 0.1 p[3] + 1. p[4]),

           {10 - 2. p[1] + 0.2 p[2] + 0.2 p[3] + 0.2 p[4],

           20 + 0.2 p[1] - 2. p[2] + 0.2 p[3] + 0.2 p[4],

           30 + 0.2 p[1] + 0.2 p[2] - 2. p[3] + 0.2 p[4],

           40 + 0.2 p[1] + 0.2 p[2] + 0.2 p[3] - 2. p[4]}]
```

The function **Demands [ ]** may be used to extract the vector of demand functions from any demand system.

In[60]:= **Demands[{p1,p2,p3,p4},demandsystem2]**

Out[60]= {10 - 2. p1 + 0.2 p2 + 0.2 p3 + 0.2 p4,

      20 + 0.2 p1 - 2. p2 + 0.2 p3 + 0.2 p4,

      30 + 0.2 p1 + 0.2 p2 - 2. p3 + 0.2 p4,

      40 + 0.2 p1 + 0.2 p2 + 0.2 p3 - 2. p4}

In[61]:= **Demands[{1,2,3,4},demandsystem2]**

Out[61]= {9.8, 17.6, 25.4, 33.2}

In order to compute demand compatible pricing rules for pricing mechanisms it is necessary to solve a fixed point problem. Given a demand system with demand function $Q(.)$ and a pricing rule $P(.)$, one looks for a solution to $P(Q(price)) = price$. Mirman and Tauman (1982) have demonstrated that such a fixed point exists under very general conditions as long as the cost function F is continuous.

Mathematica has a built-in fixed point function that will locate a fixed point as long as the underlying system is also stable. Convergence is not guaranteed, however, particularly in cases where there are large fixed costs and asymmetric demand systems. The procedure can be illustrated by defining a function **FP[ ]** as a composite of a particular pricing mechanism and a particular demand system. **FixedPoint[FP,price]** then repeatedly applies *FP*, with a starting value of price, until the result no longer changes. A maximum number of iterations can also be specified.

In[62]:= **demandsystem3 = LinearDemandSystem[100,{10,20,30},**
        1.1*IdentityMatrix[3]-Table[.1,{3},{3}]]

Out[62]= DemandSystem[{p[1], p[2], p[3]},

      100 - 10 p[1] - 20 p[2] +

      p[1] (1. p[1] - 0.1 p[2] - 0.1 p[3]) +

      p[2] (-0.1 p[1] + 1. p[2] - 0.1 p[3]) - 30 p[3] +

      p[3] (-0.1 p[1] - 0.1 p[2] + 1. p[3]),

      {10 - 2. p[1] + 0.2 p[2] + 0.2 p[3],

      20 + 0.2 p[1] - 2. p[2] + 0.2 p[3],

      30 + 0.2 p[1] + 0.2 p[2] - 2. p[3]}]

```
In[63]:= costfunction6 = QuadraticCostFunction[10,{1,1,1},
            Table[0,{3},{3}]]

Out[63]= CostFunction[{x[1], x[2], x[3]}, 10 + x[1] + x[2] +
            x[3]]

In[64]:= FP[z_] := N[ShapleyValuePrice[Demands[z,demandsystem3],
            costfunction6]/.x_/;x<0->0];
         svp = {1,1,1}
         Do[svp = FP[svp];Print[svp],{5}]

Out[64]= {1, 1, 1}

{1.39683, 1.18116, 1.11737}
{1.43482, 1.18375, 1.11787}
{1.43913, 1.18373, 1.11784}
{1.43964, 1.18372, 1.11783}
{1.43969, 1.18371, 1.11783}

In[65]:= FixedPoint[FP,{1,1,1}]

Out[65]= {1.4397, 1.18371, 1.11783}

In[66]:= costfunction7 = CESCostFunction[{1,1,1,1},{2,2,2,2},3]

Out[66]= CostFunction[{x[1], x[2], x[3], x[4]},

                      2       2       2       2  1/3
              (x[1]  + x[2]  + x[3]  + x[4] )      ]

In[67]:= FP[z_] := AumannShapleyPrice[Demands[z,demandsystem2],
            costfunction7]/.x_/;x<0->0;
         asp = {1,1,1,1}
         Do[asp = FP[asp];Print[asp],{5}]

Out[67]= {1, 1, 1, 1}

{0.0440507, 0.0952724, 0.146494, 0.197716}
{0.0485602, 0.0965741, 0.144588, 0.192602}
{0.0485022, 0.096542, 0.144582, 0.192621}
{0.0485028, 0.0965422, 0.144582, 0.192621}
{0.0485028, 0.0965422, 0.144582, 0.192621}

In[68]:= FixedPoint[FP,{1,1,1,1}]

Out[68]= {0.0485028, 0.0965422, 0.144582, 0.192621}
```

7.3.2 Optimal Uniform Pricing

When consumer demand functions are known, this information can be used in the computation of cost allocation and pricing rules. This section demonstrates the computation of optimal pricing rules assuming that only uniform pricing is used; that is, the per unit price of a commodity does not depend on the number of units purchased by a customer. Both profit maximizing and surplus maximizing prices may be computed using the function **KTMax[ ]**. We first consider the case of profit maximization.

```
In[69]:= Profit[p_,d_DemandSystem,c_CostFunction] :=
            p.Demands[p,d] - Cost[Demands[p,d],c];
```

```
In[70]:= costfunction8 = QuadraticCostFunction[10,{1,1,1,1},
            IdentityMatrix[4] + Table[.1,{4},{4}]]
```

```
Out[70]= CostFunction[{x[1], x[2], x[3], x[4]},

            10 + x[1] + x[2] + x[3] +

            x[1] (1.1 x[1] + 0.1 x[2] + 0.1 x[3] + 0.1 x[4]) +

            x[2] (0.1 x[1] + 1.1 x[2] + 0.1 x[3] + 0.1 x[4]) +

            x[3] (0.1 x[1] + 0.1 x[2] + 1.1 x[3] + 0.1 x[4]) +

            x[4] +

            x[4] (0.1 x[1] + 0.1 x[2] + 0.1 x[3] + 1.1 x[4])]
```

Solving for maximum profit is accomplished by the following function.

```
In[71]:= price = Array[p,4];
            KTMax[Profit[price,demandsystem2,costfunction8],
            price,{},{}]
```

```
Out[71]= {142.157, {{p[1] -> 9.25681, p[2] -> 13.092,
            p[3] -> 16.9273, p[4] -> 20.7625}}}
```

In some cases, nonnegativity constraints on price and quantity may need to be explicitly imposed in the computation of optimal prices. In addition, for some cost functions or demand systems **KTMax[ ]** may not be able to solve the first-order conditions explicitly. In these situations, an alternative method may be employed using the function **FindRoot[ ]**. **FindRoot[ ]** always finds a local optimum, but this approach is potentially sensitive to the starting values used in Newton's method. A good rule of thumb for linear demand systems is to use zero prices as starting values. For nonlinear demands and constant marginal costs, the marginal cost is a good starting value.

```
In[72]:= price = Array[p,4];
         startvals = Table[0,{Length[price]}];
         eqn = (D[Profit[price,demandsystem2,costfunction8],
             #]==0) & /@ price;
         solution = Apply[FindRoot,Join[{eqn},
             Transpose[{price,Table[0,{Length[price]}]}]]]];
         price/.solution
```

```
Out[72]= {9.25681, 13.092, 16.9273, 20.7625}
```

The computation of surplus maximizing (Ramsey) prices is similar to the computation of profit maximizing prices. The objective is now to maximize total surplus subject to the constraint that profits are equal to zero. This is accomplished by maximizing the function **IndirectUtility[ ]** subject to the profit constraint.

```
In[73]:= price = Array[p,4];
         IndirectUtility[price,demandsystem2]
```

```
Out[73]= 1000 - 10 p[1] - 20 p[2] - 30 p[3] +

         p[1] (1. p[1] - 0.1 p[2] - 0.1 p[3] - 0.1 p[4]) +

         p[2] (-0.1 p[1] + 1. p[2] - 0.1 p[3] - 0.1 p[4]) +

         p[3] (-0.1 p[1] - 0.1 p[2] + 1. p[3] - 0.1 p[4]) -

         40 p[4] +

         p[4] (-0.1 p[1] - 0.1 p[2] - 0.1 p[3] + 1. p[4])
```

```
In[74]:= KTMax[IndirectUtility[price,demandsystem2],price,{},
             {Profit[price,demandsystem2,costfunction8]}]
```

```
Out[74]= {92.0915, {{p[1] -> 7.36299, p[2] -> 10.5977,

         p[3] -> 13.8323, p[4] -> 17.067,

         lam[1] -> 0.341031}}}
```

Ramsey prices can also be computed using the function **FindRoot[ ]** as in the following example.

```
In[75]:= price = Array[p,4];
         startvals = Append[Table[0,{Length[price]}],1];
         lagrangian = IndirectUtility[price,demandsystem2]+
             lam*Profit[price,demandsystem2,costfunction8];
         eqn = (D[lagrangian,#]==0) & /@ Join[price,{lam}];
         solution = Apply[FindRoot,Join[{eqn},
             Transpose[{Append[price,lam],startvals}]]]];
         price/.solution
```

```
Out[75]= {7.36299, 10.5977, 13.8323, 17.067}
```

7.4   Optimal Nonlinear Pricing

7.4.1   Two-Part Tariffs

Nonlinear pricing methods allow the firm to charge a different marginal price for each unit sold to a given customer. Thus the outlay of a given customer is a nonlinear function of consumption rather than a linear homogeneous function as in the previous section. Under general nonlinear pricing methods, this function is allowed to take any form, in which case the customer is presented with a schedule of quantities available for consumption, and the corresponding outlays. A special case of nonlinear pricing, more frequently observed in practice, is that in which the customers are presented with a menu of two-part tariffs, consisting of a constant marginal price per unit and an entry fee. A general outlay function can be implemented by means of a set of self-selecting two-part tariffs if and only if it is concave. For additional discussion of nonlinear pricing methods, see Maskin and Riley (1984) for the general case, and Sharkey and Sibley (1993) for the case of self-selecting two-part tariffs.

As in the analysis of uniform pricing we begin by defining a system of demands. It is assumed that there is a single commodity and different types of customers who are characterized by their demand functions. In solving for optimal pricing rules, it is assumed that the firm or regulator knows the set of demand functions (i.e., the distribution of consumer types) but does not know "who is who" (i.e., cannot practice first-degree price discrimination). Because we are interested in both pricing using self-selecting two-part tariffs and general nonlinear pricing, we require both direct and indirect utility functions.

A demand system for nonlinear pricing is defined by the *Mathematica* function **DemandSystem[p_,V_,Q_,q_,U_]**, where p is a price vector, $V[p]$ is a vector of indirect utility functions, $Q[p]$ is a vector of demand functions, q is a quantity vector, and $U[q]$ is a vector of utility functions. The function **NonlinearDemand-System[ ]** generates a demand system for the analysis of nonlinear pricing.

```
In[76]:= demandsystem4 = NonlinearDemandSystem[{20,25,30,35},
            {2,2,2,2}]


Out[76]= DemandSystem[{p[1], p[2], p[3], p[4]},

                                        2
                             (20 - p[1])
            {10 (20 - p[1]) - -----------
                                   4


              25 (25 - p[2])   (25 - p[2])
              -------------- - -----------
                    2               4
```

$$15 \ (30 - p[3]) - \frac{(30 - p[3])^2}{4}$$

$$\frac{35 \ (35 - p[4])}{2} - \frac{(35 - p[4])^2}{4}$$

$$\left\{\frac{20 - p[1]}{2}, \ \frac{25 - p[2]}{2}, \ \frac{30 - p[3]}{2}, \ \frac{35 - p[4]}{2}\right\},$$

$$\{q[1], \ q[2], \ q[3], \ q[4]\},$$

$$\{20 \ q[1] - q[1]^2, \ 25 \ q[2] - q[2]^2, \ 30 \ q[3] - q[3]^2,$$

$$35 \ q[4] - q[4]^2 \ \}]$$

The functions **IndirectUtility[ ]**, **Utility[ ]**, and **Demands[ ]** may be used to extract relevant functions from any demand system. In the case of demand systems used for nonlinear pricing analysis, each of these functions returns a vector of functions.

```
In[77]:= price = Array[p,4];
         IndirectUtility[price,demandsystem4]
```

$$Out[77] = \ \{10 \ (20 - p[1]) - \frac{(20 - p[1])^2}{4}$$

$$\frac{25 \ (25 - p[2])}{2} - \frac{(25 - p[2])^2}{4}$$

$$15 \ (30 - p[3]) - \frac{(30 - p[3])^2}{4}$$

$$\frac{35 \ (35 - p[4])}{2} - \frac{(35 - p[4])^2}{4}$$

```
In[78]:= Demands[price,demandsystem4]
```

```
Out[78]=   20 - p[1]    25 - p[2]    30 - p[3]    35 - p[4]
         {----------,  ----------,  ----------,  ---------}
             2            2            2            2
```

```
In[79]:= quant = Array[q,4];
         Utility[quant,demandsystem4]
```

```
Out[79]=              2                2                2
           {20 q[1] - q[1] , 25 q[2] - q[2] , 30 q[3] - q[3] ,

                        2
           35 q[4] - q[4] }
```

In this section we compute optimal pricing rules assuming that prices are restricted to sets of two-part tariffs, which can be designed for each type of customer. We consider both profit maximizing and surplus maximizing tariffs. These objectives are defined in the functions **Profit1[ ]** and **CS1[ ]** defined in the following. In addition, optimal tariffs must satisfy "self selection" constraints, so that no consumer type wishes to consume under a tariff designed for a different consumer, and "individual rationality" constraints, so that all consumers whom the firm wishes to serve receive nonnegative utility. The self-selection constraints are defined by the functions **DIC1[ ]** and **UIC1[ ]** which give the "downward binding" and "upward binding" constraints, respectively. If consumers are indexed such that $Q_{i+1}(p) > Q_i(p)$ for every p, then the downward binding constraint requires that

$$CS_{i+1}(P_{i+1}, E_{i+1}) \geq CS_{i+1}(P_i, E_i),$$

where (P_i, E_i) and (P_{i+1}, E_{i+1}) are the tariffs designed for types i and $i+1$, respectively. As long as demand functions satisfy a noncrossing property, it is sufficient to impose only these constraints rather than the full set of self-selection constraints. Similarly, individual rationality need only be verified for the smallest consumer type. Both of these simplifying assumptions are assumed in the following constraint functions.

```
In[80]:= Profit1[p_,e_,d_DemandSystem,c_CostFunction] :=
             p.Demands[p,d] + Plus @@ e - Cost[Demands[p,d],c]
         CS1[p_,e_,d_DemandSystem] := IndirectUtility[p,d] -
             p*Demands[p,d] - e
         IR1[p_,e_,d_DemandSystem] := Take[CS1[p,e,d],1]
         DIC1[p_,e_,d_DemandSystem] := Take[CS1[p,e,d] -
             CS1[RotateRight[p],RotateRight[e],d],
             -(Length[p]-1)]
         UIC1[p_,e_,d_DemandSystem] := Take[CS1[p,e,d] -
             CS1[RotateLeft[p],RotateLeft[e],d],Length[p]-1]
```

Computation of optimal two-part tariffs is not quite as straightforward as computation of optimal uniform prices from a practical point of view. Because of the large number of constraints, the approach using `FindRoot[ ]` is not desirable due to the large number of local optima encountered. When the function `KTMax[ ]` is used it is necessary to keep the number of inequality constraints to a minimum, and some experimentation may be required in order to achieve reasonably fast but accurate results. The methodology for using `KTMax[ ]` is exactly the same as in the previous section and it is illustrated in the following examples for both profit maximizing and surplus maximizing two-part tariffs. The functions `SurplusMax2Part[ ]` and `ProfitMax2Part[ ]` in the package `Pricing` compute these respective solutions by solving these constrained optimization problems. The first example computes total surplus maximizing two-part tariffs for the previously defined demand system and a cost function which we now define.

```
In[81]:= costfunction9 = QuadraticCostFunction[400,{1,1,1,1},
            Table[0,{4},{4}]]
```

```
Out[81]= CostFunction[{x[1], x[2], x[3], x[4]},

          400 + x[1] + x[2] + x[3] + x[4]]
```

```
In[82]:= price = Array[p,4];entry = Array[e,4];
         objective = Plus @@ CS1[price,entry,demandsystem4];
         vars = Join[price,entry];
         ineq = IR1[price,entry,demandsystem4];
         eq = Join[DIC1[price,entry,demandsystem4],
             {Profit1[price,entry,demandsystem4,costfunction9]}];
         KTMax[objective,vars,ineq,eq]
```

```
Out[82]= {327.788, {{p[1] -> 4.83244, p[2] -> 3.55496,

          p[3] -> 2.27748, p[4] -> 1., e[1] -> 57.5137,

          e[2] -> 70.8035, e[3] -> 88.103, e[4] -> 109.412,

          lam[1] -> 1.37271, lam[2] -> 1.02953,

          lam[3] -> 0.686353, lam[4] -> 0.343177,

          lam[5] -> 1.34318}}}
```

A similar computation solves for the set of profit maximizing two-part tariffs.

```
In[83]:= objective = Profit1[price,entry,demandsystem4,
            costfunction9];
         vars = Join[price,entry];
         ineq = {};
         eq = Join[IR1[price,entry,demandsystem4],
             DIC1[price,entry,demandsystem4]];
         KTMax[objective,vars,ineq,eq]
```

```
Out[83]= {48.5, {{p[1] -> 16., p[2] -> 11., p[3] -> 6.,

           p[4] -> 1., e[1] -> 4., e[2] -> 32.75, e[3] -> 86.5,

           e[4] -> 165.25, lam[1] -> 4., lam[2] -> 3.,

           lam[3] -> 2., lam[4] -> 1.}}}
```

7.4.2 General Nonlinear Pricing

In the case of general nonlinear pricing, it is assumed that the firm can offer each customer a "take it or leave it" offer of a given quantity at a given total outlay. With these assumptions, the computation of optimal profit maximizing and surplus maximizing nonlinear tariffs is exactly the same as in the case of two-part tariffs. We first define the relevant objective and constraint functions.

```
In[84]:= Profit2[q_,r_,d_DemandSystem,c_CostFunction] :=
            Plus @@ r - Cost[q,c]
         CS2[q_,r_,d_DemandSystem] := Utility[q,d] - r
         IR2[q_,r_,d_DemandSystem] := Take[CS2[q,r,d],1]
         DIC2[q_,r_,d_DemandSystem] := Take[CS2[q,r,d] -
            CS2[RotateRight[q],RotateRight[r],d],-(Length[q]-1)]
         UIC2[q_,r_,d_DemandSystem] := Take[CS2[q,r,d] -
            CS2[RotateLeft[q],RotateLeft[r],d],Length[q]-1]
```

It is now straightforward to compute the optimal nonlinear pricing rules. The following computations continue to use the same demand and cost functions as before. Notice that both profits and surplus are higher under general non-linear pricing than under two-part tariff pricing. The functions **SurplusMaxNonlinear[ ]** and **ProfitMaxNonlinear[ ]** also compute these solutions.

```
In[85]:= quant = Array[q,4];outlay = Array[o,4];
         objective = Plus @@ CS2[quant,outlay,demandsystem4];
         vars = Join[quant,outlay];
         ineq = IR2[quant,outlay,demandsystem4];
         eq = Join[DIC2[quant,outlay,demandsystem4],
            {Profit2[quant,outlay,demandsystem4,
            costfunction9]}];
         KTMax[objective,vars,ineq,eq]
```

```
Out[85]= {333.494, {{q[1] -> 9.43544, q[2] -> 11.957,

           q[3] -> 14.4785, q[4] -> 17., o[1] -> 99.6813,

           o[2] -> 108.778, o[3] -> 117.766, o[4] -> 126.646,

           lam[1] -> 0.0347329, lam[2] -> 0.0260497,
```

```
              lam[3] -> 0.0173665, lam[4] -> 0.00868323,

              lam[5] -> 1.00868}}}

In[86]:= objective = Profit2[quant,outlay,demandsystem4,
            costfunction9];
         vars = Join[quant,outlay];
         ineq = {};
         eq = Join[IR2[quant,outlay,demandsystem4],
            DIC2[quant,outlay,demandsystem4]];
         KTMax[objective,vars,ineq,eq]

Out[86]= {86., {{q[1] -> 2., q[2] -> 7., q[3] -> 12.,

              q[4] -> 17., o[1] -> 36., o[2] -> 116.,

              o[3] -> 171., o[4] -> 201., lam[1] -> 4.,

              lam[2] -> 3., lam[3] -> 2., lam[4] -> 1.}}}
```

Computation of optimal nonlinear tariffs may require optimization over the set of customer types. In addition, with linear demand functions, negative quantities cannot be ruled out in the preceding optimization unless inequality constraints are explicitly included. For example, if the preceding demand system is modified, then solving for the profit maximizing set of two-part tariffs for all four customer types leads to the following outcome.

```
In[87]:= price = Array[p,4];entry = Array[e,4];
         demandsystem5 = NonlinearDemandSystem[{20,40,60,80},
            {2,2,2,2}];
         Demands[price,demandsystem5]

Out[87]= 20 - p[1]    40 - p[2]    60 - p[3]    80 - p[4]
         {---------, ---------, ---------, ---------}
             2           2           2           2

In[88]:= objective = Profit1[price,entry,demandsystem5,
            costfunction9];
         vars = Join[price,entry];
         ineq = {};
         eq = Join[IR1[price,entry,demandsystem5],
            DIC1[price,entry,demandsystem5]];
         soln = KTMax[objective,vars,ineq,eq]

Out[88]= {1361., {{p[1] -> 61., p[2] -> 41., p[3] -> 21.,

              p[4] -> 1., e[1] -> 420.25, e[2] -> 310.25,

              e[3] -> 600.25, e[4] -> 1290.25, lam[1] -> 4.,

              lam[2] -> 3., lam[3] -> 2., lam[4] -> 1.}}}
```

```
In[89]:= Demands[price,demandsystem5] /. Last[Last[soln]]
```

```
Out[89]= {-20.5, -0.5, 19.5, 39.5}
```

The optimal solution is one in which the profit maximizing prices are determined for customers 3 and 4 alone.

```
In[90]:= price = Drop[price,2];entry = Drop[entry,2];
         demandsystem6 = NonlinearDemandSystem[{60,80},{2,2}];
         costfunction10 = QuadraticCostFunction[400,{1,1},
             Table[0,{2},{2}]];

         objective = Profit1[price,entry,demandsystem6,
             costfunction10];
         vars = Join[price,entry];
         ineq = {};
         eq = Join[IR1[price,entry,demandsystem6],
             DIC1[price,entry,demandsystem6]];
         KTMax[objective,vars,ineq,eq]
```

```
Out[90]= {1440.5, {{p[3] -> 21., p[4] -> 1., e[3] -> 380.25,

             e[4] -> 1070.25, lam[1] -> 2., lam[2] -> 1.}}}
```

In the case of general nonlinear pricing, these difficulties do not arise inasmuch as the optimal set of customers to serve can be implicitly solved for as part of the optimization. (In the case of two-part tariffs and linear demand functions, a customer i can be "priced out of the market" only by setting a price P_i such that $Q_i(P_i) = 0$, and an entry fee of zero. Because this price entry combination is also available to all customers, the self-selection constraints limit the set of tariffs that can be offered to larger customer types.) The following computation explicitly includes the inequality constraints $q_1 \geq 0$ and $q_2 \geq 0$.

```
In[91]:= quant = Array[q,4];outlay = Array[o,4];
         objective = Profit2[quant,outlay,demandsystem5,
             costfunction9];
         vars = Join[quant,outlay];
         ineq = Take[quant,2];
         eq = Join[IR2[quant,outlay,demandsystem5],
             DIC2[quant,outlay,demandsystem5]];
         KTMax[objective,vars,ineq,eq]
```

```
Out[91]= {1540.5, {{q[1] -> 0., q[2] -> 0., q[3] -> 19.5,

             q[4] -> 39.5, o[1] -> 0., o[2] -> 0.,

             o[3] -> 789.75, o[4] -> 1209.75, lam[1] -> 41.,

             lam[2] -> 1., lam[3] -> 4., lam[4] -> 3.,

             lam[5] -> 2., lam[6] -> 1.}}}
```

7.4.3   Nonlinear Pricing as Ramsey Pricing

This section illustrates the relationship between Ramsey pricing and optimal
nonlinear pricing. Because both pricing methodologies are the result of surplus
maximization, this relationship should not be surprising. In order to formally
represent optimal nonlinear prices as Ramsey prices, one solves the self-selection
and individual rationality constraints and incorporates this information into the
objective function. The Ramsey optimal solution then consists of maximizing the
derived objective function subject to a profit constraint. These observations are
illustrated in the following for the case of two-part tariffs and general nonlinear
pricing, respectively.

```
In[92]:= E1[x_,d_DemandSystem] := Module[{price,entry,soln},
            price = Array[p,Length[x]];
            entry = Array[e,Length[x]];
            soln = First[Solve[(#==0) & /@
                Join[IR1[price,entry,d],DIC1[price,entry,d]],
                entry]];
            (entry /. soln) /. e[i_] :> x[[i]]
            ];
```

```
In[93]:= price = Array[p,4];entry = Array[e,4];
         objective = Plus @@ (IndirectUtility[price,
             demandsystem4] -
             price * Demands[price,demandsystem4] -
             E1[price,demandsystem4]);
         vars = price;
         ineq = {};
         eq = {Profit1[price,E1[price,demandsystem4],
             demandsystem4,costfunction9]};
         KTMax[objective,vars,ineq,eq]
```

```
Out[93]= {327.788, {{p[1] -> 4.83244, p[2] -> 3.55496,

           p[3] -> 2.27748, p[4] -> 1., lam[1] -> 1.34318}}}
```

```
In[94]:= O2[x_,d_DemandSystem] := Module[{quant,outlay,soln},
            quant = Array[q,Length[x]];
            outlay = Array[o,Length[x]];
            soln = First[Solve[(#==0) & /@
                Join[IR2[quant,outlay,d],DIC2[quant,outlay,d]],
                outlay]];
            (outlay /. soln) /. q[i_] :> x[[i]]
            ];
```

```
In[95]:= quant = Array[q,4];outlay = Array[o,4];
         objective = Plus @@ (Utility[quant,demandsystem4]-
            O2[quant,demandsystem4]);
         vars = quant;
         ineq = {};
         eq = {Profit2[quant,O2[quant,demandsystem4],
            demandsystem4,costfunction9]};
         KTMax[objective,vars,ineq,eq]

Out[95]= {333.494, {{q[1] -> 9.43544, q[2] -> 11.957,

              q[3] -> 14.4785, q[4] -> 17., lam[1] -> 1.00868}}}
```

7.5   Concluding Comments

This chapter has demonstrated how *Mathematica* can be used to implement cost allocation pricing rules in both discrete and continuous situations, and to solve for optimal pricing rules in continuous problems when consumer demand functions are known. Using the tools provided here, and in the package `Pricing`, the user will be able to independently investigate specific pricing methods in greater detail.

7.6   References

Billera, L. J. and D. C. Heath. 1982. "Allocation of Shared Costs: A Set of Axioms Yielding a Unique Procedure." *Mathematics of Operations Research*, **7**, 32–39.

Carter, M. 1993. "Cooperative Games." In *Economic and Financial Modeling with Mathematica*, H. Varian, Ed., New York, Springer-Verlag (TELOS).

Hart, S. and M. Kurz. 1983. "Endogenous Formation of Coalitions." *Econometrica*, **51**, 1047–1064.

Hart, S. and A. Mas-Colell. 1989. "Potential, Value, and Consistency." *Econometrica*, **57**, 589–614.

Kalai, E. and D. Samet. 1987. "On Weighted Shapley Values." *International Journal of Game Theory*, **16**, 205–222.

Kaplan, T. and A. Mukherji. 1993. "Designing an Incentive-Compatible Contract." In *Economic and Financial Modeling with Mathematica*, H. Varian, Ed., New York, Springer-Verlag (TELOS).

Maskin, E. and J. Riley. 1984. "Monopoly with Incomplete Information." *Rand Journal of Economics*, **15**, 171–196.

McLean, R. P. and W. W. Sharkey. 1995. "Probabilistic Value Pricing." *Zeitschrift fur Operations Research* (forthcoming).

McLean, R. P. and W. W. Sharkey. 1996. "Weighted Aumann-Shapley Pricing." *International Journal of Game Theory*, **25**, forthcoming.

McLean, R. P., A. Pazgal, and W. W. Sharkey. 1995. "Potential, Consistency and Cost Allocation Prices" (unpublished manuscript).

Mirman, L. and Y. Tauman. 1982. "Demand Compatible, Equitable, Cost Sharing Prices." *Mathematics of Operations Research*, **7**, 40–56.

Moulin, H. 1988. *Axioms of Cooperative Decision Making*. Cambridge, Cambridge University Press.

Owen, G. 1972. "Multilinear Extensions of Games." *Management Science*, **18**, 64–79.

Owen, G. 1977. "Values of Games with a Priori Unions." in *Essays in Mathematical Economics and Game Theory*, R. Hein and O. Moeschlin, Eds. New York, Springer-Verlag, 76–88.

Samet, D., Y. Tauman, and I. Zang. 1984. "An Application of the Aumann-Shapley Prices for Cost Allocation in Transportation Problems." *Mathematics of Operations Research*, **9**, 25–42.

Shapley, L. S. 1953. "A Value for n-Person Games." In *Contributions to the Theory of Games*, Vol. II, H. W. Kuhn and A. W. Tucker, Eds. Annals of Mathematics Studies No. 28, Princeton, NJ, Princeton University Press, 307–317.

Shapley, L. S. and M. Shubik. 1972. "The Assignment Game I: The Core." *International Journal of Game Theory*, **1**, 111–130.

Sharkey, W. W. 1995. "Network Models in Economics." In *The Handbook of Operations Research and Management Science: Networks*. Amsterdam, North Holland.

Sharkey, W. W. and D. S. Sibley. 1993. "Optimal Non-Linear Pricing with Regulatory Preference over Customer Type." *Journal of Public Economics*, **50**, 197–229.

Varian, H. R. 1984. *Microeconomic Analysis*. New York, W. W. Norton & Company.

Young, P. 1994. "Cost Allocation." In *Handbook of Game Theory*, Vol. 2, R. J. Aumann and S. Hart, Eds. Amsterdam, North Holland.

8 Simulating the Effects of Mergers Among Noncooperative Oligopolists

Luke M. Froeb and Gregory J. Werden

8.1 Introduction

U.S. antitrust law prohibits corporate mergers that substantially lessen competition. Because it is far easier to prevent than undo a merger, the effects of mergers are almost always predicted prior to consummation. Courts make such predictions using a "structural" analysis. Markets are delineated, market shares are assigned, and the legality of a merger turns largely on how the market shares and market concentration compare with arbitrary thresholds [see generally Horizontal Merger Guidelines (1992) and Hay and Werden (1993)]. These thresholds are not explicitly based on economic models of oligopoly, on empirical studies of the effects of mergers, or on empirical studies of the relationship between market structure and economic performance. Moreover, structural analysis makes no attempt to explicitly estimate the price or welfare effects of mergers.

Economists have criticized the structural approach taken by the courts on many grounds. Among the more telling criticisms is that structural analysis is particularly ill-suited to differentiated products industries. In such industries, the structural analysis of a narrowly delineated market ignores competition between the products or areas within the delineated market and those outside it, and the structural analysis of a broadly delineated market ignores localizations of competition within the delineated market [see Rozanski and Werden (1994)]. Consequently, structural analysis is not likely to be a good predictor of the effects of mergers in differentiated products industries.

Even for relatively homogeneous and undifferentiated goods, however, structural analysis is problematic. With no underlying estimate of the price or welfare effects of mergers, there is no systematic way in which a structural analysis can trade off potential efficiencies against potential anticompetitive effects.

We offer the package `Merger.m` as an alternative to structural analysis. Powerful high-level languages such as *Mathematica* make it relatively easy to simulate mergers using standard models of static noncooperative oligopoly. Although crude, the simulations provide a perspective on the nature and magnitudes of likely price, output, and welfare effects of mergers that is missing in structural analysis. Traditional analytical tools such as differential calculus are ill-suited to the task of analyzing large discrete changes such as mergers.

The critical insight behind the simulations is that, once demand and cost structures are specified, it is possible to infer firm-specific demand and cost parameters using only readily observable individual firm prices and outputs, and one or a few estimable demand parameters. This inference requires only the assumption that the observed prices and quantities are the product of a specified equilibrium concept. Thus the oligopoly models are precisely calibrated to fit a particular industry using only the sort of information that is currently used in structural analysis.

With the estimated and inferred parameters, it is possible to calculate a post-merger equilibrium and compare it to that pre-merger. The package contains functions for simulating mergers within the context of two standard, static, noncooperative oligopoly equilibria, the quantity-setting or Cournot equilibrium, and the price-setting or Bertrand equilibrium. The former is appropriate only for homogeneous products, as it specifies a single, market clearing price. The latter is appropriate for differentiated products, as it specifies separate demands and distinct prices for each product in the market.

Although much previous theoretical work has postulated industries of identical firms, we allow for arbitrary firm asymmetries. In both equilibria, firms are distinguished on the basis of marginal cost, and in the Bertrand equilibrium, they are also distinguished on the basis of demand. The great bulk of what follows concerns the Bertrand equilibrium because structural analysis is particularly problematic in the case of differentiated products and because the Bertrand simulations are more complex.

What follows are discussions of the demand system underlying the Bertrand simulations, the inputs to the simulation, and the four steps involved in the Bertrand simulations themselves: converting market shares into choice probabilities; recovering firm-specific demand constants; calculating firm marginal costs; and computing the post-merger equilibrium. Also illustrated is one possible way of trading merger efficiencies off against anticompetitive effects. Lastly we illustrate a Cournot merger simulation and offer concluding remarks.

8.2 Turn off Some *Mathematica* Warning Messages and Load the Package

The computational engine of the `Merger.m` package is *Mathematica*'s **FindRoot** command. When using very strong nests, the **FindRoot** function may fail to converge. When this happens, *Mathematica* generates some error and warning messages. However, it can also generate misleading warning messages when it is able to find a root. Because this can confuse a novice user of the package, we recommend turning off some warning messages. As you become more familiar with the package, or if you are attempting to extend or modify the package for your own particular application, you may want to turn them on again.

```
In[1]:=  Off[General::spell];
         Off[General::spell1];
         Off[Set::write];
         Off[Power::infy];
         Off[Infinity::indet];
         Off[Solve::dinv];
         Off[NumberForm::sigz];

In[2]:=  <<Merger'Merger'

In[3]:=  ?Merger
```

This package defines functions used to simulate mergers in differentiated and homogenous product industries. Available functions: ChoiceProbabilities, DemandConstants, MarginalCosts, PostMerger, PrintResults, DiffProdMerger, DiffProdMergerMinCost, HomoProdMerger, PostMergerC.

8.3   Simulation of Mergers in Differentiated Product Industries

DiffProdMerger simulates mergers in differentiated products industries. It is predicated on several simplifying assumptions: each product is initially sold by a single firm with constant marginal cost and no fixed costs; mergers do not affect cost, so economies of scale and scope cannot be realized through merger; and, finally, product characteristics other than price are fixed, so that a merger cannot result in any strategic effects other than those involving price. In particular, mergers cannot lead to entry or to product repositioning by established firms.

8.3.1   Logit Demand

At the heart of **DiffProdMerger** is a discrete choice, random utility model of product differentiation. For tractability and other reasons discussed in the following, the logit model is used. In the logit model, demand for product j is the probability that a consumer will choose product j. The indirect utility of consumer i associated with the choice of product j is

$$U_{ij} = a_j - bp_j + e_{ij}.$$

Consumers choose the product that gives them the highest utility. If the e_{ij}s are independently and identically distributed according to the extreme value distribution, the choice probabilities have the familiar logistic form:

$$\exp(a_j - bp_j) \Big/ \sum_k \exp(a_k - bp_k).$$

With a three-choice logit model,

```
In[4]:=   q:=Exp[#]/Apply[Plus,Exp[#]]& @
          (Array[a,n]-b Array[p,n])

In[5]:=   n=3;q
```

```
Out[5]=                              a[1] - b p[1]
                                    E
          {------------------------------------------------------,
            a[1] - b p[1]    a[2] - b p[2]    a[3] - b p[3]
           E              + E              + E


                                   a[2] - b p[2]
                                  E
          ------------------------------------------------------,
            a[1] - b p[1]    a[2] - b p[2]    a[3] - b p[3]
           E              + E              + E


                                   a[3] - b p[3]
                                  E
          ------------------------------------------------------}
            a[1] - b p[1]    a[2] - b p[2]    a[3] - b p[3]
           E              + E              + E
```

The version of the logit model used in **DiffProdMerger** and its implications for mergers are shown in far greater detail by Werden and Froeb (1994).

The logit model is characterized by the *Independence of Irrelevant Alternatives* (IIA) property. The IIA property implies that second choices are made with the same relative choice probabilities as first choices. Thus if a firm raises price, it loses customers to its rivals in proportion to their market shares. Economists have typically considered the IIA property to be an inaccurate description of choice behavior in most settings. Although that may be true, the logit model is attractive as a benchmark because the IIA property reflects a diffuse prior on substitution patterns when only first choices are known. When simulation is intended only as a substitute for structural analysis, the IIA property should not be seen as troublesome.

8.3.2   Nested Logit Demand

The package offers the user a choice between this flat logit specification and a nested logit specification. The nested logit model is quite similar to the logit, but is meant to capture localized competition among goods within a nest; goods in a nest are better substitutes for each other than they are for goods outside the nest. With a nested specification, the probability of choosing *j* conditional on it being in the nest is simply an ordinary logit, as is the marginal probability that one of the goods in nest *j* is chosen. The details of the nested logit specification can be found in Train (1986).

The nested logit specification adds two parameters to the demand system, the list of choices in the nest, for example, $\{2, 3, 5\}$, and the nest parameter d which controls the strength of the nest (1 implies no nest or a flat logit, and 0 is a very strong nest). Making the nest stronger makes the goods in the nest worse substitutes for those outside it, and it makes the goods in the nest better substitutes for each other. The package is only set up to handle a single nest, but it would be relatively straightforward to modify the package to add more nests of different strength, or "subnests" within nests. It is our experience, however, that strong nests, those with nest parameters less than .5, may cause a failure of the **FindRoot** command.

8.3.3   Inputs to the Simulation

To make the simulations useful for antitrust purposes, it is important that inputs to the simulations be observable or estimable, and familiar to antitrust practitioners. Antitrust deals in market shares, whereas discrete choice models are phrased in terms of unconditional choice probabilities. Translating from one to the other is trivial except for the no-purchase option. In order to eliminate it from the model, we specify an aggregate elasticity of demand for all the goods in the specified choice set e (Werden and Froeb 1994).

The primitives of the model, which completely characterize an industry, are market shares and prices, both of which can be observed, and demand parameters e and b, both of which can be estimated. Roughly speaking, b is the cross elasticity of the demand parameter, controlling the substitutabilities among the inside goods. Not all combinations of primitive values are possible in equilibrium, and the program checks to make sure that the values input are possible (by determining whether any of the implied marginal costs are negative). This version of the logit model is termed the Antitrust Logit Model by Werden et al. (1996), and is an extension of a model used in an oligopoly context by Anderson et al. (1990).

In the simulations, it is easiest to translate market shares into discrete choice model terms. This is done using the function **ChoiceProbabilities**

```
In[6]:=  ?ChoiceProbabilities
```

```
ChoiceProbabilities[b, p0_List, q0_List, elasticity] inputs
    the coefficient on price, pre-merger prices, pre-merger
    quantities or market shares, and the aggregate elasticity
    of demand, and ouputs a vector of choice probabilities
    constructed so that the choice probability for the 'no
    purchase' option or 'outside' good is consistent with the
    specified aggregate elasticity of demand for the remaining,
    'inside' goods.  The length of p0 and q0 must equal the
    number of firms plus one.  The price on the outside good
    can take any value, i.e., it is meaningless).
```

The construction and application of the merger simulation functions are illustrated within the context of hypothetical mergers among Japanese long distance carriers. Simulations of these mergers are more fully explored by Froeb et al. (1994). The long-distance industry in Japan resembles that in the United States before the AT&T break-up; NTT is the dominant carrier with nearly 90% of the market, and it has three minor rivals: DDI, Telecom, and Teleway.

```
In[7]:= firmData={
           FirmNames={"NTT","DDI","Telecom","Teleway",
                      "No Purchase"},
           p0={1.,.9,.9,.9,0},
           q0={.865,.088,.043,.004,0}
           };
```

```
In[8]:= demandData={b=9.557,e=.62};
```

```
In[9]:= NumberForm[TableForm[Transpose[
           {{"firm",FirmNames},
            {"price",p0},
            {"market share",q0},
            {"choice prob.",
            q00=ChoiceProbabilities[b,p0,q0,e]}}
                     ]],3]
```

Out[9]= firm	price	market share	choice prob.
NTT	1.	0.865	0.808
DDI	0.9	0.088	0.0822
Telecom	0.9	0.043	0.0402
Teleway	0.9	0.004	0.00374
No Purchase	0	0	0.0658

Note that the price of the no-purchase option is arbitrarily set to 0. Only relative prices matter, and as a reasonable approximation, NTT's price is set equal to 1, whreas the other firm's prices are set at .9.

The simulations employ an estimate of b (9.557) from Froeb et al. (1994), and an estimate of the aggregate elasticity of demand for long-distance service (0.62) from another published source.

8.3.4   Recovery of Firm-Specific Demand Constants

The firm-specific demand constants a_j can be calculated from the logit choice probabilities. The individual constants are related to the inherent attractiveness of a choice. Only relative utilities matter, so one of the constants is set equal to an arbitrary constant.

DemandConstants sets the demand constant for the no-purchase choice equal to 10, and solves for the remaining constants.

```
In[10]:= ?DemandConstants
```

DemandConstants[(nest_List), (nestparam), b, p0_List, q0_List]
   solves the n demand equations, q(p0) = q0, for the n-1
   demand constants, {a(j)}, which characterize the random
   utility model: U(i,j) = a(j) - b*p(j) + e(i,j). a[n] is
   arbitrarily set equal to 10. Nestparam is the nesting
   parameter: 0 is a strong nest; 1 is a flat logit. Nest is
   a vector with the firms that are in a nest, e.g., {1,3,4}.
   The last good is the 'no purchase' option or 'outside' good,
   and its price must be set equal to zero.

```
In[11]:= n=5;
```

```
In[12]:= rules=Flatten[{a[n]->10,Table[p[i]->p0[[i]],{i,n}]}]
```

```
Out[12]= {a[5] -> 10, p[1] -> 1., p[2] -> 0.9, p[3] -> 0.9,
          p[4] -> 0.9, p[5] -> 0}
```

```
In[13]:= eqns=Take[q00-q/.rules,{1,n-1}];
```

```
In[14]:= startingValues=Table[{a[i],20},{i,1,n-1}];
```

```
In[15]:= FindRoot @@ FlattenAt[{eqns,startingValues,
             MaxIterations->500},{2}]
```

```
Out[15]= {a[1] -> 22.0657, a[2] -> 18.8246, a[3] -> 18.1084,
          a[4] -> 15.7335}
```

```
In[16]:= NumberForm[TableForm[
               Transpose[
           {{"firms",FirmNames},
            {"p0",p0},
            {"choice prob.",q00},
            {"demand constants",
           aa=DemandConstants[{},1.,9.557,p0,q00]}}
                 ]],3]
```

```
Out[16]= firms          p0    choice prob.   demand constants

         NTT           1.     0.808          22.1
         DDI           0.9    0.0822         18.8
         Telecom       0.9    0.0402         18.1
         Teleway       0.9    0.00374        15.7
         No Purchase   0      0.0658         10
```

In equilibrium, larger firms have more preferred products and hence higher a_js.

8.3.5   Calculating Firm Marginal Costs

If the firms are maximizing profits, then the first derivative of their profit function with respect to their prices must equal zero. **MarginalCosts** uses this first-order condition to infer marginal costs from the firm prices and shares.

```
In[17]:= ?MarginalCosts
```

MarginalCosts[(nest_List), (nestparam), a_List, b, p0_List,
   q0_List] calculates n-1 marginal costs from the n-1
   pre-merger first-order conditions produced by differentiating
   each firm's profit funtion with respect to its own price.
   Nest is a vector with the firms that are in a nest, e.g.,
   {1,3,4}. Nestparam is the nesting parameter: 0 is a
   strong nest, and 1 is a flat logit. The last good is
   the 'no purchase' or 'outside' good and its price must be
   set equal to zero.

```
In[18]:= profits=(Array[p,n]-Array[c,n])q;
```

```
In[19]:= rules=Flatten[{
                  Table[a[i]->aa[[i]],{i,n}],
                  Table[p[i]->p0[[i]],{i,n}],
                  c[n]->0
                  }];
```

```
In[20]:= eqns=Table[
                  D[profits[[i]],p[i]],
                  {i,n-1}]/.rules;
```

```
In[21]:= startingValues=Table[{c[i],p0[[i]]},{i,1,n-1}]
```

```
Out[21]= {{c[1], 1.}, {c[2], 0.9}, {c[3], 0.9}, {c[4], 0.9}}
```

```
In[22]:= FindRoot @@ FlattenAt[{eqns,startingValues,
              MaxIterations->500},{2}]
```

```
Out[22]= {c[1] -> 0.454694, c[2] -> 0.785992, c[3] -> 0.790985,
          c[4] -> 0.794972}
```

```
In[23]:= NumberForm[TableForm[Transpose[{
              {"firm",FirmNames},
              {"price",p0},
              {"choice prob.",q00},
              {"marginal cost",cc=MarginalCosts[aa,b,p0,q00]}
                  }]],3]
```

```
Out[23]= firm            price    choice prob.    marginal cost

         NTT             1.       0.808           0.455
         DDI             0.9      0.0822          0.786
         Telecom         0.9      0.0402          0.791
         Teleway         0.9      0.00374         0.795
         No Purchase     0        0.0658          0
```

In equilibrium, larger firms have lower marginal costs. This is relevant to the welfare effects of mergers in that, other things being equal, mergers of larger firms reduce welfare even more than otherwise because they cause substitution away from the larger firms with lower marginal costs. By contrast, mergers of small or medium-sized firms decrease welfare less than otherwise because they cause substitution toward the larger firms with lower marginal costs.

8.3.6   Computing the Post-Merger Equilibrium

Once the firm-specific demand constants and marginal costs have been recovered, it is possible to compute the post-merger equilibrium using the function **PostMerger**. The merged firm internalizes the effects of each product's price on the sales of the other. This induces the merged firm to raise the price of both products. In response, other firms in the industry also raise prices. Werden and Froeb (1994) show that post-merger price rises tend to be highly asymmetric. This is illustrated by the simulation of a merger between the two largest Japanese long-distance carriers. Note that omitting the optional nested list and nesting parameter causes the program to use a flat logit demand structure.

```
In[24]:= ?PostMerger
```

```
PostMerger[merging_List, (nested_List), (nestParam), a_List,
    b, e_, c0_List, p0_List] inputs demand parameters from a
    logit demand system, pre-merger marginal costs, prices, and
    quantities or market shares, and outputs post-merger costs,
    prices, and choice probabilities resulting from a merger
    among firms in the merging list.
```

```
In[25]:= merging={1,2};
```

```
In[26]:= mergedProfits= Plus @@ Part[profits,merging];
```

```
In[27]:= rules=Flatten[{
                Table[a[i]->aa[[i]],{i,n}],
                Table[c[i]->cc[[i]],{i,n}],
                p[5]->0
                }];
```

```
In[28]:= eqns=Table[If[
                MemberQ[merging,i],
                D[mergedProfits,p[i]],
                D[profits[[i]],p[i]]
                ],{i,n-1}]/.rules;
```

```
In[29]:= startingValues=Table[{p[i],p0[[i]]},{i,1,n-1}]
```

```
Out[29]= {{p[1], 1.}, {p[2], 0.9}, {p[3], 0.9}, {p[4], 0.9}}
```

```
In[30]:= FindRoot @@ FlattenAt[{eqns,startingValues,
            MaxIterations->500},{2}]
```

```
Out[30]= {p[1] -> 1.04873, p[2] -> 1.38002, p[3] -> 0.902712,
            p[4] -> 0.900244}
```

```
In[31]:= NumberForm[
         TableForm[Transpose[
           {{"firm",FirmNames},
            {"P0",p0},
            {"Q0",q00},
            {"P1",p1=#[[2]]& @ PostMerger[merging={1,2},
                                          aa,b,cc,p0]},
            {"Q1",q1=#[[3]]& @ PostMerger[merging,
                                          aa,b,cc,p0]}}
                         ]],3]
```

```
Out[31]= firm           P0    Q0        P1      Q1

         NTT            1.    0.808     1.05    0.822
         DDI            0.9   0.0822    1.38    0.00136
         Telecom        0.9   0.0402    0.903   0.0635
         Teleway        0.9   0.00374   0.9     0.00605
         No Purchase    0     0.0658    0       0.107
```

The merger causes a relatively small increase in the price charged by the dominant firm, NTT, but a very large increase in the price of its merger partner, DDI, resulting in a very large reduction in its output. This is similar to the "disappearance" of DDI following the merger. Notice also that the nonmerging firms increase price in response, but relatively very little.

8.3.7 Summary Statistics for the Merger

PrintResults is used to produce summary statistics relating to the effects of a merger. The Guidelines HHI is the concentration measure used in Horizontal Merger Guidelines (1992). Its pre-merger value is that of the Herfindahl index based on pre-merger outputs. Its post-merger value is its pre-merger value plus twice the product of the shares of the merging firms. Quantity HHI is a Herfindahl index based on outputs both pre- and post-merger. Consumer Surplus is computed as a compensating variation, as is conventional in discrete choice models. Consumer Surplus is arbitrarily scaled by the arbitrary choice of one of the a_js, so only a change can be computed. To place it in perspective, it is expressed as a percentage of pre-merger industry revenues. Welfare is Consumer Surplus plus profit.

```
In[32]:= ?PrintResults

PrintResults[merging_List, (nest_List), (nestParam), a_List,
    b_, e_, c0_List, p0_List, q0_List, c1_List, p1_List, q1_List,
    firmNames_List] inputs parameters and pre- and post-merger
    marginal costs, prices, and quantities, and outputs the
    full results following a merger.  The last good is the
    'no purchase' or 'outside' good, and its price must be
    set equal to zero.
```

In[33]:= **PrintResults[merging,aa,b,e,cc,p0,q00,cc,p1,q1,FirmNames]**

Out[33]= DIFFERENTIATED PRODUCTS MERGER SIMULATION RESULTS
        Elasticity = 0.62
        B = 9.557
        Nest Parameter = 1
        @ signifies nest member
        * signifies merging firms
        Changes in profits and welfare are expressed as a % of
        pre-merger revenue.

Firms	a	q0	q1	% change q
*NTT	22.07	0.8081	0.8225	1.78
*DDI	18.82	0.08221	0.001357	-98.35
Telecom	18.11	0.04017	0.06347	58.
Teleway	15.73	0.003737	0.006045	61.77
No Purchase	10	0.06576	0.1066	62.14

Firms	mc0	mc1	p0	p1	% change p
*NTT	0.4547	0.4547	1.	1.049	4.873
*DDI	0.786	0.786	0.9	1.38	53.34
Telecom	0.791	0.791	0.9	0.9027	0.3013
Teleway	0.795	0.795	0.9	0.9002	0.0271

firms	p0-mc0	p1-mc1	elas0	elas1
*NTT	0.545	0.594	1.83	1.78
*DDI	0.114	0.594	7.89	13.2
Telecom	0.109	0.112	8.26	8.08
Teleway	0.105	0.105	8.57	8.55

firms	prof0	prof1	change prof	% change prof
*NTT	0.441	0.489	0.0479	10.9
*DDI	0.00937	0.000806	-0.00857	-91.4
Telecom	0.00438	0.00709	0.00271	61.9
Teleway	0.000392	0.000636	0.000244	62.1

vars.	pre-merger	post	change	% change
Guidelines HHI	7578.	9101.	1522.	
Quantity HHI	7578.	8527.	948.9	
Industry Price	0.9865	1.038	0.05135	5.205
Industry Quantity	0.9342	0.8934	-0.04087	-4.374
Elasticity	0.62	1.058	0.4376	70.58
Average Costs	0.4997	0.4814	-0.01828	-3.658
Merged Firm Price	0.9908	1.049	0.05851	5.905
Merged Firm Prft	0.45	0.4894	4.27	8.744

```
Industry Profits     0.4548        0.4971    4.591       9.302
Consumer Surplus                             -5.487
Welfare                                      -0.8966
```

In addition to issues relating to the welfare effects of the merger, which are discussed in the next section, there is one point of special interest in these results. The equilibrium demand elasticity for DDI (and for the industry) increases quite a bit as a result of the price and output changes induced by the merger. This is important to note because some of the estimation-based methods for predicting the effects of mergers [e.g., Hausman et al. (1994)] assume that elasticities remain constant. Such large changes suggest that these methods have the potential to overstate the price effects of mergers whenever demand elasticities are sensitive to changes in prices and quantities, and that certainly is the normal case [see Froeb and Werden (1992)].

In[34]:= **?DiffProdMerger**

```
DiffProdMerger[merging_List, (nested_List), (nestParam_),
    {b,elasticity}, {FirmNames,p0,q0}] This function calls
    all the other functions to calculate the effects of a
    merger in a differentiated product industry.  Merging is
    a list of the merging firms, e.g., {1,2,3}; nested is a
    list of the products in the demand nest, e.g., {2,3,4};
    nestParam is a value between 0 and 1 that controls the
    strength of the nest--1 is a flat logit, and 0 is a strong
    nest; b is an estimated cross elasticity of demand parameter
    from the logit model; p0 is the vector of pre-merger prices;
    q0 is the vector of pre-merger quantities or market shares;
    elasticity is the pre-merger aggregate elasticity for the
    inside goods; FirmNames is a vector of firm names.  Note
    that the last choice is the 'no purchase' option or
    'outside' good with a pre-merger price and quantity of zero.
```

8.3.8 Effects of Mergers on Consumer and Total Welfare

The welfare effects of mergers in this model are examined by Froeb et al. (1994). Because all firms raise price, consumer welfare always falls. The effects of mergers on total welfare are far more complex because the asymmetric price effects of mergers lead to a reallocation of output, and firms differ with respect to cost and product preference. There is a reallocation of output from the product with the smaller pre-merger share to the product with the larger pre-merger share, and there is a shift in output from the merging firms to the nonmerging firms. The former effect necessarily enhances welfare and the latter does as well if the merging firms are relatively small.

For example, the merger of NTT and DDI previously illustrated causes a substantial reallocation of output from DDI (cutting its output to virtually zero) to NTT, which increases its output. This reallocation of output from DDI to

NTT causes a welfare gain for two reasons. NTT's marginal cost is substantially lower than that of its rivals (.4547 versus .786 for its nearest rival). NTT also has a more preferred product than its rivals (with a demand constant of 22.07 versus 18.82 for its nearest rival). The merger nevertheless reduces total welfare because mergers involving very large firms have such large price effects, but the effect of the merger on total welfare is far less than its effect on consumer welfare.

The merger of all three of the smaller Japanese long-distance carriers increases total welfare in the simulation, even though all carriers increase price as a result of the merger. The reason is that the merged firm increases its price by more than NTT, so output is reallocated to NTT, which has a lower marginal cost and a more preferred product. Although consumer welfare decreases by .73% of pre-merger revenue, total welfare increases by .05% of pre-merger revenue.

```
In[35]:= DiffProdMerger[merging={2,3,4},nest={2,3,4},nestParam=.9,
            demandData,firmData]
```

```
Out[35]= DIFFERENTIATED PRODUCTS MERGER SIMULATION RESULTS
         Elasticity = 0.62
         B = 9.557
         Nest Parameter = 0.9
         @ signifies nest member
         * signifies merging firms
         Changes in profits and welfare are expressed as a % of
         pre-merger revenue.
```

Firms	a	q0	q1	% change q
NTT	22.07	0.8081	0.8104	0.2787
@*DDI	18.87	0.08221	0.0804	-2.208
@*Telecom	18.22	0.04017	0.03595	-10.51
@*Teleway	16.09	0.003737	0.003129	-16.28
No Purchase	10	0.06576	0.07016	6.681

Firms	mc0	mc1	p0	p1	% change p
NTT	0.4547	0.4547	1.	1.006	0.6476
@*DDI	0.7906	0.7906	0.9	0.9094	1.048
@*Telecom	0.799	0.799	0.9	0.9178	1.977
@*Teleway	0.8052	0.8052	0.9	0.9241	2.674

firms	p0-mc0	p1-mc1	elas0	elas1
NTT	0.545	0.552	1.83	1.82
@*DDI	0.109	0.119	7.89	7.99
@*Telecom	0.101	0.119	8.26	8.46
@*Teleway	0.0948	0.119	8.57	8.8

firms	prof0	prof1	change prof	% change prof
NTT	0.441	0.447	0.00648	1.47
@*DDI	0.00899	0.00955	0.00056	6.23
@*Telecom	0.00406	0.00427	0.000213	5.25
@*Teleway	0.000354	0.000372	0.0000176	4.98

vars.	pre-merger	post	change	% change
Guidelines HHI	7578.	7665.	86.16	
Quantity HHI	7578.	7685.	106.8	
Industry Price	0.9865	0.9944	0.007879	0.7987
Industry Quantity	0.9342	0.9298	-0.004393	-0.4703
Elasticity	0.62	0.6667	0.0467	7.533
Average Costs	0.5005	0.4982	-0.002232	-0.446
Merged Firm Price	0.9	0.9123	0.01233	1.37
Merged Firm Prft	0.01341	0.0142	0.08579	5.897
Industry Profits	0.4541	0.4613	0.7884	1.6
Consumer Surplus			-0.7342	
Welfare			0.05419	

8.3.9 Welfare Tradeoffs When Merger Reduces Costs

Thus far we have assumed away cost savings due to mergers, that is, the **DiffProdMerger** function assumes that marginal costs do not change following the merger. However, it is simple to incorporate various assumptions about merger synergies or cost reductions into the simulations either as fixed cost savings or as reductions in marginal cost. The package includes the function **DiffProdMergerMinCost**, which calculates the effects of a merger in which the merged firm produces at the minimum of the marginal costs of the merging firms. This cost specification is not meant to be a particularly realistic assumption, but rather just one possibility that is easily incorporated into the simulations. Particular post-merger marginal costs for the merged firm can also be specified.

```
In[36]:= ?DiffProdMergerMinCost

DiffProdMergerMinCost[merging_,nest_List,nestParam,b_,p0_,q0_,
    elasticity_,FirmNames_] This function calls all the other
    functions to calculate the effects of a merger in which the
    merged firm produces at the minimum of the marginal costs of
    the merging firms.
```

8.4 Simulation of Mergers in Homogeneous Products Industries

The **HomoProdMerger** function is used to simulate mergers involving homogeneous products, assuming a Cournot equilibrium. The function posits that both industry demand and firm marginal costs are linear. As before, it is assumed that there are no fixed costs, that economies of scale and scope cannot be realized through merger, and that mergers cannot lead to entry. Although reasonable in the case of differentiated products mergers, the assumption of constant marginal costs is unsuitable with homogeneous goods because it implies that the effect of a merger is merely to destroy the higher-cost merging firm; the lower-cost merging firm owns nothing after the merger that it did not own before it.

The application of `HomoProdMerger` is illustrated with hypothetical mergers among U.S. long-distance carriers. Simulations of these mergers are more fully explored by Werden and Froeb (1994). In the United States, AT&T is the dominant carrier with about 60% of the market, MCI and Sprint are significant rivals, and there are many very small firms. This industry is probably better suited to `DiffProdMerger`, but we use `HomoProdMerger` to illustrate the program.

8.4.1 The Cournot Model

`HomoProdMerger` is based on a version of the Cournot model employed for merger policy analysis by Farrell and Shapiro (1990), McAfee and Williams (1992), and Werden (1991). Let q_j be the output of firm j, Q be the aggregate industry output, p be the price, and $C(q_j)$ be the cost function for firm j. Industry demand and firm costs are given by

$$Q = a - bp,$$
$$C(q_j) = q_j^2/k_j,$$

where k_j is the capital stock of firm j.

The primitives of this model are the industry price, the industry elasticity of demand e, and the firm market shares, s_j. The demand and cost parameters are easily calculated from these primitives. By manipulating first-order conditions, it is straightforward to derive simple solutions for equilibrium price and quantity for the industry and equilibrium quantities for each firm. These expression, in turn, can be manipulated to yield:

$$a = p(1 + 1/e),$$
$$b = es_j/(e - s_j),$$
$$k_j = s_j/b(e - s_j).$$

It is readily apparent that this model cannot yield an equilibrium in which a firm has a share larger than the industry elasticity of demand. The program warns the user if this condition is violated in the simulation inputs.

8.4.2 Simulations with U.S. Long-Distance Carriers

Having recovered these demand and cost parameters, it is a possible to calculate a post-merger equilibrium and compare it to the pre-merger equilibrium. We illustrate **HomoProdMerger** with mergers of U.S. long-distance carriers using inputs taken from Werden and Froeb (1994). Because the long-distance carriers actually charge different prices, the program computes an average price and uses it as the pre-merger price. Because the raw output data are expressed in revenue, the program uses carrier-specific prices to convert these data into quantity market shares.

```
In[37]:= FirmNames={
                      "AT&T",
                      "MCI",
                      "Sprint",
                      "Fringe Firm",
                      "Fringe Firm",
                      "Fringe Firm"};


         Revenue0={.622,.150,.097,.131/3,.131/3,.131/3};
         p0={.1661,.1586,.1621,.1621,.1621,.1621};
         quantities=(Revenue0/p0);
         q0=quantities/Apply[Plus,quantities];
         NumberForm[
                    TableForm[
                               Transpose[
                     {{"Firms",FirmNames},
                      {"P0",p0},
                      {"Q0",q0}}
                                                            ]
                                         ]
                    ,4]
```

```
Out[37]= Firms            P0        Q0

         AT&T             0.1661    0.6142
         MCI              0.1586    0.1551
         Sprint           0.1621    0.09815
         Fringe Firm      0.1621    0.04418
         Fringe Firm      0.1621    0.04418
         Fringe Firm      0.1621    0.04418
```

8.4.3   Simulate Cournot Merger

```
In[38]:= pbar=p0.q0;
         n=Length[q0];

In[39]:= ?HomoProdMerger
```

HomoProdMerger[merging_List, elasticity_ ,p0_, s0_List,
    FirmNames_List] inputs model primitives for simulation of
    a merger in a linear Cournot model in which firms are
    distinguished on the basis of their marginal costs, which
    are determined by their capital stocks. It computes and
    outputs the effects of a merger.

In[40]:= **HomoProdMerger[{1,2},.7,pbar,q0,FirmNames]**

Out[40]= HOMOGENEOUS PRODUCTS MERGER SIMULATION
          Elasticity = 0.7
          * denotes merging firm
          Changes in consumer surplus and welfare are expressed as a % of
          pre-merger revenue.

Firms	K0	mc0	q0	cost0	prof0
*AT&T	1.31	0.02011	0.02633	0.0002647	0.004054
*MCI	0.05209	0.1277	0.006651	0.0004245	0.0006662
Sprint	0.02984	0.141	0.004208	0.0002967	0.0003935
Fringe Firm	0.01233	0.1537	0.001894	0.0001455	0.0001651
Fringe Firm	0.01233	0.1537	0.001894	0.0001455	0.0001651
Fringe Firm	0.01233	0.1537	0.001894	0.0001455	0.0001651

Firms	K1	mc1	q1	cost1	prof1
Merged Firm	1.362	0.02134	0.02906	0.00031	0.004925
Sprint	0.02984	0.1549	0.004622	0.0003579	0.0004747
Fringe Firm	0.01233	0.1688	0.002081	0.0001756	0.0001992
Fringe Firm	0.01233	0.1688	0.002081	0.0001756	0.0001992
Fringe Firm	0.01233	0.1688	0.002081	0.0001756	0.0001992

Variables	Pre	Post	Change	%Change
Guidelines HHI	4168.	6073.	1905.	
Quantity HHI	4168.	5514.	1346.	
Capacity HHI	8424.	9093.	668.6	
Industry Price	0.164	0.1801	0.01613	9.835
Industry Quantity	0.04287	0.03992	-0.002952	-6.885
elasticity	0.7	0.8257	0.1257	17.96
Merged Firm Profits	0.00472	0.004925	0.0002043	4.328
Industry Av. Costs	0.03318	0.02993	-0.003255	-9.81
Industry Profits			5.514	
Consumer Surplus			-9.497	
Total Welfare			-3.983	

The welfare effects of mergers in a Cournot model such as this are similar to those with the Bertrand model discussed previously. Merger-induced reallocation of production to large firms tends to enhance welfare because the large firms have lower marginal costs. AT&T is inferred to have a far lower marginal cost than its rivals (.0201 versus .1277 for its nearest rival). Mergers also reduce average costs simply because marginal cost curves are increasing and mergers cause output reductions. Overall increases in welfare are possible from Cournot mergers just as they are from Bertrand mergers.

8.5   Conclusions

The `Merger.m` package provides a simple means for predicting the price and welfare effects of mergers using simulations based on standard oligopoly models. Such simulations are a useful starting point in the antitrust analysis of mergers, and are far superior to traditional structural analysis. They can point to the magnitude of potential welfare changes and provide a benchmark against which merging parties' efficiency claims can be measured.

Any prior beliefs about individual preferences can be combined with the logit simulations in natural ways. For example, if it is thought that the products of the merging firms are somewhat better or worse than average substitutes for each other, the results of the simulations can be interpreted accordingly, as understating or overstating the likely effects of a merger on prices or welfare. Of course, some other specification may be more appropriate for an extensive analysis in a particular case.

The package can also be modified to analyze any large discrete change in an industry such as firm exit or entry or changes in policy regime, phenomena that are difficult to study using traditional analytical tools. Theoretically the package can be extended to accomodate multiple nests, multiple "layers" of nests, multiple product firms, and more general demand systems, such as the *Almost Ideal Demand System* (AIDS) of Deaton and Muellbauer (1980). In practice, however, these extensions may prove difficult because of convergence problems or corner solutions. It is unlikely that these forms would be as well behaved as the logit models that we have employed.

8.6   Acknowledgments

Support for this project was provided by the Dean's fund for faculty research at the Owen Graduate School of Management.

8.7   References

Anderson, Simon P., A. de Palma, and J.-F. Thisse. 1992. *Discrete Choice Theory of Product Differentiation*. Cambridge, MA, MIT Press.

Deaton, A. and J. Muellbauer. 1980. "An Almost Ideal Demand System." *American Economic Review*, **70**, 312–326.

Farrell, J. and C. Shapiro. 1990. "Horizontal Mergers: An Equilibrium Analysis." *American Economic Review*, **80**, 1, (March), 107–126.

Froeb, L. M., T. J. Tardiff, and G. J. Werden. 1994."The Demsetz Postulate and the Welfare Effects of Mergers in Differentiated Products Industries." Unpublished paper, U.S. Department of Justice, Economic Analysis Group.

Froeb, L. M. and G. J. Werden. 1992. "The Reverse Cellophane Fallacy in Market Delineation." *Review of Industrial Organization*, **7**, 241–247.

Hausman, J., G. Leonard, and J. D. Zona. 1994. "Competitive Analysis with Differenciated Products." *Annales d'Economie et Statistique*, **34, 2** (April-June), 159–180.

Hay, G. A. and G. J. Werden. 1993. "Horizontal Mergers: Law, Policy, and Economics. *American Economic Review*, **83**, 2, (May), 173–177.

Horizontal Merger Guidelines. 1992. U.S. Department of Justice and Federal Trade Commission, April 2.

McAfee, R. P. and M. A. Williams. 1992. "Horizontal Mergers and Public Policy." *Journal of Industrial Economics*, **40**, 2, (June), 181–187.

Rozanski, G. A. and G. J. Werden. 1994. "The Application of Section 7 to Differentiated Products Industries: The Market Delineation Dilemma. *Antitrust*, **8**, 3, (Summer), 40–43.

Train, K. 1986. *Qualitative Choice Analysis*. Cambridge, MA, The MIT Press.

Werden, G. J. 1991. "Horizontal Mergers: Comment." *American Economic Review*, **81**, 4, (Sept.) 1002–1006.

Werden, Gregory J. and L. M. Froeb. 1994. "The Effects of Mergers in Differentiated Products Industries: Logit Demand and Merger Policy. *Journal of Law, Economics, & Organization*, **10**, 2, (Oct.), 407–426.

Werden, G. J. and L. M. Froeb. 1996. "Simulation as an alternative to Structural Merger Policy in Differentiated Products Industries." In *The Economics of the Antitrust Process*". M. Coate and A. Kleit, eds. New York, Kluwer.

Werden, G. J., L. M. Froeb, and T. J. Tardiff. 1996. "The Use of the Logit Model in Applied Industrial Organization." *International Journal of the Economics of Business*, **3**, (Feb.), 83–105.

Willig, R. D. 1991. "Merger Analysis, Industrial Organization Theory, and Merger Guidelines." *Brookings Papers on Economic Activity, Microeconomics*, 281–332.

Part II

Finance

9 Auctions

John Dickhaut, Steve Gjerstad, and Arijit Mukherji

This chapter shows methods for studying auctions. We first discuss the determination of competitive equilibrium quantities and prices by the intersection of demand and supply schedules. Our graphical implementation in *Mathematica* produces a detailed plot from the primitives: vectors of values and costs for individual buyers and sellers. Our second section outlines rules of the common auctions (first and second price sealed bid auctions, and double auctions). The double auction is one of the most important market institutions that has been extensively studied in the experiments and applied in the field. Standard theoretical models of this auction are difficult to develop.The second section also shows how to construct models of behavior to study long run behavior in these auctions. These behavioral models specify how the participants bid as a function of their information. Our third section illustrates how to plot and analyze the data and suggests comparisons that allow researchers to calibrate models with data from controlled experiments.

9.1 Introduction

The most prevalent institutions for exchanging goods and services are auctions: the NYSE, Paris Bourse, or NASDAQ for securities; the ascending price (or English Auction) for antiques; the descending (or Dutch Auction), for tulips. Even local grocery and department stores are auctions (posted price). No one knows how many auctions exist although there are numerous surveys beginning with a classical work by Cassady, *Auctions and Auctioneering* (1967). We do not investigate every type of auction, but rather provide a set of tools that should be helpful to both the teacher and researcher who wish to examine the consequences of repeated participation in a particular auction and how such participation generates market prices.

The mechanics of how to conduct such an exercise are described in numerous places. One of the best introductions is provided by Vernon Smith in *The New Palgrave: A Dictionary of Economics* (1988). Beyond this there are computer implementations that have been used in the classroom and laboratories at the University of Arizona, the California Institute of Technology, Carnegie Mellon University, the University of Indiana, the University of Iowa, the University of Michigan, and the University of Minnesota. The Iowa Electronic Market at the University of Iowa runs a double auction in derivative securities that is open to trading by anyone affiliated with an academic institution.

We confine ourselves to the illustration of the operation of several generic auctions, namely, the first-price single unit auction, the second-price single unit auction, and the double auction. We focus on demonstrating either through experiment or classroom exercise the degree to which auctions are means of enabling the attainment of certain economic desiderata, such as competitive equilibrium and/or Pareto optimality. Although the chosen auctions have both theoretical and empirical interest in their own right, using *Mathematica* with selected auctions should serve as preparation for investigations incorporating institutional features particular to a specific course and/or research topics such as T-bill auctions. (Several modifications of the sealed bid auctions presented here can be used to produce the rules of the T-bill auction).

Generally those factors that need to be considered when studying an auction are (1) the underlying demand and supply schedules that provide a basis for judging the performance of the auction, (2) the auction rules themselves, and (3) methods for graphing the auction outcomes through several periods of the auction. For example, prior to examining an auction in the classroom we would begin with particular demand and supply schedules. These would be lists of redemption values for potential buyers as well as costs for potential sellers.

9.2 Demand and Supply

9.2.1 Graphing Demand And Supply Schedules

We begin with a simple demonstration of how to build a demand curve for eight individuals and we generalize from this example. The demonstration shows the simple mechanics that must be part of any such construction. In particular we build a Cartesian representation and a sorting function to create the line to be graphed, and then we employ a graphics function of *Mathematica*. We work with the following values, which represent the redemption values to the owner of a single unit of a fictitious asset at the end of one round of trade. These redemption values would be exogeneously specified by the teacher or experimenter.

```
In[1]:=  Values={1,3,4,5,5,6,8,9};
```

We now show how to use *Mathematica* to graph a demand curve based on these values. In the process we show how to refine the graphs by exploiting built-in functions in *Mathematica*. We refer to the useful *Mathematica* commands for building the presentation. We do not define these commands explicitly but the reader can use the ? command followed by the appropriate *Mathematica* command as a memory refresher. For example

In[2]:= **?Thread**

Thread[f[args]] ''threads'' f over any lists that
   appear in args. Thread[f[args], h] threads f over
   any objects with head h that appear in args.
   Thread[f[args], h, n] threads f over objects with
   head h that appear in the first n args.
   Thread[f[args], h, -n] threads over the last n
   args. Thread[f[args], h, {m, n}] threads over
   arguments m through n.

9.2.1.1 Relevant *Mathematica* Commands for Building Demand and Supply Graphs

In[3]:= **Thread,Range,Length,Sort,ListPlot**

Using Thread we can create a set of pairs whose first element records the
ranking of the pair (0 is the highest ranking) and the second element the value.

9.2.1.2 Construction of Cartesian Pairs

In[4]:= **z1=Thread[{Length[Values]-Range[
          Length[Values]],Values}]**

Out[4]= {{7, 1}, {6, 3}, {5, 4}, {4, 5}, {3, 5}, {2, 6},
         {1, 8}, {0, 9}}

We could just graph these points.

In[5]:= **ListPlot[z1,PlotJoined->True]**

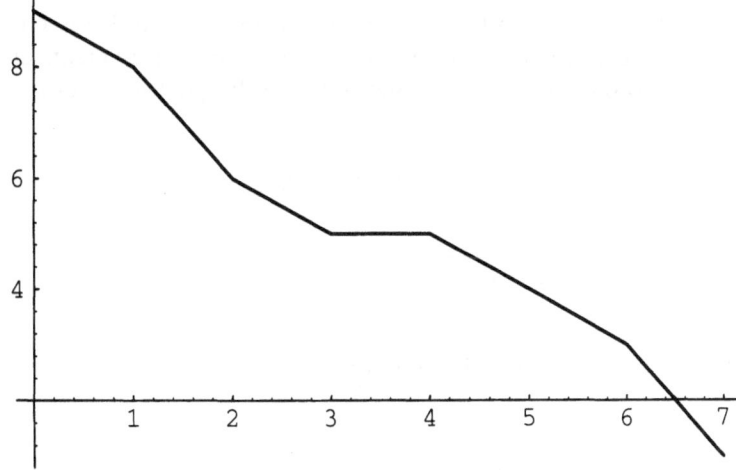

Out[5]= -Graphics-

which are roughly an inverse demand curve but if we want to capture the fact that each person has a redemption value for one whole unit (i.e. purchases are discrete and not continuous) and we want price on the vertical axis, we will need to use a few more manipulations.

9.2.1.3   Construction of Additional Points For Graphing

To capture whole units in the graph we need to add points to be plotted to produce a step function, and then sort the result to make sure the steps are plotted in the proper order.

```
In[6]:=  z1down=Thread[{Length[Values]-Range[
         Length[Values]]+1,Values}]
```

```
Out[6]=  {{8, 1}, {7, 3}, {6, 4}, {5, 5}, {4, 5}, {3, 6},
         {2, 8}, {1, 9}}
```

```
In[7]:=  z2=Join[z1,z1down ]
```

```
Out[7]=  {{7, 1}, {6, 3}, {5, 4}, {4, 5}, {3, 5}, {2, 6},
         {1, 8}, {0, 9}, {8, 1}, {7, 3}, {6, 4}, {5, 5},
         {4, 5}, {3, 6}, {2, 8}, {1, 9}}
```

9.2.1.4   Construction of Sorting Relationship

To get the points to be plotted in the right order is equivalent to creating a lexicographic ordering. *Mathematica* allows us to create an ordering g and then sort the points to be connected according to this ordering.

```
In[8]:=  g[{x1_,y1_},{x2_,y2_}]:=y1>y2
```

```
In[9]:=  g[{x1_,y1_},{x2_,y2_}]:=y1==y2&&x1<x2
```

```
In[10]:= z3=Join[Sort[z2,g],{{Length[Values],0}}]
```

```
Out[10]= {{0, 9}, {1, 9}, {1, 8}, {2, 8}, {2, 6}, {3, 6},
         {3, 5}, {4, 5}, {4, 5}, {5, 5}, {5, 4}, {6, 4},
         {6, 3}, {7, 3}, {7, 1}, {8, 1}, {8, 0}}
```

9.2.1.5   Use of Graphic Element

In[11]:= **dd'=ListPlot[z3 , PlotJoined->True]**

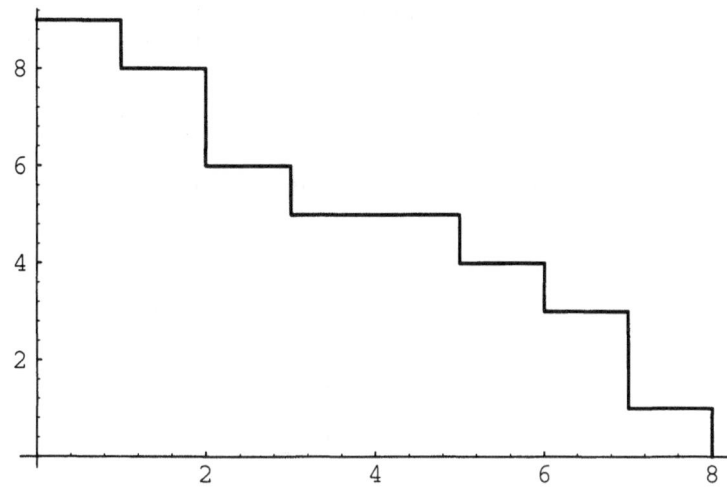

Out[11]= -Graphics-

9.2.2   More Generality–Demand and Supply

The preceding graph is a start but it does not contain relevant labels for the plot, it does not deal with supply, and it would appear to be constrained to a specific example. We enhance the graph with a few additional commands which enable us to have more control over the graphs. We distinguish the demand and supply schedules by using dashing in the graph of the supply curve. We provide common axes and we print axes labels.

9.2.2.1   Construction of Cartesian Pairs and Arrangement of Points for Plotting Purposes

To modify the preceding functions we used several additional *Mathematica* commands. The complete source code is in the package DSPack.m.

```
DSPack::usage ="DSPack.m is a package that has two versions of a
function (demandsupply) that allows the user to supply values
and costs and then graphs the demand and supply functions for
these values and costs.  The package also has functions that
compute the equilibrium quantities(eq), equilibrium prices(ep),
and computes the available surplus(surplus). It is assumed that
trades take place on a unit basis."
```

In[12]:= **<<"/Eclipse400/john/MathAuctions/DSPack.m"**

9.2.2.2   Example

The first critical function to be used is **demandsupply1**. Consider five buyers and four sellers with the following redemption values and costs. The following type of simple graph has been used extensively as a basis for research of performance in the auction as well as in classroom demonstrations.

In[13]:= **values={5,4,3,2,1};costs={2,3,4,5};**

In[14]:= **demandsupply1[values,costs]**

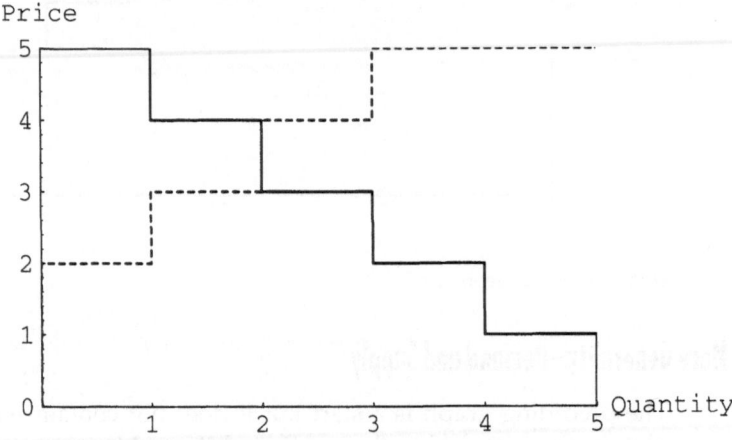

Out[14]= -Graphics-

9.2.3   More Generality–Multiple Units Per Individual

The previous schedule with each person wanting at most one unit or being able to sell at most one unit is the simplest structure researchers use to show how price formation in the double auction can result in a Pareto Optimal allocation. In most market settings we imagine the individual wants to trade more than one unit. Let us now add the ability to designate multiple units per individual and then construct the resulting graphs of the demand and supply schedules.

9.2.3.1   Modified Functions

When the functions are revised, the new structure inputs each buyer's and seller's demand and supply as n-tuples, where n denotes the amount that might be purchased by a buyer. Thus a buyer with 4 redemption values would be a 4-tuple. In our earlier example buyer 1 has redemption values of 1 and 0, as shown in the following.

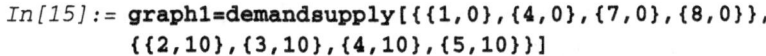

In[15]:= **graph1=demandsupply[{{1,0},{4,0},{7,0},{8,0}},**
        {{2,10},{3,10},{4,10},{5,10}}]

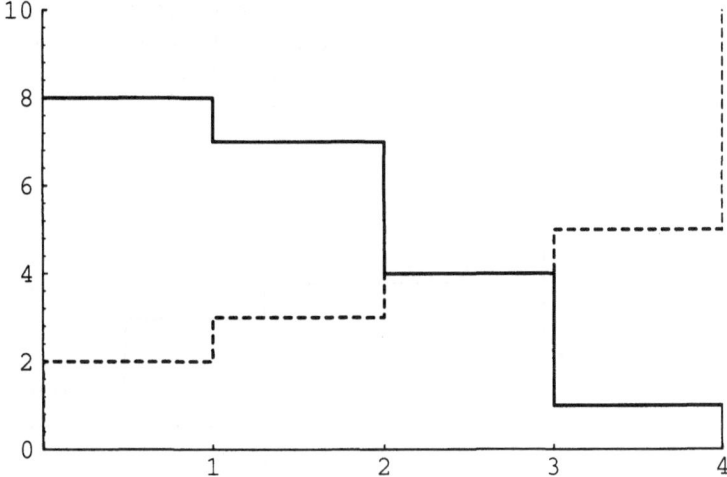

Out[15]= -Graphics-

The preceding graph allows the demonstration of multiple equilibrium quantities. This function also allows multiple purchases by one individual. To see this we simply take the last example and structure it so that the last buyer wants 2 units at 8.

In[16]:= **demandsupply[{{1,0},{4,0},{7,0},{8,8}},**
        {{2,10},{3,10},{4,10},{5,10}}]

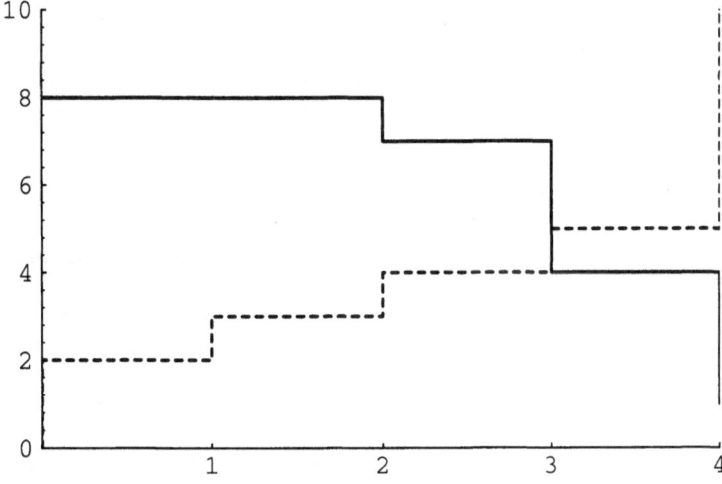

Out[16]= -Graphics-

   The function **demandsupply** allows the addition of standard graphics options from *Mathematica*.

```
In[17]:= demandsupply[{{1,0},{4,0},{7,0},{8,8}},
         {{2,10},{3,10},{4,10},{5,10}},
         AxesLabel->{Quantity,Price},
         PlotLabel->"Demand Supply"]
```

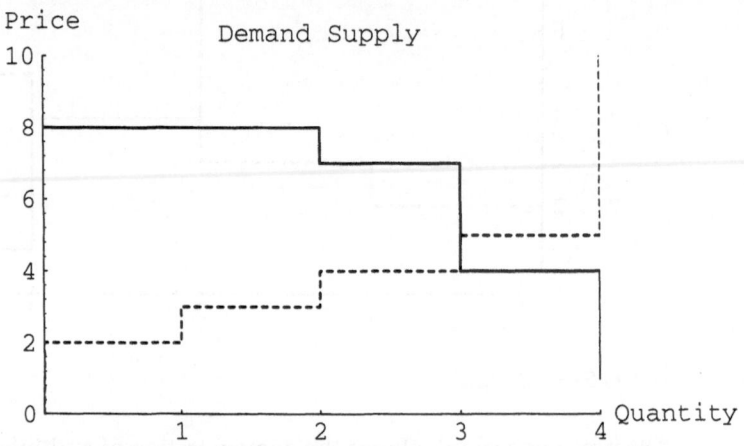

```
Out[17]= -Graphics-
```

```
In[18]:= ?demandsupply
```

```
demandsupply1::usage ="demandsupply1[v,c] is the simplest
graphical function for graphing demand and supply curves.  It
assumes that each buyer cannot buy more than one unit, and each
seller cannot sell more than one unit.The input v is a vector
of maximum prices that each buyer will buy, e.g., {2,3,5,1,3}
would denote a maximum buying price for five buyers.  Similarly
c is a vector of minimum prices at which each seller would
sell."
```

```
demandsupply::usage="demandsupply[v,c] is a more general
version of its two-element counterpart.  In this case buyers
may be able to buy more than one unit, and sellers sell more
than one unit.  A 'v' for two buyers might be {{2,1},{3,2}},
where {2,1} refers to the maximum the buyer 1 is willing to
pay for the first and second units, respectively.  A similar
notation is used for sellers.  The user may supply additional
Mathematica  Graphical options following c."
```

   In the preceding graphs it is clear what the equilibrium price and quantity are, even when these are ranges. The next set of functions allows the user to calculate the equilibrium values.

9.2.4　Equilibrium Price and Quantity

9.2.4.1　Relevant *Mathematica* Functions

In[19]:= **Reverse,Sort,Flatten,Select,Positive,Max,Min.**

To determine the equilibrium quantity we use the previous example. We are matching unit by unit the highest value demanded with the lowest cost until all positive gains are eliminated. Our first manipulation examines values from highest to lowest.

In[20]:= **Reverse[Sort[Flatten[{{1,0},{4,0},{7,0},{8,8}}]]]**

Out[20]= {8, 8, 7, 4, 1, 0, 0, 0}

Now we consider costs from lowest to highest.

In[21]:= **Sort[Flatten[{{2,10},{3,10},{4,10},{5,10}}]]**

Out[21]= {2, 3, 4, 5, 10, 10, 10, 10}

When we look at the difference of these two we find.

Out[21]= {6, 5, 3, -1, -9, -10, -10, -10}

Note that in this case three units will be traded, that is, the last positive entry in the table. If there had been a zero in the table then the quantity supplied in equilibrium would be an interval. We create a function, counter, to capture this calculation. We will find it very useful in several of the upcoming calculations.

```
In[22]:= counter[v_,c_]:=Reverse[Sort[Flatten[v
                                            ]
                                         ]
                                      ]-
                          Sort[Flatten[c
                                       ]
                                     ]
```

In[23]:= **counter[{{1,0},{4,0},{4,0},{8,8}},**
　　　　　　　{{2,10},{3,10},{4,10},{5,10}}]

Out[23]= {6, 5, 0, -1, -9, -10, -10, -10}

Now we create the equilibrium quantity function **eq**,

In[24]:= **eq[v_,c_]:=If[Position[counter[v,c],0]=={},**
　　　　　　{Select[counter[v,c],Positive][[-1]]},
　　　　　　Flatten[{Position[counter[v,c],0][[1]]-1,
　　　　　　Position[counter[v,c],0][[-1]]}]]

Here we use [[1]] and [[-1]] which represent the first and last elements of the vector. The [[ ]] notation is used extensively throughout the code presented in this chapter. The built-in *Mathematica* functions **First** and **Last** accomplish the same result as do [[1]] and [[-1]].

In the first example there is a unique equilibrium quantity,

```
In[25]:= eq[{{1,0},{4,0},{7,0},{8,8}},
           {{2,10},{3,10},{4,10},{5,10}}]

Out[25]= {3}
```

whereas in the second there is no unique equilibrium quantity.

```
In[26]:= eq[{{1,0},{4,0},{4,0},{8,8}},
           {{2,10},{4,10},{4,10},{5,10}}]

Out[26]= {2, 3}
```

This nonuniqueness is shown in the demandsupply graph.

```
In[27]:= demandsupply[{{1,0},{4,0},{4,0},{8,8}},
           {{2,10},{4,10},{4,10},{5,10}}]
```

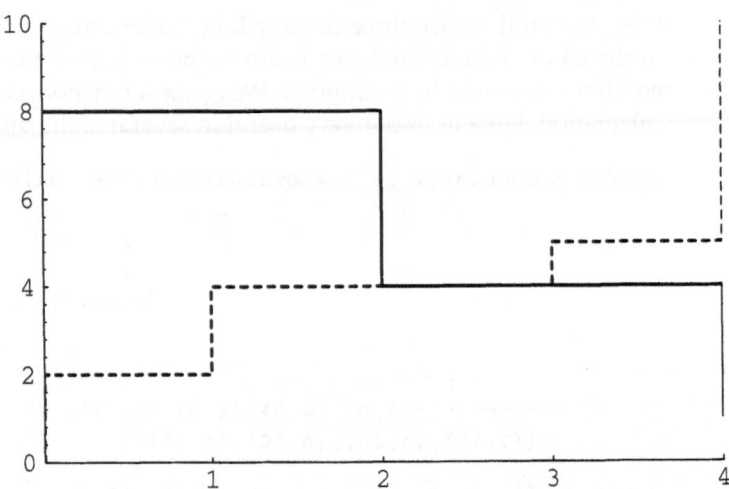

```
Out[27]= -Graphics-
```

To construct the equilibrium price range we note that when the trades are for a unique unit level there will always be an interval of prices that constitute the equilibrium. To determine this we find the possible interval for buyers and the possible interval for sellers.

The interval is constructed from **counter** because it tells where the first positive trade is. Thus we have

```
In[28]:= buyerinterval[v_,c_]:=
  {Reverse[Sort[Flatten[v]]][[
                  Length[Select[counter[v,c],Positive
                                  ]
                          ]
                             ]],
    Reverse[Sort[Flatten[v]]] [[
                  Length[Select[counter[v,c], greaterthan[0]
                                  ]
                          ]+1    ]]
     };greaterthan[x_] :=Function[z,z>=x]


In[29]:= v={{1,0},{4,0},{4,0},{8,8}}


Out[29]= {{1, 0}, {4, 0}, {4, 0}, {8, 8}}


In[30]:= c={{2,10},{4,10},{4,10},{5,10}}


Out[30]= {{2, 10}, {4, 10}, {4, 10}, {5, 10}}


In[31]:= Length[Select[counter[v,c],Positive
                                      ]
                          ]


Out[31]= 2


In[32]:= buyerinterval[{{1,0},{4,0},{4,0},{8,8}},
          {{2,10},{4,10},{4,10},{5,10}}]


Out[32]= {8, 4}
```

For sellers we have

```
In[33]:= sellerinterval[v_,c_] :=
  {Sort[Flatten[c]][[
                  Length[Select[counter[v,c],Positive
                                  ]
                          ]
                             ]],
    Sort[Flatten[c]][[
                  Length[Select[counter[v,c], greaterthan[0]
                                  ]
                          ]+1    ]]
     }
```

```
In[34]:= sellerinterval[{{1,0},{4,0},{4,0},{8,8}},
           {{2,10},{4,10},{4,10},{5,10}}]
```

```
Out[34]= {4, 5}
```

Then we take the **Min** of the **Max**s of these two intervals and the **Max** of the **Min**'s of these intervals.

```
In[35]:= ep[v_, c_] :=
  If[Length[eq[v,c]]==1,
  {Max[Min[sellerinterval[v, c]],
    Min[buyerinterval[v, c]]],
   Min[Max[sellerinterval[v, c]],
    Max[buyerinterval[v, c]]]},
    Reverse[Sort[Flatten[v]]][[
                Length[Select[counter[v, c],greaterthan[0]
                              ]
                         ]
                                ]]
         ]
```

```
In[36]:= ep[{{1,0},{4,0},{4,0},{8,8}},
           {{2,10},{4,10},{4,10},{5,10}}]
```

```
Out[36]= 4
```

The equilibrium price and quantity functions are described in DSPack.m as

```
eq::usage = "eq[v,c] determines the equilibrium quantity for a
supplied set of values or costs.  A v for two buyers might be
{{2,1},{3,2}}, where {2,1} refers to the maximum the buyer 1
is willing to pay for the first and second units respectively.
A similar notation is used for sellers. The output of this
function may be an interval, i.e., a set of quantities that
would be consistent with the equilibrium price and the v, c.
vectors."
```

```
ep::usage="ep[v,c] determines the equilibrium price for a
supplied set of values or costs.  A v for two buyers might be
{{2,1},{3,2}}, where {2,1} refers to the maximum the buyer 1 is
willing to pay for the first and second units respectively.  A
similar notation is used for sellers.  The output of this
function may be an interval, i.e., a set of prices that would
be consistent with the equilibrium quantity and the v, c.
vectors."
```

9.2.5 Surplus

A bonus from this construction is the easy calculation of surplus. Notice that it is just the positive elements of the function counter.

```
In[37]:= surplus[v_,c_]:=Apply[Plus,Select[counter[v,c],Positive
                                                                        ]
                                                              ]
```

```
In[38]:= surplus[{{1,0},{4,0},{4,0},{8,0}},
              {{2,10},{4,10},{4,10},{5,10}}]
```

```
Out[38]= 6
```

```
In[39]:= surplus[{{1,0},{4,0},{4,0},{8,8}},
              {{2,10},{4,10},{4,10},{5,10}}]
```

```
Out[39]= 10
```

The general description of surplus is

```
In[40]:= ?surplus
```

```
surplus::usage="surplus[v,c] determines the total surplus that
can be achieved from trade in a competitive equilibrium.  A v
for two buyers might be {{2,1},{3,2}}, where {2,1} refers to
the maximum the buyer 1 is willing to pay for the first and
second units, respectively.  A similar notation is used for
sellers.
```

9.3   Auction Mechanisms

So far we have specified the determination of the equilibrium price and quantity
in a competitive market without specifying the institution through which the
equilibrium prices and quantities were determined. In this section we discuss
three alternative institutions that fulfill this role. We program the rules for these
institutions in *Mathematica*, and then provide insight into what governs how
economic forces can lead to particular outcomes, such as a Nash Equilibrium
and a Competitive Equilibrium.

9.3.1   First Price Sealed Bid Auction–Single Unit

In our discussion of the Sealed Bid Auction we assume one side of the market has
a fixed amount to sell, one unit. The simple principle is to select the highest bid
from those bids submitted. The object is sold for the highest bid. (For a seller's
auction we would be concerned with the lowest offer.) Suppose submitted bids
are

```
In[41]:= b={1,2,3,4,5,6,7,7,8,8}
```

```
Out[41]= {1, 2, 3, 4, 5, 6, 7, 7, 8, 8}
```

It is possible to use the demand supply graphs to actually plot such submissions
of bids.

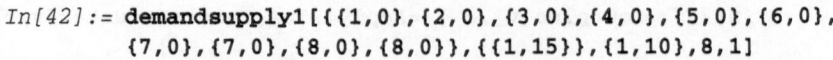

```
In[42]:= demandsupply1[{{1,0},{2,0},{3,0},{4,0},{5,0},{6,0},
         {7,0},{7,0},{8,0},{8,0}},{{1,15}},{1,10},8,1]
```

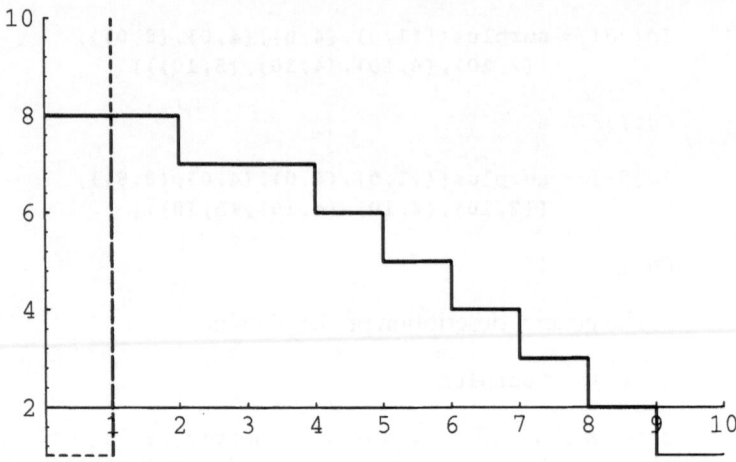

```
Out[42]= -Graphics-
```

Note in the preceding picture, although it does reveal the nature of the allocation under the bid, in fact, there is a tie between the bidders. The following procedure determines the auction winner and resolves ties by sampling from a uniform distribution. The procedure is in

```
In[43]:= <<"/Eclipse400/john/MathAuctions/Institutions.m"

In[44]:= FirstPrice[Bids_]:=
         Module[{ii,Players,TiedValues,Winner,WinnerValue
                 },
                 Players=Table[ii,{ii,1,Length[Bids]}];
                 g[i_]:=Bids[[i]]==Max[Bids];
                 TiedValues=Select[Players,g];
                 Winner=TiedValues[[Random[Integer,
                                             {1,Length[TiedValues
                                                      ]
                                             }
                                       ]
                                  ]
                                ];
                 WinnerValue=Bids[[Winner]];
                 Return[{Winner,WinnerValue
                         }
                       ]
               ]
```

Applied to the assumed vector, the winning bidder is the following.

```
In[45]:= FirstPrice[b]
```

```
Out[45]= {9, 8}
```

Here the winner is player 9 at a price of 8. Suppose we had the same sequence of bids for 40 submissions. The number of times 9 would be chosen would be:

```
In[46]:= Count[Transpose[Table[FirstPrice[b],{40}]][[1]],9]
```

```
Out[46]= 23
```

A standard approach to such auctions is to assume values are i.i.d and privately drawn from a known distribution and then ask what is an optimal bidding strategy. The theory for this model, the Independent Private Values Model, is developed by Vickrey (1961), and extended in Holt (1980) as well as Cox et al. (1982). One can use *Mathematica* to gain insight into the nature of the optimal solution. For example, suppose we were interested in the distribution of winning bids. In the case of risk neutrality a Nash Equilibrium involves each player bidding $(n-1)/n$ of value where n denotes the number of players. For our demonstration we assume that $n = 4$, and the values are drawn from the uniform interval 1–10. For a single draw we would have

```
In[47]:= draws:=Table[Random[Real,{1,10}],{4}]
```

```
In[48]:= example=draws
```

```
Out[48]= {5.23174, 6.37197, 5.79396, 5.15551}
```

The Nash-Equilibrium bids for this example will be

```
In[49]:= .75 example
```

```
Out[49]= {3.92381, 4.77898, 4.34547, 3.86663}
```

And the winning bid will be

```
In[50]:= FirstPrice[.75 example][[2]]
```

```
Out[50]= 4.77898
```

In this case if the Nash Solution is repeatedly played across a random assignment of 300 values, the distribution of winning bids will look like the following. To see how behavior might begin to be studied in such auctions, we can look at plots of outcomes when the Nash Equilibrium Strategy is followed, both in raw form and summarized as a cumulative distribution. We do more detailed analysis of possible behaviors in the next section.

```
In[51]:= table=Table[FirstPrice[.75 draws][[2]],{300}];
```

```
In[52]:= ListPlot[table,
         PlotJoined->True,PlotRange->{0,8.0},
         PlotLabel->"Winner in 300 Auctions",
         AxesLabel->{"Auction
          Number","Winning
          Bid"}]
```

```
Winning
Bid
```

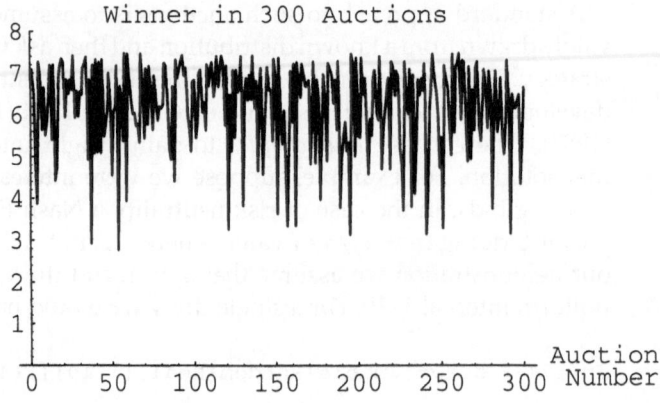

```
Out[52]= -Graphics-
```

The following use of part of the program requires one of the Standard Packages from *Mathematica*. The most reliable method of loading such packages is a **Needs** statement. We show the method that will most certainly work, but it requires that the user specify the complete path to the package being used. We illustrate the code for two different platforms.

9.3.1.1   The NextStep Method

```
In[53]:= Needs["DescriptiveStatistics'",
         "/Eclipse400/Mathematica/Packages/Statistics/\
         DescriptiveStatistics.m"]
```

9.3.1.2   The Mac Method

```
In[54]:= Needs["DescriptiveStatistics'",
         "Dickhaut's Disk:Applications:Mathematica 2.2.2:\
         Packages:Statistics:DescriptiveStatistics.m"]
```

Once the package is read in we can find, for example,

```
In[55]:= Mean[table]

Out[55]= 6.18313

In[56]:= Variance[table]

Out[56]= 1.13311
```

The reader might like to calculate these observed values for 300 draws with the theoretical expected mean bid and variance in this auction to get some sense of the sampling variation.

It is quite simple, for example, to create a cumulative distribution function (CDF) of the sample using the function **Quantile**.

```
In[57]:= ?Quantile

Quantile[list, q] gives the qth quantile of the
     entries in list.

In[58]:= Quantile[table,.01]

Out[58]= 3.13717

In[59]:= Table[{Quantile[table,q],q},{q,.01,.99,.01}]

Out[59]= {{3.13717, 0.01}, {3.26728, 0.02}, {3.35036, 0.03},
          {3.7554, 0.04}, {3.83118, 0.05}, {3.97606, 0.06},
          {4.4134, 0.07}, {4.54918, 0.08}, {4.62996, 0.09},
          {4.7004, 0.1}, {4.81634, 0.11}, {4.84589, 0.12},
          {4.93274, 0.13}, {4.97143, 0.14}, {5.05576, 0.15},
          {5.10822, 0.16}, {5.1905, 0.17}, {5.34284, 0.18},
          {5.35999, 0.19}, {5.38168, 0.2}, {5.44645, 0.21},
          {5.46104, 0.22}, {5.48481, 0.23}, {5.50736, 0.24},
          {5.58528, 0.25}, {5.6392, 0.26}, {5.65592, 0.27},
          {5.69681, 0.28}, {5.73257, 0.29}, {5.75069, 0.3},
          {5.77905, 0.31}, {5.81993, 0.32}, {5.83877, 0.33},
          {5.88571, 0.34}, {5.94509, 0.35}, {5.99199, 0.36},
          {6.02871, 0.37}, {6.05345, 0.38}, {6.08392, 0.39},
          {6.11213, 0.4}, {6.17469, 0.41}, {6.20749, 0.42},
          {6.23397, 0.43}, {6.26557, 0.44}, {6.29808, 0.45},
          {6.34564, 0.46}, {6.37866, 0.47}, {6.41354, 0.48},
          {6.46027, 0.49}, {6.47526, 0.5}, {6.49325, 0.51},
          {6.50067, 0.52}, {6.54914, 0.53}, {6.56787, 0.54},
          {6.59302, 0.55}, {6.6047, 0.56}, {6.65127, 0.57},
          {6.67598, 0.58}, {6.68229, 0.59}, {6.70149, 0.6},
          {6.74276, 0.61}, {6.79744, 0.62}, {6.83288, 0.63},
          {6.83706, 0.64}, {6.84557, 0.65}, {6.87413, 0.66},
          {6.88457, 0.67}, {6.89324, 0.68}, {6.90433, 0.69},
          {6.95466, 0.7}, {6.9652, 0.71}, {6.99739, 0.72},
```

```
{7.0135, 0.73}, {7.05893, 0.74}, {7.07083, 0.75},
{7.08243, 0.76}, {7.09496, 0.77}, {7.11285, 0.78},
{7.13267, 0.79}, {7.15145, 0.8}, {7.16361, 0.81},
{7.18408, 0.82}, {7.18916, 0.83}, {7.20361, 0.84},
{7.23138, 0.85}, {7.24448, 0.86}, {7.25214, 0.87},
{7.26604, 0.88}, {7.27235, 0.89}, {7.28247, 0.9},
{7.28428, 0.91}, {7.31392, 0.92}, {7.33169, 0.93},
{7.37287, 0.94}, {7.39043, 0.95}, {7.41438, 0.96},
{7.42916, 0.97}, {7.46402, 0.98}, {7.46999, 0.99}}
```

We find the cumulative distribution function of winning bids. when the behavior of subjects is to follow the Nash Equilibrium Strategy.

```
In[60]:= ListPlot[Table[{Quantile[
          table,q],q},{q,.01,.99,.01}],PlotJoined->True,
          GridLines->Automatic]
```

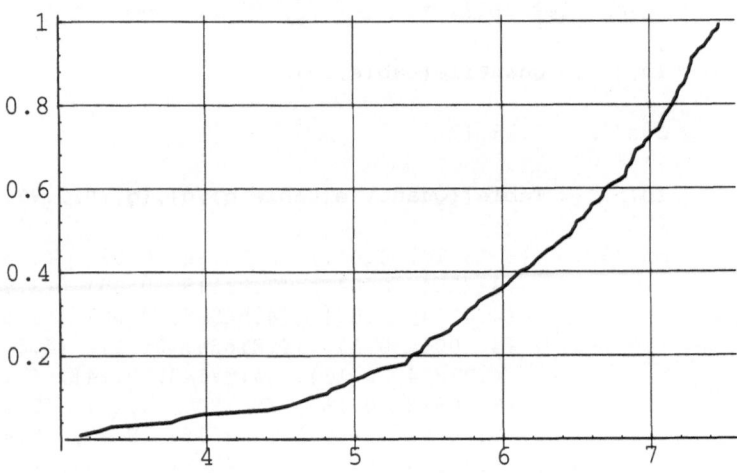

```
Out[60]= -Graphics-
```

Note: It is clear that the expected curve could be derived analytically. Thus, in and of itself, such a graph may not be useful; however, it may not always be possible to fully derive such graphs given sufficiently idiosyncratic behavior of the participants. The following example poses one form of idiosyncratic behavior.

9.3.1.3 Nash Equilibrium

In this section we show graphically why bidding 3/4 of value is a Nash Equilibrium in this setting. To do this we force three of the players to play the Nash Equilibrium strategy and one of the players to play a percentage $k.\{k >= 0\}$.

We then record the observed profits over 500 draws for the player who plays
strategy k.

```
In[61]:= draw[k_]:=Flatten[{k Random[Real,{1,10}],
                            3/4 Table[Random[Real,{1,10}
                                                    ],{3}
                                      ]
                           }
                          ]
```

```
In[62]:= x1=Function[x,x[[1]]==1]
```

```
Out[62]= Function[x, x[[1]] == 1]
```

```
In[63]:= ?x1
```

```
Global'x1
```

```
x1 = Function[x, x[[1]] == 1]
```

```
In[64]:= payoff[k_] :=
                  ((1 - k)*
                           Apply[Plus,
                                 Transpose[Select[
                                                  Table[FirstPrice[draw[k]
                                                        ], {500}
                                                       ], x1
                                                  ]
                                           ][[2]]
                                ]/k)
```

```
In[65]:= payoff[.85]
```

```
Out[65]= 198.684
```

```
In[66]:= payoff[.65]
```

```
Out[66]= 189.507
```

```
In[67]:= payoff[.75]
```

```
Out[67]= 270.943
```

```
In[68]:= ListPlot[Table[{k,payoff[k]},{k,.60,.80,.05}],
         PlotJoined->True,AxesLabel->{"Payoff","Proportion"}]
```

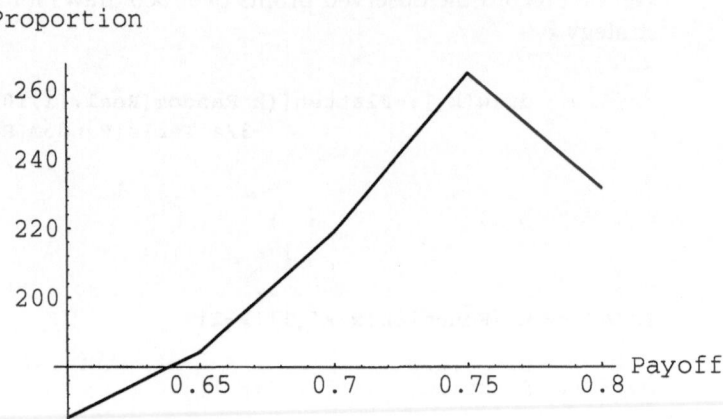

```
Out[68]= -Graphics-
```

We see that for large deviations from best response the choice of .75 is apparent. However, because of the noise in the sampling you can get disconfirming data close to optimum a reasonable proportion of the time, even though a best response is not played. Such graphs are useful in another sense. They give some insight into what the opportunity loss is to not playing an optimal strategy. Note, for example, that for a sample of 500 the amount of difference between the optimal and a strategy that is .05 away is a little less than 45. We have not stated whether we are talking about 45 cents, or 45 francs (where francs in an experiment could be 1/10 of a cent). Obviously, if it were the latter, the subject does not lose much by deviating from best response.

9.3.2   Second Price Auction

In the second price or Vickrey auction the highest bidder purchases at the second highest price. Ties are resolved randomly. One formulation of this auction procedure is the following.

```
In[69]:= SecondPrice[Bids_]:=
         Module[
              {ii,Players,TiedValues,Winner,WinnerValue},
              Players=Table[ii,{ii,1,Length[Bids]}];
              g[i_]:=Bids[[i]]==Max[Bids];
               TiedValues=Select[Players,g];
              Winner=TiedValues[[Random[Integer,
                           {1,Length[TiedValues]}]
                                ]
                            ];
              LowerSet=Complement[Players,{Winner}];
              WinnerValue=Max[Bids[[LowerSet]]];
```

```
          Return[{Winner,WinnerValue
                     }
                  ]
          ]
```

Consider the following example.

In[70]:= **bids={1,2,3,4,5,6,7,7,7,8}**

Out[70]= {1, 2, 3, 4, 5, 6, 7, 7, 7, 8}

Under the second price auction the last player, player 10, will win the auction at the second highest price, 7.

In[71]:= **SecondPrice[bids]**

Out[71]= {10, 7}

9.3.2.1 Dominant Strategy Properties

A well-known property of this auction is that it is a dominant strategy for an individual to bid the individual's true value, that is, regardless of the bidding behavior of the opponents the individual should bid value. We construct a procedure similar to the preceding. Again let k be a proportional bid where k might be different from 1. We would like our picture to demonstrate that 1 yields the highest payoff. To add to the generality we can allow inputs of proportional strategies .5, .2, and 1.0 for the other players. Notice that if $k = 1$ maximizes the player's payoffs regardless of the other players' bids, it is a dominant strategy. We have

```
In[72]:= secondpricedraw[k_]:=
              Flatten[{k Random[Real,{1,10}],
                      .5 Random[Real,{1,10}],
                      .2 Random[Real,{1,10}],
                      .8 Random[Real,{1,10}]}
                  ]
```

```
In[73]:= secondpayoff[k_] :=
         Apply[Plus,
              Transpose[Select[Table[SecondPrice[
              secondpricedraw[k]],
                  {1000}], x1]][[2]]]]/k
```

In[74]:= **secondpayoff[.93]**

Out[74]= 2359.9

In[75]:= **secondpayoff[.99]**

Out[75]= 2326.32

In[76]:= **ListPlot[Table[{k,secondpayoff[k]},{k,.84,.99,.05}],**
          PlotJoined->True]

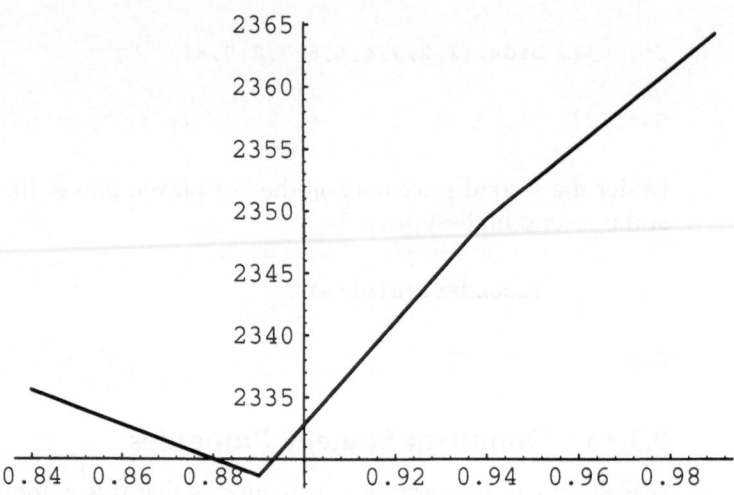

Out[76]= -Graphics-

In[77]:= **ListPlot[Table[{k,secondpayoff[k]},{k,.95,.99,.02}],**
          PlotJoined->True]

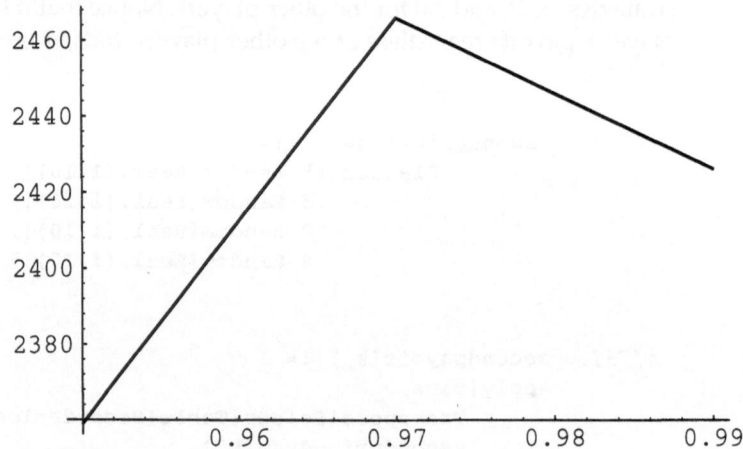

Out[77]= -Graphics-

The latter graphs once again suggest some of the inherent difficulty in testing
theoretical predictions. Major deviations from theory appear fairly easy to un-

cover. But rather close deviations from best response may actually outperform theory when the number of observations is as much as 1,000.

There are many variations on these auctions. For example, if in a k unit auction with $m > k$ bidders, all of whom want at most 1 unit, then the optimal bid is to bid one's value. Also a continuous time auction such as the Ascending Price or English (Descending Price or Dutch Auction) yield bidding strategies equivalent to the second and first price auctions, respectively. See, for instance, Myerson (1991).

9.3.3   The Double ((ommon Outcry) Auction

Many auction settings such as the NYSE, NASDAQ, and Chicago Board of Trade, operate on some form of bid-ask system accompanied by an improvement rule. Given an outstanding bid or ask, the next bid must be an improvement, that is, a higher bid for the good or a lower ask for the good. A bid that arrives that is higher than the outstanding ask clears at the prevailing ask price. It is necessary to use a different *Mathematica* package to assist in running the double auction.

```
In[78]:= Needs["DataManipulation'",
         "/Eclipse400/Mathematica/Packages/Statistics/\
         DataManipulation.m"]
```

The user will probably find it useful to embed a Needs statement of this sort in the Institution Package itself. The exact specification of the Needs statement can differ depending both on *how Mathematica is configured as well as the platform used*.

9.3.3.1 Conventions

The mechanism is built on the idea of having a history of activities. This will be a history of bids, offers, and trades. Each element of the history will be a triple indicating which seller participated, which buyer participated, and the relevant price. We use the convention of denoting an ask with a 0 in the buyer (2nd) coordinate, and a bid with a 0 in the ask (1st) coordinate. A trade has nonzero numbers in both coordinates. For example the history

```
In[79]:= {{0, 7, 2.06}, {2, 0, 4.94},
         {4, 0, 2.75}, {0, 3, 2.35}, {4, 1, 2.75},
         {0, 3, 2.6}}}
```

denotes that

buyer 7 bid 2.06
seller 2 asked 4.94
seller 4 asked 2.75
buyer 3 bid 2.35

buyer 1 took sellers ask of 2.75 (i.e., a trade took place)

buyer 3 submitted a bid of 2.6.

The role of the institution is to take a submission that might lead to a modification of the trade history to date, determine if it is a legitimate submission (i.e., it checks to see if the submission satisfies the improvement rule), and then return what would be the revised history after evaluation of this submission. We consider a series of scenarios. We begin with an initial history and then show the ramifications of a submission that does not satisfy the improvement rule, a submission that satisfies the improvement rule but does not result in a trade, and finally a submission that results in a trade.

Submission That Does Not Satisfy the Improvement Rule

Consider history1 and suppose we attach a bid that does not meet the improvement rule. What is the response of the mechanism when it receives such a history?

```
In[80]:= history1={{0, 7, 2.06}, {2, 0, 4.940000000000001},
           {4, 0, 2.75}, {0, 3, 2.35}, {4, 1, 2.75},
           {0, 3, 2.6}, {1, 0, 5.8}, {0, 4, 2.8}}
```

```
Out[80]= {{0, 7, 2.06}, {2, 0, 4.940000000000002},
           {4, 0, 2.75}, {0, 3, 2.35}, {4, 1, 2.75},
           {0, 3, 2.6}, {1, 0, 5.8}, {0, 4, 2.8}}
```

Now we attach a bid to history1 that does not satisfy the improvement rule.

```
In[81]:= candidate1=Join[history1,{{0,4,2.4}}]
```

```
Out[81]= {{0, 7, 2.06}, {2, 0, 4.940000000000002},
           {4, 0, 2.75}, {0, 3, 2.35}, {4, 1, 2.75},
           {0, 3, 2.6}, {1, 0, 5.8}, {0, 4, 2.8}, {0, 4, 2.4}}
```

The function, **message**, takes a candidate and reports what message the double auction will transmit after receiving the message.

```
In[82]:= message[candidate1]
```

```
Out[82]= {{0, 7, 2.06}, {2, 0, 4.940000000000002},
           {4, 0, 2.75}, {0, 3, 2.35}, {4, 1, 2.75},
           {0, 3, 2.6}, {1, 0, 5.8}, {0, 4, 2.8}}
```

The response is to dismiss the submission and to treat only the submissions up to the most recent submissions as consitituting the messages of the mechanism.

**Submission That Satisfies the Improvement Rule but
Does Not Result in a Trade**

```
In[83]:= candidate2=Join[history1,{{0,5,3.4}}]
```

```
Out[83]= {{0, 7, 2.06}, {2, 0, 4.940000000000002},
           {4, 0, 2.75}, {0, 3, 2.35}, {4, 1, 2.75},
           {0, 3, 2.6}, {1, 0, 5.8}, {0, 4, 2.8}, {0, 5, 3.4}}
```

```
In[84]:= message[candidate2]
```

```
Out[84]= {{0, 7, 2.06}, {2, 0, 4.940000000000002},
           {4, 0, 2.75}, {0, 3, 2.35}, {4, 1, 2.75},
           {0, 3, 2.6}, {1, 0, 5.8}, {0, 4, 2.8}, {0, 5, 3.4}}
```

Note in this case the bid was an improvement on the previous bid and therefore
satisfies the improvement rule. A similar result obtains for an ask that satisfies
the improvement rule but does not result in a trade.

```
In[85]:= candidate3=Join[history1,{{3,0,4.0}}]
```

```
Out[85]= {{0, 7, 2.06}, {2, 0, 4.940000000000002},
           {4, 0, 2.75}, {0, 3, 2.35}, {4, 1, 2.75},
           {0, 3, 2.6}, {1, 0, 5.8}, {0, 4, 2.8}, {3, 0, 4.}}
```

```
In[86]:= message[candidate3]
```

```
Out[86]= {{0, 7, 2.06}, {2, 0, 4.940000000000002},
           {4, 0, 2.75}, {0, 3, 2.35}, {4, 1, 2.75},
           {0, 3, 2.6}, {1, 0, 5.8}, {0, 4, 2.8}, {3, 0, 4.}}
```

Submission That Satisfies the Improvement Rule and Results in a Trade
Two types of submission can result in trades: the submission of a bid price
greater than or equal to the outstanding ask, and the submission of an offer
price less than or equal to the outstanding bid. We illustrate the second of these
two possibilities as follows.

```
In[87]:= candidate4=Join[history1,{{1,0,2.3}}]
```

```
Out[87]= {{0, 7, 2.06}, {2, 0, 4.940000000000002},
           {4, 0, 2.75}, {0, 3, 2.35}, {4, 1, 2.75},
           {0, 3, 2.6}, {1, 0, 5.8}, {0, 4, 2.8}, {1, 0, 2.3}}
```

```
In[88]:= message[candidate4]
```

```
Out[88]= {{0, 7, 2.06}, {2, 0, 4.940000000000002},
           {4, 0, 2.75}, {0, 3, 2.35}, {4, 1, 2.75},
           {0, 3, 2.6}, {1, 0, 5.8}, {0, 4, 2.8}, {1, 4, 2.8}}
```

9.3.3.2   Zero Intelligence Traders

A rather popular finding about the double auction is its ability to yield efficient allocations. This was demonstrated in early experiments by Smith and Plott, and the robustness of the auction is further supported by the Gode and Sunder (1993) result with so-called Zero Intelligence Traders (zits), that is, traders who are not strategic and randomly choose a bid (or offer) amount that will not result in a loss. Let us use *Mathematica* to demonstrate this result. We assume for convenience that the maximum possible value will be 12 in this scenario so that no offers above 12 would have any chance of acceptance. First consider a potential buyer with value v. Then as a zero intelligence trader the buyer would have the following representation

```
In[89]:= zitbuy[v_]:=Random[Real,{0,v}]
```

```
In[90]:= zitbuy[3]
```

```
Out[90]= 1.5123
```

```
In[91]:= zitsell[c_]:=Random[Real,{c,12}]
```

```
In[92]:= zitsell[4]
```

```
Out[92]= 6.66792
```

Now we will have traders following such strategies in our double auction. To illustrate the zero intelligence trader affect assume that any trader is just as likely to move as any other. Then assuming we begin with a set of buyer values, **values**, and seller costs, **costs**, we can construct an occurrence of a trade in the mechanism.

```
In[93]:= bidoffer[values_,costs_]:=
         Module[{d1},
         d1=Random[Integer,{1,Length[values]+Length[costs]}];
         k=If[d1<=Length[values],{0,d1,zitbuy[values[[d1]]]},
         {d1-Length[values],0,
             zitsell[costs[[d1-Length[values]]]]}]
         ];
         Return[k]
         ]
```

To see how this works, consider the following set of offers from the underlying value and cost sets

```
In[94]:= values={5,4,3,2,1};costs={2,7,8,9};
```

Assume that there is an outstanding bid and offer that are plays. Thus our beginning history is

```
In[95]:= hist={{1,0,12},{0,2,0}}
```

```
Out[95]= {{1, 0, 12}, {0, 2, 0}}
```

that is, seller 1 has offered to sell for 12 while buyer 2 is willing to buy for 0. Now let us add an element of the new history.

```
In[96]:= newhist=Join[hist,{bidoffer[values,costs]}]
```

```
Out[96]= {{1, 0, 12}, {0, 2, 0}, {3, 0, 11.8844}}
```

From this history we see what the mechanism will do with this submitted offer.

```
In[97]:= message[newhist]
```

```
Out[97]= {{1, 0, 12}, {0, 2, 0}, {3, 0, 11.8844}}
```

Building iteratively we have

```
In[98]:= histor[1]=hist={{1,0,12},{0,2,0}}
```

```
Out[98]= {{1, 0, 12}, {0, 2, 0}}
```

```
In[99]:= histor[t_]:=histor[t]=message[Join
            [histor[t-1],{bidoffer[values,costs]}]]
```

```
In[100]:= histor[2]
```

```
Out[100]={{1, 0, 12}, {0, 2, 0}, {1, 0, 2.81916}}
```

Now looking at a sequence of bids and asks, we have

```
In[101]:= hist=Table[histor[j],{j,2,800}];
```

To uncover the actual trades in history we employ select. The function determines whether a particular transaction is a trade.

```
In[102]:= trade = Function[x, !x[[1]] == 0 && !x[[2]] == 0]
```

```
In[103]:= Select[hist[[799]],trade]
```

```
Out[103]={{1, 1, 3.87311}, {1, 2, 3.28879}, {1, 1, 3.98529},
          {1, 1, 4.07317}, {1, 1, 4.26164}, {1, 2, 3.50065},
          {1, 1, 3.42808}, {1, 1, 4.16608}, {1, 1, 4.27207},
          {1, 1, 4.95113}, {1, 1, 3.36689}, {1, 1, 3.98586},
          {1, 1, 3.28882}, {1, 1, 3.15254}, {1, 1, 4.82505},
          {1, 2, 3.78062}, {1, 1, 3.92674}, {1, 1, 4.19338},
          {1, 1, 4.97558}, {1, 1, 3.08522}, {1, 1, 3.34943}}
```

It should be noted that in this example all the trades involve only three people, buyers 1 and 2 and seller 1. In fact, in all cases the goods were sold to exactly those people who were expected to receive them when we consult the supply demand graph for this set of values and costs. We later plot these to illustrate how the market works.

9.3.3.3   A More General Example

We have worked with the case in which there is only one good traded and show that it generally ends up in the hands we would expect; that is, the mechanism seems to result in efficient trades. Now we turn to the case when a number of people are expected to trade. To accomplish this, we follow the practice here of replacing a v value greater than 0 with 0 after a trade, and a cost less than 12 with 12 after a trade. Let us work with such a `history1`.

9.3.3.4   Additional *Mathematica* Functions

```
In[104]:= ReplacePart, Map
```

```
In[105]:= history1
```

```
Out[105]={{0, 7, 2.06}, {2, 0, 4.94}, {4, 0, 2.75},
          {0, 3, 2.35}, {4, 1, 2.75}, {0, 3, 2.6},
          {1, 0, 5.8}, {0, 4, 2.8}}
```

The buyers who traded are

```
In[106]:= Column[Select[history1,trade],2]
```

```
Out[106]= {1}
```

and the sellers are

```
In[107]:= Column[Select[history1,trade],1]
```

```
Out[107]={4}
```

Now we wish to alter values given this information. We use **ReplacePart** to do that.

```
In[108]:= ?ReplacePart
```

```
ReplacePart[expr, new, n] yields an expression in
   which the nth part of expr is replaced by new.
   ReplacePart[expr, new, {i, j, ...}] replaces the
   part at position {i, j, ...}. ReplacePart[expr,
   new, {{i1, j1, ...}, {i2, j2, ...}, ...}] replaces
   parts at several positions by new.
```

```
In[109]:= ReplacePart[values,0,
          Column[Select[history1,trade],2][[1]]]
```

```
Out[109]={0, 4, 3, 2, 1}
```

Similarly for sellers we have,

```
In[110]:= ReplacePart[costs,12,
          Column[Select[history1,trade],1][[1]]]
```

```
Out[110]={2, 7, 8, 12}
```

From this we can create two general functions of history,

```
In[111]:= value[history_]:=If[Select[history,trade]=={},
          values,ReplacePart[values,0,
          Map[List,Column[Select[history,trade],2]]]]
```

```
In[112]:= cost[history_]:=If[Select[history,trade]=={},costs,
          ReplacePart[costs,12,
          Map[List,Column[Select[history,trade],1]]]]
```

Now let us reconsider the problem:

```
In[113]:= histor[t_]:=histor[t]=message[Join
          [histor[t-1],{bidoffer[value[histor[t-1]],
          cost[histor[t-1]]]}]]
```

```
In[114]:= histor[1]={{1,0,12},{0,2,0}}
```

```
Out[114]={{1, 0, 12}, {0, 2, 0}}
```

```
In[115]:= histor[2]
```

```
Out[115]={{1, 0, 12}, {0, 2, 0}, {3, 0, 6.00195}}
```

```
In[116]:= histor[100]
```

```
Out[116]={{1, 0, 12}, {0, 2, 0}, {3, 0, 6.00195},
         {0, 4, 0.544341}, {0, 3, 2.86196},
         {3, 1, 6.00195}, {4, 0, 8.47432}, {1, 0, 6.54936},
         {0, 1, 0}, {0, 3, 0.554962}, {4, 0, 6.45455},
         {0, 4, 0.986474}, {1, 0, 4.57889},
         {1, 2, 4.57889}, {0, 1, 0}, {0, 3, 0.508142},
         {2, 0, 6.52924}, {2, 0, 3.01943},
         {0, 4, 0.757301}, {0, 3, 1.79473},
         {2, 3, 3.01943}, {0, 2, 0}, {4, 0, 5.24708},
         {0, 4, 0.356265}}
```

```
In[117]:= Select[histor[80],trade]
```

```
Out[117]= {{3, 1, 6.00195}, {1, 2, 4.57889}, {2, 3, 3.01943}}
```

Although this is only one set of observations, several things are important. First, all the people who would be expected to trade did. Second, the average price is

```
In[118]:= (6.00195+4.57889+3.01943)/3
```

```
Out[118]= 4.53342
```

which is in the middle of the 4 to 5 range suggested via examination of the supply-demand diagram. In addition, the surplus attained was

```
In[119]:= (8-4)+(7-2)+(4-3)=10
```

Note that the amount of surplus attained is precisely that available. Thus the double auction with zero-intelligence traders resulted in 100% efficiency. An individually rational Pareto-optimum has been achieved by our so-called zero intelligence traders.

9.4 Graphics

We have shown how to build and represent demand-supply curves used in experimentation or in classroom demonstrations. We have also looked at how an auction mechanism itself might be programmed using *Mathematica*, and how certain properties of such auctions can then be demonstrated. We now turn to the problem of displaying results.

9.4.1 Single-Sided Auctions

9.4.1.1 Price Graphs

We show here how to graphically demonstrate the results from the operation of a sequence of auctions. First we work with the Second Price Auction and generate a hypothetical set of results from that auction. We then show a basic graphic to plot such outcomes. We create 10 players, not all of whom play rationally, who play in 20 consecutive auctions.

```
In[120]:= players=Table[SecondPrice[Table[.1* k Random[Real,
             {1, 10}], {k,1,10}]],{20}]
```

```
Out[120]={{9, 5.92883}, {9, 5.52929}, {10, 8.32484},
          {7, 2.78702}, {6, 4.93561}, {9, 3.6611},
          {9, 4.51839}, {8, 4.08838}, {9, 6.99746},
```

```
{10, 8.33105}, {9, 6.38171}, {10, 6.02811},
{9, 7.82842}, {7, 5.63288}, {7, 5.0953},
{6, 4.41786}, {8, 3.45415}, {10, 5.3852},
{5, 3.10488}, {10, 7.04102}}
```

The following graph accomplishes several fundamental features that one would expect to capture in any such graph including labels for axes, labels for the plot as a whole, control of size of pointsizes that are printed, and gridline separation for periods. There is nothing very elegant here but it does capture the basic price results for the hypothetical auction.

```
In[121]:= ListPlot[Transpose[players][[2]],
          PlotStyle->PointSize[.02], PlotRange->{0,10},
          GridLines->{Range[20]+.5,None},
          AxesLabel->{Period,Price},PlotLabel->"SECOND PRICE  -
          BIASED PLAYERS"]
```

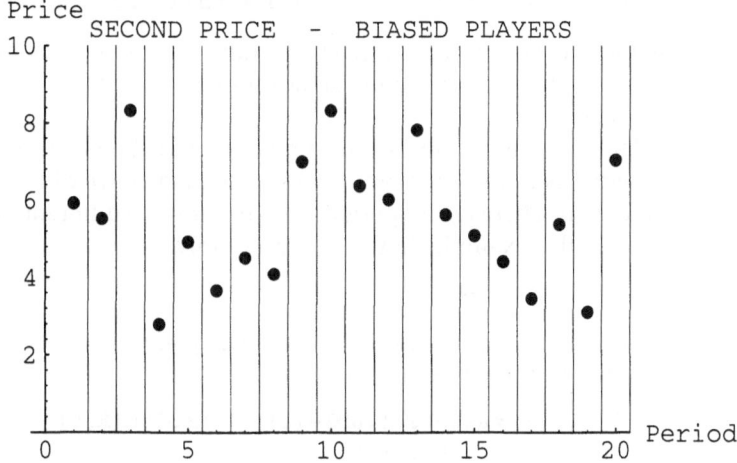

```
Out[121]=-Graphics-
```

The prior graph would certainly be useful as a simple first step at looking at any price data and is quite easy to generate using the options under **ListPlot** from *Mathematica*. However, it can be enhanced in terms of summary statistics, fonts, and text manipulation.

9.4.1.2 Bid and Ask Data

One might also like to examine bids in the second price auction, and graph the data so that it captures the distribution of the data in moving from period to period. A useful device for doing this is the sequence of box and whiskers plots. As a graphical device it works with fundamental graphics objects of *Mathematica* such as points and lines. The basic command is **boxandwhiskers**. The actual input is the set of sets in curly brackets; that is, sets must be of the form $\{\{1,2,3,6,3,\},\{3,4,5,6,9\}\}$. The rest of the items are numerical: a period is a number, recommended box width is less than one (i.e., less than a period in length), whiskerwidth must be less than box width, and `plotlabel` should be in quotes as well as vertical `axislabel`. Note in this picture the height of the box is the interquartile range and the darkened line is the median. The whiskers are the high and low values after outliers are removed. The outliers are determined in the following way. First the interquartile range is determined and then any observation is considered an outlier that is more than 1.5 times of the interquartile range removed from the high and low points of that range. This approach was adapted from Tukey's *Exploratory Data Analysis*.

```
In[122]:= Needs["DescriptiveStatistics'",
          "/Eclipse400/Mathematica/Packages/Statistics/\
          DescriptiveStatistics.m"]
```

Read in the plotters package here.

```
In[123]:= <<"/Eclipse400/john/MathAuctions/plotters.m"
```

To make the `plotters.m` package fully operational it is important to adjust the `Needs` statement in the body of the program to read `DescriptiveStatistics` package.

The most important input to box and whiskers is a collection of data from different periods. Here we generate the data as we did for the case previously described. There are 20 periods of data from 10 different people each period of time. In this example they all bid randomly.

```
In[124]:= ?Quantile
```

```
Quantile[list, q] gives the q-th quantile of the
    entries in list.
```

```
In[125]:= sets=Table[Table[.1* k Random[Real, {1, 10}],
          {k,1,10}],{20}] ;
```

```
In[126]:= ?boxandwhiskers
```

```
boxandwhiskers[sets,periods,boxwidth,whiskerwidth]
    takes a collection of sets, the total number of
    which is periods,along with specificiation for a
    boxwidth,a whiskerwidth, and returns a collection
    of boxandwhisker diagrams, one for each period.
    The actual input is the set of  sets in curlies
    i.e. sets must be of the form
    {{1,2,3,6,3,},{3,4,5,6,9}}, the rest of the items
    are numerical.  i.e. periods is a number,
    recommended box width is less than one, i.e. less
    than a period in length., and whiskerwidth must be
    less than box width. Note in this picture the
    height of the box is the interquartile range and
    the darkened line is the median.  The whiskers are
    the high and low values after outliers are removed.
```

In[127]:= **boxandwhiskers[sets,20,1,.75]**

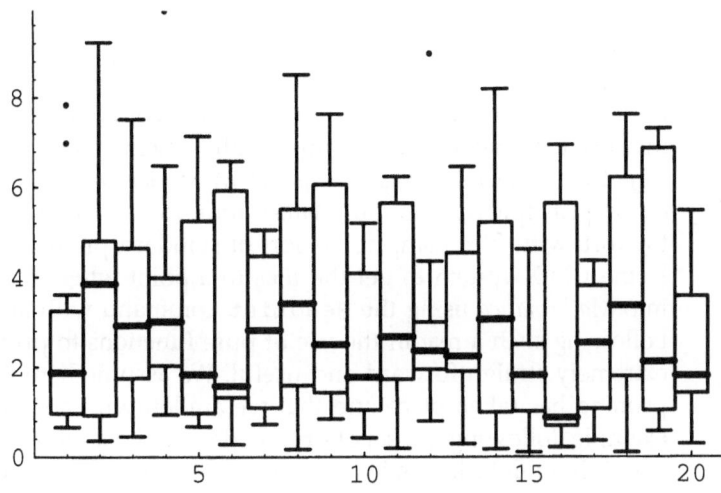

Out[127]= -Graphics-

As with other functions described in this chapter, it is possible to employ *Mathematica* Graphics Options.

In[128]:= **boxandwhiskers[sets,20,1,.75,**
      PlotLabel->"Bid Data",AxesLabel->{"Periods","$'s"}]

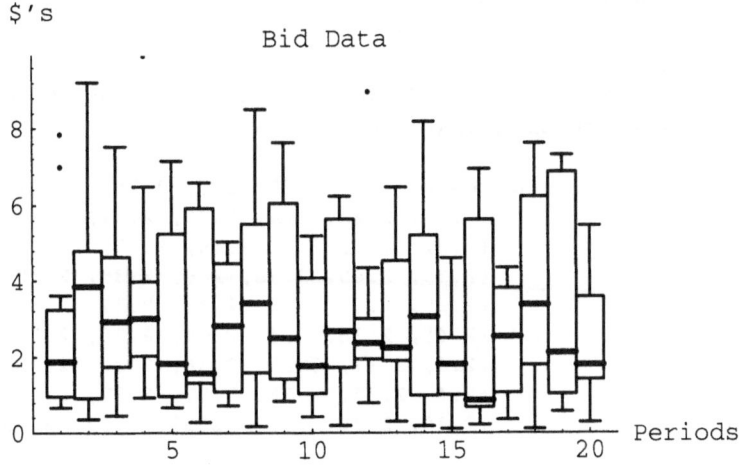

Out[128]= -Graphics-

9.4.2   Double Auctions

9.4.2.1   Price Graphs

Much of the difficulty of generating price graphs of double auctions exists because prices must be gleaned from rather long histories of bids, asks, and trades, inasmuch as a typical mechanism records the trades, bids, and asks as they occur. Usually some pruning or adjustment of the raw data file is necessary to get the data into shape to use in *Mathematica*. Although virtually any file can in principle be read into *Mathematica*, we have found that it is much easier to work with files using some sort of standard program such as awk or perl in the UNIX system to get the files to a point where they can be read easily into *Mathematica* using the **ReadList** command with an appropriate format. Following such a readin the use of pure functions to prune data can be made extremely straightforward and useful. We assume here that such editing and pruning has taken place and that we are left with a simple list of prices. For example, following is a set of pruned data that was generated by Vernon Smith and Arlington Williams in a double auctions experiment with four buyers and four sellers. The market was run in 1978 and the data were secured in private conversations with Arlington Williams and Shawn Lemaster.

```
In[129]:= v = {{3.30, 2.25, 2.10}, {2.80, 2.35, 2.20},
                {2.60, 2.40, 2.15}, {3.05, 2.35, 2.30}}

            c = {{1.90, 2.35, 2.50}, {1.40, 2.45, 2.60},
                {2.10, 2.30, 2.55}, {1.65, 2.35, 2.40}}

Out[129]={{3.3, 2.25, 2.1}, {2.8, 2.35, 2.2},
           {2.6, 2.4, 2.15}, {3.05, 2.35, 2.3}}

Out[129]={{1.9, 2.35, 2.5}, {1.4, 2.45, 2.6},
           {2.1, 2.3, 2.55}, {1.65, 2.35, 2.4}}
```

The prices reported for this experiment, where a sublist represents the prices in a particular period, were:

```
In[130]:= prices = {{3., 2.75, 2.5, 2.25, 2.35},
                {2.65, 2.22, 2.4, 2.35, 2.31, 2.35, 2.35},
                {2.5, 2.35, 2.3, 2.35, 2.35, 2.37, 2.35},
                {2.35, 2.45, 2.35, 2.4, 2.35, 2.35, 2.37},
                {2.35, 2.5, 2.36, 2.36, 2.37, 2.35},
                {2.45, 2.38, 2.4, 2.36, 2.36, 2.35, 2.35},
                {2.4, 2.37, 2.35, 2.36, 2.36, 2.35},
                {2.4, 2.37, 2.38, 2.37, 2.37, 2.35, 2.35},
                {2.39, 2.36, 2.37, 2.37, 2.37, 2.35, 2.35}}

Out[130]={{3., 2.75, 2.5, 2.25, 2.35},
           {2.65, 2.22, 2.4, 2.35, 2.31, 2.35, 2.35},
           {2.5, 2.35, 2.3, 2.35, 2.35, 2.37, 2.35},
```

```
                    {2.35, 2.45, 2.35, 2.4, 2.35, 2.35, 2.37},
                    {2.35, 2.5, 2.36, 2.36, 2.37, 2.35},
                    {2.45, 2.38, 2.4, 2.36, 2.36, 2.35, 2.35},
                    {2.4, 2.37, 2.35, 2.36, 2.36, 2.35},
                    {2.4, 2.37, 2.38, 2.37, 2.37, 2.35, 2.35},
                    {2.39, 2.36, 2.37, 2.37, 2.37, 2.35, 2.35}}
```

We have generated a graphing procedure to handle such data and combine with the demand-supply type of graph we introduced earlier. We assume the preceding v and c structures.

The graphical technique we use to graph these results is represented by the function **labexperimnt**. The structure of this function follows.

In[131]:= **labexperiment[prices,c,v,2.35]**

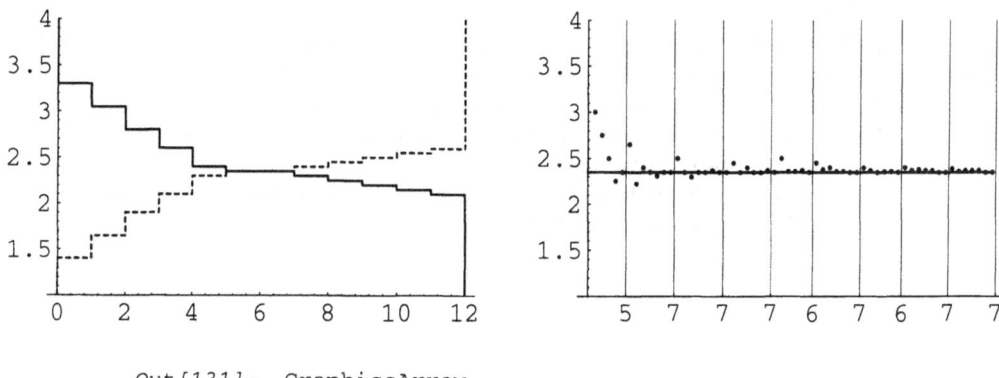

Out[131]= -GraphicsArray-

9.4.2.2   A Note on Calibration

Taking the parameters employed in an actual experiment, one can then examine the price formation process of zit traders and attempt to establish how well the price formation series of zit traders.e mimics the price series observed with real subjects.

9.5   Conclusion

We have introduced fundamental tools for studying auctions. We have focused on the generation and representation of competitive equilibrium predictions, the representation of auction rules (along with a few simulations that demonstrate properties of the auctions), and we have shown how data can be appropriately graphed.

There are some useful ways to expand the investigations begun here. For example it would be useful to study a multimarket equilibrium where one market is downstream; another route would be to add asset uncertainty. It should also prove useful to expand on the trading automata examined in this notebook. We used some of the simplest types of automata, but extensions to heuristics based on history dependent rules are feasible, and offer potential representations of rich behavior. Variations on the graphics we have described would include portraying bids and asks in double auctions. Furthermore, one may wish to microscope subintervals for the presence of isolating anomalous behavior.

9.6   References

Cassady, R. 1967. *Auctions and Auctioneering*. Berkeley, University of California Press.

Cox, J., B. Roberson, and V. Smith. 1982. "Theory and behavior of single unit auctions." In *Research in Experimental Economics*, Vol 2, Greenwich, CT, JAI Press.

Gode, D. and S. Sunder. 1993. "Allocative Efficiency of Markets with Zero Intelligence Traders: Market as a Partial Substitute for Individual Rationality." *Journal of Political Economy*, 101.

Holt, C. 1980, "Competitive Bidding for Contracts Under Alternative Auction Procedures." *Journal of Political Economy*, **88**, 3 (June), 433–445.

Myerson, R. B. 1991. *Analysis of Conflict*, Cambridge, MA, Harvard University Press.

Smith, V. L. 1988. "Auctions." In *The New Palgrave: A Dictionary of Economics*. J. Eatwell, M. Milgate, and P. Newman, Eds.

Vickrey, W. 1961. "Counterspeculation, Auctions and Competitive Sealed Tenders." *Journal of Finance*, **16**, 1 (March), 8–37.

10 Yield Management

Ward Hanson

10.1 Introduction

One of the notable innovations in pricing techniques during the past decade has been the use of yield management systems by airlines, hotels, and other service industries with recurrent but perishable capacity. Yield management is the creation of classes of service (first class, coach, supersaver, etc.) and protected capacity that allows the offering of dramatically different prices for what becomes eventually the same service. Much lower prices are charged for purchases that are correlated with high price sensitivity, normally buying early. Higher prices are charged as the service date approaches. The impact of this technique is substantial. Observers have credited yield management with raising revenues by 10 to 15%, and much more dramatic impacts on profits. Bankruptcies and even industrial espionage have been attributed to the differential abilities of some airlines in using yield management.

A related form of yield management problem arises when software can be metered and used over a network. This allows software to be treated like a shared asset, rather than an individually purchased durable good. Using technology that can track network usage exactly, organizations are matching their software purchases to actual organization-wide demand levels. Like the airline problem, the exact level of demand which will occur during a particular time slot is stochastic. Software purchases, and perhaps classes of service on the network, are optimized with regard to this uncertainty.

Kimes (1989) observes that the creation of service classes and this concern with demand uncertainty are especially relevant under conditions where (1) a firm is operating with a relatively fixed capacity, (2) when demand can be segmented into clearly identified partitions, (3) when inventory is perishable, (4) when the product is sold well in advance, (5) when demand fluctuates substantially, and (6) when marginal costs are low, but capacity change costs are high.

This chapter uses *Mathematica* to investigate some basics of yield management. These problems combine inventory rules and price setting. Industry practice uses both optimal algorithms and computationally much faster heuristic methods. *Mathematica* is a useful vehicle for demonstrating both approaches.

At the same time as analyzing perishable asset management, we demonstrate a new capability of *Mathematica* that we find generally very useful for analyzing business problems. The standard software used to analyze business problems is the spreadsheet. Among the reasons for this are the linearity of many calculations, the repeating cycle of calculations (e.g., monthly, quarterly), and the heavy use of tabular data both as inputs and outputs. However, there are fundamental difficulties with the basic spreadsheet design for the solution of complicated problems. It is far better to augment the software with a computational engine such as *Mathematica*.

Mathematica Versions 2.2 and later are client-server applications. The standard *Mathematica* front-end, the Notebook, is where the user inputs a model and receives output. Actual computation and analysis is performed in the *Mathematica* kernel. The Notebook is the client, and the kernel is the server. We substitute a spreadsheet as the client, while maintaining the kernel as the server. This is done using Mathlink, and a set of tools for communication between *Microsoft Excel* and *Mathematica* that is available from Wolfram Research. This package allows *Excel* to send and receive both data and commands to the *Mathematica* kernel. Our preferred design philosophy is to create a Mathematica package that can be run from either a notebook or a spreadsheet. Within this package are the key function definitions and function calls. Data entry and data display are separately achieved in the server applications, both of which expect the same functions to be available from the kernel package.

10.2   The Basic Framework

10.2.1   Theoretical Development

The perishable asset problems we study can be viewed as variations on a "newsboy" theme. The problem gets its name from the newsboy who must decide ahead of time how many papers to take down to the corner to sell. Too many and there will be papers unsold, and leftovers are worth only a fraction of their original price. Too few papers and there will be lost sales and consumer ill-will. Complicating this is random demand; who knows how many people will want a paper on a given day?

The newsboy problem is profit maximization subject to uncertainty, where there are specified costs of under or over supplying the market. Following the derivation in Silver and Peterson (1985), assume each unit of capacity purchased has a cost v, each sale of output generates p, each unit can be disposed of with a salvage value g, there is a penalty cost of w for each unit of demand that is not satisfied due to lack of capacity, and $p > v > g \geq 0$. Letting K be the capacity level and x the level of demand, we have profits given by

$$\Pi(K, x) = \begin{cases} -Kv + px + g*(K - x) & \text{if } x \leq K, \\ -Kv + pK - w*(x - K) & \text{if } x \geq K. \end{cases} \tag{10.1}$$

Expected profits are given by integrating over the range of possible demands. We need not choose a particular type of distribution, but assume that $f(x)$ represents a well-defined probability density function over nonnegative demands.

$$E[\Pi(K)] = \int_0^\infty \Pi(K, x) f(x)\, dx \tag{10.2}$$

$$= \int_0^K [-Kv + px + g * (K - x)] f(x)\, dx$$

$$+ \int_K^\infty [-Kv + pK - w * (x - K)] f(x)\, dx. \tag{10.3}$$

For continuous distributions, we maximize this by appropriately choosing K to make the first-order condition hold (second-order conditions also hold):

$$\frac{dE[\Pi(K)]}{dK} = -v + (p - g)Kf(K) + g \int_0^K f(x)\, dx + gKf(K)$$

$$+ wKf(K) + (p + w) \int_K^\infty f(x)\, dx - (p + w)Kf(K) = 0. \tag{10.4}$$

Letting $Pr(x \le K) = \int_0^K f(x)\, dx$, this reduces to

$$- v + g * Pr(x \le K) + (p + w) * [1 - Pr(x \le K)] = 0, \tag{10.5}$$

or

$$Pr(x \le K) = \frac{p - v + w}{p - g + w}. \tag{10.6}$$

The solution is even clearer if we introduce the concepts of *underage* and *overage* costs. Underage costs are the lost benefits of too little capacity, and are given by $c_u = p - v + w$. This is the lost revenue plus good will penalty minus the input cost. The overage cost is $c_o = v - g$, which is the input cost minus the salvage revenue. Using the preceding result, the newsboy problem is solved by setting capacity so that:

$$\text{Continuous Case:} \quad Pr(x \le K) = \frac{c_u}{c_u + c_o} = \frac{p - v + w}{p - g + w}. \tag{10.7}$$

This can be rewritten as $c_o Pr(x \le K) = c_u[1 - Pr(x \le K)]$. In other words, we choose capacity so that the expected marginal costs of overage and underage just balance.

The overage and underage formulation is also useful when we consider demands that must be integer. The expected total cost, both overage and underage, for the discrete case is given by:

$$ETC(K) = \sum_{x=0}^{K-1} c_o * (K - x)Pr(x = x) + \sum_{x=K}^{\infty} (x - K)Pr(x = x). \tag{10.8}$$

Define $\Delta ETC(K) = ETC(K + 1) - ETC(K)$, so that $\Delta ETC(K)$ is the change in expected total cost when capacity is increased from K to $K + 1$. If the expected total cost function can be verified as convex, then the best K is the smallest value for which $\Delta ETC(K) > 0$. This implies finding the smallest K such that:

$$\text{Discrete Case}: \quad Pr(x \le K) \ge \frac{c_u}{c_u + c_o} = \frac{p - v + w}{p - g + w}. \tag{10.9}$$

Let $K^*(p, v, w, g)$ be the solution to either (10.7) or (10.9). We can then investigate how expected profits $E[\Pi(K^*(p, v, w, g))]$ change as a result of changes in these arguments. This can be either as a result of further optimization, as in the case of product price, or as exogeneous shifts caused by other factors.

It is straightforward to include a budget constraint or maximum order size into this framework. Let K^* be the solution to (10.7) or (10.9) when there is no binding budget or capacity limit, B be the maximum budget or the solution to $B = \hat{K}/v$ where $\hat{K}$ is the maximum capacity, and K^{**} the optimal order when there is a budget or capacity limit. Morey and Sweeney (1984) show that

$$K^{**} = \begin{cases} \frac{B}{v} & \text{if } K^* \ge \frac{B}{v}, \\ K^* & \text{if otherwise.} \end{cases} \tag{10.10}$$

10.2.2   Implementing the Basic Framework

Mathematica's probability packages make it easy to explore the solutions for a wide range of distributions. We read in the packages for continuous and discrete distributions:

```
In[1]:=  Needs["Statistics'ContinuousDistributions'"];
         Needs["Statistics'DiscreteDistributions'"];
```

In version 2.2 this provides knowledge about 17 different continuous distributions and 8 discrete distributions.[1] In addition, the packages contain commands to yield a variety of calculations for each of these distributions (pdf, cdf, quantile, mean, etc.).

With these in hand, the solution to (10.7) or (10.9) is direct. We define **News-BoyCapacity** using both the underage/overage arguments and the underlying parameters.

---

[1] The continuous distributions are chi-square, F-ratio, normal, Student t, beta, Cauchy, chi, exponential, extreme value, gamma, half-normal, Laplace, Logistic, lognormal, Rayleigh, uniform, and the Weibull. Discrete distributions are Bernoulli, binomial, discrete uniform, geometric, hypergeometric, log series, negative binomial, and the Poisson.

```
In[2]:=  NewsBoyCapacity[dist_,underage_,overage_]:=
         Quantile[dist, underage/(underage+overage)]

         NewsBoyCapacity[dist_,v_,p_,g_,w_]:=
         Quantile[dist, (p-v+w)/(p-g+w)]
```

For continuous distributions **Quantile[ ]** returns the exact value of capacity required to satisfy (10.7). For discrete distributions it rounds up, which is what we need to ensure that the inequality holds.

We define **NewsBoyCapacityBudget** to implement the budget constraint in (10.10). We use the full parameter list version, as then marginal cost is identified.

```
In[3]:=  NewsBoyCapacityBudget[dist_,v_,p_,g_,w_,budget_]:=
         Max[ Min[Quantile[dist, (p-v+w)/(p-g+w)],budget/v],0]
```

We can investigate the sensitivity of both capacity and profits to various parameters. The profit function (10.1) is defined as:

```
In[4]:=  NewsBoyProfit[K_,x_,v_,p_,g_,w_]:=
         -K*v+p*x+g*(K-x)  /;  x <= K

         NewsBoyProfit[K_,x_,v_,p_,g_,w_]:=
         -K*v+p*K-w*(x-K)  /;  x > K
```

So far we have not had to distinguish between continuous and discrete distributions, as the definitions in the packages have parallel syntax. There is no equivalent parallel between the integration used for the continuous distributions and the summation used for the discrete. To handle this, we include an argument to indicate specifically whether the distribution is discrete or continuous, with 0 representing discrete and 1 for continuous. To speed the integration or summation, we also include a tolerance, with the integration running from the quantiles associated with *tol* and $1 - tol$. For expected profits we assume a numeric solution is wanted. For special cases where an analytic solution is possible, **NIntegrate** could be replaced with **Integrate**.

```
In[5]:=  ExpectedProfit[dist_,type_,tol_,K_,v_,p_,g_,w_]:=
         Module[{upper,lower},
           lower = If[type==0,
                     Max[0,Quantile[dist,tol]-1],
                     Quantile[dist,tol] ];

         upper = Quantile[dist,1-tol];

         If[type==0,
             Apply[Plus,
             Table[NewsBoyProfit[K,x,v,p,g,w]*PDF[dist,x],
                   {x,lower,upper}] ],
                   NIntegrate[NewsBoyProfit[K,x,v,p,g,w]*
                   PDF[dist,x],
                   {x,lower,upper}, MaxRecursion->10]]
           ]
```

To demonstrate these functions, consider the situation where an organization faces a potential daily pool of buyers U. They are influenced by price, each with a binomial purchase probability given by $a * p^{-b}$. Our demand distribution is:

```
In[6]:=  mybinomial[U_,p_,a_,b_]:= BinomialDistribution[U,
             Max[Min[a*p^(-b),1],0]]
```

With the `Max[Min[ ]]` construction we guarantee the probabilities are between zero and one. First, let us look at our capacity selection. Let $a = .1$ and $b = 1.5$.

```
In[7]:=  Plot[{
         Mean[mybinomial[Round[U],.65,.1,1.5]],
         NewsBoyCapacity[mybinomial[Round[U],.65,.1,1.5]
            ,.25,.65,.10,1.5]},{U,100,1000}]
```

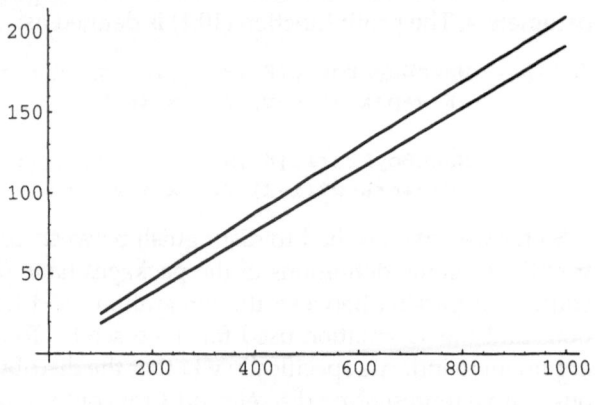

Figure 1

The profit-maximizing choice of capacity is to provide a reasonable cushion above expected demand, due to the good-will penalty and the profitability of each potential sale. We can also look at the impact of price, by graphing the expected profit as a function of various prices.

10.3   Server Management

This framework can also help an organization with a shared resource. Software metering technology can now verify in real time exactly how many users there are of a specific software application on a local area network. Among other features, this permits organizations to "block out" any use that would exceed the number of licenses that are owned. This prevents copyright violations, and effectively makes the software a network-wide resource.[2] To determine how many licenses to purchase, we can use the newsboy approach.

---

[2]Although some software publishers attempt to legally restrict this, many network-use software licenses are in place.

A software purchase is an upfront fixed fee. Often the hours of use can be classified into peak and off-peak usage, with capacity being driven by peak usage. To arrive at v, the input cost, we simply divide the license price by the number of peak hours over the relevant life of the license. If we assume there are 4 peak hours per day, 22 work days per month, 12 months per year, 2 years between upgrades, and a $750 purchase price, we would have

```
In[8]:=  v=750/(4*22*12*2);
```

For our example, we assume our users get a benefit twice this cost and there is no salvage value for the license. Peak demands are assumed to follow a binomial distribution with 100 possible users, each with a 1/3 chance of using the software any given hour.

We consider two levels of congestion penalty, 0 and $1 per hour. This gives

```
In[9]:=  p=2v;
         g=0;
         dist=BinomialDistribution[100,1/3];
```

How many licenses should an organization buy? Figure 2 presents a graph of the number of licenses the organization should buy as the congestion penalty ranges from $w = 1$ to $w = 10$.

```
In[10]:= BarChart[
         Table[
         NewsBoyCapacity[dist,v,p,g,w],
         {w,1,10}],
          PlotRange->{0,50},
          PlotLabel-> "Licenses vs. Penalty Cost" ,
          AxesLabel->{"w","L"}]
```

Figure 2

Server management, even with a high penalty cost for congestion, allows a substantial compression of license purchases while still satisfying almost all demand realizations. Experiments with different benefit levels, salvage values, or user fees are also straightforward. For example, the organization can combine user fees and the newsboy solution with a budget to simultaneously determine the best charge to apply to users and the number of licenses to purchase in a breakeven arrangement. Classes of service, such as interruptible and noninterruptible, are also possible. However, to investigate these issues we turn to the airline yield management setting.

10.4   Airline Yield Management

10.4.1   The Problem Setting

The large yield management problems facing airlines, hotels, and railroad industries are quite complex. Modeling decisions include discrete or continuous demand representations, fixed or flexible total capacity, predetermined or competitively determined prices, dynamic levels of consumer willingness to pay, cancellation possibilities, overbooking possibilities, and group reservations (Weatherford and Bodily 1992). Solving the full range of these problems has led to valuable proprietary systems which use a combination of optimization and heuristics.

Despite the complications that face large-scale applications, airline yield management problems share the basic newsboy economic structure which can be analyzed quite well using *Mathematica*. Specifically, *Mathematica*'s ability to do recursive programming and to handle probability distributions is very useful.

To make these points we use the single-leg nested allocation model of Wollmer (1992). In this framework a single airplane's flight capacity is to be allocated to a variety of fare classes, and prices for each of these classes are fixed. Demand for each fare class (e.g., first class, coach, supersaver) is uncertain with known distributions.

The initial purpose of the model is to set nested fare class protection levels k_m. This model assumes that low price customers arrive and make reservations first. For example, if there are 5 classes then customer class 5 has the first chance to book seats. However, they are only allowed to book a maximum of $C - k_5$ seats. The remaining capacity is held in reserve for later arriving potential customers. The problem is to choose the proper protection levels that result in the highest expected revenue.

10.4.2   The Revenue Function

The impact of these protection levels can be seen with the revenue function for this service. The revenue function $R[m, n, demand, klevels, fares]$, is the revenue generated by the m highest fare classes when n seats are available, when *demand* is a realized demand vector, *klevels* is the vector of nested protection levels, and *fares* is the list of prices by class.

The revenue function is defined recursively. If there is only a single fare class we get revenue which is the minimum of seats or demand:

```
In[11]:= Clear[Revenue];
         Revenue[1,n_,demand_,klevels_,fares_] :=
            fares[[1]]*n /; 0 <= n && n < demand[[1]]

         Revenue[1,n_,demand_,klevels_,fares_] :=
            fares[[1]]*demand[[1]] /; demand[[1]] <= n
```

Next we consider multiple fare classes. If capacity is less than the allocation for the higher paying fare classes, revenue will not be increased by additional fare classes.

```
In[12]:= Revenue[m_,n_,demand_,klevels_,fares_] :=
         Revenue[m-1,n,demand,klevels,fares]  /;
            0 <= n && n <= klevels[[m]]
```

Next is the case where there are some seats available, but less than the amount demanded:

```
In[13]:= Revenue[m_,n_,demand_,klevels_,fares_] :=
            (n-klevels[[m]])*fares[[m]] +
             Revenue[m-1,klevels[[m]],demand, klevels, fares] /;
               klevels[[m]] < n && demand[[m]] > n- klevels[[m]]
```

Finally, there is the case where available capacity is sufficient for class k:

```
In[14]:= Revenue[m_,n_,demand_,klevels_,fares_] :=
            demand[[m]]*fares[[m]] +
            Revenue[m-1,n-demand[[m]],demand,klevels,fares] /;
            klevels[[m]] < n && demand[[m]] <= n - klevels[[m]]
```

Using the revenue function, we can see the importance of protection levels. We need some data to see the impact:

```
In[15]:= Capacity=100;
         Demand1={x1,20,60,99};
         Demand2={15,20,60,x4};
         KLevels={0,5,35,50};
         Fares={1,.75,.6,.4};
```

Figure 3a shows how revenue increases only up to a point, and one far below flight capacity, when there is an increase in the number of highest fare customers. It flattens due to the previous reservations made by lower priced consumers. Figure 3b shows that unusually strong demand by fare class 3 can actually lead to a fall in revenue and profits, as they "snap up" the available capacity. It flattens due to protected levels for higher classes.

```
In[16]:= g1 =Plot[ Revenue[4,Capacity,Demand1,KLevels,Fares ] ,
                    {x1,1,20},
                    PlotRange-> {40,75},AxesLabel->{"x1"," "},
                    PlotLabel-> "(a)",
                    DisplayFunction->Identity ];

         g2=Plot[ Revenue[4,Capacity,Demand2,KLevels,Fares] ,
                    {x4,1,100},
                    PlotRange-> {40,75},AxesLabel->{"x4"," "},
                    PlotLabel-> "(b)",
                    DisplayFunction->Identity];

         Show[GraphicsArray[{g1,g2}]]
```

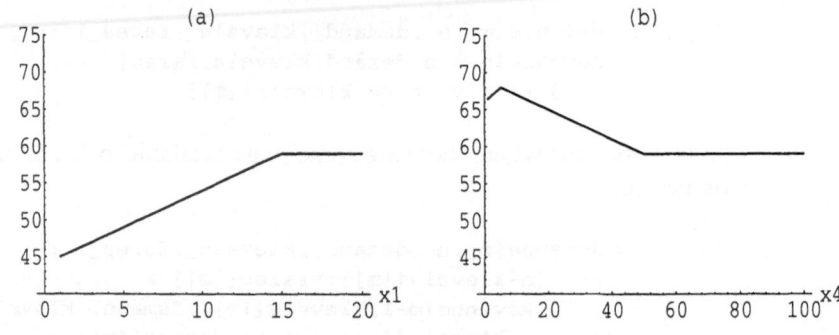

Figure 3

10.4.3   The EMSR Heuristic

Finding an optimal solution can be computationally intensive. The EMSR heuristic solution developed by Belobaba (1987) yields profits which tend to be very similar to the optimal solutions (within a percent or two) when the underlying demand is normal, although not necessarily similar in protection levels (Curry 1990). It follows a two step definition:

$$k_{ij} = [\max n \mid p_j < p_i Prob[x_j \geq n], \tag{10.11}$$

$$k_j^{EMSR} = \sum_{i=1}^{j} k_{ij}. \tag{10.12}$$

If we note that the solution to $\max K : Pr(x \geq K) \geq (p_j/p_i)$ is the same as $\min K : Pr(x \leq K) \geq 1 - (p_j/p_i)$, we can use the newsboy model to solve for the EMSR levels. The right-hand side is the newsboy solution, with

$$c_u = \text{"Underage cost"} = p_i - p_j, \text{ and} \tag{10.13}$$

$$c_o = \text{"Overage cost"} = p_j. \tag{10.14}$$

The underage cost is lost revenue from the higher price class i if the lower price class j is allowed to book a seat that would have been sold later. The overage cost is the lost revenue p_j which happens if a class j customer is turned down for the prospect of a class i customer that never materializes.

```
In[17]:= EMSRLimits[j_,Dists_,Prices_]:=
            Sum[NewsBoyCapacity[Dists[[i]],
                   Prices[[i]]-Prices[[j]],Prices[[j]],{i,1,j-1}]
```

The EMSR solution is optimal only for the two-class case. When there are three or more classes, it is not properly handling the joint probabilities in the optimal solution system of equations given before. To do that we use an algorithm developed by Wollmer (1992). However, the EMSR heuristic is often an order of magnitude or more faster than this optimal solution.

10.4.4   The Optimal Solution

Wollmer (1992) presents an algorithm for finding optimal allocation levels in a multiclass setting. The method is based on a recursive definition of the expected optimal revenue function $Z[m, n]$. These are defined with respect to optimally set protection levels k_m^* and the expectation of demand. Let k_m^* be defined by

$$k_1^* = 0. \tag{10.15}$$

$$k_m^* = [\max n \mid p_m < Z[m - 1, n] - Z[m - 1, n]] \text{ for } m > 1. \tag{10.16}$$

Equation (10.16) shows that optimal protection levels are set to equate, as closely as possible with discrete variables, the revenue from a sale to class m and the opportunity from potential higher price sales. This is the simple principle that is maintained throughout the various complications of different yield management systems. We again use the probability Packages.

```
In[18]:= Needs["Statistics`ContinuousDistributions`"]
          Needs["Statistics`DiscreteDistributions`"]
```

The optimal protection levels are determined by **KValue[ ]**. When there is only one class, there are no reserved seats. When there are just two classes, the **NewsBoyCapacity** gives a quick and accurate solution. When there are three or more classes, we set the protection level at the point where the profit from selling the seat to class m just equals the profit from reserving the seat for future customers.

```
In[19]:= KValue[m_,DistList_,PriceList_,Cap_]:=
          KValue[m,DistList,PriceList,Cap] =
          Which[m==1,  0,
                m==2,
```

```
Min[
    Ceiling[ NewsBoyCapacity[DistList[[1]],
              PriceList[[1]]-PriceList[[2]],
              PriceList[[2]] ]],
        Cap] ,
    m>2,
    Module[{x},
        For[x=KValue[m-1,DistList,PriceList,Cap] ,
        OptimalZ[m-1,x,DistList,PriceList,Cap]-
        OptimalZ[m-1,x-1,DistList,PriceList,Cap]-
            PriceList[[m]] >0 &&
            x < Cap,
        x++,   z=x]; z]
    ]
```

In all these definitions we are using the recursive formulation that stores the previously calculated values. This can dramatically increase the speed of calculation, but does require some care. This is especially true when a calculation gets interrupted, as partially determined answers may "contaminate" future calculations. The use of **Clear** and **Remove** may be necessary, followed by a re-execution of the definitions.

The **OptimalZ** function gives the expected profits from using the optimal protection levels. It is defined recursively. The key step is when there are some available seats for class m. We calculate the expected revenue from class m and the expected revenue from unsold seats that are sold to future higher price customers. This is the **Revenue** function with optimal protection levels and unknown demand.

```
In[20]:= OptimalZ[m_,n_,DistList_,PriceList_,Cap_]:=
         OptimalZ[m,n,DistList,PriceList,Cap] =
         Which[ m == 0, 0,
                m == 1, ExSingleClassRev[m,n,DistList,PriceList,
                                         Cap],
                m > 1 && n <= KValue[m,DistList,PriceList,Cap],
                    OptimalZ[m-1,n,DistList,PriceList,Cap],
                m > 1 && n > KValue[m,DistList,PriceList,Cap],
                    ExThisClassRev[m,n-KValue[m,DistList,
                                   PriceList,Cap],
                                   DistList,PriceList,Cap]+
                    ExOpportunityCost[m,n,DistList,PriceList,
                                      Cap]
              ]
```

With this formulation we are assuming a data structure for distributions of `{{ dist1, type1}, { dist2, type2}, ... { distn, typen}}`. For example, we might use `{{ BinomialDistribution[100,.2],0}, {BinomialDistribution[230,.15], 0}, {NormalDistribution [75,6.5], 1}}`. Note that we can mix continuous and discrete distributions for different classes.

The three intermediate functions `ExSingleClassRev[ ]`, `ExThisClass-Rev[ ]`, and `ExOpportunityCost[ ]` are all defined in the package that accompanies the electronic supplement. Up until here we have made no assumptions about the stochastic structure between demands for the classes. In this example, we follow Wollmer and use stochastic independence. That is, the realization of demand for class m provides no information about class $m - i$.

For many purposes the expected level of profits suffices. However, there are also situations where the distribution of profits is needed for further analysis. For some probability distributions, such as the normal, there are closed form approximations. In many cases it is necessary to resort to Monte Carlo analysis. Functions to accomplish this are included in the package, and can be called in the following Excel example . As part of Monte Carlo analysis the distribution of Spills and Load is also calculated. *Spills* are the unfilled demand that results when class k demand exceeds permitted capacity. *Loads* are the realized demand.

10.5   The Excel Implementation

10.5.1   Using the Excel Front-end

To demonstrate these commands we now turn to the spreadsheet front-end. We use *Mathlink for Excel and Mathematica* available from WRI. Once installed, this package makes the *Mathematica* kernel act like an *Excel* add-in. That is, with some manipulation the full power of *Mathematica* is available to an *Excel* user.

Although it is possible to use *Mathematica* commands interactively with Math-Link, this is fairly cumbersome. A better solution is to include all the *Mathematica* code into a package. An *Excel* user activates this package with an *Excel* macro, which can evaluate functions, read the relevant data into the kernel, and then retrieve the results back to the spreadsheet.

Figure 4 presents the first screen of a simplified yield management system. Data required from the user is shown in double outlined regions. Results returned from *Mathematica* are shown in the single outlined regions. Each of the analyses is run by clicking on their respective buttons. The user can generate the nested protection levels using either the fast EMSR heuristic or the slower optimal approach. With these protection levels established, a Monte Carlo analysis of the expected loads, spills, and revenues can be performed. The number of simulation cases variables will dictate the number of random draws used in this simulation.

The probabilities used for the calculations are generated on another spreadsheet, shown in Figure 5. This is based on a typical methodology used in market research for evaluating consumer preferences. We have shown hypothetical multinomial logit estimates for each of the fare classes and airlines. That is, observed choices are evaluated using a maximum likelihood estimation procedure where the choice probabilities are assumed to follow:

$$Prob(Choose\ airline\ i\ and\ class\ j) = \frac{E^{V_{i,j} - \beta p_{i,j}}}{\sum_{m,k} E^{V_{m,k} - \beta p_{m,k}}}. \tag{10.17}$$

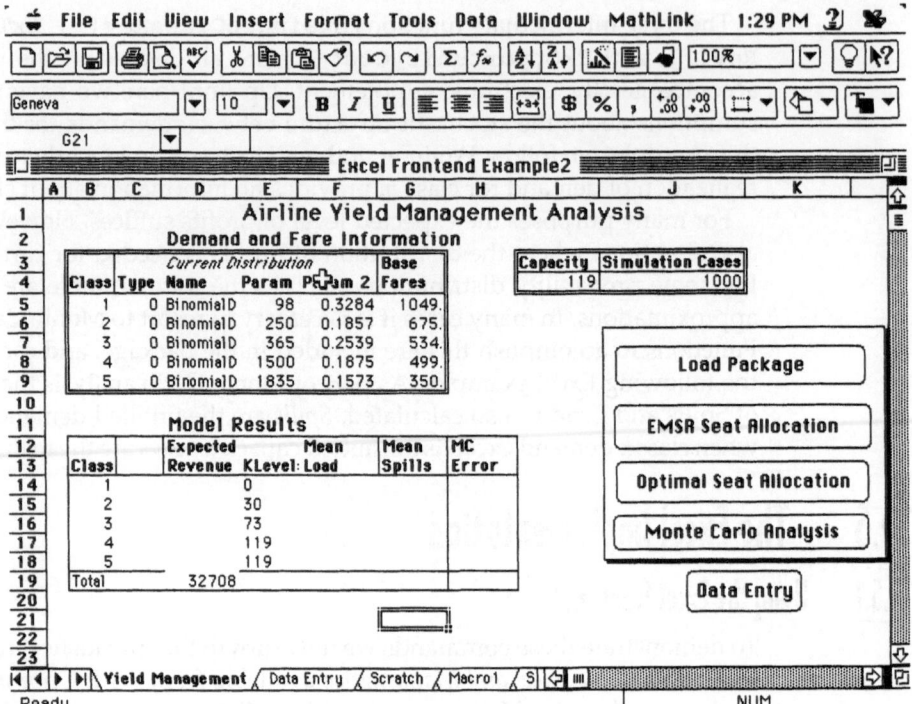

Figure 4

Figure 5

This is often justified as utility maximization with errors in measurement follow-ing a Weibull distribution [see McFadden (1974) for key original development; for comprehensive overviews see Ben-Akiva and Lehrman (1985) or Anderson et al. (1992)].

The benefits of using a spreadsheet are several. The data manipulation and checking are often easier in the tabular format than a notebook interface. Data from external sources are often available in a worksheet format, and this format may be required for further processing. Also, in areas such as education or business, there are many more users familiar with a spreadsheet than with mathematical software. This approach allows the power of a program such as *Mathematica* to be utilized in a familiar setting for many more users.

Shown in the following is the *Excel* macro which is activated when the Optimal Seat button is pushed. The electronic supplement contains the spreadsheet and the *Mathematica* package with the needed definitions. The first block of state-ments reads in the data. Range names are used, so that areas of the spreadsheet can be modified easily without having to go back and alter absolute address calls. The second block of statements calls the key functions in the *Mathematica* package, with only modest modifications to the basic *Mathematica* syntax. The third block sends the results back to the spreadsheet.[3]

```
In[21]:= OptimalKValues
        =M.SET("name1",'Yield Management'!G5)
        =M.SET("name2",'Yield Management'!G6)
        =M.SET("name3",'Yield Management'!G7)
        =M.SET("name4",'Yield Management'!G8)
        =M.SET("name5",'Yield Management'!G9)

        =M.VALUE("DistList={name1,name2,name3,name4,name5}")
        =M.SET("PriceList",'Yield Management'!G10)
        =M.SET("Cap",'Yield Management'!I4)
        =M.VALUE("Cap=Round[Cap]")
        =M.VALUE("KClass=Table[KValue[m,DistList,PriceList,Cap],
           {m,1,5}]")

        =M.EXCELPUT(KLevelRange,"KClass")
        =M.EXCELPUT(ExOptimalProfit,""OptimalZ[1,Cap,DistList,
           PriceList,Cap]")
        =RETURN()
```

Using this model, an analyst can investigate profitable price changes and likely impacts on demand structure by changing prices. For example, in a two-firm case a profit matrix for each of the airlines could be constructed and the Nash price solution calculated using the *Nash.m* package from Volume I of this series.

---

[3]The current version of *MathLink* uses *Excel* 4.0 macro notation. Future versions will use the newer Vi-sual Basic method. *MathLink* connections for other spreadsheet applications are also being planned.

10.6 Summary

A variety of problems involve costly capacity and users who differ in their needs for the product. Yield management is an approach that creates classes of service and protected capacity. *Mathematica* can be used to investigate decisions under a wide range of random environments. It can also be incorporated into pre-existing financial or operational models by linking *Mathematica* to popular spreadsheet software using *MathLink*.

Although *Mathematica* is a powerful development and analysis tool, it can also be a daunting tool. A spreadsheet interface allows an analyst to hide much of the code from users, and to analyze a range of scenarios with the power of *Mathematica*, but in the comfort of a familiar user surrounding. Another promising interface, especially for use in education, is the World Wide Web. Efforts are underway by several groups to develop a Web front-end for *Mathematica*. This can further shield the naive user, and put much more structure on the data input and output steps.

10.7 References

Anderson, S., A. de Palma, and J. Thisse. 1992. *Discrete Choice Theory of Product Differentiation*. Cambridge, MIT Press.

Belobaba, P. 1987. "Airline Yield Management: An Overview of Seat Inventory Control." *Transportation Science*, **21,2**, 63–73.

Ben-Akiva, M. and S. Lerman. 1985. *Discrete Choice Analysis: Theory and Application to Predict Travel Demand*. Cambridge, MIT Press.

Brumelle, S. and J. McGill. 1993. "Airline Seat Allocation with Multiple Nested Fare Classes." *Operations Research*, **41**, 127–137.

Curry, R. 1990. "Optimal Airline Seat Allocation with Fare Classes Nested by Origins and Destinations." *Transportation Science*, **24**, 3, 193–204.

Kimes, S. 1989. "Yield Management: A Tool for Capacity-Constrained Service Firms." *Journal of Operations Management*, **8**, 348–363.

McFadden, D. 1974. "Conditional Logit Analysis of Qualitative Choice Behavior." In *Frontiers in Econometrics*, P. Zaremka, Ed. New York, Academic Press, 105–142.

Nahmias, R. 1993. *Operations Planning*. Homewood, IL, Irwin.

Silver, E. and R. Peterson. 1985. *Decision Systems for Production Planning and Inventory Management*, second edition. New York, John Wiley & Sons.

Weatherford, L. and S. 1992. "A Taxonomy and Research Overview of Perishable-Asset Revenue Management: Yield Management, Overbooking, and Pricing." *Operations Research*, **40**, 5, 831–844.

Weatherford, L., S. Bodily, and P. Pfeifer. 1993. "Modeling the Customer Arrival Process and Comparing Decision Rules in Perishable Asset Revenue Management Situations." *Transportation Science*, **27**, 3, 239–251.

Varian, H. 1992. *Econonmic and Financial Modeling with Mathematica*, Santa Clara, CA, Telos.

Wolfram Research. 1993. *MathLink for Excel and Mathematica*, October.

Wollmer, R.. 1992. "An Airline Seat Management Model for a Single Leg Route When Lower Fare Classes Book First." *Operations Research*, **40**, 1, 26–37.

11 Implementing Numerical Option Pricing Models

Simon Benninga, Raz Steinmetz, and John Stroughair

11.1 Introduction

In a previous article in the *Mathematica Journal*, Miller (1990) showed how the Black-Scholes option pricing model could be implemented in *Mathematica*. Although the Black-Scholes model gives a closed-form solution for pricing European options, many other options cannot be priced by this model. Such options include American options and options whose terminal payoffs are dependent on the path followed by the stock price.

In this chapter we show how *Mathematica* may be used to price such options using the binary and binomial option pricing models and the Monte Carlo method. We also discuss some of the convergence and timing properties of the *Mathematica* implementations. We begin with a review of some definitions and classic option pricing results. The following sections discuss the binary and binomial option pricing models and give a simple, four-state example. We then present our *Mathematica* implementation of the models and discuss timing and convergence issues. Finally, we show how to implement the Monte Carlo method and we discuss its properties.

11.2 Review of Some Definitions and Results

In this section we give a cursory review of the definitions and major results used in this chapeter. Interested readers are referred to a standard options textbook such as Jarrow and Rudd (1983), Cox and Rubinstein (1985) or Hull (1993).

An option is an example of a *contingent security*, a financial asset whose payoff depends on the value of another financial asset. A *call option on a stock* is a security that gives the holder the right but not the obligation to buy one share of the stock on or before date T for a price K, the strike (or exercise) price. A

Reprinted with permission from *The Mathematica Journal*, 1993, **3**, 4, 66–73.

European call option gives the holder the right to purchase the share of stock only on the terminal date T, whereas an American call option gives the holder the right to purchase the share at any date up to and including the terminal date T. Although it would seem that the *early exercise* feature of an American call option should give it more value than a European option, a well-known theorem [due to Merton (1973)] states that early exercise of an American call option is not optimal if the stock on which the option is written does not pay a dividend before the option's maturity date T. It follows, therefore, that if the stock on which the option is written does not pay a dividend before the maturity date T, then an American call option written on the stock has the same value as a European call option.

A *put option on a stock* is a security that gives the holder the right to *sell* one share of the stock on or before date T for a price K. As with calls, one may distinguish between European put options, which do not allow early exercise, and American put options. The preceding result is no longer true, however. It may be optimal to exercise an American put before expiration, even if the underlying stock pays no dividends. In general, therefore, an American put option will be more valuable than the corresponding European put. This difference between puts and calls is due to the fact that the stock price is bounded below by zero but is unbounded above.

In addition to the standard European and American options previously discussed, various other "exotic" options are traded. In this chapter we consider two of these options: *lookback options* and *Asian options*. A lookback call gives the holder the right to purchase the stock for the minimum price at which the stock traded during the life of the option, and a lookback put gives the right to sell for the maximum price reached during the life of the option. For an Asian option, either the payoff or the strike price is related to the average price of the stock. Lookback and Asian options come in European and American versions. The algorithms presented in this chapter can easily be adapted to price various other exotic options.

Throughout this chapter we consider only options on stocks that do not pay dividends before the expiration date T of the option. For European options written on such stocks, the *put-call parity theorem* says that the value of a put may be expressed in terms of a call written on the same stock, the stock price itself, and the discounted exercise price.

Put-call parity theorem: Let C be the value of a European call option with maturity T and strike price K written on a stock whose current price is S_0, and let r be the continuously compounded rate of interest. Then the value of a European put option written on the same stock, with the same strike price and maturity date, is given by

$$P = C - S_0 + Ke^{-rT}.$$

In general, most of the models that price options assume a certain stochastic movement of the stock prices. The most common assumption is that the stock price S at time T will be governed by the following stochastic diffusion process:

$$ds = S\mu\, dt + S\sigma\, dZ, \tag{11.1}$$

where dS is the change in the stock price, μ is the expected logarithmic return on the stock (which, as discussed in the following, under certain circumstances can be replaced by the risk-free rate for option valuation), σ is the standard deviation of the return on the stock, and z is the standard Wiener process.

The value of an option written on a stock therefore depends on the price and stochastic properties of the stock, as well as the risk-free interest rate r. Finance theorists express this property by saying that the option may be *perfectly hedged* by the stock price and the value of a bond (which depends only on the interest rate r). This property leads to some important observations. First, the value $F(S, t)$ of a contingent security, such as an option, satisfies the partial differential equation

$$rS\frac{\partial F}{\partial S} + \frac{\sigma^2 S^2}{2}\frac{\partial^2 F}{\partial S^2} + \frac{\partial F}{\partial t} = rF \tag{11.2}$$

Although the precise derivation of this equation is beyond the purview of this chapter, its meaning can be expressed as follows: by perfectly hedging the option's change in value [the left side of (11.2)] over a short period of time, the holder of the option should earn the risk-free rate of interest on the option's value [the right side of (11.2)]. Solutions to the equation depend on the boundary condition given. For example, a European call has boundary conditions:

$$F(0, t) = 0, \qquad F(S, T) = \text{Max}(0, S - K), \tag{11.3}$$

and a European put has boundary conditions:

$$F(0, t) = 0, \qquad F(S, T) = \text{Max}(0, K - S).$$

The second observation is that because the option can be perfectly hedged, its value does not depend on the risk aversion of investors. It can thus be valued using the assumption that all investors are indifferent to risk (risk-neutral). Risk neutrality lets us express the value of the option today as the discounted expected value of the payoffs from the option using the formula

$$F = E\{e^{-rt}F_t\}.$$

The third observation is that under the stochastic process (11.1), the terminal stock price follows a lognormal distribution, and thus the logarithm of the stock final price follows the normal distribution with mean $S_0(r - \sigma^2/2)T$ and standard deviation $\sigma\sqrt{t}$. For a discussion of the properties of the lognormal distribution, see Aitchison and Brown (1966).

In a well-known paper, Black and Scholes (1973) prove that the price of a European call option [i.e., the solution to eq. (11.2) subject to the boundary conditions (11.3)] is given by:

$$C = S_0 \Phi(d_1) - Ke^{-rT}\Phi(d_2),$$

where Φ is the cumulative standard normal distribution and d_1 and d_2 are defined by:

$$d_1 = \frac{\ln(S_0/K) + (r + \sigma^2/2)T}{\sigma\sqrt{T}}$$

$$d_2 = d_1 - \sigma\sqrt{T}.$$

The Black-Scholes theorem combined with the put-call parity theorem allows us to price both European puts and calls.

In practice, many options do not have closed-form solutions. In those cases, we try to estimate the value of the option by numerically solving the differential equation. We illustrate two methods in this chapter. Binary option pricing models approximate the expected price of the option by using the lattice method, which simulates the Wiener process of the stock price. Monte Carlo methods simulate possible price paths the stock might take.

11.3   The Binary Option Pricing Model

The binary option pricing model was developed by Cox et al. (1979) and Rendleman and Bartter (1979). In the option literature, this model is usually referred to as the *binomial* option pricing model; we use this terminology for the case when the binary tree of stock prices recombines, and we refer to the more general case as the binary option pricing model. For a non-path-dependent option, the *binary* option pricing model, with appropriately chosen parameters, will converge to the standard Black-Scholes formula. The binary option pricing model is more general than Black-Scholes. It may be used to price a variety of path-dependent options for which no analytic pricing formulas exist.

The binary option pricing model assumes that at any time there are two possible future states of the world that define security returns, and that the price of any security in the economy can be expressed as a linear combination of the prices of two basic securities known as the *stock* and a *risk-free asset*. The stock's return (defined as the percentage of return plus one) over a short period of time is either up (denoted u) or down (denoted d). Thus if the stock price at time t is S, the stock price at time $t + 1$ will be either Su or Sd. If the risk-free interest rate over the same period of time is r, then a risk-free asset whose value is 1 at time t will be $R = 1 + r$ at time $t + 1$. The price of an arbitrary security that returns x if the stock price is up and y if the stock price is down will be given by $px + qy$ for some values of p and q. These values, called *spanning state prices*, can be found by expressing the value of the stock and the risk-free asset. For the stock, $pSu + qSd = S$. Therefore

$$\begin{cases} pu + qd = 1 \\ pR + qR = 1 \end{cases}.$$

It follows that

$$p = \frac{R - d}{R(u - d)}, \qquad q = \frac{u - R}{R(u - d)} = \frac{1}{R} - p.$$

Because $Rp + Rq = 1$, asset valuation in a binomial framework may be viewed as taking the *discounted expected asset payoff* when probabilities are assigned to payoffs using a particular set of pseudoprobabilities. This property, which has an extension to continuous time, is often referred to as pricing by using an *equivalent martingale measure*, and underlies the risk-neutral pricing model.

When an option's price is not path dependent, we may use the *binomial option pricing model* to price it. When it is path dependent, we use the *binary option pricing model*. Although both models use the same equivalent martingale measure approach, the binary model is much more computationally intensive than the binomial option pricing model. The following figure shows a four-date binary tree. At any time $t = 0, 1, 2, \dots$, the possible states are $u^i d^j$, where $i + j = t$. For each state, the corresponding *state price*, that is, the value at time zero (today) of a future dollar, is $p^i q^j$.

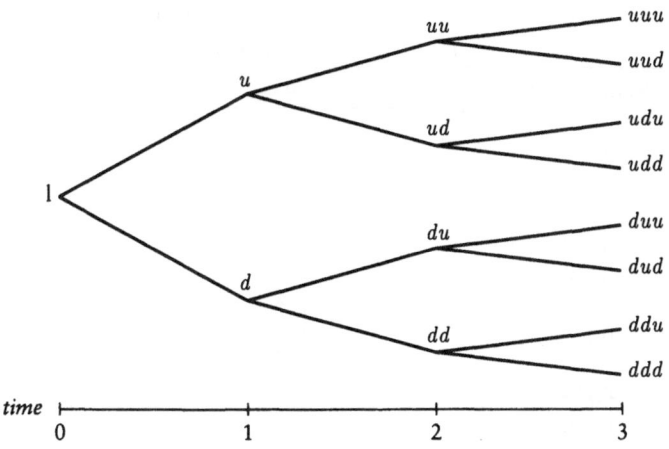

Figure 11.1   A binary tree showing the possible states from time $t = 0$ to $t = 3$.

For clarity, we present a four-date example of the binary and binomial option pricing models. In Table I the stock price over a single period can change by $u = 1.04$ or $d = 0.98$; when the risk-free interest rate is $r = 2\%$ (per period), this gives *one-period* prices for "up" and "down" states of $p = 0.6536$ and $q = 0.3268$, respectively.

All the options in Table I have an exercise price $K = 50$ and an initial stock price $S_0 = 50$. The value of any option is the dot product of the vector of state prices for states $\{1, u, d, uu, \ldots, dddd\}$ and the vector of security payoffs in these states (the corresponding columns). If an option shows *NA* in some state, it means that the state is never reached because of early exercise of the option. Early exercise values are indicated by *italics*.

Security A is a European put, which is exercised only in states *ddd, ddu, dd, udd*, and consequently has value today of 0.115. Security B is an American put, which is exercised early in state *d*. The test for early exercise is that immediate exercise is more valuable than the value of the next period's put price. For example, in state *u*,

$$k - price(u) > p \max[price(du) - K, 0] + q \max[price(dd) - K, 0].$$

Table 11.1   Four Period Example

Paramter	Value	Security	Description	Intrinsic Value Formula
K	50.00	A	European Put	$\max[0, K - S_3]$
u	1.04	B	American Put	$\max[0, K - S_t]$
d	0.98	C	European Lookback Put	$\max[0, K - \min(S_0, S_1, S_2, S_3)]$
r	1.02	D	American Lookback Put	$\max[0, K - \min(S_0, \ldots, S_t)]$
p	0.6535	E	European Call	$\max[0, S_3 - K]$
q	0.3268	F	American Call	$\max[0, S_t - K]$

State	State Prices	A	B	C	D	E	F
today							
u	0.654						
d	0.327		*1.000*				
uu	0.427						
ud	0.214						
du	0.214		NA		*1.000*		
dd	0.107		NA				
uuu	0.279					6.243	6.243
uud	0.140					2.998	2.998
udu	0.140					2.998	2.998
udd	0.070	0.059	0.059	0.059	0.059		
duu	0.140		NA	1.000	NA	2.998	2.998
dud	0.070	0.059	NA	1.000	NA		
ddu	0.070	0.059	NA	1.980	1.980		
ddd	0.035	*2.940*	NA	2.940	2.940		
Price Today		**0.115**	**0.331**	**0.454**	**0.458**	**2.998**	**2.998**

Option C is a European lookback put, in which the owner receives the difference between the strike price and the lowest price reached by that security on the path to the exercise point. Option D is a corresponding American lookback put. Finally, we use Options E and F to illustrate that an American call option will never be exercised early.

The binomial option pricing model is an extension of the Black-Scholes result in the following sense: for appropriate choices of u and d, the binomial process underlying the stock price development in the binary option pricing model converges to a lognormal distribution. It can be shown that the option price determined from the binomial option pricing model converges to the Black-Scholes option pricing formula.

There are two components to any option's value. The *exercise value* (or *intrinsic value*) is the value associated with exercising the option and is denoted EV. The value associated with letting the option run on unexercised is called the *option value* and denoted OV. (Because a European option can only be exercised at maturity, it does not have an exercise value except at maturity.) At any time, an option will trade for a price equal to the higher of these two components:

$$Option\ price = \max[EV, OV].$$

At maturity, the option has only exercise value. Thus on the terminal nodes of the tree of stock prices, a call option will have a value equal to the maximum of zero or $S - K$, and a put will have a value equal to the maximum of zero or $K - S$, where K is the strike price.

We can now price an option in terms of the state prices p and q by proceeding recursively down through the tree of stock prices starting with the terminal nodes. The recursive formula for valuing an option is:

$$OV(S_t, t) = \text{Max}[p \cdot OV(uS_t, t - \Delta t) + q \cdot OV(uS_t, t - \Delta t), EV(S_t, t)] \qquad t > 0$$

$$OV(S_0, 0) = EV(S_0, 0)$$

$$p = \frac{(R - d)}{R(u - d)}$$

$$q = \frac{1}{R} - p$$

$$R = e^{r\Delta t}$$

Under the assumption that the stock price follows the stochastic process defined in eq. (11.1), the distribution of stock prices at any time is lognormal. The stock price distribution generated by the binomial model converges to the same lognormal distribution. Therefore u and d can be related to the observed stock price volatility and to the risk-free interest rate r [see Hull (1993)]. One convenient set of parameters for which this convergence is assured [see Omber (1987)] is given by

$$u = e^{\sigma \sqrt{\Delta t}}$$
$$d = e^{-\sigma \sqrt{\Delta t}}$$
$$R = e^{r \Delta t}.$$

The following graph illustrates the convergence of the distribution of stock prices at the final nodes for various tree sizes.

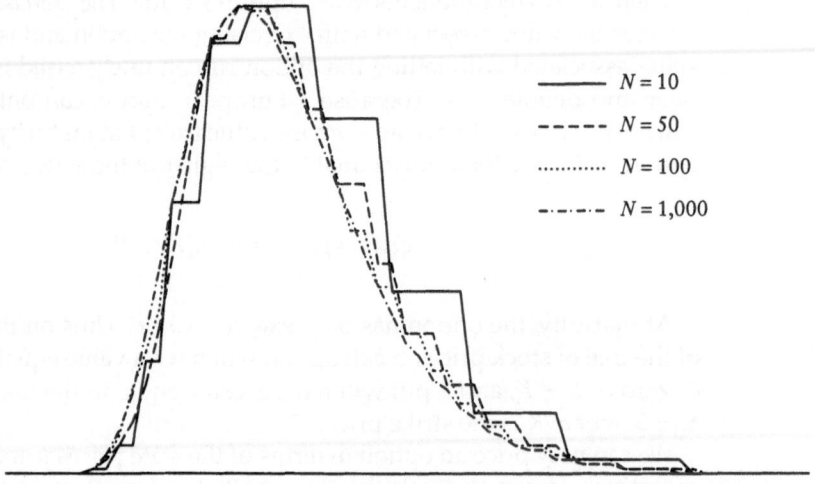

—— $N = 10$
- - - - $N = 50$
.... $N = 100$
-··-··- $N = 1,000$

Figure 11.2 The distribution of stock prices at the final nodes for various tree sizes. For appropriately chosen parameters, the distribution converges to a lognormal distribution as the size of the tree increases.

11.4 Implementing Binomial Option Pricing

In this section we present *Mathematica* functions to value American and European options of various kinds. We first consider a European option that is not path dependent. Such options include the European calls and puts. Because a European option's value depends only on the option value at the ending nodes of the tree, we may calculate the option's value by using the state prices p and q, without recursing through the tree. The European option price is the sum of the state prices of the terminal nodes of the tree times the option value at each terminal node, that is,

$$Option\ Value = \sum_{i=0}^{n} \left\{ \frac{n!}{i!\,(n-i)!} p^i q^{n-1} EV(u^j d^{n-j} S) \right\}.$$

This formula can be implemented easily in *Mathematica*. We define auxiliary functions to compute $u, d, p, q,$ and r:

```
In[1]:=  up[n_, sigma_, T_] := N[ Exp[ Sqrt[T / n] sigma] ];
         down[n_, sigma_, T_] := N[ 1/up[n, sigma, T] ];
         R[n_, Rf_, T_] := N[ Exp[ Rf T / n] ];
         P[up_, down_, r_] := N[ (r - down)/(up - down)/r ];
         Q[up_, down_, r_] := N[ 1/r - P[up, down, r] ];

         mean[l_List] := Apply[Plus, l]/Length[l];
```

The function **EuropeanOption** calculates the preceding summation.

```
In[2]:=  EuropeanOption[S0_, n_, sigma_, T_, Rf_,
             exercise_Function] :=
         Module[
         {u = up[n, sigma, T], d = down[n, sigma, T],
           r = R[n, Rf, T], p, q},
         p = P[u, d, r];
         q = Q[u, d, r];
         Sum[ exercise[S0 u^j d^(n-j)] Binomial[n, j]
               p^j q^(n-j), {j, o, n}] ]
```

The arguments of the function are the current stock price S0, the exercise price K, the number of periods n, the standard deviation sigma of the stock price, the time T to maturity (in years), the annual risk-free interest rate Rf, and the option exercise function **exercise**. Using the function **EuropeanOption**, we define pricing functions for a European put and call.

```
In[3]:=  EuropeanCall[K_, S0_, n_, sigma_, T_, Rf_] :=
             EuropeanOption[S0, n, sigma, T, Rf, Max[# - K, 0]& ]
```

```
In[4]:=  EuropeanPut[K_, S0_, n_, sigma_, T_, Rf_] :=
             EuropeanOption[S0, n, sigma, T, Rf, Max[K - #, 0]& ]
```

Here is an example of the valuation of European put and call options.

```
In[5]:=  EuropeanCall[50, 50, 300, 0.4, 5/12, 0.1]
```

```
Out[5]=  6.11227
```

```
In[6]:=  EuropeanPut[50, 50, 300, 0.4, 5/12, 0.1]
```

```
Out[6]=  4.07174
```

The function **AmericanOption** uses the binary pricing model to evaluate American options. Although the valuation is based on the expected value of the option, we must value the option at every lattice point to check for early exercise.

```
In[7]:=  AmericanOption[S0_, n_, sigma_, T_, Rf_,
             exercise_Function]:=
         Module[
         {u = up[n, sigma, T], d = down[n, sigma, T],
           r = R[n, Rf, T], p, q, OpRecurse, res},
         p = P[u, d, r];
         q = Q[u, d, r];
         OpRecurse[node_, level_]:= OpRecurse[node, level] =
           If[ level==n, exercise[S0 d^node u^(level - node)],
             Max[{p, q}.{OpRecurse[node, level+1],
               OpRecurse[node+1, level+1]},
               exercise[S0 d^node u^(level - node)] ] ];
         res = OpRecurse[0, 0];
         Clear[OpRecurse];
         res ];
```

```
In[8]:=  AmericanCall[K_, S0_, n_, sigma_, T_, Rf_]:=
             AmericanOption[S0, n, sigma, T, Rf, Max[# - K, 0]&]
```

```
In[9]:=  AmericanPut[K_, S0_, n_, sigma_, T_, Rf_]:=
             AmericanOption[S0, n, sigma, T, Rf, Max[K - #, 0]&]
```

For example,

```
In[10]:= AmericanCall[50, 50, 30, 0.4, 5/12, 0.1]
```

```
Out[10]= 6.07425
```

```
In[11]:= AmericanPut[50, 50, 30, 0.4, 5/12, 0.1]
```

```
Out[11]= 4.26343
```

```
In[12]:= EuropeanCall[50, 50, 30, 0.4, 5/12, 0.1]
```

```
Out[12]= 6.07425
```

```
In[13]:= EuropeanPut[50, 50, 30, 0.4, 5/12, 0.1]
```

```
Out[13]= 4.03372
```

Notice that the American call is worth the same as a European call, whereas a European put is worth less than the equivalent American put because of the possibility of early exercise of the American put.

We now consider path-dependent options. An example is an Asian average strike call option, which gives its owner the right to buy a share of stock for the average price (either geometric or arithmetic) during the past month. For simplicity, we assume that the average is calculated over the whole price path and not over a subset of prices (as is usually the case for path-dependent options). The European version of such options can be valued using the Monte Carlo techniques that we discuss later, but the American Asian option must be valued using the binary option pricing model. The number of nodes in the tree grows exponentially so only small trees can be computed in reasonable time.

The recursive technique is the same as was used previously. However, the exercise value EV is a function of a list of stock prices $\{S_0, S_1, S_2, \ldots, S_t\}$. For example, an American average option will have the following exercise value:

$$OV(S_0, S_1, \ldots, S_t) = \begin{cases} EV(S_0, S_1, \ldots, S_n), & \text{for } t = n \\ Max \begin{bmatrix} EV(S_0, S_1, \ldots, S_t), \\ p \cdot OV(S_0, S_1, \ldots, S_t, u \cdot S_t) + q \cdot OV(S_0, S_1, \ldots, S_t, d \cdot S_t) \end{bmatrix} \\ \qquad \text{for } t = 1, \ldots, n - 1. \end{cases}$$

The function **AsianOption** implements this formula:

```
In[14]:= AsianOption[S0_, n_, sigma_, T_, Rf_,
            expired_Function, alive_Function]:=
        Module[
        {u = up[n, sigma, T], d = down[n, sigma, T],
          r = R[n, Rf, T], p, q, Op},
        p = P[u, d, r];
        q = Q[u, d, r];
        Op[prices_List, level_]:=
          If [level == n, expired[prices],
            Max[{Op[Append[prices, u Last[prices]], level+1],
                 Op[Append[prices, d Last[prices]], level+1]}
               .{p, q},
               alive[prices]]];
        Op[{S0}, 0] ]
```

As examples, here are functions to value American and European average-price options that pay the difference between the final stock price and its arithmetic average over the period.

```
In[15]:= AmerAvgCall[S0_, n_, sigma_, T_, Rf_]:=
        AsianOption[S0, n, sigma, T, Rf,
          Max[0, mean[#] - Last[#]]&,
          Max[0, mean[#] - Last[#]]& ]
```

```
In[16]:= EurAvgCall[S0_, n_, sigma_, T_, Rf_]:=
        AsianOption[S0, n, sigma, T, Rf,
          Max[0, mean[#] - Last[#]]&, 0&]
```

```
In[17]:= AmerAvgPut[S0_, n_, sigma_, T_, Rf_]:=
            AsianOption[S0, n, sigma, T, Rf,
               Max[0, Last[#] - mean[#]]&,
               Max[0, Last[#] - mean[#]]& ]

In[18]:= EurAvgPut[S0_, n_, sigma_, T_, Rf_]:=
            AsianOption[S0, n, sigma, T, Rf,
               Max[0, Last[#] - mean[#]]&, 0&]

In[19]:= AmerAvgCall[50, 10, 0.4, 5/12, 0.1]

Out[19]= 3.3323

In[20]:= EurAvgCall[50, 10, 0.4, 5/12, 0.1]

Out[20]= 2.41693
```

Note that early exercise of American Asian calls may be optimal, so that the value of the American call is higher than that of the European call.

11.5   Timing and Convergence of the Binary Method

The algorithm for valuing European options has a complexity of $o(n)$, compared with $o(n^2)$ for American options. This results in a much longer calculation time for American options. We used *Mathematica* to plot the evaluation time (in seconds) as a function of n for both types of option.

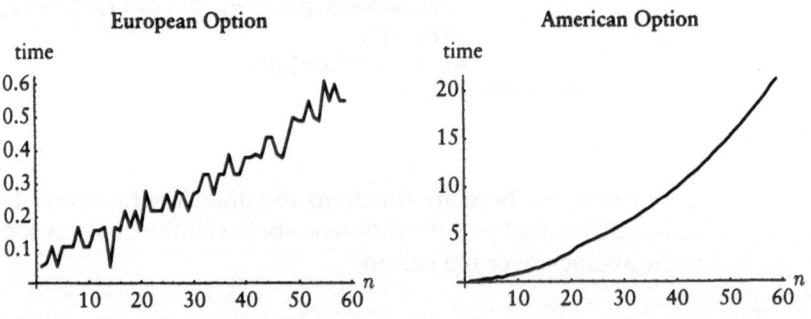

Figure 11.3   Evaluation time for European and American options as a function of the number of periods in the binary model.

The times were measured with *Mathematica 2.2.1* running under *Windows* on a 486DX 25 MHz machine. Although one can reduce these times using a faster CPU, the ratio between timings for the two types would not be changed. Because of the exponential nature of the algorithm for Asian options, we did not plot its timing; clearly, however, the user should not try trees with more than about 15 levels.

An interesting aspect of the binomial approximation is the speed of convergence to the final result. We used the function **EuropeanPut** to price a European option with several values for the volatility (the parameter that most strongly affects convergence). Figure 4 shows the convergence for 10, 20, 30, and 40% volatility.

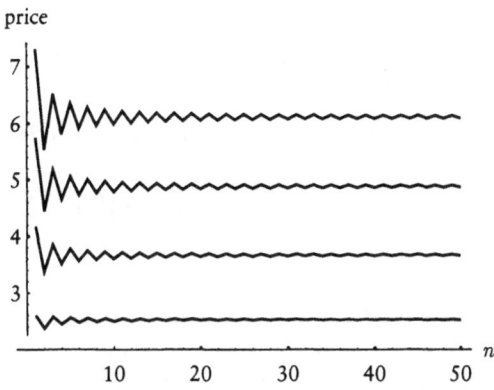

Figure 11.4   The result of the binomial option algorithm for a European option, as a function of the number of terminal nodes of the tree. Convergence is shown for four values of the volatility parameter, from 40% (top) to 10% (bottom).

Another way to look at convergence is to compute the absolute change from each iteration to the next. Figure 5 shows the change (labeled "error") for a volatility of 40%.

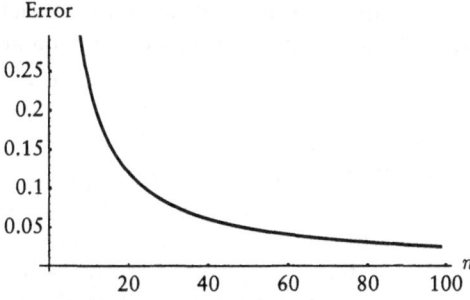

Figure 11.5   The absolute change ("error"), from one iteration to the next, in the result of the European option algorithm for an option with 40% volatility.

Notice that even after 100 iterations, the result still changes by a few cents every iteration, which is rather disturbing. We can see that for American options, a larger number of iterations must be performed to produce accurate results and the computation time will be rather long.

We found that the geometric mean of two successive iteration results provides a rather accurate approximation of the actual value, without going through the valuation of very large trees. However, we could not check this estimate for all possible options (especially path-dependent ones). Another useful method, which can be implemented easily, is the control variate technique explained in the next section.

11.6   The Monte Carlo Approach

The value at time zero of a European option that pays off F_T at time T is:

$$F = E\{F_T e^{-rT}\},$$

where E denotes the expectation operator in a risk-neutral world and r is the risk-free interest rate. In general, F_T depends on the value of an underlying stochastic variable, usually the stock price or some simple function of the stock price such as the average over the last n days before maturity. If we make the simplifying assumption that the risk-free rate is known with certainty (as we did in the binomial models), we can rewrite this equation as:

$$F = B_0 E\{F_T\} = e^{-rT} E\{F_T\},$$

where B_0 is the price of a zero-coupon discount bond that matures at time T.

In the risk-neutral world, the stock price follows the stochastic process (11.1) with the expected logarithmic return μ equal to the risk-free interest rate r. The Monte Carlo technique simulates the path of the stochastic variable. Using a large number of random paths, we expect to achieve a large enough sample that the mean of the sample will be close to the actual mean of the possible stock prices. In practice, approximately 5,000 runs are required to achieve option prices accurate to within a few cents.

The function **MCEuropean** implements the Monte Carlo method for a European option that depends only on the price of the stock at expiration. Because we only require the distribution of terminal stock prices, and not the complete path throughout time, we save a considerable amount of computation time by simulating the terminal prices directly, rather than the entire path. It can be shown that the terminal stock price, in the risk neutral world, is lognormally distributed. The Monte Carlo approach has the additional benefit of providing an estimate of the error by giving the standard error of the sample mean. The function **MCEuropean** computes the option price and the standard error:

```
In[21]:= Needs["Statistics`NormalDistribution`"]

In[22]:= nor[mu_, sig_]:= Random[NormalDistribution[mu, sig]];
```

```
In[23]:= MCEuropean[s_, n_, sigma_, T_, Rf_,
             exercise_Function]:=
         Module[
            {m = N[Log[s] + (Rf - 1/2 sigma^2) T],
             sg = N[sigma Sqrt[T]],
             tbl},
            tbl = Table[nor[m, sg], {i, n}];
            Exp[-Rf T] Map[exercise, Exp[Join[tbl, 2m - tbl]]] //
              {Mean[#], StandardErrorOfSampleMean[#]}& ]
```

The *Mathematica* function **Random** allows us to generate random variables distributed according to any distribution function. Our program uses a method called the antithetic variable technique to improve the accuracy of the result. The idea is to use each random number ρ to generate two samples: ρ and $2m - \rho$, where m is the mean. Thus the total variance is reduced. Unfortunately, these two samples are not perfectly negatively correlated because of the lognormal transformation, and the actual reduction in variance is only moderate.

The Monte Carlo technique requires a much larger value of n than the binomial method. If n is large enough, we can safely assume that the correct option price lies within an interval of six standard errors centered on the estimate. To illustrate, we apply the function to value the call option we have used in previous examples.

```
In[24]:= MCEuropeanCall[k_, s_, n_, sigma_, T_, Rf_]:=
         MCEuropean[s, n, sigma, T, Rf, Max[# - k, 0]&]
```

```
In[25]:= MCEuropeanCall[50, 50, 300, .4, 5/12, .1]
```

```
Out[25]= {6.05954, 0.401488}
```

Although it is interesting to use the Monte Carlo approach to value standard European options, the pricing of these options does have a closed form solution, or they can be accurately valued using numerical integration. The Monte Carlo approach is most useful for valuing options that do not have an analytic solution. In the following example, we show how another type of average price Asian call may be valued. The payoff from this option is $Max[0, \bar{S} - K]$ where $\bar{S}$ is the average price reached by the stock during a specified period before the option matures.

The function **paths** generates a random sample of price paths for the averaging period. It returns a list of n random paths, each consisting of **navg** prices over the period from time **T1** to time **T**. The prices at the start of the period are given by the appropriate lognormal distribution for time **T1**.

```
In[26]:= paths[s_, sigma_, T1_, T_, Rf_, n_, navg_]:=
         Module[
           {mdist = Log[s] + (Rf - sigma^2/2) T1,
            sdist = sigma Sqrt[T1],
            mpath = 1 + Rf (T - T1)/(navg - 1),
            spath = sigma Sqrt[(T - T1)/(navg - 1)]},
           Table[
             NestList[# nor[mpath, spath]&,
               Exp[nor[mdist, sdist]],
               navg - 1], {i, n}] ];
```

The function **MCAsianCall** evaluates the exercise function of the average of the prices in each path and then computes the average and the standard error of this sample.

```
In[27]:= MCAsianCall[s_, k_, sigma_, T1_, T_, Rf_, n_, navg_]:=
         (Exp[-T Rf] *
           Map[Max[0, Mean[#] - k]&,
               paths[s, sigma, T1, T, Rf, n, navg]]) //
           {Mean[#], StandardErrorOfSampleMean[#]}&
```

Here is a valuation of an Asian call option with five months till maturity, for which the strike price will be compared with the average price of the stock over the last 30 days:

```
In[28]:= MCAsianCall[50, 50, .4, 4/12, 5/12, .1, 300, 30]
```

```
Out[28]= {5.41183, 0.472882}
```

Notice that this average call option is less valuable than a normal call option because the average tends to be less volatile compared to the actual stock price.

We can improve the accuracy of this Monte Carlo estimate by using a method known as the control variate technique [see Hammersley and Handscomb (1964)]. We modify the result of the function **MCAsianCall** by adding the difference between the Black-Scholes valuation at time **T1** and the (path-independent) Monte Carlo estimate for a European call expiring at **T1**. The function **BSCall** evaluates the Black-Scholes formula.

```
In[29]:= cnorm[x_]:= N[CDF[NormalDistribution[0, 1], x]];
```

```
In[30]:= BSCall[k_, s_, sigma_, T_, Rf_]:=
         Module[
           {d1 = (Log[s/k] + T (Rf + sigma^2/2))/(sigma Sqrt[T])},
           N[s cnorm[d1] - k Exp[-Rf T] cnorm[d1-sigma Sqrt[T]]]];
```

The function **MCAsianCall2** computes the corrected Monte Carlo estimate.

```
In[31]:= MCAsianCall2[s_, k_, sigma_, T1_, T_, Rf_, n_, navg_]:=
         Module[
           {path = paths[s, sigma, T1, T, Rf, n, navg],
            sample, call},
           sample = Exp[-T Rf] Map[Max[0, Mean[#] - k]&, path];
           call = Mean[sample];
           {call, StandardErrorOfSampleMean[sample],
             call + BSCall[k, s, sigma, T1, Rf] -
               Exp[-Rf T1] *
                 Mean[Map[Max[0, # - k]&, Map[First, path]]]} ]

In[32]:= MCAsianCall2[50, 50, .4, 4/12, 5/12, .1, 300, 30]

Out[32]= {5.41183, 0.472882, 5.68827}
```

In general, we note that the Monte Carlo method can be used to give crude estimates of option prices. Because of the inability to value American options, the need to develop a new program for each option type, and the relative speed (at least under *Mathematica*), we found this method to be inferior to the binomial approach. One of the main advantages of the Monte Carlo method is the ability to price options using different stochastic assumptions, even observed probabilities, and to include multiple stochastic variables (such as interest rate and jump process) without the need to develop a formal model.

11.7   Conclusion

A number of recent papers such as Kemna and Vorst (1990) and Ritchken et al. (1993) discuss approximations to pricing formulas for options that are difficult to price. In this chapter we have shown that *Mathematica* may be used to price many of these options directly, using the parsimonious code that is its hallmark.

11.8   Acknowledgment

The authors thank Bruce Grundy, Bob Korsan, Troels Petersen, and Robert Reider for helpful comments.

11.9   References

Aitchison, J. and J. A. C. Brown. 1966. *The Lognormal Distribution*. New York, Cambridge University Press.

Black, F. and M. Scholes. 1973. "The Pricing of Options and Corporate Liabilities." *Journal of Political Economy*, **81**, 659–673.

Cox, J., S. Ross, and M. Rubinstein. 1979. "Option Pricing: A Simplified Approach." *Journal of Financial Economics*, **7**, 229–264.

Cox, J. and M. Rubinstein. 1985. *Option Markets*. Englewood Cliffs, NJ, Prentice-Hall.

Hammersley, J. M. and D. C. Handscomb. 1964. *Monte Carlo Methods*. London, Methuen.

Hull, J. C. 1993. *Options, Futures, and Other Derivative Securities*. Englewood Cliffs, NJ, Prentice-Hall.

Jarrow, R. A. and A. Rudd. 1983. *Option Pricing*. Homewood, IL, Irwin.

Kemna, A. and T. Vorst. 1990. "A Pricing Method for Options Based on Average Asset Values." *Journal of Banking and Finance* (March), 113–129.

Merton, R. C. 1973. "Theory of Rational Option Pricing." *Bell Journal of Economics and Management Science* (Spring), 141–183.

Miller, R. M. 1990. "Computer-Aided Financial Analysis: An Implementation of the Black-Scholes Model." *Mathematica Journal*, 1, 1, 75–79.

Omberg, E. 1987. "A Note on the Convergence of Binomial-Pricing and Compound-Option Models." *Journal of Finance*, 42 (June), 463–469.

Rendleman, R. and B. Bartter. 1979. "Two State Option Pricing." *Journal of Finance*, 34 (December), 1093–1110.

Ritchken, P., L. Sankarasubramanian, and A. M. Vijh. 1993. "The Valuation of Path Dependent Contracts on the Average." *Management Science* (forthcoming).

12 YieldCurve

Mark Fisher and David Zervos

12.1 The Term Structure of Interest Rates

The term structure of interest rates occupies a central position in both macroeconomics and finance. The fundamental relationship is the *discount function*, $\delta(t, \tau)$, which gives the price at time t of a default-free zero-coupon bond that pays one unit at time τ. Hereafter we assume that the current time is 0, suppress the first index, and write $\delta(\tau)$. Thus $\delta(\tau)$ is the present value of one unit to be delivered with certainty in τ periods hence. We find it convenient to look at the *log of the discount function*, $\ell(\tau) := \log[\delta(\tau)]$.

Interest rates are derived from bond prices. The *zero-coupon (yield) curve*, $z(\tau) := -\log[\delta(\tau)]/\tau = -\ell(\tau)/\tau$, gives the yield-to-maturity on a zero-coupon bond that matures at time τ. The *forward rate curve*, $f(\tau) := -d\log[\delta(\tau)]/d\tau$, gives the marginal return at maturity τ of extending one's investment. We can write the forward curve in terms of the zero curve by first writing $\delta(\tau) = e^{-\tau z(\tau)}$ and then applying the definition for forward rates: $f(\tau) = z(\tau) + \tau z'(\tau)$. Thus we see that the relationship between the zero and forward curves is that of average and marginal curves.

The techniques embodied in the YieldCurve package are designed to extract the term structure from a set of bonds (*i*) that are default-free and (*ii*) whose prices are determined by the present value of their stated payments. All U.S. Treasury securities meet the first criterion, but some do not reasonably meet the second criterion, such as callable bonds, "flower" bonds, and bonds "on special" in the repo market.

Consider a set of n bonds. Let p_i be the price of bond i, c_{ij} be its jth payment, paid at time τ_{ij}, and m_i be the number of remaining payments. Then[1]

$$p_i = \sum_{j=1}^{m_i} c_{ij}\, \delta(\tau_{ij}) + \varepsilon_i = c_i{}^\top \widetilde{\delta}(\tau_i) + \varepsilon_i,$$

---

[1] "$\top$" denotes transpose. In addition, the prices p_i include accrued interest.

where c_i is the vector of payments for bond i, τ_i is the vector of maturities of those payments, ε_i is a random error, and

$$\widetilde{\delta}(\tau_i) := (\delta(\tau_{i1}), \ldots, \delta(\tau_{im_i}))^\top$$

is the $m_i \times 1$ column vector that results from applying δ to each element of τ_i. Thus the present value of the payments is given by $\pi_i = c_i^\top \widetilde{\delta}(\tau_i)$.

12.2   Fitting the Term Structure

Estimating the term structure from bond prices is not, however, a trivial matter. A variety of techniques have been proposed over the past twenty-five years. McCulloch (1971, 1975) was the pioneer in this field. Essentially, McCulloch parameterized $\delta(\tau)$ as a cubic spline and estimated the spline coefficients with linear regression. Following McCulloch, Vasicek and Fong (1982), Shea (1984), Jordan (1984), Chambers et al. (1984), and Coleman et al. (1992), among others, extended the spline-based estimation technique to explore tax-related effects on bond pricing, to consider different parameterizations of the splines, and to analyze potential sources of heteroskedasticity in the residuals. Other authors have pursued alternative estimation techniques based on parsimonious parameterizations of the discount function. For instance, Nelson and Seigel (1987) and Bliss (1993) consider a functional form with only four unknown parameters. (In contrast, for a sample of 150 securities, McCulloch would typically choose a spline with 18 parameters.)

Fisher et al. (1995) present an extension of the spline-based techniques (see that paper for the specifics). In particular, they fit smoothing splines instead of regression splines. Smoothing splines have a penalty for excess "roughness" with a single parameter that controls the size of the penalty. An increase in the penalty reduces the effective number of parameters. Hence a single value controls the entire parameterization of the spline. For regression splines, the number of parameters must be chosen in advance. By contrast, they use *generalized cross validation* to choose adaptively the roughness penalty—and hence the effective number of parameters. In other words, they let the data determine the appropriate number of parameters. In addition, Fisher et al. place the spline directly on the log of the discount function $\ell(\tau)$ and on the forward rate function $f(\tau)$, as well as on the discount function $\delta(\tau)$. Based on their simulations and on their estimation results (using daily data on U.S. Treasury coupon securities from December, 1987 through September, 1994), they found that splining the forward rate function with a smoothing spline and choosing the effective number of parameters via generalized cross validation produced the most accurate and least biased results on average.

This chapter describes the *Mathematica* package YieldCurve that implements the techniques described in Fisher et al. (1995). YieldCurve contains commands to estimate the term structure of interest rates using regression splines and smoothing splines—with or without generalized cross validation. YieldCurve also has functions to display and analyze results and produce reports. YieldCurve calls a number of other *Mathematica* packages—both standard packages and other included packages.

12.2.1   File Names: Packages and Data

To install the packages, one should create a subdirectory, for example, \ycurve. The following files should be copied to this subdirectory: YieldCurve.m, ShowTime.m, PageLayout.m, BSplineBasis.m, CommaDelimited.m, TriangularPlot3D.m, MakeCalendar.m, and daycount.m.[2] The first seven files contain *Mathematica* packages. The file daycount.m contains information for determining the number of days until a payment is made. In addition, there are seven files with names of the form yyyymmdd.dat that contain data on Treasury securities, as well as strips.dat and openmkt.dat. Two other files will be created in the working directory as the main package is used: LStart.m and DLStart.m. If FunctionalForm -> LogDelta or FunctionalForm -> DLogDelta, DiscountFunction will create the file LStart.m or DLStart.m in the default directory (if it does not already exist). It is possible that bad starting values in LStart.m or DLStart.m could lead to difficulty in estimation. In any case, either file can always be deleted, causing internal defaults to be used.

Also included are the files CRSPDailyBonds.m and CRSPMonthlyBonds.m. These files contain packages that provide access to the Center for Research in Security Prices (CRSP) Daily and Monthly U.S. Government Bond Files. Each package contains (among other things) the function MassageCRSPData, which reads the (ASCII) data files and produces an MD object. Interested users should read the files for additional information.

12.3   B-Spline Bases

A spline is a piecewise polynomial joined at so-called knot points. Let the order of the polynomial be given by r. Thus a cubic B-spline is order 3, whereas a step function is order 0. At each knot point, the polynomials that meet are restricted so that one additional independent parameter is added. For example, a step function has only one parameter, and thus there are no restrictions between adjacent step functions for a 0-order spline. By contrast, a cubic polynomial has four parameters; thus for a cubic spline, the level and first two derivatives of each cubic are restricted to be identical at the knot points.

A numerically stable parameterization of a spline is provided by a B-spline basis. Let $\{s_k\}_{k=1}^{K}$ denote the knot points with $s_k < s_{k+1}, s_1 = 0$, and $s_K = M$, the

---

[2]If using DOS or Windows, truncate the file names as follows: yieldcur.m, showtime.m, pagelayo.m, bsplineb.m, commadel.m, triangul.m, and makecale.m.

maximum maturity of any bond in the sample.[3] The knot points define $K - 1$ intervals over the domain of the spline $[0, T]$. For the purpose of defining a B-spline basis, it is convenient to define an augmented set of knot points $\{d_k\}_{k=1}^{K+2r}$ where $d_1 = \cdots = d_r = s_1$, $d_{K+r+1} = \cdots = d_{K+2r} = s_K$, and $d_{k+r} = s_k$ for $1 \le k \le K$. Then a B-spline basis is a vector of $\kappa = K + r - 1$ order-r B-splines defined over the domain.

Here is an example.

```
In[1]:=  SetDirectory["/tr/data1/m1mef00/math/ycurve"]; (* your
                    directory here *)
         Needs["YieldCurve`"]; (* loads BSplineBasis as well *)
         Off[ShowTime]; (* turn off timings *)
```

0. Second

```
In[2]:=  knots = Range[0, 5];
         basisknots = PadKnots[knots, 3]

Out[2]=  {0, 0, 0, 0, 1, 2, 3, 4, 5, 5, 5, 5}
```

A B-spline is defined by the following recursion, where $1 \le k \le \kappa$.[4]

```
In[3]:=  (* i-th spline, r-th order, evaluated at tau *)
         phi[i_, r_, tau_] :=
           ((tau - k[i]) phi[i, r - 1, tau])/(k[i + r] - k[i]) +
            ((k[i + r + 1] - tau) phi[i + 1, r - 1, tau])/
                (k[i + r + 1] - k[i + 1])

         (* terminal condition *)
         phi[i_, 0, tau_] := d[i]

         (* i-th spline, j-th region, r-th order,
            evaluated at tau *)
         phi[i_, j_, r_, tau_] :=
           phi[i, r, tau] /. {d[j] -> 1, d[_] -> 0}
```

We can see that the fourth cubic B-spline is a function of five knot points beginning with k[4].

```
In[4]:=  Cases[phi[4, 3, tau], k[_], Infinity] //Union

Out[4]=  {k[4], k[5], k[6], k[7], k[8]}
```

The functional form for the fourth cubic spline over the sixth region (between k[6] and k[7]) is given by

---

[3] In all cases, we distribute the knot points according to the distribution of the final maturities of the bonds. For example, with three knot points, we place the single interior knot point s_2 at the median maturity.

[4] For a more detailed discussion of B-spline bases and their properties, see de Boor (1978).

```
In[5]:=  phi[4, 6, 3, tau]
```

```
Out[5]=                                       2
              (tau - k[4]) (-tau + k[7])
        ------------------------------------------ +
        (-k[4] + k[7]) (-k[5] + k[7]) (-k[6] + k[7])

                        (tau - k[5]) (-tau + k[7])
          ((-tau + k[8]) (--------------------------- +
                          (-k[5] + k[7]) (-k[6] + k[7])

          (tau - k[6]) (-tau + k[8])
          ----------------------------)) / (-k[5] + k[8])
          (-k[6] + k[7]) (-k[6] + k[8])
```

The function **MakeBSpline** will produce a **BSplineFunction**:

```
In[6]:=  ?MakeBSpline
```

MakeBSpline[knots, d:0] takes a list of knot points and
    returns an InterpolatingFunction that represents a
    B-spline of order Length[knots] - 2. Valid orders are 0
    (step function), 1 (linear), 2 (quadratic), and 3
    (cubic), or higher. (Higher order splines use less
    efficient routines.) If the optional second argument is
    given as 1, then the derivative of the spline is
    returned. If the optional third argument is given as -1,
    then the integral of the spline is returned.
    Differentiation is supported to any order; integration is
    supported to order -2.

We can construct a cubic **BSplineFunction** for the fourth B-spline over the sixth region:

```
In[7]:=  bs463 = MakeBSpline[Take[basisknots, {4, 8}]]
```

```
Out[7]=  BSplineFunction[{0, 4}, <>]
```

```
In[8]:=  Plot[bs463[tau], {tau, 0, 4}];
```

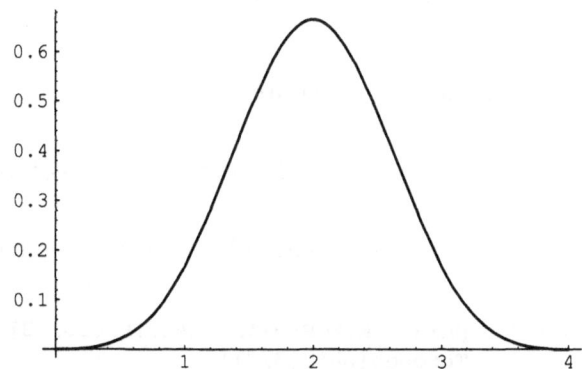

The internal structure of a **BSplineFunction** can be seen to be an **Interpo-latingFunction** wrapped in a **Which**.

```
In[9]:=  InputForm[bs463]

Out[9]=  BSplineFunction[{0, 4}, Which[#1 < 0, 0, #1 <= 4,
             InterpolatingFunction[{0, 4},
               {{0, 0, {0, 0}, {0}},
                {1, 0, {1/6, 1/2, 1/3, 1/6}, {0, 0, 1}},
                {2, 1, {2/3, 0, -1/2, -1/2}, {0, 0, 1}},
                {3, 2, {1/6, -1/2, 0, 1/2}, {0, 0, 1}},
                {4, 3, {0, 0, 1/6, -1/6}, {0, 0, 1}}}][#1],
               True, 0]\
             & ]
```

The **InterpolatingFunction** contains information about the polynomials that make up the B-spline. We can see the polynomials with **PlotIFPolynomials**.

```
In[10]:= PlotIFPolynomials[bs463];
```

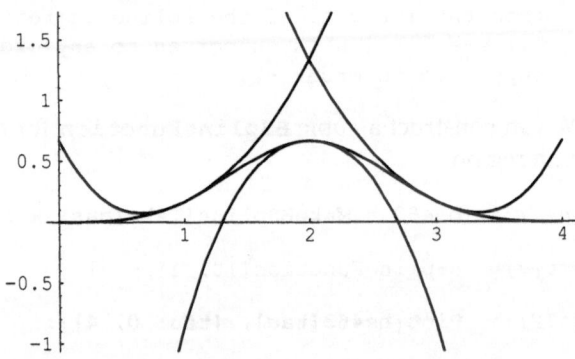

A *B-spline basis* is a row vector:

$$\phi^r(\tau) := (\phi_1^r(\tau), \ldots, \phi_\kappa^r(\tau)).$$

For example, we can make a cubic B-spline basis and evaluate it at $\tau = 3/2$.

```
In[11]:= phi3 = MakeBSplineBasis[knots, 3]
         Through[phi3[3/2]]
```

```
Out[11]= {BSplineFunction[{0, 1}, <>],
          BSplineFunction[{0, 2}, <>],
          BSplineFunction[{0, 3}, <>],
          BSplineFunction[{0, 4}, <>],
          BSplineFunction[{1, 5}, <>],
          BSplineFunction[{2, 5}, <>],
          BSplineFunction[{3, 5}, <>],
          BSplineFunction[{4, 5}, <>]}
```

$$Out[11]= \left\{0, \frac{1}{32}, \frac{15}{32}, \frac{23}{48}, \frac{1}{48}, 0, 0, 0\right\}$$

Over any interval between adjacent knot points s_k and s_{k+1} there are $r+1$ nonzero B-splines, with adjacent intervals sharing r. This gives $\phi^r(\tau)$ a semi-orthogonal structure from which it gets its numerical stability.

Here we plot $\phi^r(\tau)$ for r from 0 to 3 and τ from 0 to 5 over the knot points.

```
In[12]:= bases = Table[MakeBSplineBasis[knots, i], {i, 0, 3}];
         Show[GraphicsArray[Partition[
           PlotBSplineBasis[#,
             DisplayFunction -> Identity]& /@ bases, 2],
             DisplayFunction -> $DisplayFunction]];
```

Any r-order spline can be constructed from linear combinations of the B-splines, $\phi^r(\tau)\beta$, where $\beta := (\beta_1, \ldots, \beta_\kappa)^\top$ is a vector of coefficients. Now we plot $\phi^r(\tau)\beta$ for the given bases, where the βs are given by **Range[r + 5]**:

```
In[13]:= betas = Table[Range[r + 5], {r, 0, 3}];
         splines = MapThread[Through[#1[tau]] . #2 &,
             {bases, betas}];
         Show[GraphicsArray[Partition[
           Plot[#, {tau, 0, 5}, PlotRange -> {0, 8},
```

```
            Ticks -> {Automatic, {2,4,6,8}},
            DisplayFunction -> Identity]& /@ splines, 2]],
            DisplayFunction -> $DisplayFunction];
```

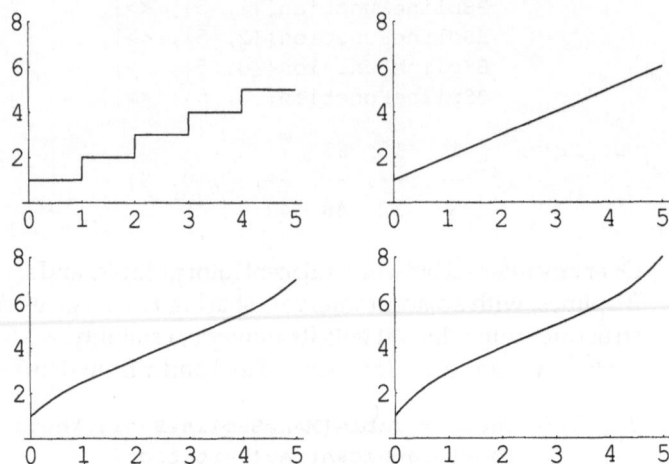

As an alternative, we can construct the linear combination directly with **Make-FinalSpline**:

```
In[14]:= fsplines = MakeFinalSpline[knots, #]& /@ betas;
         Plot[Evaluate[Through[fsplines[tau]]], {tau, 0, 5}];
```

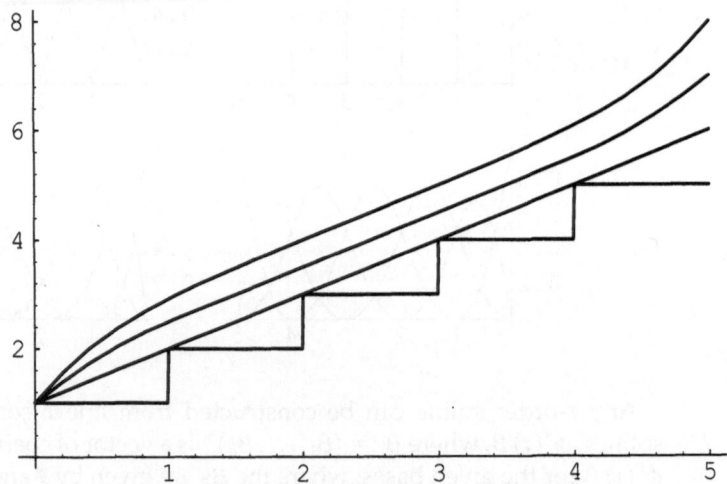

As is stands, $\phi^r(\tau)$ is a vector-valued function of a scalar argument, τ. In what follows, it proves useful to have notation for a B-spline basis as a function of vector-valued argument τ_i. To that end, define $\tilde{\phi}_k^r(\tau_i) := (\phi_k^r(\tau_{i1}), \ldots, \phi_k^r(\tau_{im_i}))^\top$, an $m_i \times 1$ column vector, and $\tilde{\phi}^r(\tau_i) := (\tilde{\phi}_1^r(\tau_i), \ldots, \tilde{\phi}_\kappa^r(\tau_i))$, an $m_i \times \kappa$ matrix.

The function **SplineMatrix** returns the matrix $\widetilde{\phi}^r(\tau_i)$. The quasi-orthogonal structure is evident in a plot.

```
In[15]:= taui = Table[i, {i, 0, 5, 1/3}];
         phi3mat = SplineMatrix[knots, taui, 3];
         ListPlot3D[phi3mat];
```

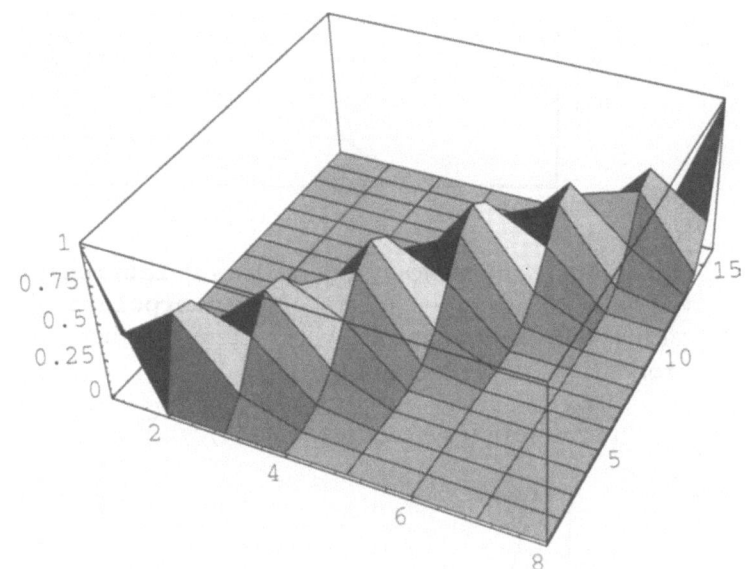

12.4   Splining Functional Forms

Consider splining each of the three functional forms: let $\delta_s(\tau) := \phi^r(\tau)\beta$, $\ell_s(\tau) := \phi^r(\tau)\beta$, and $f_s(\tau) := \phi^r(\tau)\beta$. In the latter two cases, we can transform the splined functional form to produce a discount function that can be used to represent present values—$\delta_s^\ell(\tau) := \exp(-\ell_s(\tau)) = \exp(\phi^r(\tau)\beta)$ and $\delta_s^f(\tau) = \exp(-\int_0^\tau f_s(u)\,du) = \exp(-\int_0^\tau \phi^r(u)\,\beta du) = \exp(-\psi(\tau)\beta)$, where $\psi(\tau) := \int_0^\tau \phi^r(u)\,\beta du$ is the integral of a B-spline basis.

We replace $\widetilde{\delta}(\tau_i)$ in the present value expression with the spline representation; where we had $\pi_i = c_i^\top \widetilde{\delta}(\tau_i)$, we now have (i) $\pi_i^\delta(\beta) = (c_i^\top \widetilde{\phi}^r(\tau_i))\beta$, (ii) $\pi_i^\ell(\beta) = c_i^\top \exp(-\widetilde{\phi}^r(\tau_i)\beta)$, and (iii) $\pi_i^f(\beta) = c_i^\top \exp(-\widetilde{\psi}^r(\tau_i)\beta)$.

In order to spline the forward rate curve, all spline-making functions can produce the integral of B-splines. For example,

```
In[16]:= bs463i = MakeBSpline[Take[basisknots, {4, 8}], -1];
         Plot[bs463i[x], {x, 0, 4}];
```

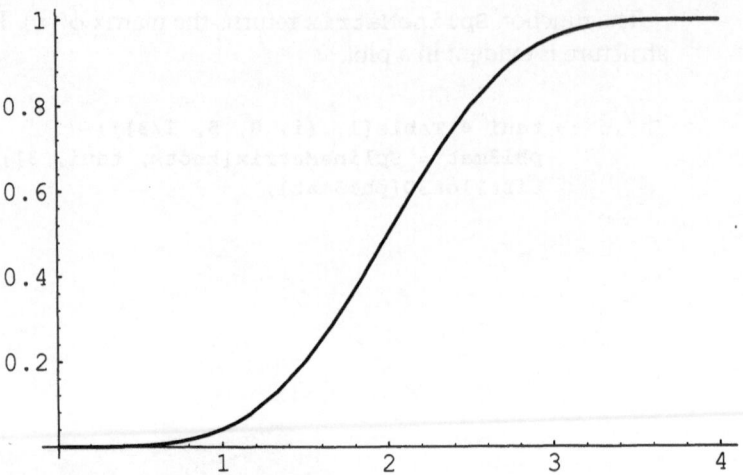

Mathematica automatically differentiates an **InterpolatingFunction**, but will not integrate it. The integral of an **InterpolatingFunction** is instead calculated by **IntegrateIF**, which returns another **InterpolatingFunction**.

In[17]:= **PlotIFPolynomials[bs463i];**

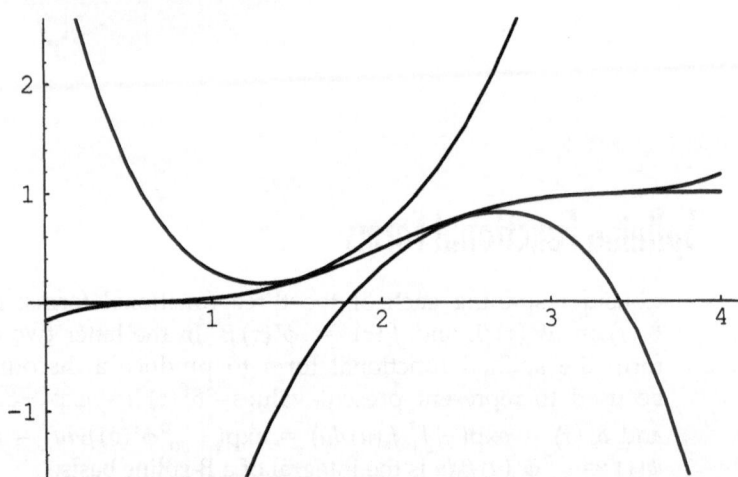

SplineMatrix can return $\widetilde{\psi}''(\tau_i)$, where the last argument indicates the order of differentiation (in this case integration).

In[18]:= **phi3int = SplineMatrix[knots, {1, 3/2, 4.2}, 3, -1]**

Out[18]=   1   7   13   1
          {{-, --, --,   --, 0, 0, 0, 0},
           4   16   48   24

$$\{-\frac{1}{4}, \; \frac{127}{256}, \; \frac{141}{256}, \; \frac{77}{384}, \; \frac{1}{384}, \; 0, \; 0, \; 0\},$$

$$\{-\frac{1}{4}, \; -\frac{1}{2}, \; -\frac{3}{4}, \; 1, \; 0.982933, \; 0.587867, \; 0.1288, \; 0.0004\}\}$$

Note that the integral of a B-spline basis does not retain the orthogonality of the B-Spline basis.

12.5 Regression Splines

Because neither $\pi_i^\ell(\beta)$ nor $\pi_i^f(\beta)$ is linear in β, we must use some sort of nonlinear least squares to find β^* for regression splines when we choose either of these functional forms.

Let P be an $n \times 1$ vector of bond prices p_i, and $\Pi(\beta)$ be the corresponding vector of present values of the bonds $\pi_i^j(\beta)$. Then for a regression spline, we choose β as follows.

$$\min_{\beta} [(P - \Pi(\beta))^\top (P - \Pi(\beta))].$$

Following Chow (1983), we linearize $\Pi(\beta)$ around an initial guess β^0,

$$\Pi(\beta) \approx \Pi(\beta^0) + (\beta - \beta^0) \frac{\partial \Pi(\beta)}{\partial \beta^\top} \bigg|_{\beta = \beta^0},$$

and define $X(\beta^0) := \partial \Pi(\beta)/\partial \beta^\top |_{\beta=\beta^0}$ and $Y(\beta^0) := P - \Pi(\beta^0) + \beta^0 X(\beta^0)$.
Rearranging the minimization problem using these definitions yields

$$\min_{\beta} \left[\left(Y(\beta^0) - X(\beta^0)\beta \right)^\top \left(Y(\beta^0) - X(\beta^0)\beta \right) \right].$$

The minimizer for the previous expression is

$$\beta^1 = \left(X(\beta^0)^\top X(\beta^0) \right)^{-1} X(\beta^0)^\top Y(\beta^0),$$

where β^1 is an updated β^0. We can use β^1 as the initial guess for the next iteration, obtaining β^2. We iterate until convergence. The solution is the fixed-point $\beta^* = (X(\beta^*)^\top X(\beta^*))^{-1} X(\beta^*)^\top Y(\beta^*)$.

On the other hand, $\pi_i^\delta(\beta)$ is linear in β, which is why splining the discount function is so attractive. The relationship between bond prices and present values can be written $p_i = x_i \beta + \varepsilon_i$, where the "independent variables" are the bond payments evaluated according to the B-spline basis; that is, $x_i := c_i^\top \widetilde{\phi}^r(\tau_i)$.

Now let X be the matrix corresponding to the x_i. We can use ordinary least squares (OLS) to determine $\beta^* = (X^\top X)^{-1} X^\top P$. This produces a regression spline of the discount function of the sort McCulloch used.

12.6 Smoothing Splines

A smoothing spline is a regression spline with a penalty for roughness. With a smoothing spline, one can use a large number of knot points but penalize excess variability in the estimated discount function. This results in reducing the effective number of parameters because the penalty forces implicit relationships between the parameters of the spline. The penalty we describe here applies only to a cubic spline. Let $h(\tau)$ be the function being splined. The penalty is defined as

$$\lambda \int_0^T h''(\tau)^2 d\tau,$$

a constant times the integral of the squared second derivative of the function being splined.

The penalty can be written in terms of the B-spline basis as follows:

$$\lambda \int_0^T \left(\frac{\partial^2 \phi^3(\tau) \beta}{\partial \tau^2} \right)^2 d\tau = \lambda \beta^\top \left(\int_0^T \phi^{3\prime\prime}(\tau)^\top \phi^{3\prime\prime}(\tau) d\tau \right) \beta = \lambda \beta^\top H \beta.$$

H is a $\kappa \times \kappa$ matrix that is band diagonal by the structure of a B-spline basis. Because any β that makes $h_s(\tau, \beta)$ linear in τ is not penalized, H has two zero eigenvalues. Also note that H is completely determined by the knot points. For example, we can construct H for the knots previously given.

```
In[19]:= H = PenaltyMatrix[knots, 3];
         NullSpace[H]

Out[19]= {{-14,  -13,  -11,  -8,  -5,  -2,  0,  1},
          {15,  14,  12,  9,  6,  3,  1,  0}}
```

We see the the null space of H is indeed two-dimensional.

The minimization problem can be stated as follows for a given λ.

$$\min_{\beta(\lambda)} \left[\left(P - \Pi(\beta(\lambda)) \right)^\top \left(P - \Pi(\beta(\lambda)) \right) + \lambda \, \beta(\lambda)^\top H \beta(\lambda) \right].$$

In general, the minimizer is found by nonlinear least squares as described in the previous section, iterating on

$$\beta^{i+1}(\lambda) = \left(X(\beta^i(\lambda))^\top X(\beta^i(\lambda)) + \lambda H \right)^{-1} X(\beta^i(\lambda))^\top Y(\beta^i(\lambda))$$

until convergence:

$$\beta^*(\lambda) = \left(X(\beta^*(\lambda))^\top X(\beta^*(\lambda)) + \lambda H\right)^{-1} X(\beta^*(\lambda))^\top Y(\beta^*(\lambda)).$$

(Note that when splining $\delta(\tau)$, $\beta^*(\lambda) = (X^\top X + \lambda H)^{-1} X^\top P$.)

Formally, the previous expression is a ridge regression estimator. By employing a roughness penalty, we can over-parameterize the spline, making $X(\beta^*(\lambda))^\top X(\beta^*(\lambda))$ nearly singular, and use the penalty to reduce the effective number of parameters. The penalty thus "solves" the multicollinearity problem. The advantage of this technique is that the shape of the spline is controlled by a single parameter λ.

One common measure of the effective number of parameters is the trace of $A(\lambda)$, denoted $\text{tr}(A(\lambda))$, where

$$A(\lambda) := X(\beta^*(\lambda)) \left(X(\beta^*(\lambda))^\top X(\beta^*(\lambda)) + \lambda H\right)^{-1} X(\beta^*(\lambda))^\top.$$

Note that $A(\lambda) Y(\beta^*(\lambda))$ is the vector of fitted Y values which in the linear case is the vector of fitted prices. The extreme cases are $\text{tr}(A(0)) = \kappa$ (with no penalty the number of effective parameters equals the number of B-splines), and $\text{tr}(A(\infty)) = 2$ (with an infinite penalty the number of effective parameters equals 2).

12.7 Generalized Cross Validation

In this section, we provide a technique for choosing the appropriate value for λ. We choose the value of λ that minimizes the *generalized cross validation* (GCV) value,

$$\gamma(\lambda) := \frac{\left((I - A(\lambda))Y(\beta^*(\lambda))\right)^\top \left((I - A(\lambda))Y(\beta^*(\lambda))\right)}{\left(n - \theta\,\text{tr}(A(\lambda))\right)^2}.$$

The numerator of the previous expression is the residual sum of squares. When $\theta = 1$, the denominator is the squared effective degrees of freedom (the difference between the number of observations and the effective number of parameters). The parameter θ is called the cost. It controls the tradeoff between goodness-of-fit and parsimony. In plain-vanilla GCV, $\theta = 1$. However, θ can be increased to reduce the signal extracted, thereby stiffening the spline.

When the discount function is splined directly, $A(\lambda) = X(X^\top X + \lambda H)^{-1} X^\top$ and there is a simplified expression for $\gamma(\lambda)$ that can be minimized directly. In general, however, a new $X(\beta^*(\lambda))$ matrix must be formed for each value of λ. Thus for each value of λ we test, we must solve for $\beta^*(\lambda)$ and then calculate

$\gamma(\lambda)$. The overall solution is given by

$$\beta^*(\lambda^*) = \left(X(\beta^*(\lambda^*))^\top X(\beta^*(\lambda^*)) + \lambda H \right)^{-1} X(\beta^*(\lambda^*))^\top Y(\beta^*(\lambda^*)),$$

where λ^* minimizes $\gamma(\lambda)$.

12.8   Implementing the Estimators

For smoothing splines, we need starting values for λ. However, λ is not free of units, thus it is not easy to know in advance what a good starting value is. At extreme values of λ (both large and small) the GCV function becomes flat and optimizers can get stuck at nonminimums. Experimenting with different values is important to find out where good starting values are for a given data set. We have found that starting near 10^{10} usually (but not always) converges to the true global minimum. In addition, one may need to "tune" the FindMinimum routine. For example, one may need to boost the accuracy goal; for example, AccuracyGoal -> 10.

When splining either $\ell(\tau)$ or $f(\tau)$, we need starting values for β as well. The fixed point problem will not converge with bad starting values. Fortunately, good starting values for β are easy to calculate. One of the properties of B-splines is that $\sum_{k=1}^{K} \phi(\tau) = 1$. As a consequence, the coefficients β track the value of the function $\phi(\tau)\beta$. Thus any reasonable estimate of the function to be splined can be used to form starting values. For example, suppose a crude estimate of the function to be splined is $\widehat{h}(\tau)$. Let the starting value for β_k be $\beta_{k0} = \frac{1}{3} \sum_{i=k}^{k+2} \widehat{h}(d_i)$. With these starting values, the fixed point problem converges rapidly. The internal default for the yield curve is a flat 5% curve. If DLStart.m or LStart.m is used, the yield curve stored in there is used.

12.9   Usage Overview

A typical session will include reading data, calculating when the coupon payments occur, and estimating the yield curve. In addition a session may include calculating yields and yield errors, and producing graphs and reports.

We start by reading some data.

```
In[20]:= md = ReadData["19880719.dat"]
```

```
Out[20]= -MD[{1988, 7, 19}]-
```

ReadData reads the data in 19880719.dat and creates an MD object, which in this case is named md. The MD object contains information about the bonds found in the input file. ReadData requires the data be in a particular format, which we can see as follows.

```
In[21]:= First @ ReadList["19880719.dat", String]
```

```
Out[21]= 7/19/1988,912794PY4,8/4/1988,0.5,0,99.7321
```

The order of fields is quote date, I.D. number, maturity date, original term to maturity (in years), coupon rate, and price per $100 of face value (not including accrued interest for coupon bonds).

Let us see what options **ReadData** takes.

```
In[22]:= Options[ReadData]
```

```
Out[22]= {Description -> {}}
```

One can add a description (a string or list of strings) to help keep track of different MD objects.

A list of information the object contains can be had by entering **MDSelectors**. The selectors can be used to extract information the bonds included.

```
In[23]:= MDSelectors
```

```
Out[23]= {CouponRate, Description, IDNumber, MaturityDate,
           NumberOfSecurities, Price, QuoteDate, SettlementDate,
           Term}
```

Here are two examples.

```
In[24]:= NumberOfSecurities[md]
         CouponRate[md] //Short
```

```
Out[24]= 224
```

```
Out[24]= {0, 0, 0, 0, 0, 0, 0, 0, <<212>>, 8.75, 8, 8.25, 8.875}
```

The next step is to construct all the payments (c_i) and the number of days to each payment (τ_i) for each of the bonds in the sample. We use **ConstructPayments**. First, let us see what the options are.

```
In[25]:= Options[ConstructPayments]
```

```
Out[25]= {FullPrice -> False, PaymentsPerYear -> 2}
```

These are the appropriate options for our data: U.S. Treasury coupon securities pay coupons every six months, and our coupon-bond price data does not include accrued interest (and therefore must be added by **ConstructPayments**). Neither of these options has an effect on bills or strips.

```
In[26]:= cp = ConstructPayments[md]
```

```
Out[26]= -CP[{1988, 7, 19}]-
```

ConstructPayments calculates the number of days to each coupon payment for each bond in the sample, using information in daycount.m. It takes an MD object as an argument and returns a CP object that contains a reference to the MD object used to create it. Thus CouponRate[cp] will return the same list of coupon rates for the bonds in the sample. **CPSelectors** will return a list of additional information stored in CP objects.

```
In[27]:= CPSelectors
```

```
Out[27]= {AccruedDays, AccruedInterest, DaysInPeriod,
          DaysToPayments, FullPriceQ, LastPayment, NextPayment,
          Payments, PaymentsPerYear, QuoteDate,
          RemainingPayments}
```

```
In[28]:= DaysToPayments[cp] //Shallow
         Payments[cp] //Shallow
         CouponRate[cp] //Shallow
```

```
Out[28]= {{15}, {43}, {71}, {99}, {128}, {155}, {1}, {8}, {22},
          {29}, <<214>>}
```

```
Out[28]= {{100}, {100}, {100}, {100}, {100}, {100}, {100},
          {100}, {100}, {100}, <<214>>}
```

```
Out[28]= {0, 0, 0, 0, 0, 0, 0, 0, 0, 0, <<214>>}
```

We see that each of the first 10 securities is a Treasury bill with one remaining payment of 100.

We are now ready to fit the term structure. **DiscountFunction** is the main estimation function. It takes a CP object as an argument and returns a DF object. The default functional form is DLogDelta, which indicates that the forward rates should be splined. The default LambdaValue is Automatic, which indicates the generalized cross validation should be used to determine the value of λ, the weight on the penalty. The DF object contains the results of the estimation including, for example, the estimated spline (FinalSpline[df]) and the difference between the actual and fitted bond prices (PriceError[df]).

First look at the options available for **DiscountFunction**.

```
In[29]:= Options[DiscountFunction]
```

```
Out[29]=                                        #2 - #1
         {BetaConvergenceTest -> (Max[Abs[-------]] < 0.0001 & ),
                                           #2
```

```
                          30
         Bounds -> {0., 1. 10  }, DropByTerm -> 0,
         FunctionalForm -> DLogDelta, IDNumberDropList -> {},
         InitialCurve -> Automatic, Knots -> Automatic,
         LambdaValue -> Automatic, Lambda0 -> Automatic,
```

```
                    MaximumMaturity -> 30,
                    ObservationWeights -> Automatic,
                    OvernightForwardRate -> Automatic,
                    Restriction -> True, ShowLambdaProgress -> True,
                    SplineOrder -> 3, TuningParameter -> 2}
```

In addition to the options listed, one can pass options for **FindMinimum** (such as AccuracyGoal -> 10).

It is always a good idea to read the usage statement.

In[30]:= **?DiscountFunction**

```
DiscountFunction[cp] estimates a discount function for a
    given day.  Run MassageData and ConstructPayments first
    to create the CP object. The default options are Knots ->
    (number of securities)/3, DropByTerm -> 0 (drop the 0
    most recently issued securities of each term),
    MaximumMaturity -> 30. The default FunctionalForm is
    DLogDelta, which uses a nonlinear routine to estimate the
    forward rate function; other functional forms are
    LogDelta and Delta. If DLogDelta or LogDelta is used,
    DiscountFunction takes options to set the starting values
    (Lambda0, Bounds, and options to tune FindMinimum) and
    looks for a file named "LStart.m" or "DLStart.m" to find
    starting values for beta0 and lambda0.  If the
    appropriate file cannot be opened, internal default
    values are used.
```

In[31]:= **df1 = DiscountFunction[cp, FunctionalForm -> Delta,
           LambdaValue -> 10^10]**

Out[31]= -DF[{1988, 7, 19}]-

Setting LambdaValue -> 10^10 fixes the value of λ without minimizing the GCV function. The **DFSelectors** can be used to extract information from the DF object.

In[32]:= **DFSelectors**

Out[32]= {AverageAbsoluteError, BetaHat, BetaHatCovarianceMatrix,
           Delta, DropByTerm, EffectiveParameters, FinalSpline,
           FixedLambdaQ, ForwardCurve, GCVMinimizedQ, GCVValue,
           KeepList, Knots, Lambda, MaximumMaturity,
           NumberOfObservations, ObservationWeights,
           PredictedPrice, PriceError, QuoteDate,
           ResidualVariance, RestrictionQ,
           SemiAnnualForwardCurve, SemiAnnualZeroCurve,
           Significance, SplineOrder, TuningParameter, ZeroCurve}

For example, we can find the average absolute pricing error.

In[33]:= **AverageAbsoluteError[df1]**

Out[33]= 0.82538

This is an error of 82.5 basis points per $100 of face value—which is not very good. We see why in a moment.

There are other functions that take DF objects as arguments as well. For example,

In[34]:= **DFSummaryStatistics[df1]**

Out[34]= no. of obs.........   224
       longest payment....   29.82 years
       no. dropped.......   0
       functional form.... Delta
       restriction....... True
       minimize GCV....... False
       tuning parameter...   2
       no. of knots.......   74
       no. of parameters..   31.8
       lambda............   1.00e10
       residual variance..   7.53003
       avg. abs. error....   0.8254

We see that the number of knot points (chosen automatically) is 74, but with the penalty we used, $\lambda = 10^{10}$, the effective number of parameters is only 31.8. Here are the forward rate (dashing) and zero-coupon rate curves (if a color screen is available, use the option Color -> True in **ShowGraph**).

In[35]:= **ShowGraph[df1, PlotStyle -> {Dashing[{.02, .01}],{}}];**

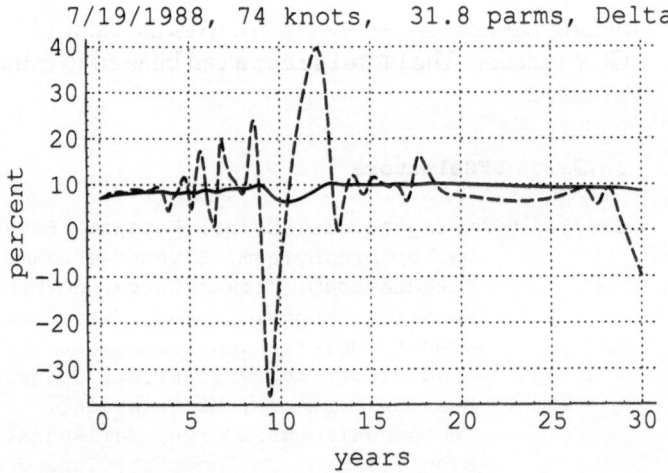

Both **ShowGraph** and **DFSummaryStatistics** can be combined with **DFSummaryPage**, which is especially useful for sending reports to a printer:

```
In[36]:= DFSummaryPage[df1,ShowPageBorders -> False,
            PlotStyle -> {Dashing[{.02, .01}],{}},
            Title -> "Way over-parameterized"];
```

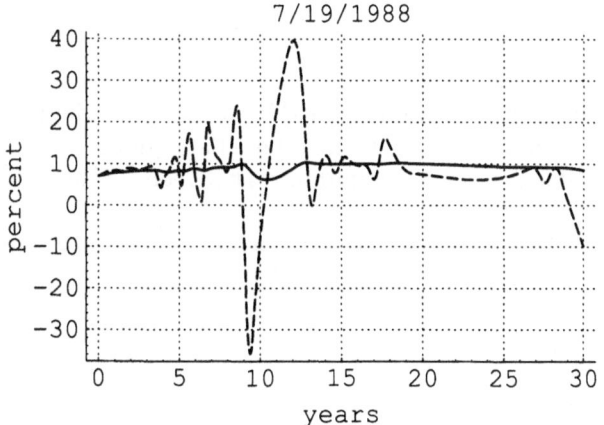

Way over-parameterized

```
no. of obs.........    224
longest payment....    29.82 years
no. dropped........    0
functional form....    Delta
restriction........    True
minimize GCV.......    False
tuning parameter...    2
no. of knots.......    74
no. of parameters..    31.8
lambda.............    1.00e10
residual variance..    7.53003
avg. abs. error....    0.8254
```

This looks bad—the term structure is over-parameterized. Let us examine the generalized cross-validation function:

```
In[37]:= Plot[GCVFunction[10^x], {x, 0, 20}];
```

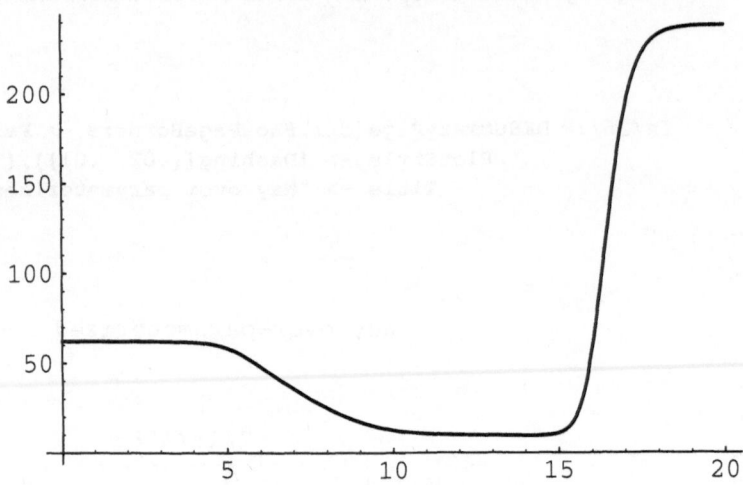

Notice the function is flat at both ends. An adaptive optimizer (such as **Find-Minimum**) can get stuck in these flat regions.

It looks as if the minimum is between 10^{10} and 10^{16}.

```
In[38]:= Plot[GCVFunction[10^x], {x, 10, 16}];
```

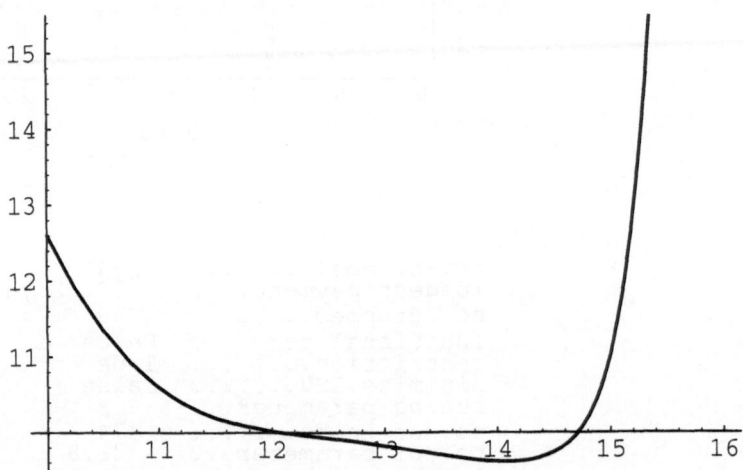

The minimum appears to be close to 10^{14}. Let us use that as a starting value to apply GCV. Note that a pair of starting values is required.

```
In[39]:= df2 = DiscountFunction[cp, FunctionalForm -> Delta,
            DropNumber -> 0, Lambda0 -> {10^14, 1.1 10^14}];
        {Lambda[df2], EffectiveParameters[df2],
            AverageAbsoluteError[df2]}
```

Out[39]=   14
                    {1.16709 10   , 4.14526, 0.919242}

We see that λ^* is close to our guess, and that the number of parameters has fallen to 4.1 whereas the average absolute error has risen a bit to 92 basis points. Let us look at the yield curves.

In[40]:= **ShowGraph[df2, PlotStyle -> {Dashing[{.02, .01}],{}}];**

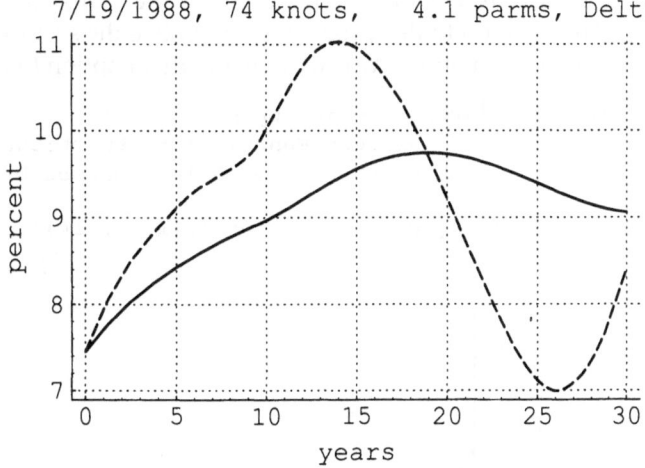

These curves are much more well-behaved. But recall that the average pricing error is large (for Treasury bonds). Let us look at the pricing errors.

In[41]:= **MaturityPlot[PriceError[df2]];**

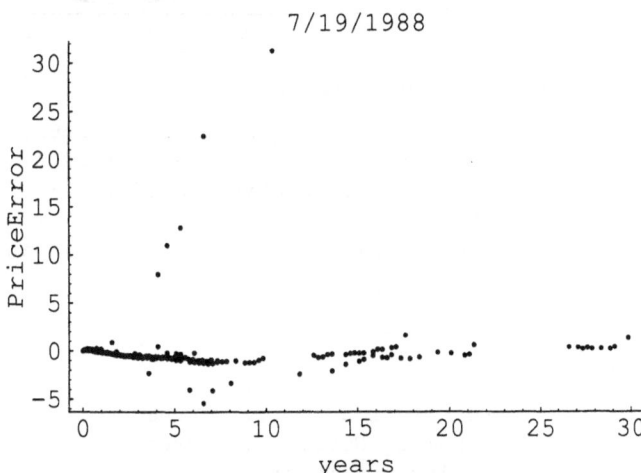

There are a few enormous outliers. What is wrong with these securities? The answer is that we have included some callable bonds and some flower bonds in the sample. The prices of these bonds reflect features that are not captured directly in the present value function. Including them in the estimation will affect the results as follows. First, their inclusion will affect the value of β^*, the estimated spline coefficients, conditional on the value of λ. But perhaps more important, their inclusion will affect the value of λ chosen via GCV. This is because minimizing the GCV function is a signal-extraction technique. Therefore when there is more noise in the data, a larger penalty will be chosen for a smoother curve at the expense of the sum-of-squares fit.

The solution to this problem is to remove the securities with special features from the estimation. We can do that with an option to **DiscountFunction**:

```
In[42]:= iddrop = << iddrop.m;
         df3 = DiscountFunction[cp, FunctionalForm -> Delta,
            LambdaValue -> 10^10, IDNumberDropList -> iddrop];
```

```
In[43]:= Plot[GCVFunction[10^x],{x, 8, 14}];
```

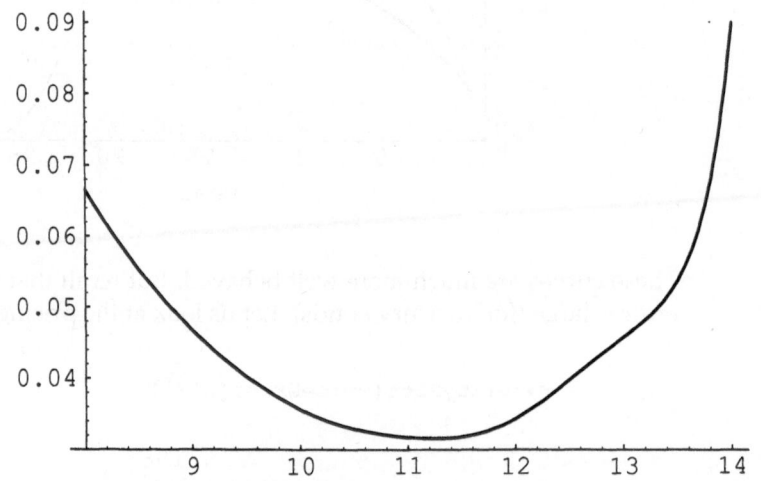

Now the minimum is between 10^{11} and 10^{12}.

```
In[44]:= df4 = DiscountFunction[cp, FunctionalForm -> Delta,
            Lambda0 -> {10^11.5, 1.1 10^11.5},
            IDNumberDropList -> iddrop];
         DFSummaryStatistics[df4]
         ShowGraph[df4, PlotStyle -> {Dashing[{.02, .01}],{}}];
```

```
Out[44]= no. of obs.........    196
         longest payment....      29.82 years
         no. dropped........        0
         functional form....    Delta
         restriction........    True
         minimize GCV.......    True
         tuning parameter...        2
```

```
no. of knots.......      65
no. of parameters..      15.4
lambda.............      1.74e11
residual variance..      0.02436
avg. abs. error....      0.0990
```

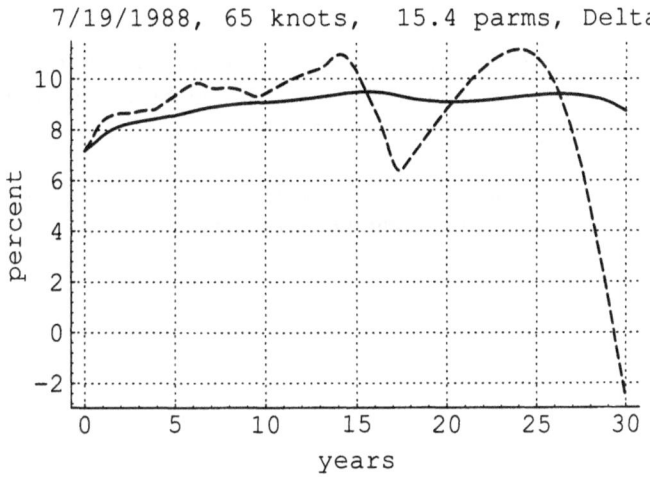

7/19/1988, 65 knots, 15.4 parms, Delta

The number of effective parameters is 15.4 and the average absolute error is down to about 10 basis points. This is quite an improvement from the previous fit.

It turns out that there is another class of securities that tends to have another additional feature that is not captured in the present value of the stated payments. The one or two most recently issued securities of a given original term-to-maturity are often on special in the repo market. As such, an additional stream of payments can be obtained in the financing market by the holder. We can screen out the most recently issued securities by term with another option to **DiscountFunction**, DropByTerm.

```
In[45]:= df5 = DiscountFunction[cp, FunctionalForm -> Delta,
           DropByTerm -> 2,
           Lambda0 -> {10^11.5, 1.1 10^11.5},
           IDNumberDropList -> iddrop];
```

Having dropped the two most recently issued securities of each original term to maturity, the pricing errors are a bit smaller. And although the number of knots chosen was 7 fewer, the number of effective parameters dropped by less than 4.

Let us use this discount function for an illustrative digression (even though it could probably be improved on by using a different functional form). Consider a coupon bond with a face value of $1 that pays its coupon as a continuous stream—an instantaneous coupon bond. Let this bond mature at time τ. The (instantaneous) swap rate is the coupon rate that makes the value of this bond equal $1 today. The (instantaneous) forward swap rate is the coupon rate that

makes the forward value of the bond equal the forward value of $1 at time t'.
Here is the formula for the forward swap rate.

$$s(t, t', \tau) = \frac{\delta(t') - \delta(\tau)}{\int_{t'}^{\tau} \delta(u)\, du}.$$

We can plot the instantaneous forward swap surface as follows. First extract
$\delta(\tau)$ from the DF object (otherwise the plotting routine will run much slower)
and then run **PlotSwapSurface**:

```
In[46]:= delta = Delta[df5];
         PlotSwapSurface[delta];
```

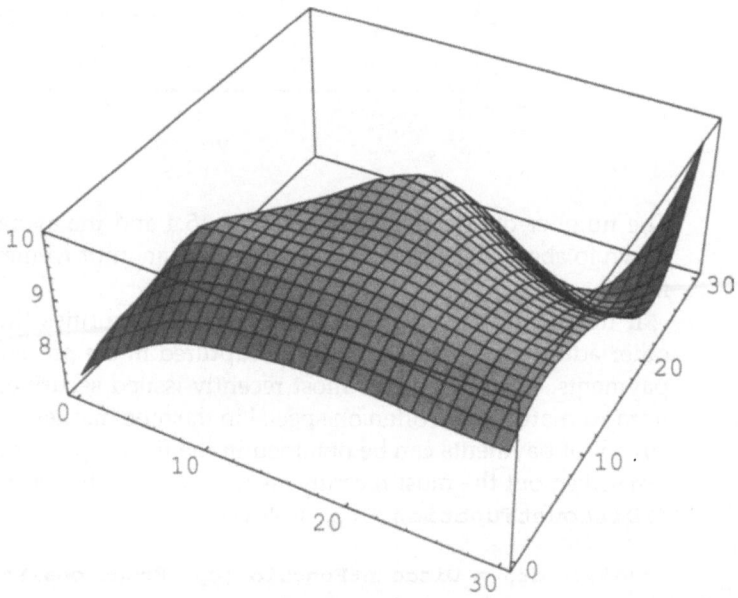

The spot swap curve (also known as the par coupon yield curve) is on the nearest
face, whereas the forward rate curve runs along the diagonal. **PlotSwapSurface** calls **TriangularPlot3D**, a package that is included in the distribution.
   Now let us calculate the actual and fitted yields. First consider how to compute
the compounding. The default uses the Securities Industry Association Standard
Securities Calculation Methods.

```
In[47]:= Options[YieldCalc]
         ?Compounding
```

```
Out[47]= {Compounding -> SIACompounding}
```

Compounding is an option for YieldCalc that specifies how to
handle the compounding of yields. The Default is
Compounding -> SIACompounding, which specifies the use of
the Securities Industry Association formulas. Currently
this handles zeros incorrectly. The other valid setting
is Compounding -> ContinuousCompounding, which specifies
the use of continuous compounding for bills and zeros.
Compounding is also a YCSelector. It returns the setting
used for the constructions of the YC object.

SIACompounding is useful for comparisons with yields quoted in the news-
paper. On the other hand, to compare the yields on bills or strips to the
continuously compounded **ZeroCurve**, it is useful to use Compounding ->
ContinuousCompounding. (As an alternative, one can use **SemiAnnualZe-
roCurve** instead.)

Now let us calculate the actual and fitted yields.

In[48]:= **yc = YieldCalc[df5]**

Out[48]= -YC[{1988, 7, 19}]-

YieldCalc calculates yield to maturity for each of the bonds in the sample
(Yield[yc]) and the difference between that yield and the predicted yield
(YieldError[yc]), among other things. **YieldCalc** can be run on a CP object,
in which case it will not attempt to calculate predicted yields.

In[49]:= **MaturityPlot[Yield[yc]];**

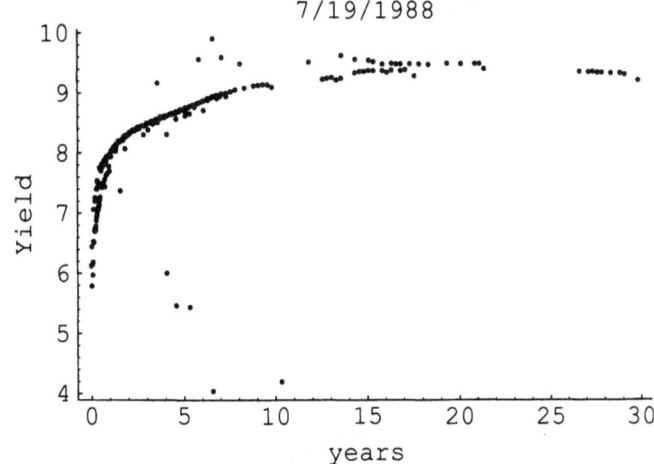

Although yields are plotted in percent, yield errors are plotted in basis points.

In[50]:= **MaturityPlot[YieldError[yc]];**

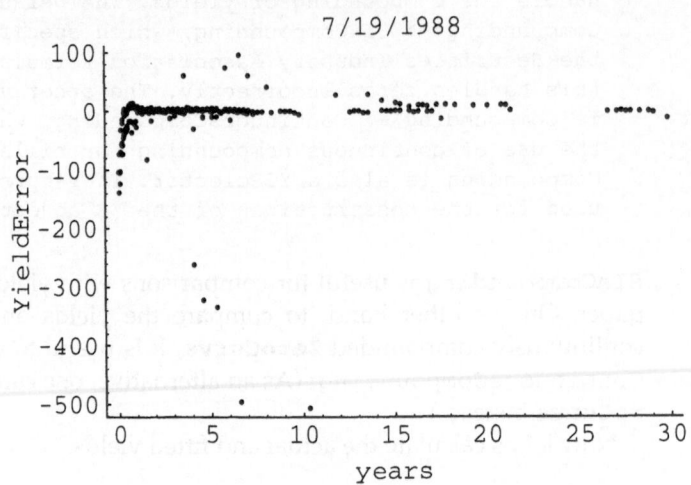

So far we have restricted ourselves to splining the discount function directly, largely for speed considerations. With a large number of securities, the nonlinear routines run quite slowly. So to speed things up, we spline only Treasury bills.

In[51]:= **pos = Flatten @ Position[CouponRate[md], 0|0.];**
          mdbills = MDSubset[md, pos];
          cpbills = ConstructPayments[mdbills];

For comparison purposes, we spline the discount function first with no penalty.

In[52]:= **dfbills1 = DiscountFunction[cpbills,**
              FunctionalForm -> Delta, MaximumMaturity -> 1,
              LambdaValue -> 0]

Out[52]= -DF[{1988, 7, 19}]-

In[53]:= **PlotGCVFunction[];**

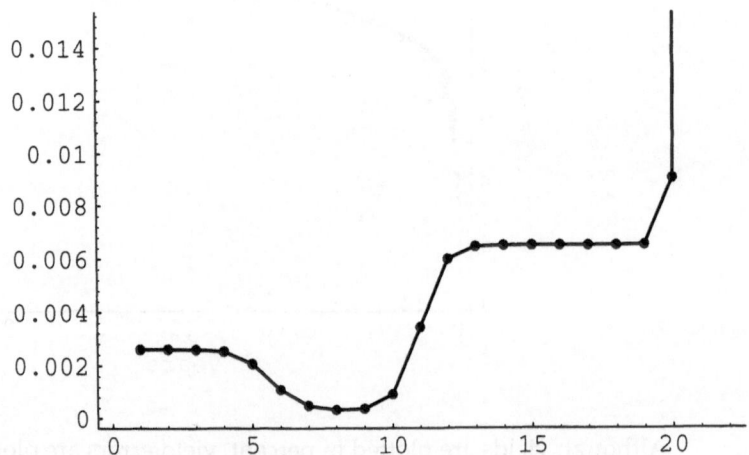

```
In[54]:= dfbills2 = DiscountFunction[cpbills,
            FunctionalForm -> Delta, MaximumMaturity -> 1,
            Lambda0 -> {10^8, 10^9}];

Out[54]= -DF[{1988, 7, 19}]-

In[55]:= dfbills3 = DiscountFunction[cpbills, DropNumber -> 0,
            FunctionalForm -> DLogDelta, MaximumMaturity -> 1,
            LambdaValue -> 0];

lambdastar = 0

Out[55]= -DF[{1988, 7, 19}]-

In[56]:= PlotGCVFunction[];
```

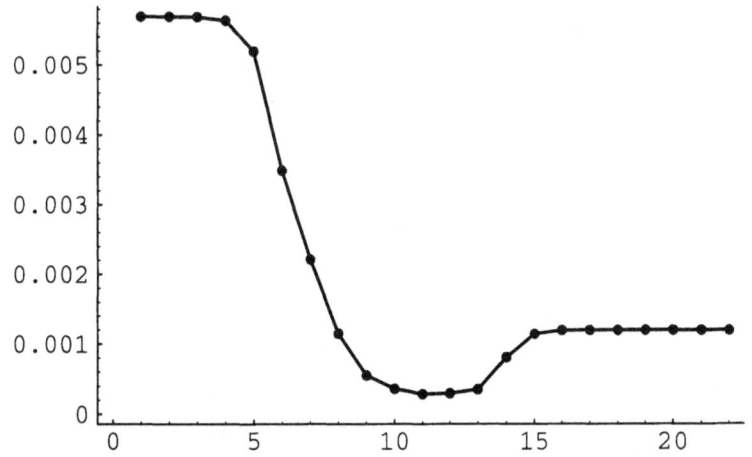

```
In[57]:= dfbills4 = DiscountFunction[cpbills,
            FunctionalForm -> DLogDelta, MaximumMaturity -> 1,
            Lambda0 -> {10^11, 10^12}];

lambda = 1.*10^11
lambda = 8.*10^10
lambda = 1.12360679775*10^11
lambda = 1.11014526840039*10^11
lambda = 1.200000000000047*10^11
lambda = 1.076393202250034*10^11
lambda = 1.152786404500073*10^11
                           11
lambdastar = 1.15279 10

Out[57]= -DF[{1988, 7, 19}]-
```

Note that when the functional form is either LogDelta or DLogDelta, the option ShowLambdaProgress controls whether the adaptive search routine reports its progess. For long calculations involving many securities and many knot points, it is useful to see how λ evolved and where it ended if the calculation was ultimately aborted or if it bombed.

Now let us compare the graphs of the two estimation techniques:

```
In[58]:= ShowGraph[dfbills2];
         ShowGraph[dfbills4];
```

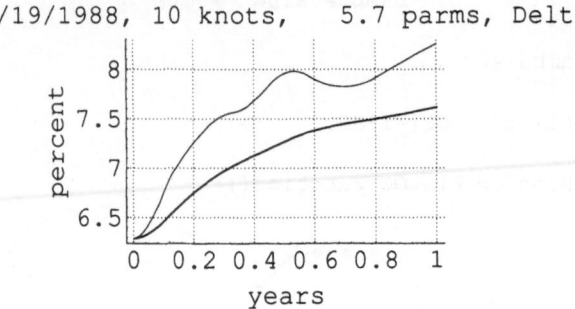

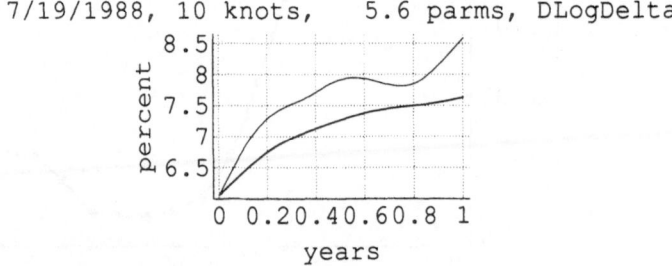

These results are very similar looking in this case. In other cases, the results may differ substantially.

12.10   Two Ways to Use the Program

12.10.1   Interactive

The program was designed to facilitate an interactive examination of how well different splining methods fit the term structure. To that end, we have built in flexibility as to the number and placement of knot points, the functional form to be splined, and the size and technique of choosing the penalty. The way in which we have stored the output at each stage (in a self-contained, insulated object) allows the user to have multiple estimates of the term structure available at once, making comparisons easy. For example, one can run **DiscountFunction** with different settings on the same data as we have done previously. All of this is easily accomplished by giving different objects different names.

12.10.2   Estimation Loop

Some users may wish to run the same settings on many different days of data and save some of the results to a file. Here are some suggestions as to how to do that. In a separate subdirectory (for convenience) create the data files, one per day. Name them in such a way that they are in calendar order (for convenience). Use **SetDirectory** to change the directory. Use **FileNames** to get a list of the file names. Write a function that (*i*) estimates the term structure according to the chosen settings and (*ii*) extracts the wanted information and appends it to a file. Map that function onto the list of filenames.

Here is an example of such a function. It takes two arguments, an input file name (where to find the data), and an output file name (where to append the results).

```
In[59]:= EstimationLoop[in_String, out_String] :=
         Module[{md, cp, df, qd, zc, fc, zeros, forwards},
         (* estimate the term structure *)
         md = ReadData[in]; (* or use a version of
            MassageData *)
         cp = ConstructPayments[md];
         df = DiscountFunction[cp]; (* use your settings *)
         (* extract the zero and forward curves *)
         zc = ZeroCurve[df];
         fc = ForwardCurve[df];
         (* read off zero and forward rates every 6 months *)
         zeros = Table[{m, zc[m Years]}, {m, .5, 30, .5}];
         forwards = Table[{m, fc[m Years]}, {m, 0, 30, .5}];
         (* get the instantaneous zero rate from the forward
            curve *)
         PrependTo[zeros, First @ forwards];
         (* prepare data for file *)
         qd = DateToString @ QuoteDate[md];
         zeros = Join[{qd, "z"}, #]& /@ zeros;
         forwards = Join[{qd, "f"}, #]& /@ forwards;
         (* append data to output file *)
         AppendDelimited[out, #]& /@ {zeros, forwards}]
```

Here is the usage: **EstimationLoop[#, "output.dat"]& /@ fn**, where fn is the list of input data file names. A typical row in output.dat will look like the following.

```
In[60]:=  9/29/1993,z,7.5,5.21428
```

```
Syntax::sntxf:
   " 9/29/1993" cannot be followed by ",z,7.5,5.21428".
```

This file can be read back into *Mathematica* using

```
In[61]:= data = ReadDelimited["output.dat",
              {Date, String, Number, Number}];
```

It can also be searched using **FindList**. (Note that **AppendDelimited** and **WriteDelimited** are defined in the package CommaDelimited, which is distributed with YieldCurve.)

12.11 The Structure of MD, CP, and DF Objects

In this section we describe the structure of MD, CP, and DF objects. These objects are merely "wrappers" that contain (and hide) the data and results. This section serves two purposes: it helps those who wish to write their own version of **ReadData** (or its older cousin, **MassageData**), and it introduces the overall structure of the YieldCurve package.

12.11.1 MD Objects

The structure of the flat file can be seen as follows. We select a few rows from the file.

```
In[62]:= pos = {1, 30, 60, -1};
         ReadList["19880719.dat", String][[ pos ]]
```

```
Out[62]= {7/19/1988,912794PY4,8/4/1988,0.5,0,99.7321,
          7/19/1988,912794SC9,6/8/1989,0.5,0,93.5669,
          7/19/1988,912810CM8,2/15/2005,25,11.75,118.719,
          7/19/1988,912827WK4,7/15/1995,7,8.875,99.625}
```

The fields in the file are quote date, identification number, maturity date, original term to maturity (in years), coupon rate, and price per hundred dollars of face value (in decimal form). The price does not include accrued interest for coupon bonds. Note that fields are separated by commas with no intervening spaces. The identification number and the term are both required, but neither need be meaningful nor unique. (In fact, in the preceding data , the term for all bills is set to 0.5, which is not true because some bills have an original term to maturity of 1 year.) The identification number is useful for IDNumberDropList and the term is useful for DropByTerm, both options of **DiscountFunction**.

We can easily create a mini-MD object of these five securities to see what it looks like internally.

```
In[63]:= ?MDSubset
```

```
MDSubset[md, poslist] creates an MD object that contains a
    subset of bonds from another MD object according to the
    list of positions given.
```

```
In[64]:= mdsub = MDSubset[md, pos];
         InputForm[mdsub]

Out[64]= MD[{1988, 7, 19}, {{1988, 8, 4}, {1989, 6, 8},
            {2005, 2, 15}, {1995, 7, 15}}, {0.5, 0.5, 25, 7},
            {0, 0, 11.75, 8.875}, {99.7321, 93.5669, 118.719,
            99.625}, {"912794PY4", "912794SC9", "912810CM8",
            "912827WK4"}, {}]
```

The MD object contains seven items, each of which is accessible via an MDSelector: **QuoteDate, MaturityDate, Term, CouponRate, Price, ID-Number**, and **Description**. An additional MDSelector, **SettlementDate**, is not contained in the MD object; instead, it is calculated on demand.

```
In[65]:= First @ ReadList["openmkt.dat", String]

Out[65]= {1993,10,27} 912810DP0 {2015,2,15} 11.250 10957 159.13
```

```
In[66]:= mdopen = MassageData[OpenMarket]

Out[66]= -MD[{1993, 10, 27}]-
```

MassageData[OpenMarket] reads the file openmkt.dat. That file has a different structure. In particular, security price quotes are given; bills are quoted as banker's discounts and coupon securities are quoted in 32nds.

MassageData[Strips] looks for the flat file strips.dat in the working directory and assumes it has the following structure.

```
In[67]:= Take[ReadList["strips.dat", String], 3]

Out[67]= {9/30/1994,11/15/1994,99.46875,
            9/30/1994,11/15/1994,99.46875,
            9/30/1994,2/15/1995,98.09375}
```

Note the following differences in structure from the previous input flat files. There are only three fields per record: quote date, maturity date, and price as a decimal. The missing information, which is not necessary to run **Discount-Function**, is simply "made up" by **MassageData**.

In this case, the terms-to-maturity are arbitrarily set to −1 and the **IDNumbers** are set to "N/A". The **Description** is set to {"Strips"}. The term of −1 is used by **ConstructPayments** to distinguish strips from bills for the purposes of the Security Industry Association's standard securities yield calculations, which treat bills and strips separately.[5]

---

[5]Bills and strips are treated the same when yields are calculated continuously using **Compounding** -> **ContinuousCompounding**.

If one wanted to distinguish between principal and coupon strips, one could add a fourth column to `strips.dat` with an **IDNumber** that took on two values, say, "P" for principal and "C" for coupon. Then one could use the option `IDNumberDropList -> "P"` to specify that only principal should be used in the estimation.

The user may write a different **ReadData** or **MassageData** function to read data in a different form. What is required for the program to work properly is to have the new **MassageData** produce an MD object with the correct internal structure. More on this in the following.

Here is the relevant *Mathematica* code that sets up the **MDSelectors** and formats the MD objects.

```
In[68]:= MD /: QuoteDate[md_MD]          := md[[1]]
         MD /: MaturityDate[md_MD]       := md[[2]]
         MD /: Term[md_MD]               := md[[3]]
         MD /: CouponRate[md_MD]         := md[[4]]
         MD /: Price[md_MD]              := md[[5]]
         MD /: IDNumber[md_MD]              := md[[6]]
         MD /: Description[md_MD]        := md[[7]]
         MD /: NumberOfSecurities[md_MD] := Length[Price[md]]
         MD /: SettlementDate[md_MD] := FirstBusinessDay @
             DaysPlus[QuoteDate[md], BusinessDaysToSettlement]
         MD /: WhenceMD[md_MD]           := md

         Format[md_MD] := StringForm["-MD['1']-", QuoteDate[md]]

         MDSelectors = Sort @ {QuoteDate, MaturityDate, Term,
             CouponRate, Price, IDNumber, Description,
             SettlementDate}
```

12.11.2 CP Objects

Here is the `InputForm` of the CP object created by **ConstructPayments** from mdsub.

```
In[69]:= cpsub = ConstructPayments[mdsub];
         InputForm[cpsub]

Out[69]= CP[{1988, 7, 19}, {{100}, {100},
             {5.875, 5.875, 5.875, 5.875, 5.875, 5.875, 5.875,
             5.875, 5.875, 5.875, 5.875, 5.875, 5.875, 5.875,
             5.875, 5.875, 5.875, 5.875, 5.875, 5.875, 5.875,
             5.875, 5.875, 5.875, 5.875, 5.875, 5.875, 5.875,
             5.875, 5.875, 5.875, 5.875, 5.875, 105.875},
             {4.4375, 4.4375, 4.4375, 4.4375, 4.4375, 4.4375,
             4.4375, 4.4375, 4.4375, 4.4375, 4.4375, 4.4375,
             4.4375, 104.4375}}, {{15}, {323},
```

```
{26, 210, 391, 575, 756, 940, 1121, 1308, 1489,
 1672, 1853, 2036, 2217, 2401, 2582, 2766, 2948,
 3135, 3313, 3499, 3680, 3863, 4044, 4227, 4409,
 4593, 4774, 4958, 5139, 5326, 5504, 5690, 5871,
 6054},
{181, 362, 545, 726, 909, 1090, 1274, 1456, 1640,
 1821, 2008, 2186, 2372, 2553}}, {0, 0, 155, 5},
{2, 2, 2, 2},
False, Hold[mdsub]]
```

There are seven items contained in the object, all of which can be extracted (i.e.,
selected) by the CPSelectors: **QuoteDate**, **Payments**, **DaysToPayments**,
AccruedDays, **PaymentsPerYear**, **FullPrice**, and **WhenceMD**. The other
CPSelectors calculate what they return on demand.

12.11.3   DF Objects

Here is the InputForm of the DF object created by DiscountFunction from
the CP object previously given.

```
In[70]:= dfsub = DiscountFunction[cpsub, MaximumMaturity -> 16.6,
           Knots -> 0, FunctionalForm -> Delta,
           LambdaValue -> 0]


Out[70]= -DF[{1988, 7, 19}]-


In[71]:= InputForm[dfsub]


Out[71]= DF[{1988, 7, 19}, InterpolatingFunction[{0, 6064},
          {{0, 0, {1, 0}, {0}},
           {6064, 0, {0.2117929536117513,
             -0.00001535208454085584, 1.890324679160249*10^-8,
             1.195289841813016*10^-12}, {0, 0, 6064}}}], 0, 3,
         Delta, {0.03298646745656697, -0.001870960109926045,
          -(2.131225215862287*10^-6), 0.00003979571182810559},
         {1, 2, 3, 4}, 0.001091609115236887,
         0.00872483862588425,
         {0.996796948422626, -0.04007415733109442,
          -0.00004561217393878103, 0.000851702378932987},
         {0, 6064}, {{0, 0, 0, 0},
          {0, 0.005933603944256982, -0.01007417955412868,
           0.001370051508054565},
          {0, -0.01007417955412868, 0.01787216815776105,
           -0.002587323349510649},
          {0, 0.001370051508054565, -0.002587323349510649,
           0.0004489482759882174}},
         {1, 0.5944046122549978, 0.2428246338303346,
          0.2117929536117513}, True, 0, True, 2, Automatic, 3,
         0.001091609116883774, Hold[cpsub]]
```

There are 21 items contained in the object, all of which can be extracted (i.e., selected) by the DFSelectors: **QuoteDate**, **FinalSpline**, **Lambda**, **EffectiveParameters**, **FunctionalForm**, **PriceError**, **KeepList**, **ResidualVariance**, **AverageAbsoluteError**, **Significance**, **Knots**, **BetaHatCovarianceMatrix**, **BetaHat**, **Restriction**, **DropByTerm**, **FixedLambda**, **TuningParameter**, **ObservationWeights**, **SplineOrder**, **GCVValue**, and **WhenceCP**. The remaining DFSelectors calculate what they return on demand.

12.12   References

Adams, K. J. and D. R. Van Deventer. 1994. "Fitting Yield Curves and Forward Rate Curves with Maximum Smoothness." *Journal of Fixed Income*, June, 52–62.

Bliss, R. R., Jr. 1993. "Testing Term Structure Estimation Methods." Working Paper, Indiana University.

Chambers, D., W. Carleton, and D. Waldman. 1984. "A New Approach to Estimation of Term Structure of Interest Rates." *Journal of Financial and Quantitative Studies*, **19**, 3, 233–252.

Chow, G. C. 1983. *Econometrics*. New York, McGraw-Hill.

Coleman, T. S., L. Fisher, and R. Ibbotson. 1992. "Estimating the Term Structure of Interest From Data That Include the Prices of Coupon Bonds." *The Journal of Fixed Income*, September, 85–116.

de Boor, C. 1978. *A Practical Guide to Splines*. New York, Springer-Verlag.

Fisher, M., D. Nychka, and D. Zervos. 1995. "Fitting the term structure of interest rates with smoothing splines." Federal Reserve Board Working Paper 95-1.

Gilles, C. 1994. "Forward Rates and Expected Future Short Rates." Working paper, Federal Reserve Board.

Jordan, J.V. 1984. "Tax Effects in Term Structure Estimation." *Journal of Finance*, **39**, 2, 393–406.

McCulloch, J. H. 1971. "Measuring the Term Structure of Interest Rates." *Journal of Business*, **44**, 19–31.

McCulloch, J. H. 1975. "The Tax-Adjusted Yield Curve." *Journal of Finance*, **30**, 811–830.

Nelson, C. and A. Siegel. 1987. "Parsimonious Modeling of Yield Curves." *Journal of Business*, **60**, 4, 473–489.

Shea, G. 1984. "Pitfalls in Smoothing Interest Rate Term Structure Data: Equilibrium Models and Spline Approximations." *Journal of Financial and Quantitative Studies*, **19**, 3, 253–269.

Shea, G. 1985. "Interest Rate Term Structure Estimation with Exponential Splines: A Note." *Journal of Finance*, **40**, 1, 319–325.

Vasicek, O. and G. Fong. 1982. "Term Structure Estimation Using Exponential Splines." *Journal of Finance*, **38**, 339–348.

Wahba, G. 1990. *Spline Models for Observational Data*. Philadelphia, SIAM.

Part III

Statistics

13 Log Spectral Analysis: Variance Components of Asset Prices

Luke M. Froeb

13.1 Introduction

The variance of a stationary time series can be decomposed into two distinct components: that part which is due to the innovation variance of the series, and that part due to the pattern of autocorrelation in the series. Innovations, sometimes called "shocks," are the part of the series which is "new" or uncorrelated with the past. A large innovation variance means that shocks to the series are large, and strong autocorrelation means that shocks are relatively persistent. Both lead to large variance.

As an example, consider the first-order autoregressive process, $x_t = c*x_{t-1}+e_t$, with "innovation," $e_t = x_t - E[x_t \mid x_{t-1}, x_{t-2}, x_{t-3}, \ldots]$, and variance, $\text{Var}(x_t) = \sigma^2/(1 - c^2)$; $\sigma^2 = \text{Var}(e_t)$. The innovation variance contribution to variance is σ^2, and the autocorrelation contribution is $1/(1 - c^2)$. A large $|c|$ implies strong autocorrelation and consequently a large variance. Conversely, if $|c|$ is small, autocorrelation is relatively weak. If $c = 0$, there is no autocorrelation in the series. In this case, the series is "white noise" and the innovation variance is equal to the series variance. In general, if a series exhibits any autocorrelation, the innovation variance will be smaller than the series variance.

The availability of high frequency data in finance (daily, hourly, or trade-by-trade) means that researchers now confront data that are likely to exhibit significant autocorrelation because observations "close" in time are likely to be related to one another, that is, exhibit serial dependence. In some applications researchers draw inference from the strength and size of the autocorrelation, whereas in others they are focused on the variance. Decomposing variance into its component pieces allows researchers greater flexibility and precision in framing and testing hypotheses without relying on tenuous assumptions necessary to identify structural models. When the implications of theoretical models are not dependent on the exact structural form of the empirical model, hypothesis testing always presents the researcher with a dilemma: either reject the hypothesis or reject the empirical model. In such cases it is often better to frame hypotheses using less formal structure.

In this *Mathematica* notebook, we illustrate the variance decomposition, and its application to some financial hypotheses. *Mathematica* is one of the few languages with both analytic and numeric capabilities strong enough to allow users to build, as well as test, models. We formulate and test restrictions on variance components using the package `LogSpec`, short for log spectral analysis. The variance decomposition is comparatively easy to compute using the log spectrum.

We illustrate how to use the package with two different examples: the futures/spot price relationship where we derive restrictions from the cost-of-carry relationship on the relative sizes of the variance components, and test the restrictions using S&P 500 spot and futures data; and a "comparative dynamics" experiment where we estimate the elasticity of the noisiness of stock prices with respect to spread size surrounding a drop in the quoted spread.

13.2 Turn off Some *Mathematica* Warning Messages and Load the Packages

```
In[1]:=  Off[General::spell];
         Off[General::spell1];
         Off[NIntegrate::ncvb];
         Off[NIntegrate::ploss];
         Off[Part::partd];
         Off[Show::gtype];

In[2]:=  <<LogSpec`LogSpec`

In[3]:=  ?LogSpec
```

LogSpec.m defines functions used to test whether one time series is "smoother" or has a larger innovation variance than another. Detrending, spectrum computation, and Differencing functions are also defined. Available functions are: Difference, DeMean, DeTrend, Periodogram, Smoothness, LogInnovationVariance.

```
In[4]:=  <<Graphics`Legend`
```

13.3   Representations of Stationary Series

In this section, we present background material on the moving average, autoregressive, and autocovariance representations of stationary time series. We illustrate how variance can be decomposed into two distinct components using each representation. The purpose of this section is to provide background material for readers. The same material can be found in most time series or econometrics textbooks, such as Hamilton (1994) or Judge et al. (1985). If the reader is already familiar with these representations, he or she may skip to the next section.

By stationary, we mean that the first two moments of the series are finite, and are not dependent on calendar time, that is, $\mathrm{Cov}(x_t, x_{t-s}) = f(s)$. In words, the covariance between any two observations depends on how far apart they are in time, but not on what time it is. Usually observations that are closer together will tend to have stronger covariance than observations that are further apart. In the limit, the covariance between two observations dies out as the distance between them increases.

13.3.1   Moving Average Representation

Every covariance-stationary process has a nonunique moving average representation:

$$x_t = \mu + \sum_{j=0}^{\infty} a_j e_{t-j}.$$

The first coefficient of the moving average process is normalized to have a value of one, that is, $a_0 = 1$. Without loss of generality, we assume that $\mu = 0$. Moving average representations are often expressed using lag-operator notation:

$$x_t = A(L)e_t; \; A(L) = \sum_{j=0}^{\infty} a_j L^j \qquad \text{where } L^j x_t = x_{t-j}$$

The moving average representation relates the observed X process to an underlying white noise process (the time series equivalent of an i.i.d. process) and the characteristics of the lag polynomial $A(L)$. The lag polynomial gives the process its autocorrelation pattern.

The variance of a moving average process is:

$$\mathrm{Var}(xt) = \sigma^2 \sum_{j=0}^{\infty} a_j^2 \qquad \sigma^2 = \mathrm{Var}(e_t).$$

Note that the variance of a series is comprised of two separate components: the innovation variance σ^2, and the autocorrelation component of variance $\sum_{j=0}^{\infty} a_j^2$.

If $A(L) = 1$, the series is white noise and the innovation variance equals the series variance.

13.3.2 Autoregressive Representation

Some, but not all, series also possess autoregressive representations. Autoregressive representations are unique.

$$x_t = \sum_{j=1}^{\infty} c_j x_{t-j} + e_t.$$

Like the moving average representation, the autoregressive representation can be expressed using lag-operator notation:

$$C(L)x_t = e_t \qquad C(L) = 1 - \sum_{j=1}^{\infty} c_j L^j$$

and has a corresponding moving average representation:

$$C(L) = A(L)^{-1}.$$

If $C(L) = 1$, the series is white noise.

13.3.2.1 Example: $x_t = c * x_{t-1} + e_t$

```
In[5]:=  f[0]=0;
         autoregress1[c_,e_List]:=Table[
                                        f[i]=c f[i-1]+e[[i]],
                                        {i,Length[e]}]
```

The autoregression is defined recursively, with a starting value equal to the unconditional mean of the process, that is, zero. We generate data from a first-order autoregressive process by "filtering" the innovations e into a first-order autoregression. The transformed series has a different variance and autocorrelation structure than the original series.

```
In[6]:=  T=200;
         e=Table[Random[Real,{0,12^.5}]-12^.5/2,{T}];
```

We generate innovations (i.i.d variates) using the *Mathematica* random number generator. Because the variance of a uniform (a, b) random variable is $(a-b)^2/12$, we choose the range $\{0, 12^{.5}\}$ and subtract the mean, to give the innovation process a variance of one and a mean of zero.

In[7]:=   **Show[ListPlot[autoregress1[.5,e]+3,**
                 PlotStyle->Thickness[.001],
                 PlotJoined->True,
                 DisplayFunction->Identity],
                 ListPlot[autoregress1[-.8,e]+8,
                 PlotStyle->Thickness[.001],
                 PlotJoined->True,
                 DisplayFunction->Identity],
                 ListPlot[autoregress1[.2,e]+13,
                 PlotStyle->Thickness[.001],
                 PlotJoined->True,
                 DisplayFunction->Identity],
                 DisplayFunction->$DisplayFunction,
                 Ticks->{Automatic,None},
                 AxesLabel->{"time"," "},
                 PlotLabel -> "Three Autoregressions"]

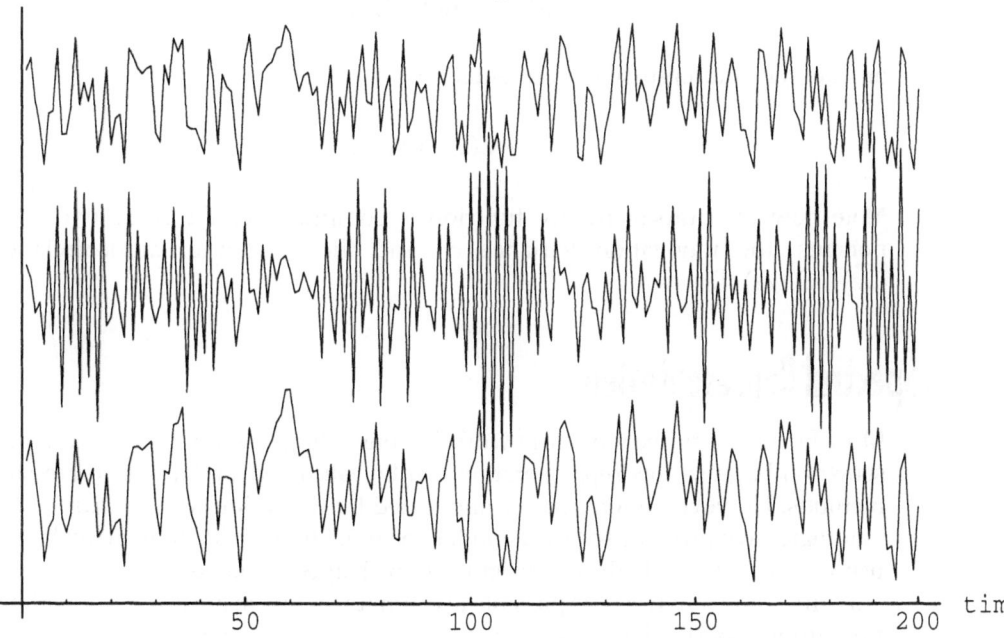

Out[7]= -Graphics-

In the preceding graph, three autoregressive processes are derived from the same innovation process. The bottom series is a slowly moving, or positively autocorrelated process ($c = .5$), whereas the middle is a quickly moving, or negatively autocorrelated process ($c = -.8$). We say that the middle series exhibits more high frequency variation than the bottom series. The middle series also has more autocorrelation than the bottom series, and this leads to a bigger variance. Like the bottom series, the top series ($c = .2$) is positively autocorrelated, but exhibits less autocorrelation than the first two, and consequently has a smaller variance.

13.3.3 Autocovariance Representation

A stationary time series can also be represented by its autocovariance function. The autocovariance generating function is

$$g_x(z) = \sum_{j=0}^{\infty} \text{Cov}(x_t, x_{t-j})z^j$$

and can be derived from the moving average representation:

$$g_x(z) = A(z)A(1/z)\sigma^2$$

or from the autoregressive representation:

$$g_x(z) = C(z)^{-1}C(1/z)^{-1}\sigma^2.$$

Note how the autocovariance function is comprised of the same two components: the innovation variance σ^2 and the pattern of autocorrelation $C(z)^{-1}C(1/z)^{-1}$.

13.4 Spectral Representation

Most financial and econometric work is done using the autoregressive representation because this representation can be estimated by familiar regression methods. However, inference is complicated by the unknown structure of the autoregressive process. To "fit" a model one must first decide how many lags to use, and then estimate the coefficients on the lagged variables.

With spectral analysis it is possible to estimate the spectrum directly—without first fitting a particular model to the series. Every stationary time series has a spectral representation, and it is possible to move between the spectral and the other representations without any loss of information. Good introductions to spectral analysis are found in Chapter 6 in Hamilton (1994), Chapter 11 in Sargent (1979), and Chapter 7 in Chatfield (1979).

The spectrum is the Fourier transform of the autocovariance function

$$s_x(w) = \sum_{j=0}^{\infty} \text{Cov}(x_t, x_{t-j})E^{-ijw}$$

and can be derived from the autocovariance generating function

$$s_x(w) = g_x(E^{-iw}) = A(E^{-iw})A(E^{iw})\sigma^2.$$

Like the variance, the spectrum is comprised of an innovation variance component σ^2 and an autocorrelation component, $A(E^{-iw})A(E^{iw})$.

```
In[8]:=  spectrum[A_,w_]:=A[z]*A[1/z]/.{z->E^(-I*w)}
```

In the preceding formula, the spectrum is computed at a particular frequency w for a process with moving average polynomial $A(L)$. We suppress the σ^2 term, implicitly assuming that the innovation variance of the series is one.

13.4.1   Frequency Decomposition of Variance

It is possible to invert the spectral representation to recover the autocovariance function:

$$\text{Cov}(x_t, x_{t-j}) = \int_{-\pi}^{\pi} E^{ijw} s_x(w)/(2\pi)\, dw.$$

Of particular interest is the zero order autocorrelation, or variance,

$$\text{Var}(x_t) = \int_{-\pi}^{\pi} s_x(w)/(2\pi)\, dw.$$

```
In[9]:=  Var[A_]:=NIntegrate[spectrum[A,w]/Pi,{w,0,Pi}]
```

Because the spectrum is symmetric around the zero frequency, we have suppressed the negative frequencies in the preceding formula. The integral of the spectrum provides a frequency decomposition of variance. The spectrum can be thought of as measuring the contribution to variance, or "power," from each frequency. Inasmuch as frequency is inversely related to periodicity = $2*\pi$/frequency, the low frequency components of variance are associated with long-run changes in the series, and the high frequency components of variance are associated with short-run changes in the series. For example, the highest observable frequency π corresponds to a periodicity of 2; the middle frequency $\pi/2$ corresponds to a periodicity of 4; $\pi/4$ to a periodicity of 8, and so on.

By measuring the shape of the spectrum, it is possible to infer the "sign" and strength of the autocorrelation component of variance. A flat spectrum corresponds to no autocorrelation, or white noise. Loosely speaking, a negatively sloped spectrum is "positively autocorrelated," with most of its power in the low frequencies, and a postively sloped spectrum is "negatively autocorrelated," with most of its power in the high frequencies.

13.4.2 The Smoothness Coefficient

The smoothness coefficient (Froeb and Koyak 1994) is designed to measure the degree of autocorrelation, or "smoothness" in a series by measuring the shape of the log spectrum. Any frequency between zero and π partitions the spectrum into long-run (low frequency) and short-run (high frequency) components. By measuring the relative size of the two components, we measure the "shape" of the log spectrum. For a cutoff frequency w_0 in the interval $(0, \pi)$, the smoothness coefficient is defined as follows:

$$\text{Smoothness Coefficient} = \int_0^{w_0} (1/w_0) \, \text{Log}[s_y(w)] \, dw$$

$$- \int_{w_0}^{\pi} (1/(\pi - w_0)) \, \text{Log}[s_y(w)] \, dw.$$

```
In[10]:= smoothness[A_,w0_]:=N[
            NIntegrate[Log[spectrum[A,w]],{w,0,w0}]/w0 -
            NIntegrate[Log[spectrum[A,w]],{w,w0,Pi}]/(Pi-w0)
            ]
```

The smoothness coefficient measures the difference between the average low and high frequency variance components of a series. For "positively" autocorrelated, or "smooth" series, the measure is positive and for "negatively" autocorrelated, or "bumpy" series, the measure is negative. For white noise series, the measure is zero. The smoothness coefficient uses the information contained in all the covariances, rather than just the first-order autocovariance, as is commonly done. In addition, as discussed in the following, it is easy to estimate and has good statistical properties.

13.4.3 The Log Innovation Variance

For a series possessing an autoregressive representation, the innovation variance is unique and can be interpreted as the one-step-ahead forecast error variance when X is regressed on its own past.

$$\sigma^2 = E[x_t - E[x_t \mid x_{t-1}, x_{t-2}, \ldots]]^2.$$

The integral of the log spectrum provides a way to recover the log innovation variance without estimating $E[x_t \mid x_{t-1}, x_{t-2}, \ldots]$.

$$\text{Log}[\sigma^2] = \int_0^{\pi} \text{Log}[S_x(w)] \, dw/\pi.$$

```
In[11]:= logInnovationVariance[A_]:=Chop[
            NIntegrate[Log[spectrum[A,w]]/Pi,{w,0,Pi}],
                                    0000001]
```

13.4.4   Example: Three AR(1) Processes

Three different spectra are plotted as follows.

```
In[12]:= A[L_]=1/(1-.5L);
         B[L_]=1/(1+.8L);
         F[L_]=1/(1-.2L);

In[13]:= Plot[{spectrum[A,w],spectrum[B,w],
            spectrum[F,w]},{w,0,Pi},
            PlotStyle->{Thickness[.007],
                    {Thickness[.004],Dashing[{.01}]},
                    {Thickness[.004],Dashing[{.02}]}},
            PlotLabel->"Spectra",
            PlotLegend->{"1/(1-.5L)",
                    "1/(1+.8L)",
                    "1/(1-.2L)"},
            LegendPosition->{0,0},
            LegendShadow->.0,
            LegendSize->{.6,.3},
            AxesLabel->{"freq"," "}];
```

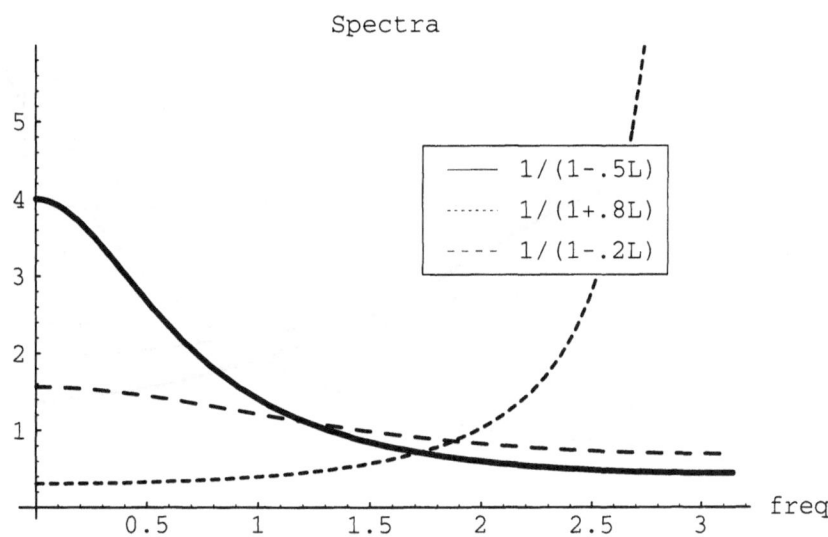

Notice how in the preceding graph the spectra flatten out as the "degree" of autocorrelation is decreased in each series. The smaller dashed line, representing very strong autocorrelation, is very steep with most of its power, or variance, in the high frequencies. The other two series are "positively" autocorrelated, or "smooth," with most of their power in the low frequencies. The solid line, representing an autoregression with a parameter of $c = .5$, is more autocorrelated than the dashed line ($c = .2$).

The area under the spectrum represents variance. The strongly autocorrelated series, represented by the smaller dashed line, has the largest variance, followed by the solid, and then the dashed line. The dashed line is the closest to white noise, which has a flat spectrum.

```
In[14]:= Plot[{Log[spectrum[A,w]],Log[spectrum[B,w]],
             Log[spectrum[F,w]]},{w,0,Pi},
             PlotStyle->{Thickness[.007],
                     {Thickness[.004],Dashing[{.01}]},
                     {Thickness[.004],Dashing[{.02}]}},
             PlotLabel->"Log[Spectra]",
             PlotLegend->{"1/(1-.5L)",
                         "1/(1+.8L)",
                         "1/(1-.2L)"},
             LegendPosition->{0,0},
             LegendShadow->.0,
             LegendSize->{.6,.3},
             AxesLabel->{"freq"," "}];
```

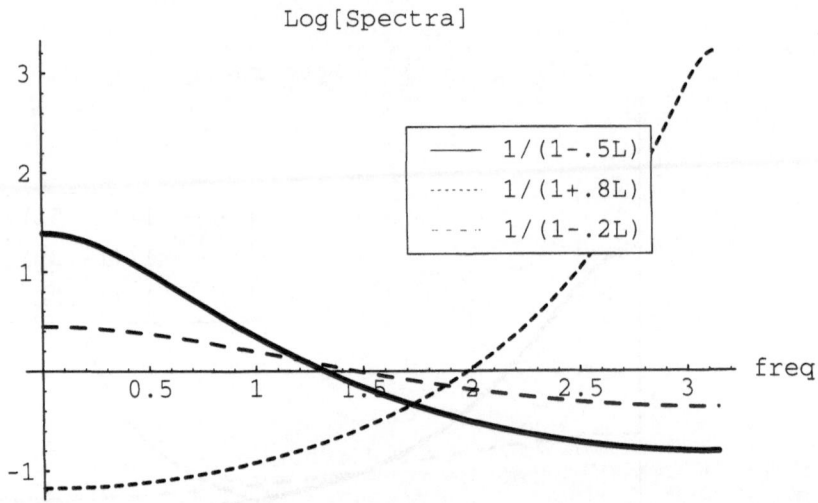

Although the series have different variances, they all have the same log innovation variance, as represented by the area under the log spectrum. In the following we formally compute the innovation variances and the smoothness coefficients of each of the series.

```
In[15]:= NumberForm[TableForm[{
             {"A[L]","Var.","Innov. var.", "Smoothness coeff."},
             {A[L],Var[A],
             Exp[logInnovationVariance[A]],smoothness[A,Pi/2]},
```

```
{B[L],Var[B],
Exp[logInnovationVariance[B]],smoothness[B,Pi/2]},
{F[L],Var[F],
Exp[logInnovationVariance[F]],smoothness[F,Pi/2]}
      }],2]
```

```
Out[15]= A[L]          Var.    Innov. var.    Smoothness coeff.


        1
     ---------
     1 - 0.5 L    1.3      1                1.2


        1
     ---------
     1 + 0.8 L    2.8      1               -1.9


        1
     ---------
     1 - 0.2 L    1.       1                0.51
```

For series with weaker autocorrelation, the smoothness coefficient is smaller in absolute value. Because the series have the same innovation variance, the difference in the magnitudes of the smoothness coefficients (different "amounts" of autocorrelation) accounts for the different variances.

The sign of the smoothness coefficient indicates whether the series is "positively" or "negatively" autocorrelated. A positive smoothness coefficient indicates that the series is slowly moving, with most of its power or variance in the low frequencies, like the first and third series. A negative smoothness coefficient indicates that the series bounces around in relatively short periods, with most of its variance in the high frequencies.

13.5 Comparing Variance Components in Different Series

Many financial and economic relationships can be thought of as filters, relating one series to another. Filtering in the time domain, that is, $y_t = A(L)x_t$, corresponds to multiplication in the frequency domain,

$$s_y(w) = s_A(w)s_x(w) \quad \text{where} \quad s_A(w) = A(E^{-iw})A(E^{iw}),$$

or addition using the log spectra,

$$\text{Log}[s_y(w)] = \text{Log}[s_A(w)] + \text{Log}[s_x(w)].$$

Here $s_A(w)$ is the spectrum of the filter $A(L)$. By studying the properties of the filter $A(L)$, it is possible to derive restrictions on the relative shapes of $\text{Log}[s_x(w)]$

and $\text{Log}[s_y(w)]$. Or to turn this around, it is possible to infer properties of the filter $A(L)$ by comparing the log spectra of X and Y. We can do this without estimating the filter directly.

One series is "smoother" than another, or has a larger innovation variance, if the difference in their smoothness coeffficients, or in their log innovation variances, is greater than zero. This method of comparing series has some desirable properties. The smoothness comparison is not affected by prefiltering, as long as both series are passed through the same filter. Likewise, the innovation variance comparison is not affected by prefiltering, even if the series are passed through different filters, as long as the filters share the same normalization, $A[0] = 1$.

13.5.1   Example: An Autoregression of an Autoregression

We consider an X series that has a first-order autoregressive representation and then pass it through another first-order autoregressive filter to turn it into the Y series.

$$A(L)x_t = e_t \quad \text{or} \quad x_t = a(L)e_t \quad \text{where} \quad a(L) = 1/A(L)$$

$$B(L)y_t = x_t \quad \text{or} \quad y_t = b(L)x_t \quad \text{where} \quad b(L) = 1/B(L)$$

$$y_t = F(L)e_t; \quad F(L) = 1/(A(L)B(L)) = a(L)b(L).$$

The purpose of this section is to show that it is possible to recover the properties of the $B(L)$ filter, which describes the relationship between X and Y, by comparing the properties of the X and Y processes.

```
In[16]:= A[L_]:=(1-.5 L);    a[L_]=A[L]^-1;
         B[L_]:=(1+.8 L)/2; b[L_]=B[L]^-1;
         F[L_]:=1/(A[L]*B[L]);


In[17]:= Plot[{Log[spectrum[a,w]],
              Log[spectrum[b,w]],
              Log[spectrum[F,w]]},{w,0,Pi},
              PlotStyle->{Thickness[.007],
                         {Thickness[.004],Dashing[{.01}]},
                         {Thickness[.004],Dashing[{.02}]}},
              PlotLabel->"Log spectra",
              PlotLegend->{"X","filter (Y-X)","Y"},
              LegendPosition->{-.8,0},
              LegendShadow->.0,
              LegendSize->{.8,.3},
              AxesLabel->{"freq"," "}];
```

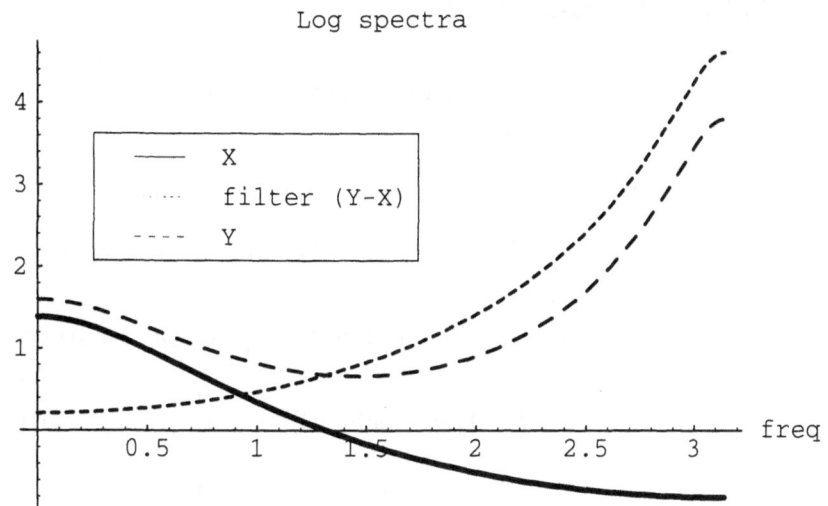

Notice that the larger dashed line (Y) is the sum of the solid (X) and smaller dashed (filter) lines. Or to turn this around, the spectral properties of the filter (smaller dashed) can be recovered by subtracting the log spectrum of X (solid) from the log spectrum of Y (larger dashed).

13.5.2 Innovation Variance of a Filter

As with the log spectrum, by subtracting the innovation variance of the observed X processes from that of the Y process, the innovation variance of the filter can be recovered. Note that if $A(0) = 1$, the log innovation variance of the filter is zero, and the log innovation variances of the X and Y processes are the same. In words, filtering a process may change its variance and autocorrelation pattern, but not its innovation variance. Here we draw a distinction between "scaling" and "filtering," where the former involves multiplying one series by a scaling factor.

Log innovation variance of Y

$$= \int_0^\pi \mathrm{Log}[s_y(w)]/\pi \, dw$$

$$= \int_0^\pi \mathrm{Log}[s_A(w)]/\pi \, dw + \int_0^\pi \mathrm{Log}[s_x(w)]/\pi \, dw$$

$= \mathrm{Log}$ innovation variance of A + Log innovation variance of X.

13.5.3   Smoothness Coefficient of a Filter

As with the innovation variance, the smoothness coefficient of a filter can be recovered by subtracting the smoothness coefficient of the observed X processes from that of the Y process.

Smoothness coefficient of Y

$$= \int_0^{w_0} (1/w_0) \, \mathrm{Log}[s_y(w)] \, dw - \int_{w_0}^{\pi} (1/(\pi - w_0)) \, \mathrm{Log}[s_y(w)] \, dw$$

$$= \int_0^{w_0} (1/w_0) \, \mathrm{Log}[s_A(w)] \, dw - \int_{w_0}^{\pi} (1/(\pi - w_0)) \, \mathrm{Log}[s_A(w)] \, dw$$

$$+ \int_0^{w_0} (1/w_0) \, \mathrm{Log}[s_x(w)] \, dw - \int_{w_0}^{\pi} (1/(\pi - w_0)) \, \mathrm{Log}[s_x(w)] \, dw$$

$$= \text{smoothness coefficient of } A + \text{smoothness coefficient of } X.$$

In the following we illustrate this relationship explicitly using our autoregression of an autoregression example.

```
In[18]:= NumberForm[TableForm[Transpose[{
           {" ","Log innov. var.", "Smoothness Coeff."},
           {"Y series",
           logInnovationVariance[F],smoothness[F,Pi/2]},
           {"X series",
           logInnovationVariance[a],smoothness[a,Pi/2]},
           {"filter (Y-X)",
           logInnovationVariance[b],smoothness[b,Pi/2]}
                }]],2]
```

```
Out[18]=                          Y series   X series   filter (Y-X)
           Log innov. var.         1.4        0          1.4
           Smoothness Coeff.      -0.68       1.2       -1.9
```

The filter characteristics (smoothness and innovation variance) are recovered from the difference between the characteristics of the observed X and Y processes. This theoretical exercise illustrates the estimation strategy that follows. We recover characteristics of filters (economic relationships) by examining the differences between innovation variances and smoothness coefficients of two observed series.

13.6   Estimation

13.6.1   The Periodogram

The periodogram is the sample analogue of the theoretical spectrum. It is computed by taking the finite Fourier transform of the original series, and "squaring" it (multiplying by its complex conjugate). This is equivalent to taking the finite

Fourier transform of the sample autocovariance function.

$$d_x(w) = \sum_{t=1}^{T} x_t E^{-itw}.$$

$$I_x(w) = |d_x(w)|^2$$

In[19]:= **?Periodogram**

Periodogram[list] takes a (usually detrended and demeaned) time
series, 'list' (less the first observation in the case of an
even number of observations), and returns the periodogram.
The periodogram is normalized so that its mean is the
variance of the time series.

There is a large body of literature dealing with the stochastic properties of the periodogram as $T \to \infty$. We mention the following.

(i) $I_x(w_i)/s_x(w_i)$ is asymptotically distributed as $Z^2/2$, where Z^2 is distributed as a chi-square with 2 degrees of freedom.

(ii) $I_x(w_i)$ is asymptotically independent of $I_x(w_j)$ for $i \neq j$.

13.6.2 The Innovation Variance and Smoothness Coefficient

There is a smaller body of literature dealing with the asymptotic properties of the log periodogram, and in particular with sums of log periodogram ordinates. For the special case where X is a normally distributed random variable, it is possible to show that:

(i) $\sum_{i=1}^{n} \text{Log}[I_x(w_i)]/n + $ Euler's gamma $(= .57721)$ is asymptotically distributed as

$$N(\text{Log}[\sigma^2], \pi^2/(6n))$$

(Davis and Jones 1968).

(ii) $\sum_{i=1}^{n_1} \text{Log}[I_x(w_i)]/n_1 - \sum_{j=n_1+1}^{n} \text{Log}[I_x(w_j)]/n_2$ is asymptotically distributed as

$$N(\text{SmoothnessCoeff}, (\pi^2/6)/(1/n_1 + 1/n_2))$$

(Froeb and Koyak 1994)

In the preceding formulas, "n", "n_1", and "n_2" refer to the number of periodogram ordinates in each average. When X is not normally distributed the estimators are still consistent, and Monte Carlo results in Froeb and Koyak (1994) suggest that the normal approximation to the asymptotic distribution works well for nonnormal distributions and in small samples.

13.6.3   Example: An Autoregression of an Autoregression

We calculate the sample innovation variance and smoothness coefficients of the first-order autoregressive processes previously illustrated.

```
In[20]:= X=autoregress1[.5,e];
         Y=2*autoregress1[-.8,X];

In[21]:= NumberForm[TableForm[{
              {" ","Y Series","X Series","filter (Y-X)"},
              Prepend[
                   LogInnovationVariance[
                        Log[Periodogram[Y ]],
                        Log[Periodogram[Drop[X,1] ]]
                   ],{"Log innov. Var.","std. err."}],
              Prepend[
                   Smoothness[Pi/2,
                        Log[Periodogram[Y ]],
                        Log[Periodogram[Drop[X,1] ]]
                   ],{"Soothness Coef.","std. err."}] }],2]
```

Out[21]=	Y Series	X Series	filter (Y-X)
Log innov. Var.	1.3	-0.1	1.4
std. err.	0.13	0.13	0.15
Soothness Coef.	-0.77	1.2	-2.
std. err.	0.26	0.26	0.31

A two-σ confidence interval around the estimated innovation variance and smoothness coefficients will contain the true values (calculated in the previous table) 95% of the time.

13.7   Spot and Futures Prices

13.7.1   Theory: The Cost-of-Carry Relationship

One of the simplest relationships in finance is the cost-of-carry relationship between futures and spot prices:

$$f_t = s_t E^{cT},$$

where c is the "cost of carry," and T is the time to maturity. For a stock index, as we use in our empirical section, the cost of carry is the interest rate less the income earned by the index (Hull, 1995). "Tests" of this relationship can be framed around the means (the mean of the spot price is smaller than the mean of the futures price), around the variances (the variance of the spot price is smaller than the variance of the futures price), or around the smoothness coefficients and the innovation variances. We illustrate the latter approach by first examining the filter relating spot to futures prices.

```
In[22]:= A[L_]:=E^(c T)
```

```
In[23]:= c=.1;
         T=1;
         Plot[Log[spectrum[A,w]],{w,0,Pi},
             PlotLabel->"Log spectrum:  cost-of-carry filter",
             AxesLabel->{"freq"," "}]
```

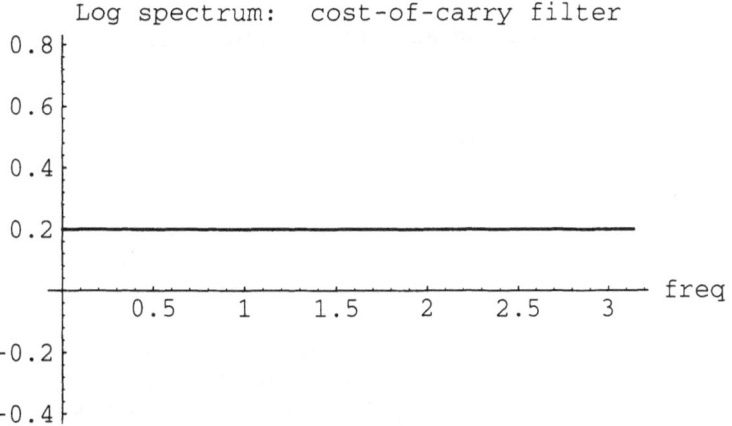

```
Out[23]= -Graphics-
```

The positive log spectrum of the cost-of-carry filter implies that spot prices have a lower innovation variance than futures prices, and the flat filter implies that they have the same smoothness coefficient.

13.7.2   Empirics: Testing the "Cost-of-Carry" Model Using S&P 500 Spot and Futures Prices

The purpose of this section is to "test" the cost-of-carry relationship between spot and futures prices. Previously we derived two implications for the relationship between the series: the innovation variance of the futures series is larger; and the smoothness coefficients of the spot and futures series are the same. We test these predictions using spot and futures data for the S&P 500 stock index.

13.7.2.1   Read Data and Plot Series

Daily futures and spot prices for 1989 are in a file called "**data89.dat**". The columns of the data file are the date, opening spot price, closing spot price,

opening futures price, and closing futures price. We use the closing prices for
the two series.

```
In[24]:= myPath="Luke's 500MB:Mathematica 2.2.2:\
          Packages:LogSpec:";
```

```
In[25]:= Clear[dataFile];
          dataFile=myPath<>"data89.dat";
```

```
In[26]:= data=ReadList[dataFile][[1]];
```

```
In[27]:= Show[GraphicsArray[
               {{
               ListPlot[Transpose[data][[3]],
                  PlotJoined->True,
                  DisplayFunction->Identity,
                  PlotLabel->"spot"]
               },{
               ListPlot[Transpose[data][[5]],
                  PlotJoined->True,
                  DisplayFunction->Identity,
                  PlotLabel->"futures"]
               }}],
               PlotLabel->"1989 S&P 500"]
```

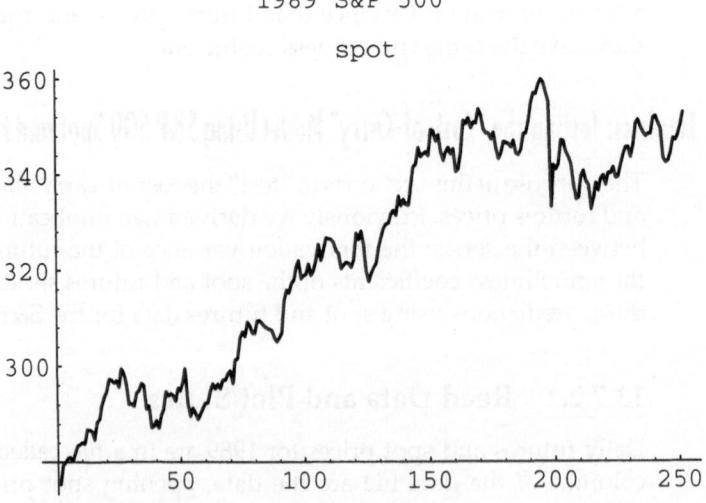

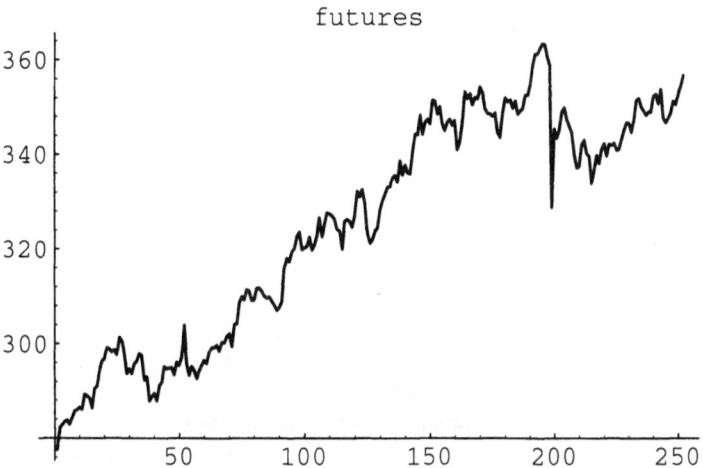

Out[27]= -GraphicsArray-

The two series look very similar, but it is difficult to discern important differences by simply eyeballing the series, although it is something that should always be done to check for outliers and errors in the data.

13.7.2.2   Compute Innovation Variances and Smoothness Coefficients

We first difference the log data, as is customary, to make the series stationary. The log first difference of a series can be interpreted as a period-by-period growth rate in the series.

In[28]:= **?Difference**

```
Difference[list,(k)] returns the kth difference of a time
    series, list.  Default value of k is 1.  The output vector
    has length N-k, where N = number of observations in list.
```

In[29]:=   **spot=Difference[Log[Transpose[data][[3]]]];**
          futures=Difference[Log[Transpose[data][[5]]]];

In[30]:= **?LogInnovationVariance**

```
LogInnovationVariance[Log[periodogram1],
    (Log[periodogram2]),(twoPeriods->False)] inputs 1, or 2 log
    periodograms and returns a list of doubles, {Log Innovation
    Variance [i], standard-error[i]}.  If called with two log
    periodograms, the 3 doubles correspond to #1, #2, (#1-#2).
    When called using the twoPeriods->True option, the standard
    errors are computed by assuming the series are from different
    time periods.
```

```
In[31]:= ?Smoothness
```

Smoothness[frequency, Log[periodogram1],
    (Log[periodogram2]),(twoPeriods->False)] inputs 1 or 2 log
    periodograms and returns a list of triples, {frequency[i],
    smoothness coefficient[i], standard error[i]}. If called
    with two log periodograms, the 3 triples correspond to #1,
    #2, (#1-#2). When called using the twoPeriods->True option,
    the standard errors are computed by assuming the series are
    from different time periods.

```
In[32]:= NumberForm[TableForm[{
                {" ", "spot","futures","difference"},
                Prepend[
            LogInnovationVariance[
                        Log[Periodogram[spot]],
                        Log[Periodogram[futures]]
                    ],{"Innovation Variance","std. err."}],
                Prepend[
            Smoothness[Pi/2,
                    Log[Periodogram[spot]],
                    Log[Periodogram[futures]]
                ],{"Smoothness Coefficient","std. err."}]
        }],2]
```

```
Out[32]=                              spot    futures   difference

        Innovation Variance          -9.7     -9.3       -0.41
        std. err.                    0.11     0.11        0.073

        Smoothness Coefficient       0.022    -0.44       0.46
        std. err.                    0.23     0.23        0.15
```

The spot price innovation variance is significantly lower than the futures price innovation variance, as predicted by theory. The second prediction, that the smoothness coefficients are the same, is rejected by the data. The spot prices are essentially white noise (their smoothness coefficient is not significantly different from zero) whereas the futures prices exhibit marginally significant negative autocorrelation. Their difference is statistically significant.

The negative autocorrelation in the futures series is probably due to the "bid-ask bounce" on the Chicago exchange, as the futures contracts "bounce" between the bid and the ask. Because the spot price of the index is an average of underlying NYSE stock prices, rather than a single traded contract, the spot price does not exhibit such short-run volatility. We conclude that smoothness test rejection of the cost-of-carry relationship is due to the institutional differences between an index price (spot), and a single contract (futures), rather than a rejection of the fundamental cost-of-carry relationship. Computing this "test" with variances or means would not have rejected the model, but would have missed this feature of the data.

13.8   Tick Size and the Information Content of Stock Prices

13.8.1   Theory: Measuring "Spread Noise" in Prices

Price changes in most financial securities have a lower bound called the "tick size." The minimum tick size in U.S. financial markets has recently received considerable regulatory attention as have the related issues of spread size and decimal trading. In this section, we use a natural experiment to estimate the effects of a sudden decrease in tick size on the behavior of stock prices. The advantage of a natural experiment over a structural approach such as that of Huang and Stoll (1994) is that it does not depend on structural identifying assumptions—inference is drawn directly from the data before and after the change. In particular, we are interested in whether a change in the tick size increases the informativeness of stock price with respect to spread sizes.

By "information" we mean the extent to which intraday stock price movements reflect events related to the value of a company. Formal statistical inference would be called an event study, but informal inference depends on the same basic principles: better information about the timing of the event, that is, a smaller event window, and a better estimator of the normal stock price reaction make it possible to draw better inferences about how events affect the value of a company. With more or better information of this type, for example, stockholders can more closely monitor the actions of managers to attenuate the problems of moral hazard associated with separation of ownership and control.

Tick size, or spread size, has an obvious effect on the amount of information in stock prices. For example, with a tick size of $0.25, one would not expect to see much of a stock price reaction to an event expected to increase a company's value by only $0.10/share because it would be hard to distinguish a $0.10 movement from the normal tick-to-tick stock price adjustments. Consequently it would be very difficult to draw inference about the effects of such a small event on the value of a company. But tick size affects inferences about large events as well as small ones. A bigger tick size makes it more difficult to predict a normal stock price reaction because the confidence intervals surrounding the expected reaction are wider. Consequently the variance/bias tradeoff associated with the choice of window size is worsened for all events. Formally, a larger tick size decreases the power of hypothesis tests surrounding an event; informally, it means that stock price reactions to events will tend to get lost in the tick-to-tick price movements. *Ceteris paribus*, a larger tick or spread size increases the amount of noise in a stock's price (Chordia and Froeb 1995).

For an idealized event window of one period in length, the "abnormal" stock reaction to an event is defined to be

$$e_t = \Delta p_t - E[\Delta p_t \mid \Phi_{t-1}]$$

and we judge its significance by constructing a simple test statistic,

$$(\Delta p_t - E[\Delta p_t \mid \Phi_{t-1}]) / \mathrm{Sqrt}[\sigma^2]; \qquad \text{where } \sigma^2 = E[\Delta p_t - E[\Delta p_t \mid \Phi_{t-1}]]^2,$$

where Φ_t is the information available to the market participants at time t. From this expression it is easy to see that, *ceteris paribus*, the larger the denominator σ^2, the harder it will be for a stockholder to judge whether a given stock reaction is significantly different than what would have been expected. This reasoning motivates our measure of the uninformativeness or "noisiness" of stock prices as σ^2.

If we take Φ_{t-1} to be the history of past price changes, σ^2 becomes the innovation variance of the series, and we estimate the effects of spread size on σ^2 by estimating innovation variances before and after a dramatic narrowing of the spread. Focusing on the innovation variance allows us to ignore the autocorrelated, and predictable, component of variance. This focus also illustrates one of the main advantages of the log spectral approach—that the innovation variance can be estimated without estimating $E[\Delta p_t \mid \Phi_{t-1}]$.

13.8.2 Empirics: Estimating Innovation Variances Surrounding a Decrease in Tick Size

Surrounding press coverage of alleged collusion among NASDAQ market makers in May, 1994, several stocks, among them Microsoft, began trading at odd as well as even eighth quotes (Christie et al. 1994). This change in trading was associated with a dramatic decrease in observed bid-ask spreads from about \$0.25 to about \$0.125. We use this natural experiment to estimate the effects of spreads on "noise" in stock prices. These data are described more fully in Chordia and Froeb (1995).

13.8.2.1 Read the Data Files

```
In[33]:= Clear[dataFile];
         dataFile[1]=myPath<>"MSFT26.dat";
         dataFile[2]=myPath<>"MSFT27.dat";

In[34]:= z[1]=ReadList[dataFile[1]] [[1]];

In[35]:= z[2]=ReadList[dataFile[2]] [[1]];
```

13.8.2.2 Graph Data

```
In[36]:= MSFT26=Transpose[z[1] ][[1]];
         MSFT27=Transpose[z[2] ][[1]];

In[37]:= Show[GraphicsArray[
                {{
                ListPlot[MSFT26,
                  PlotJoined->True,
                  DisplayFunction->Identity,
```

```
                                   PlotRange->{51.3, 53},
                                   PlotLabel->"MSFT 5/26/94"]
                                },{
                                ListPlot[MSFT27,
                                   PlotJoined->True,
                                   DisplayFunction->Identity,
                                   PlotRange->{51.3, 53},
                                   PlotLabel->"MSFT 5/27/94"]
                                }}],
                                PlotLabel->"MSFT stock prices"]
```

MSFT stock prices

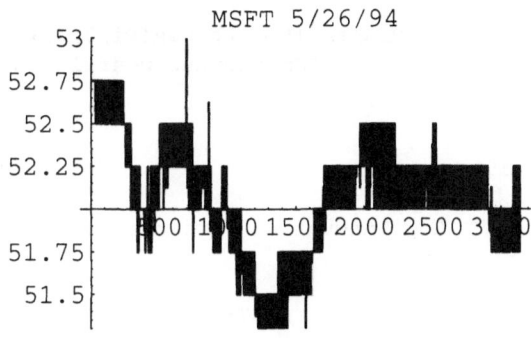

Out[37]= -GraphicsArray-

The drop in the spreads is easily seen in the preceding graphs. On 5/26, the stock is bouncing between bid and ask quotes that are $0.25 apart, but on 5/27, the bid-ask difference narrows to $0.125.

By examining the graphs, we see two suspicious observations, one at about observation 800 on 5/26, and one at about observation 2200, on 5/27. It is difficult to believe that such large tick-to-tick movements are not errors in reporting, so we remove these observations from the following series using the **Select** command.

13.8.2.3 Compute Innovation Variances and Smoothness Coefficients

```
In[38]:= X=Log[Periodogram[Select[Difference[MSFT26],
            Abs[#]<=.5&]]];
         Y=Log[Periodogram[Select[Difference[MSFT27],
            Abs[#]<=.5&]]];

In[39]:= NumberForm[
         TableForm[{{" ", "5/26/94","5/27/94","difference"},

         Prepend[LogInnovationVariance[X,Y,twoPeriods->True],
            {"Log Innovation Variance","std. err."}],

         Prepend[Smoothness[Pi/2,X,Y,twoPeriods->True],
            {"Smoothness Coefficient","std. err."}]
            }],3]
```

```
Out[39]=                              5/26/94  5/27/94  difference

         Log Innovation Variance     -4.2     -5.48    1.27
         std. err.                   0.0324   0.0384   0.0502

         Smoothness Coefficient      -1.91    -2.08    0.163
         std. err.                   0.0648   0.0768   0.1
```

The log innovation variance exhibits a large and significant decrease. Roughly, a halving of the spreads caused a fourfold decrease in the innovation variance. The smoothness coefficient does not change. This is somewhat surprising because many structural models of the bid-ask "bounce," for example, Huang and Stoll (1994), would predict an increase in the smoothness coefficient, that is, less relative short-run variation in the series, unless there is relatively little real information driving the price movements.

13.9 Conclusions

By decomposing variance into its component pieces, we have demonstrated a flexible hypothesis testing framework that does not rely on structural model estimation. This can be an advantage when the distinguishing features of models are not dependent on the particular autoregressive or moving average structure of the time series.

13.10 Acknowledgments

Support for this project was provided by the Dean's fund for faculty research at the Owen Graduate School of Management at Vanderbilt University. I wish to acknowledge useful comments from James Baker, Roger Huang, Eduardo

Ley, James Overdahl, and brown bag seminars at the Owen School and at the Economics Department at Vanderbilt. A large part of the original code for the LogSpec.m package was written by Steve Sweeney.

13.11 References

Chatfield, C. 1979. *The Analysis of Time Series, an Introduction*. London, Chapman and Hall.

Chordia, T. and L. Froeb. 1994. "Tick Size and the Information Content of Stock Prices." Owen Graduate School of Management, working paper #94-06.

Christie, W., J. Harris, and P. Schultz. 1994. "Why did Nasdaq Market Makers Stop Avoiding Odd-Eighth Quotes?" *Journal of Finance*, **49**, (Dec.), 1841–1860.

Davis, H. T. and R. H. Jones. 1968. "Estimation of the Innovation Variance of a Stationary Time Series." *JASA*, **63**, (March), 141–149.

Froeb, L. 1994. "An Innovation Variance Ratio Test." Manuscript.

Froeb, L. and R. Koyak. 1994. "Measuring and Comparing Smoothness in Time Series: The Production Smoothing Hypothesis." *Journal of Econometrics*, **64**, 97–122.

Hamilton, J. 1994. *Time Series Analysis*. Princeton, NJ, Princeton University Press.

Huang, R. and H. Stoll. 1994. "The Components of the Bid-Ask Spread: A General Approach." Owen Graduate School of Management, working paper #94–33.

Hull, J. 1995. *Introduction to Futures & Options Markets*. Englewood Cliffs, NJ, Prentice-Hall.

Judge, G., W. Griffiths, R. C. Hill, H. Lutkepohl, T. C. Lee. 1985. *The Theory and Practice of Econometrics*. New York, John Wiley & Sons.

Sargent, T. 1979. *Macroeconomic Theory*. New York, Academic Press.

14 Data Analysis Using *Mathematica*

Robert A. Stine

14.1 Introduction

The package **DataTools** offers a collection of statistics functions that one can use to explore and summarize data in various ways. These tools are inherently graphical, with analytic helpers included as needed, such as in the case of density estimates and scatterplot smooths. The programming makes extensive use of the built-in functions of *Mathematica*, and this package makes selective use of a subset of the supplemental *Mathematica* packages that are part of the standard distribution. Interested readers may also find more specialized packages of interest. For example, there are specialized packages for time series analysis (He 1995) and econometrics (Belsley 1993).

The tools divide into five broad functional categories defined by a given task. The tasks and noteworthy tools are:

- reading data from an external file (**ReadDataFile, WriteDataFile**),
- grouping data for descriptive summary statistics (**Bin, Average, Median,** etc.),
- plotting a single collection of data (univariate plots, via **Histogram, KernelDensity, Boxplot,** and **QQPlot**),
- plotting several variables (**Scatterplot**), and
- smoothing and regression functions (**Smooth, OLS,** and **RobustRegression**).

The functions in each category allow missing data as distinguished by symbols of the user's choosing. All these functions are defined by loading the package **DataTools** as follows. (The file **DataTools.m** found on the disk with this volume needs to be located on the search path that *Mathematica* uses when looking for files on a system.)

```
In[1]:=   <<DataTools.m
```

To present these functions in a bit more realistic (and it is hoped, interesting) context, I introduce them over the course of a small exploratory analysis of the daily return on General Motors common stock over the two years 1987 and 1988. This span includes the turbulent period around October, 1987. The data are in the file **gm8788.dat** included on the disk that comes with this volume.

The analysis of these data progresses in a fashion intended to introduce the functions of this package, and might seem a bit contrived. After reading the data, the analysis begins with some simple descriptive statistics that use binning to summarize the data one month at a time. The next two sections use univariate and bivariate plots that augment the graphical functions of *Mathematica* with histograms, boxplots, and kernel density estimates. The last section explores how the volatility in these data tracks using basic regression tools that are perhaps more useful than the built-in **Fit** command, but less comprehensive (and faster) than the **Regression** function found in the supplemental **Statistics** package. Throughout, the emphasis is upon graphical displays that reveal interesting features of the data.

14.2   Reading Data Files

The function **ReadDataFile** reads data from an external file into *Mathematica*. This function expects the file to possess a very simple text format that is often used by commercial statistics packages for interchanging data. The first line of the file is a quoted string used to document the file; this allows users to insert a comment into the file to remind them of its contents. The second line of the file is a list of variable names separated by one or more spaces. The remaining lines of the file are the observation records, with as many values per line as there are variable names. For example, here is how a file with 2 variables and 3 observations would appear:

```
"A simple file example"
Var1   Var2
2   3
12 na
1 3
```

Missing data can be denoted by whatever symbol one chooses, such as the **na** symbol used here or some other symbolic tag such as **missing**.

In picking the symbol to denote missing data, one must be careful to avoid symbols that are predefined in *Mathematica*. The functions of this package skip over symbolic values using casewise deletion methods prior to calculations, so any symbolic value will do. The familiar symbol **na** will work most of the time. However, if the symbol **na** had been defined to be, say, 27 in the session before the file was read, the second value for **Var2** would be 27 rather than distinguished as missing data. A choice that is sure to work is the reserved *Mathematica* symbol **Indeterminant** as used in the econometrics package of Belsley (1993).

ReadDataFile makes use of the underlying *Mathematica* code for reading files and thus inherits the built-in error messages associated with file manipulations. For example, if the file name is entered incorrectly, the underlying *Mathematica* function **OpenRead** gives an error message.

```
In[2]:=  ReadDataFile["gmprice.87"]

OpenRead::noopen: Can't open gmprice.87.
```

The data file **gm8788.dat** contains the day, month, year, price, and daily return for General Motors common stock for the 506 trading days during 1987 and 1988. Each line of the file (after the first two header lines) contains five values that define these variables. To help distinguish the names of variables read from the file from other symbols, upper-case characters have been used in the name for each (as, for example, **DAY** for the day of the month).

```
In[3]:=  ReadDataFile["gm8788.dat"]

File documentation: "Returns on General Motors Stock during
    1987-1988"
    Variables to be read: {DAY, MONTH, YEAR, PRICE, RETURN}
    506 cases were read.
```

A list named by the associated symbol extracted from the second line of the input file holds the data for each variable. For example, an abbreviated list of the return data is

```
In[4]:=  Short[ RETURN ]

Out[4]=  {0.01325758, 0.02429906, 0.003649635, <<501>>, 0,
            -0.02052786}
```

This output shows the first three daily returns, then indicates 501 values are hidden, and then shows the last two daily returns.

ReadDataFile will not overwrite data previously defined during the active *Mathematica* session. If some of the symbols that are to denote variables (in this example, the symbols **DAY, MONTH, YEAR, PRICE**, and **RETURN**) are already defined in the active session, a warning message is printed. This feature avoids accidentally replacing an important piece of data by new data read from the external file. For example, a second attempt to read the same file generates a message but does not define any variables.

```
In[5]:=  ReadDataFile["Dave:Work:Varian II:gm8788.dat"]
```

```
File documentation: "Returns on General Motors Stock during
    1987-1988"
```

```
ReadDataFile::defined:
    Variable symbol(s) {DAY, MONTH, YEAR, PRICE, RETURN}
        already defined. Clear and read again.
```

To reread the data, use **Clear** to remove the old definitions of the conflicting symbols (as in **Clear[DAY, MONTH, YEAR, PRICE, RETURN]**) and repeat the file read.

   With the data defined, we can now turn to some basic plots and summary statistics.

14.3   Descriptive Statistics, Sequence Plots, and Binning

14.3.1   Descriptive Statistics and Missing Values

The **DataTools** package includes a few simple summary statistics. These functions are mostly of value in conjunction with others that plot or group the data. The names of the functions, following *Mathematica* convention, are not abbreviated. For example, the average and standard deviation over these two years are

```
In[6]:=  ave = Average[ RETURN ]
```

```
Out[6]=  0.000933401
```

```
In[7]:=  sd = StandardDeviation[ RETURN ]
```

```
Out[7]=  0.0200948
```

Other summaries include **Variance, Median, InterquartileRange**, and **MAD**, which computes the median absolute deviation about the median. As promised, each of these functions omits symbolic data from calculations. When one or more symbolic items are found, a message is printed and the calculation continues with the remaining numerical values.

```
In[8]:=  Average[ Join[RETURN,{miss}] ]
```

```
DataTools`Private`dataFilter::found: 1 missing values removed.
```

```
Out[8]=  0.000933401
```

The filtering of missing data is controlled by the predicate **okQ** defined internally within **DataTools**. Alternative data filters are easily obtained by editing the definition of this function within the package.

Before moving on, the programming of these simple functions offers some insight into the speed of *Mathematica* calculations. Functions such as **Average** make extensive use the function **Dot** rather than **Plus**. Although this choice might seem odd, this approach produces faster summaries in typical applications even though it involves some overhead. For example, consider the time that it takes to compute the average of 1,000 uniform random numbers.

```
In[9]:=  x = Table[Random[],{1000}];
```

The obvious way to compute the average is to use the function **Plus**. Repeating the calculation 10 times takes about half a second. (The command **Plus@@x** is read as the summation of the list **x**.)

```
In[10]:= Timing[ Table[(Plus@@x)/Length[x], {10}]  ]  // First
```

```
Out[10]= 0.516667 Second
```

In comparison, the function **Average** builds a constant vector and then computes the dot product, as in the following calculation which takes less than a quarter of a second.

```
In[11]:= Timing[ Table[one=Table[1,{1000}];
              Dot[one,x]/1000,{10}] ] // First
```

```
Out[11]= 0.233333 Second
```

Even with the overhead of having to build the constant vector, **Dot** yields a faster calculation. In this case, the explanation is that **Plus** sorts its arguments into canonical order; **Dot** does not. Hayes (1995) offers a variety of other suggestions that are useful for speeding up *Mathematica* calculations. (Notice that the function **Average** does several other things, such as check for missing values, that slow its calculation.)

14.3.2   Sequence Plots and Dates

A careful analysis of any time series begins with sequence plots. To use the built-in function **ListPlot** requires some simple but tedious manipulations that **Scatterplot** provides automatically when given a single list as its argument. **Scatterplot** is basically a call to **ListPlot**, but **Scatterplot** adds features that are important in data analysis, including a transposed argument list, the option **PlotRange** set to show all the data, and missing values. The options of **Scatterplot**, such as adding a label to the plot, are a superset of those of **ListPlot**.

In[12]:= **Scatterplot[PRICE, PlotLabel->"Daily GM Stock Price"]**

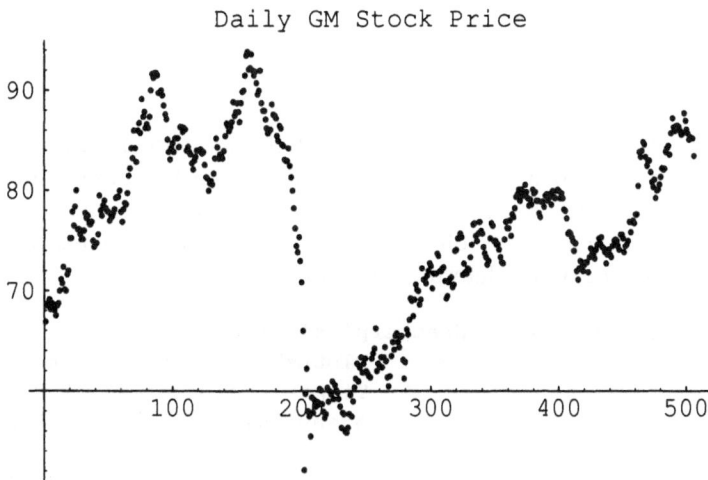

Daily GM Stock Price

Out[12]= -Graphics-

In contrast to the drift seen in the daily stock prices, the associated daily returns (i.e., the change in price from the previous trading day divided by the price on the previous day) show no evident trend. With a little extra effort, we can give the horizontal time axis a more useful set of labels. The first step is to associate dates with the axis labels. Because October 19, 1987 (day number 202), is the day the stock market fell substantially, it is useful to label this specific date.

In[13]:= **Position[RETURN, Min[RETURN]]**

Out[13]= {{202}}

Having a function that forms the labels makes the calculations easier to follow. Here is a simple version that builds a date string. The result is a (numerical value, date string) pair. This form is expected by the internal functions that label the axes of a plot.

In[14]:= **calDate[index_] :=**
```
        With[ {m={"Jan", "Feb", "Mar", "Apr", "May", "Jun",
                  "Jul", "Aug", "Sep", "Oct", "Nov", "Dec"}
              },
              {index,
                  StringJoin[ToString[DAY[[index]]]," ",
                             m[[MONTH[[index]]]]," ",
                             ToString[YEAR[[index]]] ]}
        ]
```

For example, the first day in these data is

```
In[15]:= calDate[1]
```

```
Out[15]= {1, 2 Jan 1987}
```

These labels are compatible with the standard **Ticks** option. It is probably also a good idea with these extended tick marks to move the axis beneath the data and make the plot relatively longer. Also, because such date labels will crowd on the axis, the following **Tick** option provides just three dates. The ticks for the y-axis are determined automatically.

```
In[16]:= sp = Scatterplot[RETURN,
                PlotLabel->"Daily GM Stock Return",
                Ticks->{calDate/@{1, 202, 506},Automatic},
                AxesOrigin->{0,-0.25}, AspectRatio->.5]
```

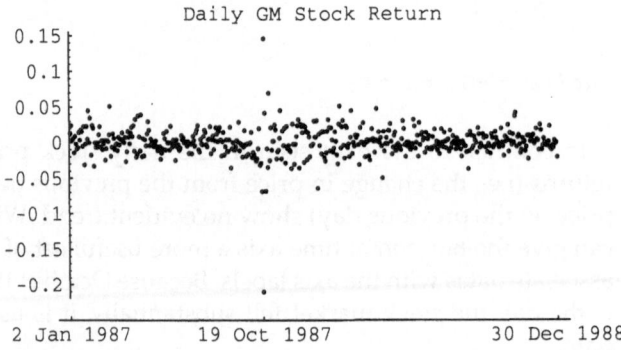

```
Out[16]= -Graphics-
```

We can further refine this plot by adding, for example, grid lines based on the average and standard deviation of the returns.

```
In[17]:= Show[sp, GridLines->{None, {ave+2 sd, ave-2 sd}}]
```

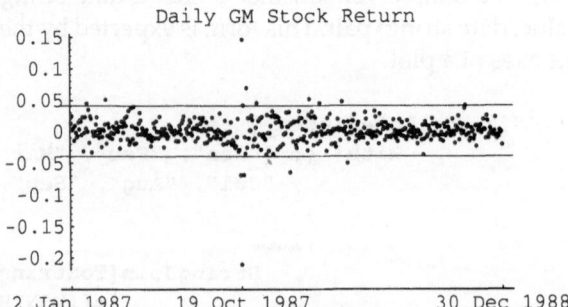

```
Out[17]= -Graphics-
```

It appears that the outlying values have inflated the standard deviation so that more than the usual 95% of the returns fall within two standard deviations of the mean. The actual percentage within this interval is about 97%.

```
In[18]:= withinQ[x_] := (ave-2sd <= x <= ave+2sd)
```

```
In[19]:= N [ (Count[RETURN, x_?withinQ])/Length[RETURN] ]
```

```
Out[19]= 0.970356
```

14.3.3   Binning

Simple descriptive functions such as **Average** and **StandardDeviation** become more interesting and powerful when combined with the grouping function **Bin**. As with built-in functions, each of the functions in **DataTools** has an accompanying description accessed by the query function "**?**". The first argument defines the "binning axis" and the second gives the values to be split into the associated bins.

```
In[20]:= ?Bin
```

```
Bin[x_List, y_List] returns a nested list of the values of y
    which share a common value of x. The first element in each
    item of the result is the binning value.
```

Here is a simple example of how to use **Bin**.

```
In[21]:= Bin[{1,1,1,2,2,2}, {1,2,3,4,5,6}]
```

```
Out[21]= {{1, {1, 2, 3}}, {2, {4, 5, 6}}}
```

Binning makes it easy to summarize the daily stock returns by calendar month. In the following examples, the trailing semicolon is important to avoid a lengthy printout on the screen. Also, **Bin** will print a warning message if, as illustrated in the next command, the arguments appear in the wrong order and thereby attempt to create a substantial number of bins (the cutoff in the code is 90% of the length of the input list).

```
In[22]:= byMonth = Bin[RETURN, MONTH];
```

```
Bin::TooMany: Appear to have too many (464) bins.
```

The next command groups the data by month into a list with 24 two-term lists.

```
In[23]:= byMonth = Bin[N[YEAR+(MONTH-1)/12], RETURN];
         Length[ byMonth ]
```

```
Out[23]= 24
```

The first member of each paired list in **byMonth** is the numerical date, and the second member is the list of associated values. Here is the paired list for January, 1987.

```
In[24]:= First[byMonth]
```

```
Out[24]= {1987., {0.01325758, 0.02429906, 0.003649635,
          0.005454545, -0.01446655, 0.009174312, -0.001818182,
          -0.009107468, -0.007352941, 0.01481481, 0.003649635,
          0.01818182, 0.01607143, -0.005272408, 0.0229682,
          -0.03108808, -0.001782531, 0.02321429, 0.005235602,
          0.04513889, 0}}
```

With the returns grouped into monthly subsets, function mapping gives summary statistics for each month. In the next command, **Average** and **Standard-Deviation** are applied to the returns for each month (second member of each list), and each date (the first member) is converted into a string, dropping the redundant characters "19".

```
In[25]:= summary   = {Average[ #[[2]] ],
                      StandardDeviation[ #[[2]] ],
                      StringDrop[ToString[#[[1]]], 2] }&
                 /@ byMonth;
         Short[summary]
```

```
Out[25]= {{0.00639151, 0.0163335, 87.}, <<23>>}
```

The format of this summary as a list of $\{x, y, \text{string}\}$ triples is ideal for the plotting functions that come with *Mathematica*. These functions expect data to be organized as a list of observations, with each element of the list denoting the values for one observation. The function **LabeledListPlot** from **Graphics'Graphics'** gives a nice plot. The default *Mathematica* scaling, however, conceals the large outlier from October, 1987; the option **PlotRange->All** forces the plot to show all the data.

```
In[26]:= LabeledListPlot[summary,
                         AxesLabel->{"Ave Return", "SD Return"},
                         PlotRange->All]
```

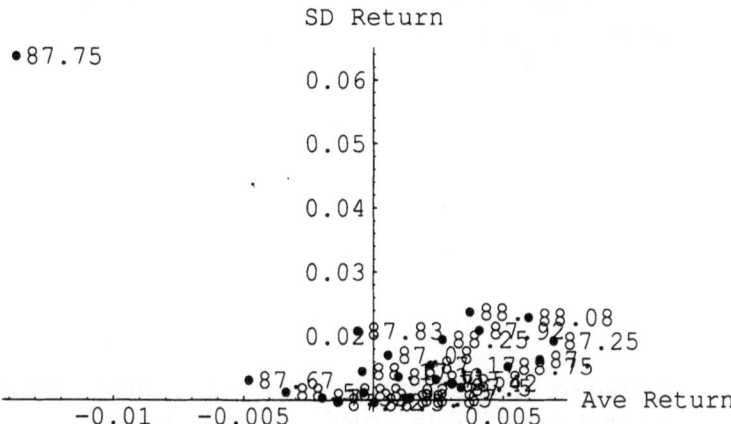

Out[26]= -Graphics-

To see the pattern in the cluster of the other 23 months, we need to manually set the range.

In[27]:= **LabeledListPlot[summary,**
                AxesLabel->{"Ave Return", "SD Return"},
                PlotRange->{{-.005, .010}, {0.005, .025}}]

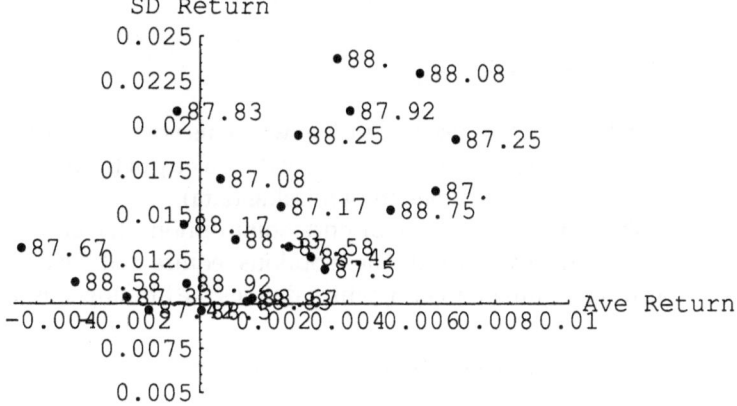

Out[27]= -Graphics-

As financial theory would suggest, months with higher average return also tend to have higher standard deviation. That is, risk and return are positively correlated if we set aside October, 1987.

To compute the correlation explicitly, first transpose the list of means and standard deviations so that the columns are easily accessed. With October, 1987 included in the data, the correlation is negative.

```
In[28]:= trans = Transpose[summary];
         avg = trans[[1]];
         sd  = trans[[2]];
```

```
In[29]:= Correlation[avg, sd]
```

```
Out[29]= -0.515415
```

We can set aside October, 1987 (the tenth month) without losing its value by simply tagging it with a symbolic value. The tagging is done by multiplying this observation in place using the "C-like" expression *=.

```
In[30]:= avg[[10]] *= na
```

```
Out[30]= -0.0137414 na
```

With this outlier set aside, the correlation is virtually the same as before, only positive.

```
In[31]:= Correlation[avg, sd]
```

```
DataTools'Private'dataFilter::found: 1 missing values removed.
```

```
Out[31]= 0.542882
```

Functions such as **Correlation** which use two or more values associated with an observation exclude that observation if any of the needed values are symbolic (i.e., use casewise deletion of missing data).

The function **Bin** also supports some options that are useful when the binning factor is not categorical. These options require that the data be sorted so that the leading argument to **Bin**, which defines the binning axis, is in the desired order.

```
In[32]:= Options[Bin]
```

```
Out[32]= {BinPercentage -> 0.2, BinWidth -> Automatic}
```

The resulting bins hold either a fixed proportion of the elements of the second argument as ordered by the first argument, or group the data over intervals of a fixed width. The leading element of the resulting bin lists is the average of the associated values defined by the first argument. For example, the next command splits the data into two bins.

```
In[33]:= Bin[{10,20,30,40,50,60},{1,2,3,4,5,6},
            BinPercentage->0.5]
```

```
Out[33]= {{20, {1, 2, 3}}, {50, {4, 5, 6}}}
```

To illustrate these types of binning methods, let us first quickly build a numerical date variable by combining the day, month, and year information. Ignoring the lengths of the months, we have

```
In[34]:= DATE = DAY + MONTH * 30 + (YEAR-1987)*360;
         Short[DATE]
```

```
Out[34]= {32, 35, 36, 37, 38, 39, 42, 43, 44, <<492>>, 743, 747,
          748, 749, 750}
```

Following is a sequence plot of the average returns for 30-day segments. The argument to the *Mathematica* function **ListPlot** is formed by function mapping; the first element is just the first element of each list produced by bin (the "average date"), and the second is the average return. As with other built-in *Mathematica* graphing commands, we need to set the option **PlotRange -> All** to avoid hiding outlying portions of the data. (The **SetOption** command can be used to change the default for the entire session.)

```
In[35]:= ListPlot[{#[[1]], Average[#[[2]]]}& /@
                   Bin[DATE, RETURN, BinWidth->30],
                   PlotRange->All ]
```

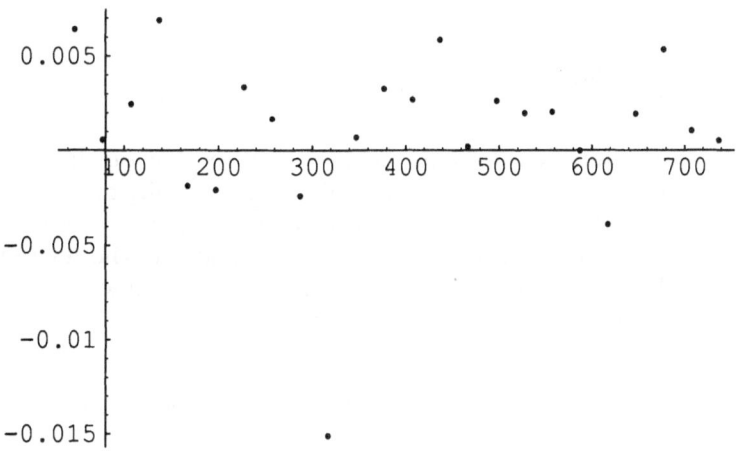

```
Out[35]= -Graphics-
```

14.4   Distribution Plots

14.4.1   Histograms

The function **Histogram** draws this familiar summary of the distribution of
a set of values. It uses the function **GeneralizedBarChart** from the supplemental *Mathematica* graphics package. The function also holds the expression
given as its input and uses this expression as a label for the plot. Continuing our
analysis of the GM returns, the default bin width is small because of the extreme
outliers noted in the initial time series plots.

```
In[36]:= Histogram[RETURN]
```

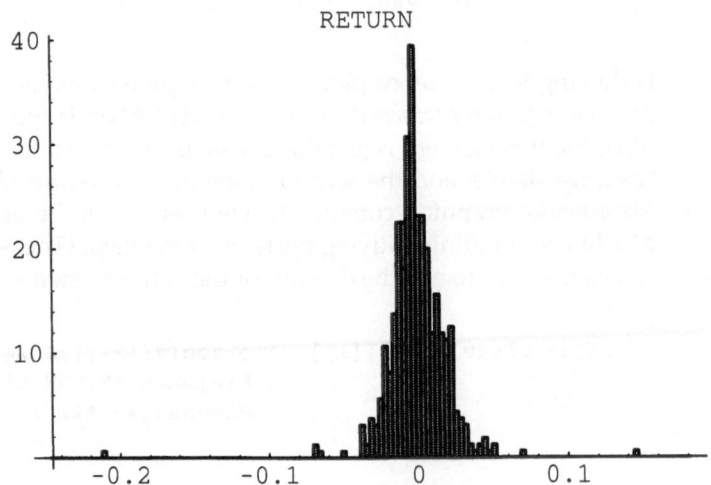

```
Out[36]= -Graphics-
```

The function **Select** makes it easy to filter out the extremes, which in this
example are associated with the large volatility of the stock market in October,
1987. We obtain a more informative histogram by selecting only those days for
which the return lies between −0.1 and 0.1. The revised plot also illustrates
how to use options to adjust the bin width and to add a more useful label. The
resulting plot is saved and named **hist**.

```
In[37]:= filteredReturn  = Select[RETURN,(Abs[#]<0.1)&];
```

```
In[38]:= hist = Histogram[ filteredReturn,
              PlotLabel->"Filtered GM Return",
              BinWidth->.005]
```

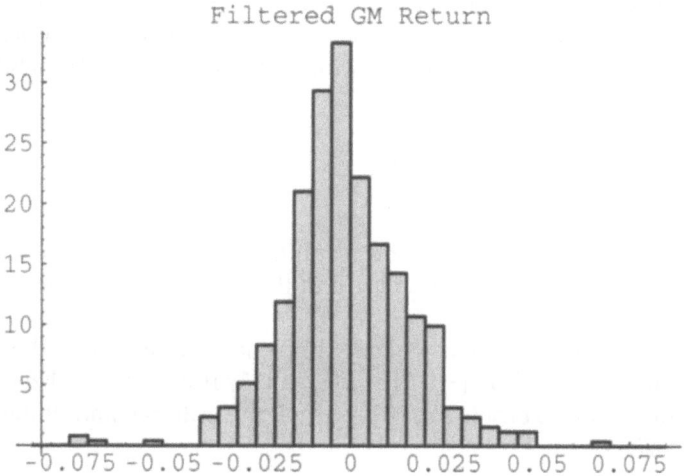

Out[38]= -Graphics-

14.4.2   Kernel Density Estimates

The histogram conveys an inadequate impression of the distribution of the underlying population. Kernel density estimates (Silverman 1986) eliminate some of these problems, such as the choice of where to position the bins and the roughness due to the rectangular bins. A kernel density estimate based on n observations $X_1, X_2, \ldots, X_n$ is defined as

$$K_h(x) = \frac{1}{n} \sum_{i=1}^{n} \frac{1}{h} S\left(\frac{x - X_i}{h}\right), \qquad (14.1)$$

where the function S is a smoothing kernel which is typically a smooth probability density such as the standard normal. The parameter $h > 0$ controls the level of smoothness: small values of h produce a rough density estimate, whereas large values of h produce a very smooth estimate. The right choice for h depends on the true underlying density function which is to be estimated, and Silverman (1986) reviews methods that have been proposed for choosing h from data.

The function **KernelDensity** computes a kernel density estimate, and returns the estimate K as a *function*. The default options for **KernelDensity** allow one to choose the kernel function S (**KernelFunction**), the number of points at which the kernel density K is evaluated (**KernelGrid**), and the smoothing parameter h (**KernelScale**).

In[39]:= **Options[KernelDensity]**

Out[39]= {KernelFunction -> BiweightKernel, KernelGrid -> 25,
        KernelScale -> Automatic}

By default, the kernel scale h is determined automatically by the function **KernelScale** which assumes the unknown density f is a normal density with standard deviation σ and evaluates Equation (3.21) from Silverman (1986),

$$h_{opt} = k_2^{-2/5} \left(\frac{\int S(t)^2 dt}{n \int f''(x)^2 dx} \right)^{1/5} , \tag{14.2}$$

where $k_2 = \int t^2 S(t) dt$. The resulting smoothing parameter h_{opt} minimizes the mean integrated squared error of the density estimate under the assumption of normality.

For example, a particularly simple kernel function is the biweight. This function is defined on $[-1, 1]$ as $S(x) = (15/16)(1 - x)^2$ and zero elsewhere. (This is the default kernel.) For this kernel, the optimal smoothing parameter is about $2.78\sigma/n^{1/5}$.

```
In[40]:= S[t_] := (15/16)(1-t^2)^2;
         KernelScale[S,-1,1]
```

```
Out[40]= 2.77794
```

Alternatively, the optimal parameter for a Gaussian kernel is approximately $1.06\sigma/n^{1/5}$.

```
In[41]:= S[t_] := (1/Sqrt[2 Pi]) E^(-t^2/2);
         KernelScale[S,-Infinity,Infinity]
```

```
Out[41]= 1.05922
```

To avoid repeated calculation of the optimal smoothing constant via (14.2), both these kernels with their optimal parameters are predefined in the **DataTools** package. Further illustration of these calculations in *Mathematica* appears in Stine (1995).

Returning to our data analysis, **KernelDensity** by default uses a biweight kernel with the optimal h as previously defined.

```
In[42]:= kd = KernelDensity[filteredReturn]
```

```
KernelDensity::scale: Kernel smoothing constant =
   2.77794 s/n^(1/5)
```

```
KernelDensity::range:
   Kernel width is 0.00621676 on interval
   [-0.0812166,0.0822533]
```

```
Out[42]= InterpolatingFunction[{-0.0812166, 0.0822533}, <>]
```

The symbol **kd** represents a function that interpolates the kernel density estimate along a default grid of 25 points that are equally spaced on the x-axis. The domain of the interpolating function is, in this example, the interval $[-0.0812, 0.0823]$. This function can be evaluated like any other within its domain of definition.

In[43]:= **kd[0]**

Out[43]= 30.3378

Plots are more interesting.

In[44]:= **kPlot = Plot[kd[x], {x,-0.06, 0.06}]**

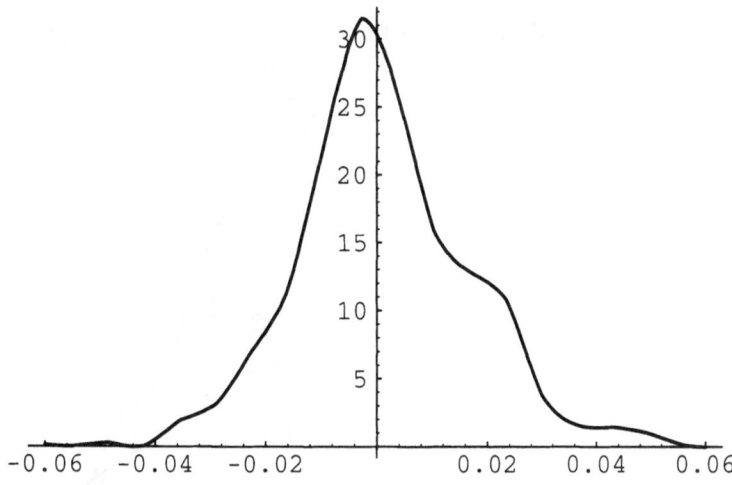

Out[44]= -Graphics-

It ought to be clear from this graph, though, that the use of a kernel density estimate with the optimal smoothing parameter does not completely avoid the question of how to choose a bin width. The calculations that lead to the optimal smoothing constant begin with the assumption that the population is normal. Some will feel that the kernel scale chosen by the optimal scheme (14.2) produces an estimate that is too "rough" in this example. In such situations, one can control the smoothness of the estimate by manually setting the option **KernelScale**. Setting the value of this option to 1 and 5 yields rougher and smoother density estimates, respectively.

In[45]:= **kd1 = KernelDensity[filteredReturn, KernelScale->1];**

KernelDensity::scale: Kernel smoothing constant = 1 s/n^(1/5)

KernelDensity::range:
    Kernel width is 0.0022379 on interval [-0.0732589,0.0742956]

```
In[46]:= kd5 = KernelDensity[ filteredReturn, KernelScale->5];
```

```
KernelDensity::scale: Kernel smoothing constant = 5 s/n^(1/5)
```

```
KernelDensity::range:
    Kernel width is 0.0111895 on interval [-0.0911621,0.0921989]
```

In this case, the resulting estimates are similar. In the figure that follows, the kernel using $h_{opt} = 2.778$ is shown as the connected line, with the alternatives using $h = 1$ (black) and $h = 5$ (gray) dashed.

```
In[47]:= kpThree = Plot[{kd[x], kd1[x], kd5[x]},{x,-.06,.06},
            PlotStyle->{GrayLevel[0],
                {GrayLevel[0] ,Dashing[{.02,.02}]},
                {GrayLevel[.5],Dashing[{.02,.02}]}} ]
```

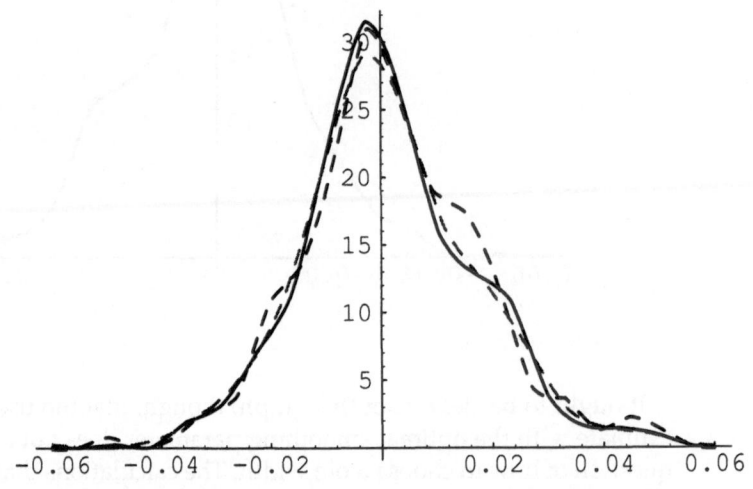

```
Out[47]= -Graphics-
```

Silverman (1986) suggests several more rigorous methods for choosing the scale, but all require further assumptions about the unknown density or substantially more computing.

When overlaid with a histogram, we see that the kernel estimator smooths out irregularities due to the rectangular bins. Most of its advantage over the histogram as an estimator of the unknown density comes from removing the rough edges of the histogram's bins. Both of the estimates, however, indicate a curious "bump" on the right side near a return of 0.025.

In[48]:= **Show[hist, kPlot]**

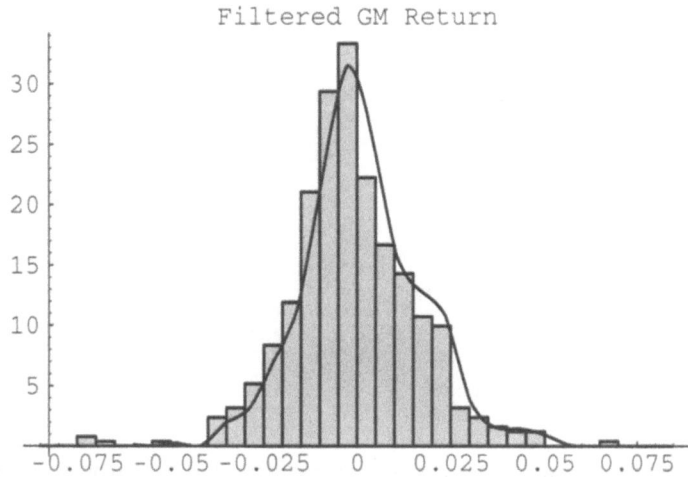

Out[48]= -Graphics-

14.4.3 Boxplots

We can further augment the plot of the kernel density estimate and histogram
by adding a boxplot to show the locations of the quartiles and outliers. The
function that draws boxplots is quite flexible and has quite a few options that
make it easy to add these summaries to other figures.

In[49]:= **Options[Boxplot]**

Out[49]= {BoxVertical -> False, BoxWidth -> 1, BoxCenter -> 1,
             BoxFill -> True, AspectRatio -> 0.5, Frame -> True}

Inasmuch as the boxplot summarizes one variable, we need to define how to
position it in a graph with two axes. **BoxCenter** is the x-axis or y-axis coordinate
that locates the image of the boxplot, and **BoxWidth** is the width of the box on
this same axis. Because the vertical scale of the histogram of the returns runs
from 0 to 35, we locate the box below the x-axis so that it will not obscure
the histogram or axis labels and set its width to 5. By default, the boxplot is
positioned horizontally.

In[50]:= **bp = Boxplot[filteredReturn, BoxCenter->-10,
                    BoxWidth->5]**

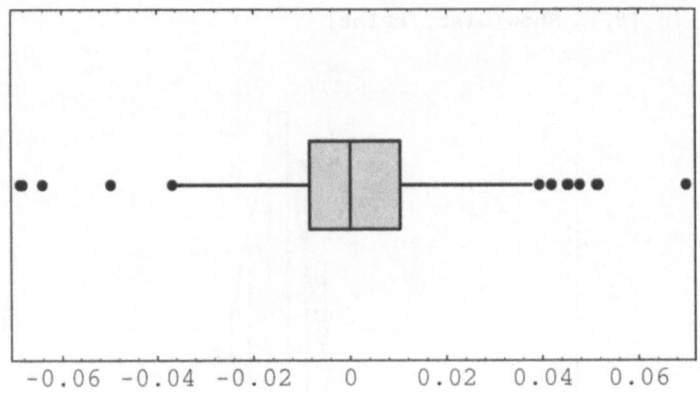

Out[50]= -Graphics-

The final summary of this subset of the daily returns combines the histogram, kernel density, and boxplot in one display.

In[51]:= **Show[hist, kPlot, bp]**

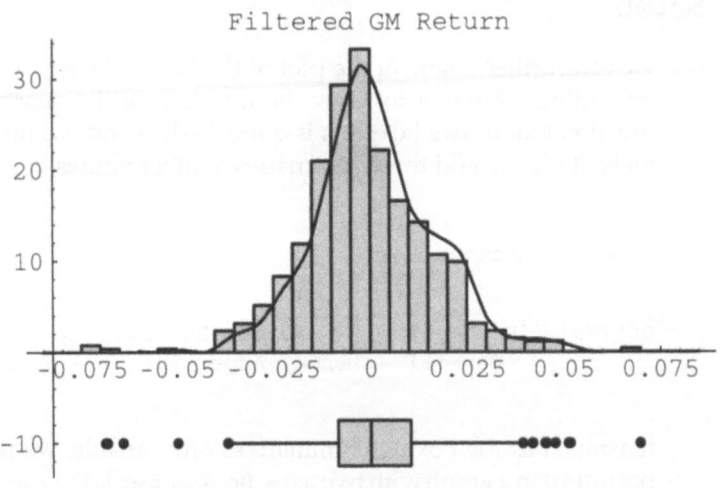

Out[51]= -Graphics-

Boxplots are particularly useful for comparison. For example, a sequence of comparison boxplots makes the periods of high variation in the returns clear. The comparison boxplots are constructed by using a pure function applied to the data binned into 20 cells. Setting **DisplayFunction->Identity** avoids having to see the 20 individual boxplots as they are generated.

```
In[52]:= boxes = Boxplot[#[[2]], BoxCenter->#[[1]], BoxWidth->25,
                        BoxVertical->True, AspectRatio->2,
                        DisplayFunction->Identity]& /@
                Bin[DATE,RETURN,BinPercentage->.05];
```

```
In[53]:= Show[boxes, PlotRange->Automatic,
              DisplayFunction->$DisplayFunction]
```

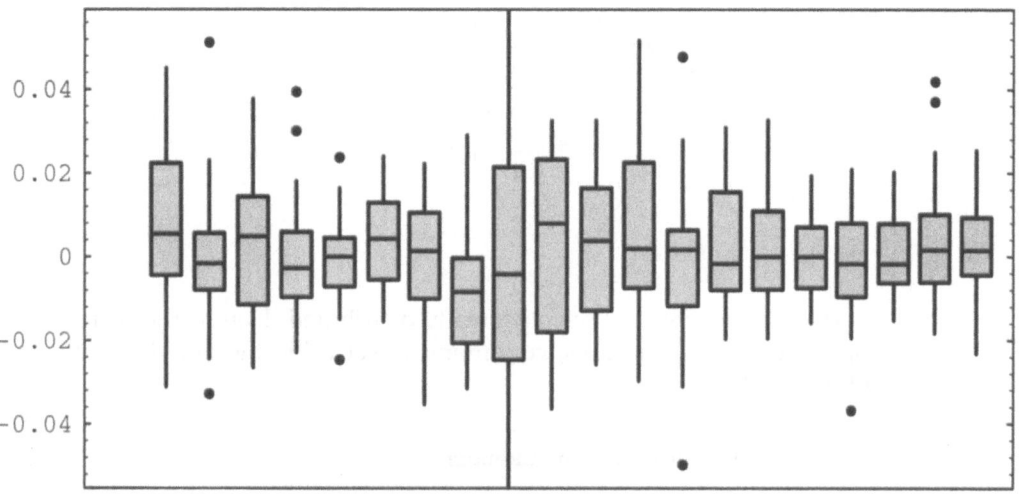

```
Out[53]= -Graphics-
```

14.4.4 Quantile Plots

As mentioned before, a weakness of the automatic algorithm for choosing the amount of smoothing in **KernelDensity** is that this method *assumes* that the underlying population is normal. To see if this assumption is reasonable, here is the normal quantile plot (or QQ plot) of the filtered returns. (This is a rather slow command due to the speed of the *Mathematica* code that evaluates the inverse normal distribution.) The plot also shows a reference line; when the data are a sample from a normal population, the points lie within sampling error of this line. For example, by using **NormalSample** included in **DataTools** to generate a sample of normals, we can test this function.

```
In[54]:= norm = NormalSample[25];
        QQPlot[ norm ]
```

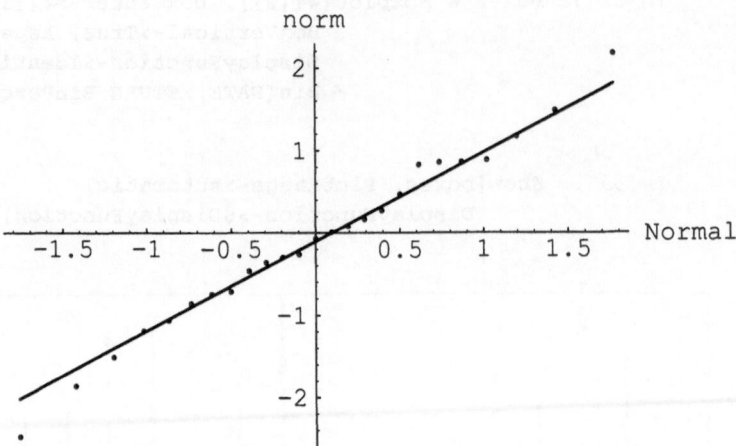

Out [54]= -Graphics-

The GM returns also seem normally distributed. Here is the corresponding figure for the GM returns, continuing to set aside the outlying values from October, 1987.

In [55]:= **QQPlot[filteredReturn]**

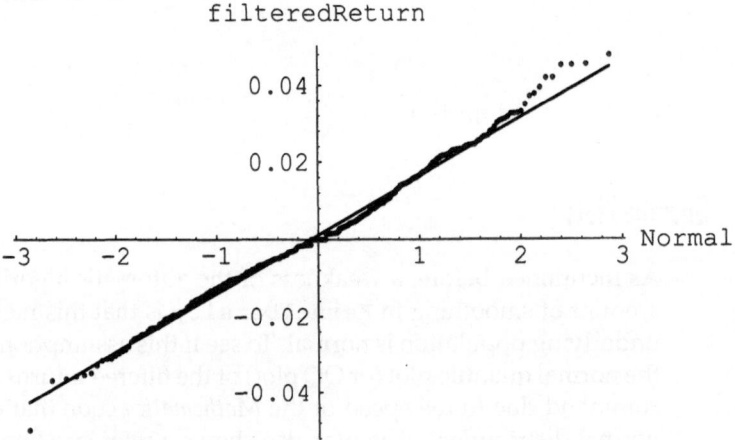

Out [55]= -Graphics-

Although the upper tail of the data slips away from the reference line at the right of the figure (a region of substantial sampling variation), the distribution of the returns (albeit without October, 1987) appears quite normal.

14.5   Scatterplots, Smoothing, and Regression

14.5.1   Scatterplot Matrix

Although there appears to be little correlation over time in the sequence of returns, one might still suspect that some correlation exists in the volatility. The binning function again comes in handy for computing means and standard deviations from the 50 periods of 10 days each. (This command does not generate 51 bins because it excludes the last incomplete bin of 6 values; also, the bin size is the floor of the length of the series times the bin percentage.)

```
In[56]:= bins = Bin[DATE,RETURN, BinPercentage->.02];
```

```
In[57]:= time   = First /@ bins;
         mean   = Average[#[[2]]]& /@ bins;
         stdDev = StandardDeviation[#[[2]]]& /@ bins;
```

To view these two sequences of summary measures, we would like to examine each versus time as well as plotted versus each other. The function **Scatter-plotMatrix** generates all three of these plots, and collects them together in an array with their associated correlations.

```
In[58]:= ScatterplotMatrix[mean, stdDev, time]
```

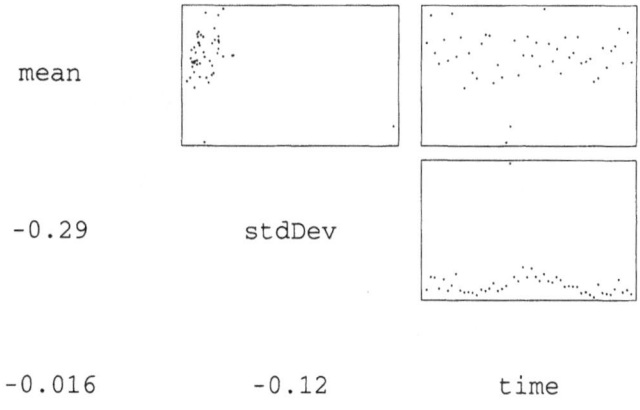

mean		
-0.29	stdDev	
-0.016	-0.12	time

```
Out[58]= -GraphicsArray-
```

The coincident timing of the outlying values of the mean and standard deviation of the returns is apparent in the last column of two plots which shows both series plotted on time. The plot of the mean versus standard deviation of the returns suggests just how volatile the market became in late 1987.

14.5.2   Scatterplot Smoothing

This section focuses upon functions that describe dependence. For these examples, the dependence is that in the sequence of 50 standard deviations computed from 10 consecutive trading days. One period dominates the sequence of standard deviations in the prior scatterplot matrix. Rather than continue with this outlier, set the extreme value to the average of its neighbors.

In[59]:= **Max[stdDev]**

Out[59]= 0.0271235

In[60]:= **Position[stdDev,Max[stdDev]]**

Out[60]= {{21}}

In[61]:= **stdDev[[21]] = Average[stdDev[[{20,22}]]]**

Out[61]= 0.0177502

Here is the sequence plot of the "cleaned" standard deviations. With the outlier no longer compressing the rest of the data, this plot shows considerable tracking. (Compare this plot to that in the lower right corner of the scatterplot matrix.)

In[62]:= **Scatterplot[time, stdDev]**

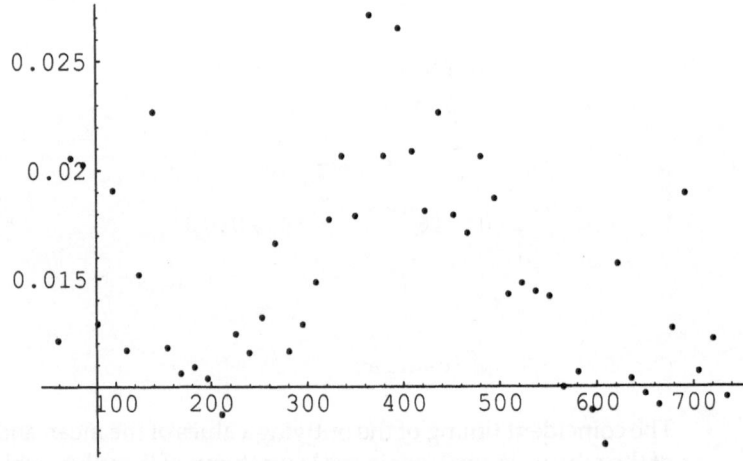

Out[62]= -Graphics-

A lag plot gives a better notion of the strength of the correlation. The scatterplot of SD_t on its lag SD_{t-1} shows a moderate level of period-to-period dependence, confirmed by the correlation estimate which is slightly above 0.5.

```
In[63]:= lagSD = Drop[stdDev,-1];
         SD    = Drop[stdDev, 1];
```

```
In[64]:= sp = Scatterplot[lagSD, SD]
```

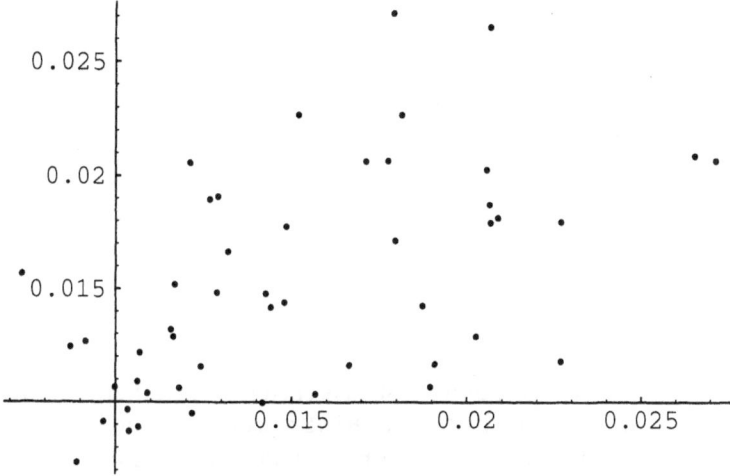

```
Out[64]= -Graphics-
```

```
In[65]:= Correlation[lagSD, SD]
```

```
Out[65]= 0.538746
```

Whereas correlation measures the strength of linear association, a scatterplot smoother offers an image of the dependence that does not presume linearity. The function **Smooth**, like **KernelDensity**, builds a function. The function constructed by **Smooth** estimates the dependence of SD_t on SD_{t-1} in the form of the conditional expectation $E[SD_t|SD_{t-1}]$. **Smooth** works by building a sequence of local linear approximations that are joined with a cubic spline. Near the edges of the data, the smooth is simply the local linear fit.

```
In[66]:= smth = Smooth[lagSD, SD]
```

```
Out[66]= InterpolatingFunction[{0.0073308, 0.0271235}, <>]
```

The domain of the resulting function is limited to the indicated interval.

In[67]:= **Plot[smth[x],{x,0.008,0.025}]**

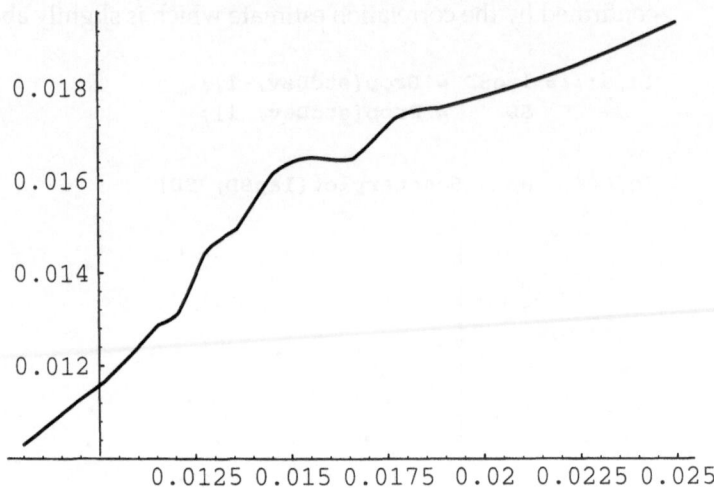

Out[67]= -Graphics-

By default, **Smooth** constructs each local linear approximation using 40% of the data as defined by **SmoothBinPercentage** and is evaluated at about 20 points along the *x*-axis (the reciprocal of **SmoothSkipPercentage**).

In[68]:= **Options[Smooth]**

Out[68]= {SmoothSkipPercentage -> 0.05,
            SmoothBinPercentage -> 0.4}

The wiggles in the smoother, like those in a kernel density which is too rough, are probably random fluctuations. As with kernel density estimates, the choice is somewhat subjective. Although computationally intensive methods exist for determining the optimal smoothing parameter, one needs to carefully examine the estimate graphically. Setting the binning percentage wider to span 60% of the data offers a smoother approximation to the conditional expectation of SD_t.

In[69]:= **smth60 = Smooth[lagSD, SD, SmoothBinPercentage->.6]**

Out[69]= InterpolatingFunction[{0.0073308, 0.0271235}, <>]

We plot the second smooth estimate using dashes so that we can superimpose it with the other initial estimate. With either smoother, the relationship appears a bit nonlinear with the slope tapering off as we move from left to right.

```
In[70]:= smthPlot = Plot[{smth[x], smth60[x]}, {x,0.008,0.025},
                    PlotStyle->{GrayLevel[0],
                        Dashing[{0.025,0.025}]}]
```

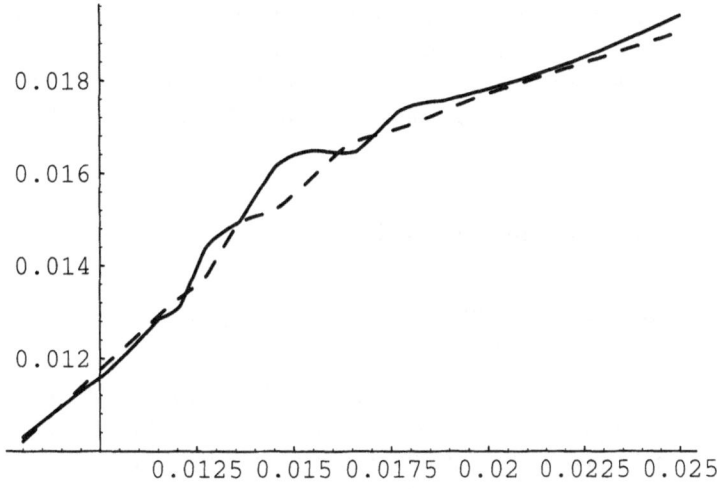

```
Out[70]= -Graphics-
```

With the data superimposed, the nonlinearity appears small relative to the variation in the sequence of standard deviations.

```
In[71]:= Show[sp, smthPlot]
```

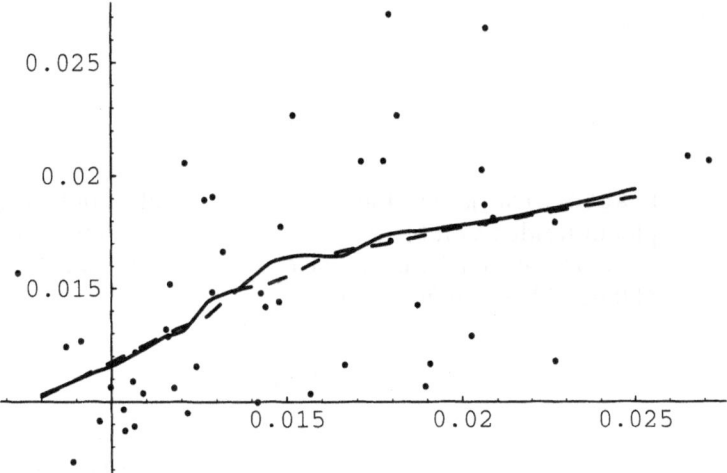

```
Out[71]= -Graphics-
```

14.5.3   Regression

Regression offers a parametric alternative to smoothing. The fitting routine **Regression** included with *Mathematica* is found in the supplemental **Statistics** package. It differs from the more basic program **OLS** described here by providing more output and taking longer to run.

One uses **OLS** in the manner of **Scatterplot**, with the covariates or predictors as the first argument, then the response. Two options control the behavior of **OLS**.

In[72]:= **Options[OLS]**

Out[72]= {Constant -> True, Residuals -> True}

By default, the result of **OLS** is a list with the fitted values and residuals. If the option **Residuals** is set to **False**, the fitted values and residuals are not returned; instead, **OLS** returns a list of the fitted coefficients. A contant term is estimated in the linear equation unless the option **Constant** is set to **False**.

In this example, the fitted slope of a simple linear regression of SD_t on its lag SD_{t-1} is quite significant.

In[73]:= **fitRes = OLS[lagSD, SD];**

Factor	Coefficient	Std. Err.	t-Stat
1	0.00683517	0.00196591	3.47685
lagSD	0.544174	0.124125	4.38409

$$s = 0.00411978 \quad R^2 = 0.290247$$

Scatterplot accepts the output of **OLS** as its input and produces the familiar plot of residuals on fitted values. We can also embellish the residual plot with a smooth function by using the **ScatterplotFunction** option and a smooth of the residuals on fitted values.

In[74]:= **sRes = Smooth @@ fitRes**

Out[74]= InterpolatingFunction[{0.0108244, 0.0215951}, <>]

In[75]:= **Scatterplot[fitRes, ScatterplotFunction->sRes]**

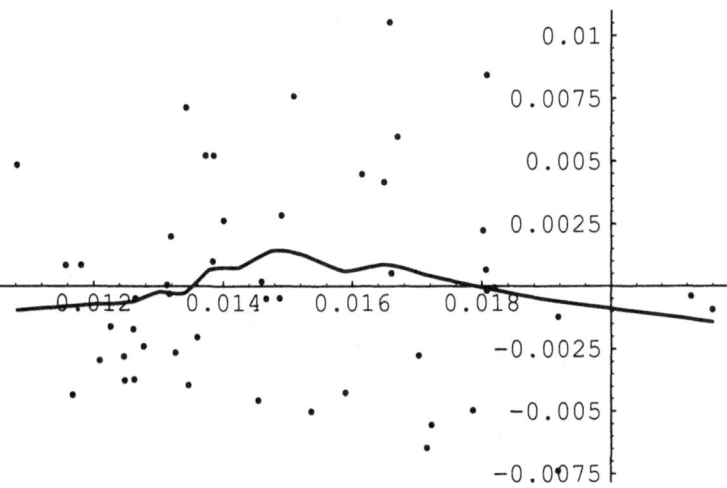

Out[75] = -Graphics-

The smooth in this residual plot suggests slight deviations from linearity, and once again one might suspect that the slope differs at the extremes of the data. For the curious, we can go further and fit a quadratic polynomial model as a means of capturing the slight curvature. The fit, as one might expect, does not improve significantly (the *t*-statistic for the added coefficient is small).

In[76] := **OLS[{lagSD, lagSD^2}, SD];**

Factor	Coefficient	Std. Err.	t-Stat
1	0.00130892	0.0061473	0.212925
lagSD	1.28057	0.785928	1.62937
lagSD^2	-22.3323	23.5346	-0.948912

$s = 0.00412416 \quad R^2 = 0.303873$

We can show this quadratic function with the data as well, once again using the **ScatterplotFunction** option to superimpose a function on the scatterplot. Though not significant, the curvature is consistent with the visual impression created by the original nonlinear smoother.

In[77]:= **quad[x_] := .0013 + 1.28 x -22.33 x^2;**
        Scatterplot[lagSD, SD, ScatterplotFunction->quad]

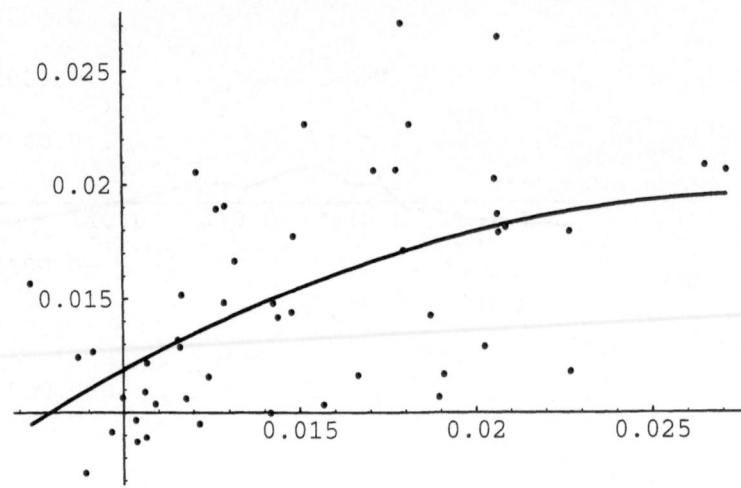

Out[77]= -Graphics-

Although very few methods can accommodate the huge outlier introduced into the analysis by the activity around October, 1987, it is often useful nonetheless to check results of a least squares analysis by using a robust regression. Street et al. (1988) give a short, readable introduction to the calculations and ideas of robust regression. A robust regression uses an iterative calculation that performs a sequence of weighted least squares regressions, here starting from an unweighted OLS fit. Each iteration attempts to downweight outlying values deemed "unusual" by the algorithm. In this example, a robust regression finds little reason to differ from a least squares analysis.

In[78]:= **rr = RobustRegression[lagSD, SD];**

RobustRegression::iter: Iteration 0 @ {0.00683517, 0.544174}

RobustRegression::iter: Iteration 1 @ {0.00669804, 0.540797}

RobustRegression::iter: Iteration 2 @ {0.00667787, 0.538616}

General::stop: Further output of RobustRegression::iter
        will be suppressed during this calculation.

Factor	Coefficient	Asym. S.E.	Coef/S.E.
1	0.0066713	0.00221112	3.01716
lagSD	0.537434	0.133268	4.03274

Robust scale = 0.00382219

The results returned by **RobustRegression** are similar to those of the *Mathematica* function **Regression** and are more extensive than those of **OLS**. To distinguish among these items, **RobustRegression** adopts the style of **Regression** and returns a list of replacement rules. The labels for each of these replacement rules are shown next.

In[79]:= **First /@ rr**

Out[79]= {Estimates, Variance, Scale, WeightFunction,
            FitResiduals, PredictedResponse, RobustC, Weights}

To plot the residuals, we have to use these rules to extract values as in the following.

In[80]:= **robFitRes = {PredictedResponse, FitResiduals} /. rr;**

The robust fit is quite similar to that from least squares even though several observations have been downweighted by the iteratively reweighted least squares algorithm used to obtain the robust estimates. The plot on the left shows the residuals and fit from the robust analysis, and that on the right is the plot of the robust residuals on the fitting weights used in the final stage of the iterations.

In[81]:= **sp1 = Scatterplot[robFitRes, DisplayFunction->Identity];**
            sp2 = Scatterplot[Weights/.rr, robFitRes[[2]],
                            DisplayFunction->Identity]

Out[81]= -Graphics-

In[82]:= **Show[GraphicsArray[{sp1,sp2}],**
                   DisplayFunction->$DisplayFunction]

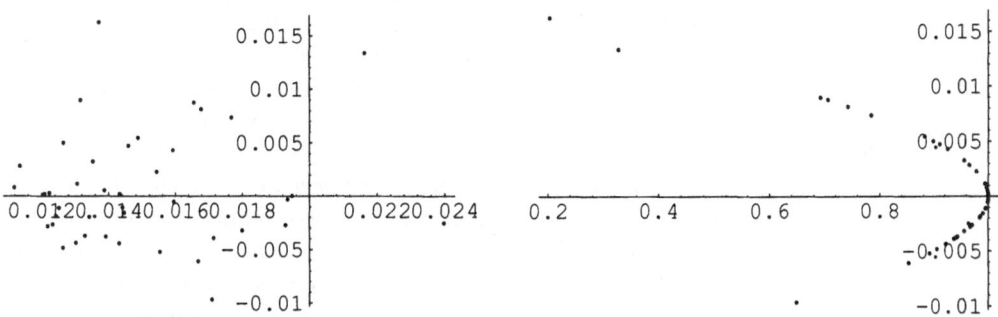

The curve evident in the plot of the robust residuals on the weights shows how the points become downweighted as they move away from the fit (represented by the horizontal line at zero in these plots). The downweighting by default is accomplished by the biweight function $b(x) = (1 - x^2)^2$ for $|x| < 1$ and zero otherwise. (The biweight function used in kernel density estimation differs by a multiplicative constant that makes the kernel integrate to one.) The robust tuning constant is a further option used to scale the residuals' defaults to the value giving 95% efficiency in a Gaussian problem.

```
In[83]:= Options[ RobustRegression ]

Out[83]= {Constant -> True, Residuals -> True,
          RobustWeightFunction -> BiweightWeightFunction,
          RobustConstant -> 4.685,
          MaxIterations -> 10}
```

Further discussion and examples of robust regression in *Mathematica* appear in Stine (1995).

14.6 Discussion

With the proliferation of many specialized packages for statistics, why should one use *Mathematica* for data analysis?

Few would dispute the claim that *Mathematica* produces superb graphics that capture the results of a statistical data analysis. Each graph can be easily modified and customized to illustrate each component of the analysis. The resulting figures are clearly suitable for inclusion in publications. These same graphics are, unfortunately, rather static.

Until true interactive graphics become standard in *Mathematica* it will remain the poor cousin of other dedicated statistical computing environments as a foundation for the actual data analysis. Modern data analysis, as powerfully illustrated by the R-Code software of Cook and Weisburg (1994), relies upon highly interactive graphics such as plot linking, slicing, and brushing. These methods are not feasible in current releases of *Mathematica* for most systems. The methods *are* feasible in alternative systems, such as the Lisp-Stat environment (Tierney 1990, 1995) used to build R-Code. Lisp-Stat provides both the capability to link plots so that high-dimensional features of the data are revealed as well as the interface tools, such as slider controls, that control these features.

Nonetheless, the notebook front-end of *Mathematica* is itself a highly interactive environment. Notebooks allow one to develop and carefully document the stages of an analysis within *Mathematica* itself, without having to resort to cutting and pasting results or thoughts on the analysis into other documents. One should also keep in mind that choices in data analysis are often guided by theory (such as the choice of the kernel smoothing parameter), and the symbolic manipulation features of *Mathematica* make such calculations routine.

14.6.1 Acknowledgments

Thanks to John Fox for comments on previous versions of this work and to Dave Belsley for numerous hints and the encouragement to use numerically stable methods when fitting regressions.

14.7   References

Belsley, D.A. 1993. "Econometrics.m: A Package for Doing Econometrics in *Mathematica.*" In *Economic and Financial Modeling with Mathematica*, H. Varian, Ed., New York, Springer, 300–343.

Cook, R. D. and S. Weisburg. 1994. *An Introduction to Regression Graphics*. New York, Wiley.

Hayes, A. 1995. "Experiments in Efficient Programming." *Mathematica Journal*, **5**, 24–31.

He, Y. 1995. *Time Series Pack: Reference and User's Guide*. Champaign, IL, Wolfram Research.

Silverman, 1986. *Density Estimation for Statistics and Data Analysis*. London, Chapman and Hall.

Stine, R. A. 1995. "Data Analysis using *Mathematica.*" *Sociological Methods and Research*, **23**, 352–372.

Street, J.O., R. J. Carroll, and D. Ruppert. 1988. "A Note on Computing Robust Regression Estimates Using Iteratively Reweighted Least Squares." *American Statistician*, **42**, 152–154.

Tierney, L. 1990. *Lisp-Stat*. New York, Wiley.

Tierney, L. 1995. "Data Analysis Using Lisp-Stat." *Sociological Methods and Research*, **23**, 329–351.

15 Doing Monte Carlo Studies with *Mathematica*

David A. Belsley

Mathematica is a highly productive environment in which to develop and perfect Monte Carlo studies. In this chapter we examine the basic notions of Monte Carlo experimentation and how they can be carried out in *Mathematica*. The procedures are exemplified with an actual Monte Carlo study that investigates the relative power of using zero-padded versus truncated residuals in testing for serial correlation with artificial regressions.

15.1 Introduction

Monte Carlo methods are becoming an increasingly important way in which we learn about the properties of statistical objects whose theoretical analysis in some way confounds current human abilities. In rough metaphor, a Monte Carlo experiment is a strenuous and systematic exercise of some statistical object that puts it through its paces so many times and under so many known conditions that we can begin to understand its typical (likely) behavior. The flexibility and power of the research environment that is *Mathematica* make it particularly easy to design, refine, and develop Monte Carlo experiments. And although the slowness of *Mathematica*'s interpreted language does not always make it an ideal environment for production runs, particularly on many desktop computers, it is not an altogether inappropriate environment for this use as well. In this chapter, without any pretense towards completeness, we examine some of the basics of conducting Monte Carlo studies, many of which are illustrated as we go with a study of the relative power of using zero-padded residuals versus truncated residuals in testing for serial correlation with artificial regressions. All this is explained in greater detail as we proceed. First let us examine more rigorously what a Monte Carlo experiment is.

15.1.1 The Monte Carlo Method

Hendry (1984) correctly makes a distinction between Monte Carlo methods used to solve analytically difficult or intractable problems and those involving sampling studies used to learn about the properties of analytically unwieldy statistics. An example of the former would be solving the integral

$$\int_D f(x)\, dx$$

for some function $f(x)$ that is analytically difficult to integrate. Situations like these arise frequently in Bayesian analyses in determining posterior densities. Suppose, however, we sample many, many times from a random variable x with known distribution $g(.)$ on D, each time calculating $f(x)/g(x)$. Then, after n such replications, the sample mean of these values

$$(1/n) \sum f(x)/g(x)$$

converges to the population mean

$$\int_D [f(x)/g(x)] g(x)\, dx = \int_D f(x)\, dx,$$

which is the desired integral. Although these uses of Monte Carlo methods are powerful and useful, they are not the methods that concern us here. Rather, our interest centers on the second type of Monte Carlo experimentation: systematic sampling experiments.

A trivial but easily understood example of this latter type of Monte Carlo study would be one that explores the statistical properties of the sample mean of random samples drawn from a known population with known mean μ and variance σ^2. Using a random number generator for this distribution, we could construct numerous samples, say, of size 30, from this population, calculating the sample mean of each. We would then amass a fairly detailed empirical distribution of the sample mean, from which we could estimate its mean and variance. We could then do the same with different values for μ and σ^2 and with different sample sizes n. Ultimately, we would begin to discover that the sample mean is distributed with a mean that equals the population mean μ and a variance that is the population variance σ^2 divided by the sample size n. This, of course, is a result that is already well known theoretically, but in more complicated instances, we can learn things from Monte Carlo studies that we are not able to determine theoretically.

Notice that the Monte Carlo procedure seems to reverse the standard estimation problem. There one uses a given sample and a given statistic to estimate a particular set of unknown population parameters. In a Monte Carlo study, however, we know the population and its parameters, and we use them to generate data with these known properties. Then, from repeated samples of such data, we investigate the ability of a particular statistic or set of statistics to use those data to tell us correctly about those properties that we know to be true. Monte Carlo experiments, then, allow us to understand the practical ability of a given statistical procedure to attain its intended objective, or to compare the relative efficiencies of different procedures that have the same objective. It becomes possible, for example, to investigate the small-sample bias of an estimator of a given parameter, because we know the true value of the given parameter that generated the data.

15.1.2   Why Use Monte Carlo Techniques?

Traditionally, Monte Carlo techniques have been used to obtain answers or partial answers when problems are either too difficult to succumb reasonably to theoretical analysis or are theoretically intractable. However, more recently, another element has given impetus to Monte Carlo techniques: they appeal to an increasing population of researchers who simply "think this way." This group of researchers thrives on the ever-enriching empirical diet offered by the laboratory that is the computer, particularly the personal computer.

15.1.2.1   Advantages

Monte Carlo techniques have one massive advantage: they are very generally applicable—as noted previously, they can be applied even for very complex notions, and can be done when theory bogs down. In many cases, this one advantage is quite capable of counterbalancing a rather imposing list of disadvantages.

15.1.2.2   Disadvantages

Monte Carlo techniques tend to lack generality of conclusions. Very often the result of a Monte Carlo study is "it all depends." Technique A, for example, appears better than Technique B for small samples, but not for large; or for certain portions of the parameter space, but not others. Correlative to this, then, is the possibility that a given Monte Carlo result does not hold for all parameter values. This is the issue of *validity*.

The dimensionality of a Monte Carlo study can also increase very quickly. If, for example, one wishes to examine r estimators over n samples sizes with k different model sizes each having p different parameter values (a not overly rich request for information), one would be considering $rnkp$ separate experiments. That is, one's desire for information causes the size of the study to increase multiplicatively, and if the requests are for more detail in all dimensions simultaneously, the size increase will be exponential.

Even modest Monte Carlo studies entail large blocks of computer time. Although this may seem like a problem that would diminish along with the large increases in computing power that we have witnessed over the last decade, in fact we find that our ambitions increase with capacity. If we find we can psychologically tolerate an eight-hour run, we respond to a ten-fold increase in computational speed with a ten-fold increase in problem complexity, augmenting our notion of "modest" and retaining the eight-hour run.

Monte Carlo studies and their results are inherently statistical in nature, and hence they do not produce exact results. This is the issue of *imprecision*. Rather generally, imprecision can be reduced by increasing n, the number of replications employed. But, typically, the precision decreases with $n^{-1/2}$, so it requires a four-fold increase in the number of replications to halve the variance. In some types of problems, variance-reduction techniques can be employed that alleviate this problem. *Quasi-random numbers* (numbers chosen systematically according to various schemes throughout the sample space) can be used instead of (pseudo) random numbers, to result in a precision that decreases as n^{-1} rather than $n^{-1/2}$. *Stratified sampling* is a technique that samples more densely only where more information is needed, thereby reducing overall variability without increasing overall effort. *Antithetical sampling* exploits negative correlation between two statistics to reduce the overall variance of their sum. And the technique of *control variates* exploits the positive correlation between two statistics to achieve the same aim relative to their difference.

Finally, the results of Monte Carlo studies can vary with the random sample, an issue known as *reliability*.

All these disadvantages, however, are often outweighed by the single advantage of doability. In the last analysis, it is easy to concede that an answer—even one that is somewhat imprecise, lacking in generality, and obtainable only over a long period of time—is far better than no answer.

15.1.3 Monte Carlo Sampling Experiments

Let us formalize somewhat this sampling-study aspect of the Monte Carlo method. Suppose a random T-vector $\mathbf{y}$ is associated with a set of T observations on data $\mathbf{x}$ (which could be a T-vector or a $T \times K$ matrix). Let

$$\mathbf{s} = \mathbf{f}(\mathbf{y}, \mathbf{x})$$

be any statistic, that is, any real-valued (vector) function of the sample values $\mathbf{y}$ and $\mathbf{x}$. Examples of $\mathbf{s}$ include the sample mean of $\mathbf{y}$ (here $\mathbf{x}$ is absent), the least squares estimator $\mathbf{b} = (\mathbf{x}'\mathbf{x})^{-1}\mathbf{x}'\mathbf{y}$, the estimated regression variance $(\mathbf{y} - \mathbf{x}\mathbf{b})'(\mathbf{y} - \mathbf{x}\mathbf{b})/T - K$, the t-statistic of the kth component of $\mathbf{b}$, or the F-statistic for the test that the kth and jth components of $\mathbf{b}$ are jointly significantly different from zero. It makes no difference what $\mathbf{s}$ is, just as long as it is a known real-valued function of the sample values $\mathbf{y}$ and $\mathbf{x}$. Now let us assume additionally that $\mathbf{y}$ is generated according to the known data-generating process (dgp)

$$\mathbf{y} = \mathbf{g}(\mathbf{x}, \mathbf{b}, \mathbf{e}),$$

where **b** is a set of parameters, and **e** is a T-variate random variable on some sample space D and having distribution

$$h(e; d)$$

with parameters **d**. Then, for given **x**, we can investigate the properties of **s** on the dgp (**g**, **h**) by repeatedly sampling **e**s randomly from **h** and amassing a large sample of values of

$$s = s(e \mid x, b, d, T, K) = f(g(x, h(e; d)), x).$$

The preceding notation is intended to emphasize that, in a Monte Carlo setting, there is a direct link between a random draw on **e** and a resulting value for the statistic **s**, and that this link is conditional on numerous items: the (predetermined) data **x**, the parameters **b** of the dgp, the parameters **d** of the distribution generating **e**, the sample size T, and the number of **x**s, K. Thus repeated draws on **e** produce a sample of values for **s**, and different samples for **s** can be obtained for different values assumed for the conditioning elements {**x**, **b**, **d**, T, K}. A series of N repetitions (or replications) of this process for given {**x**, **b**, **d**, T, K} is called a Monte Carlo *run*, and a set of runs over a judiciously chosen set of values for different {**x**, **b**, **d**, T, K} is called a Monte Carlo *experiment*. For large N, each run constitutes an empirical distribution of the statistic **s** at its given set of conditions, and from it we can investigate properties of this distribution, such as its mean, variance, bias, and so forth. Furthermore, with appropriate choices for {**x**, **b**, **d**, T, K}, we can begin to see how these statistical summaries are related to these conditions. The ultimate goal of a Monte Carlo sampling study is to summarize any stable relations that exist between relevant aspects of the distribution of **s** and its conditions {**x**, **b**, **d**, T, K}—or to be able to show that no such stable relations exist. Unfortunately, conclusions of this latter type often characterize Monte Carlo results; that is, Monte Carlo studies often conclude that "it all depends." One estimator, for example, may show greater bias than another for some parameter values but not for others, and so on.

15.1.4 The Elements of a Monte Carlo Experiment

The preceding allows us quickly to summarize the basic components of a Monte Carlo experiment. These are

- a defining question,
- the design of the experiment,
- the computer runs, and
- summarizing the results.

The first of these issues, although crucially important, is nevertheless so straightforward that we can deal with it here; the others are dealt with in turn in subsequent sections.

Most Monte Carlo experiments can be simply defined by a question, often dealing with the small-sample characteristics of some statistic. Thus one may ask what is the small-sample bias of a particular estimator, what are the relative efficiencies of various simultaneous-equations estimators, what is the size of a given test when the distribution has fat tails or when the model includes variates with unit roots, or what is the power of one test statistic relative to another.

Such questions arise naturally in conducting statistical analyses. The greater part of our knowledge about complex statistical matters often relies heavily on asymptotic (very, very large-sample) properties. In practice, of course, we rarely have such large samples, and so questions arise as to the relevance of these asymptotic results to life-sized samples. Sometimes one can gain ideas about how the small-sample properties differ from the large through approximation methods. If, for example, one does not know the distribution of the elements of a particular random sequence $\{x_t\}$ (a sequence of random variables indexed on t, such as the sample mean or the least-squares estimator based on a sample of size t), but does know that the transformation $t^{1/2}(x - c)$ converges to a nondegenerate limiting distribution with mean m and nonzero variance v, then, for moderate samples, one has $Et^{1/2}(x - c) \approx m$ or $Ex \approx c + t^{-1/2}m$. Rather than basing small-sample approximations to the mean on the asymptotic value c, one can get a better approximation by including the $t^{-1/2}m$ term. But even techniques such as this require moderate sample sizes for the approximation to be good, and they require that the relevant moments exist, which is not always the case. The Cauchy distribution, for example, has no moments, nor does the inverse of a normally distributed random variable. Thus Monte Carlo experiments have become a popular way to deal with such questions.

The heart of a Monte Carlo experiment is its design, which, in the terms of our previous anatomy, consists in defining the statistic $\mathbf{s} = \mathbf{f}(\mathbf{y}, \mathbf{x})$ and the dgp $\mathbf{y} = \mathbf{g}(\mathbf{x}, \mathbf{b}, \mathbf{e})$ with its accompanying distribution for the error structure, $\mathbf{h}(\mathbf{e}; \mathbf{d})$. We discuss these issues in the next several sections, but for the moment, let us introduce the particular Monte Carlo experiment that is used here for illustrative purposes.

15.1.5   A Monte Carlo Study of Zero-Padding in Testing for Serial Correlation

As we proceed, we illustrate some of the elements of Monte Carlo experimentation with an example: a study of the relative effectiveness of zero-padding when testing for serial correlation using artificial regressions. Let us provide the groundwork for this study now.

MacKinnon (1992) and Davidson and MacKinnon (1993) remind us of how to use artificial regressions to provide, among many other things, an amazingly simple and flexible test for serial correlation: the original regression is simply augmented by appropriate lags of the uncorrected OLS residuals, the joint significance of whose coefficients is then tested using a standard F-statistic if there are several parameters involved, or t-statistic if there is only one parameter.

Thus suppose we are dealing with the model (as we do in fact)

$$y_t = a + \mathbf{b}\mathbf{x}_t + v_t,$$

where the $\mathbf{x}_t$ are fixed regressors and the v_t are disturbance terms. Suppose further we suspect v_t may possess first-order serial correlation, that is,

$$v_t = \rho v_{t-1} + e_t,$$

where e_t has zero mean, constant variance, and is appropriately uncorrelated over different observations. Then the null hypothesis $H_0: \rho = 0$ can be tested simply by (a) regressing the y_ts on the $\mathbf{x}_t$s to obtain the residuals err_t, (b) regressing y_t on the original model augmented with the residuals lagged err_{t-1} from the first regression, that is, running the "artificial" regression

$$y_t = a + \mathbf{b}\mathbf{x}_t + c\,\mathrm{err}_{t-1} + w_t,$$

and then (c) testing the hypothesis $H_0: c = 0$ using the standard t test. An analogous procedure can be used for testing for any order or combination of orders of serial correlation. Thus if one suspects v of having simple fourth-order serial correlation $v_t = \rho v_{t-4} + e_t$, one need only substitute err_{t-4} for err_{t-1} in the preceding artificial regression. And if one suspects a more complex relationship such as $v_t = \rho_1 v_{t-1} + \rho_4 v_{t-4}$, one can test the null of no serial correlation, that is, $H_0: \rho_1 = \rho_4 = 0$, simply by forming the artificial regression

$$y_t = a + \mathbf{b}\mathbf{x}_t + c_1\mathrm{err}_{t-1} + c_2\mathrm{err}_{t-4} + w_t,$$

and examining the standard F-statistic for $H_0: c_1 = c_2 = 0$, that is, by testing that c_1 and c_2 are not jointly significantly different from zero.

This test was first proposed in essence in Durbin (1970), along with his more famous h test, and later in Breusch (1978) and Godfrey (1978a, b), but, for some reason, it has only slowly gained in popularity. However, the general applicability of this procedure for testing for serial correlation of any order or combination of orders, its validity even in the presence of lagged dependent variates, the absence of a "region of indeterminacy" in interpreting its results, and its simplicity in use promote it, in principle, to a position of dominance among the well-known battery of tests for serial correlation that otherwise apply only to special cases or only when the $\mathbf{x}$s are exogenous.

But there is a serious potential drawback in applying this procedure to small samples: each additional lag utilized in the artificial regression cuts into its limited degrees of freedom $(T - K)$ twice. First, successive lags further truncate the residual vector $\mathbf{err}$ and so reduce T in the artificial regression, and second, the inclusion of these lags as artificial regressors directly increases K. It is therefore with interest that one reads in various of the previously cited works that the first of these reductions can be eliminated by zero-padding—padding out those residuals lost to truncation with zeros, their expected value—and that the test remains valid, a result that is given asymptotic justification.

Of course, appeals to asymptotic virtues are small comfort to those whose samples are sufficiently small to be concerned with saving degrees of freedom, so the question naturally arises as to the small-sample effectiveness of this zero-padding procedure. The illustrative Monte Carlo study presented here addresses this issue by comparing the small-sample power of the test using truncated residuals to that of the test using zero-padding. Let us briefly indicate how this study pairs up with the given prototype.

Because we are interested in small-sample properties, pick $T = 20$ and take a fixed vector of 20 exogenous observations **x**. The data generating process **g** for **y** is

$$\mathbf{y} = 8 + .6\mathbf{x} + \mathbf{v},$$

$$\mathbf{v} = \rho\mathbf{v}_{-1} + \mathbf{e},$$

where **e** is a sample of independent normals with mean zero and variance 36. Exactly how all this is done is explained later. For the moment, just note that the preceding process **g** transforms any random pick on **e** into a vector **y**, the "dependent variate." The parameters of **g** are **b** = $\{8, .6, \rho\}$, only the last of which is subject to change here, and the distribution **h** of the error structure **e** in this case has parameters **d** = $\{0., 36\}$. The statistic **s** = **f**(**y**, **x**) for this study becomes a pair of t- (or F-) statistics derived as follows:

The process **s** = **f**(**y**, **x**):

(a) **y** is regressed on an intercept and **x** to obtain the residuals **err**;

(b) **err** is lagged in the following ways:

    (1) **errtrunc**$_{-1}$ simply loses the observation lost to lagging (it has 19 numeric values),

    (2) **errzp**$_{-1}$ uses zero-padding to replace this lost element with zero (it has 20);

(c) two artificial regressions are run:

    (1) **y** is regressed on an intercept, **x**, and **errtrunc**$_{-1}$, and

    (2) **y** is regressed on an intercept, **x**, and **errzp**$_{-1}$; and

(d) the t-statistics t_{trunc} and t_{zp} from these regressions are calculated and stored.

Once again, note for the moment that this four-step process is **f**(**y**, **x**), the mapping that describes exactly how one goes from a given **y** and **x** to the pair of t-or F-statistics $\{t_{\text{trunc}}, t_{\text{zp}}\}$. Now, putting the **g** process into the **f** process, we see that for each **e** we generate, we get a pair of ts, $\{t_{\text{trunc}}, t_{\text{zp}}\}$ = **s**(**e**|**x**, **b**, **d**, T, K) = $f(\mathbf{g}(\mathbf{x}, \mathbf{h}(\mathbf{e}; \mathbf{d})), \mathbf{x})$. The conditions for this process are $\{\mathbf{x}, \mathbf{b}, \mathbf{d}, T, K\}$, and for specific choices on these conditions we can repeatedly draw **e**s and thereby generate a sample of $\{t_{\text{trunc}}, t_{\text{zp}}\}$s. After many replications of this (we use 5,000 in this study), we can use this sample to investigate the relative power of these two tests.

The power of a test is simply its ability to reject a null hypothesis when it is wrong. So we need only to determine the proportions of the t or F values in the sample that exceed critical values relevant to the two tests and compare them. In this study we have fixed most of the conditions for x, b, d, T, and K. The only condition that is varied from run to run in this Monte Carlo experiment is that of ρ, but broadly interpreted. For we not only change the value of ρ, but the number of ρs, that is, the nature of the lag structure characterizing the process generating the **vs**. We assume different orders of lag for the serial correlation (first, fourth, and twelfth), and some multiple orders (first and fourth together), and we also examine the process under the more realistic assumption that the exact order of the serial correlation is not known, so that redundant lags of **err** are included in the artificial regressions.

Like many Monte Carlo studies, the results seem to be: "it all depends." But as shown in the following, it does seem fair to conclude from these experiments that zero-padding helps very little. Indeed in many simple but important cases, zero-padding actually results in marginally reduced power, and although there may be an increase in power in some more complex autoregressive structures, the increase is slight and the situations in which it might occur are difficult to predict. For those of us who would kill to save a degree of freedom, this is a disappointing, but nevertheless very interesting, result—which, it should be emphasized, in no way otherwise reduces the value of the suggested test procedure based on artificial regressions. It merely reestablishes in our minds the unlikelihood of ever being able to get something for zero.

15.2   Design

As noted previously, the design of a Monte Carlo experiment consists in defining the statistic $s = f(y, x)$ and the dgp $y = g(x, b, e)$ with its associated error distribution $h(e; d)$. Little need be said regarding the choice of the statistic s, for, as should be clear from the examples of the defining question given in the preceding section, this choice typically arises naturally and completely from the question itself. The statistic s *is* the estimator whose small-sample bias is to be assessed, or the test statistic whose power or size is of interest. The defining question also greatly affects the choice of the model g of the dgp and its accompanying distribution h, but not completely so, and some interesting issues arise in this regard. We examine some of these issues now.

15.2.1   The Model of the dgp: $y = g(x; b; e)$

The basic elements to be specified for the model $y = g(x, b, e)$ are the functional form of g, the nature of the variates x, and the values for the parameters b. Important aspects of the functional form are usually imposed by the defining question, which typically makes clear whether one is working with a single equation, simultaneous equations, linear or nonlinear equations, stationary or evolutive models, random walks, VARs, and so on. Not so clear, however, are questions relating to the detailed structure of these equations. In investigating the small-sample bias of a simultaneous-equations estimator, for example, the number of endogenous and exogenous variables, the degree of overidentification, the nature of the variates (trended, first differences, etc.) are all issues that can affect the results, and it is usually necessary to make stringent choices that balance getting useful results with the need to keep the study within practical bounds.

In dealing with choices of this sort, it is often useful to keep in mind whether one is interested in understanding the behavior of the statistic **s** in particular cases or in knowing if there are cases where particular things can happen. Clearly, if the former is true, then one chooses the **xs** and **bs** to reflect the particular of interest. In some instances (say, when one is interested in knowing the behavior of a statistic in a situation akin to a particular real-life situation), this can greatly reduce the scope of the needed Monte Carlo experiments. But if one were interested in obtaining information on the more general behavior of the statistic, the **xs** and **bs** must reflect this generality, and the scope of the experiments will necessarily be larger. By contrast, if one is interested in knowing only if there are situations where particular things can happen (that one estimator, for example, could be more efficient than another), then the specific **xs** and **bs** that are used may be of much less importance. If one can observe the required outcome with any reasonably chosen **xs** and **bs**, that may suffice.

15.2.1.1 The xs

Different notions can be employed in choosing the particular **xs** to be used. The **xs** can be generated randomly, they can be actual data, or they can be generated to emulate actual data. The preceding discussion helps in making this decision. If a particular real-life situation is to be investigated, then it makes sense to use the actual data from this situation. This may, in fact, be one of the best uses of Monte Carlo experiments: to try to determine, for example, which estimator is most effective in a given situation. If more general behavior is of interest, however, then it may not make sense to use actual data. One of the major drawbacks of Monte Carlo experiments is that the results can depend greatly on the particular **xs** that are chosen. In choosing actual data, one is often warping the results to a particular case. In these instances, it is preferable to generate data that emulate particular types of real life data. This allows one to control more completely the generality of the results and to check more easily whether the results are particularly sensitive to the nature of the data. In economic and financial models, for example, the data are often trended. By generating different, but related data series, one can do small trial studies to see if the results are sensitive to different data types, say, those that are highly trended, moderately so, or even untrended. Because the data are being generated, these different series can be made similar in certain respects such as levels, but different in other ways that matter. One cannot do this easily with actual data. Similarly, to take another example, in investigating the behavior of a statistic under differing degrees of collinearity, it would be virtually impossible to find actual data that become systematically more collinear so that the nature of the relation between the statistic and the degree of collinearity can be assessed, but one can readily generate data series that exhibit the desired characteristics. Finally, if one is only interested in seeing if there are situations in which the statistic can behave in certain ways, it may make little difference whether one uses actual data or picks the xs randomly; it is necessary here only to find an acceptable x that produces the desired result. If a few short trials fail to achieve this goal, however, one may wish to switch to data generated to emulate specific characteristics so that it will be easier to search systematically for a possible x with the desired properties.

15.2.1.2   Number of xs (K) and Sample Size (T)

One cannot, of course, choose the xs without also selecting a number of variables K and the sample size T, although their choices involve separate issues. If the number of variates is central to the defining question, then one would usually do separate runs with a well-chosen spectrum of values for K. In investigating the properties of a simultaneous-equations estimator, for example, the degree of overidentification could be an important factor. Here one could vary the number of excluded exogenous variables used in generating the data, or vary the number of included endogenous variates, or both. When K is to vary, the object should initially be to employ as few alternatives as needed to get an idea of what happens. Once some idea of whether or how the results depend upon K, additional runs could be considered if greater refinement is desired. When the magnitude of K is not a central issue, a universally good rule would be to make it as small as possible. This not only speeds up the runs, but introduces less fog in general.

Similar considerations apply to the choice or choices of the sample size T. For the most part, T will be chosen small for Monte Carlo studies. And if the general small-sample behavior of the statistic is at issue, a range of Ts that is suggestive of real-life samples is clearly appropriate. Truly small samples for regression equations are 12-20. Moderate sizes are 50, whereas larger small-sample values are closer to 100-200. Such a spread is likely to provide information that will be of use to most who read the study. One could also use larger samples of 1,000 or even orders-of-magnitude larger if interest centers on how fast the statistic of interest converges to its asymptotic behavior. It should also be clear that T and K cannot be chosen completely independently: one must preserve positive degrees of freedom.

15.2.1.3   The bs

Choosing the coefficient values can be one of the biggest headaches in designing a Monte Carlo experiment because the results can be so sensitive to the choice and the range of choice can be so great. Again, if general results are desired, the guiding principle should be as few choices as possible to gain as wide a range of information as possible. This greatest-good-for-the-greatest-number principle has as great a chance of attaining complete success here as it does in politics, but the idea is straightforward. If, by contrast, one is trying only to find whether certain results are possible, then the overriding principle should be to keep the number of choices as small as possible.

Clearly if there are special values for some of the parameters that greatly affect the behavior of the model, they should either be directly examined or avoided, as the goals of the study dictate. Thus, for example, if a model becomes unstable or unstationary when a certain coefficient equals 1, and one is interested in the behavior of **s** with a stable model, this value should be avoided. On the other hand, if one were interested in the behavior of **s** as the model approaches instability, then values near unity would reasonably be added to some of the parameter sets defining the different runs.

15.2.1.4   xs and bs in the Example

Recall that our illustrative study is attempting to examine whether it is reasonable or worthwhile to use zero-padding when conducting tests of serial correlation using artificial regressions. The statistic **s** here is a pair of t-tests or F-tests (to be discussed later). The dgp consists of a regression equation, $\mathbf{y} = g(\mathbf{b}) + \mathbf{v}$ along with an accompanying model defining the serial correlation in the error term **v**. It is clear that the important element of this study is the nature of the serial correlation and not so much the nature of the regression equation. As a first crack, then, it seems appropriate to specify as simple a regression equation as possible; that is, linear, intercept, and maybe one x variate. If in this case one finds zero-padding is worthwhile, it may be of interest to go further and find out if it is more or less worthwhile in different situations. But if one finds that zero-padding is not worthwhile here, and indeed could be detrimental, then there is less interest in widening the study.

So a very simple regression equation

$$\mathbf{y} = 8 + .6\mathbf{x} + \mathbf{v}$$

is specified along with its parameters, which are just chosen to be typical. The real interest here is in the specification of the rest of the model: the part that deals with the serial correlation in **v**. The most common forms of serial correlation are first-order, quarterly, and annual. So the given data can be treated in concept three ways; as annual data, quarterly data, and monthly data. A 1st-order lag can therefore be viewed as an annual lag, a quarterly lag, or a monthly lag. A 4th-order lag can be viewed as an annual lag on quarterly data, and a 12th-order lag an annual lag on monthly data. This leads to the following basic structures for the serial correlation

Model 1: $\mathbf{v} = \rho\mathbf{v}_{-1} + \mathbf{e}$, (simple 1st-order serial correlation),

Model 2: $\mathbf{v} = \rho\mathbf{v}_{-4} + \mathbf{e}$, (simple 4th-order serial correlation),

Model 3: $\mathbf{v} = \rho\mathbf{v}_{-12} + \mathbf{e}$, (simple 12th-order serial correlation).

These choices emulate standard economic situations while also providing evidence spanning a variety of numbers of degrees of freedom lost to lagging. In the case of the 12th-order lag, for example, the test with zero-padded residuals will have 12 more degrees of freedom than the test using truncated residuals. In addition, to see if things change much in a slightly more complicated situation, the following model is included having both 1st- and 4th-order serial correlation,

Model 4: $v = \rho_1 v_{-1} + \rho_4 v_{-4} + e$, (1st- and 4th-order serial correlation).

We discuss how these disturbance terms, including the **es**, are generated later.

As for the sample size, I take $T = 20$, a figure that is ever etched in my mind as being small, because, during my graduate school days, we were painfully aware that even when we should become lucky enough to have post-war (annual) data series this long, it would hardly be enough. And as for the x data, I could either generate them or use actual data. Because my concern is in seeing whether there is a benefit or a cost to using zero-padding to augment the residual terms, there is no particular choice for the xs that stands out, so I simply took annual disposable income figures for 1947-1966 from Belsley (1991). Further, since the **y** data are being generated by the model, these xs can be viewed simply as generic economic-type data.

```
In[1]:=  x = {218.075, 229.7, 230.925, 249.65, 255.675, 263.25,
              275.475, 278.4, 296.625, 309.35, 316.075, 318.8,
              333.05, 340.325, 350.475, 367.25, 381.225, 408.1,
              434.825, 458.875};
```

Later on there is some interesting behavior of the test statistics in the first-order case that could be due to the trended character of these data. As a result, I also ran several trial runs using a set of randomly generated xs of roughly similar magnitude

```
In[2]:=  xR = {167.628, 299.205, 147.2815, 144.790, 357.968,
               397.229, 188.895, 105.129, 332.846, 387.844,
               345.603, 215.358, 175.627, 220.927, 207.116,
               288.873, 237.548, 276.829, 173.479, 103.990};
```

The actual numbers were generated as

```
In[3]:=  SeedRandom[4]
         xR = Table[Random[Real, {100,400}], {20}];
```

but different versions of *Mathematica* use different random-number algorithms, so I have included the values (rounded to three places) for convenience. Although the use of **xR** instead of **x** causes some change in the levels of the powers, the essential story of the relative powers remains unchanged.

A single set of parameters is chosen for the regression equation itself; a value of 8 for the intercept and a value of .6 for the coefficient of the single variate x. Again, the emphasis of this study is in different values for ρ (or ρ_1 and ρ_4) determining the nature of the serial correlation. In Models 1-3, one can reasonably bracket the field by choosing values for ρ that suggest modest, moderate, and strong serial correlation, both positive and negative. Thus each of the first three models is run using six different values assumed for ρ: 0.3, 0.7, 0.9, −0.9, −0.7, and −0.3. Runs for Model 4 are made for the following 12 $\{\rho_1, \rho_4\}$ pairs: $\{-0.3, 0.5\}$, $\{0.5, -0.3\}$, $\{0.9, 0.03\}$, $\{0.03, 0.9\}$, $\{-0.8, 0.1\}$, $\{0.1, -0.8\}$, $\{-0.4, -0.5\}$, $\{-0.5, -0.4\}$, $\{0.5, 0.4\}$, $\{0.4, 0.5\}$, $\{0.2, 0.3\}$, $\{0.3, 0.2\}$. These values are chosen (a) to provide a sprinkling about the four quadrants of the two-dimensional parameter space, (b) to ensure that Model 4 will be stationary (i.e., have roots lying outside the unit circle), and (c) to provide some linkage of the results of this model with those of the others. Thus the pair $\{0.9, 0.03\}$ makes Model 4 close to Model 1 with $\rho = 0.9$; the pair $\{0.1, -0.8\}$ allows comparison to Model 2 with $\rho = -0.9$, and so on.

Stationarity is ensured by picking ρs that produce roots for each model's characteristic equation that lie outside the unit circle. For the first three models this is achieved simply by picking ρ so that

$$\text{Abs}[\rho] < 1.0.$$

For Model 4, things are slightly more complicated, but easily handled within *Mathematica*. Letting L be the lag operator $L^k x_t = x_{t-k}$, Model 4 can be written as $(1 - \rho_1 * L - \rho_4 * L^4)v_t = e_t$. And the fourth degree polynomial equation

$$(1 - \rho_1 * L - \rho_4 * L^4) == 0.0$$

is the model's characteristic equation. For each candidate pair of ρs, it is necessary to check that the moduli of the four roots to this equation are larger than unity. This is simply accomplished in *Mathematica* using the routine

```
In[4]:=  CheckRoots[r1_,r2_]:=
            Abs[b]/.{ToRules[Roots[1-r1*b-r2*b^4==0.0,b]]}
```

The heart of this is the *Mathematica* routine Roots[eqn, var], which produces a list of values of var that satisfy a given equation eqn containing var. This solution list has the form {var == expr1,..., var == expr4} and is not of a form that can be used directly for replacement (substitution) in another function, such as Abs[]. But another *Mathematica* function, ToRules[], is designed explicitly to do this. Thus when ToRules[] is finished, the list is of the form {var -> expr1, . . ., var -> expr4}. This list is then used with ReplaceAll[] (infix /.) to produce the desired values from Abs[b], which returns the absolute value of a real number and the modulus of a complex one. Thus, for example, we have

```
In[5]:= CheckRoots[.5,.4]
Out[5]= {1.44002, 1.2888, 1.2888, 1.04521}
```

(Note: the code needed to enact this function can take a bit of time to read in the first time it is evoked, but subsequent calls will be amazingly rapid.)

15.2.2   The Sampling Distribution of the dgp: h(e; d)

The model **g** that we just discussed is only one part of the dgp; the random element **e** and its distribution complete it. We begin here with some basic considerations in generating random variables and random numbers, and then turn to the specifics of generating the serially correlated **vs** used in the illustrative study.

15.2.2.1   Generating Random Numbers

We have seen that the main purpose of a Monte Carlo experiment is to exercise a given specification of a model about its sample space so that either its range of behavior can be assessed or its typical behavior estimated, notions summarized in the statistic **s** or elements of its distribution. To do this it is clearly necessary to generate large numbers of random variables suitable to the model's sample space. In the illustrative study, for example, we consider 2 variants of 4 models, each with 6 parameter values (two with 12), giving 60 runs of 5,000 replications, each one needing at least 21 random normals requiring two uniform random draws each—thus accounting for a minimum of 12.6 million random numbers!—and this is a relatively small study.

In general, the distribution **h(e; d)** required of the random variables will be dependent upon the particular Monte Carlo experiment. There is a massive literature on generating random variables of any particular distribution. However, the facility exists in *Mathematica* for great flexibility here, particularly using the *inverse-transformation technique*. The principle of this technique is simple, for if a random variable x is distributed according to the cumulative distribution function $F(x)$, then clearly the random variable $y = F(x)$ is distributed uniformly on the interval $(0, 1)$, that is, $U(0, 1)$. We can therefore get random draws on a variable distributed with $F(x)$ simply by taking $x = F^{-1}(y)$, where y is a random number drawn from $U(0, 1)$, that is, through an appropriate inverse-transformation of a random draw on $U(0, 1)$. The *Mathematica* function Random[ ] produces random numbers drawn from $U(0, 1)$, and the package InverseStatistical Functions.m possesses the inverse functions for most encountered random variables. However, in many Monte Carlo studies, including the one here, it is reasonable to assume a normal distribution and the normal does not have a closed-form inverse. The inverse could be approximated numerically to any desired degree of accuracy, but there are simpler ways to proceed.

Box and Muller (1958) show that the random variable $(-2\text{Log}[y_1])^{1/2} \times \text{Cos}[2\pi y_2]$ is distributed as a standard normal when y_1 and y_2 are independent draws from $U(0, 1)$. Thus,

```
In[6]:=  Gaussian[mean_:0, variance_:1] := N[mean +
             Sqrt[variance]
             Sqrt[-2 Log[Random[]]] Cos[2Pi Random[]]]
```

does the trick of generating random normals with given mean and variance. This code appears as part of StatUtilities.m, used in this study, and a very similar form is found in the *Mathematica* notebook NormalDistribution.m packaged in the Statistics folder. Evoking Gaussian[] without arguments results in a standard Normal, that is, one with default mean zero and variance one.

StatUtilities.m also has variants on this theme to allow for lists of independent standard normals and lists of multivariate normals. Thus

```
In[7]:=  SphericalStandardGaussian[size_,seriesLength_:1]:=
             If[seriesLength>1,
                Return[Table[Gaussian[],{size},{seriesLength}]],
                Return[Table[Gaussian[],{size}]]
             ]
```

uses Gaussian[ ] to return either a list of size independent Gaussians, or a size by seriesLength matrix of them. Further, if one needs an r-variate Normal (multivariate Normal of size r) with mean **m** and variance/covariance matrix **V**, this is readily obtained by taking the square root of **V** (any square matrix **C** such that $V = CC'$), and forming $z = m + Cx$, where x is an r-variate standard normal, obtainable as x = SphericalStandardGaussian[r]. This is precisely what the code for MultivariateGaussian[] found in StatUtilities.m does. It uses the *Mathematica* function Singular-Values[] to determine the square-root matrix **C**. The **R** matrix from the QRDecomposition[] could also be used.

Another procedure for generating random variables is the *rejection method*. This procedure has the advantage of complete generality, for in principle it can be used to produce a random variable having any given density function $f(x)$. Here a *comparison function* $g(x)$ is chosen to dominate $f(x)$ over its domain and to possess a well-defined indefinite integral G that is easily inverted. Then two uniform variates are drawn, one from the range of G to be transformed via G^{-1} to determine a point x_0 in the domain, and a second from $U(0,1)$ to accept or reject this draw in proportion to $0 < f(x_0)/g(x_0) < 1$. Although this procedure has the advantage of complete generality, it has the disadvantage of requiring unused random draws every time a rejection occurs—a problem that looms larger the worse the approximation is of $g(x)$ to $f(x)$. Thus the ease with which one can define special functions in *Mathematica*, taking different simple shapes over different regions of the domain, combines well with *Mathematica*'s excellent facility for both numerical and symbolic integration and its ability to solve for inverses to make *Mathematica* a particularly fertile environment for developing random variable generators of this type.

We see that behind both of these methods for generating random variables is a means for generating a sequence of random numbers uniformly on [0, 1], and so any environment friendly to Monte Carlo studies must have a good random number generator. *Mathematica* does.

Random numbers are ideally a sequence displaying no patterns, no predictability, and admitting of no simple description. Of course, any iterative scheme is a simple description, so this last condition is usually weakened to allow for randomness if no computations carried out on the sequence can reveal the simple description. There are several commonly used procedures for generating random numbers from $U(0, 1)$ that come close to these ideals: linear congruential generators, shift-register generators, and lagged-Fibonacci generators. The *linear congruential* generator produces numbers sequentially according to a scheme like $x_n = z_n/k$, where $z_n = (mz_{n-1} + b) \bmod k$, with an initial seed x_0. Because z_n is taken mod k, x_n must lie between zero and one. The *shift-register generator* forms its sequence of binary numbers according to $x_{n+1} = xT^n$, where x is a binary k-vector seed, T is a $k \times k$ binary matrix, and all arithmetic is done modulo 2. The *lagged-Fibonacci generator* forms its sequence from r seeds $\{x_1, \ldots, x_r\}$ used along with an operation @ (typically + or −) (modulo m) and a rule $x_n = x_{n-r} @ x_{n-s}$. (Regular Fibonacci numbers are modulo infinity, @ = +, $r = 2$, and $s = 1$.) Although the numbers that these generators produce are called random, it is clear that once started the processes are completely deterministic. For appropriate configurations, however, their resulting values act very much like random numbers and so are called pseudorandom numbers. Unfortunately, with the exception of the lagged-Fibonacci generator, these procedures fail some tests of randomness. The linear congruential generator, for example, exhibits latticing; that is, for sufficiently high dimensional spaces, the points generated will lie on equispaced hyperplanes. And none of these generation procedures possesses extremely long periodicity (the length of sequence before repetition occurs) unless configured to require excessive computational costs or memory needs (e.g., thousands of bits for the shift-register generator, or many hundreds of lags for the lagged-Fibonacci generator).

To overcome these shortcomings, the function `Random[]` that is built into *Mathematica* has been selected from a "new class" of random number generators [Marsaglia and Zaman (1991)] that appears to pass most tests of randomness and have fantastically long periodicities. The procedure is called the *subtract-with-borrow* (SWB) generator and is a generalization of the lagged-Fibonacci process. Here there is a number base b, two lags r and s with $r > s$, r nonnegative "digits" or seeds $\{x_1, \ldots, x_r\}$ of base b, and a borrow bit $c = 0$ or 1, initially chosen randomly. Let $z_n = x_{n-r} - x_{n-s}. - c$. Then the nth element of this random sequence is determined as $x_n = z_n$ if $z_n \geq 0$ (and then the borrow bit is set to $c = 0$), or $x_n = z_n + b$ if $z_n < 0$ (and then the borrow bit is set to $c = 1$). `Random[]` tunes this procedure with $r = 48$, $s = 8$, and $b = 2^{31}$, and each invocation calls it twice to fill out a machine double. The result is a generator that can produce any of 210 separate cycles of random numbers (depending on the seed used), each of which has a period of roughly 10^{445}. In short, it would appear that *Mathematica* offers an excellent random number generation facility for the

Monte Carlo experimenter. (The function Random[] picked with non-default parameter values, however, may or may not draw on this subtract-with-borrow procedure.)

It is of interest to note, however, that recent research of Tezuka et al. (1993) and Couture and L'Ecuyer (1994) has shown that this new class is not all that new. Indeed, they show that the series produced by the subtract-with-borrow generator (and its closely related cousin, the add-with-carry (AWC) generator) can be closely approximated by a standard linear congruential generator with a very large prime modulus. This generator should, therefore, exhibit the same latticing problem as the linear congruential generator, and Tezuka et al. show this to be the case for dimensions exceeding the largest lag—48 for the situation in *Mathematica*. This is somewhat disappointing, for it now appears that the real advance with this new class is not that it is truly a new system with thoroughly desirable properties, but rather that it is a computationally efficient means for producing series from a linear congruential generator with a massively large prime moduli, a configuration that would otherwise be either very expensive or completely impractical to implement. This is certainly an important step forward, and it means that the random number generator in *Mathematica* is among the best currently available. But one hopes there will be advances, possibly combining the output from such generators with others, that can avoid the latticing problem.

It is an interesting question just how important the latticing problem actually is to any particular Monte Carlo study. If the purpose of the generation mechanism is merely to spread out the conditions under which the statistical object of interest is investigated, such regularity may be of no consequence whatsoever. This is often the case for Monte Carlo type experiments conducted in, say, econometrics. If, however, the studies are comparing large numbers of objects, greater in number than the dimensionality above which latticing occurs, the latticing could indeed impose structure in the results that is unwarranted and possibly unfortunate.

Now each of the preceding random number generators requires a seed value to start the process rolling. One sets the seed in *Mathematica* with the built-in function

```
In[8]:=  SeedRandom[n]
```

where the integer n is chosen by the user. Any method can be used to choose n, but a reasonable procedure is to select it randomly, say, with code such as

```
In[9]:=  RandomPick[]  := Random[Integer, {1,100000}]
```

Resetting the seed to the same value causes the same sequence of pseudo-random numbers to repeat exactly. This is a tremendous advantage in doing statistical experiments in general, and Monte Carlo studies in particular, because it means that a given experiment can be repeated if need be, or a new experiment can be given the same set of random numbers—a facility that allows one to check readily if peculiar results are due to the model itself or to the particular random numbers that occurred. It is important therefore to store the seed with the experiment that uses it, and it is a good idea to use a different seed for each run. It should be noted, however, that the process invoked by Random[] has evolved through the several releases of *Mathematica*, leaving one with the less than desirable situation that a given seed used in earlier versions will not produce the same sequence as it does in a later version.

Beginning with version 2.2 of *Mathematica*, the current state of the random number generator is stored in the global variable $RandomState. And so, although it has always been possible to reinitiate the random number generator from the same point by using the same seed, it has only recently become possible to record the state of the random number generator in order to pick up a sequence where it stopped. This desirable facility allows one to break up a run as often as desired, restarting each time exactly where you left off, despite what may happen in between. Thus should one wish to break up a run into smaller groups of replications instead of doing all at once (which can take a bit of time), one could use a process such as

```
In[10]:= Model1[.9,1000,"Mod1(.9)"]
         keepState = $RandomState
```

where the function Model1[] conducts a Monte Carlo run of a number of replications given by its second argument, in this case 1,000. Then, at some later time, to start up again where one left off for another, say, 2,000 replications, use

```
In[11]:= $RandomState = keepState;
         Model1[.9,2000,"Mod1(.9)"]
```

It should be recalled that the value for keepState is in volatile memory and will last only as long as the current *Mathematica* session. Thus if the value is to be preserved for a future session, be sure not to place a semicolon after $RandomState. Its value will then print out on the screen and can be saved with the notebook. Thus

```
In[12]:= keepState = $RandomState
```

```
Out[12]= 113611003623663467547574951866646444641495976983547345\
         473033190820470344245205573231689675998164634291955 8\
         295055167565398525515984496775612642133054627901027 9\
         761825728425583300718637848150587651643031455427858 6\
         055879365385382841158268590045470920354692474693157 9\
         262963093365093187198651329801982649872743219042135 4\
         297751948154713459885804755427208200841523750743226 8\
         735933240480508149661727307415813430974009509742840 0\
         684546149626431016461390438878390804389903131698430 8\
         076950929973687398586290256573078412204276781117205 2\
         415231769389239759475657876706184200 6
```

To reuse it, select its cell and change it to an editable form, such as text. Then edit out the backslashes and extra spaces and precede it with $RandomState = , so one has

```
$RandomState =
11361100362366346754757495186664644464149597698354734547303319082
0470344245205573231689675998164634291955829505516756539852551598
4496775612642133054627901027976182572842558330071863784815058765
1643031455427858605587936538538284115826859004547092035469247469
3157926296309336509318719865132980198264987274321904213542977519
4815471345988580475547270820084152375074322687359332404805081496
6172730741581343097400950974284006845461496264310164613904388783
9080438990313169843080769509299736873985862902565730784122042767
8111720524152317693892397594756578767061842006
```

Now this cell, with its information, may be saved with the notebook for future needs. To start the random number generator where it left off, one need only select this cell, convert it to input form, and enter it.

15.2.2.2 Initializing and Generating the Autocorrelated vs in the Example

In our illustrative model, the **es** are generated as standard normals with mean 0 and variance 36 using the previously described routines Gaussian[], SphericalStandardGaussian[], and MultivariateGaussian[]. The choice of 36 for the variance here is immaterial because the t- and F-statistics used for this study are invariant to this value [this is a good theoretical exercise for the reader (or one that can be verified empirically with a few trials)], so there is nothing particularly special here. The real interest arises in initializing and generating the serially correlated disturbances **v** in the four models. For each replication of each Monte Carlo run of each model we require a set of initial values to generate a list **v** containing $T = 20$ random variables displaying the appropriate autoregressive structure. In Model 1, for example, we require 1 initial value for **v**. Models 2 and 4 require 4, and Model 3 needs 12. A typical ploy is to begin with initial values set equal to the expected value of the **v**s, that is, zero. But this is not a very desirable method to use for Monte Carlo studies in general, as it forces an unwarranted similarity upon the nature of the **v**s for each repetition, particularly in small samples. And it is an especially bad method to use in this particular Monte Carlo study, which examines zero-padding, as it produces **v**s that begin with values that are not as far removed from zero as they typically could be, clearly biasing the results in zero-padding's favor.

One means of alleviating this problem is to start the process with zeros, but then allow it to run for some large number of iterations to "settle in" before eventually taking a string of 20 to use for **v**. The cost of this, however, is the computer time needed to generate a multitude of unused random numbers, and such costs can become significant in Monte Carlo experiments with their large

numbers of replications, particularly if one wishes to reseed the generator for
each run.

Rather, in this study we draw the needed number of initial values randomly
from an appropriate marginal distribution for the **v** process. For Models 1
through 3, these processes are of the form

$$v_t = \rho v_{t-n} + e_t, \quad \text{for } n = 1, 4, \text{ and } 12.$$

Let us denote by μ the mean of v_t. Because $\mu = E v_t = E v_{t-k}$ for all k in a
stationary process, we have

$$(1 - \rho)\mu = E e_t = 0,$$

which implies $\mu = 0$, since $\rho > 1$. Further, stationarity implies $\text{Var}(v_t) = \text{Var}(v_{t-k})$ for all k. Let us call this common variance σ_v^2. Then we have

$$\sigma_v^2 = E(\rho v_{t-k} + e_t)^2 = \rho^2 \sigma_v^2 + \sigma_e^2, \text{ or}$$
$$\sigma_v^2 = \sigma_e^2 / (1 - \rho^2),$$

where σ_e^2 is the common variance of the **es**. And the lagged covariances $E v_t v_{t-k}$
will be zero for $k = 1, \dots, n - 1$. This means that we can produce a set of n initial
values consistent with the process of the **vs** simply by taking n random draws
from a normal distribution with mean zero and variance $\sigma_e^2 / (1 - \rho^2)$. In Model 1
we need only one such draw, 4 for Model 2, and 12 for Model 3. In the case of
Model 1 this is done with the following code:

```
In[13]:=    v = 6*SphericalStandardGaussian[21];
            v[[1]] /= Sqrt[1-rho^2];
            Map[(v[[#]] += rho*v[[#-1]])&,Range[2,21]];
            y = 8 + .6x + Drop[v,1];
```

SphericalStandardGaussian[21] produces 21 independent standard normals (mean 0, variance 1). Although initially called **v** here, these actually are
the **es**, soon to become the **vs**. Multiplying by 6 causes them to have a variance
$\sigma_e^2 = 36$, as desired. The first element of **v**, the single initial condition needed
for Model 1, is then divided by the square root of $1 - \rho^2$, so that it is now a draw
from a normal distribution with mean zero and variance $\sigma_v^2 = 36/(1 - \rho^2)$, as
desired. (Note that the C-like code a /= b means a = a/b.) The next line uses
the Map[] function to make each element in **v** beyond the first equal to itself
plus ρ times the previous element (+=), thus carrying out the first-order autoregressive process. The & at the end of the first argument transforms the expression
in the parenthesis into a function that carries out that expression. And the place-
holder # becomes the argument for this function that takes on successive values
determined by the list that is the second argument to Map[], in this case the
range of integers going from 2 to 21. This exemplifies a particularly elegant
way *Mathematica* allows one to write certain iterative procedures without using

`Do[]` or `For[]` statements, with all their extra baggage. The result of all this, of course, is 21 **vs**, of which the first is an initial condition to be discarded. This is done with the `Drop[]` expression used in the next statement that also generates the actual **y** values incorporating the serially correlated residuals that will be used in the Monte Carlo replication.

The corresponding set of operations is done slightly differently in Models 2 and 3. The code for Model 2 is

```
In[14]:= v = Join[(1./Sqrt[1.-rho^2])*
         6*SphericalStandardGaussian[4],
         6*SphericalStandardGaussian[20] ];
       Map[(v[[#]] += rho*v[[#-4]])&,Range[5,24]];
       y = 8 + .6x + Drop[v,4];
```

The principle is the same, but, because it now requires 4 initial values for **v**, each independent and having mean zero and variance $\sigma_e^2/(1 - \rho^2)$, it is more efficient to generate them on their own and `Join[]` them to 20 additional random draws with variance 36 that constitute the **e**s. Of course, **v** now has `Length` = 24, and 4 initial values must be dropped. This part of the code for Model 3 is the same, except modified for 12 initial values.

New issues arise in initializing the somewhat more complicated Model 4. Here again we need 4 initial values for **v**, but they are no longer independent. We must first calculate the variance/covariance matrix for the marginal distribution of this process, and then make draws from a multivariate normal distribution with this variance/covariance matrix. This is done as follows: because **v** is now generated according to

(1) $v_t = \rho_1 v_{t-1} + \rho_4 v_{t-4} + e_t,$

the variance and first four covariances, $c_k = E v_t v_{t-k}$ $(k = 0, \dots, 4)$, must obey

(2a) $c_0 = E v_t(\rho_1 v_{t-1} + \rho_4 v_{t-4} + e_t) = \rho_1 c_1 + \rho_4 c_4 + \sigma_e^2$
(2b) $c_1 = E v_{t-1}(\rho_1 v_{t-1} + \rho_4 v_{t-4} + e_t) = \rho_1 c_0 + \rho_4 c_3$
(2c) $c_2 = E v_{t-2}(\rho_1 v_{t-1} + \rho_4 v_{t-4} + e_t) = \rho_1 c_1 + \rho_4 c_2$
(2d) $c_3 = E v_{t-3}(\rho_1 v_{t-1} + \rho_4 v_{t-4} + e_t) = \rho_1 c_2 + \rho_4 c_1$
(2e) $c_4 = E v_{t-4}(\rho_1 v_{t-1} + \rho_4 v_{t-4} + e_t) = \rho_1 c_3 + \rho_4 c_0.$

Substituting (2e) into (2a) produces

(2a′) $c_0 = 1/(1 - \rho_4^2)[\rho_1 c_1 + \rho_1 \rho_4 c_3 + \sigma_e^2]$

and (2a′), along with (2b)-(2d), gives a system of four equations

(3a) $c_0 - 1/(1 - \rho_4^2)\rho_1 c_1 - 1/(1 - \rho_4^2)\rho_1 \rho_4 c_3 = 1/(1 - \rho_4^2)\sigma_e^2$
(3b) $c_1 - \rho_1 c_0 - \rho_4 c_3 = 0$
(3c) $c_2 - \rho_1 c_1 - \rho_4 c_2 = 0$
(3d) $c_3 - \rho_1 c_2 - \rho_4 c_1 = 0$

from which to solve for $c_0, c_1, c_2,$ and c_3 in terms of $\rho_1, \rho_4,$ and σ_e^2. And from these four values we can construct the variance/covariance matrix of the marginal

distribution of four successive values for v_t from the process (1). The function
VarMat [] accomplishes this task.

```
In[15]:= VarMat[r1_,r4_,se2_] :=
          Block[{c,n},
              c = Inverse[{{1.,-r1/(1.-r4^2),0.,-r1*r4/(1.-r4^2)},
                    {-r1, 1., 0., -r4}, {0.,-r1,1.-r4,0.},
                    {0.,-r4,-r1,1.}}].{se2/(1.-r4^2),0.,0.,0.};
              n = Length[c];
              c = Drop[Join[Reverse[c],c],{n}];
              Map[Take[c,{#,#+n-1}]&,Reverse[Range[n]]]
          ]
```

VarMat [] works by first inverting the system (3) and solving for **c**, then creating
a vector which is **c** preceded by itself reversed and with the double element of
c_0 removed, that is, $\{c_3, c_2, c_1, c_0, c_1, c_2, c_3\}$. From this, Map[] can select the four
rows need to form the variance/covariance matrix

```
In[16]:= S = {{c[[0]],c[[1]],c[[2]],c[[3]]},
                {c[[1]],c[[0]],c[[1]],c[[2]]},
                {c[[2]],c[[1]],c[[0]],c[[1]]},
                {c[[3]],c[[2]],c[[1]],c[[0]]}}
```

It is now possible to generate four normal variates with mean zero and vari-
ance/covariance matrix **S** by taking **M**, the square root of **S**, calculated via a
Cholesky or QR Decomposition or the Singular-Value Decomposition and forming

```
In[17]:= M.SphericalStandardGaussian[4]
```

which is precisely what the function MultivariateGaussian[] found in
StatUtilities.m does. All the preceding is therefore accomplished, along
with the generation of the appropriate **y** variate, with the following code in
Model 4, the general nature of which should now be familiar.

```
In[18]:= sige = 6.0;
          varMatrix = VarMat[rho1,rho2,sige^2];
          v = Join[MultivariateGaussian[4,1,,varMatrix],
              sige*SphericalStandardGaussian[20]];
          Map[(v[[#]] += rho1*v[[#-1]]+rho2*v[[#-4]])&,
              Range[5,24]];
          y = 8 + .6x + Drop[v,4];
```

15.3   Runs

The pieces are now together so that we can start the runs. The pieces consist
of the statistic **s**, the dgp **g** with its sampling distribution **h**, and a collection of
conditioning values $\{x, b, d, T, K\}$. For any one set of conditioning values, we

need only draw **es** repeatedly from **h(e; d)**, generate **y** = **g(x, b, e)** and calculate the statistic from **s** = **f(y, x)**. Only one question lingers: How many replications for each run?

15.3.1 Number of Replications

We have seen that the purpose of a Monte Carlo experiment is to exercise a given model to see how it behaves, and this typically takes lots of trials. Determining how many trials is often a balancing act. Most Monte Carlo studies use in excess of 1,000 replications, frequently employing numbers such as 2,000, 5,000, 10,000, and even 50,000. Sometimes theoretical considerations can provide guidance for the number of replications needed to achieve a given objective, as is shown shortly. And one can always play it by ear, doing sequential test runs of, say, 1,000, 3,000, 5,000, and so on replications and assessing the results after each to determine how stable they are becoming. But often practical considerations come to the fore, and mundane matters such as computer availability, time, and cost become the determining factors.

In a study such as our illustrative one, assessing the power of a test, we can get some idea of an appropriate number of replications as follows: basically we are doing this Monte Carlo study to estimate of the probability that a given test will reject the null hypothesis, and to compare such estimates for two different tests. Each replication produces a test statistic that either rejects the null hypothesis or does not, and so can be viewed as an outcome of a Bernoulli trial with probability p of success (rejection) and $1 - p$ of failure. After n such replications, we have a sample of n independent Bernoulli trials with a number, say, x successes, which is distributed as a binomial distribution with mean np and variance $np(1 - p)$. The estimated power x/n therefore has mean p and variance $p(1 - p)/n$, and for large n this is approximately normally distributed. If, therefore, we wish to determine n so that a band about our estimated power $x/n \pm r$ has a probability q of containing the true power, we need to determine the n such that

$$c_q[p(1 - p)/n]^{-1/2} = r,$$

where c_q is the appropriate q-critical value of the standard normal. For a 95% range, $c_{.95}$ is 1.96, and we can determine appropriate values for n with

```
In[19]:= nValue[p_,r_] := 1.96 Sqrt[p(1-p)/n] == r
```

We note this depends on p, and we do not know p. So we can experiment with a range of values. Let us first suppose we set $r = .01$; that is, we are basically asking for a precision for our probability estimates of .02. Then values of n for ps equal to .03, .3, .5, and .9 are simply determined in *Mathematica* with

```
In[20]:= TableForm[Map[{#,Solve[nValue[#,.01],n]}&,
                       {.03,.3,.5,.9}]]
```

```
Out[20]= 0.03    n -> 1117.91
         0.3     n -> 8067.36
         0.5     n -> 9604.
         0.9     n -> 3457.44
```

This indicates upwards of 10,000 replications for some values of p. Of course, a fixed range of .02 may be appropriate in the neighborhood of $p = .5$, but not around $p = .03$. Thus we might want ranges that are a fixed proportion of the probability, say, ±5%. The previous code is readily modified to solve this problem:

```
In[21]:= TableForm[Map[{#,Solve[nValue[#,.05#],n]}&,
                                     {.03,.3,.5,.9}]]
```

```
Out[21]= 0.03    n -> 49684.7
         0.3     n -> 3585.49
         0.5     n -> 1536.64
         0.9     n -> 170.738
```

From this, we see that approximately 3,600 replications would be adequate for the most part, but we could consider runs with as many as 50,000 replications for tests with powers near zero. One must, of course, temper justice with mercy; such figures are beyond reasonableness with a desktop computer running in *Mathematica*. Larger numbers could become possible either using faster code (say, *MathLink* to appropriate C code) or a remote kernel running on a significantly faster machine. In the current study, 5,000 is chosen as a compromise that is both possible and not unreasonable relative to the study's goals. We are not interested here in gaining a thoroughly refined estimate of the power of these tests. Rather, we are interested in seeing if there is a stable relationship in their relative powers, and a little trial shows that 5,000 replications is more than adequate for this purpose. In every case tested, by the way, things settled down after 2,000 replications, and, indeed, the overall results would be very little different had 1,000 replications been used.

15.3.2 The Runs in the Example

In our illustrative example, then, each run consists of 5,000 replications of a given model with a given value or set of values for ρ. In each replication one must

(a) generate a list **v** of 20 appropriately serially correlated error terms, as described in the previous subsection,

(b) use them to construct the variate **y = 8 + .6x + v** using the **x** data previously described,

(c) regress **y** on **x**, storing the resulting residuals **err**,

(d) run a regression of **y** on **x** and the appropriate truncated lag(s) of **err** (no zero-padding),

(e) run a regression of **y** on **x** and the appropriate zero-padded lag(s) of **err**, and

(f) calculate the appropriate *t*- or *F*-statistics for the coefficient(s) of the lagged **err**(s) from the preceding two regressions, and file them for later processing to determine the relative power of truncation versus zero-padding.

15.3.2.1 A Tutorial Look at Model1[]

In our illustrative example, a run doing the preceding tasks for Model 1 (simple first-order serial correlation) with a ρ of 0.9 would be effected with

```
In[22]:= Model1[0.9, 5000, "Mod1(.9)"]
```

Let us take a moment to look at the code behind this function call in some detail. Parts of it should by now be familiar. Those who already have substantial *Mathematica* experience are welcome to skim or skip the following detail.

```
In[23]:= Model1[rho_,trials_,filename_String] :=
         Block[{count,v,y,err,beta1,beta2,se1,se2,yhat},
             OpenAppend[filename];
             yhat = 8 + .6x;
             Do[
                 v = 6*SphericalStandardGaussian[21];
                 v[[1]] /= Sqrt[1-rho^2];
                 Map[(v[[#]] += rho*v[[#-1]])&,Range[2,21]];
                 y = yhat + Drop[v,1];
                 err = Reg[y,{"const",x},
                     displayOutput->False][[2]];
                 {beta1,se1} = Reg[y, {"const",x,lag[err]},
                     returnValues->Level2,displayOutput->
                     False][[{1,5}]];
                 {beta2,se2} = Reg[y, {"const",x,
                     lag[err,,,lagValue->0.0]},returnValues->
                     Level2,displayOutput->False][[{1,5}]];
                 Write[filename,{beta1[[3]]/se1[[3]],
                     beta2[[3]]/se2[[3]]}];
                  If[DivHundQ[count],Print[count]]
               , {count,trials}
               ];
             Close[filename];
           ]
```

Because of the number of symbols used in this function, it is best to give them local scoping (so they disappear from memory after the function has done its task) by placing them in a Block[] statement. A Module[] statement could also be used, but Block[] produces faster code, which is important here. The symbols appearing in the opening set of braces in Block[{}, body] get local scoping.

The first statement in the body of the code, the OpenAppend[], creates a file (if it does not already exist) with name "filename" and makes sure that anything written into it is appended to the end of the file rather than starting anew from the beginning. One also must include in this name a path to the disk and folders that are relevant. The actual run file that accompanies this chapter shows how this is done on the Macintosh. Writing results to a file on disk is much slower than maintaining them in core, but there are certain reasons for doing so here. First, one may ultimately decide to evaluate the results in several different ways at different periods of time. To do this, they must be made permanent. Second, these runs take a long time, during which problems such as power failures could occur. It is therefore advisable to save what has been done as soon as it is done.

The next four lines, determining **v** and **y**, have been explained in the previous subsection. The result is a dependent variate **y** that possesses first-order serial correlation with the given ρ.

In the next line, the function Reg[], located in the package Econometrics.m, is used to regress **y** on **x** along with an intercept term "const". The latest version of Econometrics.m is 2.3.4 and is available from the author. An earlier version 2.2.6 was released with the first volume of the *Mathematica Journal* and with the predecessor to this volume. After loading Econometrics.m with

```
In[24]:= <<Econometrics.m
```

we get the information about Reg[] with

```
In[25]:= ?Reg
```

```
Reg[y_,x_,opts___] runs a regression of y on x.  y is a vector
   or list of vectors, x is a matrix, a list of vectors or
   matrices, or a tensor of lists of vectors. Include "const"
   (quotes are essential here) in x list if there is to be an
   intercept.  y and x may contain missing observations (any
   non-numeric entries).

Options[Reg] = {displayOutput -> True, varDCom ->
   False, displayDigits -> 3, varCovMatrix -> OLS (White),
   algorithm -> QR (SVD), returnValues -> Level1 (Level2)}

returnValues Options
   Level1 = {beta,err,yhat,sig2} (default)
   Level2 = {beta,err,yhat,sig2,se,vcMat}
```

In this first regression, we need only to retain the residuals **err**, the second element of the list of default values returned by Reg[]. This is accomplished by tacking [[2]] onto the end of the function call. It is also unnecessary (indeed highly undesirable) that the regression output be displayed on the screen, so this is turned off with the option `displayOutput->False`. Note also that the entire call to `Reg[]` is followed by a semicolon in order to prevent the list **err** from being printed on the screen (which would occur 5,000 times in each run).

Recall that the test for serial correlation requires that we rerun this initial regression with the lagged residuals included as a regressor. And to compare the effect of truncation versus zero-padding, we must do so twice, first using lagged residuals that ignore the observation lost to lagging (truncation), and second using residuals that replace this lost observation by zero (zero-padding). The basis of this comparison is done for this model by examining (and storing) the *t*-statistics of the lagged residual term in each regression. The next two calls to `Reg[]` do this. Note that `lag[err]` (the truncated lagged residuals) occurs among the regressors in the first regression and `lag[err,,,lagValue->0.0]` (the zero-padded lagged residuals) occurs among the regressors in the second.

The function `lag[]` is a very flexible lag/lead operator that is packaged along with `Econometrics.m`. We examine its information with

```
In[26]:= ?lag
```

```
lag[list_,n_,m_] creates lags (leads) of list. Negative values
    denote leads. lag[list] is list lagged once. lag[list,n] is
    list lagged n times. lag[list,n,m] creates a matrix of list
    lagged n through m>n times.

Options[labels -> True, lagValue -> Indeterminate].

Attributes: HoldFirst.
```

One might want to make a simple list and experiment with what `lag[]` does to and with it. The default for the values lost to lagging is `Indeterminate`, which is equivalent to truncation, because this *Mathematica* symbol is designed to retain its value through all calculations. When `Reg[]` encounters any nonnumeric value in an observation, that observation is deleted from the regression calculations. We can cause `lag[]` to replace values lost to lagging with zeros instead of `Indeterminate` simply by using the option `lagValue->0.0`, which is what is done in the second of these regressions. Note that the three commas are needed in `lag[err,,,lagValue->0.0]` so that `lag[]` knows this last expression is the fourth argument and not the second (which is now given its default value of 1).

Because we need to obtain the *t*-statistics for the lagged residual terms in each of these regressions, `Reg[]` must return both the estimated coefficients (`beta`) and their estimated standard deviations (`se`). This requires the second output level, which is obtained using the option `returnValues->Level2`. Noting from the information for `Reg[]` that `beta` is the first element of this list and `se` is the fifth, we append `[[{1,5}]]` to these function calls to return only these elements as `{beta1,se1}` in the first regression and `{beta2,se2}` in the second. The desired *t*-statistics are the ratios of the third elements in each of these lists (the information corresponding to the lagged residual term), which, as can be seen from the Write[] statement, are appended to filename on disk.

One other aspect of these regressions needs discussion. Note that the same **err** is used to form both the truncated and zero-padded lagged residuals used in the two artificial test regressions. Alternatively, separate **err**s could be used for each test regression. This would be appropriate if one were interested in gaining independent power assessments of each technique. Our interest here, however, is in learning how these two tests fare against one another when confronted with the same situation, to see if one is able to make better use of the given information in rejecting the null hypothesis of serial correlation. For this, using the same **err** is appropriate.

The final statement in the body of this function merely checks to see if count, the number of the replication, is evenly divisible by 100, and prints this number to the screen. This allows one to monitor the progress of the run, which can be quite lengthy on a desktop, even a quite powerful one. A function such as

```
In[27]:= DivHundQ[num_] := num - 100*Floor[num/100.] == 0
```

must, of course, be defined before Model1[] can be run. This is made global so that it can be used by all the different Model functions.

15.3.2.2   Models 2 through 4

Model2[] and Model3[] are essentially the same as Model1[].

```
In[28]:= Model2[rho_,trials_,filename_String] :=
        Block[{count,v,y,err,beta1,beta2,se1,se2,yhat},
            OpenAppend[filename];
            yhat = 8 + .6x;
            Do[
                v = Join[(1./Sqrt[1.-rho^2])*6*
                    SphericalStandardGaussian[4],
                    6*SphericalStandardGaussian[20] ];
                Map[(v[[#]] += rho*v[[#-4]])&,Range[5,24]];
                y = yhat + Drop[v,4];
                err = Reg[y,{"const",x},
                    displayOutput->False][[2]];
                {beta1,se1} = Reg[y, {"const",x,lag[err,4]},
                    returnValues->Level2,displayOutput->
                    False][[{1,5}]];
                {beta2,se2} = Reg[y, {"const",x,
                    lag[err,4,4,lagValue->0.0]},returnValues->
                    Level2,displayOutput->False][[{1,5}]];
                Write[filename,{beta1[[3]]/se1[[3]],
                    beta2[[3]]/se2[[3]]}];
              If[DivHundQ[count],Print[count]]
```

```
            ,{count,trials}
            ];
            Close[filename];
    ]


In[29]:= Model3[rho_,trials_,filename_String] :=
         Block[{count,v,y,err,beta1,beta2,se1,se2,yhat},
            OpenAppend[filename];
            yhat = 8 + .6x;
            Do[
                v = Join[(1./Sqrt[1.-rho^2])*6*
                    SphericalStandardGaussian[12],
                    6*SphericalStandardGaussian[20] ];
                Map[(v[[#]] += rho*v[[#-12]])&,Range[13,32]];
                y = yhat + Drop[v,12];
                err = Reg[y,{"const",x},
                    displayOutput->False][[2]];
                {beta1,se1} = Reg[y, {"const",x,lag[err,12]},
                    returnValues->Level2,displayOutput->
                    False][[{1,5}]];
                {beta2,se2} = Reg[y, {"const",x,
                    lag[err,12,12,lagValue->0.0]},
                    returnValues->Level2,
                    displayOutput->False][[{1,5}]];
                Write[filename,{beta1[[3]]/se1[[3]],
                    beta2[[3]]/se2[[3]]}];
                If[DivHundQ[count],Print[count]]
              ,{count,trials}
            ];
            Close[filename];
    ]
```

The lag structures for these models are generated differently, as we know from before. And thus different lags of **err** are required in the two test regressions. For the quarterly Model2[], for example, the fourth-order lag for the truncated residuals is obtained with lag[err,4], whereas this lag for the zero-padded residuals is obtained with lag[err,4,4,lagValue->0.0], and analogously for Model3[] with 12 lags.

Differences again arise with Model4[], but they are not major.

```
In[30]:= Model4[rho1_,rho2_,trials_,filename_String] :=
         Block[{count,v,y,beta,err,sig2,vcMat,varMatrix,f,
                sigu,yhat},
            OpenAppend[filename];
            yhat = 8 + .6x;
            sigu = 6.0;
            varMatrix = VarMat[rho1,rho2,sigu^2];
```

```
Do[
    v = Join[MultivariateGaussian[4,1,,varMatrix],
        sigu*SphericalStandardGaussian[20]];
    Map[(v[[#]] += rho1*v[[#-1]]+rho2*v[[#-4]])&,
        Range[5,24]];
    y = yhat + Drop[v,4];
    err = Reg[y,{"const",x},
        displayOutput->False][[2]];
    {beta,sig2,vcMat} = Reg[y, {"const",x,lag[err],
        lag[err,4]},returnValues->Level2,
        displayOutput->False][[{1,4,6}]];
    f = Fstat[beta,sig2*vcMat,{"na","na",0.,0.}];
    {beta,sig2,vcMat} = Reg[y, {"const",x,
        lag[err,,,lagValue->0.0],lag[err,4,4,
        lagValue->0.0]},returnValues->Level2,
        displayOutput->False][[{1,4,6}]];
    Write[filename,
        {f,Fstat[beta,sig2*vcMat,
        {"na","na",0.,0.}]}];
      If[DivHundQ[count],Print[count]]
    ,{count,trials}
    ];
    Close[filename];
]
```

The generation of **v** and **y** has been explained before. And **err** is determined exactly as in the previous models. But in our test regressions, we now have two lags: first- and fourth-orders. And it is the joint significance of their estimated coefficients that constitutes the test for serial correlation. Thus the *t*-statistic used in Models 1 through 3 will not suffice, and we must turn to an *F*-statistic. The function Fstat[], packaged with StatUtilities.m, does this job. The latest version of StatUtilities.m is 2.2.2, and it is available from the author. An earlier version (2.1) is packaged with the predecessor to this volume. We read it in with

In[31]:= **<<StatUtilities.m**

and check for the information on Fstat[] with

In[32]:= **?Fstat**

```
Fstat[estBetas_,VarCovMatrix_,hypothValues_:Null] calculates
    the F test of Ho: beta = hypothValues vs. H1: beta
    != hypothValues.  estBetas can be the full set of regression
    estimates; VarCovMatrix would then be sig2*xx from the
    regression output.  hypothValues is a list. The dimensions
    of these arguments must be p, pxp, and p, respectively.  If
    an element of hypothValues is a number, that becomes the
    hypothesized value for that coefficient in the test.  If an
```

element is a non-number, such as an NA, that coefficient is ignored in the test (i.e., the test is marginal with respect to that coefficient). If hypothValues is omitted, Fstat assumes the first coefficient is a constant term and tests that all slope coefficients are zero.

We see that, once we feed Fstat[] a set of estimates and their variance/covariance matrix, we can obtain the F-statistic relevant to any null hypothesis on any subset of these estimates. Thus we can get the F-statistic relevant to the null hypothesis that the coefficients of the two lagged residual terms in the test regressions are jointly equal to zero by giving Fstat[] the full set of four betas, their variance/covariance matrix, and the list of hypothesized values {"na","na",0.0,0.0}. For each of the two test regressions in Model4[], then, we first hang on to {beta,sig2,vcMat}, which constitute the first, fourth, and sixth elements in the list returned with Level2 of returnValues. The variance/covariance matrix of beta is sig2*vcMat. Because we want only to test that the coefficients for the two lagged residual terms are jointly zero, we want the test to be marginal relative to the first two coefficient estimates (those of the intercept and **x**), and this is accomplished by placing a nonnumeric entry in the first two positions of the list of hypothesized values and zeros in the last two. The value returned by Fstat[] for the first test regression is retained in **f**. That for the second is calculated directly in the Write[] statement, which also stores both these F values in filename.

15.3.2.3 The "A" Models: Rerunning Models 1–4 with Redundant Lags

In Models 1 through 4, we test for serial correlation exactly in the form that it is known to exist. Model 1 has first-order serial correlation, and our test regressions have one lag; Model 2 has fourth order, and the test regressions have a single fourth-order lag, and so on. Typically, however, the investigator does not know a priori exactly what the order or orders of the serial correlation are. At best it is known that the order is up to, say, the nth. Thus, in testing, one tends to include a spectrum of lags, and it is of interest therefore to investigate the relative power of truncation to zero-padding when the test regressions use additional redundant orders. To do this, we rerun each of the previously described four models in an "A" version that includes redundant test lags. With Models 1A, 2A, and 4A, we include the first four lags of **err** in the test regressions; that is, we add to the list of regressors lag[err,1,4] for the truncated version and lag[err,1,4,lagValue->0.0] for the zero-padded version. lag[err,1,4] is equivalent to {lag[err,1], lag[err,2], lag[err,3], lag[err,4] }. Here we are pretending the investigator suspects there may be up to fourth-order serial correlation, but does not know its exact form. This of course increases the number of coefficients whose joint significance is being tested, requiring, rather generally, an F-test. And it further reduces the degrees of freedom because the number of regressors has increased.

This game cannot be played the same way with the A version of Model 3 with its 12th-order lag. If we were to pretend that the investigator suspects up to 12th-order serial correlation and includes the first 12 lags, the number of degrees of freedom for the regressions with truncated residuals would be reduced to negative numbers and so could not be done. There are only 20 observations. If one tests for 12 lags, each increasing the number of regressors by 1 and simultaneously reducing the number of observations by 1, one would lose 24 degrees of freedom beyond the 2 already required for the intercept and x, ending up with −6 degrees of freedom. (This, then, is a case that would seem to speak greatly in the favor of zero-padding, for there would be no truncation and no loss of the 12 additional degrees of freedom on this account; there would still be 20 − 14 = 6 degrees of freedom, and the test could still be accomplished. We shall see, however, that this promise is illusory.) Thus for this case we alter the rules slightly but realistically. Instead of testing for the full spectrum of 12 lags relevant to this model, a subset of the 4 most typical lags is assumed, namely, the 1st, 3rd, 6th, and 12th. That is, the data are treated as monthly with lags of one-month, one-quarter, semi-annual, and annual. This allows for both the truncated and zero-padded versions to be tested and compared, the first having 20 − 6 − 12 = 2 degrees of freedom and the second having 20 − 6 − 0 = 14 degrees of freedom. These figures are $T - K - L$, where T is the size of the original data series, K is the number of regressors, and L is the loss in observations due to lagging. In addition, this model is run a third time using zero-padding with the full spectrum of 12 lags, just to see how it fares. As noted, this model has 20 − 14 − 0 = 6 degrees of freedom.

Here is the code for the four A models for those who are interested in the details. They are very similar to their non-A counterparts and need no additional explanation.

```
In[33]:= Model1A[rho_,trials_,filename_String] :=
        Block[{count,v,y,err,beta,sig2,vcMat,f,yhat},
            OpenAppend[filename];
            yhat = 8 + .6x;
            Do[
                v = 6*SphericalStandardGaussian[21];
                v[[1]] /= Sqrt[1-rho^2];
                Map[(v[[#]] += rho*v[[#-1]])&,Range[2,21]];
                y = yhat + Drop[v,1];
                err = Reg[y,{"const",x},
                    displayOutput->False][[2]];
                {beta,sig2,vcMat} = Reg[y, {"const",x,
                    lag[err,1,4]},
                    returnValues->Level2,displayOutput->
                    False][[{1,4,6}]];
                f = Fstat[beta,sig2*vcMat,
                    {"na","na",0.0,0.0,0.0,0.0}];
                {beta,sig2,vcMat} = Reg[y, {"const",x,
                    lag[err,1,4,lagValue->0.0]},returnValues->
                    Level2,displayOutput->False][[{1,4,6}]];
```

```
            Write[filename,{f,Fstat[beta,sig2*vcMat,
                {"na","na",0.0,0.0,0.0,0.0}]}];
              If[DivHundQ[count],Print[count]]
             ,{count,trials}
            ];
            Close[filename];
        ]


In[34]:= Model2A[rho_,trials_,filename_String] :=
         Block[{count,v,y,err,beta,sig2,vcMat,f,yhat},
            OpenAppend[filename];
            yhat = 8 + .6x;
            Do[
                v = Join[(1./Sqrt[1.-rho^2])*
                    6*SphericalStandardGaussian[4],
                    6*SphericalStandardGaussian[20] ];
                Map[(v[[#]] += rho*v[[#-4]])&,Range[5,24]];
                y = yhat + Drop[v,4];
                err = Reg[y,{"const",x},
                    displayOutput->False][[2]];
                {beta,sig2,vcMat} = Reg[y, {"const",x,
                    lag[err,1,4]},
                    returnValues->Level2,displayOutput->
                    False][[{1,4,6}]];
                f = Fstat[beta,sig2*vcMat,
                    {"na","na",0.0,0.0,0.0,0.0}];
                {beta,sig2,vcMat} = Reg[y, {"const",x,
                    lag[err,1,4,lagValue->0.0]},returnValues->
                    Level2,displayOutput->False][[{1,4,6}]];
                Write[filename,{f,Fstat[beta,sig2*vcMat,
                    {"na","na",0.0,0.0,0.0,0.0}]}];
                  If[DivHundQ[count],Print[count]]
                 ,{count,trials}
                ];
            Close[filename];
        ]


In[35]:= Model3A[rho_,trials_,filename_String] :=
         Block[{count,v,y,err,beta,sig2,vcMat,f1,f2,f3,yhat},
            OpenAppend[filename];
            yhat = 8 + .6x;
            Do[
                v = Join[(1./Sqrt[1.-rho^2])*
                    6*SphericalStandardGaussian[12],
                    6*SphericalStandardGaussian[20] ];
                Map[(v[[#]] += rho*v[[#-12]])&,Range[13,32]];
                y = yhat + Drop[v,12];
                err = Reg[y,{"const",x},
                    displayOutput->False][[2]];
```

```
            {beta,sig2,vcMat} = Reg[y, {"const",x,lag[err],
                lag[err,3],lag[err,6],lag[err,12]},
                returnValues->Level2,
                displayOutput->False][[{1,4,6}]];
            f1 = Fstat[beta,sig2*vcMat,
                {"na","na",0.0,0.0,0.0,0.0}];
            {beta,sig2,vcMat} = Reg[y, {"const",x,
                lag[err,,,lagValue->0.0],
                lag[err,3,3,lagValue->0.0],
                lag[err,6,6,lagValue->0.0],
                lag[err,12,12,lagValue->0.0]},
                returnValues->Level2,
                displayOutput->False][[{1,4,6}]];
            f2 = Fstat[beta,sig2*vcMat,
                {"na","na",0.0,0.0,0.0,0.0}];
            {beta,sig2,vcMat} = Reg[y,{"const",x,
                lag[err,1,12,lagValue->0.0]},returnValues->
                Level2,displayOutput->False][[{1,4,6}]];
            f3 = Fstat[beta,sig2*vcMat,Join[{"na","na"},
                Table[0.0,{12}]]];
            Write[filename,{f1,f2,f3}];
              If[DivHundQ[count],Print[count]]
            ,{count,trials}
            ];
        Close[filename];
    ]


In[36]:= Model4A[rho1_,rho2_,trials_,filename_] :=
        Block[{count,v,y,beta,err,sig2,vcMat,varMatrix,f,
                sigu,yhat},
            OpenAppend[filename];
            yhat = 8 + .6x;
            sigu = 6.0;
            varMatrix = VarMat[rho1,rho2,sigu^2];
            Do[
                v = Join[MultivariateGaussian[4,1,,varMatrix],
                    sigu*SphericalStandardGaussian[20]];
                Map[(v[[#]] += rho1*v[[#-1]]+rho2*v[[#-4]])&,
                    Range[5,24]];
                y = yhat + Drop[v,4];
                err = Reg[y,{"const",x},
                    displayOutput->False][[2]];
                {beta,sig2,vcMat} = Reg[y, {"const",x,
                    lag[err,1,4]},
                    returnValues->Level2,
                    displayOutput->False][[{1,4,6}]];
                f = Fstat[beta,sig2*vcMat,
                    {"na","na",0.,0.,0.,0.}];
                {beta,sig2,vcMat} = Reg[y, {"const",x,
```

```
                        lag[err,1,4,lagValue->0.0]},
                        returnValues->Level2,
                        displayOutput->False][[{1,4,6}]];
                   Write[filename,{f,Fstat[beta,sig2*vcMat,
                        {"na","na",0.,0.,0.,0.}]}];
                   If[DivHundQ[count],Print[count]]
                 ,{count,trials}
                 ];
             Close[filename];
        ]
```

15.3.3 Run Times

Mathematica's interpreted language is not the speediest of environments, and is therefore not ideally suited to the actual running of Monte Carlo studies which by their very nature are computationally intensive. *Mathematica*, however, is a fantastically flexible environment, making it an ideal platform in which to develop a Monte Carlo study. I opted in this case to do everything in *Mathematica*, runs and all, because *Mathematica* was available with all the tools needed in an immediately accessible form, and because I wanted to see what it was like. And it took a lot of running time. Most of the runs were done on a Mac IIfx which is no longer the fastest Macintosh, but it is still right up there. A single run (5,000 repetitions) of Model 1, for example, could take upwards of 5 hours. Model 4 took even more time, and Model 3A, with its three regressions, one including up to 14 variates, could drag on for 11 hours. These timings could be reduced by one-quarter or more with a Quadra 840, a significant difference, and, of course, it is hoped that the new PowerMacs will open entirely new vistas. (Indeed, since doing these studies, I have acquired a PowerMac 8100/110. On this machine, the 11-hour run takes roughly 1 hour. This is over three times faster than the same run on an IBM RS 6000.) However, even with slow machines, one is aware that there are large blocks of the day when a computer is idle, and so a bit of patience and management allows one to make even lengthy runs such as these without too great inconvenience. It is slow, but possible.

Then too, one must recall that one's ambitions increase directly with one's possibilities. If it is found that an 11-hour run is psychologically acceptable, the acquisition of a faster machine will probably not decrease overall run time. Rather, one will simply undertake larger projects (with more replications or more cases) still requiring lengthy runs. But, then, when you think about it, this is as it should be.

One important hint: if you are using a screen saver, be sure to turn it off. The constant communication required by it can cause a significant drag on the speed of the number-crunching engine. If you are concerned with screen burn during the long runs, simply turn the monitor's brightness control down manually.

As a matter of interest, I thought I could save myself some time by doing some of the runs on an accessible Mac II si, also equipped with a coprocessor. But I soon found that what could be done overnight on the fx needed a full weekend on the si, and so its efforts did little to shorten the overall running time. Such runs as these are not for the average machine.

Of course, there are several alternatives that would allow one to continue being able to take advantage of *Mathematica*'s flexible and productive development environment while gaining considerable speed on the production runs. If one is running on a network linked to a speedier machine, it is always possible to run the kernel remotely on the fast machine, feeding off the number crunching to it. A second possibility, that can be done with one's own machine, is to make use of *MathLink* to allow the heavy calculation functions to be written in a compiled language such as C or Pascal that will run significantly faster. This alternative is clearly advantageous only if the needed functions are already developed or if the total running time is so large that it will pay to develop them. Fortunately, however, desktop computers do not need to sleep, and we humans do. This situation opens many possibilities.

15.4   Results

Once the runs are done, it is possible to assess the results of the Monte Carlo experiment. This typically consists of examining a property or set of properties of the empirical distribution of the statistic **s** that has been stored away in such large numbers during the runs. In the case of our illustrative example, it is the relative powers of the t- or F-statistics for the tests involving the truncated residuals and the zero-padded residuals.

15.4.1   Estimating Power

In our illustrative example, each run produces 5,000 sets of t or F values stored on disk in the file `filename`. The power of the test generating those values is by definition the probability that that test will reject the null hypothesis (H_0: no serial correlation) when it is in fact wrong. Of course, we know this null is incorrect in every case here, because we generated the data with a specific serial correlation. So we need to determine the proportion of the repetitions that have test statistics that reject the null, and our interest is in comparing this proportion for the tests arising from the regressions using the truncated residuals to that for the tests using zero-padded residuals. A test rejects the null if it exceeds the relevant critical value for the t- or F-test. Critical values for Student's t are relevant to Models 1 through 3, where the coefficient for only one lagged residual is involved, and critical values for the F are relevant to all the others.

15.4.1.1   Critical Values

The following table reports for each test in each model the appropriate degrees of freedom and the corresponding 5% critical values. In the case of the t-tests, these are one-sided tests, assuming one knows a priori whether to test for positive or negative serial correlation (which, by the way, is certainly not always the case).

Obviously, in the case of a one-sided test for negative serial correlation, the negative of the critical value is appropriate. F-tests are by their very nature two-sided. Because the test results are stored, it is possible to go back and re-evaluate them under alternative assumptions.

5% one-sided critical values for the *t*-test

	Truncated residuals d. of f. / critical value		Zero-padded residuals d. of f. / critical value (+ or −)	
Model 1	16	1.746	17	1.740
Model 2	13	1.771	17	1.740
Model 3	5	2.015	17	1.740

5% critical values for the *F*-test

	Truncated residuals ds. of f. / critical value		Zero-padded residuals ds. of f. / critical value		
Model 4	(2, 12)	3.89	(2, 16)	3.63	
Model 1A	(4, 10)	3.48	(4, 14)	3.11	
Model 2A	(4, 10)	3.48	(4, 14)	3.11	
Model 3A	(4, 2)	19.25	(4, 14)	3.11	(selected lags)
			(12, 6)	4.00	(full lags)
Model 4A	(4, 10)	3.48	(4, 14)	3.11	

15.4.1.2 Power Calculations

The following code produces the power estimates, and it is worth a look in detail for those who are just becoming familiar with the wonders of functional programming in *Mathematica*.

```
In[37]:= power[series_,critValue_] :=
           Block[{temp},
               {temp = Length[Select[series,If[critValue>=0,
                   (#>=critValue)&, (#<=critValue)&]]],
                   N[temp/Length[series]]}]

           CalculatePowers[file_String,critValues_List] :=
               TableForm[MapThread[power,
               {Transpose[ReadList[file]],
               critValues}]]
```

The first function, power[], counts the number of items in the list series that exceed the specified critValue and returns this number and its proportion of the overall number of entries in the list. Counting the number of items in a list is accomplished with the *Mathematica* function Length[], and producing a list of items satisfying a given criteria is accomplished with the *Mathematica* function Select[], which is the heart of the power[] function. Thus suppose we have a list of *t* values

```
In[38]:= tValues = {2.3,1.2,1.8}
```

```
Out[38]= {2.3, 1.2, 1.8}
```

Those that exceed 1.740 are found with

```
In[39]:= Select[tValues, (#>=1.740)&]
```

```
Out[39]= {2.3, 1.8}
```

Again, note here that the postfix & turns the expression it follows into a pure function that carries out that expression, and # is the argument to the function. Select[] in turn applies this function to each element of tValues (substituting each element of tValues in turn for #), returning the list of all those for which it is True. Although it is clear that Select[] carries out its activities iteratively on the elements of the list tValues, there is no need for the programmer to set up this iterative structure or specify its limits; this is done automatically by the function Select[] itself. These are several examples of the *functional programming* that characterizes much of *Mathematica*'s programming environment and show its power. We will see more shortly.

The number of elements in tValues satisfying this criterion is

```
In[40]:= Length[%]
```

```
Out[40]= 2
```

and their proportion of the total is

```
In[41]:= %/Length[tValues]//N
```

```
Out[41]= 0.666667
```

The N[] function is employed to prevent *Mathematica* from presenting a fractional answer (2/3), because both numerator and denominator here are integers.

The power[] function carries out this sequence of operations in a single statement but it has one additional feature. A criterion function like (# >= 1.740) & is appropriate for a positive critical value such as 1.740, but would not be appropriate if we had negative serial correlation and wished to examine how many *t*-values were less than, say, −1.740. Here we would need the criterion function (# <= -1.740) &. Thus the second argument of Select[] in power[], the criterion function argument, is an If[] statement that first checks to see if the critical value is positive or negative and returns *the function* (#>= critValue) & if it is positive and (# <= critValue) & if it is negative. That is, the second slot of Select[] (the criterion- function slot), is here an If[] statement that returns to its own position the appropriate criterion function to employ. This is an even more powerful example of functional programming, in which functions are treated just like other objects and can be both input (arguments) and output (return values) of other functions.

Now we have a power[] function that works very well for determining the proportion of *t*- or *F*-values in a given list that satisfy a specified criterion. But we typically will be applying this, not to a single list of *t*-values, but to the two or three that have been written to each run's file, one for the test applied to truncated residuals and one (or two in the case of Model 3A) for the test applied to zero-padded residuals. Since each of these series will have its own criterion (because they have different degrees of freedom), they must be treated separately. Suppose then we were to analyze the results from the run for Model 1 with $\rho = 0.9$. On disk, in a file, say, "Mod1(.9)", sit 5,000 pairs of *t*-values, each pair consisting of one replication's *t*s using the truncated residuals and the zero-padded residuals. One way to proceed would be something like

```
In[42]:= output = Transpose[ReadList["Mod1(.9)"]];
         power[output[[1]], 1.746]
         power[output[[2]], 1.740]
```

ReadList[] is a *Mathematica* function that reads the items from a file and places them in a list. In this case this results in a list of 5,000 pairs of *t*s, that is, a 5000 × 2 matrix. We, of course, want 2 lists of 5000 *t*-values each, so we Transpose[] the result of ReadList[] and store it in output. Now output's first element output[[1]] is the list of *t*s for the truncated residual test, and this is to be compared to its criterion of 1.746 and similarly for output[[2]] for the zero-padded residual test *t*s relative to its criterion 1.740. This procedure is, however, ungainly and unnecessarily extravagant of memory. One of *Mathematica*'s virtues is that each output cell is kept in memory so it can be recalled for use at any time during the session, but this virtue can become a vice when one allows massive amounts of unneeded intermediate output to be retained. Thus every time one evokes the preceding code, a 2 × 5000 matrix of values is kept in storage, and if these items are needed only once during the session, this can be a large price to pay. The function CalculatePowers[] provides a single statement that combines the effect of the preceding three lines and it avoids retaining the intermediate output.

The heart of CalculatePowers[] is the *Mathematica* function Map-Thread[], which is yet another example of functional programming, in which the functions themselves embody much of the detail that would have to be spelled out explicitly in structural programming languages such as C. MapThread[f,{{a1,...,an},{b1,...,bn},...}] forms the list {f[a1,b1,...],...,f[an,bn,...]}; that is, MapThread[] threads the head f in a parallel fashion across a set of lists, producing a list of fs. If f happens to be a function of several arguments, then it produces a list of function values where the first arguments are drawn from the first list, and the second from the second, and so on. CalculatePowers[] simply threads power[] across two lists, the first bing the list of sets of *t*-values and the second a list of the criteria relevant to each. There is no need to tell it how many series it must work with; it figures this out for itself simply from the size of the lists with which it is working. On top of all this, it is wrapped in a function `TableForm[]` that formats the output for easy reading. The result is

```
In[43]:= CalculatePowers["Mod1(.9)",{1.746, 1.740}]

Out[43]= 3855    0.771
         3796    0.7592


In[44]:= CalculatePowers["Mod3A(.7)",{19.25,3.11,4.00}]

Out[44]= 578    0.1156
         646    0.1292
         119    0.0238
```

15.4.1.3   Doing a Run

Runs and their results are effected with a sequence of instructions pulling together the various items discussed. Let us suppose we want to do a run of 5,000 replications on Model 2 with a ρ of -0.7 and store the results in a file called "`Mod2(-.7)`". We decide to seed the random number generator with 894. Thus we write

```
In[45]:= SeedRandom[894]
         Model2[-.7,5000,"Mod2(-.7)"]
         CalculatePowers["Mod2(-.7)",{-1.771,-1.740}]
```

Recall also that `Model2[]` requires various functions found in the packages `Econometrics.m` and `StatUtilities.m`, and so it is assumed they have already been loaded.

A notebook, `MonteCarlo.nb`, providing the complete set of runs, accompanies this chapter.

15.4.2   Summarizing the Results

For smaller Monte Carlo experiments, or those that have relatively simple output, there is little need to do anything more than tabulate and interpret the results. We can certainly do that here for Models 1 through 3 and Models 1A through 3A.

15.4.2.1   Models 1 and 1A: Simple 1st-Order Serial Correlation

Let us look first at the results in columns 2 and 3 of Table 1 relevant to the exact test specification. Here the artificial regressions test for serial correlation exactly in the form in which it is present (i.e., the test has an exact specification): in

Table 1 Results for Models 1 and 1A

ρ (1)	Exact test specification		Redundant regressors	
	truncated (2)	zero-padded (3)	truncated (4)	zero-padded (5)
.3	.115	.113	.047	.058
.7	.586	.578	.171	.262
.9	.771	.759	.301	.429
-.9	.991	.991	.893	.930
-.7	.932	.929	.601	.694
-.3	.416	.413	.115	.147

this case, first-order. It is clear that there is very little difference whether one uses the truncated or the zero-padded residuals, regardless of ρ. The truncated residuals seem to have a very slight edge, but it is very slight. In any event, we can certainly conclude that there is no advantage here to attempting to save degrees of freedom by using zero-padded residuals in the artificial regressions.

An interesting result is also apparent here: although it is clear that the power of both these tests increases with absolute ρ, this power is asymmetric with respect to positive versus negative values for ρ. Both test statistics are far more powerful for negative ρ's than for positive. This is the kind of result that could be due to other aspects of the problem that are not being investigated. One important possibility here is the fact that the x data are themselves rather trended (which is akin to a strong positive serial correlation), and the tests may be confounding the positive serial correlation in the disturbance term with that in the x variate. Thus it is reasonable to do a quick study to see if using a nontrended x produces substantially different results.

To this end, Model 1R is constructed identically to Model 1 except that it uses x-data picked randomly with a range similar to that used in Models 1 and 1A. The **xR** variate used here, as noted before, is

```
In[46]:= xR = {167.628, 299.205, 147.2815, 144.790, 357.968,
               397.229, 188.895, 105.129, 332.846, 387.844,
               345.603, 215.358, 175.627, 220.927, 207.116,
               288.873, 237.548, 276.829, 173.479, 103.990}
```

Using these data produces the following results in runs that otherwise correspond exactly to those for Model 1 (except that only 1,000 replications are used).

Things look a bit better in Table 1a, but the same tendency is observed: there is still an asymmetry with respect to negative versus positive serial correlation, but it is less than before. And the truncated residuals still demonstrate very slightly superior power across the board. It is interesting to note that the major changes have taken place for positive ρs; the figures for negative ρs are virtually unchanged. For those who are interested, this is an issue that might be clarified by more extensive experiments. For the current study we can rest content in noting that zero-padding continues to show no advantage.

Table 1a Results for Model 1R

	Exact test specification	
ρ	truncated	zero-padded
(1)	(2)	(3)
.3	.204	.201
.7	.733	.723
.9	.901	.900
-.9	.994	.992
-.7	.936	.931
-.3	.415	.405

Looking next to the A-test, where there are redundant regressors—four orders of lag are used in the test regression even though only one order is used to generate the data—we see in columns 4 and 5 of Table 1 that there is a slight edge toward using zero-padded residuals for all values of ρ. Here then is a hint that when the exact nature of the serial correlation is not known a priori, and so there is a strong likelihood that redundant regressors will be used in the test, there may be some advantage to the use of zero-padded residuals. But clearly the advantage is small. It is also to be noted that the asymmetry mentioned is exacerbated in this case. The testing procedure seems, in general, to have quite poor power against positive serial correlation when using redundant regressors, even for values of ρ near unity. This suggests that a priori knowledge that allows narrowing the specification for which serial correlation is to be tested is valuable; the wholesale addition of redundant regressors is to be avoided.

15.4.2.2 Models 2 and 2A: Simple 4th-Order Serial Correlation

Table 2 shows the results for the case of simple fourth-order serial correlation. Once again, in the case of exact test specification shown in columns 2 and 3, the power increases with absolute ρ, although the increase is more nearly symmetrical here, positive to negative. Likewise, the test based on truncated residuals has marginally higher power than that based on zero-padded residuals. It is noted, however, that in the case of $\rho = -0.3$, this result reverses, giving zero-padding

Table 2 Results for Models 2 and 2A

	Exact test specification		Redundant regressors	
ρ	truncated	zero-padded	truncated	zero-padded
(1)	2)	(3)	(4)	(5)
.3	.174	.157	.100	.105
.7	.779	.747	.506	.500
.9	.969	.960	.897	.878
-.9	.993	.992	.936	.916
-.7	.904	.906	.570	.564
-.3	.331	.349	.091	.090

a very slight edge. In essence then these results are very similar to those for Model 1.

However, the use of redundant regressors in this case, shown in columns 4 and 5, does not give the edge to zero-padding. In fact, for the most part, the test based on truncated residuals does better here too. But the difference between the two tests, here as elsewhere, is little to write home about. It is also of interest to note that the deterioration in power against positive ρ's due to redundant regressors that is witnessed in the case of Model 1's first-order serial correlation is nowhere near as dramatic when testing for fourth-order serial correlation with redundant regressors.

15.4.2.3 Models 3 and 3A: Simple 12th-Order Serial Correlation

The results for simple 12th-order serial correlation are shown in Table 3. Here too we note in columns 2 and 3 that the test based on truncated residuals does slightly better than that based on zero-padded residuals when the test takes exactly the form appropriate to the nature of the serial correlation. A modest curiosus arises here, however, because zero-padding does take the edge for ρs small in absolute value but not otherwise. Furthermore the symmetry of the tests, positive to negative values of ρ, is striking here in comparison to the previous results.

The results using redundant regressors shown in columns 4 and 5 again demonstrate the overall deterioration of the power of both tests on this account. Here too the test using truncated residuals modestly outperforms that using zero-padded residuals for ρs near unity in absolute value but the reverse holds otherwise. The results in column 6 are as striking as they might be unexpected. It appears that using the full spectrum of redundant regressors with zero-padding produces a test with uniformly lousy power, less than 3 percent. Thus, although zero-padding allows this test to be carried out (whereas the test based on truncated residuals would have negative degrees of freedom and be impossible to conduct), it is wholly without power and virtually useless.

Table 3 Results for Models 3 and 3A

ρ spectrum (1)	Exact test specification truncated (2)	Exact test specification zero-padded (3)	Redundant regressors truncated selected (4)	Redundant regressors zero-padded selected (5)	Redundant regressors zero-padded full (6)
.3	.155	.161	.056	.055	.026
.7	.600	.589	.116	.129	.024
.9	.950	.913	.297	.269	.026
−.9	.947	.878	.305	.299	.028
−.7	.603	.591	.114	.158	.029
−.3	.164	.180	.052	.056	.030

15.4.2.4   Models 4 and 4A: 1st- and 4th-Order Serial Correlation

An examination of columns 2 and 3 of Table 4 shows that the results for exact test specification for the model having both first- and fourth-order serial correlation are a mixed bag indeed. In some cases the test based on truncated residuals does slightly better and in other cases zero-padding barely wins—in no case is the difference very striking. Although these results are clear from Table 4, any patterns in the relation are not so clear. Here then one might want to employ some more clever form of summary technique that is better able to capture any systematic relations that might exist. A *response surface* approach is certainly one way to proceed here, that is, a regression of the statistic of interest on the parameters. This is very easily accomplished in *Mathematica*. Thus let us enter the powers and ρ values from columns 1, 2, and 3 as data.

```
In[47]:= powers = {{.563, .5826}, {.422, .4868}, {.4094, .5378},
                   {.907, .8884}, {.8834, .9248}, {.8998, .8864},
                   {.687, .7232}, {.6842, .7282}, {.0694, .0618},
                   {.1216, .0962}, {.042, .0392},
                   {.0352, .0304}};
```

```
In[48]:= rho1={-.3, .5, .9, .03, -.8, .1, -.4, -.5, .5, .4,
              .2, .3};
         rho4={.5, -.3, .03, .9, .1, -.8, -.5, -.4, .4, .5,
              .3, .2};
```

Now we can regress the powers on the ρs descriptively. The exact form of the regression can be determined through trial, but a full quadratic (linear, squares, and cross-products) would seem to be a good start. So, assuming Econometrics.m is already in place, or entered now with

```
In[49]:= <<Econometrics.m
```

Table 4   Results for Models 4 and 4A

$\rho1\ \rho4$ (1)	Exact test specification		Redundant regressors	
	truncated (2)	zero-padded (3)	truncated (4)	zero-padded (5)
{-.3, .5}	.563	.583	.480	.514
{.5, -.3}	.422	.487	.262	.329
{.9, .03}	.409	.538	.269	.389
{.03, .9}	.907	.888	.880	.856
{.-8, .1}	.883	.925	.821	.874
{.1, -.8}	.900	.886	.787	.773
{-.4, -.5}	.687	.723	.544	.588
{-.5, -.4}	.684	.728	.521	.588
{.5, .4}	.069	.062	.093	.101
{.4, .5}	.122	.096	.147	.143
{.2, .3}	.048	.039	.069	.068
{.3, .2}	.035	.030	.048	.051

we can do the appropriate regression with

```
In[50]:= {btrunc,bzpad} = Reg[Call[powers,truncpower,
            paddedpower],{"const",rho1@,rho4@,rho1^2@,rho4^2@,
            rho1*rho4@}][[1]];
```

```
Dependent variable is truncpower
RSquared = 0.976073  RBarSquared = 0.956134
R2uncentered = 0.992251  SER = 0.0722138
Num of Observations = 12    Degrees of Freedom = 6
dw = 1.72434 with 0 missing obs.
```

	coef.	st. err.	t
Const	0.094	0.050	1.854
rho1	-0.372	0.045	-8.230
rho4	-0.175	0.045	-3.866
rho1^2	0.801	0.108	7.387
rho4^2	1.155	0.108	10.649
rho1 rho4	-0.525	0.162	-3.237

```
Dependent variable is paddedpower
RSquared = 0.957229  RBarSquared = 0.921586
R2uncentered = 0.986488  SER = 0.0991422
Num of Observations = 12    Degrees of Freedom = 6
dw = 1.58841 with 0 missing obs.
```

	coef.	st. err.	t
Const	0.094	0.069	1.350
rho1	-0.361	0.062	-5.826
rho4	-0.199	0.062	-3.208
rho1^2	0.926	0.149	6.219
rho4^2	1.139	0.149	7.654
rho1 rho4	-0.577	0.223	-2.591

These regressions look as if they are capturing the spirit of the data, and can be used to summarize how the powers depend on the parameter pair {rho1, rho4}. The clearest way to do this is graphically. Thus let us first form the regression equation

```
In[51]:= truncpower   = btrunc.{1, r1, r4, r1^2, r4^2, r1 r4}
```

```
Out[51]=                                                    2
         0.0935387 - 0.37188 r1 + 0.800977 r1   - 0.174682 r4 -
                                                    2
         0.525051 r1 r4 + 1.15464 r4
```

```
In[52]:= Plot3D[truncpower, {r1, -1.0, 1.0}, {r4, -1.0, 1.0},
         AxesLabel->{"rho1","rho4","truncpower"}]
```

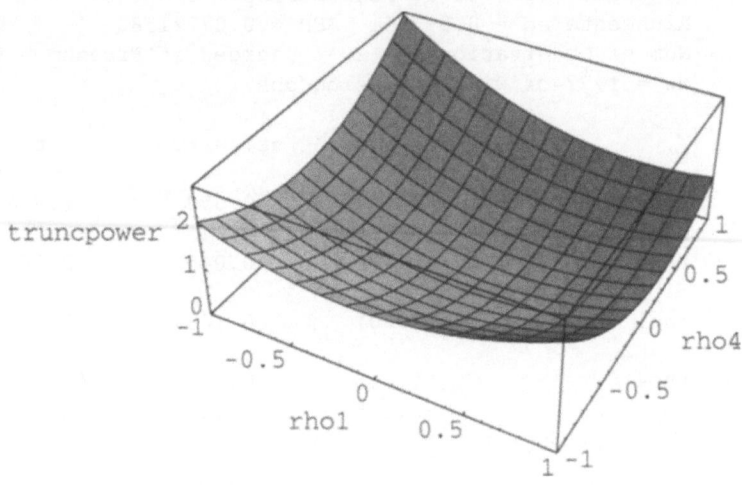

```
Out[52]= -SurfaceGraphics-
```

Here we see that the power of this test is clearly minimal near the origin and increases as we move outward in widening circles. We must be careful, however, in interpreting this graph for it looks as if it predicts powers greater than one in several of its corners. But of course the combinations in the corners are not really allowable because they produce nonstationary models, having roots lying inside the unit circle. Furthermore, we must note that this descriptive regression is based on only 12 observations and has only 6 degrees of freedom. At most we hope to gain some notion of tendencies from it. We could do a similar response surface for the power of the test based on zero-padded residuals, but it is clear it would be extremely similar. Anyway, our real interest is in the differences in power between these two tests, so let us consider

```
In[53]:= difpowers = powers.{1, -1}
```

```
Out[53]= {-0.0196, -0.0648, -0.1284, 0.0186, -0.0414, 0.0134,

         -0.0362, -0.044, 0.0076, 0.0254, 0.0028, 0.0048}
```

```
In[54]:= bdif  = Reg[difpowers@,{"const", rho1@, rho4@,
                   rho1^2@, rho4^2@, rho1 rho4@}][[1]];
```

```
Dependent variable is difpowers
RSquared = 0.758005   RBarSquared = 0.556342
R2uncentered = 0.808654   SER = 0.0295007
Num of Observations = 12     Degrees of Freedom = 6
dw = 1.47708 with 0 missing obs.
```

	coef.	st. err.	t
Const	0.000	0.021	0.001
rho1	-0.010	0.018	-0.566
rho4	0.024	0.018	1.316
rho1^2	-0.125	0.044	-2.819
rho4^2	0.015	0.044	0.344
rho1 rho4	0.052	0.066	0.784

In[55]:= **difpowers = bdif.{1, r1, r4, r1^2, r4^2, r1 r4}**

Out[55]=
$$0.0000223872 - 0.0104488\ r1 - 0.124872\ r1^2 +$$
$$0.0242941\ r4 + 0.0519376\ r1\ r4 + 0.0152207\ r4^2$$

In[56]:= **Plot3D[difpowers, {r1, -1.0, 1.0}, {r4, -1.0, 1.0},**
AxesLabel->{"rho1","rho4","difpowers"}]

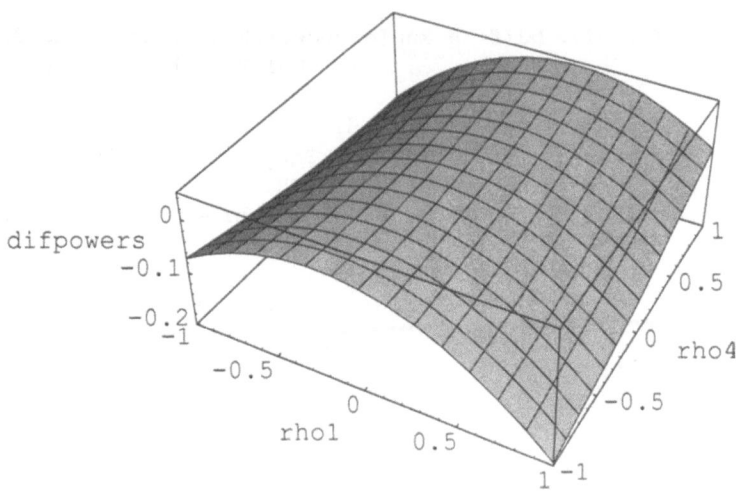

Out[56]= -SurfaceGraphics-

Now we can note very clearly that the relative power of the two tests has less to do with the value of rho4, but does move toward the advantage of zero-padding (values < 0) as rho1 increases in absolute value. Recalling again that values in the corner extremes are not relevant, we can also see that the advantage is not great, rarely exceeding 0.1. We also see the loss of information that can accompany such summarizing procedures, for this graph seems to indicate a uniform advantage for the test based on zero-padded residuals over that based on truncated residuals. The actual data, however, indicate this to be by no means the case; there are situations in which the reverse is noted to be true.

Comparing columns 4 and 5 to 2 and 3 in Table 4 shows that a very similar picture applies to the redundant-regressor results except, for the most part, the overall power level has been reduced. Of course, a similar response-surface analysis could be conducted for this case. This exercise is left to the reader.

15.4.2.5   Exercise for Reader

```
In[57]:= powers = {{.480, .5142}, {.2624, .3294}, {.269, .389},
                   {.880, .856}, {.821, .8742}, {.7874, .7728},
                   {.544, .588}, {.5212, .5876}, {.0932, .1012},
                   {.147, .1434}, {.0688, .068}, {.0482, .0508}};
```

This exercise will be left to the reader.

```
In[58]:= difpowers = powers.{1, -1}

Out[58]= {-0.0342, -0.067, -0.12, 0.024, -0.0532, 0.0146, -0.044,

          -0.0664, -0.008, 0.0036, 0.0008, -0.0026}

In[59]:= bdif  = Reg[difpowers@,{"const", rho1@, rho4@,
                   rho1^2@, rho4^2@, rho1 rho4@}][[1]];
```

Dependent variable is difpowers
RSquared = 0.765649 RBarSquared = 0.570356
R2uncentered = 0.846202   SER = 0.0277802
Num of Observations = 12   Degrees of Freedom = 6
dw = 1.19725 with 0 missing obs.

	coef.	st. err.	t
Const	-0.014	0.019	-0.747
rho1	-0.001	0.017	-0.042
rho4	0.022	0.017	1.243
rho1^2	-0.112	0.042	-2.683
rho4^2	0.036	0.042	0.854
rho1 rho4	0.023	0.062	0.374

```
In[60]:= difpowers = bdif.{1, r1, r4, r1^2, r4^2, r1 r4}
```

```
Out[60]=                                              2
              -0.0144985 - 0.000726586 r1 - 0.111905 r1   +


                                                      2
              0.0215978 r4 + 0.0233378 r1 r4 + 0.0356309 r4
```

```
In[61]:= Plot3D[difpowers, {r1, -1.0, 1.0}, {r4, -1.0, 1.0},
            AxesLabel->{"rho1","rho4","difpowers"}]
```

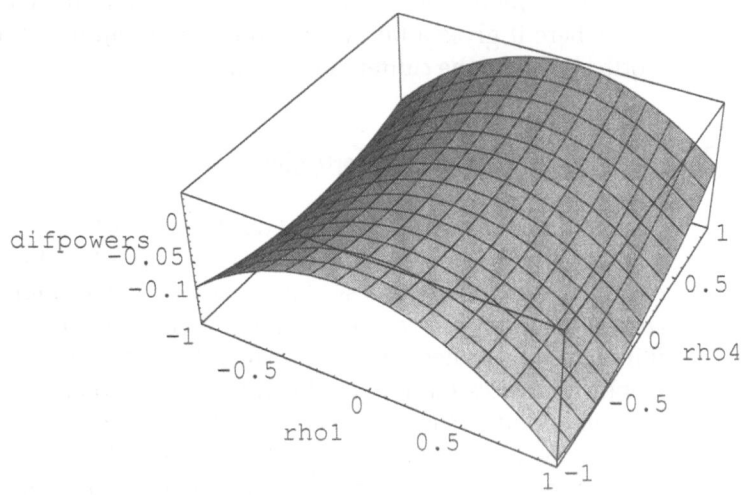

```
Out[61]= -SurfaceGraphics-
```

15.4.2.6   Summary of the Experimental Results

With the type of serial correlation most often subjected to test—simple 1st-
or 4th- or even 12th-order lags—the test using artificial regressions with zero-
padded residuals used to preserve degrees of freedom appears to buy nothing,
and indeed typically results in very slightly less power than the test based
on truncated residuals, even with its smaller degrees of freedom. In the case of
simple 1st-order serial correlation, some mileage can be had out of zero-padding
when one overparameterizes the test model, attempting to blanket a wider
spectrum of serial correlation, but the benefits are small. For higher-order simple
serial correlation, there are basically no benefits to zero-padding. For models
with a more complex pattern of serial correlation, such as the combination of
first and fourth investigated here, some advantage does go to zero-padding in

some but not all instances, which, for the most part, are not readily predictable. Again, the advantages in either direction are small. All in all, then, it seems reasonable to conclude that there is reason to avoid using zero-padding for testing for patterns of simple serial correlation, and that there is little reason to use it otherwise: you certainly will not hurt yourself much by not doing so, and you could if you do. In terms of economy and consistency of testing procedure, the standard tests based on truncated residuals seem a reasonable choice in small samples. As noted, this is a result that flies somewhat in the face of those of us whose ears perk up at any suggestion for saving a degree of freedom.

If this procedure seemed rather generally to buy something, so that one did not need to think very much about when and where to use it, then it would be a worthwhile addition to our everyday bag of tricks. But instead we find few situations where it buys very much, and quite to the contrary, very common ones where it gives a bit away. It does not seem therefore to be a procedure worth adding to the clutter of the toolbox.

15.4.3   Determining the Sign of the Serial Correlation

Having tucked away the results of our Monte Carlo runs on disk, we can return to them at any time for further analysis. An interesting question arises, for example, as to the usefulness of the t-tests for determining the sign of the serial correlation. Suppose we suspect first-order serial correlation, but are not sure if it is positive or negative. Informally, researchers often use the same statistic employed for testing for serial correlation as a diagnostic of its sign. Thus if the null hypothesis $H_0: \rho = 0$ is rejected in favor of first-order serial correlation because the t-statistic, say, is less than the negative cutoff, one might use this as diagnostic evidence that there is negative serial correlation. Notice that this sort of diagnostic is relevant only for Models 1, 1R, 2, and 3, which have test statistics that are both positive and negative. The remaining models make use of F-tests, which are always positive and therefore allow for no discrimination as to sign. Furthermore, because we are assuming ignorance of the sign of the serial correlation, the relevant tests would be two-sided as would the appropriate critical values.

We could therefore reanalyze the results for Models 1, 1R, 2, and 3 asking two questions: how often would the sign of the t-test correctly indicate the sign of the serial correlation, and how often would it incorrectly indicate this sign? The answer to the first question is of course directly related to the power of these tests, which we have already investigated (except that we used one-tail critical values rather than two-tail) and there is little to be gained redoing these. Thus we concentrate on answering the second question here, which requires that we determine the proportion of times the t-statistic is significantly in the direction opposite that of the sign of the serial correlation. This is readily done using the `CalculatePowers[]` function previously introduced, but this time we would use critical values that are for a two-sided 5% region and are of the opposite sign as that of the serial correlation.

The appropriate 5% two-sided critical values for the *t*-test here are

	truncated residuals d. of f. / critical value	zero-padded residuals d. of f. / critical value (+ or −)
Models 1 and 1R	16 2.120	17 2.110
Model 2	13 2.160	17 2.110
Model 3	5 2.571	17 2.110

Thus for Model 1 with $\rho = .3$ we would use

```
In[62]:= CalculatePowers["Mod1(.3)",{-2.120,-2.110}]
```

```
Out[62]= 18    0.0036
         21    0.0042
```

thereby determining that we would be misled as to the sign of the serial correlation less than 0.4% of the time using truncated residuals and slightly more than 0.4% of the time using zero-padded residuals. Table 5 summarizes these results for Models 1, 1R, 2, and 3.

It is clear that both tests do quite well in not misleading us about the sign of the serial correlation, virtually regardless of the magnitude of ρ (but particularly when ρ has at least moderate absolute value). In the cases of first-order serial correlation in Model 1 and fourth-order serial correlation in Model 2, a slight

Table 5 Proportion of times test incorrectly determines sign of serial correlation

ρ (1)	Model 1 truncated (2)	zero-padded (3)	@ truncated (4)	Model 1R zero-padded (5)
.3	.0036	.0042	.0030	.0020
.7	.0002	.0002	.0000	.0000
.9	.0000	.0000	.0000	.0000
−.9	.0000	.0000	.0000	.0000
−.7	.0000	.0000	.0000	.0000
−.3	.0004	.0004	.0000	.0000

ρ (1)	Model 2 truncated (2)	zero-padded (3)	Model 3 truncated (4)	zero-padded (5)
.3	.0028	.0036	.0066	.0064
.7	.0002	.0002	.0002	.0000
.9	.0000	.0000	.0000	.0000
−.9	.0000	.0000	.0000	.0000
−.7	.0000	.0000	.0000	.0000
−.3	.0004	.0008	.0060	.0044

edge goes to truncated residuals. In the cases of Models 1R and 3, a slight edge goes to zero-padding. But again in no case are the differences—or their absolute levels—of substance.

15.5 Summary

Mathematica provides an environment for developing Monte Carlo experiments that is fantastically flexible and fertile. Its built-in resources can help to reduce development time even for very complex studies in major ways. One can often be up and running with trial studies in an amazingly short period of time. Furthermore, the all-important task of providing a good quality random number generator comes with the territory.

The interpreted language of *Mathematica*, however, leaves much to be desired for speed in production runs, particularly on a personal computer. Although modest studies, such as the one illustrated here, are possible using a personal computer that ranks in the speedier categories, more ambitious studies would certainly want access to a kernel running, possibly remotely, on a machine of the workstation variety, such as an RS 6000, a PowerMac, or faster. But all this is possible in *Mathematica*.

Alternatively, one can take advantage of the remarkable facilities provided by *MathLink*, a means for communicating either with other programs or with one's own *Mathematica* functions written in a speedier compiled language such as C. *MathLink* allows *Mathematica* output to be fed to, say, a speedy statistical package and receive its output in return. And it allows a sequence of C language statements to be named and treated just like any other *Mathematica* function. The number-crunching portion of a production run, then, can be accomplished in a computationally more efficient setting and fed back reasonably seamlessly within the *Mathematica* session. Although such facility is nice, it initially requires much more awkward communication or much more outside development, and thereby defeats somewhat the purpose of using *Mathematica* for its inherent resources and flexibility.

In short, *Mathematica* is one amazingly flexible research environment in general, which, when linked to a computationally speedy kernel if necessary, offers the same attractions to Monte Carlo experimenters in particular.

15.6 References

Belsley, D. A. 1991. *Conditioning Diagnostics*, New York, John Wiley & Sons.

Box, G. E. P. and M. E. Muller. 1958. "A Note on the Generation of Random Normal Deviates." *Annals of Mathematical Statistics*, **29**, 610–611.

Breusch, T. S. 1978. "Testing for Autocorrelation in Dynamic Linear Models." *Australian Economic Papers*, **13**, 334–355.

Couture, R. and P. L'Ecuyer. 1994. "On the Lattice Structure of Certain Linear Congruential Sequences Related to AWC/SWB Generators." *Mathematics of Computation*, **62**, 799–808.

Davidson, R. and J. G. MacKinnon. 1993. *Estimation and Inference in Econometrics*. New York, Oxford University Press.

Durbin, J. 1970. "Testing for Serial Correlation in Least-Squares Regression When Some of the Regressors are Lagged Dependent Variables." *Econometrica*, **38**, 410–421.

Godfrey, L. G. 1978a. "Testing against General Autoregressive and Moving Average Error Models when the Regressors Include Lagged Dependent Variables." *Econometrica*, **46**, 1293–1301.

Godfrey, L. G. 1978b. "Testing for Higher Order Serial Correlation in Regression Equations when the Regressors Include Lagged Dependent Variables." *Econometrica*, **46**, 1303–1310.

Hendry, D. F. 1984. "Monte Carlo Experimentation." In *Handbook of Econometrics*, Vol. II, Z. Griliches and M. D. Intrilligator, Eds. Amsterdam, North-Holland.

Kiviet, J. F. 1986. "On the Rigor of Some Misspecification Tests for Modelling Dynamic Relationships." *Review of Economic Studies*, **53**, 241–261.

MacKinnon, J. G. 1992., "Model Specification Tests and Artificial Regressions." *Journal of Economic Literature*, **30**, 102–146.

Marsaglia, G. and A. Zaman. 1991. "A New Class of Random Number Generators." *The Annals of Applied Probability*, **1**, 462–480.

Press, W. H., S. A. Teukolsky, W. T. Vetterling, and B. P. Flannery. 1992. *Numerical Recipes in C*, 2nd Ed. Cambridge, Cambridge University Press.

Tezuka, S., P. L'Ecuyer, and R. Couture. 1993. "On the Lattice Structure of the Add-with-Carry and Subtract-with-Borrow Random Number Generators." *ACM Transactions on Modeling and Computer Simulation*, **3**, 315–331.

16 Random[Title]: Manipulating Probability Density Functions

Colin Rose and Murray D. Smith

Perhaps as a result of the information and uncertainty revolution of the 1970s, economists spend much of their time manipulating probability density functions. This chapter provides a symbolic toolset to make that job easier. At one extreme, it empowers even the "statistically challenged" with the ability to perform complex operations (without realizing it). At the other extreme, the power of *Mathematica* is such that it should also appeal to the professional theoretical statistician working with messy n-dimensional multivariate distributions, characteristic functions, inversion theorems, and so on. Discrete density functions are not considered. The toolset for this chapter is the package pdf.m, available on disk. It should be loaded up before proceeding further.

Structure

Mathematica v3 users: Users of *Mathematica* v3 (or later) should type the following before proceeding further:

```
In[1]:= SetOptions[ Integrate, GenerateConditions -> False ]
```

16.1   Getting Started

This chapter adopts a standardized user interface. The common starting point is always to specify a density function (say, f) *and* its domain. For instance, let us consider a logistic probability density function (pdf), defined on the set of real numbers:

```
In[2]:=           f  =  E^-x  (1 + E^-x)^-2
          domain[f] = {x, -Infinity, Infinity}
```

```
Out[2]=         1
          -------------

            x        -x 2
          E   (1 + E  )
```

```
Out[2]=  {x, -Infinity, Infinity}
```

The word **domain[ ]** is a special package-defined function that passes useful information on to *Mathematica*—it must always be specified along with the pdf. Having done so, *Mathematica* can get to work. Here is the distribution function (**DF**) of f, namely, the $P(X < x)$:

```
In[3]:=  DF[x, f]
```

```
Out[3]=     1
          -------

              -x
          1 + E
```

We shall also refer to this as the cumulative distribution function (cdf). The expectation of, say $3x^4$, is given by:

```
In[4]:=  Expect[3 x^4, f]
```

```
Out[4]=        4
          7 Pi
          -----
            5
```

This may take a few seconds to evaluate, because the necessary integration packages have to be loaded up first. Subsequent calculations will be much faster. Expectations are discussed in much greater detail in Section 16.2 where the **Expect** function is used to derive a smorgasbord of moments.

The package also performs transformations. For instance, if we wanted to find the density of $u = 2\exp(x/3)$ where x is a random variable with density $f(x)$, we would first specify the transformation equation:

```
In[5]:=  eqn = {u == 2 Exp[x/3]}
```

```
Out[5]=            x/3
         {u == 2 E   }
```

The density of u is then given by:

```
In[6]:=  Transform[eqn, f]   // Simplify
```

```
Out[6]=        3      3
          8 u  Abs[-]
                   u
         {-----------, {u, 0, Infinity}}
                3 2
           (8 + u )
```

Note that the **Transform** function has also worked out the domain of u. Transformations are discussed in much greater detail in Section 16.3.

These tools extend naturally to a multivariate setting. Although the package automatically handles trivariate and higher order density functions, we consider here a (comparatively) simple bivariate pdf $g(x, y)$, defined on the positive domain:

```
In[7]:=          g  =  9/2 (1+x+y) (1+x)^-4 (1+y)^-4
         domain[g] = {{x, 0, Infinity}, {y, 0, Infinity}}
```

```
Out[7]=     9 (1 + x + y)
         --------------------
                4       4
         2 (1 + x)  (1 + y)
```

```
Out[7]=  {{x, 0, Infinity}, {y, 0, Infinity}}
```

Here is its distribution function, namely, the $P(X < x, Y < y)$:

```
In[8]:=  G = DF[{x, y}, g]   // Factor
```

```
Out[8]=  x y (3 + 3 x + 3 y + 2 x y) (6 + 3 x + 3 y + 2 x y)
         -----------------------------------------------------
                                    3         3
                             4 (1 + x)  (1 + y)
```

Here is a plot of G:

```
In[9]:=  Plot3D[G, {x, 0, 2}, {y, 0, 2}];
```

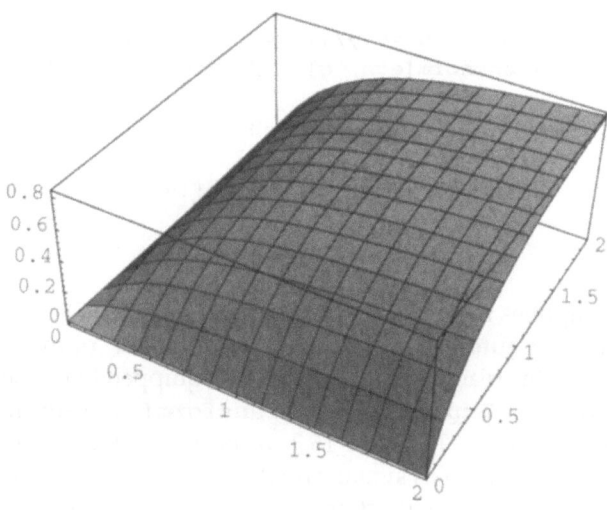

Here is the expectation of $y/(y + 2)$:

```
In[10]:= Expect[y/(y+2), g]
```

```
Out[10]= 5 - 6 Log[2]
         ------------
              4
```

Here is the marginal pdf of x:

```
In[11]:= Marginal[x, g] // Simplify
```

```
Out[11]= 3 (3 + 2 x)
         -----------
               4
         4 (1 + x)
```

Here is the pdf of y, conditional on $X = x$:

```
In[12]:= Conditional[x, g] // Simplify
```

```
Here is the conditional pdf g(y | x).
```

```
Out[12]=    6 (1 + x + y)
         -------------------
                      4
         (3 + 2 x) (1 + y)
```

Now consider the transformation $u = y/(1 + x)$ and $v = 1/(1 + x)$. We can calculate the joint pdf of u and v.

```
In[13]:= eqn = { u == y/(1+x), v == 1/(1+x) };
         Transform[eqn, g]    // Simplify
```

```
Out[13]=              7        -3
           9 (1 + u) v  Abs[v  ]
         {----------------------, {{u, 0, Infinity}, {v, 0, 1.}}}
                     4
              2 (u + v)
```

This simplifies further if we note that v is positive. Once again, the **Transform** function has automatically derived the "domain" or extremes of u and v.

By now, the reader should already be equipped to use such functions in his or her own work. **Expect[ ]** and **Transform[ ]** are examined in much greater depth in Sections 16.2 and 16.3, respectively. In a multivariate setting, little idiosyncracies such as syntax and dependence necessitate devoting a section to multivariate analysis (Section 16.4). Before proceeding further, we round this section off with an economic application of our new toolset.

16.1.1   Example: The Gini Coefficient and the Lorenz Curve

In statistics, the Gini coefficient has been used to measure dispersion. Its advantage over, say, the variance, is that it is unitless, and lies within the unit interval. In economics, the Gini coefficient is often used to measure the extent of inequality in the distribution of income, with the Lorenz curve providing a visual perspective. If income X is Pareto distributed (as is often assumed), then its pdf is

```
In[14]:=        f  =  a b^a x^-(a+1);
          domain[f] = {x, b, Infinity};
```

for parameters $a > 0$ and $b > 0$. In our context, we require that the mean of f exists and is positive, where:

```
In[15]:= mean = Expect[x, f]
```

```
Out[15]=  a b
         ------
         -1 + a
```

and thus we impose the tighter restriction $a > 1$. The distribution function and the first moment distribution function (fmdf) are given, respectively, by

```
In[16]:=    F = DF[x, f]
          fmdf = mean^-1 Integrate[x f, {x, b, x}] // Simplify
```

```
Out [16] =        a
               b
         1  -  --
                a
               x
```

```
Out [16] =       a              a
             -(b   x) + b  x
             --------------
                          a
               b  x
```

The Lorenz curve is simply a plot of fmdf against F [see, for example, Stuart and Ord (1994), sec. 2.25]. This is easily done with **ParametricPlot**. We shall assume $a = 2$ and $b = 1$, and thus generate a standard Lorenz curve diagram.

```
In[17]:= a=2; b=1;
         ParametricPlot[{{F, fmdf}, {F, F}}, {x, b, 100},
             PlotRange -> All, AspectRatio -> 1,
             Frame -> True];
```

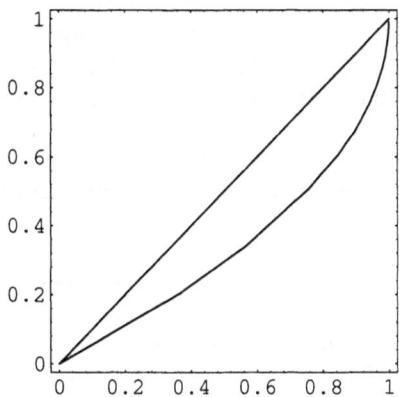

The Gini coefficient is equivalent to twice the area between the two curves. A general method of deriving it is to use mean, F and fmdf from the preceding as follows.

```
In[18]:= a = .; b = .;
         Gini = mean^-1 Expect[x F - mean fmdf, f] // Simplify
```

```
Out[18] =       1
             --------
             -1 + 2 a
```

This corresponds to a value of a 1/3 for the preceding plot.

16.2   Special Expectations: Moments, Generating Functions and More

Comment

It is worth noting that *Mathematica*'s ContinuousDistribution package can also "derive" the mean, variance, skewness, and kurtosis (as well as a few other measures) for a number of well-known density functions. However, it is important to realize that *Mathematica*'s ContinuousDistribution package does NOT calculate these results. Rather, it knows these results in exactly the same way as a textbook appendix knows them: that is, because someone typed them in there. By contrast, this section actually calculates the mean or variance or any other expectational measure from first principles. As such, it is not limited to the set of well-known distributions, nor to the set of well-known measures.

16.2.1   Deriving Moments

In statistics, one problem can usually be handled in several different ways—the appropriate technique often depends on the problem. When using *Mathematica*, the same variety applies. This section discusses two alternative ways of deriving moments about the origin: a direct approach, and a generating function approach (moment generating functions and characteristic functions). Attention is also focused on Fourier and Laplacian transforms. For our first example, we consider a normal pdf, for its familiarity allows us to focus on *Mathematica*, rather than the functional form. In this vein, let x be $N(\mu, \sigma^2)$ with pdf g:

```
In[19]:=          g = Exp[- (x-mu)^2 / (2 sig^2)]/ (Sqrt[2Pi] sig)
            domain[g] = {x, -Infinity, Infinity}
```

```
Out[19]=                           1
            -----------------------------------
                          2       2
            (-mu + x) / (2 sig )
          E                       Sqrt[2 Pi] sig
```

```
Out[19]= {x, -Infinity, Infinity}
```

We can set up a simple function to directly evaluate the kth moment as follows:

```
In[20]:= Moment[k_] = Expect[x^k, g]
```

```
Out[20]=                                                              2
                                              k   3    mu
                      Sqrt[2] mu Hypergeometric1F1[1 + -, -, ------]
                                              2   2         2
  1 k/2   k    k                 k                        2 sig
((-)   2   sig  Gamma[1 + -] (--------------------------------------------------- -
  4                       2                      sig
```

```
                                                      2
       k                                   k  3   mu
    (-1)  Sqrt[2] mu Hypergeometric1F1[1 + -, -, ------]
                                           2  2      2
                                                 2 sig
    -------------------------------------------------- +
                          sig


       2      2                                         2
     mu /(2 sig )                           k   1   -mu
    E              Sqrt[Pi] LaguerreL[-, -(-), ------] +
                                      2   2       2
                                              2 sig


              2      2                                        2
       k   mu /(2 sig )                         k   1   -mu
    (-1)  E              Sqrt[Pi] LaguerreL[-, -(-), ------])) /
                                            2   2       2
                                                     2 sig


             2      2
     1 k/2  mu /(2 sig )
    (2 (-)   E             Sqrt[Pi])
       2
```

Mathematica has found the *k*th moment in terms of inbuilt functions such as the Laguerre polynomial, and generates an output only a *Mathematica* fan could love. We can use this result to find any arbitrary moment. Here is the eighth one:

```
In[21]:= Moment[8]

Out[21]=   8          6   2         4    4         2   6
         mu  + 28 mu  sig  + 210 mu  sig  + 420 mu  sig  +

                 8
         105 sig
```

Rather than deriving the *k*th moment directly (as before), we can proceed by finding the moment generating function (mgf) instead:

```
In[22]:= mgf = Expect[E^(t x), g] // ExpandAll

Out[22]=              2  2
          mu t + (sig  t )/2
         E
```

We can quickly write up a function to derive the *k*th moment from any specified generating function (gf):

```
In[23]:= M[k_, gf_] := D[gf, {t, k}] /. t -> 0
```

Note, though, that the function assumes that the argument variable is t. Let us try it out: here are the first nine moments of the normal pdf, obtained from the preceding mgf.

```
In[24]:= Do[ Print[M[i, mgf]], {i, 9}]
```

```
mu
    2     2
mu  + sig
    3             2
mu  + 3 mu sig
    4       2   2       4
mu  + 6 mu  sig  + 3 sig
    5        3   2           4
mu  + 10 mu  sig  + 15 mu sig
    6        4   2        2   4         6
mu  + 15 mu  sig  + 45 mu  sig  + 15 sig
    7        5   2          3   4            6
mu  + 21 mu  sig  + 105 mu  sig  + 105 mu sig
    8        6   2          4   4         2   6         8
mu  + 28 mu  sig  + 210 mu  sig  + 420 mu  sig  + 105 sig
    9        7   2          5   4          3   6            8
mu  + 36 mu  sig  + 378 mu  sig  + 1260 mu  sig  + 945 mu sig
```

The mgf approach can be surprisingly fast: the following cell contrasts the time taken to derive the 30th moment using both the direct approach and the mgf approach:

```
In[25]:= Moment[30];     // Timing
         M[30, mgf];      // Timing
```

```
Out[25]= {3.15 Second, Null}
```

```
Out[25]= {0.333333 Second, Null}
```

However, the mgf does not exist for every distribution. By contrast, characteristic functions are theoretically guaranteed to exist, though this is not to say that *Mathematica* can always derive it. For our example, the characteristic function (cf) is given by

```
In[26]:= cf = Expect[ E^(I t x), g]
```

```
Out[26]=                                      2       2
                             I t x - (-mu + x) /(2 sig )
           Integrate[E

                {x, -Infinity, Infinity}] / (Sqrt[2 Pi] sig)
```

Unfortunately, *Mathematica* v2.2 cannot evaluate this integral, although v3 can. However, this lapse is only momentary (!), for we can take advantage of the powerful Fourier transform package instead. We can do so because a Fourier transform is identical to a characteristic function, *provided* the pdf $g(x)$ is defined over $(-\infty, \infty)$. To proceed, we need to load in the Fourier transform package:

```
In[27]:= <<Calculus'FourierTransform'
```

Having done so, the characteristic function (cf) of pdf $g(x)$ is given by:

```
In[28]:= cf = FourierTransform[g, x, t]

Out[28]=                  2  2
            I mu t - (sig  t )/2
          E
```

So, with these additional integration rules, *Mathematica* has found the solution. The use of the Fourier transform has a second advantage: it is often fast, and it is fast because this package has been designed purely for this kind of problem. In fact, if one does the appropriate timings, it transpires that the Fourier transform is about 20 times faster at doing this type of integration than *Mathematica* would be without it. Once we have the cf, we can derive moments from it by modifying the **M[ ]** function slightly to account for the addition of the imaginary number **I**. We call the new function **MI**:

```
In[29]:= MI[k_, gf_] := I^-k M[k, gf] // Expand
```

Once again, the eighth moment is given by:

```
In[30]:= MI[8, cf]

Out[30]=   8          6    2          4    4          2    6
          mu  + 28 mu  sig  + 210 mu  sig  + 420 mu  sig  +

                8
          105 sig
```

It is worth stressing the caveat again: it is only appropriate to use the Fourier transform package to derive characteristic functions *if* the pdf is defined over the set of real numbers.

A similar trick exists for densities $g(x)$ defined on the positive domain $(0, \infty)$. In such cases, one can use Laplace transforms to derive generating functions. Of course, one would first have to load up the Laplace transform package in the normal way:

```
<<Calculus'LaplaceTransform'
```

The following expression would then yield the characteristic function:

```
LaplaceTransform[ g, x, -I t ]
```

One can also use the Laplace transform to derive the mgf. The following expression would do this:

```
LaplaceTransform[ g, x, -t ]
```

These are powerful (and memory hungry) tools, and it often pays to exploit them.

16.2.2 Deriving Central Moments

Instead of deriving the kth moment $E(x^k)$, we can also derive the kth central moment $E(x - \mu)^k$, or the kth standardized central moment $E((x - \mu)/\sigma)^k$. Doing so provides a general way of deriving measures such as the variance, skewness, kurtosis, and so on, rather than writing specific functions for each of these measures. This section briefly applies the techniques of the previous section. We consider three approaches: the direct approach, the generating function approach, and a "moment about the origin" approach. To illustrate, let y have Gamma density with pdf $h(y)$ over the positive domain:

```
In[31]:=            h  =  y^(a-1) E^(-y/b) b^-a / Gamma[a]
          domain[h] = {y, 0, Infinity}

Out[31]=       -1 + a
           y
          ----------------
            a  y/b
           b  E     Gamma[a]


Out[31]= {y, 0, Infinity}
```

(1) Direct approach:
To get things going, let us derive the mean (say, μ) first:

```
In[32]:= mu = Expect[y, h]


Out[32]= a b
```

We can now find any arbitrary central moment $E(y - \mu)^k$. For instance, the standard deviation (sd) is given by:

```
In[33]:= sd = Expect[(y-mu)^2, h] // Sqrt

Out[33]=              2
          Sqrt[a b ]
```

We are now armed to find any central moment, whether it be standardized or not. For instance, a kurtosis measure is given by:

```
In[34]:= Expect[((y-mu)/sd)^4, h]
```

```
Out[34]= 3 (2 + a)
         ---------
             a
```

(2) Generating function approach.

Whereas the mgf $E(e^{ty})$ generates raw moments, the "centralized mgf" $E(e^{t(y-\mu)})$ generates central moments (moments about the specified mean μ):

```
In[35]:= cmgf  = Expect[ E^( t (y-mu) ), h]
```

```
Out[35]=              1
         ------------------
          a   a b t  1      a
          b   E      (- - t)
                       b
```

We can now apply our **M[ ]** function (defined above in Section 16.2.1) to derive any desired central moment. Here is the fifth central moment:

```
In[36]:= M[5, cmgf] // PowerExpand // Expand
```

```
Out[36]=        5       2 5
          24 a b  + 20 a  b
```

Instead of deriving the mgf, we can alternatively derive the centralized cf. This too generates a useful expression:

```
In[37]:= ccf  = Expect[E^(I t (y-mu)), h]
```

```
Out[37]= Cos[a (b t - ArcTan[b t])]     I Sin[a (b t - ArcTan[b t])]
         --------------------------  -  ----------------------------
                   2  2 a/2                       2  2 a/2
              (1 + b  t )                    (1 + b  t )
```

Applying the **MI[ ]** function (defined above in Section 16.2.1) derives any desired central moment. Here is the fifth central moment again:

```
In[38]:= MI[5, ccf]
```

```
Out[38]=        5       2 5
          24 a b  + 20 a  b
```

(3) Deriving central moments from moments about the origin.
For this Gamma pdf example, the mgf is:

```
In[39]:= mgf = Expect[ E^(t y), h]
```

```
Out[39]=        1
           -----------
            a  1      a
           b  (- - t)
                b
```

Hence, the kth moment is known and is given by **M[k, mgf]**. By contrast, let us suppose that we cannot get *Mathematica* to calculate the central moments. In such a hypothetical (though not unrealistic) example, we can derive the unknown central moments from the known moments about the origin. The function that does this is entitled **CentralM[ ]**. Here is the fifth central moment:

```
In[40]:= cm = CentralM[5, Z]
```

```
Out[40]=        5              5            3
          5 Z[1]  - Z[0] Z[1]  - 10 Z[1]  Z[2] +

                   2
          10 Z[1]  Z[3] - 5 Z[1] Z[4] + Z[5]
```

The answer is expressed in terms of **Z[k]**, where **Z[k]** denotes the kth moment about the origin. For reasons of efficiency, it is best to leave this as a function of Z (an unevaluated moment), rather than expressing it in terms of **M[k, mgf]** (which would evaluate **M[k, mgf]** each time it appears).
To calculate cm for our example, we can replace all occurrences of **Z[1]** with **M[1]**, **Z[2]** with **M[2]**, and so on.

```
In[41]:= cm /. Table[ Z[k] -> M[k, mgf], {k, 0, 5}]
              //PowerExpand//Expand
```

```
Out[41]=         5       2 5
           24 a b  + 20 a b
```

16.2.3 Deriving Cumulants

This section discusses two possible ways of deriving cumulants. We consider, by example, the following little known pdf (after Kaplansky), defined on the set of real numbers. A plot illustrates:

```
In[42]:=                f = (9/4 + x^4) Exp[- x^2] / (3 Sqrt[Pi] )
          domain[f] = {x, -Infinity, Infinity};

          Plot[f, {x, -3, 3}];
```

```
Out[42]=       9    4
            - - + x
              4
          ---------------
               2
              x
          3 E    Sqrt[Pi]
```

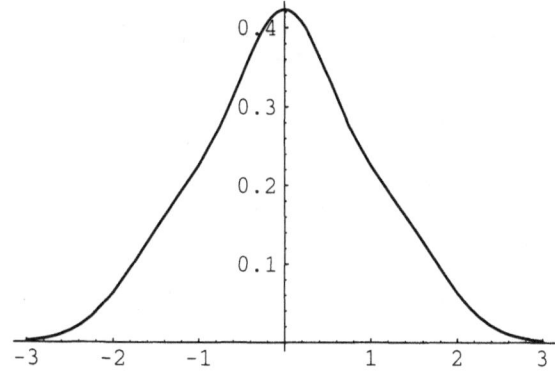

(1) Derive the cumulant generating function.

The cumulant generating function is just the log of the characteristic function.

```
In[43]:= cgf = Log[ Expect[ E^(I t x), f] ]
```

```
Out[43]=               2    4
              48 - 12 t  + t
          Log[---------------]
                     2
                   t /4
               48 E
```

Applying the **MI[ ]** function derives any desired cumulant from this generating function. Here are the first four even-valued cumulants:

```
In[44]:= Table[ MI[i, cgf], {i, 2, 8, 2}]
```

```
Out[44]=        1         35
          {1, -(-),  0,  --}
                4         8
```

(2) Deriving cumulants from known moments.

If *Mathematica* cannot determine the characteristic function, we can still evaluate the kth cumulant, if we know the first k moments (either about the origin *or* central). The package function `CumulantM[k, Z]` does this, for some specified integer k. Here is the eighth cumulant expressed as a function of the first eight moments `Z[k]` about the origin.

```
In[45]:= cm = CumulantM[8, Z]
```

```
Out[45]=            8                6                  4    2
        -5040 Z[1]   + 20160 Z[1]  Z[2] - 25200 Z[1]  Z[2]  +

                2    3          4              5
        10080 Z[1]  Z[2]  - 630 Z[2]  - 6720 Z[1]  Z[3] +

                3                        2      2          2    2
        13440 Z[1]  Z[2] Z[3] - 5040 Z[1] Z[2]  Z[3] - 1680 Z[1]  Z[3]  +

              2                   4                2
        560 Z[2]  Z[3]  + 1680 Z[1]  Z[4] - 2520 Z[1]  Z[2] Z[4] +

              2                                       2          3
        420 Z[2]  Z[4] + 560 Z[1] Z[3] Z[4] - 35 Z[4]  - 336 Z[1]  Z[5] +

                                                    2
        336 Z[1] Z[2] Z[5] - 56 Z[3] Z[5] + 56 Z[1]  Z[6] - 28 Z[2] Z[6] -

        8 Z[1] Z[7] + Z[8]
```

Such formulae can be found in advanced statistical texts for values of k up to 10; for example, see Stuart and Ord (1994). Of course, with *Mathematica*, one is not constrained to the first 10 cumulants, and it is much easier to apply the results. If `M[k, gf]` denotes the kth moment about the origin, we would just proceed to derive:

```
cm /. Table[ Z[k] -> M[k, gf], {k, 0, 8}]
```

If we want the cumulant formula in terms of moments about the mean, simply set `Z[1]` to 0:

```
In[46]:= cm /. Z[1] -> 0
```

```
Out[46]=           4                2                2                2
        -630 Z[2]  + 560 Z[2] Z[3]  + 420 Z[2]  Z[4] - 35 Z[4]

        - 56 Z[3] Z[5] - 28 Z[2] Z[6] + Z[8]
```

where each `Z[i]` value now denotes a central moment.

16.3   Transformations

Let x be a random variable with density $f(x)$, and let u denote some transform $u(x)$. We seek the pdf of u, say, $h(u)$. Two standard methods for solving such problems are:

- The Method of Transformations: this applies to monotonic transformations; and
- The MGF Approach: this is less restrictive, but requires some input from the user. It is based on the uniqueness theorem relating moment-generating functions to densities.

16.3.1   The Method of Transformations

• *Automated Examples*
The function **Transform[eqn, f]** automates the task of finding the pdf of u. It also calculates the domain of u (univariate case) or the extremities of u (multivariate case) if it can do so. It is best illustrated by example; for instance,

Let x have uniform density $f = 1/\pi$, defined on $(-\pi/2, \pi/2)$. Show that the transform $u = \tan(X)$ is Cauchy.

We first specify the pdf f and its domain, as always. In addition, we also need to specify the transformation equation:

```
In[47]:= f = 1/Pi;
         domain[f] = {x, -Pi/2, Pi/2};

         eqn = {u == Tan[x]};
```

Note the double equal sign in the transformation eqn. If, by mistake, you enter $u =$ Tan[x] (or if u was previously given some value), you will need to clear u (**Clear[u]**) before continuing. In fact, it is always a good idea to **Clear[u]** at the very start.
The solution to this problem is easily obtained:

```
In[48]:= Transform[eqn, f]

Out[48]=           1
            Abs[------]
                  2
             1 + u
         {-----------, {u, -Infinity, Infinity}}
              Pi
```

Note that the output has two parts: the first part provides the density of u (which is Cauchy), whereas the second part provides the domain of u. The domain is only provided if *Mathematica* and the **Transform** function think they can determine it. Even so, it is always a good idea to check the domain by doing a quick plot of u (here, by plotting `Tan[x]` over the relevant domain).

The **Transform[ ]** function extends naturally to a multivariate setting. Care must be taken to ensure that the problem is set up so that the number of transformations is equal to the number of variables. An example illustrates:

Let x_1 and x_2 be defined on the unit interval with joint pdf $f(x_1, x_2) = 1$. That is,

```
In[49]:= f = 1;
         domain[f] = { {x1, 0, 1}, {x2, 0, 1} };
```

Find the joint pdf of $y_1 = x_1 + x_2$, and $y_2 = x_1 - x_2$.
The transformation eqn here is:

```
In[50]:= eqn = {y1 == x1+x2, y2 == x1-x2};
```

Note the bracketing here—it takes the same form as *Mathematica*'s **Solve** function. Here is the solution.

```
In[51]:= Transform[eqn, f]
```

```
Out[51]=  1
          {-, {{y1, 0, 2.}, {y2, -1., 1.}}}
          2
```

So, the joint pdf of y_1 and y_2 is a 1/2. It should be stressed that, in the multivariate case, the stated "range" for y_1 and y_2 denotes the extremeties of the domain—not the domain itself! This is because in a multivariate setting, the transformation often introduces dependence between y_1 and y_2. We can see this easily by plotting out the space of the transformed variables y_1 and y_2. To do so, we use a 3D parametric plot to plot $y_1 = x_1 + x_2$, and $y_2 = x_1 - x_2$, for all possible values of x_1 and x_2.

```
In[52]:= ParametricPlot3D[ {x1+x2, 0, x1-x2}, {x1, 0, 1},
             {x2, 0, 1}, ViewPoint -> {0, -3, 0},
             AxesLabel -> {"y1", "", "y2"},
             AxesEdge -> {Automatic, None, Automatic} ];
```

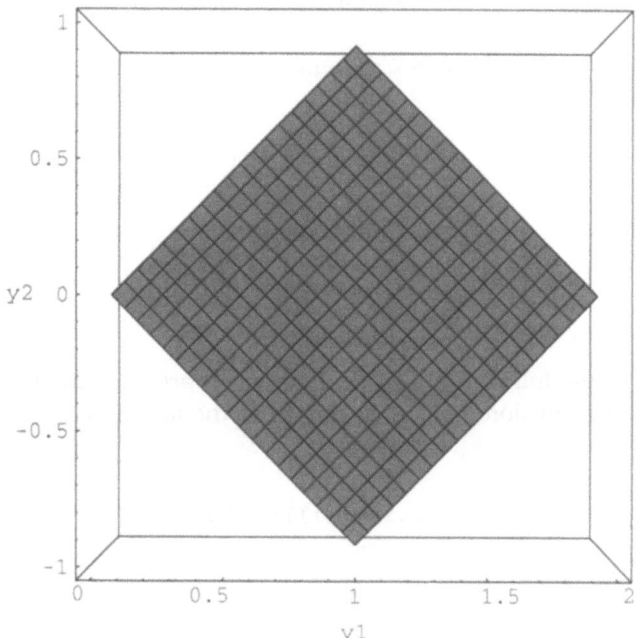

It is worth stressing that it is only appropriate to use the Method of Transformations if the transform itself is monotonic (univariate setting) or one-to-one (multivariate setting). The **Transform[ ]** function does not (and can not) check for this, so some care must be taken in using it.

• *Manual Examples*
If the transformation function has more than one possible inverse (e.g., a transformation from x to y of form $y = x^2$), *Mathematica* cannot automate the task, because it does not know which inverse to use. For instance, consider the following transformation equation.

```
In[53]:= f = 2x; domain[f] = {x, 0, 1}; eqn = {y == 27 x^3};
```

If we try the automated approach:

```
In[54]:= Transform[eqn, f]
```

```
Transform::m: Multiple Solutions. Please try manual approach.
```

The **Transform** function recognizes that there are multiple possible solutions and so provides a warning message. In such cases, a manual approach can help *Mathematica* on its way. We proceed in two stages:

Step 1: Find the inverse function, as a function of x

```
In[55]:= inv = Solve[eqn, x]
```

```
Out[55]=         1/3                      1/3  1/3                    2/3  1/3
                y                     -((-1)    y   )             (-1)    y
        {{x -> ----},  {x -> ---------------},  {x -> ------------}}
                 3                       3                         3
```

Clearly, we are only interested in the first solution, namely, `inv[[1]]`.

Step 2: Apply the Method of Transformations

In the following, we select the appropriate solution from the preceding `inv`. The function `J[ ]` then calculates the Jacobian of Transformation (in absolute value).

```
In[56]:= z = (f/.inv[[1]])  J[x/.inv[[1]], y]
```

```
Out[56]=     1/3            1
          2 y      Abs[------]
                         2/3
                        9 y
        -------------------
                 3
```

We can simplify this further by noting that y is positive, given the domain of x. Unfortunately, *Mathematica*'s **Abs[ ]** value function is a little primitive at present, and will not do this for us, even if we tell it the sign of y. This is mildly irritating, primarily because *Mathematica* has difficulty integrating expressions that contain the **Abs[ ]** function. If we want to work further with z, we will need to get rid of the **Abs[ ]** component. One solution (albeit a banal one) is simply to re-input z via the keyboard. Alternatively, **ComplexExpand** or **PowerExpand** may help, but some care should be taken using **PowerExpand** as it ignores branch cuts. The neatest solution is probably to pass a replacement rule over z. For instance, if we are dealing with **Abs[expr]**, and expr is known to be positive, we can write a replacement rule as follows:

```
In[57]:= myrule := Abs[qq_] -> qq
```

We can try this out:

```
In[58]:= z /. myrule
```

```
Out[58]=     2
          -------
              1/3
          27 y
```

In multivariate cases, the same two-step manual procedure still applies except that x would be replaced by the vector $\{x_1, x_2, \ldots, x_n\}$, and y by $\{y_1, y_2, \ldots, y_n\}$. There is an example in Section 16.5.

16.3.2   The MGF Approach

The mgf approach is based on the "uniqueness theorem" which states that if two mgfs are the same, then they share the same density. As before, x has density $f(x)$, u denotes some transform $u(x)$, and we seek the pdf of u. To do so, we find the mgf of $u(x)$—call this w. We then compare the functional form of w with well-known moment-generating functions (typically, this is done with the appendix in a statistics text, unless one has a fine memory for such things). If we can find a match, then the pdf is identified by the uniqueness theorem. As such, it is a flexible technique, though the matching is not always easy.

Example: show that if x is $N(0,1)$, then x^2 is chi-squared with 1 degree of freedom.

Solution: As always, we set up x and its domain.

```
In[59]:=           f   =  Exp[-x^2/2]/Sqrt[2 Pi];
            domain[f] = {x, -Infinity, Infinity};
```

We now find the mgf of x^2. That is, find $E(e^{tx^2})$.

```
In[60]:= mgf = Expect[ Exp[t x^2], f]
```

```
Out[60]=          1
            --------------
            Sqrt[1 - 2 t]
```

Referring to any standard statistics textbook, we see that this output is identical to a moment-generating function of the chi-squared type, with 1 degree of freedom. Hence x^2 is chi-squared with 1 degree of freedom.

The "uniqueness theorem" applies equally to both the moment-generating function *and* the characteristic function. As such, instead of deriving the mgf of u, we could just as well have derived the characteristic function of u, and looked *it* up in a textbook. Indeed, using the cf has two advantages: for many densities, the mgf does not exist, whereas the cf does; and once we have the cf, we can (in theory) derive the pdf that is associated with it by means of the inversion theorem [see Stuart and Ord (1994, sec. 4.3)], rather than looking up the cf in a statistics textbook. This is important if the derived cf is not of a standard (or common) form. The following example highlights the latter benefit.

Example: The Product of Two Normal Variates

```
In[61]:= ClearAll[g, z]
```

Let x_1 and x_2 be independent $N(0, 1)$ random variables. We wish to find the density of the product $z = x_1 x_2$. Each normal variate has density g of form:

```
In[62]:= g[x_] = Exp[-x^2/2]/Sqrt[2 Pi];
```

Then the joint pdf $f(x_1, x_2)$ is:

```
In[63]:=            f  = g[x1] g[x2];
          domain[f] = {{x1, -Infinity, Infinity},
                       {x2, -Infinity, Infinity} };
```

The cf of $z = x_1 x_2$ is given by:

```
In[64]:= cf = Expect[ Exp[I t (x1 x2)], f]
```

```
Out[64]=        1
          ------------
                    2
          Sqrt[1 + t ]
```

Inverting the cf yields the pdf of z:

```
In[65]:= pdf = Integrate[ Exp[-I t z] cf,
               {t, -Infinity, Infinity}]/(2Pi)
```

```
Out[65]=                 2
          BesselK[0, Sqrt[z ]]
          --------------------
                   Pi
```

where **BesselK[ ]** denotes the modified Bessel function of the second kind. The following diagram contrasts the pdf of z with that of the normal pdf.

```
In[66]:= Plot[{pdf, g[z]}, {z, -2.5, 2.5},
             PlotLabel -> "Space Shuttle"];
```

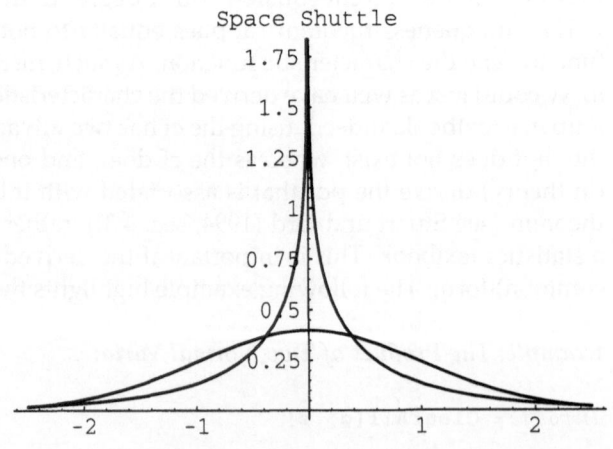

The only downside to this approach is that *Mathematica* (v2.2) often has some difficulty in deriving both characteristic functions and their inversions (however, see the discussion on Fourier and Laplace transforms in Section 16.2).

16.4   Multivariate Analysis

The "Getting Started" section showed that functions such as **Expect, DF,** and **Transform** extend naturally to a multivariate setting. Nevertheless, a brief discussion of multivariate analysis is warranted, in part because multivariate analysis introduces idiosyncracies such as syntax and dependence, and in part because it requires some special functions such as **Marginal** and **Conditional**. We illustrate by example. Consider the following joint pdf.

```
In[67]:=        g  = k Exp[x1] x1 (x2+1) (x3-3)^2 x4^-2
         domain[g] = { {x1, 0, 1},
                       {x2, 1, 2},
                       {x3, 2, 3},
                       {x4, 3, 4} };

Out[67]=  x1                                2
         E   k x1 (1 + x2) (-3 + x3)
         ---------------------------
                    2
                  x4
```

where *k* is a constant.

16.4.1   Marginal and Conditional

Marginal[var, g] derives the marginal joint pdf of the variable(s) specified in var. If there is more than one variable in var, then it must take the form of a list. The ordering (syntax) of the variables in this list is irrelevant. For example, the marginal bivariate distribution of x_2 and x_4 is given by

```
In[68]:= Marginal[{x2, x4}, g]

Out[68]= k (1 + x2)
         ----------
               2
            3 x4
```

whereas the marginal distribution of x_4 is

```
In[69]:= Marginal[x4, g]

Out[69]=  5 k
         -----
             2
          6 x4
```

The constant $k > 0$ is determined such that g integrates to unity over its domain. We can use **Marginal** to determine k, by letting var be an empty set:

```
In[70]:= Marginal[{}, g]
```

```
Out[70]= 5 k
         ---
          72
```

Thus, if g is well defined, k must equal 72/5.

Conditional[var, g] derives a conditional pdf, conditional upon var. As before, if there is more than one variable in var, then it must take the form of a list, the syntax of which is irrelevant. To eliminate any confusion, a message clarifies what is being conditioned on (and what is not). Here is the joint conditional pdf of x_2, x_4, given x_1 and x_3.

```
In[71]:= Conditional[{x1, x3}, g]
```

```
Here is the conditional pdf g(x2, x4 | x1, x3).
```

```
Out[71]= 24 (1 + x2)
         -----------
              2
           5 x4
```

Note that this output is the same as the first **Marginal** example (given $k = 72/5$). This is because $x_1, \ldots, x_4$ are mutually independent. To ascribe a particular value to the conditioning variable, one would proceed as follows.

```
In[72]:= h = Conditional[x1, g] /. x1 -> 1
```

```
Here is the conditional pdf g(x2, x3, x4 | x1).
```

```
Out[72]=                             2
           72 (1 + x2) (-3 + x3)
         ----------------------
                    2
                 5 x4
```

In order to apply package functions to this pdf, we need to declare the domain over which h is defined. Recall that a pdf derived by a user will only be recognized by the package IF its domain is specified by the user. Thus to recognize the previous output as a pdf, enter

```
In[73]:= domain[h] = Delete[domain[g], 1]
```

```
Out[73]= {{x2, 1, 2}, {x3, 2, 3}, {x4, 3, 4}}
```

We can now use package functions on h; for example:

```
In[74]:= Expect[x2 x3, h]
```

```
Out[74]= 69
         --
         20
```

A further feature is afforded by the use of the function **Convert**. If S denotes the set of variables $\{x_1, x_2, x_3, \ldots, x_n\}$ on which g is defined, and var is a subset of S, then **Convert[var, g]** provides the complement of var. If there is more than one variable in var, then it must take the form of a list, the syntax of which is irrelevant. Thus if one does not like the structure of the **Conditional** function, one can set up a new version.

```
In[75]:= My[x_, f_] := Conditional[Convert[x, f], f]
         SetAttributes[My, HoldRest]
```

And then contrast it

```
In[76]:= My[x3, g]
```

```
Here is the conditional pdf g(x3 | x1, x2, x4).
```

```
Out[76]=              2
              3 (-3 + x3)
```

with the original:

```
In[77]:= Conditional[x3, g]
```

```
Here is the conditional pdf g(x1, x2, x4 | x3).
```

```
Out[77]=       x1
           24 E    x1 (1 + x2)
           ------------------
                    2
                5 x4
```

16.4.2   DF and Probability

Given some joint pdf $f(x_1, x_2, \ldots, x_n)$, the function **DF[{x1, x2, ..., xn}, f]** calculates the multivariate distribution function $P(X_1 < x_1, X_2 < x_2, \ldots, X_n < x_n)$. Here syntax is important, as the position of each element $\{x_1, x_2, \ldots\}$ must correspond to the ordering specified in the domain. For instance, we defined the domain of g as follows.

```
In[78]:= domain[g]
```

```
Out[78]= {{x1, 0, 1}, {x2, 1, 2}, {x3, 2, 3}, {x4, 3, 4}}
```

So the distribution function of *g* would be given by:

```
In[79]:= cdf[x1_,x2_,x3_,x4_] = DF[{x1,x2,x3,x4}, g]      // Factor

Out[79]=
         x1     x1                                                              2
k (1 - E    + E   x1) (-1 + x2) (3 + x2) (-2 + x3) (13 - 7 x3 + x3 ) (-3 + x4)
-----------------------------------------------------------------------------
                                 18 x4
```

Note that we have set up cdf as a *Mathematica* function of x_1 through x_4, and can thus apply it in the standard way. Here, we find *k* (again), this time by evaluating cdf at the upper boundary of the domain

```
In[80]:= cdf[1,2,3,4]

Out[80]= 5 k
         ---
          72
```

which once again yields a value of $k = 72/5$. If we require the probability content of a closed region within the domain, we could just re-type the whole integral. For instance, the probability of being within the region

$$S = \{0 < x_1 < .5, \qquad 1 < x_2 < 1.5, \qquad 2 < x_3 < 2.5, \qquad 3 < x_4 < 3.5\}$$

is given by:

```
In[81]:= k = 72/5;
         pr = Integrate[g, {x1, 0, 0.5},
                           {x2, 1, 1.5},
                           {x3, 2, 2.5},
                           {x4, 3, 3.5}  ] // N // Timing

Out[81]= {0.533333 Second, 0.0395189}
```

Although this is straightforward, it is by no means the fastest solution. In particular, the probability content of a closed region can be found purely by using the function cdf[ ] (which we have already found) and the boundaries of the region, without any need for further integration. WARNING: the solution is NOT cdf[0.5, 1.5, 2.5, 3.5] - cdf[0, 1, 2, 3]! Rather, one must evaluate cdf[ ] at every possible extremum defined by set *S*. The package function MrSpeedy[cdf, S] does this.

```
In[82]:= MrSpeedy[cdf_, S_] :=
            (Apply[Outer, Prepend[S, cdf]] // Flatten)
            (Nest[{-#, #}&, 1, Length[S]] // Flatten)
```

It does not need to be typed in because it is a package function. For our example

```
In[83]:= S={{0,.5}, {1,1.5}, {2,2.5}, {3,3.5}};
         MrSpeedy[cdf, S] // Timing
```

```
Out[83]= {0.0166667 Second, 0.0395189}
```

MrSpeedy has provided a 30-fold speed increase over direct integration. To see how **MrSpeedy** works, replace cdf with, say, df:

```
In[84]:= MrSpeedy[df, S]
```

```
Out[84]= df[0, 1, 2, 3] - df[0, 1, 2, 3.5] - df[0, 1, 2.5, 3] +

         df[0, 1, 2.5, 3.5] - df[0, 1.5, 2, 3] +

         df[0, 1.5, 2, 3.5] + df[0, 1.5, 2.5, 3] -

         df[0, 1.5, 2.5, 3.5] - df[0.5, 1, 2, 3] +

         df[0.5, 1, 2, 3.5] + df[0.5, 1, 2.5, 3] -

         df[0.5, 1, 2.5, 3.5] + df[0.5, 1.5, 2, 3] -

         df[0.5, 1.5, 2, 3.5] - df[0.5, 1.5, 2.5, 3] +

         df[0.5, 1.5, 2.5, 3.5]
```

Note that this approach applies to any n-variate distribution. We examine **MrSpeedy** again in Section 16.5.

16.4.3 Concerning Domains: Rectangular Versus Nonrectangular

This section has considered (multivariate) examples in which the domain defines an independent product space. By this we mean that the domain of the joint pdf does not involve any of its constituent random variables. If the product space is independent, then in a bivariate setting, for example, the domain over which a joint pdf is defined would appear rectangular. As such, we refer to this class of problem as having rectangular domains. A typical example is $\{0 < x < 2, -3 < y < 3\}$. By contrast, the domain may depend on random variables. Examples are $0 < x < y < \infty$, or $x^2 + y^2 < 1$.... We refer to such examples as having nonrectangular domains.

The package functions in this chapter were designed for the class of problems with rectangular domains. There does not appear to be any unified or automated way of dealing with nonrectangular domains. As such, if the domain is nonrectangular, the package functions can not be "guaranteed", and are not recommended.

16.5   The Multivariate Normal Distribution

In[85]:= **ClearAll[pdf, cdf]**

The multivariate normal distribution is so pervasive throughout economics and statistics that we devote an entire section to it and (some of) its properties; see also Rose and Smith (1996). The package function **MVN[xvec, muvec, varcov]** automatically calculates the n-dimensional multivariate normal pdf defined on xvec$\{x_1, x_2, \ldots, x_n\}$, with mean vector muvec and positive-definite variance-covariance matrix varcov. Even so, the multivariate normal is still a beast to set up, because one still has to define xvec, muvec, and varcov: a messy business for $n > 2$. To overcome this problem, the package function **Template[n]** fully automates this task, for any positive integer n.

```
In[86]:= Template[2]

     xvec = {x1, x2};

   muvec = {mu1, mu2};

  varcov = {{s11, s12}, {s21, s22}};

       f = MVN[xvec, muvec, varcov]

domain[f] = {{x1, -Infinity, Infinity},
             {x2, -Infinity, Infinity}}
```

To be useful, we have to convert this "Output" into an "Input." The easiest way to do this is: (1) select the preceding cell bracket with the mouse, by clicking at the right edge of the screen window, and (2) change the cell-style to "Input" either by using the menu or by using the appropriate keyboard shortcut (command-9 on a Macintosh). This immediately produces usable input. Users of Windows will need to unformat the cell first. We can now edit it so as to set up any particular problem in which we are interested.

16.5.1   The Bivariate Normal

Let us suppose our particular interest is the bivariate normal with zero mean vector, variance elements unity, and correlation coefficient r. After a few quick edits, we end up with the following input. The function **MVN** then constructs the pdf we desire, namely $n2$:

```
In[87]:=        xvec = {x1, x2};
              muvec = {0, 0};
             varcov = {{1, r}, {r, 1}};
                 n2 = MVN[xvec, muvec, varcov]      // Simplify
          domain[n2] = {{x1, -Infinity, Infinity},
                        {x2, -Infinity, Infinity}}
```

```
Out[87]=      2                    2              2
            (x1   - 2 r x1 x2 + x2 )/(2 (-1 + r ))                1
           E                                               Sqrt[------]
                                                                   2
                                                                 1 - r
          -------------------------------------------------------------------
                                   2 Pi
```

```
Out[87]= {{x1, -Infinity, Infinity}, {x2, -Infinity, Infinity}}
```

The shape and orientation of $n2$ is dependent on r. We illustrate this with the following set of contour plots.

```
In[88]:= lis = Table[ContourPlot[n2/.r->i, {x1,-2,2}, {x2,-2,2},
                Contours->4,
                DisplayFunction -> Identity],
                {i,-.99,.99,.22}];

         Show[GraphicsArray[Partition[lis,5]],
              DisplayFunction->$DisplayFunction];
```

Each plot corresponds to a specific value of r. In the top left corner, $r = -.99$ (almost perfect negative correlation), whereas in the bottom right corner, $r = .99$ (almost perfect positive correlation). In any given plot, on any given contour k, $n2$ will always be constant on all two-dimensional ellipses defined by $(x_1^2 - 2rx_1x_2 + x_2^2)/(1 - r^2) = k$, for every constant $k > 0$. One can show that the ellipses are centred at the origin with major axis of length $2\sqrt{k(1 + \text{Abs}(r))}$ and minor axis of length $2\sqrt{k(1 - \text{Abs}(r))}$, with orientation along the 45 degree line when $r > 0$, or the 135 degree line when $r < 0$.

We can try out our toolset on pdf *n2*. The marginal distribution of x_1 is well-known to be $N(0, 1)$, as we confirm with:

```
In[89]:= Marginal[x1, n2] // PowerExpand // Simplify
```

```
Out[89]=              1
              -------------------
                   2
                 x1 /2
              E         Sqrt[2 Pi]
```

The conditional distribution of x_1 given x_2 is $N(rx_2, 1 - r^2)$, as we confirm with:

```
In[90]:= Conditional[x2, n2] // PowerExpand // Simplify
```

```
Here is the conditional pdf n2(x1 | x2).
```

```
Out[90]=               2                2
              (x1 - r x2) /(2 (-1 + r ))
          E
          ---------------------------
                            2
          Sqrt[2 Pi] Sqrt[1 - r ]
```

And here is the expectation of $(x_1 x_2)$:

```
In[91]:= Expect[x1 x2, n2] // PowerExpand // Simplify
```

```
Out[91]= r
```

When $r = 0$, the **DF** function can find a solution for the distribution function in terms of the inbuilt error function:

```
In[92]:= r = 0;    N2 = DF[{x1, x2}, n2]    // Simplify
```

```
Out[92]=          x1                    x2
          (1 + Erf[-------]) (1 + Erf[-------])
                  Sqrt[2]              Sqrt[2]
          -------------------------------------
                            4
```

We can now compare the zero correlation pdf (n2/.r->0) with its cdf:

```
In[93]:= Plot3D[ n2, {x1, -3, 3}, {x2, -3, 3}];
         Plot3D[ N2, {x1, -3, 3}, {x2, -3, 3}];
```

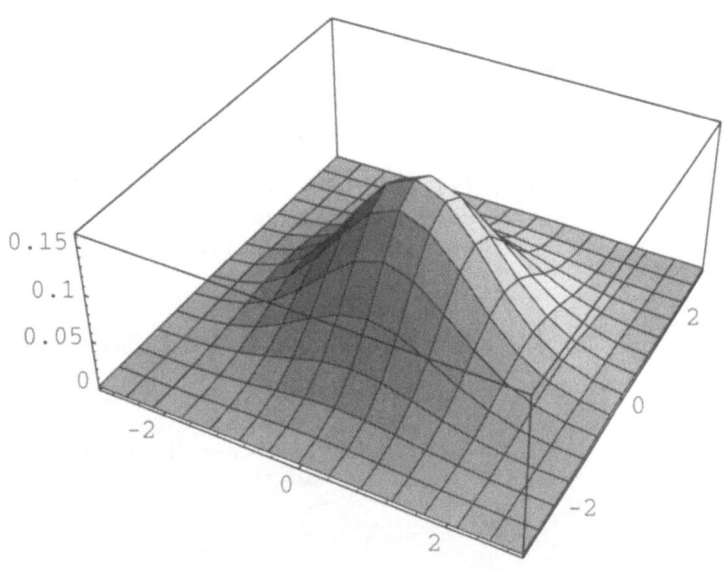

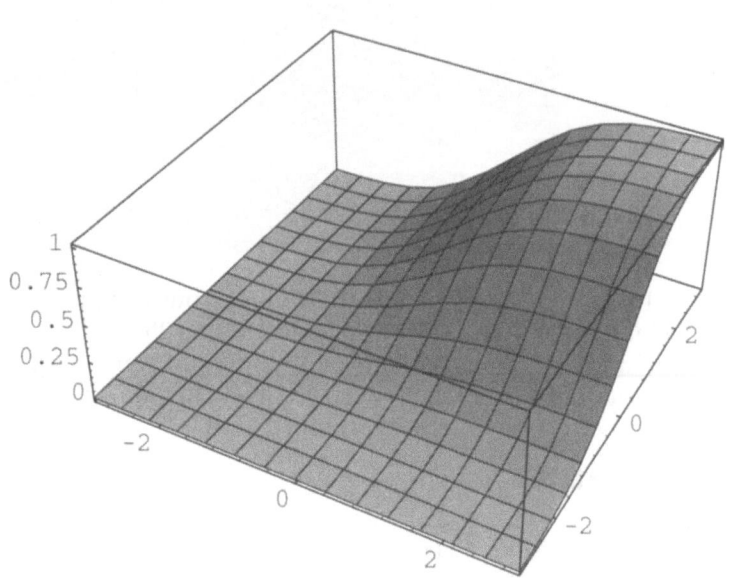

One can generate some interesting pictures using the multivariate normal. For instance, the diagram below is just the bivariate normal pdf plotted at 9 points on a flat grid. The plots are alternatively positive and negative valued, corresponding with the positive and negative indentations on the surface of the grid.

```
In[94]:= z = Sum[(-1)^(i+j)
              MVN[{x1, x2}, {i, j}, {{1, 0}, {0, 1}}],
              {i,0,10,5}, {j,0,10,5}]//N;

         Plot3D[z, {x1, -3, 13}, {x2, -3, 13}, PlotPoints -> 200,
              Ticks -> None, Mesh -> False,
              ViewPoint ->{0, 0, 4}];
```

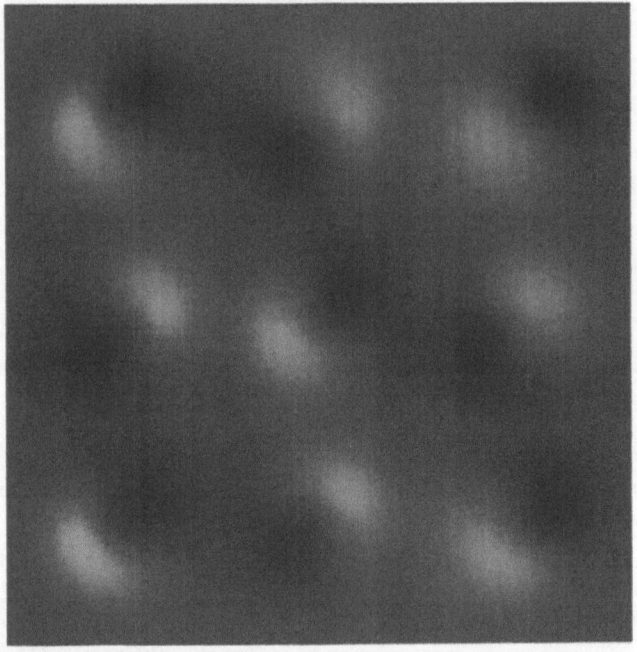

To appreciate this plot in all its glory, your computer should support 24 bit colour, you will need plenty of RAM (around 25M split evenly between the front end and the kernel), and about 3 minutes of computing time on a PowerMac 8500 (or about 45 minutes or so on a 68040 or equivalent).

16.5.2   The Trivariate Normal

```
In[95]:= ClearAll[r, s, t]
```

The trivariate normal can be set up with:

In[96]:= **Template[3]**

Let us suppose we are interested in the standardized trivariate normal, but with correlation coefficients *r*, *s*, and *t*. After a little editing, we obtain:

In[97]:=
```
        xvec = {x1, x2, x3};
       muvec = {0, 0, 0};
      varcov = {{1, r, t}, {r, 1, s}, {t, s, 1}};

          n3 = MVN[xvec, muvec, varcov] // Simplify
   domain[n3] = { {x1, -Infinity, Infinity},
                  {x2, -Infinity, Infinity},
                  {x3, -Infinity, Infinity} };
```

Out[97]=
```
            2     2   2                                  2     2   2
(Power[E, (x1  - s  x1  - 2 r x1 x2 + 2 s t x1 x2 + x2  - t  x2  +


                                                   2     2   2
   2 r s x1 x3 - 2 t x1 x3 - 2 s x2 x3 + 2 r t x2 x3 + x3  - r  x3 )/

          2    2       2                         1
   (2 (-1 + r  + s  - 2 r s t + t )))] Sqrt[-------------------------]) /
                                               2    2           2
                                           1 - r  - s  + 2 r s t - t


            3
   (2 Sqrt[2 Pi ])
```

We saw that a contourplot of the bivariate pdf *n2* yielded an ellipse, or a circle given zero correlation. To obtain similar contourplot diagrams for the trivariate pdf *n3*, we first need to load up the following package,

In[98]:= **<< Graphics'ContourPlot3D'**

We can now obtain 3D contourplots of *n3*, for any allowable set of correlation coefficients. Once again, the shape and orientation of the plot will be affected by the choice of correlation coefficients. The plot may take up to 7 minutes or so to generate on something like a 68040 machine, or about a minute on a PowerPC or high-end Pentium. Reduce the resolution to **PlotPoints-> {3, 5}** if working with anything slower.

In[99]:= **z = n3 /.{r->.2, s->.3, t->.4};**

```
      ContourPlot3D[z, {x1, -1.3, 1.3}, {x2, -1.3, 1.3},
                    {x3, -1.3, 1.3},
                    PlotPoints -> {4, 6},
                    Contours -> {0.05}] ;
```

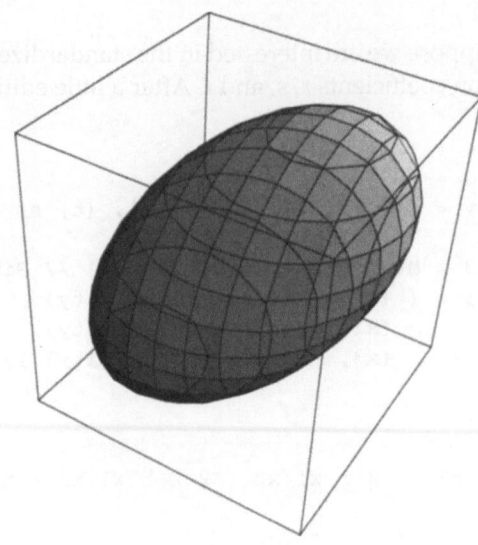

Thus, whereas the bivariate case yields elliptical contours (or a circle given zero correlation), the trivariate case yields the intuitive 3D equivalent, namely, the surface of an ellipsoid (or that of a sphere given zero correlations). Here, parameter r alters the "orientation" of the ellipsoid in the x_1-x_2 plane, just as s does in the x_2-x_3 plane, and t does in the x_1-x_3 plane.

We can put our toolset to work. Once again, in the case of zero correlations, the pdf (say, o3) and cdf (O3) simplify neatly:

```
In[100]:=domain[o3] = domain[n3];

        o3 = n3 /. {r -> 0, s -> 0, t -> 0}
        O3 = DF[{x1, x2, x3}, o3] // Simplify
```

```
Out[100]=        2     2     2
            (-x1  - x2  - x3 )/2
          E
          ---------------------
                    3
            2 Sqrt[2 Pi ]
```

```
Out[100]=          x1                x2                x3
            (1 + Erf[-------])  (1 + Erf[-------])  (1 + Erf[-------])
                    Sqrt[2]            Sqrt[2]            Sqrt[2]
          ------------------------------------------------------------
                                      8
```

16.5.3   Numerical Analysis

Finding the numerical value of a multivariate pdf is usually straightforward. For instance, we can set up the trivariate pdf (*n3*), for arbitrarily selected parameter values, as a *Mathematica* function of x_1, x_2, and x_3:

```
In[101]:= pdf[x1_, x2_, x3_] = n3 /. {r -> .5, s -> .5, t -> .5}
          // N;
```

and then apply it in the standard way.

```
In[102]:= pdf[0, 1, 2]
```

```
Out[102]= 0.00574031
```

Although it is straightforward to find numerical values for any multivariate pdf, it is not quite as easy to do so for the cdf. Prior to *Mathematica*, the standard approach for doing this required writing lengthy programs in languages such as FORTRAN; see, for example, Schervish (1984). With *Mathematica*, one can forget all this messing about and work directly with the original density—much like a bull at a red cape! We can distinguish possible scenarios: (a) the case of zero correlation, and (b) nonzero correlation.

(a) Zero correlation

Given zero correlation, *Mathematica* can find a symbolic solution to the required integral in terms of the inbuilt error function, **Erf**. In fact, we have already found the zero correlation cdf for both the bivariate and trivariate cases (see the preceding N2 and O3). Writing O3 as a *Mathematica* function of x_1, x_2, and x_3 yields

```
In[103]:= cdf[x1_, x2_, x3_] = O3 // N;
```

which we can apply in the ordinary way to obtain results that are virtuous in being both super accurate and super fast.

```
In[104]:= cdf[-2, 0, 2]
          cdf[Infinity, Infinity, Infinity]
```

```
Out[104]= 0.0111163
```

```
Out[104]= 1.
```

If we require the probability content of a closed region within the domain, we could just retype the whole integral. For instance, the probability of being within the region

$$S = \{1 < x_1 < 2, \qquad 3 < x_2 < 4, \qquad 5 < x_3 < 6\}$$

is given by:

```
In[105]:= pr = Integrate[o3, {x1, 1, 2}, {x2, 3, 4}, {x3, 5, 6}]
              // N // Timing
```

```
Out[105]=                                        -11
              {2.13333 Second, 5.1178 10    }
```

Alternatively, we can use **MrSpeedy** (see Section 16.4.2). For this example:

```
In[106]:= S = {{1, 2}, {3, 4}, {5, 6}};
              MrSpeedy[cdf, S]  // Timing
```

```
Out[106]=                                  -11
              {0. Second, 5.1178 10    }
```

So, **MrSpeedy** has provided a 200-fold speed increase over direct integration! To see how **MrSpeedy** works, replace cdf with, say, df:

```
In[107]:= MrSpeedy[df, S]
```

```
Out[107]= -df[1, 3, 5] + df[1, 3, 6] + df[1, 4, 5] -

              df[1, 4, 6] + df[2, 3, 5] - df[2, 3, 6] -

              df[2, 4, 5] + df[2, 4, 6]
```

(b) Non-zero correlation

In the case of nonzero correlation, *Mathematica* v2.2 cannot find a solution to cdf in terms of inbuilt functions. Users of *Mathematica* v3 or later should use the MultinormalDistribution package, specially designed for this purpose. Users of *Mathematica* v2.2 can resort to simply using numerical integration directly. For suitably complex problems (and anything higher than a trivariate pdf is potentially a candidate here) over suitably large domains, the calculation of the numerical integral can be horribly slow (measured in hours), on even a "fast" machine. Here is an easy trivariate example with correlation coefficients set to .5:

```
In[108]:= h =  n3 /. {r -> .5, s -> .5, t -> .5} //N
```

```
Out[108]=                                                            2
              0.0897936 / Power[2.71828, 1. (0.75 x1  - 0.5 x1 x2 +

                          2                                    2
              0.75 x2  - 0.5 x1 x3 -  0.5 x2 x3 + 0.75 x3 )]
```

The $P(-2 < x_1 < 0, 0 < x_2 < 1, -1 < x_3 < 1)$ is given by:

```
In[109]:= NIntegrate[h, {x1, -2, 0},  {x2, 0, 1}, {x3, -1, 1}]
          // Timing
```

```
Out[109]= {9.23333 Second, 0.102401}
```

For more difficult problems, it is possible to speed things up by sacrificing some accuracy. One way of doing this is to change the parameter **Precision-Goal**. The default setting is equal to your computer's **$MachinePrecision** minus 10 (i.e.. **PrecisionGoal** is 9 on Macs, and 6 on Intel platforms). To illustrate, let us suppose we are interested in the probability content of the positive quadrant, that is, $P(x_1 > 0, x_2 > 0, x_3 > 0)$. Theoretically, this volume is equal to $1/8 + [\arcsin(r) + \arcsin(s) + \arcsin(t)]/(4\pi)$ [cf. Stuart and Ord (1994, eq.15.42)]. This simplifies to $1/4$ for our example. Note the tradeoff between accuracy and time, as one alters the **PrecisionGoal**:

```
In[110]:= Table[ NIntegrate[h, {x1, 0, Infinity},
                               {x2, 0, Infinity},
                               {x3, 0, Infinity},
                    PrecisionGoal -> i] // Timing,
                  {i, 1, 4}] // TableForm
```

```
Out[110]= 1.26667 Second    0.252152

          3.6 Second        0.24977

          7.86667 Second    0.249975

          26.2 Second       0.249999
```

Some care should be taken, as setting **PrecisionGoal->1** can yield grossly incorrect results.

How does *Mathematica* compare with highly specialized multivariate normal computer programs such as Bohrer-Schervish, MULNOR, and MVNORM [see Schervish, (1984)]? In the case of zero-correlation, *Mathematica* can easily outperform such programs in both accuracy and speed, due to its symbolic engine. In the case of nonzero correlation, *Mathematica* performs very well on accuracy grounds. However, using brute force numerical integration is computationally intensive, and it would be euphemistic to say that a fast computer is desirable.

16.5.4   Applied Example: Darts Hitting a Target

Darts are flung at a vertical circular target of unit radius. The distribution of horizontal and vertical deviations from the centre of the target is bivariate normal, with zero means, equal variances v, and correlation p. We wish to derive the probability of hitting the target.

We begin by setting up the appropriate bivariate normal distribution.

```
In[111]:= f = MVN[{x1, x2}, {0, 0}, {{v, p v}, {p v, v}}]   // Simplify
```

```
Out[111]=        2              2       2
          (-x1  + 2 p x1 x2 - x2 )/(2 (v - p  v))                1
         E                                              Sqrt[-----------]
                                                                 2   2
                                                              (1 - p ) v
         ---------------------------------------------------------------
                                   2 Pi
```

The solution requires a transformation to polar coordinates. Thus

```
In[112]:= inv = {x1 -> r Cos[t],    x2 -> r Sin[t]};
```

Here $r = \sqrt{x_1^2 + x_2^2}$ represents the distance of (x_1, x_2) from the origin, while $t = \arctan(x_2/x_1)$ represents the angle of (x_1, x_2) with respect to the x_1 axis. Thus, $r > 0$ and $0 < t < 2\pi$. We seek the joint pdf of r and t. We thus apply the method of transformations (see Section 16.3):

```
In[113]:= g = (f/.inv)  J[{x1,x2}/.inv, {r,t}]
                //PowerExpand//Simplify
```

```
Out[113]=     2                               2
          (r  (-1 + p Sin[2 t]))/(2 (v - p  v))
         E                                              Abs[r]
         ----------------------------------------------------
                              2
                      2 Sqrt[1 - p ] Pi v
```

Recall that J[ ] denotes the Jacobian of transformation in absolute value. *Mathematica* does not simplify **Abs[r]** to r, but we can do this with a quick replacement.

```
In[114]:= g = g /. Abs[x_] -> x
```

```
Out[114]=     2                               2
          (r  (-1 + p Sin[2 t]))/(2 (v - p  v))
         E                                                r
         ----------------------------------------------------
                              2
                      2 Sqrt[1 - p ] Pi v
```

The probability of a dart hitting the target is given by $P(r < 1)$. In the simple case of zero correlation ($p = 0$), this is

In[115]:= **pr = Integrate[g /.p->0, {r, 0, 1}, {t, 0, 2 Pi}]**

Out[115]=   -1/(2 v)
          1 - E

As expected, this probability is decreasing in the variance v, as the following plot illustrates.

In[116]:= **Plot[pr, {v, 0.001, 5}];**

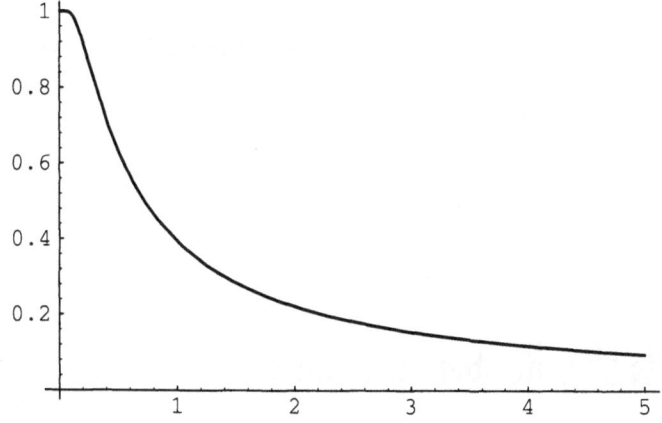

More generally, in the case of nonzero correlation ($p \neq 0$), *Mathematica* cannot solve the integral with respect to t. This is not surprising as the solution does not have a convenient closed form. Nevertheless, for given parameters v and p, one can use numerical integration to find a solution. For instance, if $v = 1$, and $p = .7$, the probability of a hit is:

In[117]:= **NIntegrate[g/.{v->1, p->.7}, {r, 0, 1}, {t, 0, 2 Pi}]**

Out[117]= 0.459866

16.5.5   Random Number Generation for the MVN

The package function **MVNRandom[n, varcov]** generates n pseudorandom k-dimensional drawings from the multivariate normal distribution with zero mean vector, and variance covariance matrix varcov($k \times k$). Once again, varcov is required to be symmetric and positive-definite. The function has been optimised for speed. To illustrate, we generate 6 drawings from a trivariate normal:

```
In[118]:= v3 = {{1, 0.2, 0.4}, {0.2, 1, 0.3}, {0.4, 0.3, 1}};

          ww = MVNRandom[6, v3]

Out[118]= {{0.972332, 0.0831734, 0.520824},
           {-0.171588, -1.74339, 0.568195},
           {-0.094059, -1.19412, -1.22568},
           {0.425176, -0.741486, -0.0691181},
           {0.674832, 0.18416, 0.0838228},
           {1.70836, -0.745775, 0.0320709}}
```

In the case of a non-zero mean vector, simply proceed as follows:

```
In[119]:= mu = {10,0,-20};  Map[(mu+#)&, ww]

Out[119]= {{10.9723, 0.0831734, -19.4792},
           {9.82841, -1.74339, -19.4318},
           {9.90594, -1.19412, -21.2257},
           {10.4252, -0.741486, -20.0691},
           {10.6748, 0.18416, -19.9162},
           {11.7084, -0.745775, -19.9679}}
```

16.6 Random Number Generation

An intrinsic component of simulation studies involves generating pseudorandom drawings from some specified distribution. The inbuilt *Mathematica* function **Random** allows a user to generate pseudorandom drawings from a uniform distribution. Generally, however, pseudorandom drawings from distributions other than uniform will be required. In this respect, the most commonly used approach is to invert the cdf; hereafter, we refer to this approach as the Inverse Method. The *Mathematica* Statistics package uses well-known textbook results (derived using the Inverse Method) to implement random number generation for common densities. By contrast, we show how to derive the well-known textbook results for both common and not so common densities. For the Inverse Method to work efficiently, the inverse cdf should be reasonably straightforward to compute. Unfortunately, it is often the case that the inverse cdf is not computationally clear-cut, therefore impairing the performance of a simulation algorithm; this is illustrated in the following in the case of the $N(0, 1)$ distribution. An alternative procedure in this situation is to overlay the desired distribution with another distribution that possesses a tractable inverse cdf. This latter distribution is sampled and a test then conducted to decide whether to accept the pseudorandom drawing as one that might originate from the desired distribution; term this the Rejection Method. Next, we offer brief details of each generation method; a suitable reference for extensive details is Stuart and Ord (1994, chapter 9).

16.6.1   Inverse Method

Let $g(x)$ denote the pdf of X, and $y = G(x)$ the corresponding cdf, with inverse $x = G^{-1}(y)$. Let u be a pseudorandom drawing from $U(0, 1)$, and then compute $G^{-1}(u)$. The resulting value, say, $x_g = G^{-1}(u)$ is regarded as a pseudorandom drawing from $g(x)$. For this method to work efficiently, the inverse function of G should be computationally tractable. Here is a quick example with a Cauchy density.

```
In[120]:= Clear[g]
```

```
In[121]:=        g   =  1/(Pi (1+x^2));
           domain[g] = {x, -Infinity, Infinity};
```

The distribution function is given by

```
In[122]:= G = DF[x, g]

Out[122]= 1   ArcTan[x]
          - + ---------
          2      Pi
```

whereas the inverse distribution function is

```
In[123]:= inv = Solve[ u == G, x]

Out[123]=             Pi (-1 + 2 u)
          {{x -> Tan[-------------]}}
                           2
```

When $u = $ **Random[ ]**, this formula generates pseudorandom Cauchy drawings. More generally, if the inverse yields more than one possible solution, we would have to select the appropriate solution before proceeding. In our case, it is just:

```
In[124]:= x /. inv

Out[124]=        Pi (-1 + 2 u)
          {Tan[-------------]}
                     2
```

Typically, one generates thousands upon thousands of random numbers. As such, it is worth optimizing this output for repetitive numerical work. To do so, we replace all symbolic arguments with their numerical counterparts. Thus, Pi is replaced with, say, 3.14159, and the symbols 1 and 2 are replaced by 1. and 2., respectively. Finally, we replace u with **Random[ ]**. It is easiest just to type this in manually:

```
In[125]:= xg := Tan[3.14159 (Random[]-.5)]
```

This should provide numerical output, as is easily verified.

In[126]:= **xg**

Out[126]= 1.46874

We now generate, say, 4000 random numbers from the Cauchy pdf.

In[127]:= **data = Table[xg, {4000}];   // Timing**

Out[127]= {0.783333 Second, Null}

It is always a good idea to check the data set before continuing. The output should consist only of real numbers. Here are the last 10 values:

In[128]:= **Take[data, -10]**

Out[128]= {2.20615, 0.773992, -0.146404, 1.6003, 4.02796,

          -0.0552739, -0.256995, -1.00623, 8.70962, -1.79319}

which seems fine. We use the package function **Monty** to inspect fit.

Monty[datalist, {min, max, stepsize}, g] plots the relative frequency of datalist between the values of min and max. The empirical pdf is built by counting the relative frequency of observations falling in intervals of length stepsize, and is plotted at the midpoint of each interval. If the optional argument g is specified, this plot is then superimposed on top of the parent pdf (g) to facilitate a visual comparison.

In[129]:= **Monty[data, {-5, 5, .1}, g];**

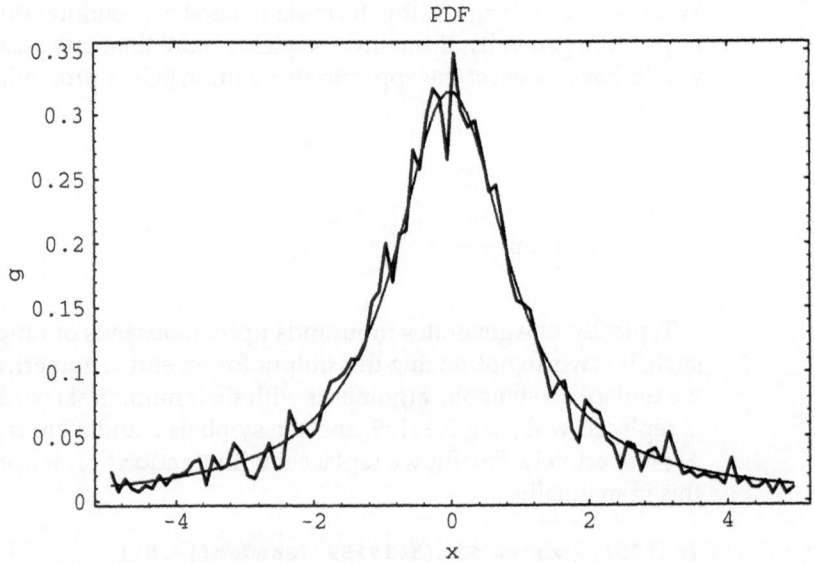

(Recall that g is only a valid pdf if domain[g] has been specified.)

Some caveats: the Inversion Method can only work if *Mathematica* can determine both the **DF** and its inverse. Inverse functions are tricky, and *Mathematica* may occasionally experience some difficulty in this regard. Because one ultimately has to work with a numerical density (i.e., numerical parameter values) when generating random numbers, it is often best to specify parameter values at the very start; this makes it easier to calculate **DF** and its inverse.

16.6.2   Rejection Method

Suppose we wish to generate pseudorandom numbers from some density $f(x)$. We try the Inverse Method, but it fails because for some reason *Mathematica* cannot invert the cdf $F(x)$. Let us suppose, however, that we know how to generate random numbers from some density $g(x)$ where:

- g is defined over the same domain as f
- there exists a constant $c > 0$ such that $f(x)/g(x) \le c$ for all x. Let $c = \sup(f(x)/g(x))$.

The Rejection Method then provides a way of generating pseudorandom drawings from $f(x)$. It does so as follows:

(1) generate a pseudorandom drawing from $g(x)$, call this number x_g;

(2) accept x_g as a random selection from $f(x)$ iff $v \le t(x_g)$, where:

- v is a pseudorandom drawing from $U(0,1)$,
- $t(x_g) = f(x_g)/(c\,g(x_g))$;

(3) if x_g is rejected, return to step (1).

Although this 3-step procedure may seem complex, it can be modeled in just one line when using *Mathematica*. Let us suppose we wish to generate pseudorandom numbers from the standard normal pdf (f). One standard way of doing this would be to use Wolfram's statistics package which comes with *Mathematica* (and includes the normal pdf), and which thus serves as a useful reference point. Instead, we present a Rejection Method approach, and show that it is almost twice as fast as Wolfram's package approach (v2.2).

```
In[130]:=        f = Exp[-x^2/2]/Sqrt[2Pi];
           domain[f] = {x, -Infinity, Infinity};
```

If we try the Inverse Method, it will fail because *Mathematica* cannot invert the normal cdf. However, we already know that we can generate pseudorandon numbers from the Cauchy pdf $g(x)$ (see the preceding Inversion Method). This is defined over the same domain as the normal (f), and we can easily check whether $c = \sup(f(x)/g(x))$ exists, by doing a quick plot of f/g.

```
In[131]:= Plot[f/g, {x, -4, 4}];
```

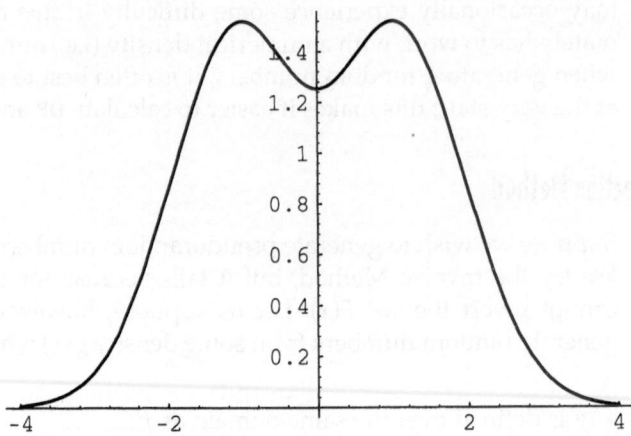

This suggests that c is roughly equal to 1.5. We can check the "exact" value using numerical methods (in the following line, the negative signs have been added in order to find the maximum, rather than the minimum).

```
In[132]:= c = -FindMinimum[-f/g, {x, 0.8, 1.2}] [[1]]
```

```
Out[132]= 1.52035
```

Stage (2) defined a function called "$t(x)$". This is simply given by:

```
In[133]:= t[x_] = f/(c g)   // N
```

```
Out[133]=                    2
            0.824361 (1. + x )
            ------------------
                      2
                 0.5 x
            2.71828
```

Then steps (1) through (3) can be modeled in just one line, by setting up a recursive function. Note how x_g (a pseudorandom Cauchy as previously defined) is used to generate x_f (a pseudorandom normal).

```
In[134]:= xf := ( z = xg;  If[Random[] < t[z], z, xf] )
```

So, let us try it out.

In[135]:= **dd = Table[xf, {2000}]; // Timing**

Out[135]= {2.43333 Second, Null}

To check the fit:

In[136]:= **Monty[dd, {-3, 3, .1}, f];**

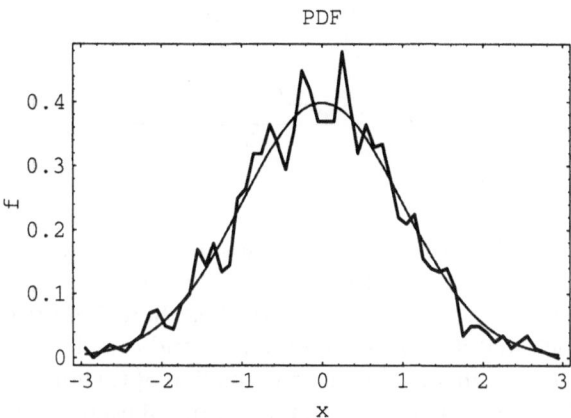

We end our analysis by establishing a benchmark, namely, the length of time it takes to obtain a sample of size 2,000 from the $N(0, 1)$ distribution using Wolfram's statistics package that accompanies *Mathematica* v2.2. To make this comparison, we first load up the master package

In[137]:= **<<Statistics'Master'**

and then generate 2,000 drawings from $N(0, 1)$ using the package:

In[138]:= **ndist = NormalDistribution[0,1];**

            ee = Table[Random[ndist], {2000}]; // Timing

Out[138]= {5.25 Second, Null}

In this example, it is evident that the Rejection Method has resulted in improved speed relative to the Statistics package; in fact, it is almost twice as fast. Both methods are "exact" solutions that accurately fit the desired $N(0, 1)$ distribution. We have already verified this for the Rejection Method, and can quickly do so for the Statistics package.

In[139]:= **Monty[ee, {-3, 3, .1}, f];**

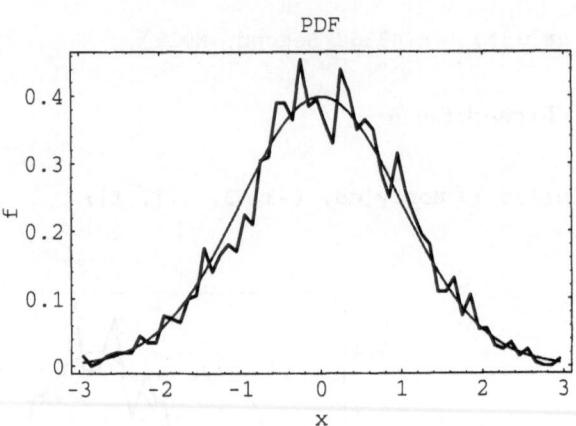

The Rejection Method is most useful when working with densities $f(x)$ that are not covered by the `Statistics` package, and for which the Inverse Method does not work. When using the Rejection Method, density $g(x)$ should be chosen such that it is easily computable, and easy to generate from using the Inverse Method; that is, the inverse function of G should be computationally tractable. It is also worth checking that output at each stage of the process is numerical.

16.7   Example: Statistical Curvature and Maximum Likelihood Estimation

Suppose we have a statistical problem involving a family of pdfs $F = \{f(x; \theta), \theta \in \Theta\}$ indexed by the single parameter $\theta \in \Theta$, a possibly infinite interval of the real line. It is known that if F is an exponential family, then standard linear methods will usually solve the problem in neat fashion. For example, the maximum likelihood estimator (MLE) for θ is a sufficient statistic in an exponential family, and achieves the Cramer-Rao Lower Bound (CRLB) if we have chosen the right function of θ to estimate.

But suppose we consider arbitrary one-parameter families F and try to quantify how nearly "exponential" they are. This can be done by using a quantity g_θ called "the statistical curvature of F at θ," defined such that $g_\theta = 0$ if F is exponential and $g_\theta > 0$, for at least some θ values, otherwise. Families with small curvature enjoy, nearly, the good statistical properties of exponential families. Large curvature indicates a breakdown of this favorable situation. For example, the variance of the MLE exceeds the CRLB in approximate proportion to g_θ^2.

To illustrate, we shall derive the curvature of the Weibull distribution,

In[140]:=   **f = q x^(q-1) Exp[-(x^q)];**
          domain[f] = {x, 0, Infinity};

Denote the score and Hessian, respectively, by

```
In[141]:= s = D[Log[f], q]       // Simplify
          h = D[Log[f], {q,2}]   // Simplify
```

```
Out[141]= 1               q
          - + Log[x] - x  Log[x]
          q
```

```
Out[141]=   -2    q       2
          -q    - x  Log[x]
```

Fisher's Information, i_θ, is given by

```
In[142]:= iq = -Expect[h, f]     // Simplify
```

```
Out[142]=                                     2       2
          6 - 12 EulerGamma + 6 EulerGamma  + Pi
          --------------------------------------
                           2
                        6 q
```

The statistical curvature of F at θ is defined as $g_\theta = \sqrt{\det(M_\theta)/i_\theta^3}$, where M_θ is the (2×2) covariance matrix of (s, h):

$$M_\theta = \begin{bmatrix} i_\theta & E(sh) \\ E(sh) & E(h^2) - i_\theta^2 \end{bmatrix}$$

To evaluate g_θ, we therefore require the following expectations:

```
In[143]:= esh = Expect[s h, f]
          eh2 = Expect[h^2, f]
```

```
Out[143]=                                   2             3
          (-24 EulerGamma + 30 EulerGamma  - 6 EulerGamma  +

                 2                2             3
            5 Pi  - 3 EulerGamma Pi  - 12 Zeta[3]) / (6 q )
```

```
Out[143]=                                             2
          (30 - 120 EulerGamma + 420 EulerGamma  -

                           3              4
            360 EulerGamma  + 60 EulerGamma  +

                 2                2              2   2
            70 Pi  - 180 EulerGamma Pi  + 60 EulerGamma  Pi  +

                 4
            9 Pi  - 720 Zeta[3] +

                                    4
            480 EulerGamma Zeta[3]) / (30 q )
```

```
In[144]:= Mq = {{iq, esh},{esh, eh2 - iq^2}};
          gq = Sqrt[Det[Mq]/iq^3] // N
```

```
Out[144]= 0.838732
```

For a random sample of size n, the curvature of the joint density is $G_\theta = g_\theta/\sqrt{n}$; thus as n increases the curvature becomes smaller. It has been suggested that if a distribution has squared curvature greater than $1/8$ then the degree of curvature is "large" (Efron 1975). In terms of random sampling, it is possible to establish the value of n, say, n_0, for which the distribution's curvature is reduced below the worrisome point for sample sizes equal to and larger than n_0. In the case of the Weibull distribution we find $n_0 = 6$, viz.:

```
In[145]:= Solve[gq^2/n0 == 1/8, n0]
```

```
Out[145]= {{n0 -> 5.62777}}
```

How sure can we be that with some minimal sample size obtained from a curved distribution (thus the curvature of the sampling distribution of the data would now be "less-than-worrisome") that this will necessarily translate through to the sampling distribution of a statistic that may be of interest? Reflecting on the example given in the very first paragraph of this section, we might test this proposition by examining the empirical distribution of the MLE:

```
In[146]:= F = DF[x, f]
```

```
Out[146]=      q                    q
          -x                   -x
       -E     + Limit[E    , x -> 0, Direction -> -1]
```

For $\theta > 0$, this Limit = 1. Inverting F then yields:

```
In[147]:= x /. Solve[u == 1-Exp[-x^q], x]
```

```
Out[147]=          1    1/q
           {Log[-----]   }
                1 - u
```

For $u =$ **Random[ ]**, this generates pseudorandom Weibull drawings. Thus, for a sample of size n, generated assuming $\theta = 1$:

```
In[148]:= xg := Table[(-Log[1 - Random[]])^(1/q), {n}]    /. q->1
```

The log-likelihood (LLH) function (which is globally concave in $\Theta = \{\theta : \theta > 0\}$) based on a random sample of size n is:

```
In[149]:= LLH := n Log[q] + (q-1)Apply[Plus, Log[xx]] -
             Apply[Plus, xx^q]
```

We now generate the empirical distribution of the MLE of θ:

```
In[150]:= n = 6;  nsim = 1000;
          eMLE = Table[xx=xg; q/.FindMinimum[-LLH,
             {q,1,.01,10}][[2]], {nsim}];
```

We may now use **Monty** to visually inspect the accuracy of the asymptotic approximation $N(\theta, 1/(n\, i_\theta))$, to the empirical distribution of the MLE for the case $n = n_0$.

```
In[151]:=                mean = q            /. q->1;
                          var = 1/(n iq)   /. q->1  // N;

                 asydist = (2 Pi var)^(-.5) Exp[-(x - mean)^2 /
                              (2 var)];
          domain[asydist] = {x, -Infinity, Infinity};

          Monty[eMLE, {0, 2, .10}, asydist];
```

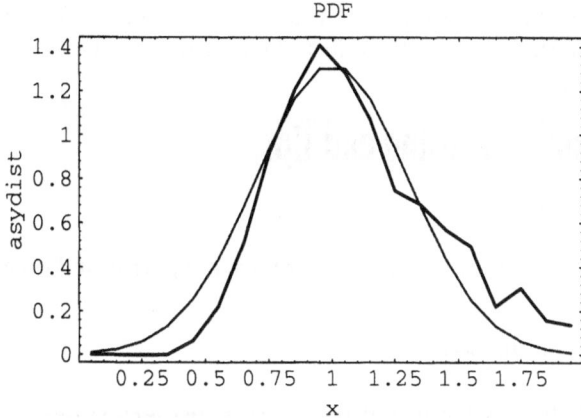

The empirical distribution shows distinct evidence of skewness. It is apparent that the asymptotic distribution is not a good approximation when $n = n_0 = 6$. The "less-than-worrisome" curvature of the $n = 6$ sampling distribution has not resulted in the asymptotic distribution of the MLE being a useful approximation at this sample size.

At a larger sample size, $n = 30$, the following result occurred:

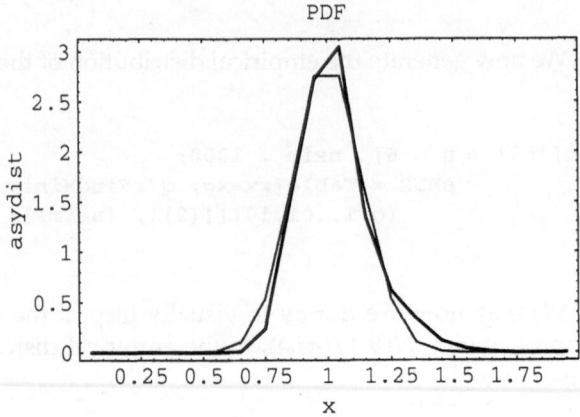

A very fine fit indeed! When $n = 30$ the curvature of the sampling distribution is

```
In[152]:= gq^2/30
```

```
Out[152]= 0.0234491
```

which is approximately $1/40$; that is, five times smaller than the "worrisome" level $1/8$. Insofar as parameter estimation is concerned, more conservative views on the extent of the effect of curvature must be entertained.

16.8   Trouble-Shooting and Tips

Timings

- The Timings in this chapter were performed on a PowerMac 8500.

Domain Tips

- If a function returns an error message containing the word domain, check that the domain of the relevant pdf has been specified. It is easy to forget to do so.
- To work simultaneously with a general pdf $f = f(x;a)$, and a special case $g = f(x;a = 1)$, one can proceed as follows:

```
In[153]:= f = a Exp[-a x];        domain[f] = {x, 0, Infinity};
          g = f /. a ->1;         domain[g] = domain[f];
```

One can then use the package functions in the normal way:

```
In[154]:= Expect[3x^2, f]
          Expect[3x^2, g]
```

```
Out[154]= 6
          --
          2
          a
```

```
Out[154]= 6
```

- If doing multivariate analysis, is the domain rectangular or nonrectangular? Note that package functions should generally not be used with nonrectangular domains such as $x^2 + y^2 < 1$ or $0 < x < y < \infty$ (see Section 16.4).

Transform Tips

- If, by mistake, one enters eqn = {u = expr}, rather than {u == expr}, the **Transform** function will not work. To fix this up, first **Clear[u]**, then try the example again (Section 16.3).
- The **Transform** function generates output containing the **Abs[ ]** function. *Mathematica* cannot integrate over such output, so one will need to remove **Abs[ ]** manually. Section 16.3 discusses this.
- Using Transform in a multivariate setting often induces dependence between the transformed variables. If so, it may be inappropriate to use the package functions on the transformed pdf. Of course, this is only relevant to multivariate examples (see Sections 16.3 and 16.4).

Multivariate Normal Tips

- The function **MVN[xvec, muvec, varcov]** requires that varcov is both symmetric and positive definite. If varcov is numerical, the **MVN** function will automatically check that these criteria are satisfied. If varcov contains parameters in symbolic form, it cannot perform this test. As such, if you specify numerical values ex-post, your **varcov** matrix will not be checked. The following example illustrates:

```
In[155]:= Clear[r]
          MVN[{x1,x2}, {0,0}, {{.9, .5}, {.5, .2}}]
```

```
MVN::pd: Your variance-covariance matrix is not positive
    definite.
```

```
In[156]:= MVN[{x1,x2}, {0,0}, {{.9, r}, {r, .2}}] /. r -> .5
```

```
Out[156]= ((0. + 1.88982 I) E
              (-((7.142 x1-12.85 x2) x2) -
              x1 (-2.857 x1 + 7.14 x2))/2) / Pi
```

Random Sampling Tips

- In the Rejection Method, the function **xf** makes use of recursion. *Mathematica* has a default limit that stops recursion after 256 iterations (if it did not, one could get stuck in an infinite loop). On certain problems, the default setting of 256 iterations may not be sufficient. If so, *Mathematica* will generate **$RecursionLimit** error messages. If this happens, raise the limit (to, say, 4,000 iterations) by entering the following input:

  In[157]:= `$RecursionLimit = $IterationLimit = 4000;`

- Problem: **Monty[x, {a, b, c}, f]** does not work for me. Solution: set **domain[f]**.

- Problem: **Monty** still does not work for me. Solution: try setting slightly different values for 'a' and 'b' (e.g., set a = 0.0001 instead of 0).

Discontinuous PDFs

Consider a discontinuous pdf such as:

In[158]:= `f = If[x<b, Exp[-x]/2, Exp[-x] (1+Exp[b])/2];`
      `domain[f] = {x,0,Infinity};`
      `Plot[f/.b->1, {x, 0, 5},`
          `PlotLabel -> "Discontinuity at b"];`

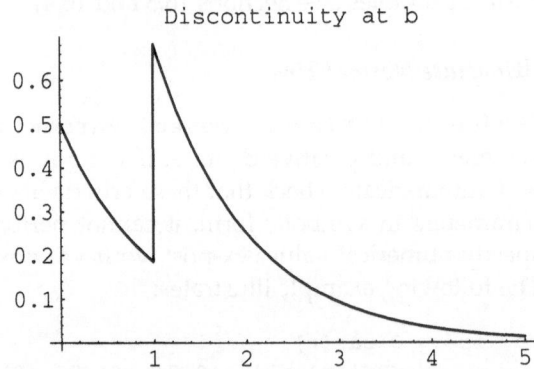

In[159]:= **Expect[x, f]**

Out[159]=
```
                                    Exp[-x]   Exp[-x] (1 + Exp[b])
        Integrate[x If[x < b, -------, --------------------],
                                    2                 2

            {x, 0, Infinity}]
```

Obviously `Expect` just does not work. What we need to do is split the pdf into its components and apply our commands to each component separately. Thus

```
In[160]:= f1 = Exp[-x]/2; domain[f1] = {x,0,b};
          f2 = Exp[-x] (1+Exp[b])/2;
                                domain[f2] = {x,b,Infinity};

          Expect[x, f1]  +  Expect[x, f2]  // Simplify
```
```
Out[160]=      b
          1 + -
               2
```

Generally, some thought is required. For example,

```
In[161]:= DF[x, f1]
```
```
Out[161]= 1     1
          - - ----
          2      x
               2 E
```

is the cdf provided $x < b$, whereas if $x \geq b$ we would derive the cdf as:

```
In[162]:= DF[b, f1] + DF[x, f2]    // Simplify
```
```
Out[162]=             b
                  1 + E
          1 - ------
                    x
                 2 E
```

16.9   Acknowledgments

We thank Eduardo Ley and an anonymous referee for some helpful suggestions.

16.10   References

There is a wealth of bibliographic sources for the material examined in this chapter. Rather than clutter the text with copious citations, we refer the interested reader to what is, in our opinion, the pre-eminent work in this field, namely Stuart and Ord (1994).

Efron, B. 1975. "Defining the Curvature of a Statistical Problem (With Applications to Second Order Efficiency)." *The Annals of Statistics*, **3**, 1189–1242 (with comments).

Rose, C. and Smith, M. D. 1996. "The Multivariate Normal Distribution." *The Mathematica Journal*, 6, 32–37.

Schervish, M.J. 1984. "Multivariate Normal Probabilities With Error Bound." *Applied Statistics*, **33**, 81–94. (See also: "Corrections." *Applied Statistics*, **34**, 103–104, 1985.)

Stuart, A. and Ord, J.K. 1994. *Kendall's Advanced Theory of Statistics*, Vol. 1, 6th ed. London, Charles Griffen.